Office XP
Brief Edition

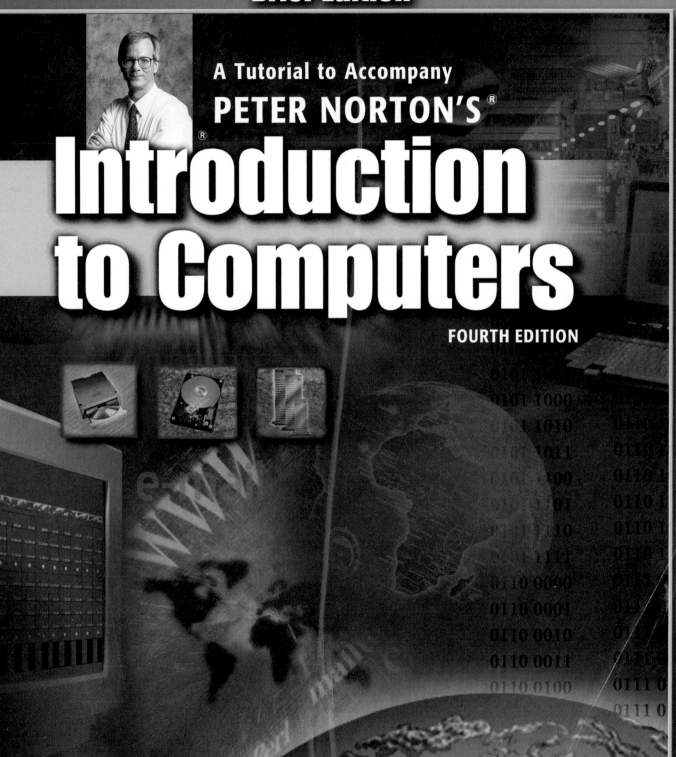

A Tutorial to Accompany

PETER NORTON'S®

Introduction to Computers

FOURTH EDITION

Glencoe
McGraw-Hill

New York, New York   Columbus, Ohio   Chicago, Illinois   Peoria, Illinois   Woodland Hills, California

Office XP: Brief Edition
A Tutorial to Accompany
Peter Norton's® Introduction to Computers

Glencoe/McGraw-Hill

A Division of The **McGraw·Hill** Companies

Send all inquiries to:
Glencoe/McGraw-Hill
21600 Oxnard St., Suite 500
Woodland Hills, CA   91367-4906

ISBN: 0-07-829789-3
Development: FSCreations, Inc.

Peter Norton, Peter Norton's stylized signature, and Peter Norton's crossed-arms pose are registered trademarks of Peter Norton.

Microsoft Office, Office XP, Excel 2002, PowerPoint 2002, Word 2002, Access 2002, Outlook, Windows, Windows 98, Windows Millennium Edition (Windows Me), Windows 2000, Windows NT, Windows XP, and *Internet Explorer* are registered trademarks of Microsoft Corporation. All brand names and product names are trademarks or registered trademarks of their respective owners. Glencoe/McGraw-Hill is not associated with any product or vendor mentioned in this tutorial.

Between the time that Web site information is gathered and published, it is not unusual for some sites to have closed. URLs will be updated in reprints when possible.

All individuals and companies named in this tutorial are fictitious.

Printed in the United States of America

4 5 6 7 8 9   027   06 05 04

Preface

Office XP: Brief Edition, one of the instructional tools that complements *Peter Norton's*® *Introduction to Computers,* covers the basic features of Office XP. Glencoe and Peter Norton have teamed up to provide this tutorial and its ancillaries to help you become a knowledgeable, empowered end user. After you complete this tutorial, you will be able to create and modify documents, explore the World Wide Web, and produce Web pages.

Objectives of the *Office XP: Brief Edition* Tutorial

Office XP: Brief Edition A Tutorial to Accompany Peter Norton's Introduction to Computers presents hands-on instruction on *Office XP.* The objectives of the *Office XP: Brief Edition* tutorial are:

◆ To introduce the basic concepts of Windows 2000. No computer knowledge is assumed in this tutorial.

◆ To introduce the basic concepts of Microsoft Internet Explorer 5.5.

◆ To introduce the basic concepts and skills of Microsoft Office XP, using Word, Excel, Access, PowerPoint, and Outlook.

◆ To provide hands-on tutorial exercises and realistic applications of the Office XP features.

◆ To help you develop proficiency in using Office XP.

◆ To help you explore and navigate the World Wide Web, search the Internet, create a Web page, communicate via e-mail, and more.

◆ To empower you to accept responsibility for learning.

◆ To help you demonstrate the skills and knowledge you have acquired by creating a personal portfolio.

Organization of the *Office XP: Brief Edition* Tutorial

The *Office XP: Brief Edition* tutorial is divided into six sections: (1) a *Getting Started* section that includes three lessons covering the basic concepts of Windows 2000, Internet Explorer 5.5, and Office XP; (2) the *Word 2002* tutorial; (3) the *Excel 2002* tutorial; (4) the *Access 2002* tutorial; (5) the *PowerPoint 2002* tutorial; and (6) a *Managing Information* section that includes two lessons covering the basic concepts of Outlook and Office XP integration.

◆ *Getting Started*—**Lesson 1: Windows 2000 Basics.** This lesson presents the basic features of the Windows 2000 operating system to enable you to work more effectively with application programs, such as Office XP.

◆ *Getting Started*—**Lesson 2: Internet Explorer 5.5 Basics.** This lesson presents the basic features of Microsoft Internet Explorer 5.5, a program designed to help you explore the Internet, search the Internet, and view your newly created Web pages.

- *Getting Started*—Lesson 3: Office XP Basics. This lesson presents an overview of the Microsoft Office XP program—a suite of applications that allows you to create and modify documents, worksheets, databases, and presentations, along with managing information.

- The *Word 2002* tutorial. In the *Word 2002* tutorial, you will learn the basic features of Microsoft Word 2002 and be able to create and modify documents. You also will learn to use Word 2002 to explore the World Wide Web and create hyperlinks.

- The *Excel 2002* tutorial. In the *Excel 2002* tutorial, you will learn the basic features of Microsoft Excel 2002 and be able to create and modify worksheets. You also will learn to use Excel 2002 to collaborate on the Web and create hyperlinks in a worksheet.

- The *Access 2002* tutorial. In the *Access 2002* tutorial, you will learn the basic features of Microsoft Access 2002 and be able to create and modify databases. You also will learn to use Access 2002 to explore the World Wide Web and create hyperlinks in a database.

- The *PowerPoint 2002* tutorial. In the *PowerPoint 2002* tutorial, you will learn the basic features of Microsoft PowerPoint 2002 and be able to create and modify presentations. You also will learn how to use PowerPoint 2002 to create hyperlinks in a presentation and publish a presentation on the Web.

- *Managing Information*—Lesson 1: Outlook Basics. This lesson presents the basics of Outlook 2002, a personal information management program that helps you manage messages, appointments, contacts, and tasks.

- *Managing Information*—Lesson 2: Integrating Office XP. In this lesson, you will improve your productivity skills by learning more about integrating Outlook 2002 data with Word 2002, Excel 2002, Access 2002, and PowerPoint 2002 documents in numerous hands-on activities and exercises.

In addition to the lessons and tutorials, the *Office XP: Brief Edition* tutorial includes these items to reinforce learning:

- Appendices. Two appendices provide additional information. *Appendix A: Portfolio Builder* gives an overview of portfolios and provides tips on creating your personal portfolio. *Appendix B: Self Check Answers* provides the answers to all Self Check exercises in the entire tutorial.

- Glossary. Use the Glossary to look up terms that you don't understand.

- Index. Use the Index to find specific information in the *Office XP: Brief Edition* tutorial.

- Office Data CD. Attached to the inside back cover of the *Office XP: Brief Edition* tutorial you will find the Office Data CD. This CD contains all the files you need to complete the activities in the entire *Office XP: Brief Edition* tutorial. A separate Data folder appears on the CD for each of the four individual tutorials (Word, Excel, Access, and PowerPoint), plus one folder for the Integration lesson. You must copy the folders and files from the Office Data CD to a folder on your hard drive or network drive. (Instructions for copying these folders and files from the Office Data CD are provided on pages 87–91.)

Structure and Format of the
Office XP: Brief Edition Tutorial

Office XP: Brief Edition covers a range of functions and techniques and provides hands-on opportunities for you to practice and apply your skills. Each lesson includes the following:

◆ **Contents and Objectives.** The Contents and Objectives provide an overview of the features you will learn in the lesson.

◆ **Explanations of Important Concepts.** Each section of each lesson begins with a brief explanation of the concept or software feature covered in that section. The explanations help you understand "the big picture" as you learn each new feature.

◆ **In the Workplace.** In the Workplace, which appears in the margin at the beginning of each lesson, presents a real-world overview of how the lesson material may be applied within an organization.

◆ **New Terms.** An important part of learning about computers is learning the terminology. Each new term in the tutorial appears in bold type and is defined in the Glossary.

◆ **Hands On Activities.** Because most of us learn best by doing, each explanation is followed by a Hands On activity that includes step-by-step instructions that you complete at the computer. Integrated in the steps are full-screen figures to guide you along the way, as well as notes and warnings to help you learn more about the features.

◆ **Office XP Basics.** This element appears in the margin next to Hands On activities. Office XP Basics lists the general steps required to perform a particular task. Use Office XP Basics as a reference to quickly and easily review the steps to perform a task.

◆ **Hints & Tips.** This element, which appears in the margin, provides tips for increasing your effectiveness while using the Office XP program.

◆ **Another Way.** This margin element provides alternate ways to perform a given task.

◆ **Did You Know?** Read each Did You Know?, another element that appears in the margin, to learn additional facts related to the content of the lesson or other interesting facts about computers.

◆ **Web Note.** Web Notes, which also appear in the margin, contain interesting facts and Web addresses that relate to the content of the lesson and to your exploration of the World Wide Web.

◆ **Illustrations.** Many figures are provided to point out the specific features on the screen and illustrate what your screen should look like after you complete important steps.

◆ **Using Help.** Using Help activities encourage you to access online Help to explore topics related to the lessons in more depth.

◆ **Self Check Exercises.** To check your knowledge of the concepts presented in the lesson, a Self Check exercise is provided at the end of each lesson. After completing the exercise, refer to *Appendix B: Self Check Answers* to verify your understanding of the lesson material.

◆ **On the Web.** The On the Web sections teach important concepts relating to the use of the World Wide Web.

◆ **Summary.** At the end of each lesson, a Summary reviews the major topics covered in the lesson. You can use the Summary as a study guide.

◆ **Concepts Review.** Lessons may include four types of questions: True/False, Matching, Completion, and Short Answer; in addition, an Identification exercise provides you with an opportunity to identify screen elements relating to the lesson. Complete these objective-type exercises to review the concepts and skills that have been presented in the lesson.

◆ **Skills Review.** The Skills Review section provides guided hands-on exercises to practice each skill you learned in the lesson.

◆ **Lesson Applications.** The Lesson Applications provide additional hands-on practice. These exercises combine multiple skills learned in the lesson.

◆ **Projects.** The projects provide additional hands-on practice to apply your problem-solving and critical thinking skills. Each project allows you to apply multiple skills learned in the lesson. Additional *On the Web* projects reinforce the skills learned in the lesson's *On the Web* section, as well as a *Project in Progress* that builds from one lesson to the next in the Word 2002, Excel 2002, Access 2002, and PowerPoint 2002 tutorials.

◆ **Case Study.** Appearing after the last lesson in the Word 2002, Excel 2002, Access 2002, and PowerPoint 2002 tutorials, the Case Study is a capstone activity that allows you to apply the various skills you have learned to plan, create, and modify documents.

New Features of Microsoft Office XP®

Below is a selective list of the new features of Microsoft Office XP:

◆ **Task Panes.** Using the task panes in Microsoft Office XP, you can perform efficiently varied tasks such as opening files, formatting a document, or conducting searches.

◆ **Speech Recognition.** You can dictate text directly into a file using speech recognition, or you can format text using voice commands.

◆ **Handwriting Recognition.** This feature allows you to enter handwritten text into a file using your mouse or to convert your handwritten text to typed characters.

◆ **Ask a Question Box.** You can get immediate online help and avoid using the Office Assistant by typing your Help question directly into the Ask a Question box. (The Office Assistant is now hidden by default.)

◆ **Smart Tags.** The smart tags feature allows you to access contextual information directly from your file. A smart tag typically appears embedded in your file after you complete a task such as pasting data. (This feature is not applicable for Access.)

◆ **Microsoft Design Gallery Live.** Every Office XP user can access Clips Online and choose among thousands of images and animations available for download over the Web. (Clips Online cannot be accessed directly from the Access application.)

◆ **Document Recovery.** The document recovery feature ensures that you don't have to worry about losing your documents. If your computer should crash or a program error should occur while you are working with Office XP, the document recovery feature allows you to save and recover your current files.

◆ **Web Discussions.** Discussions about documents are now so easy. The Web Discussions feature allows you to use a Local Area Network or the Internet to discuss the content of a document with other members of a team.

About Peter Norton

Acclaimed computer software entrepreneur Peter Norton is active in civic and philanthropic affairs. He serves on the boards of several scholastic and cultural institutions and currently devotes much of his time to philanthropy.

Raised in Seattle, Washington, Mr. Norton made his mark in the computer industry as a programmer and businessman. *Norton Utilities*™, *Norton AntiVirus*™, and other utility programs are installed on millions of computers worldwide. He is also a best-selling author of computer books.

Mr. Norton sold his PC software business to Symantec Corporation in 1990, but he continues to write and speak on computers, helping millions of people better understand information technology. He and his family currently reside in Santa Monica, California.

Reviewers

Many thanks are due to the following individuals who reviewed the manuscript and provided recommendations to improve this tutorial:

Kenneth Wallace
Craven Community College
New Bern, North Carolina

Rhonda Davis
Isothermal Community College
Spindale, North Carolina

Nancy Jobe
Ivy Tech State College
Evansville, Indiana

Katherine Burkhart
Star Technical Institute
Lakewood, New Jersey

Tommy Davis
Gulf Coast Community College
Panama City, Florida

Sherri Brinkley
MVC Business School
Arnold, Missouri

Acknowledgment

Glencoe would like to acknowledge tom white.images for contributing illustrations to this program.

SYSTEM REQUIREMENTS FOR MICROSOFT OFFICE XP

Below is a list of the system requirements for Microsoft Office XP. For additional information, see the Microsoft Office XP Web site at **www.Microsoft.com/Office/**.

Hardware

Pentium III processor, 133-megahertz (MHz) or higher; CD-ROM drive; super VGA (800 x 600) or higher-resolution monitor with 256 colors; and compatible pointing device

Memory Requirements

◆ Windows 98 or Windows 98 Second Edition: 24 MB RAM, plus 8 MB RAM for each Office program running simultaneously

◆ Windows Millennium Edition (Windows Me), or Windows NT®: 32 MB RAM, plus 8 MB RAM for each Office application running simultaneously

◆ Windows 2000 Professional: 64 MB RAM, plus 8 MB RAM for each Office application running simultaneously

◆ Windows XP Professional or Windows XP Home Edition: 128 MB RAM, plus 8 MB RAM for each Office application running simultaneously

Minimum Hard Disk Space

Note: Hard disk space requirements will vary, depending upon your system configuration and custom installation choices.

Office XP Standard: 210 MB

Office XP Professional and Professional Special Edition: 245 MB

Operating System

Windows 98, Windows 98 Second Edition, Windows Millennium Edition (Windows Me), Windows NT 4.0 with Service Pac 6 (SP6) or later, Windows 2000, or Windows XP.

Table of Contents

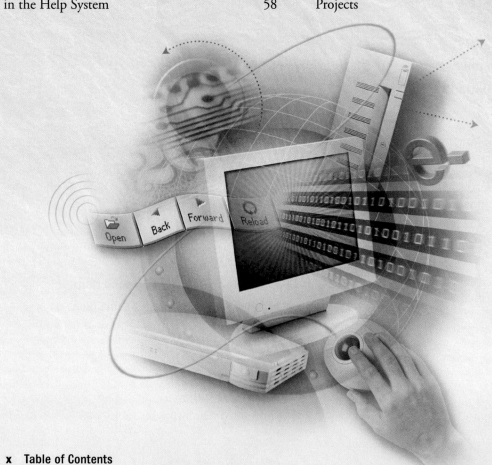

Word 2002   121

Access 2002   369

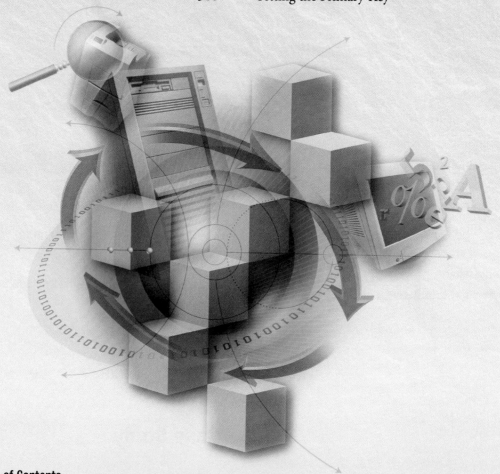

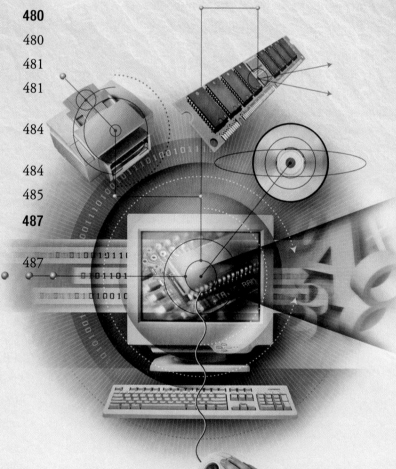

PowerPoint 2002   525

Managing Information 649

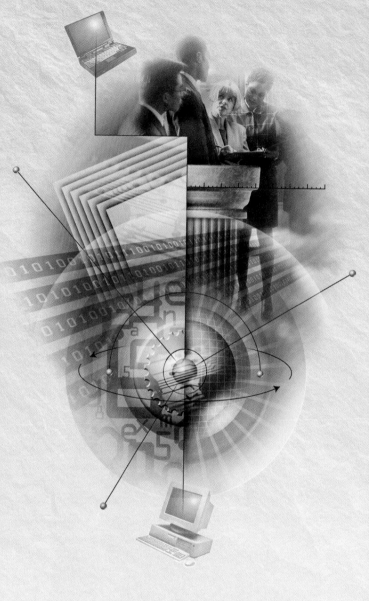

Contents

Understanding Online Help Systems

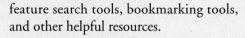

Help is everywhere . . .

Have you noticed that online help systems have almost completely replaced printed manuals for many types of computer products? Why is this? First, online help systems are cheaper to produce than printed materials. Second, online help systems can be updated and distributed much more quickly. Third—and equally as important—online help systems can be interactive and intuitive, making them far more instructive and easier to use than any printed manual.

Don't let program-related questions or problems stump you. And don't give up on learning other program features that will allow you to gain efficiencies. By "reaching out" to available online help options, you may find answers galore—and just a click or two away. You can use any combination of these online help forms:

- **Electronic Documents.** An electronic document is a computer-based version of a printed manual. It may be included with software, even when no printed manuals are provided. Such documents look like printed books but are used on-screen, as seen in utilities such as Adobe's Acrobat Reader. Electronic documents may feature hyperlinked index and contents entries, as well as hyperlinked cross-references. You can click a heading, page number, or reference and jump to the appropriate section. Electronic documents also may

feature search tools, bookmarking tools, and other helpful resources.

- **Application Help Systems.** Most software applications feature an online help system installed with the product. Windows-based application help systems use a standard interface; so, after you learn how to use one of them, you can use another with ease. Application help systems can include audio, animation, video-based demonstrations, links to Internet resources, and much more.

- **Web Help.** You can use newer-generation help systems over the World Wide Web or over a corporate intranet through a standard Web browser. The advantage of Web help is that it is centralized—located on a single server—instead of being stored on each user's system. This centralization enables administrators to update the information quickly and frees customers from making duplicate copies on individual user machines.

- **FAQs.** Many companies post electronic documents containing frequently asked questions (FAQs) on their Web or intranet sites, on newsgroups, and on bulletin boards. As their name implies, FAQs provide answers to the most commonly asked questions about a product, and a FAQ may be the first place to look when you have a problem with a product.

- **Knowledge Bases.** Knowledge bases can help you find information and technical support online. You can find many knowledge bases at the Web sites of companies that produce software and hardware products. To use a knowledge base, type a question or a term into the site's search box. The knowledge base then will provide you with one or more possible solutions to your problem.

- **E-Mail Support.** Some software companies provide technical support via e-mail. You compose an e-mail message describing your question or problem and submit it to the manufacturer. The manufacturer then responds within twenty-four hours,

in most cases. Depending on the nature of your problem, you may receive a standard document or a customized response from a technical support person.

- **Real-Time Communication.** Online chatting and instant messaging technology is becoming an easy way for companies to offer improved real-time customer interaction and technical support. Some software companies offer real-time or live online technical support—with experts on standby just waiting to help you solve your problems. After you type your question, you can begin chatting online with a live expert, who can help you directly on your computer. Some technology even lets the expert see your computer screen and share your mouse and keyboard.

It's easy to become an empowered, independent end user. Just be resourceful and access the available online Help options—the answers you need may be only a click away!

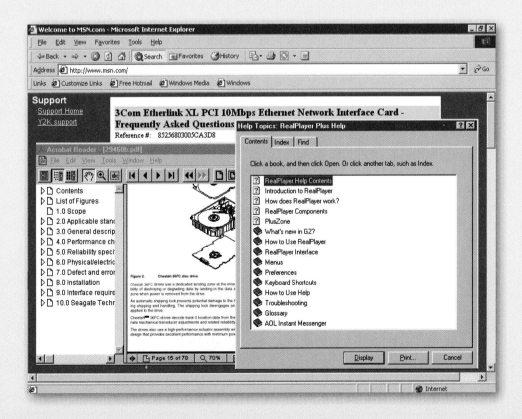

LESSON 1

Windows Basics

CONTENTS

- The Windows 2000 Operating System
- Starting the Computer With Windows 2000
- Using the Windows 2000 Desktop
- Using the Mouse
- Working With Windows
- Running Programs
- Choosing Program Options From the Menu Bar
- Using Dialog Boxes
- Printing Your Work
- Getting Help
- Using Windows Explorer
- Shutting Down Your Computer
- On the Web: Getting Online Help

OBJECTIVES

After you complete this lesson, you will be able to do the following:

- ► Define the Microsoft Windows 2000 operating system.
- ► Start your computer.
- ► Use your mouse to point, click, double-click, right-click, select, drag, and display objects.
- ► Activate and move desktop icons.
- ► Identify the common window elements.
- ► Size, minimize, maximize, restore, and scroll windows.
- ► Run more than one program, switch between programs, and close programs.
- ► Use menus and dialog boxes.
- ► Set a default printer.
- ► Find help on Windows 2000 topics.
- ► Use Windows Explorer to view and modify the structure of a disk; create folders and subfolders; and rename, delete, copy, and move files.
- ► Change attributes of files and folders.
- ► Quit Windows 2000 and shut down your computer.
- ► Search the Internet for online support.

THE WINDOWS 2000 OPERATING SYSTEM

The computer system you work with consists of hardware and software. Usually, the hardware includes these components:

◆ A processor to manage, interpret, and manipulate the flow of data

◆ A keyboard to type information

◆ A mouse (or trackball) to point to objects and select options on the screen

◆ A monitor to see what you are doing

◆ A printer to produce hard copy output

◆ Disks to store information

Your computer system also needs both task-specific and general operational **software.** Software that helps you accomplish a specific task is called an **application program** (or **application**). You might use different applications to type a letter, to manage a budget, to balance a checkbook, or to organize a mailing list. When you are able to run more than one application program at a time, **multitasking** results. With a few quick keystrokes or a click of the mouse, you can switch from one application to another. Software that allows you to operate your hardware and use applications is called **operating system software,** or an **operating system,** for short.

Sometimes the operating system manages your computer automatically. When you turn on your computer, the operating system looks up the current date and time, sets your preferred speaker volume, and displays the selected screen color scheme. At other times, your operating system follows your instructions, such as when you duplicate a specific file or start a particular application. These computer instructions are called **commands.**

Not all personal computers use the same operating system software. Your computer's operating system determines not only the specific commands your system can execute, but also the manner in which you give those commands and otherwise interact with your computer. This human-computer interaction is called the **user interface.** It determines the look and feel of your computing experience.

Windows 2000 continues the process of combining pleasing and easy-to-use operating systems, such as Windows 98, with robust, security-conscious networking operating systems, such as Windows NT 4. Windows 98 and its predecessor, Windows 95, support a variety of hardware and software, and integrate Internet access with the basic operating system. Windows NT 4 gives corporate, network users an operating system that protects sensitive documents within a stable computing environment. To effectively combine these features, Windows 2000 utilizes a **graphical user interface** (or **GUI**), that enables you to use on-screen pictures to operate your computer.

STARTING THE COMPUTER WITH WINDOWS 2000

The operating system software oversees every operation you perform on your computer. When you turn on your computer, the computer gives itself a complex set of instructions to start up. This start-up process is called **booting the system,** and is derived from the expression "pulling oneself up by the bootstraps." First, a built-in program tests the computer. This **Power On Self Test (POST)** checks the memory, keyboard, display, and disk drives of the computer system. Next, files from the hard disk containing essential operating system components are loaded. Because computer systems and setups vary greatly, you may see a series of screens informing you of the progress of the start-up procedure. Finally, the opening screen appears.

HANDS on

Booting Windows 2000

In this activity, you will start the computer and boot the Windows 2000 operating system. All activities and figures in this tutorial were developed using the Windows 2000 operating system. If you are using a different version of Windows, the information appearing on your screen may vary slightly from the activities and figures in this tutorial.

> **WARNING** *If Windows 2000 is not the operating system on the computer you are using, or if your computer is already on, ask your instructor, computer lab assistant, or network administrator how to boot your system.*

1. **Press the power button or flip the power switch to turn on the computer. If the monitor connected to the system has a separate power switch, turn on that switch as well.**

2. **Observe the booting process.**

   a. **Listen for the POST sound. A single beep means the system passed all the tests; a series of beeps indicates a hardware problem. If you hear a series of beeps, check your keyboard and monitor connections, read the message on the screen, or consult your computer manual to fix the problem. You may need technical help from the manufacturer, a lab assistant, or a technician. (Your computer may not make any sounds while booting.)**

   b. **Watch the screen. After a few moments, you may see a memory indicator while the system checks the random access memory. Then some information appears on the screen, followed by the Windows 2000 copyright screen. A progress indicator gives you a visual clue as to how much more of the operating system needs to be loaded into memory. The Log On to Windows screen may appear next, requesting your user name and password.**

When you **log on** to a computer with Windows 2000, you inform the operating system who you are. The operating system then loads your personal settings to complete the booting process. Systems that have multiple users, such as networks, keep track of who is allowed to access the computer by assigning unique **user names** and **passwords.** You may not be able to select your own user name; rather, a network administrator may assign the name to you. To provide security, each user must have a secret code or password known only to the user. In Windows 2000, each user chooses a password (up to 14 characters) that is entered along with the user name during the log-on procedure. When choosing a password, you should choose a series of letters, numbers, or special characters that

Windows **BASICS**

Booting the System

1. Turn on the computer and the monitor, if necessary.

2. Enter your user name and password.

3. Click OK.

would be difficult for someone else to guess. If you suspect that someone else knows your password, you should change your password immediately.

3. If you are prompted for a user name and/or password, type your user name in the User name text box and/or press ⎡Tab⎤ and type your password. If you do not know your user name and/or password, ask your instructor for help.

Asterisks appear as you type your password. This way, others who may see your log-on screen will not learn your password.

4. Click OK.

The system completes the booting process. You may see the Getting Started with Windows 2000 window, as shown in Figure 1.1. A **window** is a rectangular on-screen frame in which you do your computing work. The name, Windows, comes from the visual image of these frames. The Getting Started with Windows 2000 window displays options that allow you to register your operating system with Microsoft Corporation, to explore a description of new features in Windows 2000, and to set up a connection to the Internet.

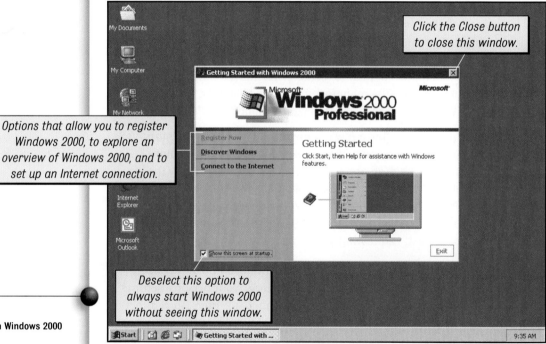

Figure 1.1
Getting Started with Windows 2000 window

5. If necessary, click the Show this screen at startup check box to clear the option; this will prevent the Getting Started with Windows 2000 window from appearing each time you boot your computer. Click the Close button ☒ in the upper-right corner of the window.

Now your screen should resemble Figure 1.2. This screen, called the Windows 2000 **desktop,** is the background for your computer work. The desktop contains many of the tools for working with Windows 2000.

> **NOTE** *Your desktop details may vary, but you still will see the basic features discussed in this lesson.*

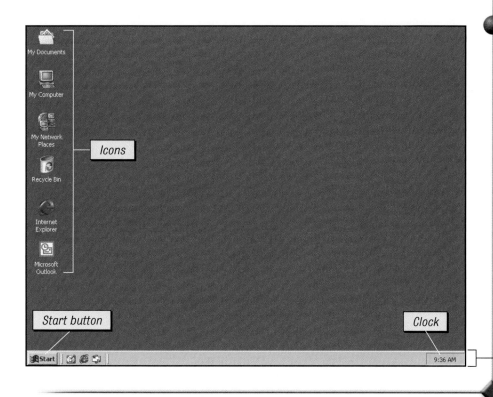

Figure 1.2
Windows 2000 Desktop

GETTING STARTED

USING THE WINDOWS 2000 DESKTOP

Windows 2000 has many features that integrate the operating system with the Internet. The **Web style desktop** lets you use your mouse and view your screen just as you would when you run Internet Explorer, a **browser** program that lets you access the World Wide Web. Users may choose to retain the former Windows 95 user interface, now called the **classic style desktop.**

Additionally, when you set up your screen as the **active desktop,** information is sent to your desktop via the Internet. This information may be news articles, weather reports, stock market quotations, or sports scores. You can get this information by specifically requesting it or subscribing to a service that sends you information on a regular basis.

Due to Window's high degree of customization, it is rare for two desktops to look exactly the same. The following desktop elements, however, are common to almost all screens.

◆ Several small, labeled pictures or **icons,** such as My Documents, My Computer, My Network Places, Recycle Bin, and Internet Explorer appear on the desktop. These icons represent some of the resources that are available on your system, such as programs, data files, printers, disk drives, and others. Your desktop may include a large number of icons, or just a few.

◆ The **taskbar,** the bar across the bottom of the desktop, contains buttons that you can click to perform various actions, including the Start button  on the left and the Clock button on the right.

◆ The Start button , when clicked, displays a menu of programs installed on the computer. A **menu** is a list of items you can choose from to select a command, set software features, or choose options.

◆ When you elect to run a program or select an option, a window usually appears on your desktop.

Did you know?

Before Windows 95, Windows was really an operating *environment*. The operating *system* was DOS; Windows changed the look and feel of the operating system.

USING THE MOUSE

You will use the **mouse** extensively in Windows 2000. The mouse is the key to the graphical user interface because it lets you choose and manipulate on-screen objects without having to type on the keyboard. Although the mouse is the most popular pointing device, you also may use several other pointing devices. **Trackballs** have buttons like the mouse, but instead of moving the mouse over the desktop, you spin a large ball. Laptops often employ either a small **joystick** in the middle of the keyboard or a **touch-sensitive pad** below the keyboard. Each of these devices lets you point to items on the screen and click buttons to perform actions on those items.

You can perform several actions with the mouse:

◆ An arrow on the screen pointing toward the upper left is called the **pointer** (or **mouse pointer**). Moving the mouse to position the pointer on the screen is called **pointing**. Table 2.1 shows several shapes you may notice as you point to objects on the screen. When you rest your pointer on some icons on the desktop, a description may appear.

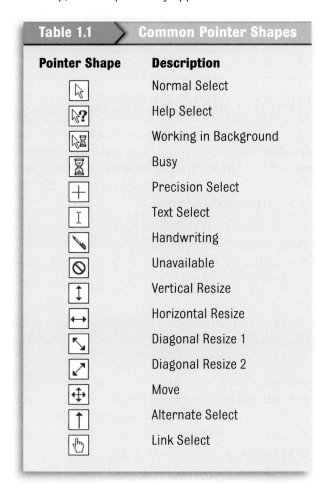

Table 1.1	Common Pointer Shapes
Pointer Shape	**Description**
⬚	Normal Select
⬚	Help Select
⬚	Working in Background
⬚	Busy
⬚	Precision Select
⬚	Text Select
⬚	Handwriting
⬚	Unavailable
⬚	Vertical Resize
⬚	Horizontal Resize
⬚	Diagonal Resize 1
⬚	Diagonal Resize 2
⬚	Move
⬚	Alternate Select
⬚	Link Select

◆ To **click** the mouse, point to an object and quickly press and release the left mouse button.

◆ To work with an object on the screen, you usually must **select** (or **choose**) the item by clicking the object—pressing and quickly releasing the mouse button.

◆ To **double-click,** point to an object and click the left mouse button twice in rapid succession without moving the pointer.

◆ To **right-click,** point to an object, press the right mouse button, and then quickly release it.

◆ To **drag** (or **drag-and-drop**), point to an object you want to move, press and hold the left mouse button, move the mouse to drag the object to a new location, and then release the mouse button.

Your mouse probably has two or three buttons. Whenever the directions in this tutorial say *click,* use the left mouse button. If you must use the right mouse button, the directions will say *right-click* or *click the right mouse button.* (Windows 2000 lets you reassign the mouse buttons so that the right button performs the actions ordinarily performed by the left button. See Help for specific information.)

HANDS on

Practicing Mouse Techniques

In this activity, you will become familiar with using the mouse to select, open, and move objects on the desktop.

1. On the desktop, point to the My Computer system icon.

A description of the icon appears.

2. To select the icon, click My Computer.

Notice that the selected icon highlights (changes color).

3. To deselect the icon, point to an empty area of the desktop and click.

The icon deselects or returns to its original color.

4. Point to the My Computer icon and double-click.

The My Computer window appears, as shown in Figure 1.3. When you double-click an object on the screen, such as an icon or a file name, the object's window **opens** on the screen.

5. Double-click the Control Panel icon.

The Control Panel window opens. It contains a series of icons that lets you customize your computing environment.

6. Click the Close button ☒ — the X located in the upper-right corner.

The Control Panel window disappears from the desktop. Clicking a window's Close button ☒ **closes** the window and removes the window from the screen.

GETTING STARTED

Windows BASICS

Using the Mouse

• To select an object, point to the object and click.

• To deselect the object, click an area away from the selected object.

• To open an icon, double-click the icon.

• To double-click, click the left mouse button twice rapidly without moving the pointer.

• To right-click, click the right mouse button.

• To drag-and-drop, press and hold the left mouse button over a selected object, move the mouse where desired, and release the mouse button.

Figure 1.3
My Computer window

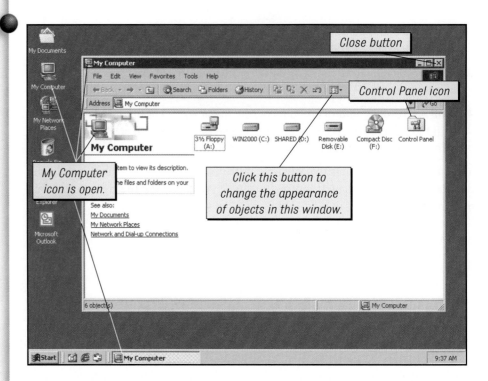

7. Point to the **My Computer icon** and press and hold the left mouse button. Move the mouse down and away from you to drag the icon from its current position to the lower-right corner of the screen but do *not* place it on top of another icon. Then release the mouse button.

The icon should appear somewhere near the lower-right corner of the screen, as shown in Figure 1.4.

Figure 1.4
Moved My Computer icon

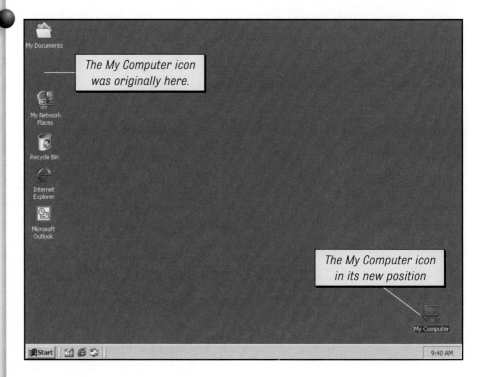

NOTE *If the My Computer icon won't stay where you drop it, right-click the desktop and click Arrange Icons. If a check mark appears by Auto Arrange, click Auto Arrange to remove the check mark. Then, repeat step 7.*

8. **Drag the My Computer icon to its original location. Click anywhere on the screen to deselect the icon.**

WORKING WITH WINDOWS

A window provides a view into your work and is designed to simplify tasks you perform on the computer. Options and information for each application are contained in the window, and you easily can access and use them. You can position a window on the screen and change its size using the mouse.

Two types of windows exist: application windows and document windows. An **application window** opens when you run a program. **Document windows** let you perform separate jobs within an application window. Figure 1.5 illustrates elements common to most windows. Each window contains some or all of the tools shown in Table 2.2.

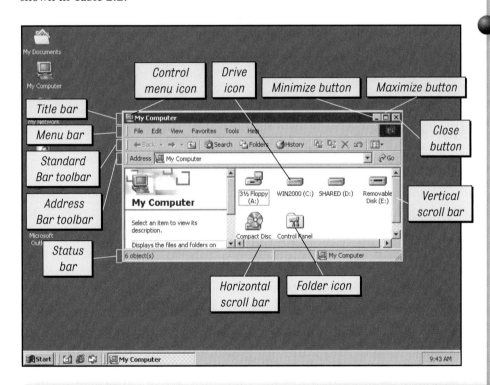

Figure 1.5
Components of a typical window

Table 1.2	Common Window Elements	
Tool	**Description**	
Title bar	The shaded bar at the top of a window that displays the name of the window and contains buttons for manipulating the window.	
Control menu icon	The icon 🖳 at the left end of the title bar that displays the Control menu when clicked. The Control menu contains options for manipulating windows. Double-clicking the icon closes the active window.	

Table 1.2 ▶ **Common Window Elements (continued)**

Tool	Description
Minimize button	The first button ▬ near the right end of the title bar that contains a horizontal line. Clicking this button reduces the window to a taskbar button.
Maximize button	The second button ☐ near the right end of the title bar that contains a box. Clicking this button enlarges the window to fill the entire screen.
Restore Down button	The second button ▤ near the right end of the title bar that replaces the Maximize button when the window is maximized. Clicking this button returns the window to its previous size.
Close button	The button ✕ at the far right end of the title bar. This button closes the application and the window.
Window borders	The edges, or borders, of the window that you can drag to resize a window.
Window corners	The corners of a window that you can drag to enlarge or shrink both the height and width of a window at the same time.
Menu bar	The area below the title bar that displays menu names, such as File, Edit, View, and Help.
Workspace	The area in the window that displays the information with which you are working.
Scroll bars	Horizontal and vertical bars along the bottom and right sides of a window that allow you to move to and view the hidden portion of your workspace when it doesn't all fit in the window.

Moving and Sizing Windows

To move a window to a new location, point to the title bar, click and hold the left mouse button, move the mouse to drag the window, and release the button when the window is at the desired location. Some computers are set to show an outline of the window while it is being dragged. When the mouse button is released, the contents of the window appear in place of the outline.

When you point to the edge of a window, the pointer changes shape to indicate the direction in which the window edge can move. A pointer on the left or right edge of a window becomes a horizontal double-headed arrow ↔; moving the pointer to the top or bottom edge of the window changes the pointer to a vertical double-headed arrow ↕. By moving the pointer to one of these locations, you can drag that window edge to change the size of the window. For example, dragging the left edge of the window to the right makes a narrower window; dragging the bottom edge down makes a longer window.

If you point to one of the four corners of the window, the pointer becomes a diagonal double-headed arrow (⬉ or ⬈). Dragging a corner of the window stretches or shrinks two sides simultaneously. You can move a window by clicking the control menu icon ▣ and selecting the Move command. A four-way arrow appears, and you then can move the window.

HANDS on

Practicing Moving and Sizing a Window

In this activity, you will practice moving and resizing a window.

1. **Double-click the My Computer icon**. If the window is maximized, click the **Restore Down button** 🗗 on the title bar.

2. Point to the title bar, press and hold the left mouse button, and then drag the My Computer window down to the lower-right corner of the screen, as shown in Figure 1.6. Release the mouse button to set the position of the My Computer window.

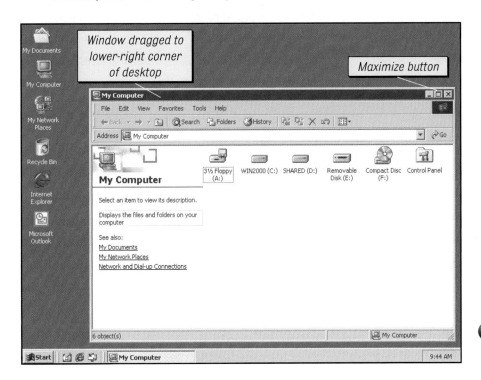

Window dragged to lower-right corner of desktop

Maximize button

Figure 1.6
Moved window

Windows BASICS

Moving and Sizing Windows
To move a window:

1. Point to the title bar.

2. Drag the window to the desired location.

To size a window, do one of the following:

- Click the Maximize button, the Minimize button, or the Restore Down button.

- Drag the border or corner of the frame to the desired size.

3. Click the **Maximize button** 🗖 on the Title bar.

The selected window enlarges to cover the full screen. The Maximize button 🗖 changes to a Restore Down button 🗗.

4. Click the **Minimize button** 🗕 on the Title bar.

The My Computer window closes and its button on the taskbar appears raised, as shown in Figure 1.7.

NORTON
ONLINE

Visit **www.glencoe.com/norton/online/** for more information on Windows.

Figure 1.7
My Computer taskbar button

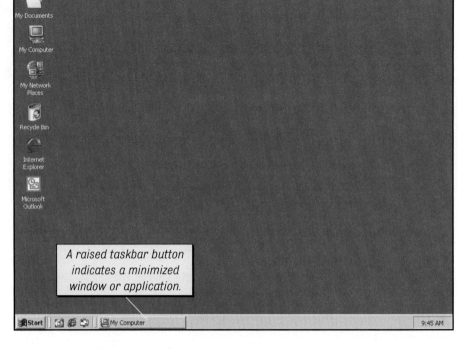

A raised taskbar button indicates a minimized window or application.

5. Click the **My Computer taskbar button**.

The window reappears on the desktop.

6. Click the **Restore Down button** 🗗 on the My Computer window.

The window reduces to its original size before it was maximized to full-screen size.

7. Point to the top border of the My Computer window until the pointer changes to a vertical, double-headed arrow ↕.

8. Drag the top border outline up to near the top of the screen and release the mouse.

The window expands vertically.

9. Point to the left border of the window until the pointer changes to a horizontal, double-headed arrow ↔.

10. Drag the left border near to the left edge of the screen so that the window expands horizontally to nearly fill the desktop.

HINTS & TIPS

When you size a window, drag the corner to maintain the relative dimensions (height and width) of the window. If you drag the top or sides, you will be stretching or shrinking only one dimension at a time.

Arranging Icons

In an earlier activity, you learned how to use the mouse to drag an icon to a new location. You also can display icons in neat rows, using the Arrange Icons command on the **shortcut menu** that appears when you right-click the desktop or a window. Within most windows, you can change the size of the icons as well. Windows 2000 allows you to view icons in two different sizes. **Large icons** are easy to distinguish, but they take up more room. **Small icons** are about a quarter of the size of large ones.

HANDS on

Changing the Size of a Window's Icons

In this activity, you will modify the size of icons displayed in an open window.

1. In the My Computer window, double-click **Control Panel** and size the window so that it occupies one-fourth of the screen.

2. Right-click an empty area in the Control Panel window, point to **View**, and click **Large Icons** on the shortcut menu.

The icons are displayed in the large display size.

3. Right-click an empty area in the Control Panel window, point to **Arrange Icons**, and then click **by Name** on the shortcut menu.

The icons are arranged to conform to the shape of the window. Notice that they also are arranged alphabetically by name.

4. Right-click an empty area in the Control Panel window, point to **View**, and click **Small Icons**.

The icons appear in a smaller display size.

5. Right-click an empty area in the Control Panel window, point to **View**, and click **Large Icons**.

Changing the Size of an Icon

1. In an open window, right-click an empty area.

2. Point to View and click Large Icons or Small Icons.

Using Scroll Bars

A **scroll bar** appears along the right and/or bottom side of a window when there is not enough room to display all the contents of the window. If the hidden information is above or below what is viewed in the window, you will see a **vertical scroll bar;** if the information is to the left or right, you will see a **horizontal scroll bar.** Both types of scroll bars are illustrated in Figure 1.8 on the next page.

Within the scroll bar is the **scroll box,** which indicates the relative position of the screen information within its window. If the scroll box is at the top or left of the scroll bar, you are viewing the top or left part of the information. If the scroll box is at the bottom or right of the scroll bar, you are viewing the bottom or right of the information. Clicking the scroll bar shifts the display to view another screen of information. Clicking below or after the scroll box displays the next screen of information. Clicking above or before the scroll box displays the previous screen. You also can drag-and-drop the scroll box to move quickly to the desired position within a document or list of information. **Scroll arrows** at either end of the scroll bar allow slow window navigation. Clicking a scroll arrow moves one line up or down on a vertical list or right or left on a horizontal scroll bar. Pressing and holding a scroll arrow permits line-by-line scrolling in the direction the arrow points.

Figure 1.8
Scroll bars, arrows, and boxes

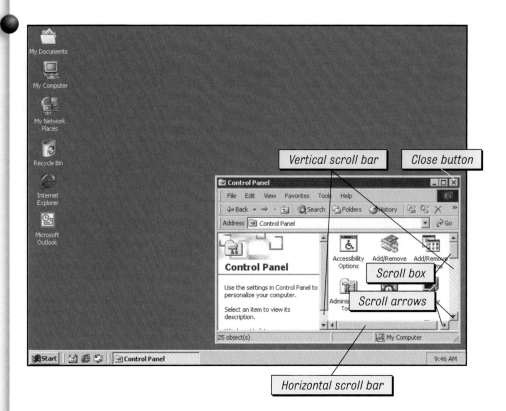

Vertical scroll bar

Close button

Scroll box

Scroll arrows

Horizontal scroll bar

HANDS on

Scrolling a Window

In this activity, you will practice using scroll bars to scroll the contents of a window.

Scrolling a Window

- Click the scroll bar to view hidden information.

- Click below or after the scroll box to view more information.

- Click above or before the scroll box to view the previous screen of information.

- Click a scroll arrow to move one line up or down vertically or right or left horizontally.

1. **Verify that the Control Panel window is still open and sized as shown in Figure 1.8. Point to the vertical scroll bar—anywhere below its scroll box—and click.**

The column of icons appears to scroll upward as the scroll box moves downward.

2. **If the scroll box is not already at the bottom of the vertical scroll bar, point to the vertical scroll bar below the scroll box and click as many times as is necessary to move the scroll box to the bottom of the scroll bar.**

As you click the scroll bar below the scroll box, the column of icons continues to scroll until the last icon is visible at the bottom of the window.

3. **Point to the scroll arrow at the top of the vertical scroll bar. Press and hold the left mouse button until the scroll box moves to the top of the vertical scroll bar.**

4. **Right-click an empty area of the window, point to View, and click List. The icons change to a smaller size in multiple columns.**

5. Click to the right of the scroll box in the horizontal scroll bar.

The contents of the window scroll to the left as the scroll box moves to the right on the horizontal scroll bar.

6. Point to the scroll arrow to the left of the horizontal scroll bar, and then press and hold the left mouse button until the scroll box moves to the left end of the horizontal scroll bar.

The contents of the window scroll to the right as the box moves to the left.

7. Click the **Close button** ☒ in the Control Panel window.

RUNNING PROGRAMS

The Windows taskbar is located at the bottom of the computer screen (by default). It displays the names of the programs that currently are running. The taskbar also contains the Start button ![Start]. Although you can start programs by double-clicking their icons in the My Computer window, the Start button provides a convenient way to start programs and open documents, search for files, change system settings, access the Help feature, and shut down the computer.

Before you can run or **launch** a program, it must be installed. Windows 2000 includes a set of programs—called **accessories**—that lets you perform simple tasks. WordPad—a word processing program—and Notepad—a text editing program—are two of these accessories.

In Windows 2000 you can have many programs running at once, but only one window can be active (that is, in control) at a time. The **active window** is in front of any inactive windows and has a taskbar button that looks sunken or pressed in. In addition, the title bar of an active window is highlighted. If you want to switch between programs that are running in Windows, you need to activate the window for the program you want to use. The quickest way to switch between programs is to click the appropriate taskbar button.

> **WARNING** *It's easy to keep opening applications on top of one another without closing them. When you finish using an application, however, get into the habit of closing it. Unnecessarily running multiple applications will clutter your desktop and deplete system memory—which can result in slower processing times.*

HINTS & TIPS

Before running a program from the Start menu, verify whether the program is open but minimized on the taskbar. Running the program a second time may cause a second copy to be opened.

HANDS on

Starting and Closing a Program

In this activity, you will start two Windows 2000 accessory programs, switch between them, and close them.

1. Click the **Start button**  on the Windows taskbar.

The Start menu appears.

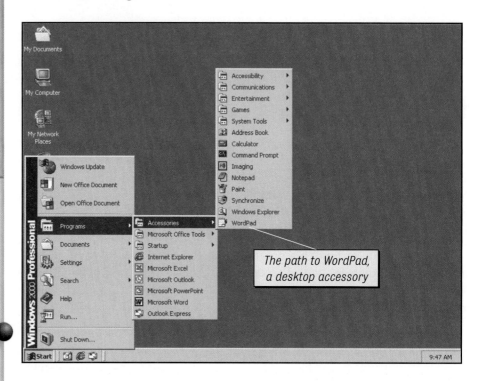

Windows BASICS

Launching, Switching Between, and Closing Programs

To launch a program:

1. Click the Start button.

2. Point to Programs.

3. Point to submenus until you can click the desired program.

To switch between programs:

Click the program's taskbar button.

To close a program:

Click the Close button.

Figure 1.9
Accessories menu

2. **Point to Programs. If necessary, click the double arrow at the bottom of the menu to list all the items on the Programs menu.**

The Programs submenu appears. This menu contains the Windows 2000 accessories and applications available on your computer.

3. **Point to Accessories and the Accessories submenu appears, as shown in Figure 1.9.**

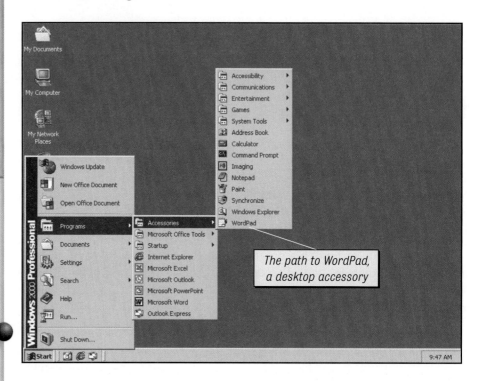

The path to WordPad, a desktop accessory

4. **Click WordPad.**

The WordPad program is loaded into memory, its window opens, and a WordPad button appears on the taskbar.

5. **If the WordPad window doesn't cover the entire screen, click the Maximize button ▢ on the title bar.**

Your screen should look similar to Figure 1.10. Now WordPad is ready for you to type your text in the window's workspace. If you typed text, you would save the text as a **document,** a data file that the application lets you create and modify.

6. **Click the Start button ⊞Start, point to Programs, point to Accessories, and click Notepad.**

The Notepad program starts. Its window opens, covering the WordPad window. You now have two programs running: WordPad and Notepad.

7. **If the Notepad window covers the entire screen, click the Restore Down button ⧉.**

8. **Click the WordPad taskbar button.**

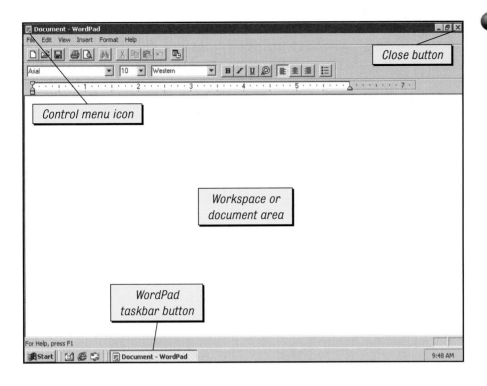

Figure 1.10
Blank WordPad window

The WordPad window once more fills the screen and becomes the active window, hiding the Notepad window.

9. Click the Notepad taskbar button.

Notepad is again in the foreground. Notice that part of the WordPad window remains visible, but the Notepad window is active.

10. Click outside the Notepad window on the WordPad window.

The WordPad window once again fills the screen, hiding the Notepad window.

11. Click the Close button ☒ in the WordPad window. If a box appears asking if you want to save any changes you have made to the document, click No.

The WordPad window closes, and the Notepad window reappears.

12. Click the Control menu icon ▣ in the Notepad window and click Close.

The Notepad window closes, and you return to the desktop.

Another Way

- You also may switch between programs by holding down [Alt] and pressing [Tab]. Continue pressing [Tab] until the desired program name appears, and then release both keys.

- You may close a program by clicking Exit or Quit on a File menu.

CHOOSING PROGRAM OPTIONS FROM THE MENU BAR

In Windows, many program features, options, and commands are hidden within a menu bar. You already have used two kinds of menus—those within the Start menu and shortcut menus. On a menu bar, menu options appear when you open the menu. When a menu is open, you can view and click the menu option you want. Menu options followed by three dots, called **ellipsis marks** (…), open a dialog box that contains additional choices. Clicking anywhere outside the menu closes it.

Using the Menu Bar

In this activity, you will practice choosing from a menu bar.

1. Launch WordPad. Maximize the window, if necessary.

The WordPad window opens. The menu bar appears directly below the window's title bar.

2. Click View on the menu bar.

The View menu appears, as shown in Figure 1.11.

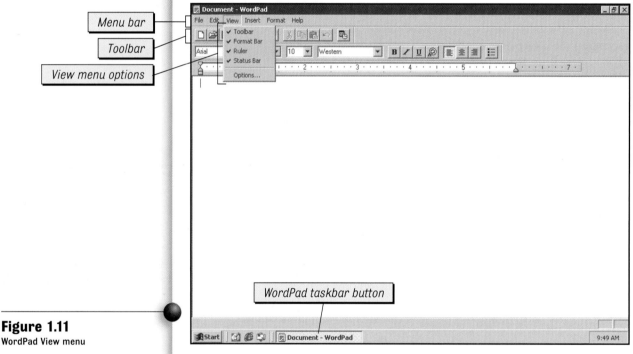

Figure 1.11
WordPad View menu

3. Slowly move the mouse pointer down the View menu.

Notice that each menu option is highlighted as the pointer passes over it. If you wanted to select an option, you would click when the desired option is highlighted.

4. Click outside the View menu to close it.

USING DIALOG BOXES

A good portion of your interaction with Windows-based programs will involve the use of **dialog boxes.** A dialog box is a special window that prompts the user for information to perform a command. You cannot proceed until you have responded to the questions in the dialog box, even if it is only to accept the suggested answers. The title bar shows the name of the dialog box. The following types of controls may appear in dialog boxes.

◆ **Tabs,** similar to the tabs on paper file folders, represent different sections or categories of options you may choose. To select a category, click the tab and that portion of the dialog box will appear in front of the other tab categories.

◆ **Option buttons** are small circles that indicate a list of mutually exclusive options. In a set of option buttons, you can choose only one at a time. Clicking a different button changes your choice. The chosen option button contains a black dot.

◆ **Check boxes** are small boxes that allow you to switch an option off or on. A check mark in the box means the option is on; an empty box indicates the option is off. Clicking an empty box changes the response in a check box.

◆ **Command buttons** are small labeled rectangles. You click a command button to choose an action. A button with a heavy border around it is the default button. Pressing Enter⏎ does the same thing as clicking the default button. Some command buttons open dialog boxes that offer additional choices or expand the current dialog box with advanced options.

◆ **Triangle buttons** and **drop-down lists** let you choose from a predetermined set of options. You click the triangle button, point to the desired option in the list that appears, and click.

◆ **Text boxes** are rectangles in which you can type information.

◆ **Spinner buttons** may appear in text boxes that contain numbers. Spinner buttons allow you to change numbers by clicking an up arrow or a down arrow. Clicking the up arrow increases the displayed number; clicking the down arrow decreases the displayed number.

◆ A **slider control** is a horizontal or vertical line with progressive values and an indicator. Dragging the indicator increases or decreases the value.

Another Way

To expand a menu, double-click the menu name.

GETTING STARTED

HINTS & TIPS

To avoid distractions by other windows or by the desktop, you may want to maximize the window of the application in which you're working.

HANDS on

Examining Controls in a Dialog Box

In this activity, you will change the default options in WordPad.

1. With WordPad still open, click the **View menu**, and then click **Options**.

The Options dialog box appears on the WordPad window.

2. Click the **Options tab**, as shown in Figure 1.12.

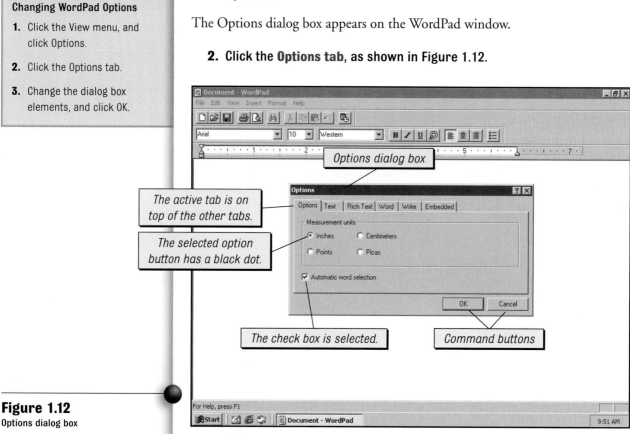

Figure 1.12
Options dialog box

3. In the *Measurement units* area of the Options dialog box, click the **Centimeters option button** (or another option if Centimeters is already selected).

Notice that the black dot moves from one option to another. Remember that you can select only one option button at a time.

4. Point to the **Automatic word selection check box** and click to clear the Automatic word selection check box.

The check mark in the box disappears, indicating that you have turned off the option.

5. Click the **Cancel command button** to cancel the changes and close the Options dialog box.

6. Click **File**, and then click **Page Setup**.

The Page Setup dialog box appears.

7. Click the **Size triangle button**.

A drop-down list appears showing available paper sizes, as shown in Figure 1.13.

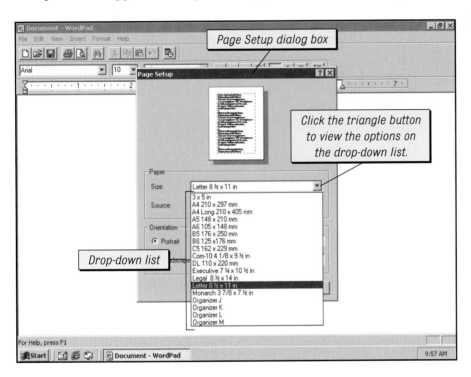

Figure 1.13
Page Setup dialog box

8. Click a blank area on the window to close the drop-down list.

9. Click **Cancel** to close the Page Setup dialog box.

10. Click **File**, and then click **Print**.

The Print dialog box appears.

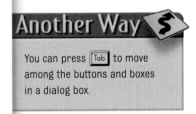

You can press Tab to move among the buttons and boxes in a dialog box.

11. In the *Page Range* area of the Print dialog box, click the **Pages option button** and type 1 in the text box.

This tells WordPad to print only the first page of the current document.

12. In the Number of copies box, click the **Number of copies up arrow** until it changes to 5.

This tells WordPad to print five copies of the first page.

13. Click **Cancel** to cancel your changes and close the Print dialog box. Then, click **File** and click **Exit**.

WordPad is closed, and the desktop reappears.

PRINTING YOUR WORK

Before you print from a Windows-based program, always make sure that Windows 2000 and the application program you are running are set to print to the same printer. If your computer is currently connected to just one printer, someone probably already has set up that printer as the default printer. The term **default** applies to a printer (or folder or disk drive, for that matter) that your system automatically uses. Setting a default printer saves time, because you don't have to specify the printer each time you want to print something. At any time, you can use a different printer and change the default printer. If you are connected to more than one printer, occasionally you may need to switch between them.

HANDS on

Selecting a Default Printer

To select a printer, you can use the Control Panel or the Start button [Start] to go directly to the Printers window. In this activity, you will learn how to set a default printer using the Printers window.

1. Click the **Start button** [Start], point to **Settings**, and click **Printers**.

The Printers window opens, as shown in Figure 1.14. The icons in this window represent the printers that have been installed on your computer or that you can access over a network. One of the printers will have a check mark next to its icon—this is the default printer.

2. Right-click the default printer—the printer with the check mark next to the icon.

The Set as Default Printer option has a check mark beside it. If you wanted to set another printer as the default printer, you would click this option.

3. Click anywhere outside the menu to close the shortcut menu.

4. Click the **Close button** [X] in the Printers window.

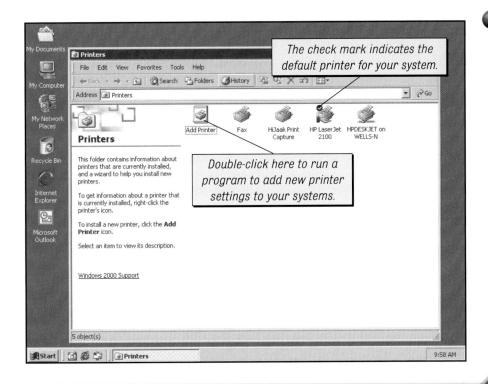

Figure 1.14
Printers window

The check mark indicates the default printer for your system.

Double-click here to run a program to add new printer settings to your systems.

GETTING HELP

Now that you know how to manipulate windows and dialog boxes, you are ready to use the powerful Windows 2000 **online Help** system. If you are not sure how to do something, you can look it up using Help, one of the Start menu choices. This command displays the Windows 2000 Help window, as shown in Figure 1.15.

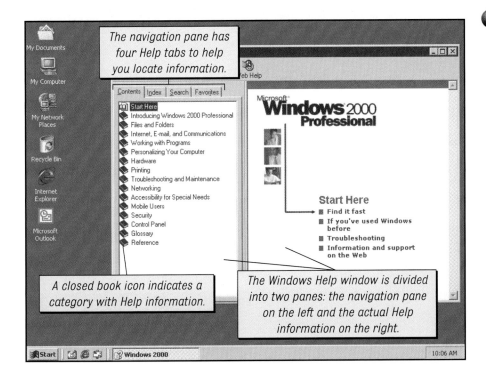

Figure 1.15
Windows 2000 Help window

The navigation pane has four Help tabs to help you locate information.

A closed book icon indicates a category with Help information.

The Windows Help window is divided into two panes: the navigation pane on the left and the actual Help information on the right.

GETTING STARTED

The Help window is divided into two **panes.** A pane is a portion of a window. You use the navigation pane of the Help window to locate the topic on which you want help. The right pane of the Help window displays the actual information.

The navigation pane of the Windows Help window has four tabs: Contents, Index, Search, and Favorites. These tabs represent pages. The front tab is the page that is currently open, and the contents are displayed below it. In this case, the **Contents** tab is open, and you see Help topics in the window. If you click one of the topics, you either display help on that subject or a list of books contained within that book. You can click the desired book to display the contents. Sometimes, more topics are available than what fits on the screen. The vertical scroll bar lets you find these topics.

Clicking the **Index** tab allows you to see an alphabetical listing of Help topics. You can navigate quickly to the desired topic by typing it in the text box at the top of the Index window. When you type a letter, the display scrolls to the first topic beginning with that letter. As you continue typing, you will get closer to the topic for which you are searching. You also can use the scroll bar to find the desired topic. When you've highlighted the topic you want, click the Display button to show the information on that subject. The **Search** tab lets you search for words in the description of the Help information, rather than searching by topic. The **Favorites** tab lets you save particularly useful Help topics for later review.

Figure 1.16 shows the Windows 2000 Help window that appears when you click the *Working with Program* category and then select the *Start a program* topic. You can use the vertical scroll bar to scan the Help text. You may see underlined words and phrases in the Help text; your pointer changes shape when you are pointing to underlined text. Some of these terms are **glossary terms** or keywords. Clicking a glossary term displays (or hides) a definition of the word or phrase. Clicking other underlined words or phrases may jump to related Help windows or dialog boxes.

Figure 1.16
Glossary term

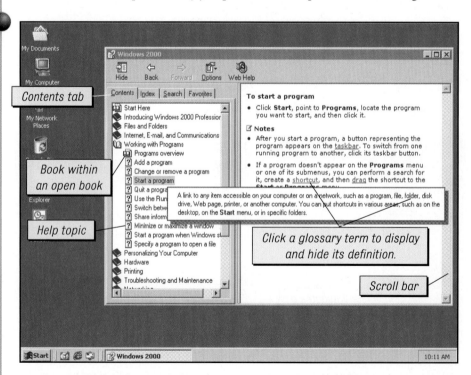

Windows 2000 Help also provides the Web Help button ![Web Help] that connects you directly to a Microsoft Web page. There you can search for additional online information by asking specific questions.

HANDS on

Using Windows Help

In this activity, you will practice using the Windows 2000 Help system to discover how to perform various tasks.

1. Click the **Start button**  and click **Help**.

The Help files load and the Windows 2000 Help window opens, as shown in Figure 1.15 on page 27.

2. If necessary, click the **Contents tab** to display the list of topics.

3. Click the **closed book icon** in front of the Working with Programs category.

The closed book icon changes to an open book icon, and the category expands to show a subcategory (indicated by another book icon) and numerous individual Help topics (indicated by a question mark).

4. Click the **Start a program topic**.

The Help topic information appears in the right pane of the Help window, as shown in Figure 1.16 on page 28.

5. In the Help information, click **shortcut** to display its definition.

6. Click anywhere on the screen to hide the definition.

7. Click the **Index tab**.

The Windows Help set of index topics appears.

8. In the *Type in the keyword to find* box, type printing.

As you type each letter, the highlight within the list of Help topics jumps to the next word that contains the letter you just typed. In this instance, Help jumps to *printing* and displays the related printing subtopics.

9. Click the **common tasks subtopic**, and then click the **Display button**.

A Help window appears on the right pane with information about the common tasks of printing files and documents.

10. Click the **Search tab**.

The Help Search window appears.

11. In the *Type in the keyword to find* box , type cascade and click the **List Topics button**.

The results of the search are listed in the *Select Topic to display* box.

Windows **BASICS**

Using Help
1. Click Start.
2. Click Help.
3. Click the tab you want to use.
4. Explore for help.

HINTS & TIPS

You can get help on items within a dialog box by right-clicking the item and selecting *What's this?*

12. Double-click the **Arrange all open windows topic**.

The Help information appears in the right pane, as shown in Figure 1.17.

Figure 1.17
Windows Help Search tab

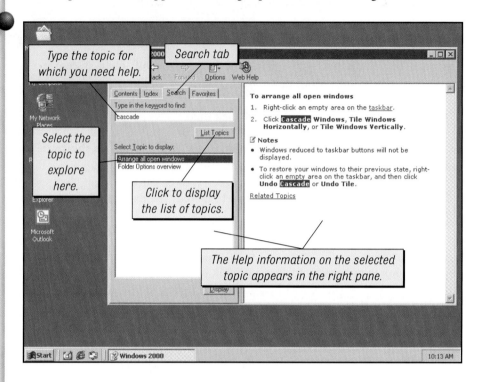

13. Click the **Close button** ☒ in the Help window.

USING WINDOWS EXPLORER

In Windows, the Programs menu is your main tool for launching programs. However, all of those programs are stored on your hard drive as files or programs. The documents that you create using applications also are stored as files or documents. Windows Explorer is the program you use to organize all of the files stored on your hard drive and disks.

One of the primary goals of file maintenance is to keep your file structure organized so you can find and open files easily when you need them. You can organize files by setting up **folders**—organizational structures that can contain files and subfolders. Many of the folders on your computer system are created during the installation of software. You can use Windows Explorer to create your own folders.

The Explorer window consists of two panes—the Folders pane and the Contents pane. The Folders pane displays the organization of the drives, folders, and subfolders available on your computer. A plus sign (+) in a box to the left of a folder or **drive icon** indicates that the folder or drive contains one or more subfolders. When you click a drive icon or folder name in the Folders pane (the left pane), the folders (or subfolders) and files contained in that drive or folder appear in the Contents pane (the right pane).

> **NOTE** *You must have a blank, formatted floppy or removable disk to complete the activities in this section.*

Early DOS users made fun of Mac users with their friendly-looking icons, *WYSIWYG* windows, and mouse clicks. These same users now have a very similar GUI in Windows 2000.

HANDS on

Creating a Subfolder

In this activity, you will create a new folder on a floppy or removable disk.

1. **Click the Start button** ⬛Start, **point to Programs, point to Accessories, and click Windows Explorer.**

The Explorer window opens and displays the name of the default location (such as My Documents) in the title bar.

2. **If the window is not maximized already, click Maximize** 🔲.

3. **If you want your Explorer window to match the activities and figures in this tutorial (and if you have permission to change the settings on the computer you are using), click Folder Options on the Tools menu.**

   a. **In the Folder Options dialog box, click the General tab, if it is not on top. If necessary, click the option buttons to select these settings:**

      In the *Active Desktop* area, select Use Windows classic desktop.

      In the *Web View* area, select Enable Web content in folders.

      In the *Browse Folders* area, select Open each folder in the same window.

      In the *Click items as follows* area, select Double-click to open an item (single-click to select).

   b. **In the Folder Options dialog box, click the View tab. Click to select *only* the following options on the View tab (make sure no other options are selected on the View tab):**

      Do not show hidden files and folders

      Hide file extensions for known file types

      Hide protected operating system files (Recommended)

      Show and manage the pair as a single file

      Show My Documents on the Desktop

      Show pop-up description for folder and desktop items

4. **Click OK to close the Folder Options dialog box.**

5. **In the Explorer window, click List on the View menu, if it is not already selected.**

6. **If a plus sign (+) appears beside the My Computer icon in the Folders pane of the Explorer window, click the plus sign to expand the sublevels.**

Your screen looks similar to Figure 1.18. Your list of files will be different.

Windows BASICS

Creating Folders and Subfolders

1. Click the drive and/or parent folder.

2. Click File, point to New, and click Folder.

3. Type the name of the new folder and press ⌷Enter⏎⌷.

Figure 1.18
Windows Explorer

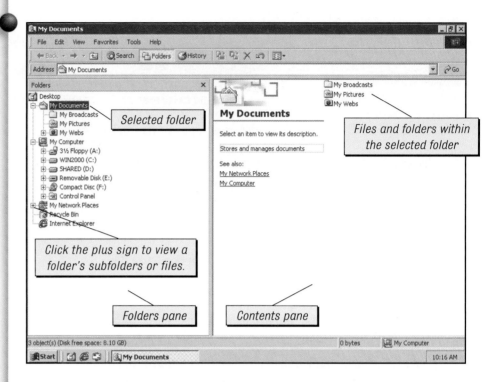

7. Insert a blank floppy or removable disk into the appropriate drive.

8. In the Folders pane, find and click the drive icon that represents the drive you are using (either the floppy drive or the removable disk drive).

The contents of the selected drive appear in the Contents pane.

9. Click **File**, point to **New**, and click **Folder**.

A new folder with the name *New Folder* appears in the Contents pane.

10. Type Temporary to replace *New Folder*, and then press Enter⏎.

Now you will create a folder within the *Temporary* folder.

11. In the Folders pane, click the **plus sign** next to the drive icon for your disk.

The subfolders and files (if any) contained on the disk appear in the Folders pane, including the folder you just created.

12. Click the *Temporary* subfolder in the Folders pane.

Notice that the subfolder icon changes to an open folder to indicate that you can view the contents of the folder. However, as shown in the Contents pane, the folder is currently empty.

13. Click **File**, point to **New**, and click **Folder**.

14. Type Second Folder to replace the *New Folder* name, and then press Enter⏎. Double-click the *Temporary* subfolder in the Folders pane to view its contents.

The new folder (*Second Folder*) is displayed in the Contents pane, as shown in Figure 1.19.

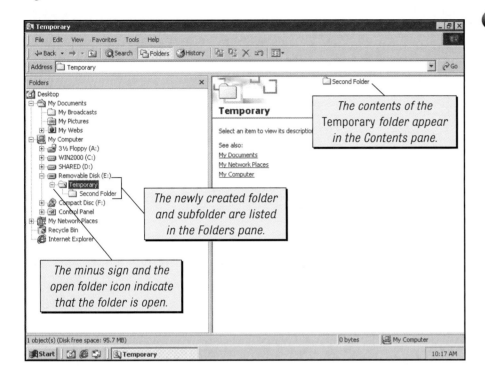

Figure 1.19
New folder and subfolder
in Windows Explorer

GETTING STARTED

HANDS on

Moving and Copying Folders and Files

The tasks most frequently performed with Windows Explorer are copying and moving files or folders within a folder structure or from one disk or drive to another. You can complete these actions simply by dragging file and folder icons from one place to another in the Explorer window. Dragging a file or folder to a different place on the <u>same</u> disk or drive physically moves the file. Dragging a file or folder to a <u>different</u> disk or drive copies the file. In this activity, you will move a folder from one location on a disk to a new location.

1. Verify that your disk is still in its drive, and the *Temporary* Folder is selected in the Folders pane of the Explorer window.

2. Click the **Second Folder icon** in the Contents pane.

3. Drag the **Second Folder icon** in the Contents pane to the drive icon you are using in the Folders pane. When the drive icon for the drive you are using is highlighted, release the mouse button.

An information box may appear briefly while you are moving the folder. You can see by looking in the Contents pane that the *Temporary* folder is now empty. The folder named *Second Folder* now appears in the Folders pane, on the same level as the *Temporary* folder, as shown in Figure 1.20.

Windows **BASICS**

Moving a Folder or File

1. Open Windows Explorer.

2. In the Contents pane, click to select the file or folder that you want to move.

3. Scroll the Folders pane until you can see the destination folder.

4. To move, drag the selected item to its new destination.

Windows BASICS

Copying a Folder or File

1. Open Windows Explorer.

2. In the Contents pane, select the folder or file that you want to copy.

3. Press and hold `Ctrl` and drag the selected item to its destination.

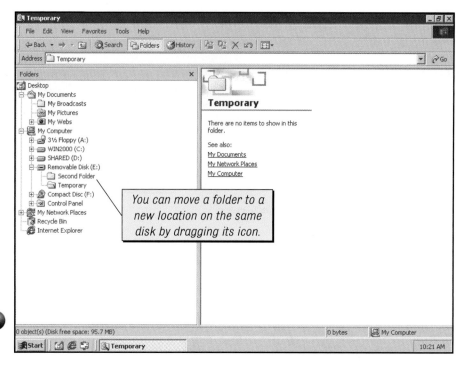

> You can move a folder to a new location on the same disk by dragging its icon.

Figure 1.20
New location for a folder

Windows BASICS

Renaming and Deleting Folders and Files

To rename a folder or file:

1. In Windows Explorer, select the file or folder name to rename.

2. Click the file or folder name again.

3. Type a new name for the file or folder and press `Enter↵`.

To delete a folder or file:

1. In Windows Explorer, select the file or folder to delete.

2. Press `Delete`.

3. Click Yes to confirm.

HANDS on

Renaming and Deleting Folders and Files

You can rename a file or folder at any time. Be careful, however, not to rename files or folders that you did not create—maintaining their original name may be essential to the Windows 2000 operating system. When you delete files from the hard disk drive, they are temporarily stored in the Recycle Bin. You can restore the deleted file by double-clicking the Recycle Bin desktop icon. In this activity, you will rename a folder and delete folders that you no longer need.

1. **With your disk still in its drive, click the Second Folder icon in the Folders pane.**

2. **Click within the folder name *Second Folder,* not on the icon itself.**

A frame surrounds the selected folder name, and a text pointer appears within the frame, as shown in Figure 1.21.

3. **Type Introduction Exercise and press `Enter↵`.**

The words you type replace the highlighted name, and the folder has the new name.

4. **Click the *Temporary* folder on your disk and press `Delete`.**

The Confirm Folder Delete dialog box asks you to confirm that you want to delete the folder.

5. **Click Yes or press `Enter↵` to remove the folder from your disk.**

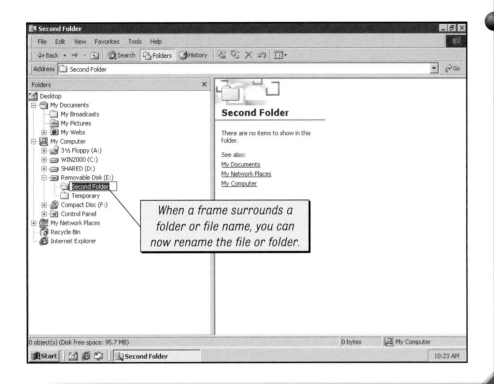

Figure 1.21
Rename a folder or file

File Attributes

An **attribute** is a property that controls the use of a folder or file. Windows 2000 files and folders can have up to four attributes: read-only, hidden, archive, and system. Hidden and system attributes are primarily used to protect those folders and files the operating system needs. The archive attribute identifies files and folders that have not been copied onto a backup storage medium. The read-only attribute lets you view files but does not allow you to change or delete the files.

Setting File Attributes

In this activity, you will add the read-only attribute to a folder and then remove the attribute.

NOTE *You must have a blank, formatted floppy or removable disk to complete this activity.*

1. **Verify that your disk is still in its drive and that the Explorer window is open.**

2. **In the Contents pane, right-click the *Introduction Exercise* folder on your disk.**

3. **On the shortcut menu that appears, click Properties.**

The Introduction Exercise Properties dialog box appears with the General tab on top.

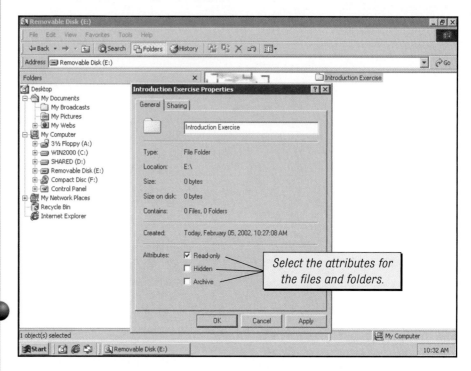

Windows BASICS

Setting File Attributes

1. In Windows Explorer, select the file(s) or folder(s) that have attributes you want to change.

2. In the Folders pane, right-click the selected file or folder. On the shortcut menu, click Properties.

3. In the Attributes area of the Properties dialog box for the selected folder/file, click to clear and/or select the check boxes for the desired attributes. Click Apply.

4. Close the Properties dialog box and the Explorer window.

Figure 1.22
General tab of the Properties dialog box

---

4. In the *Attributes* area of the Introduction Exercise Properties dialog box, click the **Read-only box** so the check mark appears, as shown in Figure 1.22. Then, click **Apply** and click **OK**.

The folder's attribute is now set to read-only.

5. In the Explorer window, right-click the *Introduction Exercise* folder and click **Properties**.

6. In the *Attributes* area of the Introduction Exercise Properties dialog box, click to clear the **Read-Only check box**. Then, click **Apply** and click **OK**.

You now have removed the read-only attribute from the *Introduction Exercise* folder.

7. Delete the *Introduction Exercise* folder.

8. Close the Explorer window. Remove your disk from its drive.

SHUTTING DOWN YOUR COMPUTER

When you are finished working with the computer, you should develop the habit of closing all open applications and using the proper procedure to log off or to shut down Windows 2000. In fact, turning off the computer while applications are running is dangerous. Some of the work you have been doing may not have been saved onto a disk and will be irretrievably lost. In addition, you will not have given the operating system the opportunity to erase information it may have stored temporarily on disk.

WARNING *Check with your instructor or computer lab assistant for the shut down procedures in your lab or school environment.*

HANDS on

Shutting Down

In this activity, you will shut down the computer you are using, following the procedures for your lab or school environment.

NOTE *If you plan to proceed directly to the* On the Web *activity, do not complete this activity.*

1. **Follow the shut down procedures for your lab or school environment or continue with step 2.**

2. **Click the Start button ⊞ Start.**

3. **Click Shut Down.**

The entire screen darkens a bit, and the Shut Down Windows dialog box appears.

4. **Click the Shut down option in the drop-down list (if it isn't already selected) and click OK.**

After a few moments, a message may appear, indicating that you may turn off your computer.

5. **Turn off your computer and monitor, if necessary.**

Windows **BASICS**
Shutting Down the Computer
1. Click Start.
2. Click Shut Down.
3. In the Shut Down Windows dialog box, click Shut down and click OK.
4. If a message appears, turn off your computer and monitor.

Self Check ☑

Test your knowledge by answering the following questions. See Appendix B to check your answers.

1. Dragging a file from one folder to another folder on the same drive __moves__ the file.

2. The process of loading the operating system is called __booting__.

3. The __file__ attribute is used to protect files on a disk.

4. A(n) __dialog__ box appears when you click a menu item followed by ellipses.

5. The __folder__ pane of the Windows Explorer window displays the organization of the drives, folders, and subfolders available on your computer.

GETTING ONLINE HELP

Every day, computer users around the world use the Internet for work, play, and research. The **Internet** is a worldwide network of computers that connects each Internet user's computer to all other computers in the network. Vast quantities of infinitely varied information—from simple text in the form of an e-mail message to extremely complex software—can pass through these connections. The most popular tool used to access the Internet is the **World Wide Web** (**WWW** or the **Web**). A document published on the Web is referred to as a **Web page** and is stored in a specific place on the Web called a **Web site**.

Using your Web **browser**—a software tool used to navigate the Web—you can jump instantly from Windows 2000 Help to the Microsoft Corporation Web site. In this activity, you will explore Microsoft's Web site for assistance.

1. Click the **Start button** 🏁 Start and click **Help**.

After a few moments, Windows Help opens.

2. Click the **Web Help button** 🔳 on the Help toolbar.

Read the Help information that appears in the right pane of the Help window.

3. Connect to the Internet using your Internet Service Provider (ISP). If necessary, type your user name and password. If you are not sure how to connect to the Internet, or you do not know your user name and password, ask your instructor for assistance.

4. In the Windows 2000 Help window, click the **Windows 2000 home page link**. Click the **Maximize button** 🔲, if necessary.

Your Web browser connects you to the Microsoft Windows 2000 Web site, and the Windows 2000 home page appears, as shown in Figure 1.23.

5. In the Search This Site box, type **printing**, and then click **Go**.

> **WARNING** *You may see Security Alert and/or Security Warning windows informing you that you are about to send information over the Internet. If you do not trust the organization to which you are connected, click No. Otherwise, click Yes and continue.*

6. Read the page, noting the various hyperlinks related to printers.

Figure 1.23
Windows 2000 home page

Figure 1.24 shows a series of helpful articles that might appear, prompted by your search. As new solutions and problems occur, Microsoft frequently updates this list, so don't be surprised if your list is quite different.

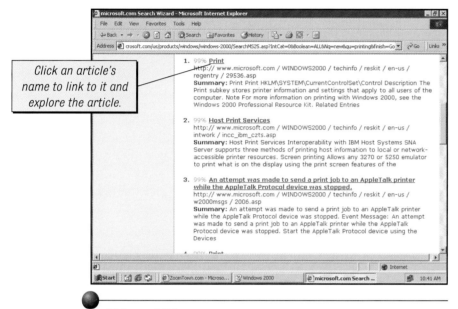

> Click an article's name to link to it and explore the article.

Figure 1.24
Result of a Web search

7. Click and explore an article of interest.

8. When you are finished exploring, click the **Close button** ☒ in your browser window.

9. Click the **Close button** ☒ in the Windows 2000 Help window.

10. Close any open browser windows, and disconnect from the Internet if your instructor tells you to do so. (To quickly close an open window, right-click its taskbar button and click **Close** on the shortcut menu.)

WARNING *You may proceed directly to the exercises for this lesson. If, however, you are finished with your computer session, follow the shut down procedures for your lab or school environment.*

SUMMARY

Every computer needs an operating system. The operating system is a vital component in the computer system that includes the hardware, programs, and you. In this lesson, you learned how to interact with the Windows 2000 operating system so that you can boot up and shut down your computer, run application software, and manage the computer's data filing system. You also learned that you can explore online help from Windows 2000 and from Microsoft.

Now that you have completed this lesson, you should be able to do the following:

- Define the components and function of the Windows 2000 operating system. (page 5)
- Start the Windows 2000 operating system. (page 6)
- Use your mouse to point, click, double-click, right-click, select, drag, and display objects. (page 10)
- Identify common window elements, such as the title bar, the menu bar, drive icons, and buttons. (page 13)
- Move and resize a window. (page 14)
- Change the size of icons using the View menu. (page 16)
- Use the scroll bars. (page 17)
- Launch, activate, and close programs. (page 19)
- Select options from a menu bar. (page 21)
- Identify, select, and enter data into dialog boxes using tabs, option buttons, check boxes, command buttons, triangle buttons, text boxes, spinner buttons, and slider controls. (page 23)
- Set your default printer. (page 26)
- Explore online help on Windows 2000 topics. (page 27)
- Create a folder. (page 30)
- Move or copy a folder or file. (page 33)
- Rename or delete a folder or file. (page 34)
- Change a file's attribute(s). (page 35)
- Shut down your computer. (page 36)
- Get online help for Windows 2000 from Microsoft. (page 38)

CONCEPTS REVIEW

1 TRUE/FALSE

Circle T if the statement is true or F if the statement is false.

T   F   **1.** The Power On Self Test checks the memory, keyboard, display, and disk drives of the computer system.

T   F   **2.** An application window opens when you run a program.

T   F   **3.** A scroll bar appears when there is not enough room to display all the contents of the window.

T   F   **4.** A Windows 2000 taskbar button means that a program is open.

T   F   **5.** Command buttons allow you to choose an action.

T   F   **6.** Check boxes are small boxes used for switching an option off and on.

T   F   **7.** The Active Desktop lets you use your mouse and view your screen just as you would when you run Internet Explorer.

T   F   **8.** When you click a glossary term in Windows Help, its definition appears.

T   F   **9.** You must rename a file before you can change its attributes.

T   F   **10.** The desktop is the background for your computer work.

2 MATCHING

Match each of the terms on the left with the definition on the right.

TERMS

1. clicking
2. dialog box
3. drag-and-drop
4. active window
5. icons
6. default
7. mouse
8. taskbar
9. window
10. folder

DEFINITIONS

a. A container for files and other icons

b. The key to the graphical user interface that lets you choose and manipulate on-screen objects

c. Rectangular object that displays an application program, a document, and other features and that can be sized and positioned anywhere on screen

d. Element that contains the Start button, the clock, and a button for an open application

e. Mouse technique that moves an object on the screen

f. The window you are currently using; the one with the colored title bar

g. Value, option, or item that is assumed if no other is specified

h. Rectangular object that displays one or more options a user can select to carry out a command

i. Mouse technique in which a button is pressed and released once very quickly

j. Graphic pictures or on-screen objects which carry out an operation when selected with the mouse

SUMMARY AND EXERCISES

GETTING STARTED

3 COMPLETION

Fill in the missing word or phrase for each of the following statements.

1. For some elements displayed on screen in the Windows 2000 environment, you can view a shortcut menu by clicking the _____ mouse button.

2. To help you remember and choose them, lists of commands and options appear on _____ .

3. _____ appear as small images on the desktop or in windows.

4. A(n) _____ setting is one that the computer, or an applications program, uses automatically until the user specifies another.

5. To view information that exists below the last visible line at the bottom of a window, you can use the _____ .

6. Click the _____ to enlarge a window as much as possible.

7. To _____ a file or folder, select the file or folder and then type the new name.

8. _____ a file or folder's icon from one location to another to move the file or folder.

9. The _____ attribute prevents a file from being changed.

10. In Windows Help, the _____ tab displays book icons to help you find the information you need.

4 SHORT ANSWER

Write a brief answer to each of the following questions:

1. Describe the difference between the Web style desktop and the classic style desktop.

2. Describe the procedure for logging on to Windows 2000 and for shutting down your computer.

3. Identify common window elements.

4. Explain the difference among these terms: scroll bar, scroll box, and scroll arrow.

5 IDENTIFICATION

Label each of the elements of the Windows 2000 desktop in Figure 1.25.

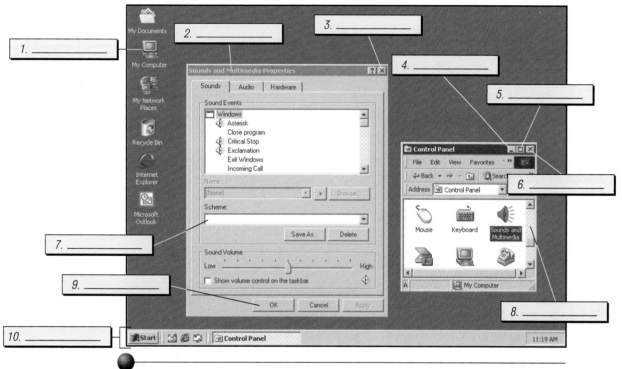

Figure 1.25

SKILLS REVIEW

Complete each of the Skills Review problems in sequential order to review your Windows 2000 skills to boot the computer; master mouse skills; move and resize windows; rearrange objects within windows; scroll windows; launch, close, and switch between programs; change settings with dialog boxes and menus; set a default printer; use Windows 2000 Help features; create, move, rename, and delete folders; change attributes of folders; and shut down your computer.

1 Boot Windows 2000 and Practice Mouse Techniques

1. Turn on your computer and monitor.

2. Enter your user name and password, if necessary.

3. Close the Getting Started with Windows 2000 window, if necessary.

4. On the Windows 2000 desktop, select the **My Computer icon**.

5. Drag the **My Computer icon** to the middle of the desktop.

6. Double-click the **My Computer icon**.

7. Double-click the **Control Panel icon**.

8. Click the **Close button** ☒.

9. Drag the **My Computer icon** back to its original location.

2 Move and Size a Window

1. On the Windows 2000 desktop, double-click the **My Computer icon**.

2. Click the **Maximize button** ▢, if necessary.

3. Click the **Restore Down button** ▣, if necessary.

4. Point to the **My Computer window title bar**. Press and hold the left mouse button and drag the window to the upper-right corner of the desktop.

5. Point to the window's borders and/or corners, press and hold the left mouse button, and drag to change the dimensions of the window. Size the window so that it occupies about half the horizontal desktop area (Figure 1.26).

6. Maximize the window. Then, restore the window.

7. Close the My Computer window.

3 Change View, Resize a Window, and Resize and Rearrange Icons

1. On the Windows 2000 desktop, open the My Computer window.

2. Double-click the **Control Panel icon**.

3. On the View menu, click **Small Icons**.

4. Right-click an empty area of the Control Panel window, point to **Arrange Icons** and click **by Name**.

5. Change the View to Large Icons.

6. Rearrange the icons by Comment.

7. Close the open window.

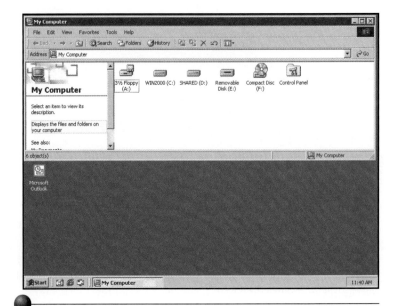

Figure 1.26

4 Use Scroll Bars

1. On the Windows 2000 desktop, open the My Computer window.

2. Double-click the **Control Panel icon**.

3. Resize the Control Panel window so that both vertical and horizontal scroll bars appear.

4. Drag the horizontal scroll box to the right.

5. Click the vertical scroll arrow.

6. Close the My Computer window.

5 Launch, Switch Between, and Close Programs

1. Click the **Start button** ![Start], point to **Programs**, point to **Accessories**, and click **Notepad**.

2. Click the **Maximize button** □.

3. Click the **Start button** ![Start], point to **Programs**, point to **Accessories**, and click **Calculator**.

4. Click the **Notepad button** on the taskbar.

5. Click the **Calculator button** on the taskbar.

6. Close the Calculator window.

7. Click the **Control menu icon** 🖥 in the Notepad window. Then, click **Close**.

6 Use Menu Options and Dialog Boxes

1. Click the **Start button** ![Start], point to **Programs**, point to **Accessories**, and click **Calculator**.

2. Click the **View menu** and click **Scientific**.

3. Click the **Close button** ✕.

4. Click the **Start button** ![Start], point to **Programs**, point to **Accessories**, and click **WordPad**.

5. On the View menu, click **Options**.

6. Click the **Word tab**. Then, click the **Wrap to window option button**.

7. Verify that the Ruler check box has a check mark in it. Uncheck the other check boxes, if necessary (Figure 1.27).

8. Click the **Cancel button**; then close WordPad.

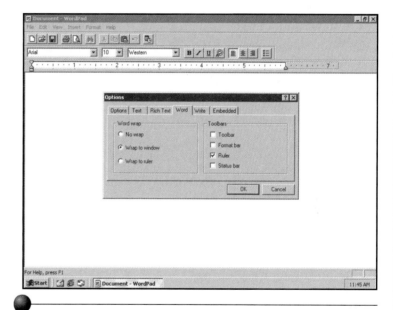

Figure 1.27

7 Select a Default Printer

1. Click the **Start button** ![Start], point to **Settings**, and click **Printers**.

2. Right-click the printer with the check mark by its icon.

3. Click the **Set as Default Printer option** and close the Printers window.

8 Use Windows 2000 Help

1. Click the **Start button** ![Start] and click **Help**.

2. In the navigation pane, click the **Contents tab**.

3. Click the **Introducing Windows 2000 Professional topic**.

4. Click the **What's new? category**.

5. In the Help information, click the **Easier to use link**.

6. Read the Help information that appears in the right pane.

7. In the navigation pane, click the **Index tab**, and type **desktop** in the *Type in the keyword to find* box.

8. Double-click the words *display settings*.

9. Read the Help information.

10. Click the **Search tab**, and then type **print** in the *Type in the keyword to find* box.

11. In the *Select Topic to display* box, double-click the **Add a printer that is attached to your computer topic**.

12. Read the Help information.

13. Close Windows 2000 Help.

9 Create and Move Folders in Windows Explorer

NOTE *You must have a blank, formatted floppy or removable disk to complete Skills Review 9 and 10.*

1. Click the **Start button** Start, point to **Programs**, point to **Accessories**, and click **Windows Explorer**.

2. Maximize the Explorer window, if necessary.

3. Insert a blank floppy or removable disk in the appropriate drive.

4. In the Folders pane, expand My Computer and click the drive icon for your disk.

5. Click the **File menu**, point to **New**, and click **Folder**.

6. Type **Memos** and press Enter⏎.

7. In the Folders pane, click the **plus sign (+)** next to the drive icon for your disk.

8. Click the *Memos* folder.

9. Click the **File menu**, point to **New**, and click **Folder**.

10. Type **October** and press Enter⏎.

11. Click the *October* folder in the Contents pane.

12. Drag the *October* folder to the drive icon you are using.

13. Click the *Memos* folder.

10 Rename and Delete Folders and Change Attributes

1. With your disk still in its drive and the Explorer window open, click the *October* folder on your floppy or removable disk.

2. Click the *October* folder again, type **Letters**, and press Enter↵ .

3. Click the *Memos* folder and press Delete . Click **Yes** to delete the folder.

4. Right-click the *Letters* folder and click **Properties**.

5. Click the **Read-only check box**. Then click **Cancel**.

6. Click the *Letters* folder and press Delete . Click **Yes** to delete the folder.

7. Close Windows Explorer.

8. Remove your disk from its drive.

11 Shut Down the Computer

1. Click the **Start button** Start and click **Shut Down**.

2. In the drop-down list, click the **Shut down option**.

3. Click **OK**.

LESSON APPLICATIONS

1 Change the Date and Time

Change the time zone setting on your computer.

1. Double-click the clock on the Windows taskbar.

2. In the Date/Time Properties dialog box, click the Time Zone tab.

3. Change the system date and the time zone setting to the (GMT-10:00) Hawaii option.

4. Verify the change to the new time setting.

5. Reset the date and time zone setting to the correct information for your location and close the Date/Time Properties dialog box.

2 Explore Windows 2000 Help

Explore Windows 2000 Help to find the definition of a glossary term.

1. Open Windows Help and click the Contents tab.

2. Click the *Introducing Windows 2000 Professional* category and click the *How to Use Help* category.

3. Click the *Help overview* topic.

4. Read the definition of the glossary term; hide its definition.

5. Close Help.

SUMMARY AND EXERCISES

3 Use Windows Explorer

Customize the appearance of the Explorer window.

1. In the Explorer window, modify the appearance so that the Explorer window looks similar to Figure 1.28.

2. Customize the appearance of the window to suit your preferences.

3. Close the Explorer window.

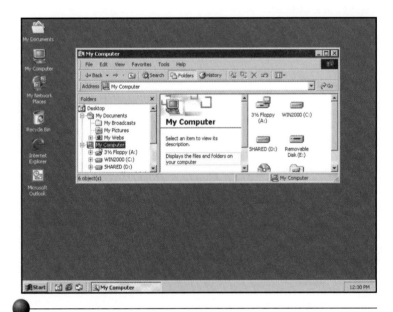

Figure 1.28

4 Work With Folders on a Disk

Create folders and subfolders on your floppy or removable disk. Then move, copy, and rename the folders.

> **NOTE** *You must have a blank, formatted floppy or removable disk to complete this activity.*

1. Create three new folders on your floppy or removable disk: *Budgets*, *Expenses*, and *Work Log*.

2. In the *Budgets* folder, create a subfolder named *January*.

3. Move the *January* subfolder in the *Budgets* folder to the *Expenses* folder.

4. Copy the *January* subfolder in the *Expenses* folder and paste it to the *Work Log* folder. (*Hint:* Press and hold down [Ctrl] while dragging the folder.)

5. Rename the *January* subfolder in the *Expenses* folder as *February*.

6. Delete the *January* subfolder in the *Work Log* folder.

PROJECTS

1 Set Up a Folder Structure on a Disk

Imagine you work for an advertising company that has four clients. For each of these clients you develop brochures, radio ads, and television commercials. On a floppy or removable disk (or another location assigned by your instructor), create folders and subfolders that meet the following specifications:

1. Create a new folder for each of your clients: *Abrams Hardware, Best Electronics, A1 Cleaners,* and *Midcity Auto.*

2. Create three subfolders within the *A1 Cleaners* folder: *Brochures, Radio Ads,* and *Television Commercials.*

3. Change the name of the *Brochures* subfolder in the *A1 Cleaners* folder to *Newspaper Ads.*

4. Delete the *Radio Ads* subfolder.

2 Explore the Windows 2000 Home Page

The company for which you work wants you to find out if the HP 870 printer is compatible with Windows 2000.

1. Start Web Help from Windows 2000 Help.

2. Follow the Search for Windows 2000-compatible hardware link to the Search for Compatible Hardware Devices page.

3. Scroll down to the search section, type **HP** as the Company name, type **870** as the Model, and select *Printers* as the Device Type, as shown in Figure 1.29.

Which HP 870 models are Windows 2000-compatible?

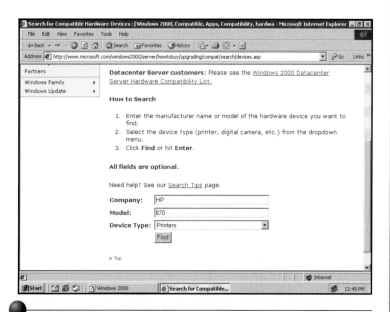

Figure 1.29

LESSON 2

Internet Explorer Basics

CONTENTS

- What Is Internet Explorer 5.5?
- Starting the Internet Explorer Browser
- Exploring the Internet Explorer Browser Window
- Navigating the World Wide Web
- Returning to Favorite Places
- Searching the Web
- Using Outlook Express
- Exploring Internet News
- Exiting the Browser

OBJECTIVES

After you complete this lesson, you will be able to do the following:

- Describe the components of Internet Explorer.
- Start and exit the Internet Explorer browser.
- Identify the elements of the browser window.
- Display and hide toolbars and the Search, Favorites, and History bars.
- Use the Help system and add a Favorites topic.
- Navigate the Web using links and toolbar buttons.
- Type URLs to move to a Web page.
- Print a Web page.
- Add a favorite place and later return to a favorite place.
- Use a search engine to find information on a topic.
- Start and exit Outlook Express.
- Send, read, and reply to mail.
- Understand how Internet news is organized.

WHAT IS INTERNET EXPLORER 5.5?

Every day, computer users around the world use the Internet for work, play, and research. The **Internet** is a worldwide network of computers that connects each Internet user's computer to all other computers in the network. The most popular tool used to access the Internet is the **World Wide Web** (**WWW** or the **Web**). The Microsoft Internet Explorer 5.5 suite includes programs that allow you to explore all parts of the Internet using the Internet Explorer browser and to communicate with others using Outlook Express.

Computer users access the
Internet every day. Employers
value employees who are capable
of efficiently using this vast
source of information. Internet
Explorer 5.5 will allow you to
explore the Web and use it to
communicate with others.

Internet Explorer Browser

To access most Internet services and all World Wide Web pages, you need a
browser—a software tool used to navigate the Web. The Internet Explorer browser
is the primary program in the Internet Explorer 5.5 suite. The Internet Explorer
browser lets you view Web pages in their visual format, search for information, set
bookmarks to jump quickly to favorite pages, download software, and much more.

Outlook Express

Outlook Express takes care of your communication needs on the Internet. Outlook
Express allows you to create and send new e-mail messages, read and reply to messages from others, attach files to or download files from e-mail messages, and read
and post messages to newsgroups. Although Outlook Express is automatically
loaded when you install Internet Explorer, you also can use other programs to read
and send e-mail and newsgroup messages.

STARTING THE INTERNET EXPLORER BROWSER

When you start your computer, Windows will launch, and you will see the desktop of your computer, as shown in Figure 2.1. If Internet Explorer is installed, you
should see the icon on the desktop and on the Quick Launch bar.

Figure 2.1
Windows desktop

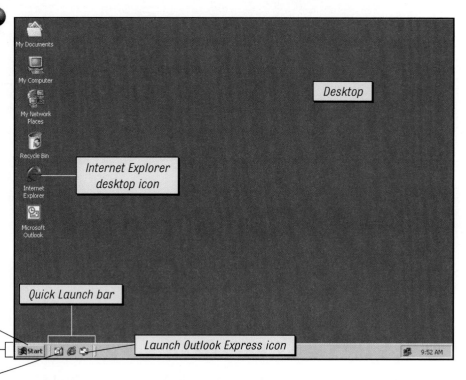

WARNING *You must use Microsoft Internet Explorer 5.5 to complete the
activities in this lesson. If you use a different Internet Explorer version,
the steps in the Hands On activities may still work; but you will undoubtedly see differences in the menus, toolbars, and functions, as well as the
figures in the lesson. Access the Help menu within Explorer to determine
relevant information if differences exist.*

HANDS on

Launching Internet Explorer

In this activity, you will launch Internet Explorer and connect to the Internet (if necessary).

1. **Double-click the Internet Explorer icon** 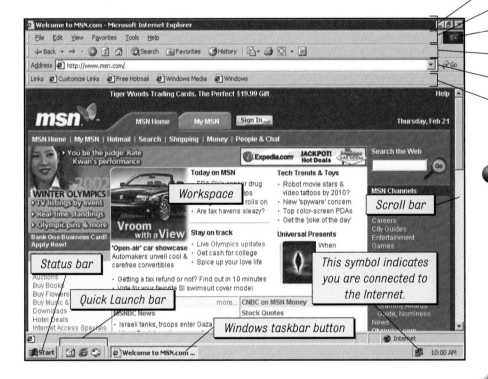 **on the desktop.**

2. **Connect to the Internet using your Internet service provider (ISP). If necessary, type your user name and password. If you are not sure how to connect to the Internet, or you do not know your user name and password, ask your instructor or lab assistant for assistance.**

You connect to the Internet, and the Internet Explorer browser launches. When the browser launches, the default home page appears in your browser window. The **home page** is the Web page that your browser uses as a starting point. Although your default home page may vary from the one shown in Figure 2.2, the elements on your screen will be similar.

3. **Click the Maximize button** ▢ **on the title bar, if necessary.**

Explorer **BASICS**

Starting the Browser

1. Double-click the Internet Explorer icon on the desktop.

2. Connect to your Internet service provider, if necessary.

GETTING STARTED

Title bar
Menu bar
Activity indicator
Standard Buttons toolbar
Address bar
Links bar

Workspace
Scroll bar
Status bar
Quick Launch bar
This symbol indicates you are connected to the Internet.
Windows taskbar button

Figure 2.2
Internet Explorer browser

Another Way $

To launch the Internet Explorer browser, click the Start button, point to Programs, and click Internet Explorer.

EXPLORING THE INTERNET EXPLORER BROWSER WINDOW

The Internet Explorer browser contains various elements that are always on the screen. You can hide or display other elements, depending on the options you select.

Title Bar

The title bar, which always appears at the top of the window, identifies the name of the current location. The title bar is hidden when the screen is shown in Full Screen mode. If the title bar is not visible, click the Restore Down button ⬜ in the upper-right corner of the window.

Menu Bar

The menu bar appears directly below the title bar. You can use the various options within the menus to issue commands. Many of the commands used most often also are available on the toolbars. Like the title bar, the menu bar is hidden in Full Screen mode. If the menu bar is not visible, click the Restore Down button ⬜ in the upper-right corner of the window.

Activity Indicator

The activity indicator will rotate, move, or change in appearance while a Web page is loading. Once the transaction is complete, the activity indicator is idle. Your activity indicator may use a different icon than the one shown in Figure 2.2.

Standard Buttons Toolbar

The Standard Buttons toolbar consists of buttons that issue commonly used commands. Table 2.1 shows the buttons on the Standard Buttons toolbar. If this toolbar is not visible, click the View menu, point to Toolbars, and click Standard Buttons.

Table 2.1		Standard Buttons Toolbar
Button	**Name**	**Lets you . . .**
⬅ Back ▾	Back	Display the last document or Web page that you retrieved during this session. Continue to press the Back button to view previously retrieved documents.
⇨ ▾	Forward	Display the next document or Web page that you retrieved during this session. You can click this button only if you have used the Back button.
⊗	Stop	Stop the downloading process of the current document or Web page. This button is useful if you change your mind about downloading a document or if the downloading process is taking too long.
⟳	Refresh	Download a new copy of the current document or Web page. You can use this button to check for updates on the page or if you accidentally stopped the download and want to continue.
⌂	Home	Display the page designated as the home page. It's what you see when you first start Internet Explorer.
Search	Search	Display the Search bar. The Search bar appears on the left side of the window and contains options to search the Web for information.

NORTON
ONLINE

Visit **www.glencoe.com/norton/online/** for more information on using Internet Explorer.

	Table 2.1	Standard Buttons Toolbar (continued)

Button	Name	Lets you . . .
[★ Favorites]	Favorites	Display the Favorites bar. The Favorites bar appears on the left side of the window and contains options to jump to favorite sites and documents.
[History]	History	Display the History bar. The History bar appears on the left side of the window and contains options to jump to sites and documents that you have recently visited.
[Mail icon]	Mail	Display a drop-down menu from which you can choose to read mail, create a new message, send a link, send a page, or read news. After you choose an option, your mail or newsreader program is launched.
[Print icon]	Print	Print the current Web page.
[W icon]	Edit with Microsoft Word	Change the displayed page using Microsoft Word (or Microsoft FrontPage, if installed).
[Discuss icon]	Discuss	Launch the discussion groups.

Address Bar

The Address bar appears at the top of the window under the menu bar. If the Address bar is not visible, click the View menu, point to Toolbars, and then click to select Address Bar. The most common use of the Address bar is to type an address of a specific Web site. If someone has told you to visit the Web site **http://www.collegenet.com**, you simply can type this address in the Address bar and press [Enter] to go to that site. As you navigate the Web, the text in the Address bar changes to display the address of the current page.

The Address bar stores the sites that you've visited previously. You can click the Address bar triangle button to display a list of these sites. Click any of the sites in the list to go there. You also can search for Web sites using the Address bar. You simply type a word or phrase that you are trying to find and click the Go button [Go] or press [Enter]. Internet Explorer will use one of the search engines available and display a list of sites that contain the word or phrase.

Links Bar

The Links bar provides links to preset pages and offers the quickest way to get to the Web pages you use most often. If the Links bar is not visible, click the View menu, point to Toolbars, and then click to select Links. You simply click the link to the page to which you want to go, and Internet Explorer takes you there. You can add Web pages to or delete Web pages from the Links bar. To add a page to the Links bar, drag the icon for the page from your Address bar or drag a link from a Web page to the Links bar.

Did you know?

When you link to your Internet service provider, you may not be connected at the optimum baud rate. If your modem is capable of a higher rate than your Internet service provider is capable of handling, you will not be able to use the full capacity of your modem.

Workspace

The workspace is located in the center of the window. The workspace displays the current Web page or document you are viewing. If the entire page does not fit within the window, scroll bars will appear to the right and/or bottom of the workspace so you can scroll up and down or right and left through the content of the page.

Some Web pages are broken into frames. **Frames** are panels of a page, separated by borders or scroll bars. Some framed Web pages allow you to adjust the size of each frame by dragging the border. Other framed Web pages provide scroll bars on frames so you can scroll each frame separately.

Status Bar

The status bar appears at the bottom of the window. As you work on the Web, watch the status bar for reports on the progress of an action. If the status bar is not visible, click the View menu and click to select Status Bar.

Quick Launch Bar

The Quick Launch bar appears within your Windows taskbar at the bottom of the screen. The Quick Launch bar lets you point and click to access your desktop, the Internet Explorer browser, and Outlook Express.

Explorer Bars

When activated, Explorer bars appear on the left side of the main workspace area. The Favorites and History bars allow you to move from site to site within the bar by clicking the desired link. The Search bar allows you to access a search engine to find a word or phrase on the Web. The Folders bar allows you to access your desktop.

To display the Search, Favorites, or History bar, simply click the appropriate button for the desired bar on the Standard Buttons toolbar, or click the View menu, point to Explorer Bar, and click to select the appropriate bar. To display the Folders bar, click the View menu, point to Explorer Bar, and click to select Folders.

HANDS on

Displaying and Hiding Toolbars

In this activity, you will hide and display browser toolbars.

1. **Click the View menu, and point to Toolbars.**

The Toolbars submenu lists the common toolbars. A check mark appears next to the toolbars that are currently displayed.

2. **If a check mark appears before Standard Buttons on the Toolbars submenu, go on to step 3. If you don't see a check mark in front of the Standard Buttons option on the Toolbars submenu, click to select the Standard Buttons option.**

3. Right-click the **menu bar**. If check marks do not appear before Address Bar and Links in the Toolbars submenu, click to select the two toolbar options. (You must redisplay the Toolbars submenu each time you select or clear a toolbar on the Toolbars submenu.) On the Toolbars submenu, click to clear any other toolbars that are currently displayed. If necessary, click a blank area of the application window to close the Toolbars submenu.

Displaying Explorer Bars

In this activity, you will display and close Explorer bars.

1. Click the **Search button**  on the Standard Buttons toolbar.

The Search bar appears on the left side of the window (see Figure 2.3). Notice that the Search button on the toolbar now looks raised, showing that it is active.

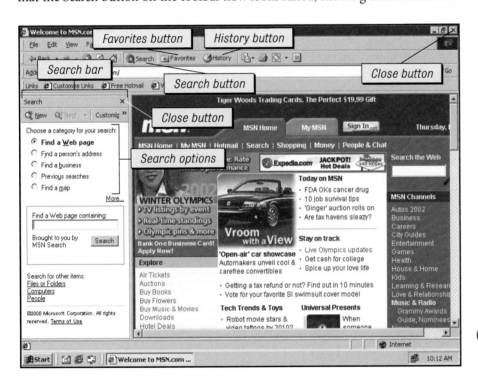

Figure 2.3
Search bar

2. Click the **Favorites button**  on the Standard Buttons toolbar.

The Search bar automatically closes, and the Favorites bar appears in its place. If you have any favorite sites stored, they will appear in the Favorites bar.

3. Click the **History button** on the Standard Buttons toolbar.

The History bar displays the recent Web sites and pages you have visited.

4. Click the **History button** again to close the History bar and expand the workspace to fill the whole window.

Exploring the Favorites Tab in the Help System

The Favorites tab is a tool that you use to create shortcuts to frequently accessed or important Help file information. In this activity, you will learn how to use the Favorites tab.

1. Click the Help menu, and click Contents and Index.

The Microsoft Internet Explorer Help window appears, revealing the navigation pane, which contains the Contents, Index, Search, and Favorites tabs. Note, too, that the Show button 🖼 changes to a Hide button 🖼 on the toolbar. You can resize and move this window as desired.

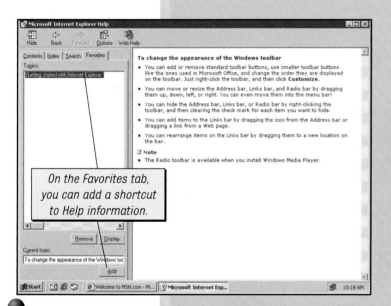

On the Favorites tab, you can add a shortcut to Help information.

2. Click Maximize ☐ in the Help window, if necessary. In the navigation pane, click the Contents tab. Then, click the closed book icon in front of Customizing Your Browser.

The closed book icon changes to an open book icon, and the category expands to show the topics related to the Help category.

3. In the navigation pane, double-click the Change the appearance of the Windows toolbar topic to display the Help topic's information in the right pane of the Help window. Read the Help information. In the navigation pane, click the Favorites tab.

Figure 2.4
Favorites tab

The Favorites tab displays (Figure 2.4). Any information previously stored in your Favorites tab will be listed in the Topics box. Notice that the *To change the appearance of the Windows toolbar* topic is still displayed in the right pane; it also appears in the Current topic box at the bottom of the navigation pane.

4. Click the Add button at the bottom of the navigation pane to add the Help information to the Topics box. Click the Contents tab, click the Printing and Saving Information category, and then click the Print a Web page topic.

5. Click the Favorites tab. In the Topics box, double-click the To change the appearance of the Windows toolbar option to jump immediately to the Help information. Click the Remove button at the bottom of the navigation pane to delete the topic from the Favorites listing. Close the Help window.

NAVIGATING THE WORLD WIDE WEB

The World Wide Web is a method for organizing the information on the Internet into a seamless system that uses links to navigate individual pages or places within pages. You can use a Web browser to explore Web pages and to transfer almost any kind of Internet resource to your own computer. A **Web page** can include a combination of text, graphic images, sound, animation, and video clips. Like a page in a book or a magazine, the layout of a Web page is limited only by the designer's imagination. A **Web site** is a collection of related Web pages.

The Web uses hypertext to provide links between resources that may be located anywhere on the Internet. **Hypertext** is an easy-to-use method for linking related information together. The rules for hypertext pages are called **Hypertext Transfer Protocol (HTTP),** and the page description format used is called **Hypertext Markup Language (HTML).** Web pages also contain **links** or **jumps** that, when clicked, take you to another section of the same Web page, another file on the same host computer, or a file on some other computer halfway around the world. When you point to any link or jump (whether the link is text or a picture), your pointer will change from an arrow to a hand with a pointing finger.

HANDS on

Navigating With Links and Buttons

In this activity, you will navigate the Web by following various links and issuing commands from the Standard Buttons toolbar.

1. **Slowly point to various items on your home page. As you point to various items (text and images), notice whether the pointer changes to the shape of a hand, indicating that this item is a link.**

2. **Click a text link.**

The browser moves to a new Web page (or to another part of the same page). As the action is taking place, you can watch the progress report in the status bar.

3. **Read the information on the new page. Then return to your home page by clicking the Back button** ⬅ Back ⮟ **on the Standard Buttons toolbar.**

Notice that the link on which you previously clicked may have changed color. This change of color differentiates the links you have used from those that you have not yet explored. Many Web pages and documents use one color to represent links that you have not yet explored and another color to represent links that you have explored.

4. **If your home page contains any links shown as an image, click one of them.**

Again, the browser moves to the related Web page (or to another part of the same page). Notice that each time you move to a new page, the text in the Address bar changes to show the exact address of that page.

GETTING STARTED

Explorer **BASICS**

Navigating With Links and Buttons

- Click a link to move to the new address.

- Click the Back button to move to previous pages, one page at a time.

- Click the Forward button to move one page forward.

- Click the Stop button to cancel the downloading of a page.

NOTE *If downloading the new page seems to be taking too long, or you change your mind about going to the page, click the Stop button* 🛑 *on the Standard Buttons toolbar. The transfer will stop, and you can click the Back button* [⇐ Back ▾] *or the Home button* 🏠 *on the Standard Buttons toolbar to return to your home page.*

5. If the current page contains links, click one.

6. Click the Back button [⇐ Back ▾] **on the Standard Buttons toolbar.**

The browser displays the previous page.

7. Click the Forward button [⇒ ▾] **on the Standard Buttons toolbar.**

The browser displays the next page. The Forward [⇒ ▾] and Back [⇐ Back ▾] buttons allow you to move between pages. The Forward button [⇒ ▾] is available only after you've clicked the Back button [⇐ Back ▾] at least once. To see updated pages, click the Refresh button 🔄 on the Standard Buttons toolbar.

Using URLs and Printing a Web Page

Hundreds of thousands of Web sites exist. Obviously, your home page doesn't contain links to all of these sites. One of the most direct routes to a specific site or page is to type the address in the Address bar. Every Web page has a unique **Uniform Resource Locator** or **URL.** A URL is an Internet address that is recognized by Web browsers. A URL has the following format: *protocol://domain name/path.*

Protocol identifies the kind of Internet resource. All URLs of Web pages start with *http.* (You can access other types of sites, such as FTP, telnet, and Gopher, through a Web browser by keying their types.) Both the colon (:) and the two forward slashes (//) are essential parts of every URL when the protocol is used; older Web browsers won't recognize a URL without them. If you type a URL without a protocol in the Address bar of a newer browser, such as Internet Explorer 5.5, the browser assumes an *http://* in front of the text. The **domain name** specifies the address of the Web site's computer. The **path** gives the exact location of a page. When you type a URL in the Address bar, be careful that you type every character correctly. If any letter or punctuation mark is wrong, you may not be able to make the desired connection.

NOTE *Internet Explorer's AutoComplete feature saves previous entries you have typed for Web addresses, forms, and passwords. When you type information in a field, AutoComplete may suggest possible matches. If you see a suggestion that matches what you want to enter in a field, such as the Address bar, click the suggestion. Otherwise, just keep typing your information.*

If you encounter information while surfing the Web that you want to print, you can produce a hard copy of the Web page or frame by clicking the Print button 🖨 on the Standard Buttons toolbar.

Use the Print dialog box (accessed by clicking Print on the File menu) to select options such as the number of copies to print.

HANDS on

Navigating and Printing a Web Page

In this activity, you will type a URL in the Address bar, navigate to that location, and print a Web page.

1. Click anywhere within the Address bar.

The entire address that currently appears in the Address bar is selected.

2. Type www.glencoe.com and press [Enter⏎].

The browser will load the Web page. Notice that the new address appears in the Address bar, as shown in Figure 2.5.

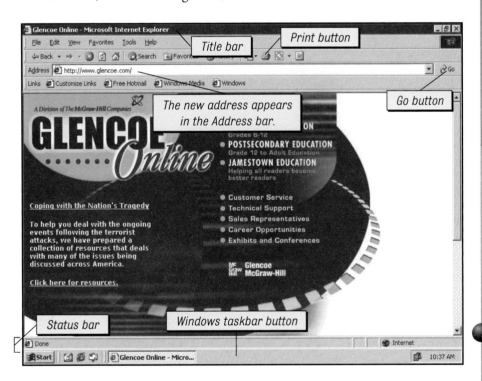

3. Browse the site by clicking links to find information about the publishing company.

4. Click the Print button 🖨 on the Standard Buttons toolbar.

If your printer is turned on and ready, the text and graphics on the current Web page will print.

Explorer BASICS

Navigating and Printing

To enter a URL:

1. Select the address in the Address bar.

2. Type the address to which you want to move and press [Enter⏎].

To print a Web page:

1. Navigate to the page you want to print.

2. Click the Print button on the Standard Buttons toolbar.

Figure 2.5
Entering a URL in the Address bar

GETTING STARTED

RETURNING TO FAVORITE PLACES

Undoubtedly, as you explore the Web, you'll find sites that you'll want to visit again. You can mark these sites by listing them on the Favorites bar. When you want to visit a site on the Favorites list, you simply click the link to return quickly to the "favorite" site.

To add a site to the Favorites list, click the Favorites button ⬛Favorites on the Standard Buttons toolbar. Then, on the Favorites bar, click the Add button ⬛Add.... In the Add Favorite dialog box, confirm or enter the name of the site and click OK to add the Web site to the Favorites list. To delete a listing on the Favorites bar, you simply right-click the item and click Delete on the shortcut menu.

Internet Explorer also allows you to make Web pages available for offline viewing; that is, you can read Web page information from your desktop when your computer is not connected to the Internet. You also can specify how you want to update the content on your computer. To make a Web page available offline, click Add to Favorites on the Favorites menu. In the Add Favorite dialog box, select the Make Available Offline check box. In the Create in box, you can create a new folder or choose a folder in which to save the shortcut to the favorite site. Click the Customize button, and the Offline Favorite Wizard will guide you through the steps to establish a schedule to update the page and to specify how much content to download to your computer. You can choose to download a Web page or a page with all its links.

HANDS on

Working With Favorites

In this activity, you will add a Web page to your Favorites list, go to your home page, and then use the Favorites bar to return to the favorite page. Finally, you will delete the favorite page from the Favorites bar.

> **1. Type** www.citysearch.com **in the Address bar and press** ⬛Enter⏎ **.**

The browser takes you to Citysearch, a Web site that provides news, weather, and other information for cities throughout the United States and the world.

> **2. When the Citysearch page has loaded, click the Favorites button** ⬛Favorites **on the Standard Buttons toolbar. Then, click the Add button** ⬛Add... **on the Favorites bar.**

The Add Favorite dialog box appears, as shown in Figure 2.6. Notice the description of the page that appears in the Name text box.

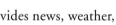

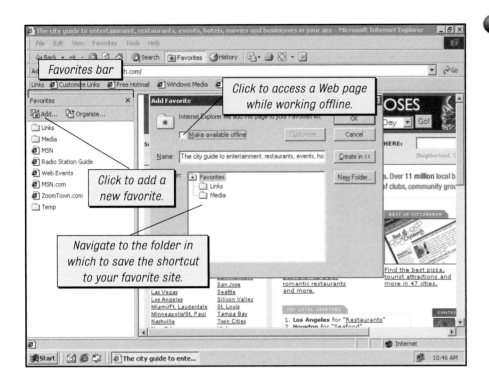

Figure 2.6
Add Favorite dialog box

Inside the figure:

Favorites bar

Click to access a Web page while working offline.

Click to add a new favorite.

Navigate to the folder in which to save the shortcut to your favorite site.

3. Click the **Create in** button to expand the Add Favorite dialog box, if necessary.

You can create a folder in which to save the shortcuts to your favorite sites.

4. In the Add Favorite dialog box, navigate to the folder in which you want to store a new folder for your favorites.

5. Click the **New Folder button**.

6. In the Create New Folder dialog box, type your name in the Folder name box and click **OK**.

A folder with your name now appears in the Add Favorite dialog box.

7. With your folder still selected, edit the description in the Name text box, if desired.

8. Click **OK** to add the page to your folder in the Favorites list.

The browser adds this Web page to the Favorites list in your folder on the Favorites bar, as shown in Figure 2.7.

Explorer **BASICS**

Working With Favorites

To add a favorite:

1. Navigate to the site you want to add as a favorite place.

2. Click the Favorites menu and click Add to Favorites.

3. Click OK to accept the name and location; or, click Create in to navigate to a folder, edit the name, and then click OK.

To return to a favorite:

1. Click the Favorites button.

2. In the Favorites bar, navigate to the favorite page.

3. Click the name of the page.

Figure 2.7

Favorites bar

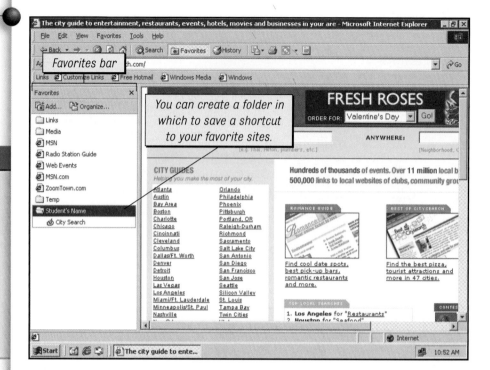

Explorer **BASICS**

Removing Favorites

1. Click the Favorites button.

2. Right-click the name of the page or folder within the Favorites bar.

3. On the shortcut menu, click Delete.

4. In the Confirm Folder Delete dialog box, click Yes.

9. In the Favorites bar, find and click your folder. Confirm that the favorite site is listed in your folder.

10. Click the **Favorites button**  to close the Favorites bar.

11. Explore the Citysearch site to find your city (or a nearby major city) and the names of at least two cinemas. Write the names and telephone numbers of the cinemas on a separate sheet of paper.

12. Click the **Home button** 🏠 on the Standard Buttons toolbar to return to your home page.

13. Click the **Favorites button** . Then, find and click your folder in the Favorites bar. Open your folder and click the Citysearch link.

The Citysearch site reappears in the workspace.

14. Close the Favorites bar. Then, explore the Citysearch site to find the names of at least two restaurants where you can meet a friend in Orlando, Florida. On a separate sheet of paper, write the names, addresses, and phone numbers of the restaurants.

15. On the Favorites bar, right-click your folder name. On the shortcut menu that appears, click **Delete**.

16. In the Confirm Folder Delete dialog box, click **Yes** to remove your folder and the Citysearch site from the Favorites list on the computer you are using.

17. Close the Favorites bar.

18. Return to your home page.

Another Way

- To add a Web page to your list of favorites, navigate to the page, right-click, and click Add to Favorites.

- To navigate to a Web site, type the address and click the Go button.

- To print, click File on the menu bar, click Print, and click OK in the Print dialog box.

SEARCHING THE WEB

Internet Explorer provides several preset links to sites that you can use to search for information on just about any topic imaginable or information on places, companies, people, and more. You also can customize your search settings and let Internet Explorer's Search Assistant do the searching for you.

Most search sites use either a subject directory method or a search engine method. A **subject directory** is a list of links to general topics arranged in alphabetical order. When you click any of the links, the links take you to a subdirectory of further links providing narrower topics. You can continue this process until you find the detailed information that you need. A **search engine** is a tool that allows you to type keywords to search for information on any topic. The result of your search displays as a list of links to Web pages. Most search engines allow you to type more than one keyword and use other symbols to narrow your search. A **keyword** is a word that you type that describes the topic for which you are searching.

When you are deciding whether to use a subject directory or search engine to find information, consider the information you already know and the number of results you want to see. For instance, if you're trying to find information on colleges located in Ohio but you don't know the names of the colleges, you might want to use a subject directory. However, if you want to find information about a specific school, you might have more success by typing the name of the school into a search engine. If you want to see the most search results possible, use a search engine. Most search engines provide methods to narrow your search and thus improve the quality of your results.

HANDS on

Searching for Information

In this activity, you will perform a search for information.

1. Click the **Search button** [🔍 Search] on the Standard Buttons toolbar.

The Search bar appears to the left of the browser window.

2. Click the **New button** [🔍 New] in the Search bar.

3. In the Choose a category for your search list, click the **Find a Web page option**, if necessary.

4. In the **Find a Web page containing text box, type** Mexican language schools **and then click the Search button in the Search bar.**

The results of your search appear in the form of links that you can click to navigate to the page described. Your search probably resulted in numerous links, as shown in Figure 2.8. Instead of muddling through all of the links, you can type additional keywords to narrow your search.

5. Click in the **Search the Web for text box** in the Search bar, type the keyword Zacatecas following *Mexican language schools* and click **Go** to process your search request.

Figure 2.8
Search results

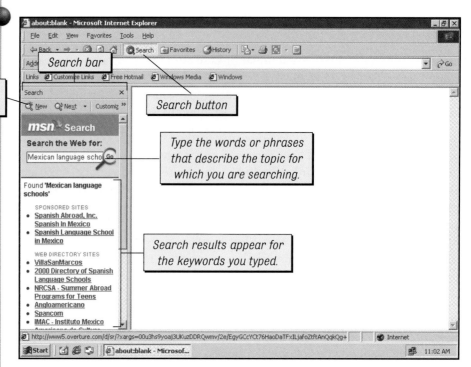

By adding the keyword *Zacatecas*, your search has been narrowed to Mexican language schools located in Zacatecas. Many search engines allow you to use special symbols (such as quotation marks, a plus symbol, or a minus sign) to narrow your results even further.

6. **Find out if the search engine you are using allows the use of special symbols. On the Search bar, look for a link to the search engine's Web site. Explore the search engine's Web site, looking for a Help or an Advanced Search link. Narrow your search as desired.**

7. **From the results of your search, click and explore one of the links that interests you.**

USING OUTLOOK EXPRESS

Outlook Express is a program (packaged with Internet Explorer) that allows you to send and receive e-mail and newsgroup messages. You can start Outlook Express from the Start button , or you can click the Launch Outlook Express button on the Quick Launch bar.

E-mail is a convenient form of communication that often saves time and money. E-mail allows you to send messages at a convenient time and allows the recipients to read the messages whenever they are ready. E-mail also provides written correspondence for future reference. And, unlike mail sent through the post office, you can receive e-mail in a matter of seconds. Depending on your Internet service provider, you may be able to send messages free of charge (or send as many messages as you want for a set price).

Click the Spelling button on the Standard Buttons toolbar of a new message window to check the spelling of your e-mail.

To send an e-mail message, you first must know the address of the person with whom you want to communicate. Then you start your mail program, choose the command to compose a new e-mail message, type the address of the recipient, type a subject (if desired), and compose the text of the message. Some e-mail programs also allow you to attach a file to the message.

Launching Outlook Express and Sending an E-mail Message

In this activity, you will launch Outlook Express and create and send an e-mail message.

1. **Click the Launch Outlook Express button** ⬚ **on the Quick Launch bar.**

Outlook Express is launched. The appearance of the main workspace in the Outlook Express area changes, depending upon the option selected in the Folders list.

2. **In the Folders list on the left, click the Local Folders option,** if necessary, and then click the **Inbox folder. Click the Maximize button** ⬚, **if necessary.**

3. **Click the New Mail button** ⬚ **on the toolbar.**

The New Message window appears, as shown in Figure 2.9.

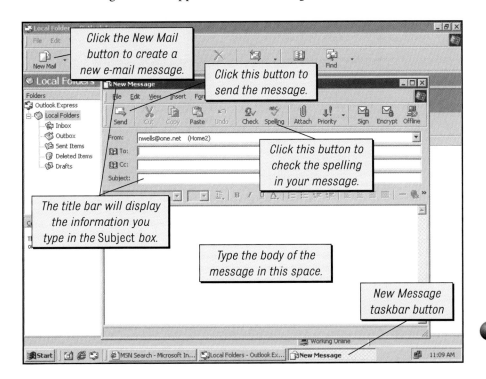

Figure 2.9
New Message window

Did you **know?**

If you see a link to a person's e-mail address on a Web page, you can click the link to start Outlook Express. The e-mail address automatically is inserted in the *To* box of a new message.

4. Click the **To box** and type the full e-mail address of a fellow student or your instructor.

NOTE *If necessary, ask your instructor for the e-mail address you should use for this activity.*

5. Press [Tab] to move the insertion point to the *Cc* box. If you want to send a copy of your message to another recipient, type the address in this field.

6. Press [Tab] again to move to the *Subject* box. Type E-mail training meetings in the *Subject* box, and press [Tab] to move to the portion of the window where the body of the message will appear.

The text that you typed in the *Subject* box appears in the title bar of the window.

7. Type the following message as the body of your e-mail message and as shown in Figure 2.10:

Training meetings to help you learn to use the advanced features of the Outlook Express mail program will be held next week. Please let me know by this Thursday which meeting time best fits your schedule:

April 20 at 3 p.m.
April 21 at 9 a.m.
April 21 at 2 p.m.
April 23 at 9 a.m.

(your name)

Figure 2.10
Completed e-mail message

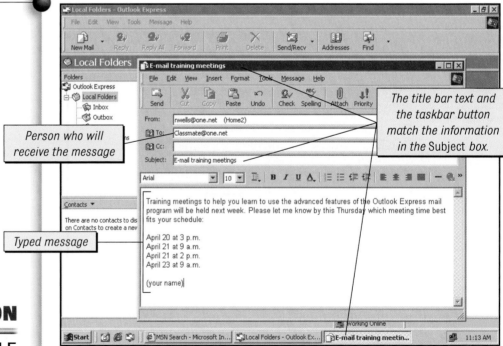

8. Click the **Send button** on the Standard Buttons toolbar.

Watch the Folders list in the left pane of the screen as your e-mail passes to the *Outbox* folder and then to the *Sent Items* folder. A number in parentheses (*1* if this is the only e-mail being sent) will appear next to the Outbox folder. When it disappears, the message has been sent.

If you are not connected to the Internet, a dialog box may appear telling you that your message will be placed in your Outbox until you click the Send and Receive All button [SendRecv]; click OK. A number in parentheses (*1* if this is the only e-mail in the Outbox) will appear next to the *Outbox* folder. Click the Send and Receive All button [SendRecv] now to send the message. If Outlook Express asks if you want to work online and/or connect, follow the dialog boxes to do so.

HANDS on

Reading and Replying to a Message

When somebody sends you an e-mail message, the message will appear in your Inbox. You can click the Send and Receive All button [SendRecv] to check for e-mail messages. To read a message, click the message in the Inbox folder in the Folders list. If you want to respond to a message you receive, you can use the Reply button [Reply] on the Standard Buttons toolbar. When you use the Reply command, the *To* and *Subject* boxes are automatically filled in for you. In this activity, you will read a message and reply to it.

1. Click the *Inbox* folder in the Folders list, as shown in Figure 2.11.

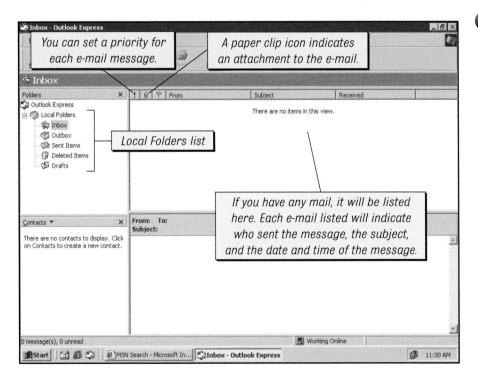

Figure 2.11
Inbox

Explorer BASICS

Reading and Replying to an E-Mail Message
To read an e-mail message:

1. Click the *Inbox* folder in the Folders list.

2. If necessary, click the Send and Receive All button.

3. Click the message that you want to read.

4. Read the message.

To reply to an e-mail message:

1. Display the message to which you want to reply.

2. Click the Reply button.

3. Type the reply and click the Send button.

A list of e-mail messages received appears in the workspace. The list displays the sender, the subject, and the date and time received. Information also may be displayed to indicate whether a file is attached (indicated by a paper clip icon) and the priority of the e-mail (indicated by an exclamation point if the message is a high priority). A new message displays a closed envelope icon in front of the sender's name when the message has not yet been read.

2. Click the message that you want to read.

The message appears in the bottom part of the window. The header shows the sender, recipient, and subject. If the message had been read, the icon in front of the sender's name would change from a closed envelope to an open envelope.

3. Click the Reply button  **on the Standard Buttons toolbar.**

A window appears with the header already completed. The blinking insertion point appears in the message area, ready for you to type your response. The original message is displayed below the point where you will type. This message is provided for reference and to those with whom you are communicating.

4. Type the following message:

> Thank you for offering the advanced features training meeting. Please accept this e-mail as confirmation that I wish to attend on April 21 at 2 p.m.
>
> (your name)

5. Click the Send button  **on the Standard Buttons toolbar to send the reply. Then close Outlook Express.**

Did you know?

Entrepreneurs often start early in life. Bill Gates, founder of Microsoft Corporation, taught himself computer programming at the age of 13. As a teenager, he and his friends rode their bikes to a local computer company to help the employees look for programming errors.

File Attachments

You also can send and receive files attached to e-mail messages. Attaching files to e-mail messages provides an easy way to move programs and files across the Internet to specific users. An attached file is not part of the message it accompanies, but the attached file travels through the Internet with the e-mail message. When you attach a file to an Outlook Express message, the file name is listed in the *Attach* box in the message header.

When you receive a message with a file attached, you simply can click the attached file icon to read it. If the file is a data file, your computer usually will choose the appropriate program to open the file.

EXPLORING INTERNET NEWS

A large and varied amount of material moves around the Internet as news. News topics range from discussions of popular television shows to announcements of new developments in every imaginable academic discipline, and from requests for help repairing 70-year-old radios to information about the latest activities in artificial intelligence. To allow people to find the discussions they want and ignore the others, Internet news is sorted into thousands of separate topics, called **newsgroups.** Some popular newsgroups might include hundreds of new messages every day, while other newsgroups devoted to more obscure subjects might handle only three or four messages a week.

With a few exceptions, newsgroups are cooperative services that do not have any formal administrators. Anybody can **post** (create and send) an **article** (also known as a message or post) that can be read by users of that newsgroup. The exceptions are **moderated newsgroups,** where all articles are screened by a person who makes sure their content is relevant to the topic of the newsgroup. To read and contribute to newsgroups on the Internet, you must use a program called a **newsreader,** which obtains news articles from a computer called a **news server.** Within the universe of Internet news, tens of thousands of separate newsgroups exist. The name of each group identifies the subject under discussion and the major category into which this particular subject falls. As a general rule, the first word (or abbreviation) of a newsgroup's name is the broad general classification, and each additional word in the name is more specific. So within the major *rec* (for recreational) group, there could be a subgroup called *rec.food* that includes separate newsgroups devoted to recipes, restaurants, and so forth. Some of these groups are themselves broken into still smaller groups; in addition to *rec.food.drink*, there also could be separate newsgroups called *rec.food.drink.tea* and *rec.food.drink.coffee*.

EXITING THE BROWSER

When you finish a session on the Web, you usually will want to close Internet Explorer. You also may want to disconnect from your Internet service provider.

HANDS on

Exiting Internet Explorer

In this activity, you will close the Internet Explorer program.

1. Click the **Close button** ☒ on the browser window.

2. If directed to do so by your instructor, disconnect from your Internet service provider.

    WARNING *You may proceed directly to the exercises for this lesson. If, however, you are finished with your computer session, follow the shut down procedures for your lab or school environment.*

> *Explorer* **BASICS**
>
> **Exiting the Browser**
>
> Click the browser's Close button. Disconnect from your Internet service provider, if necessary.

Self Check ✓

Test your knowledge by answering the following questions. See Appendix B to check your answers.

T F **1.** Internet Explorer is a program that allows you to explore the Internet.

T F **2.** Outlook Express is a program that you can use to send an e-mail message.

T F **3.** The Internet is available only to users of large companies.

T F **4.** The Standard Buttons toolbar on the browser window allows you to issue commonly used commands.

T F **5.** The rules for hypertext pages are called HTML.

SUMMARY AND EXERCISES

GETTING STARTED

SUMMARY

In this lesson, you learned that Internet Explorer 5.5 is a program that allows you to explore all parts of the Internet. The Web browser is the main component of the Internet Explorer package. The browser lets you navigate the World Wide Web. Using the Explorer bars, you can access the Search tools, review the history of your browsing, and add sites that you frequently visit to the Favorites list. Additionally with Internet Explorer, you can launch Outlook Express to send and receive e-mail messages and newsgroup messages. While working with Internet Explorer, you can access the online Help system from the Help menu.

Now that you have completed this lesson, you should be able to do the following:

- Identify the primary programs in the Internet Explorer 5.5 suite. (page 52)
- Launch the Internet Explorer browser and connect to the Internet. (page 52)
- Describe the components of the browser window. (page 53)
- Identify the buttons on the Standard Buttons toolbar. (page 54)
- Display and hide toolbars in the window. (page 56)
- Open and close the Search, Favorites, and History bars. (page 57)
- Access and use the Favorites tab of the online Help system. (page 58)
- Navigate the Web using links and buttons. (page 59)
- Navigate the Web using URLs. (page 60)
- Print a Web page. (page 60)
- Add a favorite site to the Favorites list. (page 62)
- Search the Web and add keywords to narrow the search. (page 65)
- Launch Outlook Express to send, receive, and reply to e-mail messages, and exit Outlook Express. (page 66)
- Explain how to send e-mail messages with attachments. (page 70)
- Explain the Internet News options. (page 70)
- Exit the browser and disconnect from the Internet. (page 71)

CONCEPTS REVIEW

1 TRUE/FALSE

Circle T if the statement is true or F if the statement is false.

T   F   **1.** Internet Explorer is only an Internet browser.

T   F   **2.** When the browser launches, the browser's starting point is the home page.

T   F   **3.** The Standard Buttons toolbar offers toolbar buttons to navigate the Web.

T   F   **4.** Web pages often are broken into panels of a page, which are called frames.

T   F   **5.** To open the workspace, click an option on the Standard Buttons toolbar.

T   F   **6.** Internet Explorer offers an online Help system to answer most questions.

T   F   **7.** The activity indicator will change in appearance while a Web page is loading.

T   F   **8.** To navigate to a Web page, you can use the URL.

T   F   **9.** Internet Explorer offers various search tools.

T   F   **10.** You can send and receive e-mail messages using Outlook Express.

2 MATCHING

Match each of the terms on the left with the definitions on the right.

TERMS

1. Web page
2. HTTP
3. links
4. URL
5. search engine
6. subject directory
7. keyword
8. Internet
9. newsgroups
10. post

DEFINITIONS

a. A worldwide network of computers that connects each Internet user's computer to all other computers in the network

b. An Internet address that is recognized by Web browsers

c. Any word that you type that describes the topic for which you are searching

d. Create and send an article to a newsgroup

e. A document that can include text, graphic images, sound, and animation

f. Rules for hypertext pages

g. Search tool that allows you to type keywords to search for information on any topic

h. Search tool that is a list of links to general topics arranged in alphabetical order

i. Text or an image that jumps to another section of the same document, another file on the host computer, or another file on a different computer

j. The organized news available on the Internet that allows people to find the discussions they want

SUMMARY AND EXERCISES

3 COMPLETION

Fill in the missing word or phrase for each of the following statements.

1. A Web site is a collection of related _____ .

2. Internet Explorer allows you to make Web pages available for _____ ; that is, you can read Web page information when your computer is not connected to the Internet.

3. The _____ has the following format: **protocol://domain name/path.**

4. When using search tools, use _____ to help narrow your search.

5. The page description format used for Web pages is called _____ .

6. Click the _____ button on the Quick Launch bar to start the mail program.

7. To create a new message, click the _____ button on the toolbar.

8. To send an e-mail message, you first must know the _____ of the person to whom you want to communicate.

9. In Outlook Express, the paper clip icon indicates the message has a(n) _____ .

10. To display the History bar, click the History button on the _____ toolbar.

4 SHORT ANSWER

Write a brief answer to each of the following questions.

1. What is Internet Explorer?

2. How do you start the Internet Explorer browser?

3. Name four buttons on the Standard Buttons toolbar and describe their function.

4. What is the Quick Launch bar, and where is it located?

5. Explain what happens when you click the Search, Favorites, or History buttons on the Standard Buttons toolbar.

6. How do you mark a Help topic so that you can access it quickly when you want to review the information?

7. What is the program that is used to send and receive e-mail messages, and how do you start this program?

8. How do you create a new e-mail message?

9. What are newsgroups, and who uses them?

10. How do you change the name that appears in the title bar of a new e-mail message window?

5 IDENTIFICATION

Identify each of the elements of the Internet Explorer window in Figure 2.12.

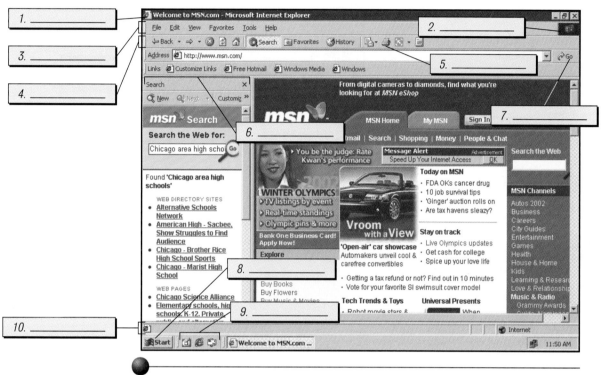

Figure 2.12

SKILLS REVIEW

Complete all of the Skills Review problems in sequential order to review your Internet Explorer skills.

1 Launch Explorer and Add a Help Topic to the Favorites Tab

1. Double-click the **Internet Explorer icon** on the desktop.

2. If necessary, connect to the Internet and maximize your browser window.

3. Click the **Help menu**, and click **Contents and Index**.

4. Click the **Index tab**. In the *Type in the keyword to find* box, type home page.

5. In the list of topics that appear, verify that *home page* is selected, and then click the **Display button**.

6. In the Topics Found dialog box that appears, select the **To change your home page topic** and click the **Display button** (Figure 2.13 on the next page).

7. Read the Help information that appears.

8. Click the **Favorites tab** in the Help window.

9. At the bottom of the Favorites tab, click the **Add button**.

10. With the *To change your home page* topic selected in the Topics box, click the **Remove button**.

11. Close the Help window.

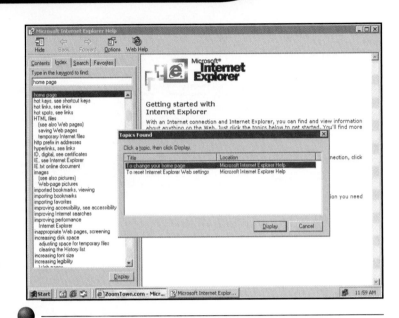

2 Navigating the Web, Printing, and Adding a Favorite

1. Click a link on your home page.

2. Click the **Back button** ⟸ Back ▾ to return to the home page.

3. Click the **Forward button** ⟹ ▾ to return to the previous page.

Figure 2.13

4. In the Address bar, type www.cnn.com and press ⏎Enter◀┘ .

5. Click the **Print button** 🖨 on the Standard Buttons toolbar.

6. Click the **Favorites button** ⭐Favorites on the Standard Buttons toolbar.

7. Click the **Add button** 📑Add... on the Favorites bar. In the Add Favorite dialog box, click **OK**.

8. In the Favorites list, find and right-click the **CNN site**. On the shortcut menu that appears, click **Delete** to remove the site from the Favorites list.

3 Searching the Web

1. Click the **Search button** 🔍Search on the Standard Buttons toolbar.

2. In the keywords box, type the name of a state that you would like to visit and perform the search.

3. Narrow your search results by typing **Amusement Parks** in the keywords box after the state name and perform another search.

4. Explore the search results.

5. Close the Search bar.

4 Using Outlook Express

1. Click the **Launch Outlook Express button** 📧 on the Quick Launch bar.

2. Click the **New Mail button** 📝 on the toolbar to create an e-mail message to a classmate or your instructor.

3. Type the e-mail address in the *To* box.

4. Type Training Meetings in the *Subject* box.

5. In the body of the e-mail message, type:

   Thank you so much for the informative training session on Outlook Express. The skills gained through this session are essential to my successful job performance.

   (your name)

6. Click the **Send button** on the Standard Buttons toolbar.

5 Closing Internet Explorer

1. Click the **Close button** ⊠ to close Outlook Express.

2. Click the **Close button** ⊠ and close the browser window.

3. Disconnect from the Internet, unless your instructor tells you to remain connected.

LESSON APPLICATIONS

1 Use the Search Bar

Use the Search bar to explore for information.

1. Launch Internet Explorer, and if necessary, connect to the Internet, and maximize the browser window.

2. Click the Search button on the Standard Buttons toolbar.

3. In the keywords box, type the name of your city (or a nearby city).

4. Use advanced search features to narrow your search; include keywords such as *digital city* and *map*.

5. Explore the search results. Create and print a map from your home to your school.

2 Search for Help on Searching

Use the Help system to learn more about searching the Web.

1. With Internet Explorer open, click Contents and Index on the Help menu.

2. On the Index tab, look for and read information about Search providers on the Internet.

3. Add the topic to the Favorites tab; then, delete the topic from the Favorites tab.

4. Close the Help window.

3 Send an E-Mail Message

Use Outlook Express to send an e-mail message.

1. Open Outlook Express.

2. Click the New Mail button ⬜ on the Standard Buttons toolbar.

3. Create an e-mail message to your instructor.

4. Type the answers to the Short-Answer questions in this lesson in the form of an e-mail.

5. Add an appropriate subject and send the e-mail. Then, close Outlook Express.

PROJECTS

1 Starting Your Language School

Assume that you are thinking about starting a summer language program in Mexico to teach Spanish to English-speaking students. You want to research the competition and also find information on teaching methods. Use Internet Explorer and the Search button to discover information on the competition (specifically in Zacatecas, if you desire to narrow your search) and also to learn about the teaching methods. Narrow your search as much as you desire using search tips for the search engine you are using. Explore the search results to find a useful site and to determine the name of at least one language school and the city or state where it is located. Print a Web page.

2 Searching for Cultural Information

Assume that with your summer language program (discussed in Project 1) you also want to provide cultural activities for the students. Using the Search tools on the Internet, discover the cultural activities that are available in the city or state of at least one school (see Project 1 for the information you recorded). Also, search for cultural or entertainment activities in this city/state. Record this information on a separate sheet of paper.

3 Searching for Exchange Rates

Use a search engine of your choice to find a Web page that computes currency exchange rates. Assume that you are considering whether to travel from the United States to Mexico or to Spain to learn Spanish. Use the Web site to convert $250 (U.S. dollars) to the currency in Mexico and in Spain.

4 Sending and Receiving E-Mails

Choose a classmate as a partner for this project. Assume that one of you is the individual who wants to create a summer language program (discussed in Projects 1 and 2) and the other is a prospective student. The prospective student should create a brief e-mail message (addressing it to the other student) expressing an interest in attending a language experience program to learn Spanish. Request information on the costs, the type of programs offered, and the available dates. Be sure to include appropriate information in the header and clearly state your request in the body of the e-mail

GETTING STARTED

(Figure 2.14). After you send the e-mail, check the *Sent Items* folder to verify the e-mail has been sent.

The second student (acting as the individual who wants to create the program) should reply with an appropriate response, answering the questions and providing the pertinent information in the header and body of the message.

Exchange additional e-mails in which the prospective student registers for the program and requests information be sent to additional classmates and the program creator verifies the registration, calculates the fees, provides confirmation information, and sends e-mails to the others who are interested.

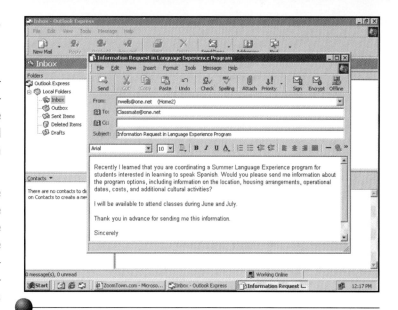

Figure 2.14

5 Testing the Students

As the plans for the language school continue to develop (discussed in Projects 1, 2, and 4), you realize that you need to have a method to test the level of each entering student. Search the Web for possible methods of testing Spanish language skills and Web sites that are in Spanish. After locating two Web sites, create and send an e-mail to your instructor listing the two sites that have content in the Spanish language.

6 Adding Favorites

While researching information to create your own language school (discussed in Projects 1–2 and 4–5), you remember that to travel to another country often requires permission. Search the Web to locate the information required for citizens of the United States to travel to another country. Also, search for any travel advisories that might be posted about U.S. citizens traveling to foreign countries, specifically Mexico. Since this information is subject to change often and you would need to verify travel advisories frequently, add this site to your Favorites list. Go to your home page and then return to this favorite site. Remember to delete this site from your Favorites list.

LESSON 3

Office XP Basics

CONTENTS

OBJECTIVES

After you complete this lesson, you will be able to do the following:

➤ Explain the purpose of the five major Office programs.

➤ Use your mouse to point, click, double-click, right-click, select, and drag.

➤ Start and shut down your computer.

➤ Copy files from a CD-ROM, and change attributes of files and folders.

➤ Start, switch between, and exit Office programs.

➤ Name the main components of the Office window, and display and hide toolbars.

➤ Open, name, save, close, and reopen files.

➤ Get help from the Office Assistant, ScreenTips, Ask a Question box, Answer Wizard, Contents, and Index.

➤ Identify buttons on the Web toolbar and get help on the Web.

➤ Connect to and disconnect from the Internet.

WHAT IS OFFICE XP?

So, just what is Office XP? The Microsoft Office XP Professional Edition suite includes these five major application programs: Word, Excel, Access, PowerPoint, and Outlook. Each **application program** in the Microsoft Office suite focuses on one aspect of computer processing; however, all five application programs are inter-active and work together to allow you to share files among the applications.

Throughout this tutorial, you will learn to use many useful tools, including word processing, worksheet, database, and presentation software. Your ability to use these programs will give you a head start in the workplace. You also will learn how to integrate data from these various programs, which you'll find to be an even greater advantage in almost any career you select.

Microsoft Word

Microsoft Word is a powerful word processing program that enables you to create a full range of business and personal correspondence. Using Word, you can create letters, resumes, e-mail messages, and other, more complex documents, such as invoices, flyers, newsletters, and Web pages. Word extends the boundaries of word processing with its ability to add graphics, charts, colors, and tables. Other Word features include step-by-step mail merge, spelling and grammar checking, and simplified table creation, to name a few. Figure 3.1 shows a Web page as it appears in Word.

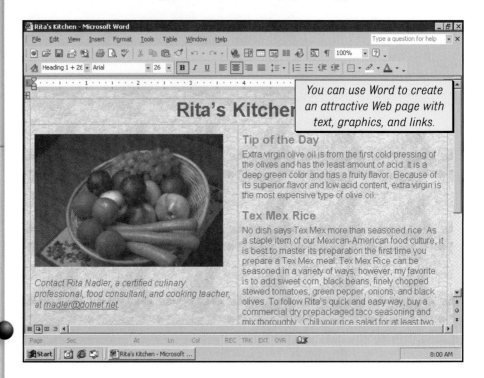

Figure 3.1
A Web page displayed in Word

WEB NOTE

You can use one of many Office programs—including Word, Excel, PowerPoint, and Access—to create a Web page. Any Web page that you create using an Office program can be viewed in your Web browser.

Microsoft Excel

Microsoft Excel is a dynamic workbook program used to track, calculate, and analyze numerical data of all kinds. You also can use Excel to build charts based on your numerical data; to sort, search, and filter data using Excel's database capabilities; and to publish data on the Web. Figure 3.2 shows a worksheet and chart as they appear in Excel.

Microsoft Access

Microsoft Access is a powerful database management program used to organize, track, and retrieve all types of data. With Access, you can use forms to enter information into a database, create queries to extract specific information from a

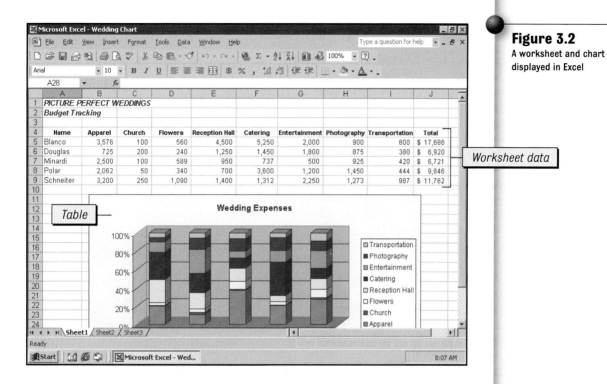

Figure 3.2
A worksheet and chart displayed in Excel

database, and print professional-looking reports based on the information contained in a database. You also can publish data stored in an Access database on the Web. Figure 3.3 shows a report created in Access.

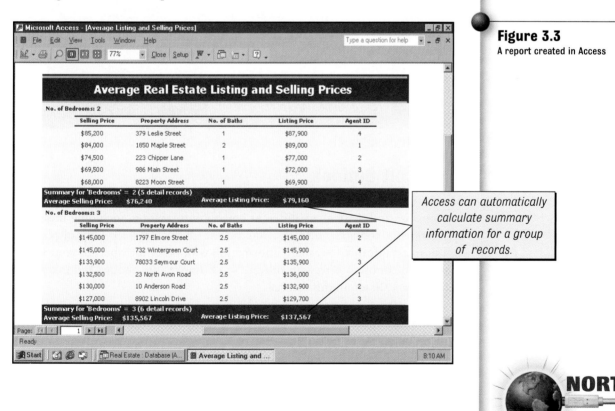

Figure 3.3
A report created in Access

NORTON
ONLINE

Visit **www.glencoe.com/norton/online/** for more information on using Office XP.

Microsoft PowerPoint

Microsoft PowerPoint is a presentation program you can use to create a series of slides—called a **presentation**—that can be shown on a computer, projected on a screen, or printed. Slides help you deliver information to an audience, using combinations of text, charts, graphics, and other types of content. PowerPoint's tools let you create detailed, dynamic slides that capture your audience's attention and make your information easier to understand and remember. PowerPoint also lets you create slides using data from other application programs, collaborate on a presentation with others, and show slides on the Web. Figure 3.4 shows a presentation slide as displayed in PowerPoint.

Figure 3.4
A slide displayed in PowerPoint

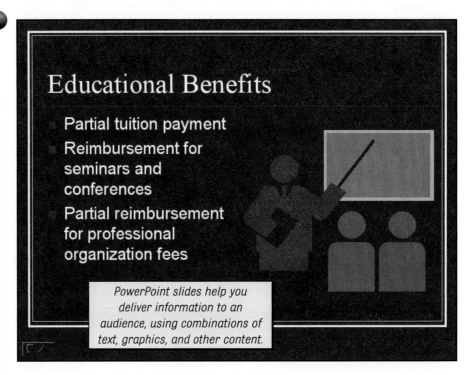

Microsoft Outlook

Microsoft Outlook is a desktop information management program in which you can organize and share many different types of information, including messages, appointments, contacts, and tasks. You can use Outlook to keep track of personal and business information, share information with other members of your workgroup, and communicate with others. You'll learn more about Outlook in the *Outlook Basics* lesson in this tutorial.

> **NOTE** *This lesson provides an overview of Word, Excel, Access, and PowerPoint, focusing primarily on the common elements among the application programs. As you work through each lesson in this tutorial, you will learn about the unique features of each application program.*

USING THE MOUSE

You will use the **mouse** extensively in the Microsoft Office application programs. The mouse is the key to the graphical user interface because it lets you choose and manipulate on-screen objects without having to type on the keyboard. Although

Did you know?

The Windows operating system provides a graphical user interface (GUI) that allows you to interact with the system by using a mouse to choose icons and menu items on the screen. GUIs are much easier to master than old-fashioned command-line interfaces, which require you to type memorized commands using the keyboard.

the mouse is the most popular pointing device, you also may use several other pointing devices. **Trackballs** have buttons like the mouse, but instead of moving the mouse over the desktop, you spin a large ball. Laptops often employ either a small **joystick** in the middle of the keyboard or a **touch-sensitive pad** below the keyboard. Each of these devices lets you point to items on the screen and click buttons to perform actions on those items.

You can perform several actions with the mouse:

◆ An arrow on the screen pointing toward the upper left is called the **pointer** (or **mouse pointer**). Moving the mouse to position the pointer on the screen is called **pointing**.

◆ To **click** the mouse, point to an object and quickly press and release the left mouse button.

◆ To work with an object on the screen, you usually must **select** (or **choose**) the item by clicking the object—pressing and quickly releasing the mouse button.

◆ To **double-click,** point to an object and click the left mouse button twice in rapid succession without moving the pointer.

◆ To **right-click,** point to an object, press the right mouse button, and then quickly release it.

◆ To **drag** (or **drag-and-drop**), point to an object you want to move, press and hold the left mouse button, move the mouse to drag the object to a new location, and then release the mouse button.

Your mouse probably has two or three buttons. Whenever the directions in this tutorial say *click,* use the left mouse button. If you must use the right mouse button, the directions will say *right-click* or *click the right mouse button.*

STARTING YOUR COMPUTER

Microsoft Office is just one of many application programs that requires **operating system** software such as Windows 2000, Windows Millennium Edition (Windows Me), or Windows 98. The operating system software oversees every operation you perform on your computer. When you turn on your computer, the computer gives itself a complex set of instructions to start up. This start-up process is called **booting the system** or performing a **system boot,** and is derived from the expression "pulling oneself up by the bootstraps." First, a built-in program tests the computer. This **Power On Self Test (POST)** checks the memory, keyboard, display, and disk drives of the computer system. Next, files from the hard drive containing essential operating system components are loaded. Because computer systems and setups vary greatly, you may see a series of screens informing you of the progress of the startup procedure. Finally, the opening screen appears.

HANDS on
Booting the System

In this activity, you will start your computer and boot the operating system. All activities and figures in this tutorial were developed using the Windows 2000 operating system. If you are using a different version of Windows, the information appearing on your screen may vary slightly from the activities and figures in this tutorial.

WARNING *If Windows 2000 is not the operating system on the computer you are using, ask your instructor, computer lab assistant, or network administrator how to boot your system.*

1. **Press the power button or flip the power switch to turn on the computer. If the monitor connected to the system has a separate power switch, turn on that switch as well.**

2. **Observe the booting process.**

   a. **Listen for the POST sound. A single beep means the system passed all the tests; a series of beeps indicates a hardware problem. If you hear a series of beeps, check your keyboard and monitor connections, read the message on the screen, or consult your computer manual to fix the problem. You may need technical help from the manufacturer, a lab assistant, or a technician. (Your computer may not make any sounds while booting.)**

   b. **Watch the screen. After a few moments, you may see a memory indicator while the system checks the random access memory. Then some information appears on the screen, followed by the Windows 2000 copyright screen. A progress indicator gives you a visual clue as to how much more of the operating system needs to be loaded into memory. The Log On to Windows screen may appear next, requesting your user name and password.**

When you **log on** to a computer with Windows 2000, you inform the operating system who you are. The operating system then loads your personal settings to complete the booting process. Systems that have multiple users, such as networks, keep track of who is allowed to access the computer by assigning unique **user names** and **passwords.**

3. **If you are prompted for a user name and/or password, type your user name in the User name text box and/or press** [Tab] **and type your password. If you do not know your user name and/or password, ask your instructor for help.**

Asterisks appear as you type your password. This way, others who may see your log-on screen will not learn your password.

4. **Click OK.**

The system completes the booting process. You may see the Getting Started with Windows 2000 window. A **window** is a rectangular on-screen frame in which you do your computing work.

NOTE *When this tutorial mentions a button, a picture of the button is displayed within the text. For instance, when a step instructs you to click the Close button ☒, the button will be illustrated as shown here.*

5. **If necessary, click the Show this screen at startup check box to clear the option to prevent the Getting Started with Windows 2000**

Office BASICS

Booting the System

1. Turn on the computer.

2. Turn on the monitor.

3. Observe the booting process.

4. Close the Getting Started with Windows 2000 window, if necessary.

Lesson 3

window from appearing each time you boot your computer. Then click the Close button ⊠ in the upper-right corner of the window.

Now your screen should resemble Figure 3.5. This screen, called the Windows 2000 **desktop,** is the background for your computer work. Several **icons** (pictures) appear on the desktop. These icons represent some of the resources that are available on your system—such as programs, data files, printers, disk drives, and others. Your desktop may include a large number of icons, or just a few. The **taskbar,** the bar across the bottom of the desktop, contains **buttons** that you can click to perform various tasks.

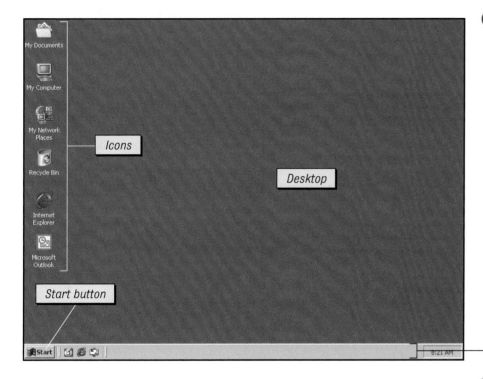

Figure 3.5
Windows 2000 desktop

CREATING YOUR *OFFICE DATA* FOLDER

The data files you need to work through this tutorial are provided on the CD-ROM housed in the back of this tutorial. CD-ROMs can hold hundreds of megabytes of data; however, as their name implies *(Compact Disc-Read-Only Memory)*, you cannot modify the data they contain. Thus, before you can begin your work, you must copy the *Office Data* folder from the Data CD to a hard drive or a network drive. You'll then use the *Office Data* folder throughout the rest of the tutorial.

Copying Folders and Files From a CD

In this activity, you will create your *Office Data* folder by copying a folder from the Data CD (in the back of this tutorial) to a hard drive or a network drive.

Office XP Basics   **87**

Copying Data From a CD

1. Insert the CD into the CD drive.

2. Open Windows Explorer.

3. In the Folders pane, click the CD drive icon. (If necessary, double-click the CD drive icon to expand the sublevels.)

4. In the Contents pane, click to select the folder that you want to copy.

5. Click Copy on the Edit menu.

6. In the Folders pane, click the drive/folder where you want to store the copied folders/files.

7. Click Paste on the Edit menu.

WARNING *Ask your instructor whether you should complete this activity. If so, confirm (1) whether to complete step 3 to change the Folder Options settings on the computer you are using and (2) the exact path and folder where you must store your* Office Data *folder.*

1. **Insert the Data CD into the CD drive of your computer.**

2. **Click the Start button** ![Start] **on the Windows taskbar. Then, point to Programs, point to Accessories, and click Windows Explorer.**

The Explorer window opens and displays the name of the default location (such as My Documents) in the title bar at the top of the window. The Explorer window consists of two **panes**—the Folders pane and the Contents pane. When you click a drive icon or folder name in the Folders pane (the left pane), the **folders** (or subfolders) and files contained in that drive or folder appear in the Contents pane (the right pane).

3. **If you want your Explorer window to match the activities and figures in this tutorial (and if you have permission to change the settings on the computer you are using), click Folder Options on the Tools menu.**

   a. **In the Folder Options dialog box, click the General tab, if it is not on top. If necessary, click the option buttons to select these settings:**

   In the *Active Desktop* area, select Use Windows classic desktop.

   In the *Web View* area, select Enable Web content in folders.

   In the *Browse Folders* area, select Open each folder in the same window.

   In the *Click items as follows* area, select Double-click to open an item (single-click to select).

   b. **In the Folder Options dialog box, click the View tab. Click to select *only* the following options on the View tab (make sure no other options are selected on the View tab):**

   Do not show hidden files and folders

   Hide file extensions for known file types

   Hide protected operating system files (Recommended)

   Show and manage the pair as a single file

   Show My Documents on the Desktop

   Show pop-up description for folder and desktop items

4. **Click OK to close the Folder Options dialog box.**

5. **In the Explorer window, click List on the View menu if it is not already selected.**

6. **If a plus sign (+) appears beside the My Computer icon in the Folders pane of the Explorer window, click the plus sign to expand the sublevels.**

Did u know?

Windows 2000 keeps track of the date and time a file was created, the date and time a file was modified, and the date a file was last opened, as well as the file type, location, and size.

7. In the Folders pane, find and click the drive icon that represents your CD drive. You may need to scroll down in the Folders pane.

The contents of the Data CD, the *Office Data* folder, appear in the Contents pane, as shown in Figure 3.6.

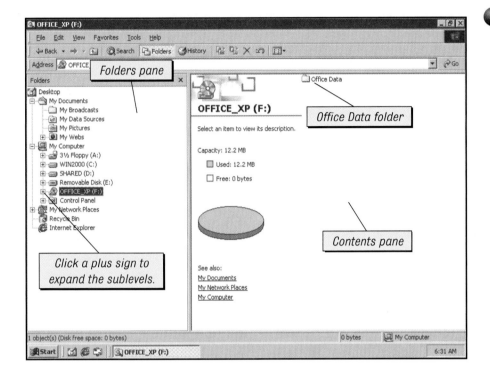

Figure 3.6
General tab of the Office Data Properties dialog box

8. In the Contents pane, click the *Office Data* folder to select it.

9. Click **Copy** on the Edit menu.

10. In the Folders pane, click the appropriate drive icon (and folder, if necessary) where you want to store the *Office Data* folder.

NOTE *Check with your instructor to determine if you should create a new folder (or subfolder) in which to store the* Office Data *folder. If so, follow these steps to create a new folder: (a) Point to New on the File menu and then click Folder; (b) Type the new folder name and press* ⟨Enter⏎⟩*; and (c) In the Contents pane, double-click the newly created folder to open it.*

11. Click **Paste** on the Edit menu.

A Copying box may appear on the screen to indicate the progress of the copying process. In a few moments, the *Office Data* folder (and all its contents) will be copied from the Data CD to the drive and/or folder you selected.

12. In the Contents pane, double-click the *Office Data* folder.

The contents of the *Office Data* folder appear, as shown in Figure 3.7. As you can see, the *Office Data* folder contains several folders and files. You'll store your work in these folders as you progress through the tutorial.

13. Remove the Data CD from the CD drive.

Another Way

To copy the contents of one folder to another folder, select the files and/or folders to copy, and then press and hold ⟨Ctrl⟩ while you drag the files and/or folders to the desired folder.

Figure 3.7
Contents of the *Office Data* folder

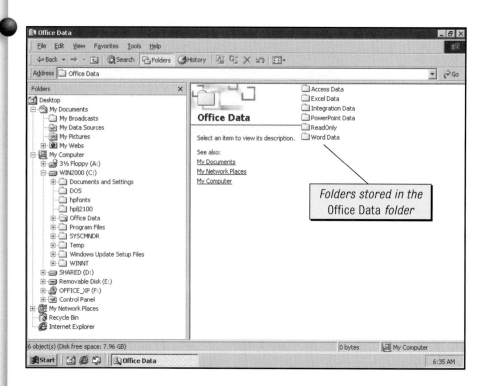

Folders stored in the
Office Data *folder*

HANDS on

Setting File Attributes

An **attribute** is a property that controls the use of a file or folder. By nature of the storage medium on which they reside, CD-ROM files and folders have a *read-only* attribute, which allows you to view files but not write to them. To actually use and save changes to the files you copied from the Data CD, you must remove the *read-only* attribute. In this activity, you will change the attributes of the files and folders in your *Office Data* folder.

NOTE *Ask your instructor if you should complete this activity.*

1. In the Folders pane of the Explorer window, right-click the *Office Data* folder.

WARNING *Carefully confirm that you have right-clicked the correct folder on your computer. You don't want to change the file and folder attributes of the wrong folder on your computer.*

2. On the shortcut menu that appears, click **Properties**.

The Office Data Properties dialog box appears with the General tab on top.

3. In the *Attributes* area of the Office Data Properties dialog box, click to clear the **Read-only check box**.

The *Attributes* area of your Office Data Properties dialog box should match Figure 3.8.

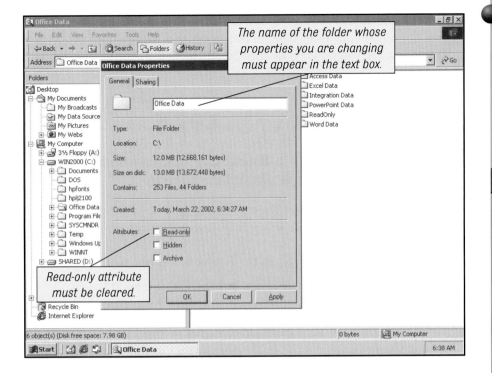

Figure 3.8
Office Data Properties dialog box

GETTING STARTED

4. Click Apply.

The Confirm Attribute Changes dialog box appears asking whether you want to unset (or remove) the read-only attribute and apply the changes to only the selected folder *or* whether you want to apply these changes to the selected folder, subfolders, and files.

5. Click the Apply changes to this folder, subfolders and files option and click OK. Click OK to close the Office Data Properties dialog box.

You have successfully removed the read-only file attributes from the files and folders in your *Office Data* folder. You are now ready to begin working with the *Office XP Brief Edition* tutorial.

6. Click the Close button ☒ in the upper-right corner of the Explorer window.

The Explorer window closes and you return to the Windows desktop.

STARTING AN OFFICE PROGRAM

Before you can start an Office application program, both Office XP and Windows 98 (or higher version) must be installed on the computer you are using. When Office is installed on a computer, its programs are added to the Programs menu so that you can use the Start button 🔳Start to launch them. Therefore, to start an Office application program, you simply click the Start button 🔳Start, point to Programs, and click the desired program (for example, Microsoft Word, Microsoft Excel, Microsoft Access, or Microsoft PowerPoint). After a few moments, the selected program is launched, its window appears, and a program taskbar button

---

Office BASICS

Setting File Attributes

1. Open Windows Explorer and navigate to the folder or file that has attributes you want to change.

2. In the Folders pane of the Explorer window, right-click the selected file or folder.

3. On the shortcut menu, click Properties.

4. In the *Attributes* area of the Properties dialog box for the selected folder/file, click to clear and/or select the check boxes for the desired attributes.

5. Click Apply.

6. In the Confirm Attribute Changes dialog box, click the desired option to apply; then click OK.

7. Click OK to close the Properties dialog box.

8. Close the Explorer window.

NORTON
ONLINE

Visit **www.glencoe.com/norton/online/** for more information on working with Office programs.

appears on the bottom of the screen. You can have more than one Office application program open at one time, if you want. To switch from one open application program to another, you simply click the appropriate taskbar button.

HANDS on

Using the Start Button to Launch the Office Applications

In this activity, you will start Word, Excel, Access, and PowerPoint using the Start button [Start], and then you will switch between application programs.

1. Click the **Start button** [Start] on the Windows taskbar.

2. Point to **Programs**. If necessary, click the double arrow at the bottom of the menu to list all of the items on the Programs menu.

The Programs menu appears; it should look similar to Figure 3.9. Depending on the applications installed on your computer, your Programs menu may be different from Figure 3.9.

Figure 3.9
Programs menu

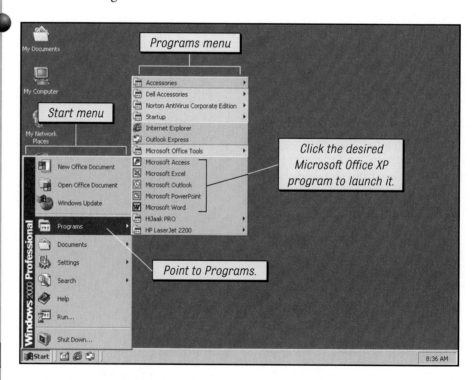

3. Click **Microsoft Word**.

The Word program starts, its window appears, and a Word taskbar button is displayed.

4. Again, click the **Start button** [Start], point to **Programs**, and click **Microsoft Excel**.

Office BASICS

Launching an Office Program

1. Click the Start button.

2. Point to Programs and click Microsoft Word, Microsoft Excel, Microsoft Access, or Microsoft PowerPoint.

The Excel program starts. Its window appears, covering the Word window, and an Excel taskbar button is displayed.

5. Click the Start button ![Start] **again, point to Programs, and click Microsoft Access.**

The Access program starts, covering the Excel window. Another taskbar button is displayed.

6. Click the Start button ![Start] **, point to Programs, and click Microsoft PowerPoint.**

The PowerPoint program starts, covering the Access window. Four buttons now appear on the taskbar, one for each open Office application program, as shown in Figure 3.10.

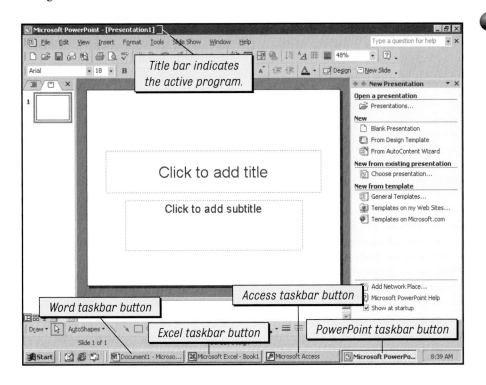

Another Way

You can start an Office program by clicking New Office Document on the Start menu. Click the General tab in the New Office Document dialog box, click the *Blank* option for the desired Office program, and click OK.

Figure 3.10
Taskbar buttons for open programs

7. Click the Excel taskbar button.

You switched from PowerPoint to Excel. Remember that you simply click the desired program's taskbar button to switch between application programs.

8. Click the Word taskbar button to return to its application window.

Did you know?

You can use the Microsoft Office Shortcut Bar to quickly start an Office program, open an existing file, or start a new file. Click the Start button, point to Programs, point to Microsoft Office Tools, and then click Microsoft Office Shortcut Bar.

EXPLORING THE OFFICE WINDOWS

The Word **application window** is shown in Figure 3.11. Your window may look slightly different, because Office allows users to **customize,** or alter, their windows to suit individual needs. However, each Office application window contains many standard Windows elements, including a title bar; the Minimize, Restore Down, and Close buttons; a menu bar; and one or more toolbars. These items should seem familiar if you have ever used a Windows 98, Windows 2000, or Windows Me application.

NOTE *The Language bar, which provides tools for handwriting and speech recognition, will appear in the upper-right corner of the application window if it has been installed on the computer you are using. To close the Language bar, point to the bar, right-click, and click Close the Language bar on the shortcut menu.*

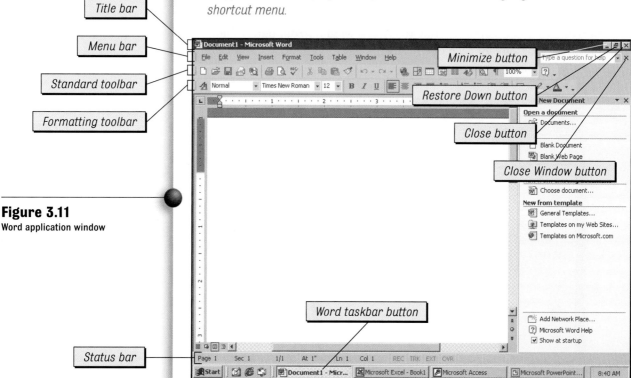

Figure 3.11
Word application window

- If your keyboard has a Start key (with a Windows symbol), press it to view the Start menu, use the arrow keys on the keyboard to make a selection, and press Enter⏎ to activate your selection.

- To switch among programs, press Alt + Tab.

Across the bottom of the screen is the taskbar, including the Start button and other buttons for **navigating** Windows. As you just learned, buttons on the taskbar show which applications are open. When a taskbar button is active, you know that program is ready to use. Across the top of the screen, the **title bar** shows the name of the application. The title bar in Word, Excel, and PowerPoint also shows the name of the current file. Word, by **default,** gives a temporary name of *Document* followed by a unique number to each unsaved file, as shown in Figure 3.11. Excel's default file name for an unsaved file is *Book1,* and PowerPoint's default file name for an unsaved file is *Presentation1.*

Working With Menus and Commands

As shown in Figure 3.11, the **menu bar** appears below the title bar. The menu bar displays menu names found in most Windows applications, such as File, Edit, and

Help. Table 3.1 provides a brief description of the common and unique menus available on the menu bars in each Office application program.

Table 3.1	The Office Menu Bars	
Menu	**Office Program**	**Contains Commands That Let You...**
File	Word, Excel, Access, and PowerPoint	Control your files by opening, saving, printing, and closing them.
Edit	Word, Excel, Access, and PowerPoint	Manipulate and rearrange elements within a file by copying, moving, and deleting them.
View	Word, Excel, Access, and PowerPoint	View files in different ways; display and hide toolbars and the task pane; and insert various other elements.
Insert	Word, Excel, Access, and PowerPoint	Insert various elements into a file.
Format	Word, Excel, and PowerPoint	Change the appearance of the elements within a file.
Tools	Word, Excel, Access, and PowerPoint	Use special tools, such as spelling, online collaboration, Web tools, and automatic correction features.
Table	Word	Insert, fill in, and format an arrangement of columns and rows as tabular information in a file.
Data	Excel	Organize data in different ways by sorting and filtering data, calculating subtotals, validating data, and creating Web queries.
Slide Show	PowerPoint	Set up a presentation for delivery; add animations or narrations to slides; set slide transitions that affect how one slide replaces another; broadcast a presentation online; and create customized presentations.
Window	Word, Excel, Access, and PowerPoint	Work with multiple files at once, in one or more windows.
Help	Word, Excel, Access, and PowerPoint	Access the online Help system, the Microsoft Office Assistance Center home page on the Web, and the Detect and Repair feature.

Menus list the **commands** available in the application. To display a menu's commands, click a menu name on the menu bar or press ⌨Alt on the keyboard plus the underlined letter in the menu name. The application will display a **short menu,** a list of the most basic commands, with arrows at the bottom. If you either hold the pointer on the menu name or point to the arrows at the bottom of the menu for a few seconds, or if you click the arrows, an **expanded menu** appears. This expanded menu shows all commands available on that menu. The most basic commands appear when a menu opens; when the list expands, less common commands also appear. Figure 3.12 shows both versions—a short menu and an expanded menu—of Excel's Tools menu.

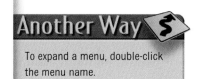

Another Way

To expand a menu, double-click the menu name.

Figure 3.12
Short and expanded Tools
menus in Excel

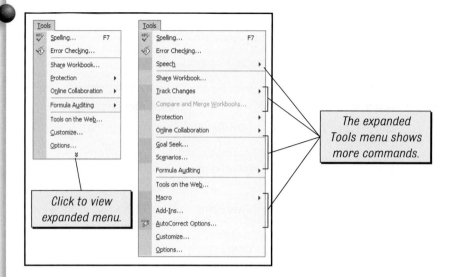

The expanded
Tools menu shows
more commands.

Click to view
expanded menu.

HINTS & TIPS

If you prefer to see expanded menus every time, turn off the expandable option by clicking Customize on the Tools menu. Then click the Options tab, click to select *Always show full menus,* and click Close.

After you use one of the additional commands from an expanded menu, the Office application adds that command to the short menu. This feature enables you to **personalize** the menus; each Office application automatically customizes menus as you work, placing the commands that you use often on the short menu.

After you display a menu, you can choose a command by clicking the desired command or by pressing the underlined letter in the command name. Ellipsis marks (…) after a command indicate that choosing the command will display a **dialog box** in which you may specify details. Pointing to a command that has an arrow to the right of it displays another list of commands called a **submenu.**

Working With Toolbars and Buttons

Below the menu bar in Word, Excel, and PowerPoint are the Standard and Formatting toolbars. In Access, the Database toolbar appears below the menu bar and is similar to the Standard toolbar in other Office applications. A **toolbar** contains buttons for many of the most frequently used commands, as shown in Figure 3.11 on page 94. Although you can access these commands on one of the menus, clicking a toolbar button is often more convenient. You quickly can identify any toolbar button by pointing to it and reading the name that appears below it in a small text box called a ScreenTip.

> **NOTE** *For the activities and figures in this tutorial, the Standard and Formatting toolbars in Word, Excel, and PowerPoint are displayed on two separate rows. If your Standard and Formatting toolbars share one row below the menu bar, you can display them as two separate rows by clicking Customize on the Tools menu. On the Options tab of the Customize dialog box, click to select the* Show Standard and Formatting toolbars on two rows *option and click Close.*
>
> *If you don't see a ScreenTip when you point to a toolbar button in an Office application, click Customize on the Tools menu. On the Options tab of the Customize dialog box, click to select the* Show ScreenTips on toolbars *option and click Close.*

Another Way

To display toolbars as separate rows, click the Toolbar Options button  and click Show Buttons on Two Rows.

The icon on each toolbar button symbolizes the command. For example, on the Standard toolbar in Word, Excel, and PowerPoint or on the Database toolbar in Access, the New button ▢ is symbolized by a piece of paper. As with the menus, you also can customize the toolbars. The most basic buttons appear on the main toolbar, while buttons used less often are accessible by clicking Toolbar Options ▾ at the end of a toolbar and navigating to the Toolbar Options list. If a button appears on the list but does not appear on the toolbar, you can open the Toolbar Options list and click the button to place a check mark beside it; the Office application then adds the button to the toolbar. To remove a button from the toolbar, open the Toolbar Options list and click the button to clear its check mark.

In Word, Excel, and PowerPoint, the Formatting toolbar appears directly below the Standard toolbar, as shown in Figure 3.11 on page 94. This toolbar includes commands for controlling the appearance of various elements within a file. For instance, using the Formatting toolbar, you can modify the font size and style, alignment, color, and other features that affect appearance.

Each Office application includes several other toolbars. Each toolbar includes specific commands to serve a unique purpose; for instance, the Web toolbar includes commands that allow you to access a Web site and navigate the Web efficiently. To view a list of the more common toolbars, point to Toolbars on the View menu to access the Toolbars submenu. A check mark next to a toolbar name indicates that toolbar is displayed. To view a list of all the available toolbars, click Customize at the bottom of the Toolbars submenu, and click the Toolbars tab in the Customize dialog box. To hide a toolbar, click the toolbar name to clear the check mark in front of the toolbar name; to display a toolbar, click the toolbar name to insert the check mark.

Working With the Status Bar and Scroll Bars

The **status bar** is the horizontal area that appears at the bottom of the application window just above the Windows taskbar. (See Figure 3.11 on page 94.) Depending on the application program you are using, the left side of the status bar provides information about a selected command, an operation in progress, or other information about the program or file. The right side of the status bar displays information about features or keys that are active. For instance, in Word, status indicator buttons turn special keys or modes (Overtype, for example) on or off. These indicator buttons display darkened when turned on and dimmed when off; just double-click the status indicator to toggle the particular key. In Excel and Access, keyboard indicators—such as CAPS or NUM—are displayed when turned on. In PowerPoint, the design template of the presentation and the language your computer is using are identified.

> **NOTE** *If the status bar is not visible on your screen when you are working with a file, click Options on the Tools menu. If necessary, click the View tab in the Options dialog box. Then, in the Options dialog box (View tab), click to select Status bar. Click OK to close the Options dialog box.*
>
> *If scroll bars are not visible on your Word or Excel screen, click Options on the Tools menu. On the View tab in the Options dialog box, click to select Horizontal scroll bar and Vertical scroll bar. Click OK to close the Options dialog box.*

HINTS & TIPS

- To move a toolbar left or right, point to the handle on the left end. When the four-way arrow appears, drag the toolbar.

- You can drag a toolbar handle to place a toolbar on another part of the screen. For example, you can "dock" a toolbar by attaching it to the left or right edge of the application window, or you can make the toolbar "float" by releasing it somewhere else in the application window.

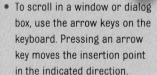

Another Way

- To scroll in a window or dialog box, use the arrow keys on the keyboard. Pressing an arrow key moves the insertion point in the indicated direction.

- To move immediately to the beginning of a file in Word, Excel, or PowerPoint, press Ctrl + Home.

- To move immediately to the end of a file in Word, Excel, or PowerPoint, press Ctrl + End.

Oftentimes a window on your screen, such as a dialog box, a Help window, or the application window, may contain more information than you can view at one time. As you work, you can move around in a window to bring the hidden portions into view. You can perform this procedure, called **scrolling,** using the scroll bars, scroll arrows, and scroll box. (See Figure 3.11 on page 94.) Use the **vertical scroll bar** to move up and down in a window, and use the **horizontal scroll bar** to move from side to side. Clicking the **scroll arrows** at each end of the bar, dragging the **scroll box** within the bar, or clicking between the scroll box and a scroll arrow allows you to navigate within a window at varying speeds. In some dialog boxes and windows, scroll bars will automatically appear when you need them so that you can display information that is hidden from view.

Working With the Task Pane

After you launched an Office program, you probably noticed a task pane on the right side of the application window. A **task pane** is a window that provides quick access to commonly used commands and features while you work with your file. Although the exact *name* of the task pane that appears at startup differs among the Office applications, the task pane commands are similar and allow you to create or access files. For instance, in Word, the New Document task pane (shown in Figure 3.13) appears by default each time you open Word. (If the task pane is not visible in an Office application, right-click any toolbar and click to select Task Pane on the Toolbars submenu that appears.) Options in a task pane that appear in colored text are **hyperlinks.** When you point to a hyperlink, the text is underlined and the pointer changes to the shape of a hand. Then, when clicked, the hyperlink activates an appropriate command or feature. For instance, if you click Blank Document in Word's New Document task pane, Word opens a new, blank document.

Figure 3.13
New Document task pane

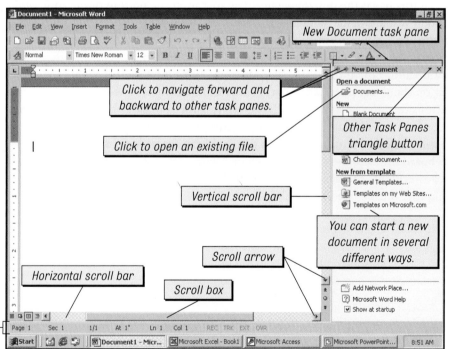

NOTE *If you click Blank Workbook in Excel's New Workbook task pane, Excel opens a new, blank workbook.*

If you click Blank Database in Access' New File task pane, Access displays a dialog box in which you could create and name a new, blank database.

If you click Blank Presentation in PowerPoint's New Presentation task pane, PowerPoint opens a new, blank presentation.

Because task pane options are also commands on menus, a task pane may open when you choose a particular menu command. For instance, clicking New on the File menu will open the New task pane for that Office application. Clicking Office Clipboard on the Edit menu will open the Clipboard task pane. To display the list of available task panes, click the Other Task Panes button ▾ in the task pane. You manually can open another task pane by choosing from the task panes list. Or, during each computer session, you also can use the Back button ◀ and Forward button ▶ in the task pane to move to the task panes you have recently accessed.

You easily can change the width of the task pane to allow more space for your work in the application window. To resize the task pane, point to the left edge of the task pane until you see a two-headed arrow. Click and drag the task pane to the left or right to the desired width. To close the task pane, click its Close button ✕.

HANDS on

Working in the Application Window

In this activity, you will explore each of the application windows.

1. **Click the Word taskbar button, if Word is not active.**

2. **Click View on the menu bar.**

The short View menu displays.

3. **Click the arrows at the bottom of the View menu.**

The expanded View menu displays all the commands on the View menu.

4. **Point to Toolbars on the View menu.**

The Toolbars submenu lists the common toolbars. A check mark appears next to the toolbars that are currently displayed.

5. **If a check mark appears before Standard in the Toolbars submenu, go on to step 6. If a check mark does not appear, click Standard.**

The Toolbars submenu closes and the Standard toolbar is displayed.

GETTING STARTED

GETTING STARTED

6. If check marks do not appear before **Formatting** and **Task Pane** in the Toolbars submenu, click to select the two toolbar options. (You must redisplay the Toolbars submenu each time you select or clear a toolbar on the Toolbars submenu.)

7. On the Toolbars submenu, click to clear any other toolbars that are currently displayed. If necessary, click a blank area of the application window to close the Toolbars submenu and the View menu.

8. In the task pane, click the **Close button** ☒ to hide the task pane.

The document area enlarges to fill the screen.

9. Verify that the Standard and Formatting toolbars are displayed as separate rows, as shown in Figure 3.14. If the toolbars are on the same row, click **Customize** on the Tools menu, click the **Options tab** if it is not on top, and click to select **Show Standard and Formatting toolbars on two rows**. Click the **Close button** in the Customize dialog box.

Standard and Formatting toolbars on separate rows

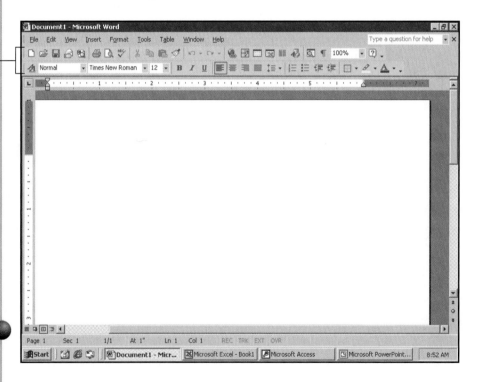

Figure 3.14
Standard and Formatting toolbars

10. Point to the **Help button** ☒ on the Standard toolbar, and read the ScreenTip. As your time permits, point to other buttons on the toolbars and read the ScreenTips.

11. Click **New** on the File menu.

The New task pane reappears.

12. Click the **Excel taskbar button**, and repeat steps 2 through 11 to explore the Excel window.

13. Switch to PowerPoint, and repeat steps 2 through 11 to explore the PowerPoint window.

NORTON
ONLINE

Visit **www.glencoe.com/norton/online/** for more information on working in the application window.

14. Switch to Access. Click **View** on the menu bar, and point to **Toolbars** on the View menu. If a check mark appears before Database in the Toolbars submenu, go on to step 15. If a check mark does not appear, click **Database**.

15. If a check mark does not appear before Task Pane in the Toolbars submenu, click to select it. Click to clear any other toolbars that are currently displayed. Close the task pane.

16. Point to the **Help button** ▣ on the Database toolbar, and read the ScreenTip. As your time permits, point to other buttons and read the ScreenTips. Finally, click New on the File menu to display the New File task pane.

WORKING WITH FOLDERS AND FILES

Any time you want to use a **file** that you or someone else created, you first must **open** it. Opening a file means copying that file from disk into the memory of your computer so that you can update or view it. As you work within each Office application, you can open a file in several ways: (1) you can click the Open button ▣ on the Standard toolbar in Word, Excel, and PowerPoint or on the Database toolbar in Access; (2) you can click the Open command on the File menu; or (3) you can click the *More* command in the New task pane (that is, *More documents* in Word, *More workbooks* in Excel, *More presentations* in PowerPoint, or *Files or More Files* in Access). In each instance, the Open dialog box is displayed, where you specify the drive, folder, and file that you want to open.

HANDS on

Opening a File

In this activity, you will open the *Creative Communications* file in the *Word Data, Excel Data, Access Data,* and *PowerPoint Data* folders in your *Office Data* folder.

1. Switch to Word by clicking its taskbar button.

2. Click the **Open button** ▣.

NOTE *In Word, Excel, and PowerPoint, the Open button ▣ is on the Standard toolbar. In Access, the Open button ▣ is on the Database toolbar.*

The Open dialog box appears. The Look in box shows the current folder or drive.

WARNING *If you're sharing a computer with one or more users in a lab or school environment, the list of files displayed in the Open dialog box may not contain the file you wish to open. Continue with steps 3 through 5 to properly navigate to your files.*

Office BASICS

Opening a File

1. Click the Open button on the Standard toolbar or on the Database toolbar.

2. In the Open dialog box, click the appropriate drive/folder in the Look In box.

3. Double-click the folder, if necessary, in which the files are stored.

4. Click the desired file and click the Open button in the Open dialog box.

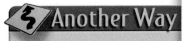

GETTING STARTED

Another Way

To open a file, double-click its name in the Open dialog box.

3. In the Open dialog box, verify that the *Files of type* list box is set appropriately for the Office program in which you want to work. For instance, to open a Word document, set the *Files of type* list box to **All Word Documents**; for an Excel workbook, **All Microsoft Excel Files**; for an Access database, **Microsoft Access**; and for a PowerPoint presentation, **All PowerPoint Presentations**.

4. Click the **Look in triangle button** to display a list of the available drives.

5. In the list of drives, click the drive that contains your *Office Data* folder. In the list of folders/files that appears, click the *Office Data* folder to select it and click the **Open button** in the lower-right corner of the Open dialog box.

NOTE *If your* Office Data *folder is not stored at the root level of the drive, you must navigate to it. If necessary, ask your instructor or lab assistant for assistance in locating your folders and files.*

Below the Look in box, you now see a list of the folders contained in the *Office Data* folder, as shown in Figure 3.15.

Figure 3.15
Open dialog box

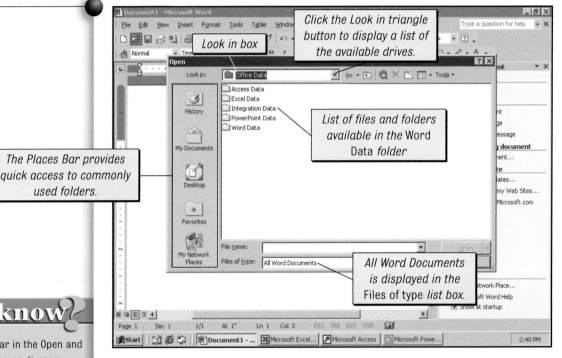

The Places Bar provides quick access to commonly used folders.

Did you know?

- The Places Bar in the Open and Save dialog boxes gives you quick access to commonly used folders. For instance, you can click the Favorites folder to see a list of files stored in this folder.

- You can access files of different formats by changing the *Files of type* setting in the Open and Save dialog boxes.

6. Double-click the *Data* folder for the Office program in which you want to work. For instance, click the *Word Data* folder to open a Word document, the *Excel Data* folder to open an Excel workbook, and so on.

Below the Look in box, you will see a list of the folders and files in the *Data* folder you opened.

7. Click *Creative Communications* in the list of file names, and click the **Open button** in the dialog box.

The application's New task pane closes and the *Creative Communications* file opens.

NOTE *If you are using Access and the Basic Search task pane opens, click its Close button ☒ to close it. Then, click the Maximize button ☐ in the Database window so the Database window will fill the entire application window.*

8. Switch to Excel and repeat steps 2 through 7 to open *Creative Communications* in the *Excel Data* folder.

9. Switch to Access and repeat steps 2 through 7 to open *Creative Communications* in the *Access Data* folder.

10. Switch to PowerPoint and repeat steps 2 through 7 to open *Creative Communications* in the *PowerPoint Data* folder.

Saving a File

NOTE *The process of naming and saving a file is the same for Word, Excel, and PowerPoint. However, the process is somewhat different for Access. A discussion on creating and naming a database file and saving data in Access is presented in Access Lesson 1.*

After working with a file for a few minutes, you should **save** it. Saving a file transfers its contents from the computer's memory to a disk for you to retrieve later. It's important to save your work frequently in case something goes wrong with the computer. For example, if you have not saved your file and your computer malfunctions or a power outage occurs, some or all of your work may be lost.

As you have already learned, Word names a new, unsaved file *Document* followed by a unique number (for example, *Document1*) as the default file name. Excel uses *Book1* as the default file name for an unsaved file; PowerPoint uses *Presentation1*. When you save a file, you should give the file a meaningful name so you can determine at a glance what information the file contains. Besides naming a file, you also must specify where to store the file (the drive and **path**). A file name, including the drive and path, can contain up to 215 characters, including spaces. The file name, however, may not include any of the following characters: \ / : * ? " < > |

When you save a new file for the first time, the Save As dialog box appears—whether you click the Save button 🖫 on the Standard toolbar or choose either the Save or the Save As commands on the File menu. However, after you've initially named and saved a file, issuing the Save command either from the File menu or by clicking the Save button 🖫 automatically updates the file on disk with the version currently in memory, without redisplaying the Save As dialog box.

If you want to save a copy of the file with a different name and/or in a different place, you must click the Save As command on the File menu. When you do this, the Save As dialog box appears so that you can specify a new file name, location, or file type. Note that when you use the Save As command, you are not renaming a file. Instead, you're saving a copy of the file under a different name, in a different place, or as a different file type. The original file with the original name, location, and file type will not be deleted, moved, or renamed.

GETTING STARTED

Did you know?

You can resize the Open and Save dialog boxes. Point to a corner of the dialog box until you see a two-headed arrow. Click and drag diagonally to the desired size.

HINTS & TIPS

You can display the three-letter file extensions (the file types) for file names that appear in the Open and Save dialog boxes. Open Windows Explorer and click Folder Options on the Tools menu. On the View tab of the Folder Options dialog box, click to clear the *Hide file extensions for known file types* check box, and then click Apply.

HANDS on

Naming and Saving a File

In this activity, you will save the *Creative Communications* file in a different location and with a different file name.

> **NOTE** *You will create and name an Access file and save data in an Access database in Access Lesson 1.*

1. Switch to Word.

2. Click **Save As** on the File menu.

The Save As dialog box appears.

3. If your *Office Data* folder does not appear in the Save in box of the Save As dialog box, click the **Save in triangle button**.

4. Click the name of the drive in which your *Office Data* folder is stored from the drop-down list (and, if necessary, double-click the folder in which your *Office Data* folder is stored).

5. Then, double-click the *Office Data* folder to open it.

6. In the *Office Data* folder, double-click the folder of the application in which you want to work. For instance, double-click the *Word Data* folder to open the folder with folders/files for Word, double-click the *Excel Data* folder to open the folders/files for Excel, and so on.

7. Click the *Tutorial* folder in the window below the Save in box.

8. Click the **Open button** in the Save As dialog box.

The *Tutorial* folder opens and appears in the Save in box.

9. In the File name box, edit the file name to be *Creative Communications-Explored* as shown in Figure 3.16.

10. Click the **Save button** in the Save As dialog box.

The program saves the file in a different folder with a different name. Now the newly created file is displayed in the application window, and the title bar and the taskbar button show the new file name.

11. Switch to Excel and repeat steps 2 through 10 to name and save your file as *Creative Communications-Explored* in the *Tutorial* folder in your *Excel Data* folder.

12. Switch to PowerPoint and repeat steps 2 through 10 to name and save your file as *Creative Communications-Explored* in the *Tutorial* folder in your *PowerPoint Data* folder.

Office **BASICS**

Naming and Saving a File in Word, Excel, and PowerPoint

To save a file with the same name and in the same location:

Click the Save button on the Standard toolbar.

To save a file with a new name and/or in a different location:

1. Click Save As on the File menu.

2. In the Save As dialog box, select the drive/folder in the Save in box.

3. Type a name for the file in the File name box.

4. Click the Save button in the Save As dialog box.

HINTS & TIPS

If the entire file name is not visible in the taskbar button, point to the button and it will appear.

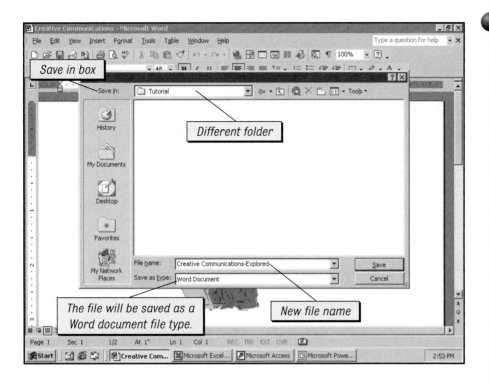

Figure 3.16
Saving a file in the Tutorial folder

Save in box

Different folder

The file will be saved as a Word document file type.

New file name

HINTS & TIPS

To quickly access your *Office Data* folder, you can add a custom folder location as a shortcut on the Places Bar of the Open and Save dialog boxes. In these dialog boxes, navigate to the folder to which you want to add a shortcut on the Places Bar. Click to select the folder, and then on the Tools menu of the dialog box, click *Add to "My Places."*

As you have just learned, you easily can use the Save As command to rename a file and save it in a different location when you are using Word, Excel, and PowerPoint.

Closing and Reopening a File

When you have finished working with a file, you should **close** the file—just as you put away file folders at the office when you're finished using them. Closing a file removes it from memory but leaves the application program running. When a file is open, two Close buttons are displayed on the screen: one for the file on the *menu bar* and one for the application program on the *title bar*. When closing a file, make sure you click the correct Close button. Clicking the Close Window button ☒ on the menu bar will close the open file, whereas, clicking the Close button ☒ on the title bar will close the application program—so be careful!

> **NOTE** *Within Word, Excel, and PowerPoint, you can have several files open at once. When more than one file is open in these applications, it is possible to click the title bar's Close button to close the displayed file without closing the application program, which can be confusing. However, you can add a Close button ☐ to the Standard toolbar; using this button avoids the problem of accidentally closing the application program when you intend to close only a file. (You can add a Close button to the Standard toolbar by accessing the Customize dialog box [Commands tab] through the Tools menu.)*

If you've used a file recently, you can reopen that file by choosing the file name from the list of recently opened files that appears in the *Open* area of the task pane (the *Open a document* area in Word, *Open a workbook* area in Excel, *Open a presentation* area in PowerPoint, or *Open a file* area in Access) or near the bottom of the File menu. By default, Office lists the last four files you've opened.

Another Way

To close a file, click Close on the File menu.

HANDS on

Closing and Reopening Files

In this activity, you will close *Creative Communications-Explored* in Word, Excel, and PowerPoint and *Creative Communications* in Access and then reopen the files.

1. Choose an Office program in which to work.

2. Click the **Close Window button** ☒ at the right end of the menu bar. If you receive a message asking whether you want to save the changes, click **No**.

The application closes the file, clearing the application window completely.

3. Click **File** on the menu bar.

The name of the file you just closed appears near the bottom of the menu, and it is listed first, as shown in Figure 3.17.

Figure 3.17
File menu listing

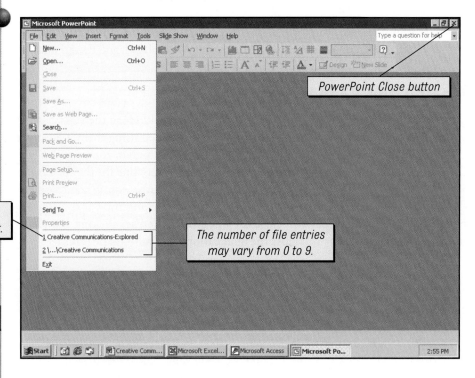

PowerPoint Close button

The most recently opened file appears first.

The number of file entries may vary from 0 to 9.

Office BASICS

Closing and Reopening a File
To close a file:

1. Click the Close Window button on the menu bar.

2. Respond to the Save prompt, if necessary.

To reopen a file:

Click the file name at the bottom of the File menu.

4. To reopen the file you just closed, click its file name (*Creative Communications-Explored* in Word, Excel, and PowerPoint or *Creative Communications* in Access), near the bottom of the File menu.

The file reappears in the application window.

5. Repeat this activity until you close and reopen *Creative Communications-Explored* in Word, Excel, and PowerPoint and *Creative Communications* in Access.

NOTE *Remember to click the Maximize button* ☐ *in the Database window to display the window at full size.*

From one Office program to the next, you can follow the same steps to close and reopen a file.

GETTING HELP WITH OFFICE

While you are using any of the Office applications, you may need to reference the extensive **online Help system**—an electronic manual that you can open with the press of a key or the click of a mouse. Office provides several different Help tools: the Office Assistant, ScreenTips, the Ask a Question box, the Answer Wizard, the Contents, and the Index.

While using the Help system, you will see many hyperlinks that provide details about a topic. When clicked, most of the hyperlinks expand to reveal explanatory text. Some hyperlinks may link to other Help frames with related topics or to Web sites. Pictures, graphic elements, and objects also may contain hyperlinks. In the Help window, you can click the hyperlink again to hide or collapse the expanded Help information.

Within a Help window, you also may see words in a sentence that are in colored text. These words are **glossary terms** and are also hyperlinks. Click the glossary term to display its definition (in green text in parentheses immediately following the term); click the term or the definition again to hide the definition.

Using the Office Assistant and ScreenTips

You can access most of the Help tools through the **Office Assistant,** an animated character that can answer specific questions, offer tips, and provide help for the program's features—sometimes even before you ask. You can activate the Office Assistant by clicking the animated character on your screen (if visible); by clicking the Help button ☒ on the Standard toolbar in Word, Excel, and PowerPoint or on the Database toolbar in Access; by clicking the Help command on the Help menu; by clicking the Help hyperlink in the New task pane; or by clicking the Show the Office Assistant command on the Help menu.

In addition to accessing the Office Assistant through the Help menu, you also can access **ScreenTips**—helpful text boxes that provide information on various program elements. When you click *What's This?* on the Help menu, the pointer changes to a question mark pointer. While the question mark pointer is displayed, you can click an element on the screen—a menu command, a toolbar button, or another element—to see its description. Click anywhere on the screen to remove the ScreenTip.

Using the Ask a Question Box

The **Ask a Question** box at the right end of the menu bar allows you to quickly access Help topics. You simply click the Ask a Question box and type a word, phrase, or question, press ⏎ Enter, and select one of the Help topics that appear. You then can explore to find the answer to your question. You can revisit Help topics you've recently explored by clicking the Ask a Question triangle button and then clicking a topic in the drop-down list.

Did you know?

To immediately display all the information on a Help topic, click the Show All hyperlink in the Help window, if there is one.

WEB NOTE

If the Office Assistant does not provide a topic that answers your question, click the *None of the above, search for more on the Web* option. A new Help window appears that allows you to connect to the Web to obtain further help. Or, you can click *Office on the Web* on the Help menu to go directly to the Microsoft Office Assistance Center site.

HANDS on

Asking for Help

In this activity, you will explore Help using ScreenTips, the Office Assistant, and the Ask a Question box.

1. Choose an Office program in which to work. If you are using Word, Excel, or PowerPoint, verify that *Creative Communications-Explored* is open. If you are using Access, verify that *Creative Communications* is open.

2. Click **What's This?** on the Help menu.

The pointer changes to a question mark pointer.

3. Click the **Open button** 📂, and read the ScreenTip that appears.

NOTE *Remember that the Open button* 📂 *is on the Standard toolbar in Word, Excel, and PowerPoint and on the Database toolbar in Access.*

4. Click anywhere on the screen to remove the ScreenTip. As your time permits, use *What's This?* to explore other elements of the application window.

5. If the Office Assistant is not currently displayed in the application window, click **Show the Office Assistant** on the Help menu. Then click the **Office Assistant**.

The Office Assistant asks what you would like to do.

6. In the Office Assistant balloon, type print a Help topic, as shown in Figure 3.18. Then click the **Search button**.

The Office Assistant lists the topics you could explore for your answer.

7. Click the **Print a Help topic option**.

A Help window appears on your screen.

8. Right-click the **Office Assistant**, and click **Hide** on the shortcut menu.

9. In the Help window, point to the **Print the current topic option**.

As you point, the pointer changes to a hand and the words become underlined, because this text is a hyperlink.

10. Click the **Print the current topic hyperlink**.

Specific information about printing a Help topic is displayed in the Help window, as shown in Figure 3.19.

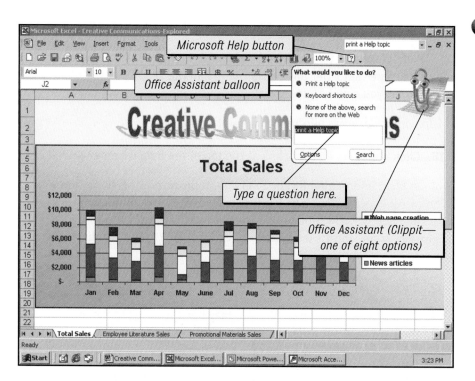

Figure 3.18
Office Assistant

 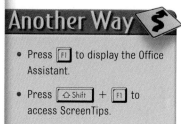
GETTING STARTED

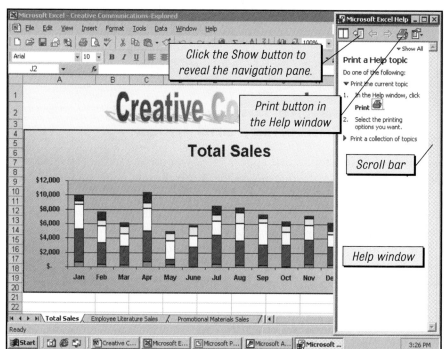

Figure 3.19
Help window

11. Read the Help information.

12. Click the **Print a collection of topics hyperlink**, and read the Help information that appears.

13. Click the two hyperlinks to hide the Help information on those topics.

HINTS & TIPS

You can print a Help topic by first displaying the topic and then clicking the Print button in the Help window.

GETTING STARTED

14. Click the **Close button** ☒ in the Help window.

15. Click the **Ask a Question box** located at the right end of the menu bar, type find a file, and press ⏎. In the drop-down list of topics you could explore, click the **Find a file topic**.

A Help window displays information about finding files.

16. Click the **Show All hyperlink** at the top of the Help window.

All of the Help information for the *Find a file* topic is revealed. (Note, too, that the Show All hyperlink has now become the Hide All hyperlink.) As you scroll down the Help window, notice that the natural language searches hyperlink is a glossary term, and its definition appears in green text immediately after the term.

17. Click the glossary term or its definition to hide the definition.

18. Click the **Hide All hyperlink**. (You may need to scroll to the top of the Help window to display the Hide All hyperlink.)

19. If desired, repeat this activity using another Office program. You'll quickly see that the Help tools are the same among the Office programs.

HANDS on

Using the Answer Wizard, Contents, and Index

Sometimes the Help topics that appear when you use the Office Assistant or the Ask a Question box do not completely answer the questions you may have. To perform a more extensive search of the online Help system, you can use these Help tools: the Answer Wizard, Contents, and Index. The **Answer Wizard** can answer specific questions in the same manner as the Office Assistant; however, it provides many more topics from which to choose for further exploration. You can use the **Contents** to view a listing of general Help topics; this method can be useful if you don't know the name of a feature. You can search for specific words or phrases or choose from a list of keywords in the **Index.** In this activity, you will continue to explore Help using the Answer Wizard, Contents, and Index.

1. If necessary, click the **Show button** in the Help window.

The Help window expands, revealing the navigation pane, which contains the Contents, Answer Wizard, and Index tabs. Note, too, that the Show button changes to a Hide button .

> **NOTE** *If the navigation pane of the Help window is somewhat narrow, the Answer Wizard tab may not be visible. In this instance, click the directional arrows near the tabs until you see the Answer Wizard tab.*

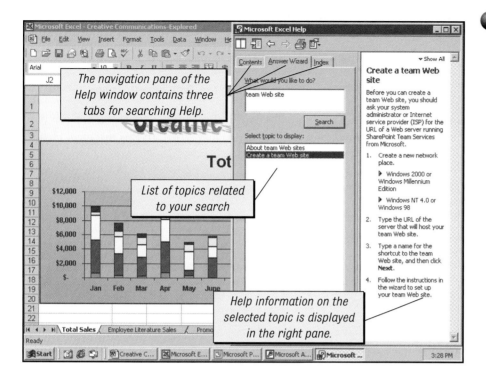

The navigation pane of the Help window contains three tabs for searching Help.

List of topics related to your search

Help information on the selected topic is displayed in the right pane.

Figure 3.20
Answer Wizard search

2. Click the **Answer Wizard tab**, if it is not on top.

3. In the *What would you like to do?* box in the navigation pane, highlight the existing text (*Type your question here and then click Search*), if it is not already selected. (You can triple-click to quickly highlight the existing text.) Then, type team Web site, **and click the Search button**.

Topics that may answer your question appear in the *Select topic to display* box. The first topic is selected, and the related Help information appears in the right pane.

4. In the *Select topic to display* box, click the **Create a team Web site topic**, as shown in Figure 3.20.

5. Read the Help information.

6. Click the **Contents tab**, scroll to the top of the navigation pane, if necessary, and double-click the closed book icon in front of the Getting Started with Microsoft Office category.

The closed book icon changes to an open book icon, and the category expands to show an individual Help topic (indicated by a question mark icon) and a subcategory (indicated by another book icon). The pane on the right still shows the previous search results.

7. In the navigation pane, double-click the **Getting Help subcategory**.

8. When the subcategory expands, click the **About getting help while you work topic**.

The Help topic's information appears in the right pane of the Help window.

Office **BASICS**

Using the Answer Wizard and Contents Tab

To use the Answer Wizard:

1. Click the Show button in the Help window, if necessary.

2. Click the Answer Wizard tab in the navigation pane, if necessary.

3. In the *What would you like to do?* box, type a search topic.

4. Click the Search button.

5. In the *Select topic to display* box, click the topic you want to read.

To use the Contents Tab:

1. Click the Show button in the Help window, if necessary.

2. Click the Contents tab in the navigation pane, if necessary.

3. Double-click the book in front of the Help category you wish to open.

4. Double-click a subcategory or click a topic you wish to read.

WEB NOTE

If you find a Help topic that begins with *WEB*, you may explore an Office Update article on the Microsoft Office Assistance Center site directly in your Help window.

GETTING STARTED

9. Click the **Back button** ⬅.

The Help information on the previous topic reappears.

10. Click the **Index tab** and type menu in the *Type keywords* box.

As you type each letter, the highlight within the *Or choose keywords* box jumps to the next word that contains the letter you just typed. In this instance, Help jumps to *menu.*

11. Click the **Search button**.

The results of the search are listed in the *Choose a topic* box, and the first topic is displayed in the right pane of the Help window.

12. In the *Or choose keywords* box, scroll to the word *customize* and double-click it so that both *menu* and *customize* appear in the *Type keywords* box.

The list of topics that contain both keywords appears in the *Choose a topic* box; as you can see, a two-word (or phrase) search results in fewer topics than a one-word (or phrase) search.

13. Click the **Hide button** 🔲.

14. Click the **Close button** ❎ in the Help window.

15. In each application, click the **Close Window button** ❎ on the menu bar to close the open file (*Creative Communications-Explored* if you are using Word, Excel, or PowerPoint or *Creative Communications* if you are using Access).

16. If a dialog box appears asking if you want to save changes to a file, click **No.**

EXITING THE APPLICATION PROGRAMS AND SHUTTING DOWN YOUR COMPUTER

When you are finished with an application program, you should exit the program properly. Failure to close an application can lead to problems the next time you want to start it. Exiting the program closes any open files and removes the application program from computer memory. You can exit an Office program by clicking the title bar's Close button ❎ or by clicking the Exit command on the File menu. After exiting the Office programs, you may choose to shut down your computer if you have no other programs running.

WARNING *Check with your instructor or computer lab assistant for the "shut down" procedures in your lab or school environment.*

HANDS on

Exiting Office Programs and Shutting Down

In this activity, you will exit each open Office program and shut down the computer you are using, following the procedures for your lab or school environment.

1. Click the **Close button** ☒ on the title bar of each open Office program.

Each Office program disappears from the screen, and you return to the Windows desktop.

2. Follow the "shut down" procedures for your lab or school environment or continue with step 3.

NOTE *If you plan to proceed directly to the* On the Web *activity, do not shut down your computer at this time.*

3. Click the **Start button** 🔊 Start.

4. Click **Shut Down**.

The entire screen darkens a bit, and the Shut Down Windows dialog box appears.

5. Click the **Shut down option** in the drop-down list (if it isn't already selected) and click **OK**.

After a few moments, a message may appear, indicating that you may turn off your computer.

6. Turn off your computer and the monitor, if necessary.

Self Check ✓

Test your knowledge by answering the following questions. See Appendix B to check your answers.

T F **1.** Both toolbars and menus can be customized for individual users.

T F **2.** To start an Office application, click the Start button, point to Programs, and click the desired Office application.

T F **3.** The task pane is a window that provides quick access to commonly used commands and features.

T F **4.** The only way to access the online Help system is through the Office Assistant.

T F **5.** To exit an Office application, click the Close Window button on the menu bar or click Close on the File menu.

GETTING HELP ON THE WEB

Every day, computer users around the world use the Internet for work, play, and research. The **Internet** is a worldwide network of computers that connects each Internet user's computer to all other computers in the network. Vast quantities of infinitely varied information—from simple text in the form of an e-mail message to extremely complex software—can pass through these connections. The most popular tool used to access the Internet is the **World Wide Web** (**WWW** or the **Web**). A document published on the Web is referred to as a **Web page** and is stored in a specific place on the Web called a **Web site.**

Using your Web **browser**—a software tool used to navigate the Web—you can access most Internet services and all World Wide Web pages directly from an Office application window. By using hyperlinks in the online Help and using other Help commands, you can instantly jump to a Web site and search for help on the Web. In this activity, you will display the Web toolbar in an application window, learn about Help on the Web, and then explore for help on the Web.

1. Start an Office program, if necessary.

2. Point to **Toolbars** on the View menu, and click **Web** on the Toolbars submenu, if it is not already selected. (If Web has a check mark next to it, the Web toolbar is displayed already. Click outside the menu to leave the toolbar selected and close the menu.)

   NOTE *If the Web toolbar appears on your screen as a* **floating toolbar**, *you can move it. Click the title bar of the floating Web toolbar and drag the toolbar to appear directly below the last displayed toolbar. When you release the mouse button, the toolbar will snap into place and become a* **docked toolbar***.*

3. Using the *What's This?* feature, read ScreenTips to identify buttons on the Web toolbar. (Use the keyboard shortcut ⇧ Shift + F1 to quickly access the *What's This?* feature.)

4. Connect to the Internet using your Internet service provider (ISP). If necessary, type your user name and password. If you are not sure how to connect to the Internet or you do not know your user name and password, ask your instructor for assistance.

Let's explore the Web Help system to learn whether Microsoft provides technical assistance for questions not answered in the online Help.

5. In the Ask a Question box, type technical assistance from Microsoft **and press** Enter ⏎. **If you are using Word, Excel, or PowerPoint, click the About Microsoft technical resources option. If you are using Access, click the Ways to get assistance while you work option. In the Help window, click Show All.**

   WARNING *Be sure to type in the Ask a Question box and not in the Address text box located on the Web toolbar that you just displayed.*

6. Scroll down the Help window and read the information about Microsoft's technical resources.

Now, let's explore the hyperlink to the Microsoft Office Web site.

7. **In the Help information, click the Microsoft Office Web site link that appears in the paragraph that explains Microsoft's Office Web site.**

Your Web browser connects you to the Microsoft Office Tools on the Web site.

8. **If necessary, click the Microsoft Office Tools on the Web taskbar button, maximize the browser window, and click the United States hyperlink on the world map.**

9. **Read the Microsoft Office Tools on the Web page, scrolling as necessary to see various hyperlinks. Look for and click the Assistance Center link. Then, click a link for assistance with an Office application.**

10. **Read the page, noting the various links that might provide additional help for the application you chose in step 9.**

11. **Explore one article of interest.**

12. **Keep clicking the Back button ⬅ Back ▾ until you return to the Tools on the Web page.**

In some instances, even though you've explored both the online Help system and the Microsoft Office Tools on the Web site, you still may not have found an answer to your question. If you need additional assistance, you can communicate directly with Microsoft by using the Search on Web feature within the online Help system.

13. **Click the Help taskbar button to return to the Help window, and then click the Show button ⬕, if necessary.**

The navigation pane with the Contents, Answer Wizard, and Index tabs appears.

14. **Click the Answer Wizard tab and click the Search on Web button at the bottom of the navigation pane. Scan the information that appears in the Help window.**

As shown in Figure 3.21, the Help window displays a form that allows you to provide specific feedback directly to Microsoft. If you have your instructor's permission and have an unanswered question, you can complete the form and click the *Send and go to the Web* button. Microsoft should then respond directly to you about the issue.

15. **Click the Close button ⊠ in the Help window. Hide the Web toolbar, and exit the Office program. Close any open browser windows, and disconnect from the Internet if your instructor tells you to do so. (To quickly close an open window, right-click its taskbar button and click Close on the shortcut menu.)**

WARNING *You may proceed directly to the exercises for this lesson. If, however, you are finished with your computer session, follow the "shut down" procedures for your lab or school environment.*

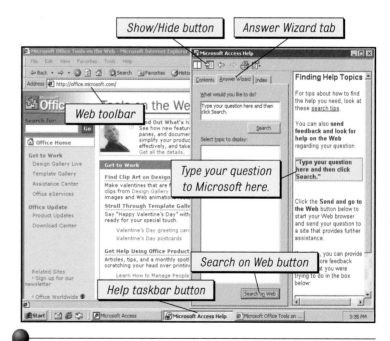

Figure 3.21
Asking Microsoft for more assistance

SUMMARY AND EXERCISES

SUMMARY

This lesson introduced basic computer and Windows-based application terms; explained how to start and exit Word; and explored menus, toolbars, the task pane, and other window objects. You learned to open, name, save, close, and reopen files. Also, you learned to get help with Office features from the online Help system. In addition, you learned to connect to the Internet and explore for help on the World Wide Web.

Now that you have completed this lesson, you should be able to do the following:

- Explain the purpose of the major Office programs. (page 81)
- Use your mouse to point, click, double-click, right-click, select, and drag. (page 84)
- Start your computer and boot the Windows 2000 operating system. (page 85)
- Copy files from a CD to a hard drive or a network drive. (page 87)
- Change file attributes. (page 90)
- Start Microsoft Word, Microsoft Excel, Microsoft Access, and Microsoft PowerPoint, and switch between programs. (page 91)
- Explore each application window and identify common window elements. (page 93)
- Open a file. (page 101)
- In Word, Excel, and PowerPoint, save a file with a different file name and in a different folder. (page 103)
- Close and reopen files. (page 105)
- Display ScreenTips for various screen elements, and use the Office Assistant and the Ask a Question box to obtain help. (page 107)
- Access and use the Answer Wizard, Contents, and Index to obtain help. (page 110)
- Exit an Office program and shut down the computer. (page 112)
- Connect to the Internet; identify buttons on the Web toolbar; explore the Web for help; and disconnect from the Internet. (page 114)

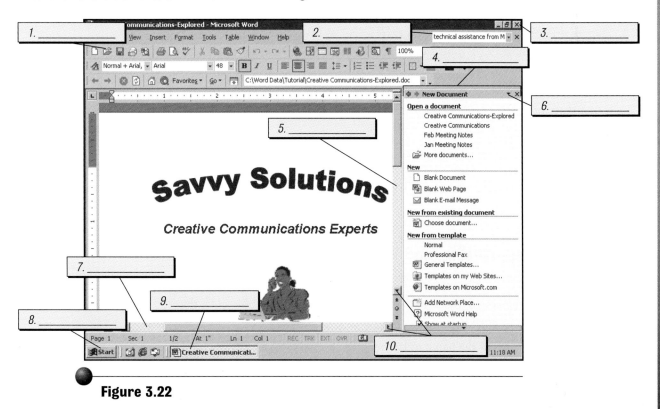

CONCEPTS REVIEW

1 TRUE/FALSE

Circle T if the statement is true or F if the statement is false.

T F **1.** Menu items are called commands because they command the computer.

T F **2.** A user may personalize toolbars and menus.

T F **3.** To display a list of the more common toolbars, click View on the menu bar and point to Toolbars.

T F **4.** A task pane can be used only when no files are open.

T F **5.** Office provides the following Help tools: the Office Assistant, ScreenTips, the Ask a Question box, the Answer Wizard, Contents, and Index.

T F **6.** To reopen a file that you recently closed, you can click the file name from the list at the bottom of the File menu.

T F **7.** The Office Assistant is controlled by a command on the Tools menu.

T F **8.** To scroll up or down in a window, use the vertical scroll bar.

T F **9.** The status bar includes the Start button.

T F **10.** To exit an Office program, click the Close button on the title bar or click the Exit command on the File menu.

2 IDENTIFICATION

Label each of the elements of the Word window in Figure 3.22.

Figure 3.22

SUMMARY AND EXERCISES

SKILLS REVIEW

Complete all of the Skills Review problems in sequential order to review your skills to start an Office program, switch between programs, and identify window elements; open, name, save, close, and reopen files; get Help; and exit Office programs.

1 Launching Office Application Programs, Opening Files, and Exploring Office Windows

1. Click the **Start button** [Start], point to **Programs**, and click **Microsoft Word**.

2. Click the **Start button** [Start], point to **Programs**, and click **Microsoft Excel**.

3. Click the **Start button** [Start], point to **Programs**, and click **Microsoft Access**.

4. Click the **Start button** [Start], point to **Programs**, and click **Microsoft PowerPoint**.

5. Click the **Access taskbar button**. Then, click the **Word taskbar button**.

6. On the Standard toolbar, click the **Open button** [icon].

7. In the Open dialog box, click the **Look in triangle button**. Then click the drive that contains your *Office Data* folder. (If your *Office Data* folder is not stored at the root level of the drive, navigate to the folder.) Then, double-click the *Word Data* folder.

8. Click *Home Page Support* in the list of file names, and click the **Open button** in the dialog box.

9. Point to various buttons on the Standard toolbar and read the ScreenTips.

10. Switch to Excel. Navigate to the *Excel Data* folder in your *Office Data* folder and open *Building Estimate*. As your time allows, point to various buttons on the Standard toolbar and read the ScreenTips.

11. Switch to PowerPoint. Navigate to the *PowerPoint Data* folder in your *Office Data* folder and open *GPS Overview*. As your time allows, point to various buttons on the Standard toolbar and read the ScreenTips.

12. Switch to Access. Navigate to the *Access Data* folder in your *Office Data* folder and open *H & L Realtors*. As your time allows, point to various buttons on the Database toolbar and read the ScreenTips.

2 Naming, Saving, Closing, and Reopening a File

1. Switch to Word. With *Home Page Support* still open, click **Save As** on the File menu.

2. In the Save As dialog box, navigate to the *Word Data* folder and double-click the *Skills Review* folder to open it.

3. In the File name box, edit the name to be *Home Page Support-Explored*. Click the **Save button** in the Save As dialog box.

4. Click the **Close Window button** [X] on the menu bar.

5. Click the **File menu**, and click *Home Page Support-Explored* in the list of files at the bottom of the File menu.

6. Switch to Excel. Save *Building Estimate* as *Building Estimate-Explored* in the *Skills Review* folder in the *Excel Data* folder. Close the file and then reopen it.

7. Switch to PowerPoint. Save *GPS Overview* as *GPS Overview-Explored* in the *Skills Review* folder in the *PowerPoint Data* folder. Close the file and then reopen it.

3 Using Help

1. Choose an Office program in which to work.

2. Click the **Ask a Question box**, type copy a file, and press [Enter]. In the list of options that you could explore, click the **Copy a file option**. In the Help window, click **Show All** and read the information.

3. Collapse the **How? link**.

4. Click the **Show button**, if necessary, to display the navigation pane. Then, in the *What would you like to do?* box on the Answer Wizard tab, type **crash recovery** and click the **Search button**.

5. In the *Select topic to display* box, click the **Recover files topic**. In the Help window, click the **Show All hyperlink** and explore all the information about document recovery.

6. Click the **Hide button**, click the **Restore Down button**, and click the **Close button** in the Help window.

4 Closing Files and Exiting Office Programs

1. In each program, click the **Close Window button** on the menu bar to close the open files. If a dialog box appears asking if you want to save changes to a file, click **No**.

2. Click the **Close button** on the title bar of each open Office program.

PROJECTS

1 Two at a Time?

Can you open two Word files with one click of the Open button? Search Help to find out if or how it can be done. Now, simultaneously open *Atlas Manual* and *Australia Tour Pricing* in your *Word Data* folder. Save *Atlas Manual* as *Atlas Manual 1* in the *Projects* folder in your *Word Data* folder; save *Australia Tour Pricing* as *Australia Tour Pricing 2* in the *Projects* folder in your *Word Data* folder. Then close the files. Reopen *Atlas Manual 1* from the File menu. Reopen *Australia Tour Pricing 2* from the appropriate task pane. Close all open files. Search Help to determine whether you can open two Excel files or two PowerPoint files with one click of the Open button. Is there any way that you can have two Access files open at the same time?

2 Button, Button, Who Has the Button?

To avoid accidentally closing an Office application program when you want only to close a file, you decide to add a Close button to the right of the Open button on the Standard toolbar in Word, Excel, or PowerPoint or on the Database toolbar in Access. Choose an Office program in which to explore Help for information on customizing a toolbar. After you've added the Close button in one of the Office programs, test it by opening a file and then closing it with the Close button. Now remove the Close button from the toolbar. Is there more than one way to add and remove a toolbar button? When would you recommend restoring the original toolbar settings?

 ## 3 Stamps or Electronic Postage?

Who isn't extremely busy? Who isn't looking for ways to be better organized? Someone recently suggested to you that you could save time by printing electronic postage instead of waiting in a line to buy postage. You decide to use the online Help system of one of the Office programs and to explore the Web for answers to your questions about electronic postage. (*Hint:* Use the Office on the Web command on the Help menu to access the Microsoft Office Assistance Center Web site and explore the Office eServices link.) Do you need to install a program to use electronic postage? Is an electronic postage program already installed on your computer? Can you print postage directly on an envelope or a label from your computer? What does it cost to get started with an electronic postage plan? Be prepared to discuss the information you discovered on the Web with your class. Close all open browser windows and disconnect from the Internet if your instructor tells you to do so. Close the Help window and exit the Office program.

Contents

Publishing on the Internet

You don't need to be a mechanic in order to drive a car . . .

You can just turn the key and go! Back in the dark ages of online communication (about seven to ten years ago!), only programming experts could post information on the Internet. But now, with the right software and an Internet account, you can publish your own materials for viewing by a worldwide audience. One of the easiest and fastest ways to publish your work online is to create your own page on the World Wide Web.

The Internet isn't limited to big business—individuals, private organizations, and small companies actually publish the vast majority of materials on the Internet. The variety of online publishing opportunities is almost limitless, and people are using these opportunities to enhance their businesses, share information, entertain, and educate others.

Do it yourself

To create a Web page, you must format a document with special tags—called Hypertext Markup Language (HTML) tags. These tags, which surround the text they affect, make the document "readable" by the Web browser, and tell it to display the text as a heading, a table, a link, normal text, and so on.

A few years ago, you would need to be (or need to hire!) a programming expert to prepare HTML tags and prepare your Web page for publication. Fortunately, now you don't

have to be a computer whiz to create HTML documents. In fact, you don't even need to know anything about HTML! With the right tools, you can quickly create attractive, interesting pages that are ready to be published on the Web.

Customize your own design

Microsoft Office XP, with its suite of applications including Microsoft Word, Microsoft Excel, Microsoft Access, and Microsoft PowerPoint, can convert ordinary documents into HTML files. This feature lets you create any type of document, save it in HTML format, and then immediately open the document in a Web browser (such as Microsoft Internet Explorer). There you can see the page just as it would appear on the Internet if you published it. You can even make changes to the original documents, resave the documents in HTML format, and view your changes in your browser—without typing a single HTML tag! In addition, many desktop applications (including those in the Microsoft Office XP suite) now have tools that let you embed graphics, create hyperlinks, and add other special features to your HTML documents.

You can also create feature-rich Web pages using your Web browser. Using a browser's editing tools, you can create new pages from scratch or use predesigned templates. Here's one quick and easy way to design a Web page: Find a Web page you like, copy it to disk, and then open it in Edit mode in the browser. You then can use that page's HTML formatting as the basis for your page! Using a browser-based editor, you work directly with HTML tags only if you want to. If you prefer, Microsoft Office XP and your browser can do all the HTML formatting for you—you don't even need to "look under the hood!"

After you have created your Web pages, simply contact your Internet Service Provider (ISP). Your ISP can provide you with space on a Web server and an address where others can find your pages. Using your chosen HTML editing tools, you can update, expand, and refresh your Web site whenever you want . . . *just turn the key and go!*

LESSON 1

Word Basics

CONTENTS

OBJECTIVES

After you complete this lesson, you will be able to do the following:

- ► Explain word processing.
- ► Start Microsoft Word.
- ► Name the main components of the Word window and display and hide toolbars.
- ► View a document in all four views.
- ► Select text and navigate a document.
- ► Edit text using Insert, Overtype, Undo, Redo, and Repeat.
- ► Rename and save a file.
- ► Move and copy text.
- ► Manage folders and change file types.
- ► Preview and print a document, labels, and envelopes.
- ► Create a document from a template.
- ► Use language and grammar tools including the Thesaurus tool.
- ► Insert text using AutoText, AutoComplete, AutoCorrect, and the Insert menu.
- ► Search for a file.
- ► Insert a hyperlink into a document.

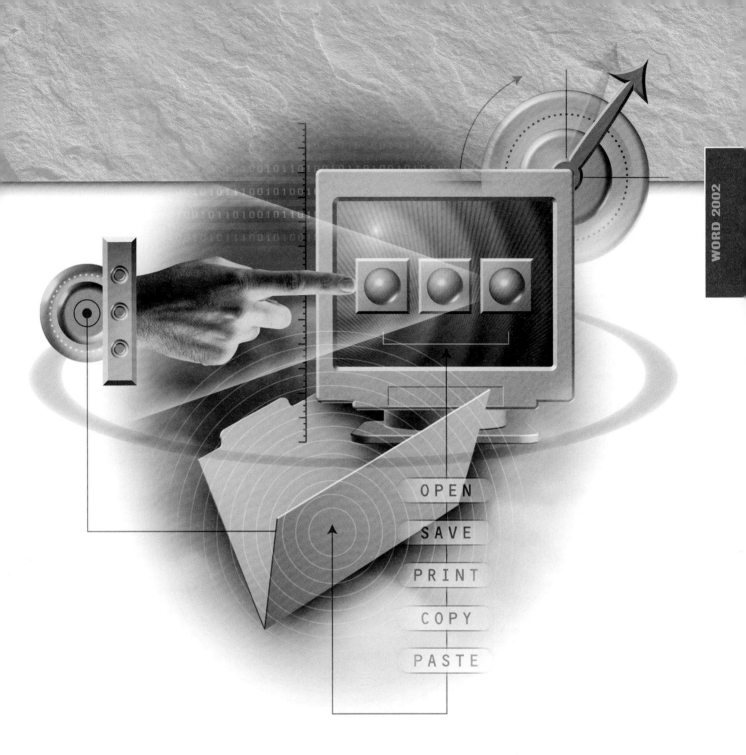

INTRODUCING MICROSOFT WORD

Microsoft Word is a powerful **word processing** program that enables you to create all kinds of documents including letters, reports, and even complicated brochures and newsletters. Using Word, you can easily perform basic word-processing functions, such as typing, editing, printing, and saving text. In addition, many features allow you to **format** (arrange) and enhance text, making it attractive and easy to read. Word will correct typing, spelling, and grammar errors. Other Word features help you find and replace text quickly and easily. Special tools allow you to add graphics, pictures, tables, sounds, and links to any document and to the Internet. Word also offers prewritten documents that you can adapt to your needs, instead of creating them from scratch.

Word provides an extensive online Help system which is always right there to answer your questions and provide tips about tasks you want to perform. You can navigate easily through your documents no matter how long or short they are. You can manage your Word files by naming and renaming files, copying and deleting files, and saving documents as various file types. You can even ask Word to convert any document to a Web page—Word will guide you step-by-step to create a Web page you can publish on an intranet or the Internet. From the Word window, you can also navigate and search the World Wide Web. You can even create an e-mail message right in the Word window, send a Word document as an e-mail message, or attach a Word document to an e-mail message.

STARTING MICROSOFT WORD

Before you can start Microsoft Word, both Microsoft Word and Windows 98 (or higher version) must be installed on the computer you are using. The figures in this tutorial use Windows 2000; if you are using a different version of Windows, the information appearing on your screen may vary slightly.

WARNING *You must create the* Word Data *folder for this tutorial from the* Data CD *located on the inside back cover of this tutorial. If you have not created the* Word Data *folder, ask your instructor for help or review* Getting Started.

HANDS on

Launching Microsoft Word

In this activity, you will start Microsoft Word.

1. Turn on your computer.

NOTE *If you are prompted for a username and/or password, enter the information at this time. If you do not know your username and/or password, ask your instructor for help.*

The Windows operating system boots the computer.

2. Click the **Start button** 🏁Start on the Windows taskbar.

3. Point to **Programs** and click **Microsoft Word**.

The Word program starts and a new, blank document appears.

EXPLORING THE WORD WINDOW

The Word application window is shown in Figure 1.1. Your window may look slightly different because Word allows users to customize, or alter, the Word window

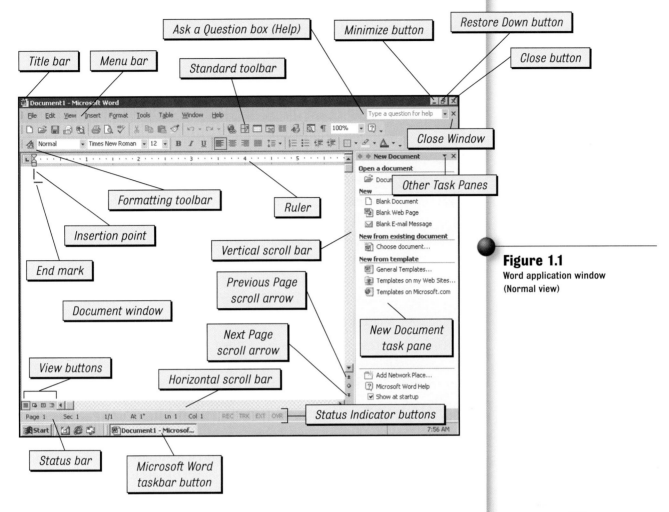

Figure 1.1
Word application window
(Normal view)

Labels (clockwise from top left):
Title bar · Menu bar · Ask a Question box (Help) · Standard toolbar · Minimize button · Restore Down button · Close button · Close Window · Other Task Panes · New Document task pane · Status Indicator buttons · Horizontal scroll bar · Next Page scroll arrow · Previous Page scroll arrow · Vertical scroll bar · Ruler · Formatting toolbar · Insertion point · End mark · Document window · View buttons · Status bar · Microsoft Word taskbar button

to suit individual needs. The Word window contains many standard Windows elements which you learned about in *Getting Started*. As shown in Figure 1.1, the document window displays the insertion point and the end mark. The **insertion point** (a blinking vertical bar) indicates where text will be inserted when you begin typing. The **end mark** (a short horizontal line) moves downward in your document each time you begin a new line. Word, by default, gives a temporary name to all documents. In Figure 1.1 the document is called *Document1*.

The task pane that appears at the right side of the application window provides quick access to commonly used commands and features. There are eight different task panes in Word (these eight options appear when you click the Other Task Panes triangle button). The New Document task pane in Figure 1.1 appears by default each time you open Word. The task pane disappears by default when you open a new blank or existing document; it can be reopened at any time by clicking Task Pane on the View menu.

Identifying Menus and Commands

As shown in Figure 1.1, the Word menu bar appears below the title bar. The menu bar displays menu names found in most Windows applications, such as File, Edit, and Help. Word also includes menus just for word processing, such as Format and Table.

Table 1.1 provides a brief description of the menus available on the Word menu bar.

HINTS & TIPS

The title of each of your open documents will appear within a Windows taskbar button. Clicking the various taskbar buttons allows you to move between the documents. If a taskbar button does not display for each open document, click Options on the Tools menu then click to activate *Windows in Taskbar* on the View tab.

Table 1.1	The Word Menu Bar

Menu	Contains Commands That Let You . . .
File	Control your document files by opening, saving, and printing them.
Edit	Rearrange text and other elements of documents by locating, copying, moving, and deleting text.
View	View documents different ways; display and hide toolbars.
Insert	Insert various elements, such as page breaks, pictures, symbols, and hyperlinks, into your documents.
Format	Determine the appearance of text in your documents; for example, the size of characters or the alignment of a paragraph.
Tools	Use Word's special word processing tools, such as a spelling and grammar checker, thesaurus, and automatic correction features.
Table	Insert, fill-in, and format an arrangement of columns and rows as tabular information in documents.
Window	Work in multiple documents at once, in one or more windows.
Help	Access Word's online Help system and Microsoft Office on the Web for word processing assistance and support.

Identifying Toolbars, Buttons, and the Ruler

Below the menu bar is Word's Standard toolbar, as shown in Figure 1.1 on page 41. A toolbar contains a row of buttons for many of the most frequently used commands. Although you can access these commands on one of the menus, clicking a toolbar button is often more convenient. You can quickly identify any toolbar button by pointing to it and reading the name that appears in a small text box called a ScreenTip.

The Formatting toolbar appears directly below the Standard toolbar. This toolbar contains buttons that control the appearance of text.

> **NOTE** *If your Standard and Formatting toolbars share one row below the menu bar, you can display them as two separate toolbars by clicking Customize on the Tools menu. On the Options tab, select the* Show Standard and Formatting toolbars on two rows *option and click Close.*

The icon on each toolbar button symbolizes the command. For example, on Word's Standard toolbar the New Blank Document button ▣ is symbolized by a piece of paper. Table 1.2 presents each button available on the Word Standard toolbar and explains its function. The Standard toolbar, like Word's menus, is adaptive. The most common buttons appear on the main toolbar, while buttons used less often are accessible by clicking Toolbar Options ▪ at the end of the toolbar. When you click a button on the Toolbar Options list ▪ that is not displayed on the toolbar, Word adds it to the main toolbar. You can also move buttons that are not frequently used from the toolbar to the Toolbar Options list.

In addition to the Standard and Formatting toolbars, the Toolbars command on the View menu provides access to many other toolbars, each arranged for a different purpose. The **ruler** displays below the Standard and Formatting toolbars, as shown in Figure 1.1 on page 41, enabling you to judge measurements, such as paragraph indentions, on document pages. (If the ruler does not appear on your screen, click Ruler on the View menu.)

WEB NOTE

The Internet connects your computer to millions of other computers all over the world. You can exchange messages, programs, and data files with every one of them.

HINTS & TIPS

By default, the ruler displays measurements in inches. You can change to another unit of measure on the General tab of the Options dialog box (Tools menu) by using the *Measurement units* list box.

Table 1.2   **The Word Standard Toolbar**

Button	Name	Action
	New Blank Document	Creates a new document.
	Open	Opens a document.
	Save	Makes a permanent copy of a document to a file on disk.
	E-mail	Opens a header to send your document as an electronic mail message.
	Search	Finds files wherever you work, such as on your computer, your local network, or your Microsoft Outlook mailbox.
	Print	Prints the entire document.
	Print Preview	Previews the document.
	Spelling and Grammar	Checks for spelling and grammar errors.
	Cut	Removes the selected item(s) from the document to the Clipboard—a temporary storage place for information that is used by all Windows applications.
	Copy	Copies the selected item(s) and places this copy on the Office Clipboard.
	Paste	Pastes the selected item(s) from the Clipboard into the current location.
	Format Painter	Copies the formatting from the selected item(s) to another item(s).
	Undo	Reverses the last command.
	Redo	Repeats the last command.
	Insert Hyperlink	Inserts a link from the current document to another part of the current document, another document, or an Internet site.
	Tables and Borders	Displays or hides the Tables and Borders toolbar.
	Insert Table	Inserts a table.
	Insert Microsoft Excel Worksheet	Inserts an Excel worksheet.
	Columns	Adjusts text to a column format.
	Drawing	Displays or hides the Drawing toolbar.
	Document Map	Turns the Document map feature on or off.
	Show/Hide ¶	Shows or hides the formatting marks.
100%	Zoom	Increases or decreases the displayed size of the document.
	Microsoft Word Help	Displays the Office Assistant—an animated character than can answer your specific questions, offer helpful tips, and provide help for any Word feature.
	Close	Closes the current document.

VIEWING A DOCUMENT

Word allows users to see all documents, including Web pages, in **WYSIWYG** (what you see is what you get). As shown in Figure 1.2, four view option buttons are located at the lower left in the Word window. A document might be created in Outline View and switched to other views for editing, formatting, and printing. The four views are identified in Table 1.3. (Point to a view button to easily identify it through a ScreenTip.) In addition, you can easily reduce or magnify the document area displayed on screen by changing the Zoom setting.

Table 1.3	Document Viewing Options	
Button	**View Type**	**Typical Use**
	Normal View	The main view used for typing, editing, and formatting text.
	Web Layout View	Used mostly for editing and formatting documents to be posted as Web pages.
	Print Layout View	Used for seeing how documents will look when printed.
	Outline View	Used only for organizing and developing the content of documents.

HANDS on

Viewing a Document in All Four Views

In this activity, you will see a document in all four views. Scrolling the document will help you observe differences in the views. You will also change the Zoom setting.

1. **Open the *Atlas* file in your *Word Data* folder, and click the Web Layout View button 🗔 in the lower-left area of the screen.**

Long lines of text and very narrow side margins characterize this view, as shown in Figure 1.2. Also, there are no horizontal lines to divide the document into separate pages.

2. **Scroll rapidly to the end of the document while watching the status bar.**

The status bar is *not* active in Web Layout View because on the Web the whole document functions as one page.

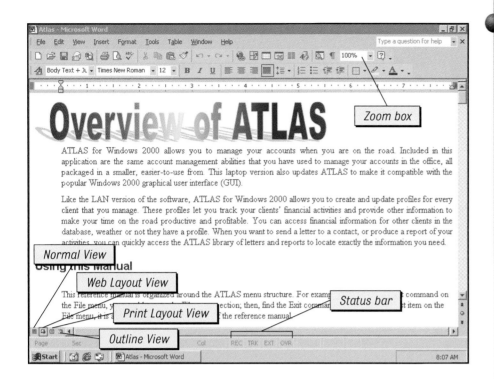

Figure 1.2
Atlas document in Web Layout View

3. Scroll to the beginning of the document then click the **Print Layout View button** 🔲.

The document takes the appearance of a printed sheet.

4. Scroll gradually to the top of page 2, and notice the break between pages 1 and 2.

5. Scroll slowly to the *Using ATLAS for Windows 2000* heading at the top of page 3.

6. Click the **Outline View button** 🔲.

The Outlining toolbar appears at the top of the document below the Formatting toolbar. A mark at the left of each paragraph of text indicates a separate unit of text that you can move above or below other units by selecting it and clicking the arrows in the Outlining toolbar.

7. Click the **Normal View button** 🔲.

In Normal View, side margins are visible on the left and right side of the text, and horizontal dotted lines divide the screen into pages.

8. Click the **Zoom box triangle button** 100% ▾ on the Standard toolbar, then click the **150% option**.

The document size enlarges to 150%.

Another Way

To view a document in a different view, click the desired View option on the View menu.

NORTON
ONLINE

Visit **www.glencoe.com/norton/online/** for more information on Microsoft Word 2002.

9. Click the **Zoom box triangle button** `100%` ▾ again, then click the **100% option**.

Word returns the document to its previous size.

10. Click **Close** on the File menu to close the document; click **No** if prompted to save changes.

SELECTING TEXT

Occasionally, you may need to select text in the form of words, sentences, lines, or whole paragraphs as you work with a document. You can select a word by double-clicking it. You can select a sentence by pressing `Ctrl` and clicking anywhere in the sentence. You can select a line of text by simply pointing to it and clicking in the **selection bar,** the invisible column between the left edge of the document window and the left margin of the page. Selecting an entire paragraph is as easy as triple-clicking anywhere in the paragraph. You can select an entire document by clicking Select All on the Edit menu.

HANDS on

Selecting Words, Sentences, Lines, and Paragraphs

In this activity, you will select a word, a sentence, a line of text, and a paragraph.

1. Open the *Home Page Support* file in your *Word Data* folder and click the Normal View button ▤, if necessary.

NOTE *Since the Normal View is the main view used for typing and editing documents, from here forward assume that all Word activities require you to be in the Normal View unless the instructions specify otherwise.*

2. Press `Ctrl` and click anywhere in the last sentence of the first paragraph.

The sentence is selected (highlighted).

3. Move the pointer to the selection bar and point to the second line of text in the second paragraph.

Your pointer becomes an arrow called the Normal Select pointer.

4. Click within the selection bar.

The line of text is selected, as shown in Figure 1.3.

Word BASICS

Selecting Text

- Double-click to select a word.
- Press `Ctrl` and click to select a sentence.
- Point to a line in the selection bar and click to select a line of text.
- Triple-click to select a paragraph.
- Click Select All on the Edit menu to select an entire document.

Figure 1.3
Selected line

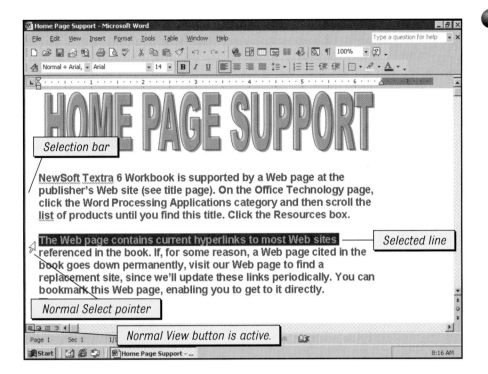

5. **Double-click the word** *Office* **in the first paragraph.**

The word *Office* is selected.

6. **Triple-click anywhere in the second paragraph.**

The entire paragraph is selected.

7. **Click Select All on the Edit menu to select the entire document.**

8. **Click anywhere in the document window to deselect the text.**

9. **Click Close Window ⊠ to close the document, and click No if prompted to save changes.**

Did you know?

Select one or more paragraphs of text in a document by dragging over the blocks of text you want to select.

Another Way

Select one or more paragraphs by selecting a line in the selection bar and dragging the pointer down or up.

NAVIGATING A DOCUMENT

Scrolling through a document to locate a specific word or phrase can be time consuming, especially in a long document. There are better methods of locating specific text. Word has several features that allow you to navigate a document more efficiently.

The Go To feature allows you to go to a specific page, line, section, heading, and so on. On the Go To tab in the Find and Replace dialog box, you can type a page number to command Word to go directly to that page. From that location, you can direct Word to go back or forward a certain number of pages.

You can quickly locate a particular word or phrase through the Find tab of the Find and Replace dialog box. Type the text you wish to find and Word will search for it and highlight the first occurrence *following* the location of your insertion point in the document. As you continue to search the entire document, Word will highlight every occurrence of the text.

HANDS on

Finding Specific Text and Pages

In this activity, you will use the Find and Replace dialog box to find specific words and you will then use the Go To feature to locate specific pages in the *Atlas* file.

1. Open *Atlas* in your *Word Data* folder and click the Normal View button ▤, if necessary.

Immediately after opening the file your insertion point will be at the beginning of the document. Word can search for specific pages and text from any point; however, if you start the search process in the middle of the document, Word will just search from that point to the end of the document. (At the end of the document, a dialog box will ask if you wish to continue the search from the document's beginning.)

2. Click the Find button 🔍.

The Find and Replace dialog box appears.

> **NOTE** *If the Find button 🔍 is not on the Standard toolbar, click Toolbar Options ▪, point to Add or Remove Buttons, point to Standard, then click a check mark next to the Find button to add it to your toolbar. You may also click Find on the Edit menu.*

3. On the Find tab, type administrator in the *Find what* box, as shown in Figure 1.4

Figure 1.4
Find and Replace dialog box

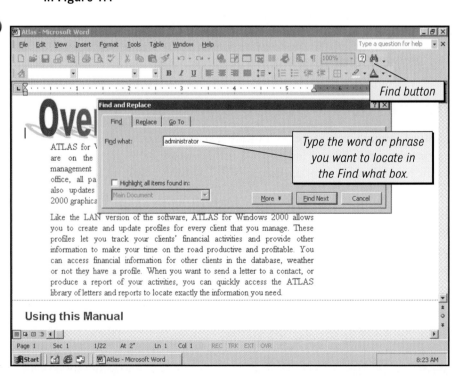

4. Click **Find Next**.

Word jumps to the first occurrence of the word *administrator* on page 5 of the document.

5. Click **Find Next** again.

A dialog box indicates Word has finished searching the document. No more occurrences of the word are found.

6. Click **OK**.

7. Click the **Go To tab** in the Find and Replace dialog box. In the *Go to what* list box, click **Page**, if it is not already selected. Then type 5 in the *Enter page number* box.

8. Click the **Go To button**.

Word jumps directly to the top of page 5, and the status bar indicates that you are now on page 5 of 22 (5/22). The insertion point is at the beginning of the page but is not blinking.

9. In the *Enter page number* box, type +4 and press Enter⏎ .

Word moves forward four pages; you are now on page 9 as indicated on the status bar (9/22).

10. In the *Enter page number* box, type −6 and click the **Go To button**.

Word moves back six pages; you are now on page 3.

11. Click **Close** ☒ on the Find and Replace dialog box.

12. Click **Close Window** ☒ to close the *Atlas* document, and click **No** if prompted to save changes.

Another Way

You can use the Bookmark feature to jump immediately to a marked location in a long document, or you can use the Document Map feature to navigate to a specific heading in your document. Explore Help for more information on these features.

EDITING TEXT AND SAVING A FILE

The power of a word processing program becomes apparent when you want to revise your document. The ease of inserting, changing, deleting, and replacing text means that you can type a rough draft of your ideas quickly and then go back later to refine, or edit, your document.

After you have edited an existing document, you can rename and save it using the Save As dialog box. This preserves the original document so you can access it later. You can change the name of any document in the Open or Save As dialog box when the file name no longer suits the document.

Inserting Text

As you point to text in a document, the pointer becomes an **I-beam pointer.** Position the pointer where you want to type, then click. The pointer becomes a blinking vertical bar called the insertion point. When you type, text will begin at the insertion point. As you type, you can delete characters to the left of the insertion point by pressing Backspace ; you can delete characters to the right of the insertion point by pressing Delete . When you type to the end of a line, the text and the insertion point

HINTS & TIPS

To view symbols representing locations where a hard return or character spaces have been entered in your document, click the Show/Hide button on the Standard Toolbar.

will move automatically to the next line. This basic word processing feature is called **word wrap.** When you wish to begin typing on a new line, press ⌈Enter←⌋ to insert a **hard return** that moves the insertion point to the next line.

> **NOTE** *Insert a hard return only to move text or the insertion point to the next line, to insert blank lines into your document, to begin a new paragraph, or to apply certain Word commands. Otherwise, allow your copy to wrap with the* soft returns *that Word inserts automatically.*

Word involves two typing modes. When you use **Insert mode,** the text you type appears on the blank screen or is inserted into existing text, pushing the characters after it to the right. When you use **Overtype mode,** your text types over the existing text. Use Insert mode—the default typing mode—to insert new text; use Overtype mode to edit text. Always determine which mode is active before you type to avoid replacing text accidentally. When Word is in Overtype mode, the status indicator button in the status bar will display OVR in black letters. When Insert mode is active, the status indicator button will display a dimmed or gray OVR button. You can switch back and forth between the modes by double-clicking the OVR button or by pressing ⌈Insert⌋.

HANDS on

Inserting Paragraphs

In this activity, you will add two paragraphs to the *Atlas* document. You will also use the Word Count toolbar to count the number of lines in your document.

1. Point to Toolbars on the View menu and click Word Count to display the Word Count toolbar, if necessary.

> **NOTE** *If the Word Count toolbar appears to float in the document window, drag its title bar up until it docks beneath the Formatting toolbar. This toolbar allows you to count the words, characters, lines, pages, and paragraphs in a document.*

2. Open *Atlas* in your *Word Data* folder.

3. On the Word Count toolbar, click the Word Count Statistics triangle button ⌈<Click Recount to view>⌋ ⌈▾⌋ and click Lines.

Notice that you have 318 lines of text in the document.

4. Scroll to page 2, click after the last character in the last line of the second paragraph, and press ⌈Enter←⌋.

The insertion point jumps down one line to begin a new paragraph. Now you will activate Insert mode to insert new text.

5. Point to the OVR status indicator button on the status bar.

The word *Overtype* appears as a ScreenTip. If OVR appears in black letters, Overtype mode is active. If OVR is gray or dimmed, Insert mode is active.

Word BASICS

Inserting Paragraphs

1. Click to position the insertion point where you want text to appear.

2. If OVR is active, double-click it to activate the Insert mode or press ⌈Insert⌋.

3. Type the text, pressing ⌈Backspace⌋ or ⌈Delete⌋ to erase errors as you type.

HINTS & TIPS

To include footnotes and endnotes in your word counts, click Word Count on the Tools menu and select *Include footnotes and endnotes.*

---

136   Lesson 1

6. If OVR is black, double-click **OVR** to activate Insert mode.

7. **Type the following text**: We have also included a small "map" in the upper-right corner of each page. This map indicates exactly where the described menu or dialog is in the program.

The insertion point moves to the right as you type and wraps to the next line when a line is full.

8. Click the **Recount button** [Recount] on the Word Count toolbar.

The Word Count toolbar shows that you now have 321 lines of text in your document.

9. Click the **Find button** [A].

10. In the Find and Replace dialog box, click the **Go To tab**.

11. In the *Go to what* list box, click **Page**, if it is not already selected. Then type **5** in the *Enter page number* box and click **Go To**.

Word jumps directly to the top of page 5, and the status bar indicates that you are now on page 5 of 22 (5/22). The insertion point is at the top of the page but not blinking.

12. Click the **Close button** in the Find and Replace dialog box.

The blinking insertion point appears to the left of the *Logging In* heading.

13. **Type the following paragraph**: If you are new to Windows 2000, look over this section to familiarize yourself with the Windows conventions.

The insertion point pushes the heading to the right as you type new text.

14. Press [Enter←].

Your document should now resemble Figure 1.5.

15. Point to **Toolbars** on the View menu and click to deselect the Word Count toolbar.

Changing a File Name and Saving a File

After making changes in an existing document, you may prefer to keep the original document intact so you can refer to it later. To preserve the original document, it is best to save your edited file under a new name. Click Save As on the File menu to access the Save As dialog box. Choose the location (drive and path) in the *Save in* box in which you want to save your file, then type a meaningful name in the *File name* text box and click the Save button.

If you decide later that the file name no longer suits the file, you can easily change it in the Open dialog box. In the *Look in* box, navigate to and open the folder in which your file is stored. Click the file, click Tools, then click Rename on the drop-down menu. When a rectangle appears around the file name, type the new name and press [Enter←].

WORD 2002

Did you know?

To learn about using Word's handwriting recognition feature as another means of inserting text into a document, explore this topic in Help.

Another Way

To rename a file in the Open or Save As dialog box, click the file name, wait a moment, then click it again. When a rectangle appears around the highlighted file name, type the new name. *Or:* Right-click the file name, then click Rename on the shortcut menu.

HANDS on

Renaming and Saving a File

In this activity, you will save the *Atlas* file with a new file name then you will rename the file in the Open dialog box. The *Atlas* document should be open in the Word application window containing the text you typed in the previous activity.

1. Click Save As on the File menu.

The Save As dialog box appears.

2. Click the Save in triangle button, and navigate to the *Word Data* folder, if necessary.

3. Double-click the *Tutorial* folder, type Atlas in Progress in the *File name* box, and click Save.

4. Close *Atlas in Progress*.

5. Click Open on the File menu.

The contents of the *Tutorial* folder appear in the Open dialog box, including your new file *Atlas in Progress*.

6. Click *Atlas in Progress*, click Tools Tools ▾ **on the dialog box toolbar, then click Rename on the drop-down list.**

A rectangle appears around the highlighted file name.

7. Type Atlas Revised as the new file name, then press Enter ↵ **.**

8. Click Cancel to close the Open dialog box.

Replacing and Deleting Text

You learned earlier in this lesson how to navigate a document and how to locate and select text. You can use these techniques when you need to insert a single word or a missing character within a word. As you learned this is best accomplished in Insert mode. Occasionally, you will need to replace incorrect characters with correct ones by *overtyping* them. You can replace text in Overtype mode.

While editing a rough draft, you will often need to **delete** characters, words, phrases, sentences, or even whole paragraphs. Deleting text is a two-step procedure. First you must select the text you want to delete. After you select text, press Delete to remove it or begin to type to replace the words. You can also replace text throughout an entire document by using the Replace feature. In the Find and Replace dialog box, type the text to find and the text to replace it. Word will jump to each occurrence, and you can choose to replace the text, skip to the next occurrence, or replace all occurrences.

HANDS on

Replacing and Deleting Letters and Words

In this activity, you will find and replace or remove incorrect letters and words in *Atlas*.

1. Open *Atlas* in your *Word Data* folder.

2. Click the **Find button** 🔍, type use from in the *Find what* box, then click **Find Next**.

The first occurrence of these characters is highlighted within *Atlas*.

3. Click anywhere in the document, and then click before the *r* in the highlighted words.

NOTE *If the Find and Replace dialog box covers the status bar or is in the way, click its title bar and drag it to another area of the window.*

4. Activate Overtype mode, if necessary, and type or to replace the letters *r* and *o*.

5. Find the word *weather* in the document and overtype it as whether, as shown in Figure 1.5.

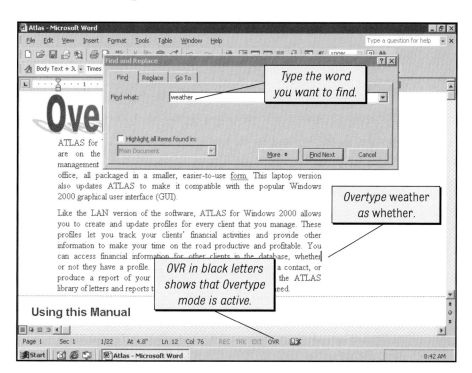

Word BASICS

Replacing Text

To overtype:

1. Click before the character you want to replace.

2. Activate Overtype mode, then type the character(s).

To insert text:

1. Click the location where you want to type.

2. Activate Insert mode and type the character(s).

To replace text:

1. Click the Find button.

2. Click the Replace tab.

3. In the *Find what* box, type the word or phrase to be replaced.

4. In the *Replace with* box, type the new text.

5. Click Find Next.

6. At each occurrence, click Replace, Replace All, or Find Next.

Figure 1.5
Word window in Overtype mode

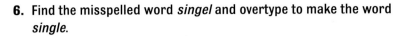

Selecting and Deleting Text

To delete a character:

1. Click before the character.
2. Press `Delete`.

To delete a word:

1. Double-click the word to select it.
2. Press `Delete`.

To delete a phrase:

1. Click before the first character.
2. Drag through the phrase to select it.
3. Press `Delete`.

6. Find the misspelled word *singel* and overtype to make the word *single*.

NOTE *A wavy red line may appear under some words (such as* singel*) to mark words or abbreviations not in the Word spelling dictionary that might be spelling errors. Similarly, a wavy green line may mark possible grammar errors. Some wavy lines will disappear as you edit the document; otherwise, ignore them for now. You will learn more about them later in this lesson.*

7. Find the phrase *than type*; overtype the *a* with e.

8. In the Find and Replace dialog box, click the **Replace tab**.

9. Type Alt in the *Find what* box. Press `Tab` and type `Alt` in the *Replace with* box. Then click the **Find Next button**.

10. At the first occurrence of *Alt*, click the **Replace button**.

Word replaces *Alt* with `Alt` and continues searching the document.

11. At the second occurrence of *Alt*, click the **Find Next button** to avoid the change.

A dialog box indicates the entire document was searched and no other occurrences were found.

12. Click **OK**.

13. Activate Insert mode. Find the words *first you* and insert the word time so the phrase reads *first time you*.

14. Click the **Find tab** and find the word *menues*.

15. Select the second *e* and press `Delete` to remove it.

The space occupied by the deleted character closes automatically.

16. Find the word *existing* and delete the *s* to make the word *exiting*.

17. Find the words *lap top* and delete the space between them.

18. Click the **Go To tab** then go to the first paragraph on page 7.

The word *the* is repeated twice in the second line.

19. Double-click the repeated word to select it and press `Delete`.

20. Go to page 10, item 2, and select and delete the words *the* and *key* to match this phrase: . . . *using backspace to erase* . . .

21. On page 12, delete the comma after the word *alerts* in the last bulleted item.

22. Close the Find and Replace dialog box, then save your document as *Atlas Edited* in the *Tutorial* folder in your *Word Data* folder. Close the document.

Visit www.glencoe.com/norton/online/ for more information on Microsoft Word 2002.

Undoing, Redoing, and Repeating Actions

As you edit documents, you may be unsure about a particular word choice or the phrasing of a sentence. Use the **Undo** or **Redo** features if you change your mind after you've edited a part of your document. The Undo button ↻ ▾ reverses actions (for example, deletes the text just typed). (The button's ScreenTip changes to Can't Undo if you cannot reverse the last action.) The Redo button ⟳ ▾ reverses an *undo* action. You can also use the Repeat command on the Edit menu to repeat an action.

HANDS on

Using Undo, Redo, and Repeat Features

In this activity, you will locate a specific word, select and replace it, then undo that action. After the word is restored, you will repeat the action.

1. **Open *Atlas* in your *Word Data* folder.**

2. **Open the Find and Replace dialog box. On the Find tab, click the More button, then click to select the Match case check box.**

Word will now skip occurrences of the text that do not match the capitalization used in the *Find what* box.

3. **Type Important: in the *Find what* box, as shown in Figure 1.6. Then, click Find Next.**

Word BASICS

Undoing, Redoing, and Repeating Actions

1. Click the Undo button to delete text just typed, or click the Undo arrow and click the action(s) you want to undo on the drop-down menu.

2. Click the Redo button to reverse an *Undo* action.

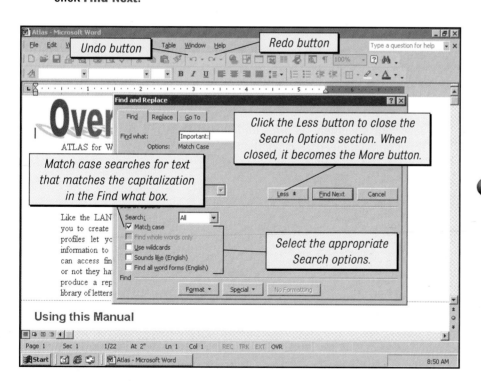

Figure 1.6
Select the Match case search option

Word jumps to *Important:* which appears highlighted in the application window.

4. **While the word is selected, click anywhere within the document and press [Delete].**

NOTE *ScreenTips for the Undo and Redo button change as actions are completed. These ScreenTips appear in parentheses after the relevant button within the following steps.*

5. Click the **Undo button**  *(Undo Clear)* to restore the word *Important:*.

The word is restored, and the Undo button's ScreenTip reads *Can't Undo*, since the action has been completed.

6. In the same sentence, select the word *checkbox* and then type button to replace it.

7. Click the **Undo button** *(Undo Typing)* to restore the word *checkbox*. Click the **Redo button** *(Redo Typing)* to restore the word *button*. Click the **Undo button** *(Undo Typing)* to restore the word *checkbox*.

8. In the Find and Replace dialog box, clear the *Match case* search option, and click the **Less button** to close the Search Options section of the dialog box.

9. Find the word *TIP:*, click two times before the word to place the insertion point at that location, then type ATLAS (no space).

10. Click **Find Next** to advance to the next occurrence of *TIP:*, then click twice before the word to activate the insertion point.

11. Click **Repeat Typing** on the Edit menu.

The word *ATLAS* is inserted before *TIP:*. The Repeat Typing command has repeated the last word you typed.

12. Close the Find and Replace dialog box.

13. Save your document as *Atlas Undone* in the *Tutorial* folder in your *Word Data* folder, then close the file.

MOVING AND COPYING TEXT

The Cut, Copy, and Paste features enable you to reword sentences and paragraphs by moving or copying text from one place to another. When you **cut** text you remove it from the document then save it on the **Office Clipboard,** a temporary holding area for text and graphics. You can then **paste** this cut text into the current document; into another document; or into a different Office application, such as Microsoft Excel or Microsoft PowerPoint. Thus, cut-and-paste is a means of moving text. Another way to move text is simply to drag it from its present location and drop it in a new location. The drag-and-drop method is handy when you want to move a small amount of text a short distance within the same document.

Cutting and deleting are different procedures. Deleting text is like erasing it; you should delete text that you have no further use for in your document. Cutting is a way to move text; you should cut text that you want to move to another location.

HINTS & TIPS

When you delete, cut, or paste text, Microsoft Word can automatically adjust the spacing around the text. To activate this feature, click Options on the Tools menu and click the Edit tab. Click to select the *Smart cut and paste* check box if necessary.

In addition to moving text, you may want to **copy** text to the Clipboard from one location and place it in another location. Copying text does not remove it from the original location. Copying can save the time and effort of retyping and avoids the risk of typing errors. You can select text, press ⌄Ctrl⌄, and use drag-and-drop to copy it to a new location. Again, drag-and-drop works best when you want to copy only a few words and drag them within the same paragraph.

The Paste Special command on the Edit menu allows you to paste (or **embed**) items from the Office Clipboard in a different format. For example, you can cut text from a Word document and paste it as a picture into another Word document or a PowerPoint slide. Similarly, you can cut data from an Excel worksheet and paste it into a Word document.

Cutting, copying, and pasting involve the Office Clipboard. You can cut or copy a single piece of text or several blocks of text. Any text you cut or copy is stored on the Office Clipboard. You can paste each text item into a different place or you can paste all the items into one location. You can paste items from the Office Clipboard individually or all at once. Click Paste to paste only the last item you cut or copied. Click Paste All to paste all of the items stored on the Office Clipboard. To view the contents of the Clipboard, click Office Clipboard on the Edit menu to activate the Clipboard task pane.

NOTE *Remember that you can reverse all of these actions—cutting, copying, and pasting—with the Undo ↶▾ and Redo ↷▾ buttons and the Repeat command on the Edit menu.*

HANDS on

Using the Office Clipboard and the Drag-and-Drop Method

In this activity, you will move a sentence to a new location and copy and paste text from one location to another.

1. **Open *Party Memo* in your *Word Data* folder then click Office Clipboard on the Edit menu.**

The Office Clipboard displays in the task pane.

2. **Click the Clear All button** 🗙 Clear All **to remove all items from the Clipboard, if necessary.**

3. **Find the words *Food and drinks* and close the Find and Replace dialog box, if necessary.**

4. **Select the sentence *Food and drinks will be provided, so come hungry*.**

5. **Click the Cut button** ✂ **on the Standard toolbar.**

The selected sentence is removed from your document and appears on the Office Clipboard, as shown in Figure 1.7.

Figure 1.7
Clipboard with one cut item

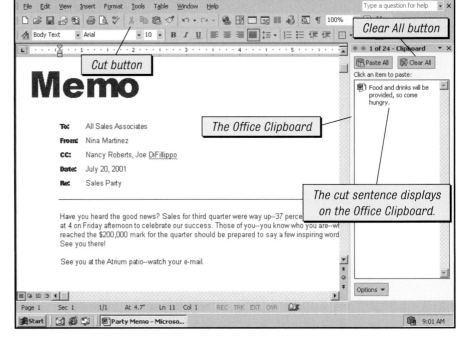

Using Drag-and-Drop

1. Select the text to be moved and point to the selected text.

2. Press and hold the left mouse button.

3. Drag the text to the new location.

4. Release the mouse button.

5. Adjust spacing between words, if necessary.

Another Way

To copy text using the drag-and-drop method, select the text, press and hold [Ctrl], then drag-and-drop the selected text.

6. In the document, click before *See you there!*, if necessary, then click the cut text on the Office Clipboard.

The cut sentence is pasted back into the document. A Paste Options button appears in your document where you inserted the cut text. Clicking the Paste Options triangle button will reveal several formatting options.

7. Press [Spacebar] to insert a space after the pasted sentence. On the Clipboard, click the **Clear All button**.

The cut text is removed from the Clipboard.

8. Select the name *Nina Martinez* after the *From:* heading and click the **Copy button** on the Standard toolbar.

The selected text remains in place and is copied to the Clipboard.

9. Select the date and click the **Copy button** on the Standard toolbar.

The date is copied to the top position on the Clipboard.

10. Click below the last line of the memo, press [Enter←] three times, and then click the **Paste All button** on the Clipboard.

The name and the date are pasted side by side at the insertion point.

11. Insert a space between the name and the date.

12. Select the phrase—*you know who you are*—in the middle of the first paragraph.

13. Point to the selected text then press and hold the left mouse button.

A faint box appears below the pointer. The message *Move to where?* appears on the status bar.

> **NOTE** *If you are not able to point to the selected text, the drag-and-drop option is turned off. To turn it on, click Options on the Tools menu. Click the Edit tab and then click Drag-and-drop text editing.*

14. Drag the selected text to position the insertion point between *quarter* and *should* which appear in the same sentence.

A faint dotted insertion point shows where the text will be dropped.

15. Release the mouse button.

The text appears in the new location, as shown in Figure 1.8.

16. Adjust space in the line before or after the text you just moved and between the words *you* and *who*, if necessary.

17. Save your document as *Revised Memo* in the *Tutorial* folder in your *Word Data* folder, then close the document.

18. Click **Close** ☒ to close the Clipboard.

Another Way

To cut or copy text, select then right-click the text and click Cut or Copy on the shortcut menu. Right-click the new location, then click Paste.

Did you know?

You can copy up to 24 items to the Office Clipboard. However, copying a 25th item will delete the first item.

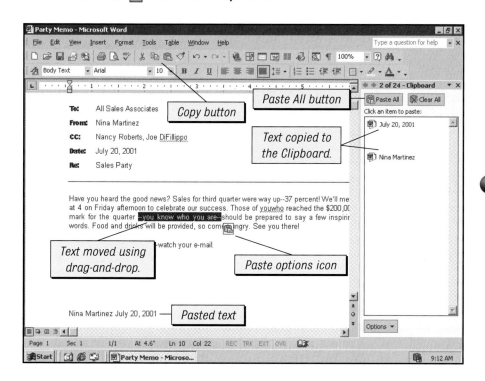

Figure 1.8
Text in new location

HANDS on

Using the Paste Special Command

In this activity, you will copy a memo header from a Word document then use the Paste Special command to paste it into another document that has been saved in a different file format. (You will learn more about file formats in the next activity.)

1. Open *Party Memo* in your *Word Data* folder.

2. Position your pointer in the selection bar at the upper-left corner of the document. When your pointer becomes an arrow, drag down in the selection bar to select all the material at the top of the document including the horizontal rule below *Re: Sales Party*.

The memo header material appears highlighted in the document.

3. Click the **Copy button** 📄, then click **Open** on the File menu and navigate to your *Word Data* folder, if necessary.

4. Click the **Files of type triangle button**, then click **Rich Text Format** to view only the files saved in that format.

5. Open the *Praise Memo* document.

The blinking insertion point appears next to the first character in the document.

6. Click **Paste Special** on the Edit menu.

7. Click the **Formatted Text (RTF) option** in the Paste Special list box and click **OK**.

The memo header is pasted into *Praise Memo* in the compatible RTF format.

8. Select *Sales Party* in the memo header and type Congratulations! to replace this text.

9. Save your document as *MKDesigns-RTF* in the *Tutorial* folder in your *Word Data* folder.

10. Close all open files; click **No** if prompted to save changes.

MANAGING FOLDERS AND CHANGING FILE TYPES

When you need to open a document, it is important to locate it quickly. One way to do that is to store related files together in a folder. Folders allow you to organize files by grouping related files together under a meaningful folder name. Creating a new folder can be accomplished in either the Save As or the Open dialog box—click the Create New Folder button 📁, enter a name for the new folder, and click OK. Change the drive letter or folder name that appears in the *Save in* text box (Save As dialog box) or the *Look in* text box (Open dialog box) to place your new folder in that location. Individual documents and folders with all their contents can also be deleted from the Save As or Open dialog box when they are no longer needed.

A **file type** or **file format** is a category or standard that is assigned to every file on a computer system. Common file types include *Word Document, Rich Text Format,* or *Text Only*. It is not unusual to save a Word file in a different file type so it can be accessed by another program. For example, if you want to share a document with a co-worker who has a different word processing program you may need to save your document in a format that is compatible with that program.

Since your Word files will usually be opened using the Word application software, in most cases you can simply accept the default file format *(Word Document)* in the

Save As dialog box. To save a document in a different file format, open the document and click Save As on the File menu to open the Save As dialog box. Then click the *Save as type* triangle button and choose a file format from the displayed list.

HANDS on

Changing File Types and Creating and Deleting Folders

In this activity, you will open a file in your *Word Data* folder then create a new folder in the *Tutorial* folder in which to save it. Before saving the file, you'll change the file format. Finally, you'll rename the folder then delete the new folder and its contents.

1. **Click Open on the File menu, navigate to your *Word Data* folder in the Open dialog box, then double-click *Australian Islands Article* to open it.**

2. **Click Save As on the File menu.**

The Save As dialog box appears containing the *Word Data* folders and files.

3. **Double-click the *Tutorial* folder.**

4. **Click the Create New Folder button 🗁 on the dialog box toolbar.**

As shown in Figure 1.9, the New Folder dialog box appears requesting a name for the new folder. Note that the *Tutorial* folder is displayed in the *Save in* box of the Save As dialog box; this is where your new folder will be stored.

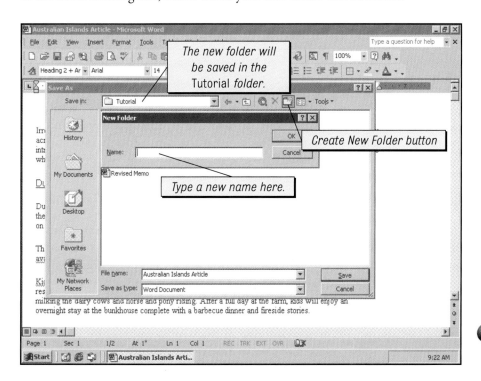

Word BASICS

Creating and Deleting Folders
Create a folder:

1. Click Open or Save As on the File menu and navigate to the location for your new folder.

2. Click the Create New Folder button, type the folder name, and press ⟦Enter◄─⟧.

Delete a folder:

1. In the Open or Save As dialog box, click the folder you want to delete.

2. Click the Delete button.

Word BASICS

Changing a File Type

1. With the document open, click Save As on the File menu.

2. In the Save As dialog box, navigate to the location where you wish to save your file.

3. Click the *Save as type* triangle button, click a file type, and click Save.

Figure 1.9
Creating a new folder

5. Type *Australian Islands Files* in the *Name* text box and click **OK**.

The *Australian Islands Files* folder displays in the *Save in* box indicating this is where the open file will be stored.

6. In the *File name* text box, edit the existing file name to read *Australian Islands Article 1*.

7. Click the **Save as type triangle button**, click **Rich Text Format** on the drop-down list, then click **Save**.

The Save As dialog box closes and *Australian Islands Article 1* is saved in Rich Text Format within the new *Australian Islands Files* folder.

8. Close *Australian Islands Article 1*.

9. Click the **Open button** .

The contents of the *Australian Islands Files* folder appear in the Open dialog box.

10. Click the **Up One Level button** .

The Open dialog box displays the contents of the *Tutorial* folder, including the *Australian Islands Files* folder.

11. Click the *Australian Islands Files* **folder**, then click the **Delete button** on the dialog box toolbar.

The Confirm Folder Delete dialog box asks if you want to remove the folder and its contents.

12. Click **Yes**.

The new folder and its contents are deleted.

13. Click **Cancel** to close the Open dialog box.

PREVIEWING AND PRINTING

Printing is a simple task in Word, whether you want to print a document, an envelope, or mailing labels. However, before you print any document, get into the habit of using the Print Preview button .

Previewing a Multi-Page Document

Print Preview lets you look at each page just as it will appear when printed. You can examine the format of up to six pages at once or one page at a time. In Print Preview, clicking a scroll arrow displays the next or previous page. You will notice that if you view the entire page at the default 40 percent size the text is too small to read; however, you can check that page breaks are satisfactory, margins are a consistent size, and headings are all the same style. You can see whether you need to make any adjustments prior to printing. If you wish to read the text at a certain place in the document, click that area to display the document at 100 percent; click the document again to return it to 40 percent.

Printing a Page and Printing Selected Pages

Clicking the Print button 🖨 on the Standard toolbar prints one copy (or **printout**) of all pages of your document. To print only certain pages, click Print on the File menu. Then, in the Print dialog box, specify whether you want to print just the current page (the page with the insertion point), only selected text (the *Selection* option), or several pages. Type page numbers with a hyphen or comma to tell Word which pages to print. To cancel a print job, double-click the printer icon (on the taskbar by the clock). In the printer window, select the job you want to cancel and click Cancel Printing on the Document menu.

Previewing and Printing a Multi-Page Document

In this activity, you will preview a multi-page document and then you will print selected pages from the document.

1. **Open *Atlas* in your *Word Data* folder.**

2. **Click the Print Preview button 🔍 on the Standard toolbar.**

The first page of *Atlas* appears at a reduced size in the Print Preview window.

3. **Click the Multiple Pages button ⊞ in the Preview toolbar.**

A drop-down display of icons representing document pages appears.

4. **Point at the third icon in the first row (1 × 3 Pages) and click.**

The first three pages appear on the preview screen, as shown in Figure 1.10.

Previewing a Document

- With the document open, click the Print Preview button.

- Click the One Page button to see one page at a time.

- Click the Multiple Pages button to see 2–6 pages at once.

- Click a scroll arrow to see the next or previous page(s).

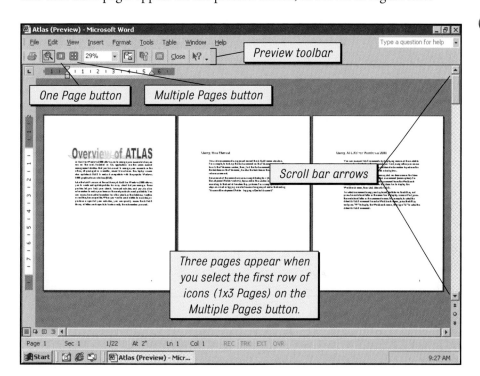

Figure 1.10
Print Preview window

Printing a Document

To print one copy of all pages:

Click the Print button on the Standard toolbar.

To print selected pages:

1. Click Print on the File Menu.

2. Click the appropriate option in the *Page range* section.

3. Enter the page numbers or page ranges, if necessary.

4. Verify the *Number of copies* setting.

5. Click OK.

Another Way

- To change the magnification setting while in Print Preview, click the Zoom arrow and select the desired option.

- To close the Print Preview window, click the Close button.

5. Click the down scroll arrow.

The next three pages display.

6. Click the **One Page button** on the Preview toolbar to view one page on the preview screen.

7. On the vertical scroll bar, click once between the scroll box and the up arrow.

The previous page displays.

8. Click the document and watch it zoom to 100 percent size then click the document again to restore it to 40 percent size.

9. Click the **Normal View button** on the View toolbar.

The Print Preview window disappears and your document displays again in Normal View. Your preview of the document indicated that the layout is fine.

10. Click **Print** on the File menu to open the Print dialog box.

11. In the *Page range* section, select the **Pages option**.

12. Type 1,6,20 in the Pages text box.

Word will print these pages of *Atlas*.

13. Verify that *Number of copies* is set to 1, as shown in Figure 1.11. If not, click the triangle button until 1 appears in the list box. Then, click **OK**.

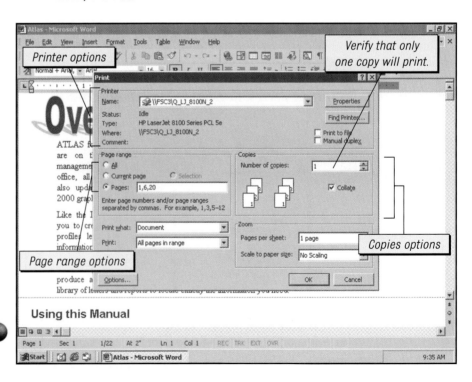

Figure 1.11
Print dialog box

14. Navigate to page 3 of *Atlas* and click an insertion point on that page.

15. Click **Print** on the File menu.

16. In the *Page range* section of the Print dialog box, select **Current Page** and click **OK**.

Word prints the third page of *Atlas*.

17. Close the document.

Printing Labels and an Envelope

Through Word you can type addresses and print them on self-adhesive mailing labels or envelopes that can be fed manually through your printer. The self-adhesive mailing labels are commonly available at office supply stores.

In this activity, you will print a sheet of labels and attach an envelope to a letter, using Word's Envelopes and Labels tool. Check that the printer is switched on and secure permission to print the labels and an envelope before you start this activity.

NOTE *If sheets of self-adhesive labels or envelopes are not available, this activity can be completed by printing on plain paper.*

1. Start Word, if necessary, then click the **New Blank Document button** ▢.

2. Point to **Letters and Mailings** on the Tools menu, and click **Envelopes and Labels** on the submenu.

3. In the Envelopes and Labels dialog box, click the **Options button** on the Labels tab.

The Label Options dialog box appears.

4. Click the **Label products triangle button** and select a label product type to match your labels.

5. In the *Product number* section, select an Address label, such as *5260 - Address*, to match the number on your mailing labels then click **OK**.

NOTE *Choose any label product type and address label if you intend to print on plain paper.*

6. Type a friend's name and address in the Address box then clear the *Use return address* check box, if necessary.

7. Click to select the *Full page of the same label* option, if necessary.

 **BASICS**

Printing a Label
To print a full page of the same label:

1. Point to Letters and Mailings on the Tools menu, then click Envelopes and Labels.

2. Click the Labels tab and the Options button.

3. Choose the label product and product number and click OK.

4. Type the address and select the *Full page of the same label* option.

5. Click the New Document button.

6. Click the Print button.

WORD 2002

8. Click the **Options button** on the Labels tab of the Envelopes and Labels dialog box. Click the **Tray triangle button** and select **Manual Feed** (for commercial labels) or a plain paper tray if commercial labels are unavailable. Click **OK**.

At this point you could click the Print button in the Envelopes and Labels dialog box to print an entire sheet with the same address; however, proceed to the next step to see how different addresses can be printed on the same sheet.

9. Click the **New Document button**. Select the text in the first label, type a different address, then press ⎯Tab⎯ to move to the next label.

From this point you could continue to type various addresses to print on the same sheet.

10. Save the document as *Labels* in the *Tutorial* folder in your *Word Data* folder, then close the document.

11. Open *AHS Workshop* in your *Word Data* folder.

12. Point to **Letters and Mailings** on the Tools menu, then click **Envelopes and Labels** on the submenu.

13. Click the **Envelopes tab** in the Envelopes and Labels dialog box.

The address from *AHS Workshop* appears in the *Delivery address* section, as shown in Figure 1.12. Without the address from an open letter, you would simply type the address in this dialog box.

Word BASICS

Printing a Label
To print a label file with different names and addresses:

1. Point to Letters and Mailings on the Tools menu, then click Envelopes and Labels.

2. Click the Labels tab and the Options button.

3. Choose the label product and product number and click OK.

4. Click the New Document button.

5. Type name and address in the first label; press ⎯Tab⎯ to move to the next label.

6. Print the label document.

Figure 1.12
Envelopes and Labels dialog box

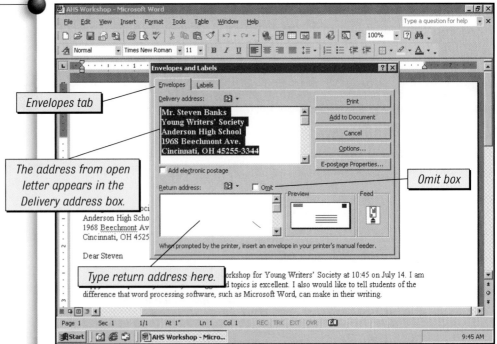

Envelopes tab

The address from open letter appears in the Delivery address box.

Type return address here.

Omit box

14. Clear the Omit box, if necessary. Type your name and address in the *Return address* box and click the **Add to Document button**.

15. Click **No** if a dialog box appears asking if you want to save the new return address as the default return address.

The envelope appears in the Word window with the delivery and return addresses.

16. Click **Print** on the File menu, select **Current page**, and click **OK** to print the envelope on plain paper.

17. Save the document as *Envelope* in the *Tutorial* folder in your *Word Data* folder then close the document.

NOTE *If you are printing on an envelope instead of plain paper, return to the Envelopes and Labels dialog box. Click Options on the Envelopes tab and choose the appropriate envelope size in the Envelope Options dialog box.*

CREATING A DOCUMENT FROM A TEMPLATE

You have learned that you can create documents by clicking the New Blank Document button ⬜. In many situations, though, you do not have to start new documents on a blank screen. Microsoft Word has preformatted **template** models that you can follow. A template includes necessary document parts, ordered and formatted. For example, the standard headings (*To:, From:,* and so on) and the current date are already displayed and properly arranged in the memo template. You replace the **variable information**—the text that is different in each memo you create. The template files are in the Templates box which you can access through the New Document task pane.

Each tab in the Templates dialog box represents a group of documents, such as *Letters & Faxes, Memos, Reports,* and *Web Pages.* To see the templates available in a group, click the tab. When you click the name of a specific template, a Preview box lets you see the template design. When you open the template you want to use, you are really working with a *copy* of it. That way, you can change the model document however you want and still have the original template unchanged.

Opening a Template and Replacing Variable Text

In this activity, you will open a memo template and use it to create a memo.

1. Start Word, if necessary, then click **New** on the File menu.

The New Document task pane displays.

2. Click **General Templates** in the New Document task pane.

3. In the Templates dialog box, click the **Memos tab**, if it is not on top.

Templates for creating memos appear.

WEB NOTE

Additional templates are available at the Microsoft Office Template Gallery. Enter the keyword *templates* into the Ask a Question box and click the *About templates* Help topic to find the hyperlink to this page or search on the keywords *template gallery* at the *Microsoft.com* Web site.

4. Click the *Contemporary Memo* icon.

A preview of this template is displayed in the Preview window.

5. Click **Document** in the Create New box, if it is not selected, and click **OK**.

NOTE *If Template is selected when you click OK, you will open the actual template, not a copy of it. Then when you type, you would change the template.*

A copy of the *Contemporary Memo* template opens and the task pane closes. *Document* appears in the title bar followed by a number, like any other new document, because you opened a copy of the template. If you opened the actual template, the title bar would indicate *Template1*.

6. Click **Normal View** ▤ then scroll and read the document.

7. Click anywhere within the brackets after *To:*.

The text within the brackets is highlighted. You have selected variable text and now need to replace it with your information.

8. Type All Sales Associates to replace the variable text.

9. After *CC:* (meaning *copies to*), click the variable text and type Nancy Roberts, Joe DiFillippo.

10. Click the variable text after *From:*, and type your name.

Notice that on the next line Word has automatically inserted the current date.

11. After *Re:* (meaning *regarding*), click the variable text and type FOURTH QUARTER CONTEST.

12. Below the horizontal line, click before the first character and drag down to the end of the last paragraph to select the heading and all three paragraphs.

When you begin typing, you will replace the selected text.

13. Type the following message exactly as shown. Remember to use [Backspace] to erase errors as you type, and allow text to wrap at the end of each line. When finished, your memo should look like Figure 1.13.

Have you heard the good news? The Fourth Quarter Sales Contest has begun. We're tracking your sales and preparing for the best quarter ever.

The top five sales performers will receive an added bonus. Check your e-mail for more details on this exciting contest, and keep selling!

14. Save your document as *Template Memo* in the *Tutorial* folder in your *Word Data* folder, then close the document.

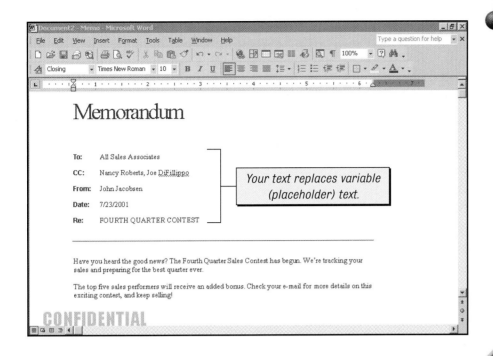

Figure 1.13
Memo created from a template

WORD 2002

USING LANGUAGE AND GRAMMAR TOOLS

Even a good writer may make occasional errors in spelling, punctuation, subject-verb agreement, word choice, typing, verb tense, and so on. Good writers proofread their documents and correct their mistakes and declare a document final only when it is free of errors. Editing and proofreading are important for two reasons: communication and image. Errors in documents may cause readers to misunderstand your message, wasting your time and theirs. Besides, the documents you prepare—whether for yourself or an employer—represent you. Their quality and appearance convey a message about your attitude and competence.

No software can edit and proofread for you. Word provides tools to help you check spelling, grammar, and usage. The Spelling and Grammar tools flag potential errors and allow you to decide if a correction is needed in each instance. When Word detects a potential spelling or grammar error, the Spelling and Grammar Status icon on the status bar displays a red **X**. Word's AutoCorrect feature helps prevent some spelling, capitalization, and grammar errors by automatically correcting such errors as you type them. (To confirm the AutoCorrect settings on the computer you are using, click AutoCorrect Options on the Tools menu and click the AutoCorrect tab. Then select the options you want Word to automatically correct and click OK.) The Thesaurus tool (point to Language on the Tools menu) can find substitutes for words that are overused or used incorrectly in your documents. With the Replace feature you learned about earlier in this lesson, you can change occurrences of words used too often and correct repeated errors.

Checking Spelling and Grammar in a Document

The wavy, red lines in your documents mark words not in the Spelling dictionary. When you right-click one of these words, a **shortcut menu** appears. If the menu lists the correct spelling, click the correct word to replace the misspelled word. If the correct spelling is not on the shortcut menu, you may correct the spelling manually or click Ignore All. Clicking Ignore All tells Word to disregard all instances

of the underlined word in the current document. (Clicking Add to Dictionary puts the underlined word into the Spelling dictionary. You must not choose the Add option unless the computer belongs to you.) The wavy, red line disappears when you click one of these options. Another option on the shortcut menu is the Spelling command. Clicking it opens the Spelling dialog box, which is useful for checking spelling in long documents.

Wavy, green lines mark grammatical forms not found in the grammar rules for U.S. English usage. When you right-click this text, a shortcut menu displays. If the menu suggests an improvement to your text, you can click the suggested change if it truly improves your text. If the text is correct as is, you may click Ignore Once to remove the green underline.

When you click the Spelling and Grammar button 🕮, you can check spelling and grammar simultaneously throughout an entire document. The Spelling and Grammar tool goes automatically to the first potential spelling or grammar error and shows the sentence, with the problem highlighted. Spelling suggestions display in the Suggestions box. For grammar errors, suggestions display in the suggestions box, but a tip also displays, providing the related grammar rule and one or more examples. As soon as you choose to change or ignore the highlighted text, Word will move to the next possible error.

HANDS on

Checking Spelling and Grammar

In this activity, you will check the spelling and grammar of words and sentences identified by the Word spelling and grammar checker.

NOTE *Before beginning this activity, check that the Spelling and Grammar features are active. If necessary, click the New Blank Document button* 🗋 *to activate the menu bar, then click Options on the Tools menu. On the Spelling & Grammar tab, click to select these check boxes:* Check spelling as you type, Always suggest corrections, Check grammar as you type, *and* Check grammar with spelling. *Clear the other check boxes. Click the Custom Dictionaries button and verify that* CUSTOM.DIC *shows in the Custom Dictionaries dialog box. Check that* Grammar Only *appears in the* Writing style *list box. After you adjust these settings, close the Options dialog box and the blank document window.*

1. **Open *Memo Draft* in your *Word Data* folder then save the document as *Memo Draft Revised* in the *Tutorial* folder in your *Word Data* folder.**

2. **Point to the underlined name *Riberts* and right-click anywhere in the name.**

A shortcut menu opens showing the suggested word *Roberts* as a possible correction. You decide that the name is misspelled and should be *Roberts*.

3. **Click *Roberts* on the shortcut menu.**

The correct name replaces the misspelled name in your memo and the red, wavy underline disappears.

Word BASICS

Checking Spelling and Grammar

1. Right-click a word underlined in red (to correct spelling) or green (to correct grammar).

2. Click an option on the shortcut menu or type the correction in the document.

Or:

1. Click the Spelling and Grammar button on the Standard toolbar.

2. Click an option in the dialog box.

---

4. Click the Spelling and Grammar button 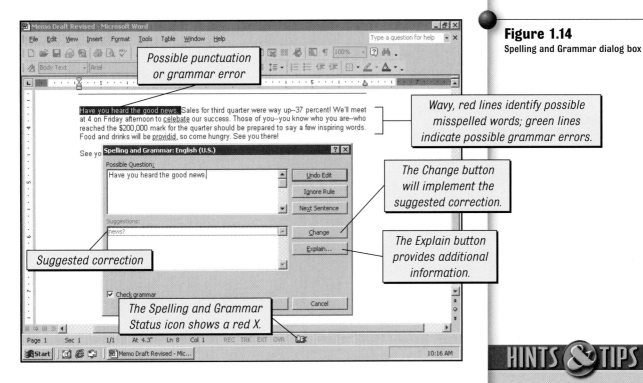 **on the Standard toolbar.**

The Spelling and Grammar dialog box appears displaying the first sentence, as shown in Figure 1.14. You may click Ignore Rule to ignore the highlighted error and similar errors (Ignore Rule can be useful in editing a long document). Click Change to implement the suggested correction. In this instance, you want more information about the possible error.

Figure 1.14
Spelling and Grammar dialog box

WORD 2002

5. Click Explain.

The Office Assistant appears with additional information and examples.

WARNING *Not all suggested grammar changes are improvements. Read the information very carefully before deciding to change your text. Also, Word may not detect some errors.*

6. Read the information, then click Change.

The sentence is corrected—a question mark replaces the period and the green line disappears. The Spelling and Grammar dialog box moves on to a misspelled word and provides suggested changes.

7. Make appropriate changes in the Spelling and Grammar dialog box to correct the next two misspelled words.

WARNING *Never add words to a dictionary (Add to Dictionary button) unless you have permission to do so or you own the computer. In any case, always check a word carefully before adding it to the Word dictionary.*

The Office Assistant states that the spelling and grammar check is complete.

8. Right-click the Office Assistant then click Hide on the shortcut menu.

9. Save and close the document.

HANDS on

Using the Thesaurus

The **Thesaurus** tool is a source of synonyms and antonyms that can help you find alternative words as you edit your document. If you tend to use the same words or phrases repeatedly, the Thesaurus tool can help you vary your vocabulary. In this activity, you will use the Thesaurus tool to find replacements for several words in the *Memo Draft Revised* document.

1. Open *Memo Draft Revised* in the *Tutorial* folder in your *Word Data* folder.

2. Select the word *good* in the first sentence of the document.

3. Click the **Tools menu**, point to **Language**, and click **Thesaurus**.

WARNING *If the Thesaurus command does not appear on the Language submenu, see your instructor. You may need to install the Thesaurus.*

The Thesaurus dialog box appears, as shown in Figure 1.15. The word *good* appears in the *Looked Up* box and its meaning is defined in the *Meanings* box below. The *Replace with Synonym* box provides words and phrases with similar meanings that could substitute for *good*. Click any word in the *Meanings* box to view a list of corresponding synonyms for that word. Type a new word in the *Replace with Synonym* box and press [Enter←] to move it to the *Looked Up* box and view a new list of meanings and synonyms for that word.

Figure 1.15
Thesaurus dialog box

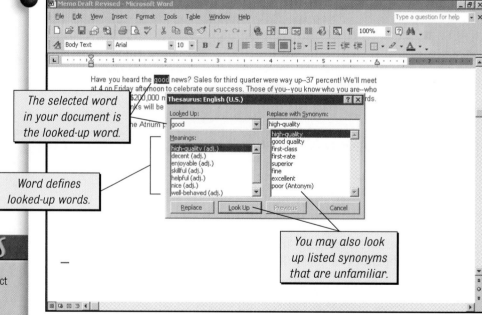

The selected word in your document is the looked-up word.

Word defines looked-up words.

You may also look up listed synonyms that are unfamiliar.

4. In the *Replace with Synonym* box, click *excellent* then click the **Look Up button**.

The word *excellent* now appears in the *Looked Up* box. As shown in the *Meanings* box, the word means outstanding—an appropriate replacement for *good*.

5. Click the **Replace button**.

The word *outstanding* replaces *good* in your document.

6. Save your changes as *Final Memo* in the *Tutorial* folder in your *Word Data* folder, then close the document.

Using AutoText, AutoComplete, and AutoCorrect

Many of your documents have repetitive elements that Word enables you to insert automatically so you can avoid typing them. AutoText is one such method of saving text or graphics for use elsewhere. When the AutoComplete feature is turned on, Word will display a ScreenTip when you type the first few characters of an AutoText entry. Pressing [Enter←] will place the AutoText suggestion in the document. In the same way, the current date and time can be easily inserted into a document using AutoComplete. Or you can use the Insert menu to choose from a large selection of various date/time formats. AutoCorrect automatically replaces typed characters with symbols or replaces incorrectly typed words with correctly spelled words as you type them.

Inserting Text Using AutoText, AutoComplete, and the Insert Menu

In this activity, you will add AutoText to the end of a document and you will use AutoComplete to insert the current date. You will then insert a new date format using the Insert menu and modify it to create a custom date/time format.

1. Open *Home Page Support* in your *Word Data* folder.

2. Press [Ctrl] + [End] to move the insertion point to the end of the document, then press [Enter←] two times.

3. Click the **View menu**, point to **Toolbars**, and click **AutoText**.

The AutoText toolbar appears below the Formatting toolbar.

4. Click the **All Entries button**  on the AutoText toolbar and point to **Header/Footer**.

The All Entries menu and the Header/Footer submenu display. (You'll learn more about creating and modifying actual headers and footers in Lesson 2.) Pointing to any of the items on the All Entries menu will display AutoText that can be inserted into your document.

5. On the Header/Footer submenu, click the **Filename option**.

The name of your file *(Home Page Support)* is inserted in the document. Whenever you change the name of this file, Word will automatically change this text in your document.

6. Click the **AutoText button** , then click the AutoText tab of the AutoCorrect dialog box, if necessary.

WORD 2002

Word BASICS

Inserting AutoText Using AutoComplete

1. Click the AutoText button and select the *Show AutoComplete suggestions* check box, if necessary.

2. As you type, watch for the AutoComplete ScreenTip to appear containing the text to be inserted.

3. Press [Enter←] if the AutoComplete text is appropriate; continue to type if it is not appropriate.

Word BASICS

Inserting a Date/Time Format

1. Click an insertion point in your document.

2. Click Date and Time on the Insert menu, and click the desired format.

3. Click to select the Update Automatically check box, then click OK.

The AutoText tab displays a list of AutoText entries; clicking an item in the list displays the item in the Preview window as it would appear in a document.

7. **Click to select the *Show AutoComplete suggestions* check box, then click OK.**

8. **Press [Spacebar] after the file name, type the current month, and press [Spacebar] again.**

An AutoComplete ScreenTip appears prompting you to press [Enter←] to insert the date.

9. **Press [Enter←] to automatically insert today's date, a comma, and the year.**

10. **Drag to select the date, then click Date and Time on the Insert menu.**

11. **In the Date and Time dialog box, click to select the Update automatically check box, if necessary.**

Update automatically will cause the date in the file to be updated to the current date each time the file is printed. Notice the variety of date and time formats.

12. **Click a different selection (a format like *Wednesday, March 20, 2001*) that does *not* display the time, then click OK to close the dialog box.**

The date is inserted in the new format. By modifying the **field codes,** the hidden codes that automatically update the date and/or time, you can create a custom format not available as a selection in the Date/Time dialog box.

13. **Right-click the date format in the document then click Toggle Field Codes on the shortcut menu.**

The underlying field code is revealed representing the day, current month, date, and year in a format like *{DATE \@ "dddd, MMMM dd, yyyyy"}*. (The exact code will vary depending upon the format you selected.)

14. **Right-click the date format code and click Edit Field on the shortcut menu.**

The Field dialog box appears with the current date format (such as *Wednesday, March 21, 2001*) highlighted in the *Field properties* list. The corresponding code for the current date format appears in the *Date formats* box.

15. **Click after the last character of the code, press [Spacebar], then type h:mm am/pm and click OK.**

The Field dialog box closes. The time has been added to the date format in your document.

> **NOTE** *Learn more about editing field codes in date/time formats by entering keywords* field formats *in the* Ask a Question *box. Click the* Date-Time Picture (\@) field switch *link.*

16. Save the file as *Home Page Support Revised* in the *Tutorial* folder in your *Word Data* folder and close the document.

17. Click **View**, point to **Toolbars**, and click **AutoText** to close the AutoText toolbar.

Using AutoCorrect While Typing

In this activity, you will add a sentence to a letter while using the AutoCorrect tool to insert a symbol and correct your misspelled words.

1. Open the *AHS Workshop* document in your *Word Data* folder.

2. Click **AutoCorrect Options** on the Tools menu to open the AutoCorrect dialog box, then click the **AutoCorrect tab**.

3. Click to select any check boxes that do not have a check mark.

The *Replace text as you type* list box contains common typographical errors or typed symbols (left column) and corresponding corrections (right column), as shown in Figure 1.16. The copyright symbol appears at the top of the list.

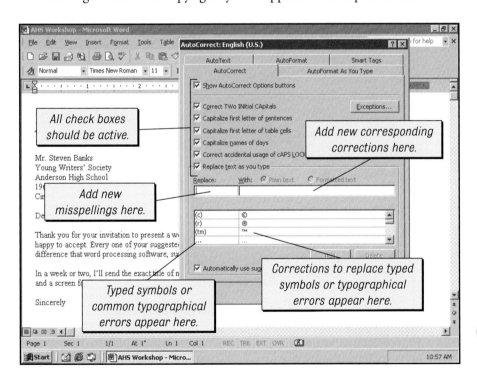

4. Scroll down in the *Replace text as you type* list box until you see the word *about* in the right column; make note of the corresponding typographical error in the left column.

5. Click **Cancel** to close the dialog box.

6. Click an insertion point at the end of the second paragraph in the *AHS Workshop* letter, then press [Enter←] twice.

Figure 1.16
AutoCorrect dialog box

NORTON
ONLINE

Visit **www.glencoe.com/norton/online/** for more information on Microsoft Word 2002.

AutoCorrect will replace a typed symbol or misspelled word as you type. To see the automatic correction, watch the Word window as you type the misspelled word *abbout* and the symbol *(c)* in the following step.

7. Type these exact words (including misspellings): I will let you know abbout the copyright (c) 2004 issue pertanning to your documents.

The misspelled word *abbout* changes to *about* as you type; the characters *(c)* are automatically replaced with the copyright symbol; however, the misspelled word *pertanning* is not corrected—it appears with a wavy, red underline. You could right-click this misspelled word and correct it on the shortcut menu; however, since you habitually type this word incorrectly it makes sense to add it to the AutoCorrect list.

8. Right-click *pertanning*, point to **AutoCorrect** on the shortcut menu, then click **AutoCorrect Options**.

9. Type pertanning in the *Replace* box, press [Tab], then type pertaining in the *With* box.

10. Click **Add**, then click **OK** to close the dialog box.

11. Select the sentence you just typed and press [Delete], then retype it (including the errors) while watching for the replacement text to be inserted as you type: I will let you know abbout the copyright (c) 2004 issue pertanning to your documents.

All the misspellings are automatically corrected and the copyright symbol is inserted.

12. Point to the middle of the word *pertaining* and when a blue horizontal bar appears under the first two characters, point to the bar.

The AutoCorrect Options button 🔄▾ appears.

13. Click the **AutoCorrect Options button** 🔄▾.

This button provides the options to restore the previous spelling or stop AutoCorrecting the word. Clicking Control AutoCorrect Options would take you back to the AutoCorrect Options dialog box.

14. Click the option to stop automatically correcting the word *pertanning*.

The incorrect spelling is restored; the red, wavy underline again appears under the word.

15. Save your document as *Autocorrect Edits* in the *Tutorial* folder in your *Word Data* folder and close the document.

HINTS & TIPS

Add a frequently used word or phrase to the AutoText tab of the AutoCorrect dialog box. Type the entry in the *Enter AutoText entries here* list and click OK. To delete an entry, click the entry and press the Delete button.

Searching for a File

In this activity, you will explore Help to learn about using the Search feature to find a file on your computer.

1. In the Ask a Question box, type find a file and press Enter←.

2. Click the Find a file link, click Show All, and read the information.

3. Close the Help window, then click the **Search button** 🔍 on the Standard toolbar.

The Basic Search task pane displays.

4. Type Atlas in the *Search text* box, and click **Search**.

5. In a few moments, all documents containing *Atlas* will display in the Search Results task pane.

6. Click one of the files to open it, and then close the file and close the task pane.

Self Check ☑

Test your knowledge by answering the following questions. See Appendix B to check your answers.

1. To count the number of lines in your document, click the _Word count statistics_ button.

2. Double-click the ___OVR___ button on the status bar to switch between Insert and Overtype modes.

3. The _Thesaurus_ can help you find alternative words as you edit a document.

4. The _clipboard_ is a temporary holding area for text that has been cut or copied.

5. To open a template, first click ___New___ on the File menu to activate the New Document task pane.

ON THE WEB

INSERTING HYPERLINKS

A hyperlink is a shortcut or jump that, when clicked, links you to another page, document, or Web site. Hyperlinks are usually easy to recognize within a document. For example, hyperlinks are often in a distinctive color and are often underlined. Typically, after you click a hyperlink, the link changes color to remind you that you already followed that link. In this activity, you will insert a hyperlink into a Web site within a document.

NOTE *Before starting this activity, connect to the Internet through your Internet Service Provider (ISP). If necessary, type your user name and password. If you are not sure how to connect to the Internet, ask your instructor for assistance.*

1. Open *Star Gazette Article* in your *Word Data* folder then point to **Toolbars** on the View menu and click **Web**.

The Web toolbar displays at the top of the document window. The Address box in the Web toolbar contains the path and file name of your open document. Table 1.4 provides a brief description of each button on the Web toolbar.

Table 1.4	The Word Web Toolbar	
Button	**Name**	**Description**
⇦	Back	Displays the previous Web site that you visited.
⇨	Forward	Displays the next Web site that you visited.
⊗	Stop	Stops the Internet connection in progress.
🔄	Refresh	Reloads the current site.
🏠	Start Page	Loads the Web site that you have specified as your starting point on the Web.
🔍	Search the Web	Loads the Web site that you have specified for launching Web searches.
Favorites ▾	Favorites	Provides access to your list of favorite Web sites.
Go ▾	Go	Allows you to access a Web site or document; also allows you to specify your Start and Search pages.
📤	Show Only Web Toolbar	Hides or displays all visible toolbars except the Web toolbar.
http://www.microsoft.com	Address	Allows you to enter the location of a Web site you wish to open.
▾	Toolbar Options	Allows you to customize the toolbar by adding or removing buttons or reset the toolbar to display the default buttons.

WORD 2002

WORD 2002

2. Click the text within the Address box to select it then type the following address: http://www.eps.mcgill.ca/~bud/craters/FaceOfVenus.html. **Verify that every character is accurate and no spaces appear between the characters, then press** Enter⏎.

Word opens your browser at the *Face of Venus* Web site.

3. **Close your browser window then scroll to the end of the open document and set the insertion point two lines below the last line.**

4. **Type** Click here for Venus on the Web. **Then select this sentence.**

5. **Click the Insert Hyperlink button** 🖦 **on the Standard toolbar.**

The Insert Hyperlink dialog box appears as shown in Figure 1.17. The text you have selected as your hyperlink appears in the *Text to display* box.

6. **Click Existing File or Web Page in the** *Link to* **bar, then click the Address box triangle button to display a list of recently visited Web sites.**

7. **Click the** *Face of Venus* **Web address which should be the first site in the list, then click OK.**

8. **Point to the hyperlink in the document, read the ScreenTip which includes the Web address, then press** Ctrl **and click the hyperlink.**

Again, Word opens your browser at the *Face of Venus* site.

9. **Close your browser to return to the Word window, then save the document as** *Venus Link* **in the** *Tutorial* **folder in your** *Word Data* **folder.**

10. **Close the Web toolbar, then close all open files and exit Word.**

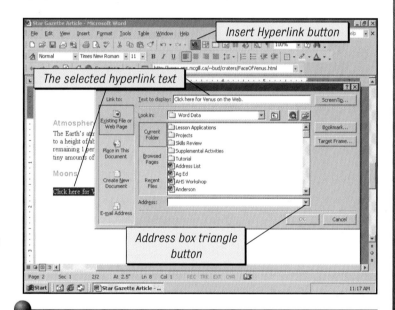

Figure 1.17
Insert Hyperlink dialog box

WARNING *You may proceed directly to the exercises in this lesson. If, however, you are finished with your computer session, follow the "shut down" procedures for your lab or school environment.*

SUMMARY AND EXERCISES

SUMMARY

More people use computers for word processing than any other task. Word is a powerful word processing application. Lesson 1 introduced basic word processing terms; explained how to start Word; and explored menus, toolbars, and other objects in the Word window. You learned to open, view, navigate, type, edit, preview, and print documents. You learned that Word offers a variety of templates that you can adapt to your needs. You used the Word language tools and the Copy, Cut, and Paste features to help edit documents. You inserted text into your document using the Insert menu, AutoText, AutoComplete, and AutoCorrect. You learned how to manage files and folders and how to change file types. Finally, you were introduced to the features of the Web toolbar and learned how to add a hyperlink to a document.

Now that you have completed this lesson, you should be able to do the following:

- Explain word processing. (page 125)
- Start Microsoft Word and name objects in the document window. (page 126)
- Provide a brief description of each menu on the Word menu bar. (page 127)
- Provide a brief description of each button on the Standard toolbar. (page 128)
- Look at documents in four different views. (page 130)
- Select single words or lines, whole paragraphs, or an entire document. (page 132)
- Find specific pages and text using the Find and Replace dialog box. (page 133)
- Edit text using the Insert and Overtype modes. (page 136)
- Rename and save a file. (page 137)
- Replace and delete text. (page 138)
- Use the Undo, Redo, and Repeat commands to edit text. (page 140)
- Use the Office Clipboard to cut, copy, and paste text. (page 142)
- Use the drag-and-drop method to move and copy text. (page 143)
- Create and delete folders and change file types. (page 146)
- Preview a document. (page 148)
- Print one page or selected pages of a multi-page document. (page 149)
- Print labels and an envelope. (page 151)
- Create a new document from a template. (page 153)
- Use the Spelling and Grammar tools to help edit documents as you type. (page 155)
- Use the Thesaurus tool to find alternate words. (page 158)
- Insert text using AutoText and AutoComplete. (page 159)
- Modify a date/time format using the Insert menu. (page 159)
- Use AutoCorrect to correct text while typing. (page 161)
- Search for a file on your hard drive. (page 163)
- Describe the Word Web toolbar features and insert a hyperlink into a document. (page 164)

CONCEPTS REVIEW

1 TRUE/FALSE

Circle T if the statement is true or F if the statement is false.

(T) F **1.** To select a sentence, press `Ctrl` and click anywhere in the sentence.

T (F) **2.** To select a paragraph, double-click anywhere within the paragraph. *Triple click*

(T) F **3.** The Normal View is the ideal choice for typing and editing text.

T (F) **4.** In Overtype mode, the text you type pushes existing text to the right. *Insert*

(T) F **5.** The Find and Replace dialog box allows you to go to a specific page in a document.

(T) F **6.** To print all pages of a document, click the Print button on the Standard toolbar.

(T) F **7.** When you type to the end of a line, *word wrap* automatically moves the insertion point to the next line.

(T) F **8.** You can right-click a word underlined in red to correct its spelling.

T (F) **9.** When you *cut* text you do not remove it from its original location.

T (F) **10.** AutoCorrect and the Spelling and Grammar tools have eliminated the need for you to edit and proofread your documents.

2 MATCHING

Match each of the terms on the left with the definitions on the right.

TERMS

1. selection bar *g*
2. Edit menu *c*
3. Word Count toolbar *a*
4. AutoComplete *i*
5. paste *e*
6. status bar *h*
7. drag-and-drop *d*
8. Print preview *j*
9. word processor *b*
10. templates *f*

DEFINITIONS

a. Allows you to quickly count characters, words, or lines of text in your document

b. Application that allows creation of text-based documents

c. Includes the Find command

d. A method of moving text without the Office Clipboard

e. To insert text stored on the Office Clipboard

f. Preformatted model documents

g. Invisible column between the left edge of the document window and the left margin of the page

h. Displays your location within a document and the typing mode

i. Automatically tries to finish what you are typing

j. Allows you to see just how your document will look when printed

SUMMARY AND EXERCISES

3 COMPLETION

Fill in the missing word or phrase for each of the following statements.

1. Use the _backspace_ key to erase errors to the left of the insertion point.

2. The Print Preview button is on the _standard_ toolbar.

3. To select a word, _double-click_ it.

4. The blinking vertical bar where text is inserted when you type is called the _insertion point_.

5. Word temporarily stores information that you have cut or copied from your document on the _office clipboard_

6. To prepare a document by following a preset format, open a _template_ .

7. The _task pane_ appears at the right side of the application window when you first open Word.

8. The _cut_ button on the Standard toolbar removes text from your document and places the text on the Clipboard.

9. The quickest way to locate a particular word or phrase in a long document is to use the _find_ command.

10. When you use _Insert mode_ , the text you type is inserted into existing text, pushing the characters after it to the right.

4 SHORT ANSWER

Write a brief answer to each of the following questions.

1. Describe how to activate and deactivate Overtype mode using the mouse.

2. Name the four document views and describe each view briefly.

3. Describe how to start Microsoft Word.

4. Explain the advantages of using a template.

5. Describe three features of the Word Web toolbar.

6. Describe two ways to navigate a document without using the scroll bars.

7. Explain why you might need to save a document as a different file type (file format).

8. Describe how to save an existing document under a new name.

9. Explain how to create a new folder and how to delete a folder.

10. Explain the advantages and limitations of using AutoCorrect and the Word Spelling and Grammar tools to edit and proofread documents.

5 IDENTIFICATION

Label each of the elements of the Word window in Figure 1.18.

Figure 1.18

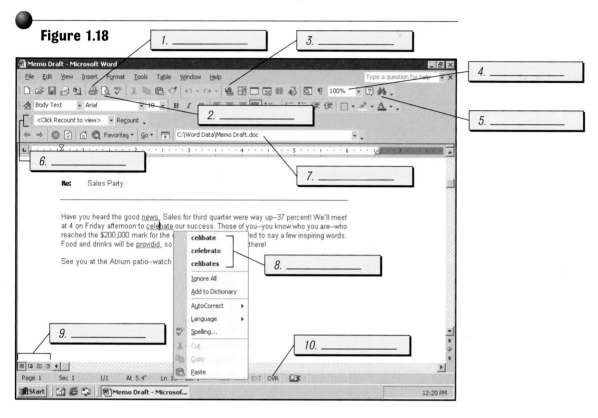

SKILLS REVIEW

Complete all of the Skills Review problems in sequential order to review your skills to start Word; identify objects in the document window; view documents; navigate a document and replace, select, and delete text; insert a paragraph; use Undo, Redo, and Repeat; move, copy, cut, and paste text; use the Paste Special command; create and delete folders and rename and save files in a new format; preview and print; create a document from a template; check spelling and grammar; use the Thesaurus; and insert text using AutoText, AutoCorrect, AutoComplete, and the Insert menu.

1 Starting Word and Viewing a File

1. Click the **Start button** 🔳 **Start**, point to **Programs**, and click **Microsoft Word**.

2. Click the **Open button** 🖼 on the Standard toolbar.

3. Click the **Look in triangle button**; then click the drive (and open the folder, if necessary) that contains your *Word Data* folder.

4. Double-click *Star Gazette Article*.

5. Click the **Print Layout View button** 🔲.

6. Scroll to the left and right and examine the width of the side margins.

7. Click the **Web Layout View button** 🔲.

8. Scroll rapidly to the end of the document; click an insertion point; then press
Ctrl + Home to go to the beginning of the document.

9. Click the **Normal View button** 📄.

2 Navigating a Document and Replacing, Selecting, and Deleting Text

1. With *Star Gazette Article* open in your document window, click the **Find button**
🔍, type **roman**, and click **Find Next**.

2. Activate Overtype mode in the status bar, and change *r* to *R*.

3. Find *nitrogen* and change the comma after it to a semicolon.

4. In the same sentence, change the comma after *oxygen* to a semicolon.

5. Search for *it's* and delete the apostrophe; click **Find Next** again and delete the
apostrophe in the second occurrence.

6. Click **Find Next**. A dialog box indicates that the search is complete; click **OK**.

7. Click the **Replace tab**. In the *Find what* box, type **Venus's**; in the *Replace with*
box, type **Venus'**. Click **Find Next** then click **Replace**. Continue searching to correct all occurrences.

8. Click the **Find tab**, scroll to the top of the document, click an insertion point,
then find the second occurrence of *drift*. Select the sentence in which it occurs and
delete it.

9. Click the **Go To tab**. In the *Go to what* list box, click **Page** and type 2 in the *Enter
page number box*. Then click the **Go To button**.

10. In the *Enter page number* box, type −1 and click the **Go To button**.

11. Close the Find and Replace dialog box, save your document as *Star Gazette Edited*
in the *Skills Review* folder in your *Word Data* folder, then close the document.

3 Inserting a Paragraph and Using the Word Count Toolbar

1. Open *Star Gazette Article* in your *Word Data* folder, and press Ctrl + End to go to
the end of the document.

2. Point to **Toolbars** on the View menu, and open the Word Count toolbar.

3. Click the **Word Count Statistics triangle button** [520 Lines ▾] and click
Words to count the number of words in the file.

4. Press Enter, and type the following paragraph using Insert mode. Correct your
errors using Backspace and Delete.

The Earth's single moon is large in comparison with the natural satellites of
all the other planets except for Pluto. Astronomers actually consider the
Earth-Moon system to be a double planet. Its size gives the moon a significant
gravitational influence on the Earth, causing our oceans to have tides.

5. Click the **Recount button** Recount to count the number of words in the file.

6. Save your document as *Star Gazette Addition* in the *Skills Review* folder in your *Word Data* folder and close the document. Close the Word Count toolbar.

4 Undoing, Redoing, and Repeating Actions

1. Open *Star Gazette Article* in your *Word Data* folder.

2. Click the **Find button** 🔍 and find the word *percent* using the Find and Replace dialog box. Select the word, then type the percent sign (%).

3. Find the next two occurrences of the word *percent* and in each instance click **Repeat Typing** on the Edit menu to replace it with the percent sign (%).

4. Close the Find and Replace dialog box.

5. Click the **Undo button** ↩ until each occurrence of the word *percent* is restored.

6. Click the **Redo button** ↪ to restore the percent sign (%) in all instances; then click Undo ↩ again to reverse those actions and restore all the occurrences of *percent*.

7. Close the document; click **No** if prompted to save changes.

5 Moving and Copying Text

1. Open *Write this Way* in your *Word Data* folder.

2. Click **Office Clipboard** on the Edit menu to display the Clipboard task pane, then click **Clear All** 🗙 Clear All .

3. Triple-click to select the next-to-last paragraph in the document, then click **Cut** ✂.

4. Paste the cut text from the Clipboard into a new line at the end of the document.

5. Type Which of these titles do you like best? and press Enter⏎.

6. Scroll to the top of the document and copy the document title and subtitle to the Clipboard as separate items. Scroll to the end of the document and click below the last line.

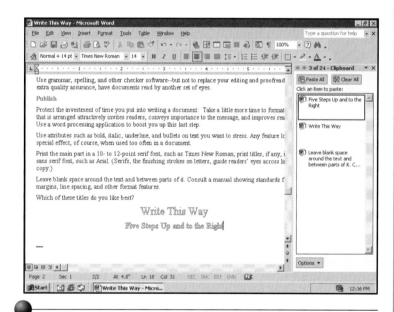

Figure 1.19

7. Click **Write This Way** on the Clipboard, then click *Five Steps Up and to the Right* on the Clipboard. (Your document should look like Figure 1.19.)

8. Next, find and select the question *Is the tone positive?*

9. Drag the sentence to the right to drop it at the end of the next sentence.

10. Save the document as *Write Revised* in the *Skills Review* folder in your *Word Data* folder then close the document and close the Clipboard.

SUMMARY AND EXERCISES

6 Using the Paste Special Command

1. Open *Australia Tour Pricing* in your *Word Data* folder.

2. Select the *Glen Travel Agency* header down to and including the date, and click **Copy** 🗈.

3. Click **Open** 🖝, then click the **Files of type triangle button** and click **Rich Text Format**.

4. Open *Glen Travel Prices* in your *Word Data* folder, click **Paste Special** on the Edit menu, then click **Formatted Text (RTF)** in the Paste Special dialog box and click **OK**.

5. Save the document as *Glen Travel Prices RTF* in the *Skills Review* folder in your *Word Data* folder, then close all documents.

6. Click **Open** 🖝, click the **Files of type triangle button**, click **All Files**, then click **Cancel**.

7 Creating and Deleting Folders

1. Click **Open** 🖝 and navigate to the *Skills Review* folder in your *Word Data* folder.

2. With the *Skills Review* folder in the *Look in* box, click **Create New Folder** 🗀.

3. Type **Star Gazette Docs** as the new folder name and click **OK**.

4. Click **Create New Folder** 🗀, type **Correspondence**, and click **OK**.

5. Click the **Up One Level button** 🗀 twice, click the *Star Gazette Docs* folder, then click **Delete** ✕. Click **Yes** to confirm the deletion.

8 Renaming and Saving Files in a New Format

1. Navigate to the *Skills Review* folder in your *Word Data* folder and click *Glen Travel Prices RTF*.

2. Click **Tools** Tools▾, click **Rename**, then type **Glen Travel Agency Prices RTF** as the new file name and press Enter↵.

3. Open *Glen Travel Agency Prices RTF* and click **Save As** on the File menu.

4. Type **Glen Travel Rates** in the *File name* box, click **Word Document** on the *Save as type* drop-down list, click **Save**, and close the document.

9 Previewing and Printing a Document

1. Open *Atlas* in your *Word Data* folder, and click the **Print Preview button** 🔍.

2. Click the **Multiple Pages button** ▦, and select **2 × 3 pages** to view pages 1–6.

3. Click the **down scroll arrow** to preview pages 7–12.

4. Click twice anywhere on page 12 (bottom right) to enlarge the page to 100 percent.

5. Click the page again to return to the 2 × 3 layout, then continue scrolling to the end of the document.

6. Click the **Print Layout View button** 🔲.

7. Scroll to page 14 and click anywhere on the page.

8. Click **Print** on the File menu.

9. In the *Print range* section, click the **Current page option**.

10. Verify that the Number of copies is set to 1, and click **OK**.

11. Close the document.

10 Printing Labels and Envelopes

1. Click the **New Blank Document button** 🔲, point to **Letters and Mailings** on the Tools menu, and click **Envelopes and Labels**.

2. Click the **Options button** on the Labels tab and select the appropriate label product and product number, if you are printing on commercial labels.

3. Click the **Tray triangle button**, click the appropriate paper tray, and click **OK**.

4. Type a relative's name and address in the Address box, select the **Full page** of the same label option, then click **Print**.

5. Point to **Letters and Mailings** on the Tools menu and click **Envelopes and Labels**.

6. Type a delivery address and return address on the Envelopes tab, and click **Add to Document**; click **No** if prompted to save the return address.

7. Click **Print** on the File menu, click the **Current Page option**, and click **OK** to print on plain paper.

8. If you are printing on an envelope, reopen the Envelopes and Labels dialog box; click **Options** on the Envelopes tab; and choose the appropriate envelope size in the Envelope Options dialog box. Print the envelope.

9. Close the document. Click **No** if asked to save changes.

11 Creating a Document From a Template

1. Click **New** on the File menu. In the New Document task pane, click **General Templates**.

2. In the Templates dialog box, click the Letters & Faxes tab, then click the **Professional Fax template** (see Figure 1.20).

3. Verify that the Document option is selected in the *Create New* box, and click **OK**. Save the document as *Template Fax* in the *Skills Review* folder in your *Word Data* folder.

Figure 1.20

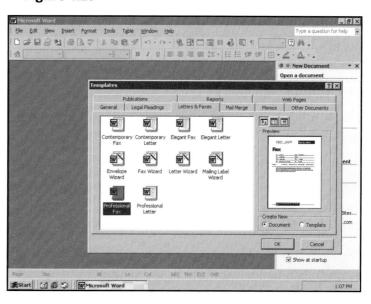

SUMMARY AND EXERCISES

WORD 2002

4. Select the *Company Name Here* header and type your name. Click the return address notation (upper left) and type your address.

5. Compose a fax message to your instructor. Click each area containing variable text (except for the current date) and type a fictional fax and phone number, if necessary. Indicate with an **X** that the material is for review. In the *Comments* section, describe the three most useful things you learned in this lesson.

6. Save and close the file.

12 Checking Spelling and Grammar

1. Open *Step Write Article* in your *Word Data* folder and save it as *Step Write Edited* in your *Skills Review* folder.

2. In the first paragraph, right-click each word underlined with a wavy, red line and make the necessary corrections.

3. Right-click the first word in the first paragraph (*paid*) and click **Grammar** on the shortcut menu. Click **Explain** to read the grammar rule. Click **Change** and change it to *Paid*, as suggested.

4. Press Ctrl + Home to move to the top of the document and click the **Spelling and Grammar button** .

5. Read the suggestion in the Spelling and Grammar dialog box and make the appropriate change.

6. Proceed through the document and study each spelling and grammar question before choosing an option. Do not add words to the spelling dictionary. Click **Ignore** if you are unsure of the correction.

7. Save and close the document.

13 Using the Thesaurus

1. Open *Ag Ed* in your *Word Data* folder then find and select the word *cogent*.

2. Click the **Tools menu**, point to **Language**, and click **Thesaurus**.

3. In the *Replace with Synonym* box, click *sound*; then click **Replace**.

4. Find and select *empirical* and replace it with a synonym.

5. Find and select *expenditure* then click **Thesaurus** on the Tools menu. Click *disbursement* in the synonym list and click **Look up**. Replace the original word with a synonym of *disbursement*.

6. Navigate to the top of page 1 using the Find and Replace dialog box. On the Replace tab, type **expenditure** in the *Find what* box, if necessary, and type **payout** in the *Replace with* box. Click **Find Next**. Follow Table 1.5 to determine in which instances to replace *expenditure*.

7. Navigate again to the top of page 1 and type **regarding** in the *Find what* box; type **about** in the *Replace with* box, and click **Replace All**. Click **OK** to acknowledge the global replacement.

8. Close the Find and Replace dialog box and save the document as *Ag Ed Revised* in the *Skills Review* folder in your *Word Data* folder. Close the file.

14 Inserting a Date/Time Format Using the AutoText Toolbar and Insert Menu

1. Open *Star Gazette Article* in your *Word Data* folder, then press [Ctrl] + [End] and press [Enter◄┘] two times.

2. Click the **View menu**, point to **Toolbars**, and click **AutoText**.

3. On the AutoText toolbar, click the **All Entries button** [All Entries ▾], point to **Header/Footer**, and click **Filename**.

4. Press [Enter◄┘] then click **Date and Time** on the Insert menu.

5. Click a month/year format *without* today's date (like *July 01*), and click **OK**.

6. Right-click the month/year format and click **Toggle Field Codes** on the shortcut menu. Right-click the code, then click **Edit Field**.

7. In the *Date formats* box, click before the first *y*, type **dd**, and press [Spacebar]. (The Field dialog box should look like Figure 1.21.) Click **OK**.

8. Close the AutoText toolbar. Save your document as *Star Gazette AutoText* in the *Skills Review* folder in your *Word Data* folder, then close the document.

15 Inserting Text Using AutoCorrect and AutoComplete

1. Open *AHS Workshop* in your *Word Data* folder.

2. Click after the last word in the second paragraph and press [Enter◄┘] twice.

3. Type the following sentence, including the typographical errors in the words *copy*, *article*, and *global*. When you press [Spacebar] after typing these words, watch the Word window to see if AutoCorrect corrects the misspellings.

   As you requested, I'll send a cpoy of my recent articel on the gloabl economy.

4. Select the word *Sincerely* then slowly type **Best regards** watching for the AutoComplete ScreenTip. Press [Enter◄┘] when prompted to insert the text.

5. Save the document as *AHS Workshop Corrected* in the *Skills Review* folder in your *Word Data* folder, then close the document.

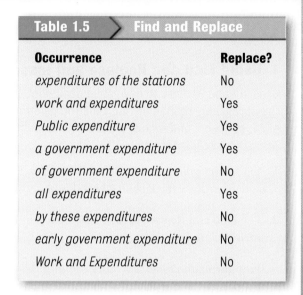

Table 1.5	Find and Replace
Occurrence	**Replace?**
expenditures of the stations	No
work and expenditures	Yes
Public expenditure	Yes
a government expenditure	Yes
of government expenditure	No
all expenditures	Yes
by these expenditures	No
early government expenditure	No
Work and Expenditures	No

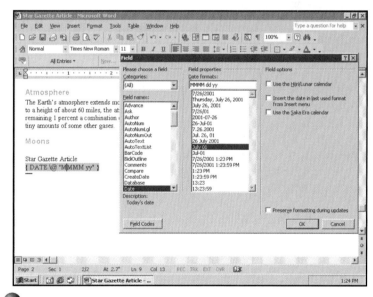

Figure 1.21

SUMMARY AND EXERCISES

LESSON APPLICATIONS

1 Using Find and Replace and Inserting a Date/Time Format

Use Find and Replace to navigate a document and find a paragraph. Select and delete the paragraph, then undo and redo the deletion. Find and replace specific words and phrases. Insert and modify a date/time format using the Insert menu. Insert AutoText using the AutoText toolbar.

1. Open *Nonprinting* in your *Word Data* folder. Find the phrase *A good approach*. Select and delete the paragraph in which this phrase occurs, then undo and redo the deletion.

2. Use Find and Replace to return to the top of the document. Go to the top of page 3, then back to page 1.

3. Find the word *entails* and replace it with the word *means*. Find the phrase *questions-and-answers* and replace it with the same phrase but without the hyphens between the words.

4. Navigate to the last page of the document and press Enter⏎ twice at the end of the last paragraph.

5. Type **This file was last updated on** then use the Insert menu to insert a date format to be updated automatically. View the field codes in the document, then edit the codes to create a new custom date/time format. Adjust spacing as necessary.

6. Activate the AutoText toolbar. On a new line, insert Header/Footer AutoText showing the file name. Close the AutoText toolbar.

7. Save your document as *Nonprinting Updated* in the *Lesson Applications* folder in your *Word Data* folder. Close the document.

2 Copying, Cutting, Pasting, and Editing Text

Copy and cut text and paste it into a new location using the Clipboard. Move text using drag-and-drop. Type and edit a new paragraph using Insert and Overtype modes.

1. Activate the Clipboard task pane and clear the Clipboard. Open *Nonprinting* in your *Word Data* folder. Find the phrase *Marginal Notes* and copy the paragraph in which it occurs to the Clipboard.

2. Find the phrase *Update the substance* and cut the paragraph in which it occurs.

3. Find the phrase *Ask a cadre*. Paste the *Marginal notes* paragraph on a new line following the *Ask a cadre* paragraph. Paste the *Update the substance* paragraph on a new line following the *Marginal notes* paragraph. Adjust vertical spacing as necessary between paragraphs (see Figure 1.22).

4. Find the two occurrences of the phrase *Copyedit the text*. In these sentences, drag-and-drop the word *wordiness* to place it before the phrase *misspelled words*. Correct punctuation and adjust spacing between words, if necessary.

5. Enter the following new paragraph on a new line at the end of the section entitled *What WPS Can Do:* WPS maintains close relationships with a number of superb outside suppliers who share our concern for quality. Select the word *close*, and type excellent using Insert mode. Activate Overtype mode and overtype the phrase *concern for quality* with the words determination to provide outstanding service.

6. Save the document as *Nonprinting Revised* in the *Lesson Applications* folder in your *Word Data* folder. Clear and close the Clipboard, then close the document.

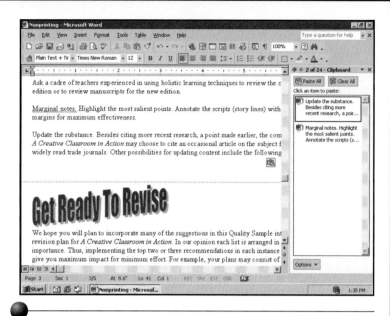

Figure 1.22

3 Copying a Header With the Paste Special Command

Copy a memo header, use Paste Special to change its file type, then paste it into another document.

1. Open *Nonprinting* in your *Word Data* folder. If necessary, open and clear the Office Clipboard.

2. Click in the selection bar to select the *A Creative Classroom in Action* header (at the top of the document), then copy the header to the Clipboard (see Figure 1.23).

3. Open the *Word Data* folder. View only those files in Rich Text Format. Open *Memo Format*. Reopen the Clipboard task pane, if necessary.

4. Use the Paste Special command to paste the header from the Clipboard into the top of the *Memo Format* document in the compatible RTF format.

5. Save *Memo Format* as *Memo Format RTF* in the *Lesson Applications* folder in your *Word Data* folder. Close all documents and clear and close the Clipboard.

4 Managing Folders and Files

Create a new folder. Change a document file type and save the file with a new name. Rename a document.

1. Open *Report Memo* in your *Word Data* folder.

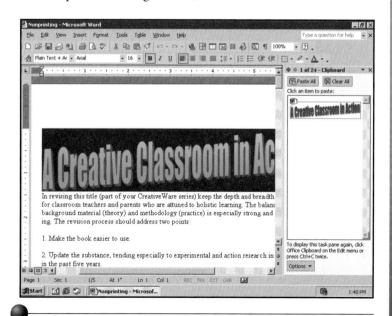

Figure 1.23

2. Change the file type to *Rich Text Format* in the Save As dialog box.

3. Save the document as *Report Memo RTF* in the *Lesson Applications* folder in your *Word Data* folder, and close the file.

4. In the Open dialog box, navigate to the *Lesson Applications* folder in your *Word Data* folder and view All Files.

5. Create a new folder within your *Lesson Applications* folder named *Sales Memos*.

6. Open *Report Memo RTF* in your *Lesson Applications* folder then save it as *Sales* in the new *Sales Memos* folder. Close the document.

7. Open the *Sales Memos* folder in the Open dialog box. Rename the *Sales* document as *Jan Sales Results*, then close the dialog box.

5 Previewing and Printing Documents, Envelopes, and Labels

Preview a document using Print Preview, then print specific pages. Print envelopes and labels.

1. Open *Ag Ed* in your *Word Data* folder and activate Print Preview. Preview pages 1–4 of the document.

2. Switch to Normal View. Click Print on the File menu and print pages 1, 3, and 4. Close the document.

3. Open a new, blank document. In the Envelopes and Labels dialog box, enter the delivery address of a friend and your return address on the Envelopes tab. Check that the Envelope size is correct. Print the envelope.

4. On the Labels tab of the Envelopes & Labels dialog box, enter the delivery address you typed for the envelope if necessary. Select the appropriate label product, product number, and paper tray. Print a single label.

6 Checking Spelling and Grammar and Using the Thesaurus

Check spelling and grammar in a document. Use the Thesaurus tool to find synonyms. Use Find and Replace to replace words throughout a document. Use AutoCorrect to correct typographical errors as you type.

1. Open the *Woodsy View News* document in your *Word Data* folder and save it as *Woodsy News Edited* in the *Lesson Applications* folder in your *Word Data* folder.

2. Check and correct spelling and grammar for the entire document. Assume that all names are spelled correctly as you respond to the spelling and grammar problems. Read the grammar rules, if necessary.

3. Navigate to the beginning of the document.

4. Find the word *capacity* and use the Thesaurus to replace it with a synonym. Find the word *trash* and replace each occurrence with a synonym.

5. Use Replace All to change *Kay Gradison* to *Kathryn Gradison* throughout the document.

6. Open the AutoCorrect tab of the AutoCorrect dialog box. Scroll through the *Replace text as you type* list. Make note of these misspelled words in the *Replace*

column and the corresponding corrections in the *With* column: *instaleld (installed)*; *int he (in the)*.

7. On a new line at the end of the *Work, Work, Work* section of the open document, type this sentence with errors to correct misspellings automatically: **Last month the Gas Co. instaleld new meters int he rear of five houses on Charles St.**

8. Save your changes and close the document.

7 Creating a Memo From a Template

Create a memo from a Word template and save it as a document.

1. Click New on the File menu and click General Templates.

2. Click the Memos tab and open *Contemporary Memo* as a new document. Save the document as *Contemporary Memo* in the *Lesson Applications* folder in your *Word Data* folder.

3. Write a short memo directed to a classmate describing two academic or career objectives you'd like to accomplish within the next five years. Save your changes, and close the document.

PROJECTS

1 Write This Way

An article you wrote needs more work before you can fax it to the publisher. Open *Step Write Article* in your *Word Data* folder. Save the document as *Step Write Released* in the *Projects* folder in your *Word Data* folder. Search for the sentence containing the word *wake*. Insert the following two paragraphs on a new line below that sentence (see Figure 1.24):

Common faults include excess words, which waste time for both writer and readers; impressive-sounding words and jargon, which often block communication; indefinite words, which are colorless and boring; long words and sentences, which raise reading difficulty; and passive voice, which hides meaning by omitting action words.

Use grammar, spelling, and other checker software—but not to replace your editing and proofreading. For extra quality assurance, have documents read by another set of eyes.

Proofread and edit the entire document using Word's spelling and grammar tools as an aid. Watch for misspelled words, incorrect words, and punctuation errors. On a new line at the end of the document, insert your name in parentheses. Insert AutoText at the end of the document in a format indicating the file name

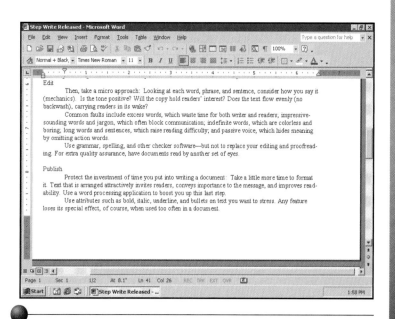

Figure 1.24

and the date the file was created and last printed. Preview the document and print it. Save and close the file.

2 Just the Fax

You need to create a cover page to fax to *The Small Business Journal* along with the article you wrote in Project 1. Open the *Elegant Fax Word* template (or another template of your choice) to create a fax cover page. In the fax template, replace the FROM information with your name; replace the Company name with *The Small Business Journal*; and replace the RE information with an appropriate subject line. Type the number of pages to be faxed. Create a name and phone numbers for the TO, PHONE, and FAX information. Create a company name and address for yourself. Delete any sample text in the header that you do not need to use. Compose a brief note as the text of the fax mentioning that you are faxing the document for publication. At the bottom of your document, insert the date (with Update Automatically activated in the Date and Time dialog box). Save the cover sheet as *Fax Article* in the *Projects* folder in your *Word Data* folder and close the document.

3 Organizing Files

You just learned that you will be writing more articles for publication in *The Small Business Journal*, so you decide to organize your files to make them easier to retrieve. Also, your editor has asked that you send your articles to the *Journal* electronically in RTF format. Open *Fax Article* (saved in Project 2) in the *Projects* folder in your *Word Data* folder (see Figure 1.25). (If you did not complete Project 2, open *Fax Info* from your *Word Data* folder.) Create a new folder named *My Faxes* in the *Projects* folder. Save *Fax Article* (or *Fax Info*) in the new folder as *Fax Article RTF* in *Rich Text Format (RTF)* so it is ready to copy to a disk to be sent to the *Journal*. Close the document.

4 My Bio From a Template

Since you often give presentations to people in your field, you need to write your biography (a brief account of your life). Then you can give a copy to program planners who may print the information in their program and/or prepare to introduce you to meeting participants. A sample bio appears in your *Word Data* folder: *Tony Denier's Bio*. Choose a Word Report template to create your own bio. (*Note:* The Word Report templates may need to be installed from your Office XP CD-ROM.) You may copy part or all of *Tony Denier's Bio* and then delete and replace text to create your own document. (*Hint:* Navigate between the two open files using taskbar buttons or use Arrange All on the Window menu.)

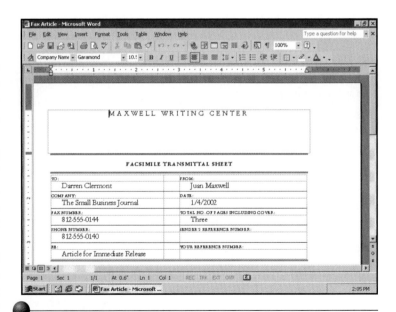

Figure 1.25

Your bio should have at least two short paragraphs and should mention your education, career achievements and/or goals, hobbies, and special interests. Edit your document carefully, checking spelling and grammar. Save the document as *My Bio* in the *Projects* folder in your *Word Data* folder. Close the file.

5 What's a Wizard?

Open a new, blank document and save it as *Wizard* in the *Projects* folder in your *Word Data* folder. Explore Help to learn more about wizards by entering *wizard* in the *Ask a Question* box, then clicking the About installing wizards link. Click Show All in the Help window to read the definition of the word *wizard*. Read the Help page and explore the links, then close the Help window. Now you will determine the types and number of wizards available on each tab of the Templates dialog box. Create a table to summarize the information you gather. (Type the entry in the first column, then press [Tab] to type the second column.) Your text should contain two columns, similar to Table 1.6. (Table 1.6 is a list of all the tabs in the Templates dialog box.)

In the Templates dialog box, count the files on each tab that contain the name *Wizard* and complete the second column of information, omitting any category (tab) that contains no wizard. Above your table, type a heading and a statement to introduce the data. Save and close the file.

Table 1.6	
Category (Tab)	**Number of Wizards**
General	
Legal Pleadings	
Letters & Faxes	
Mail Merge	
Memos	
Other Documents	
Publications	
Reports	
Web Pages	

6 AutoCorrect It

Word's AutoCorrect feature is designed to automatically correct the most common errors made while typing. However, each user makes unique errors that may not be in the AutoCorrect list. Identify common errors that you make by quickly typing a few paragraphs. (Find the text within a textbook, newspaper, or periodical.) Check to see if your errors are in Word's AutoCorrect list. Add two words to the list and type a few sentences containing the intentional misspellings to observe the AutoCorrect feature in action. For help, enter the keyword *AutoCorrect* into the *Ask a Question* box, and click the *Create or change AutoCorrect entries* Help topic (see Figure 1.26).

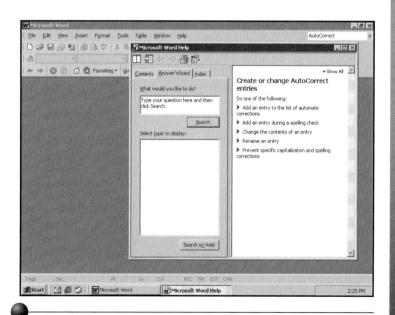

Figure 1.26

SUMMARY AND EXERCISES

7 Write This Way on the World Wide Web

Open a new, blank document and save it as *Web Link* in the *Projects* folder in your *Word Data* folder. Write a paragraph explaining why it is important to proofread a document. At the end of the document, insert hyperlinks to the following Web sites. Change the descriptive text as desired for each hyperlink.

Proofreading & Editing Tips   http://www.lrcom.com/tips/proofreading_editing.htm

Ten Proofreading Tips   http://www.ascs.org/10tips.html

Successful Proofreading Strategies   http://www.temple.edu/writingctr/cw06005.htm

Follow the links to all three sites. Of the three sites, choose two that are the most helpful to you. Delete the link to the third site. Arrange the links in the desired order in your document. Save and close the document.

If you have difficulty following one or more of the hyperlinks, it is possible the Web address may have changed. If this occurs, click Search the Web on the Word Web toolbar. Then perform a search in your browser on the keyword *proofreading*. Explore the search results to find a substitute site.

Project in Progress

8 Now You're in Business

Savvy Solutions, your new company, will provide a variety of writing, editing, and training services for small and medium-sized organizations. Today you received a letter from a local high school student asking if you would present at their annual Writer's Workshop. The letter asked you to propose a topic or to select one of these topics: Writing School Papers, Writing in Business, Writing for Newspapers and Magazines, or Writing for the Web. Use a letter template of your choice to create a new document with the following information:

Letter address:

Mr. Steven Banks
Young Writers' Society
Anderson High School
1968 Beechmont Ave.

[Your City, ST 00000]

Body:

Thank you for your invitation to present a workshop for Young Writers' Society at 10:45 on [insert a date]. I am very happy to accept.

Every one of your suggested topics is excellent, and I would love to discuss Writing in Business with the students. I will stress the importance word processing software, such as Microsoft Word, can have to their documents.

I'll send the exact title of my presentation and my bio in a week or two. Please arrange an LCD computer and a screen for my PowerPoint slides for the day of the workshop.

Insert today's date and a salutation. At the end of the letter, include a complimentary close with your name as the sender, and a title such as Writing Consultant. Add, delete, or change any information to suit your preferences. Edit and proofread with the help of the Word Thesaurus, Spelling, and Grammar tools.

Save your document as *Writing Workshop* in the *Projects* folder in your *Word Data* folder. Create a new folder in your *Projects* folder and name it *Writing Projects*. Save *Writing Workshop* in Rich Text Format (RTF) as *Writing Workshop RTF* within your *Writing Projects* folder. Save, preview, and print *Writing Workshop*. Create and print a mailing label and an envelope for your letter. Close the document and exit Word.

WORD 2002

LESSON 2

Formatting Documents

CONTENTS

- Reformatting Text
- Maintaining Consistency in a Document
- Enhancing the Appearance of a Document
- Inserting and Formatting Graphics
- Sorting Words or Numbers
- Adding Reference Features
- On the Web: Naming Favorites

OBJECTIVES

After you complete this lesson, you will be able to do the following:

▶ Insert and modify page and section breaks.

▶ Change margins and vertical alignment.

▶ Modify horizontal alignment and indentation style.

▶ Set character, line, and paragraph spacing and tab stops.

▶ Apply and modify newsletter-style formats.

▶ Use Reveal Formatting to check paragraph alignment and check for consistency of spacing in headings, between paragraphs, and in tabs.

▶ Enhance the appearance of text by applying bold, italic, and underline as well as superscripts and subscripts.

▶ Apply text animation, a border, shading, and highlighting.

▶ Use Format Painter to change text formats.

▶ Use the Style command to reformat documents.

▶ Search the Clip Organizer for an image, insert the image into a document, and edit the image.

▶ Sort a list alphabetically.

▶ Add and edit bullets, numbers, and outline numbers in a list.

▶ Add and modify page numbers in a document; insert and edit headers and footers.

▶ Insert a footnote and table of contents.

▶ E-mail a Word document.

▶ Add favorites in Word and Internet Explorer.

REFORMATTING TEXT

After you have entered and edited all text in a document, you will want to make sure the formatting of your document appears professional. The format of a document is the **layout**—the arrangement and spacing of various parts of the document in relation to the edges of the page. Much reformatting may be done with the buttons on the Formatting toolbar. The File menu, Insert menu, Format menu, and horizontal ruler are also involved in reformatting a document.

> **NOTE** *Formatting is described in relation to a* printed *document. The term* **page** *usually refers to the standard paper size (8.5 by 11 inches) on which most documents are printed.*

WORD 2002

Inserting Page Breaks and Changing Margins

In Normal View, faint, dotted horizontal lines indicate automatic **page breaks.** Page breaks are more clearly defined in Print Layout View. The blank areas forming the border from the text to the edge of the paper are called **margins.** So far, you have used the default (preset) margins for your documents. In Word, each margin (top, left, right, and bottom) is a conventional width: 1 inch. You can change these margin widths. Narrow margins let you type more text on a page, but wide margins make a page look easier to read.

Page breaks divide text into separate pages. By default, the print area is 9 inches top to bottom; and Word will fill that area unless you tell it not to. Wherever you want to start a new page you can insert a **manual page break** to override Word's **automatic page breaks.** For example, you might insert page breaks between chapters or main topics of a report. The manual page breaks you insert are labeled *Page Break* so that you can tell them from Word's automatic page breaks.

You can also control where automatic page breaks occur. By default, Word will prevent widows and orphans from occurring within a document. A **widow** is the last line of a paragraph printed by itself at the top of a page. An **orphan** is the first line of a paragraph printed by itself at the bottom of a page. If you want to prevent an automatic page break from occurring within certain text (such as a heading and the following paragraph or several paragraphs), select the text that you want to remain together and right-click. Click Paragraph on the shortcut menu and click the Line and Page Breaks tab in the Paragraph dialog box. To avoid an automatic page break within a paragraph, select the *Keep lines together* option in the Paragraph dialog box and click OK; to avoid an automatic page break between two paragraphs, select the *Keep with next* option and click OK.

Margin settings and vertical and horizontal alignment define page setup. In Word, margins may be as narrow as one-quarter inch or as wide as possible for the paper size. Margins of one inch to two inches are typical.

Setting Up Pages

The **vertical alignment**—or relationship of text to the top and bottom edges of a page—is also part of setting up (reformatting) text. Text is **top aligned** by default which means the first line of text always appears at the top margin. You can change this vertical alignment so that the last line of text prints at the bottom margin **(bottom alignment),** regardless of where the top and bottom margins are set. Another alternative is to place text an equal distance between the top and bottom margin **(centered alignment).**

The **justified** setting distributes *paragraphs* between the top and bottom margins. Justified alignment looks the same as top alignment, if the page contains only one paragraph. However, with two paragraphs on a page, one will be top aligned; the other will be bottom aligned. With three paragraphs on a page, one will be aligned at the top, one at the center, and one at the bottom.

Inserting Section Breaks

Varying the margin settings or vertical alignment within a document calls for **section breaks.** A section break shows up in Normal View as a dotted double line

NORTON
ONLINE

Visit www.glencoe.com/norton/online/ for more information on page layout.

labeled *Section Break* and either *(Next Page), (Continuous), (Odd Page),* or *(Even Page).* Table 2.1 explains the different types of section breaks. Section breaks do not show in Print Layout View or on a printed page.

Table 2.1	Types of Section Breaks
Section Break	**Description**
Next Page	The following section starts at the top of the next page.
Continuous	The following section starts on the same page.
Even page or Odd page	The following section starts on the next even- or odd-numbered page.

HANDS on

Breaking Pages

In this activity, you will insert page breaks into a document.

1. **Open *Astronomy 110* in your *Word Data* folder and save it as *Reformatted* in the *Tutorial* folder.**

With the file saved in a different folder with a new name, you can easily save changes as you work. First, you will add pages by inserting page breaks. Then you will type a few words on each new page.

2. **Click Print Layout View**  **to view the document; then click Normal View to reformat it.**

3. **Click before the first character in the first paragraph, then click Break on the Insert menu.**

The Break dialog box appears, as shown in Figure 2.1.

4. **Click Page break, if necessary, and click OK.**

You have added a page at the beginning of the document. The *Venus* heading is on page 1 and the text is now on page 2, as shown on the status bar.

5. **Click the Page Break line and type the following text**: Venus: Roman goddess of gardens and fields, of love and beauty

WARNING *Do not select the Page Break line. If you do, you will replace the line with the text you type. If this happens, click the Undo button and repeat step 5.*

Now you will add a new page in the middle of your document and another page at the end.

6. **Scroll down to locate the heading *Earth*, then click an insertion point before the first character in the heading.**

Word BASICS

Breaking Pages

1. Click the insertion point where the page is to end.

2. Click Break on the Insert menu.

3. Click Page break in the Break dialog box.

4. Click OK.

HINTS & TIPS

To delete a manual break (page or section), click the break (in Normal View) and press Delete.

Figure 2.1
Break dialog box

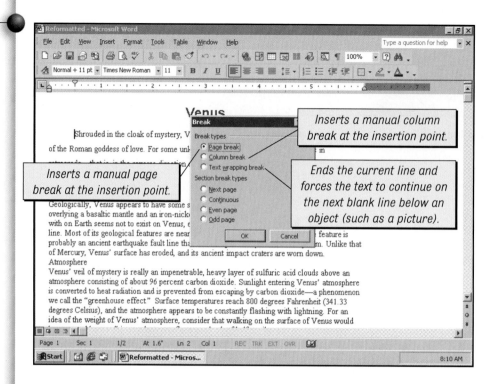

To insert a page break, press
Ctrl + Enter⏎ .

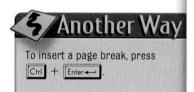

7. Click **Break** on the Insert menu, click **Page break**, then click **OK**.

8. Click **Repeat Insertion** on the Edit menu to insert another page break.

Your document looks like Figure 2.2. The insertion point is now at the top of page 4. Page 3 is represented by the narrow space between the two Page Break lines.

Figure 2.2
Manual page breaks

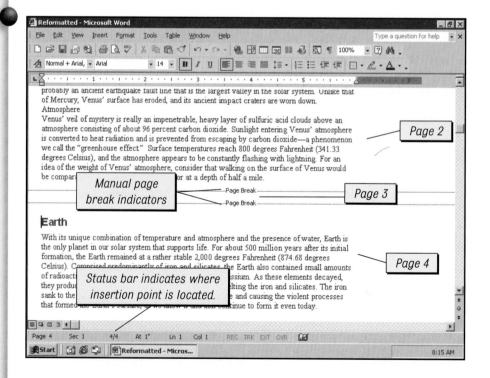

9. Click the Page Break line directly above *Earth* and press ⌨Enter←⏎.

10. Click in the middle of page 3 and type the following text, with one space before the dash: Our roots are in the dark; the earth is our country. —U. LeGuin

11. Scroll to the end of the document, insert a page break below the last line, and type Bibliography on the new page 5.

12. Click **Save** on the File menu and close the document.

HANDS on

Changing Margins, Breaking Sections, and Aligning Vertically

In this activity, you will change margins, insert section breaks, and change the vertical alignment.

1. Open *Reformatted* in the *Tutorial* folder in your *Word Data* folder, and save it as *Reformatted Margins* in the *Tutorial* folder.

2. Click **Page Setup** on the File menu, and click the **Margins tab**, if necessary.

The Page Setup dialog box appears, as shown in Figure 2.3.

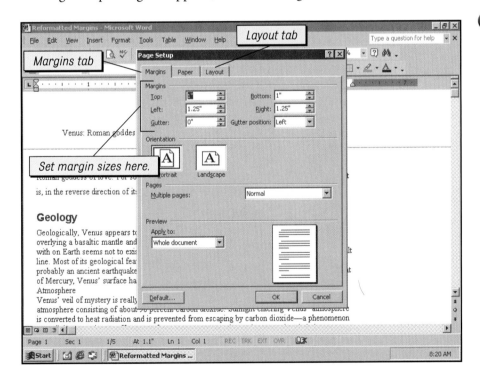

Figure 2.3
Page Setup dialog box

3. In the *Margins* section, change the top and left margins to 1.5″; change the right margin to 1″.

Reformatting Pages

To change margins:

1. Click an insertion point where a margin change is desired.

2. Click Page Setup on the File menu.

3. Click the Margins tab in the Page Setup dialog box.

4. Adjust the margin settings.

5. If necessary, choose an option in the *Apply to* box.

To change vertical alignment:

1. Click Page Setup on the File menu.

2. Click the Layout tab in the Page Setup dialog box.

3. Select a vertical alignment option.

4. If necessary, choose an option in the *Apply to* box.

To insert section breaks:

1. Click Break on the Insert menu.

2. Click one of the four section break types in the Break dialog box.

4. Click the **Layout tab** and verify that *Top* appears in the *Vertical alignment* box, then click **OK**.

5. Click **Print Layout View** 🔲 then scroll to view your new margin settings.

The margins are fine, but perhaps the single line of text on page 1 would look better if it were halfway down the page.

6. Click **Normal View** 🔳 and click at the end of the single line of text on page 1.

7. Click **Break** on the Insert menu. Under *Section break types*, click **Next page** and then click **OK**.

A Next Page section break appears in your document. Page 1 is now a separate section from the rest of the document. That means you can change the alignment on it without affecting other pages. You no longer need the manual page break.

8. Click the Page Break line under the Section Break, if necessary, then press ⌷Delete⌷.

9. Click the *Venus* heading on page 1, click **Page Setup** on the File menu, then click the **Layout tab**. In the *Vertical alignment* box, select **Center**. Verify that *This section* shows in the *Apply to* box, then click **OK**.

10. Click **Print Layout View** 🔲 and scroll to see the text on page 1 which is now centered vertically on the page between the top and bottom margins. Scroll to page 2 and note that text on this page is still top aligned (it begins at the top margin).

Page 3 also consists of a single line of text. To center it vertically, you will need a section break before and after the text to separate it from the preceding and following pages.

11. Click **Normal View** 🔳 , then go to the top of page 3.

12. Click before the first character in the text on page 3, click **Break** on the Insert menu, then click **Next Page** under *Section break types* and click **OK**.

13. Click at the end of the text on page 3 then click **Repeat Insertion** on the Edit menu.

14. Click each Page Break line (before and after the section breaks) then press ⌷Delete⌷. Your document should now resemble Figure 2.4.

15. Click before the first character on page 3, click **Page Setup** on the File menu, then click the **Layout tab**. Click **Center** on the *Vertical alignment* box, verify *This section* appears in the *Apply to* box, and click **OK**.

The text alignment is not apparent in Normal View.

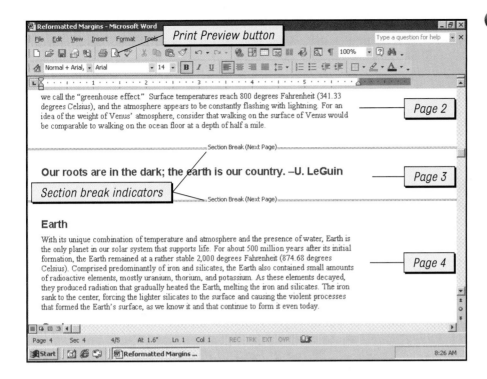

Figure 2.4
Next Page section break

Another Way

- To change margins, switch to Print Layout View. Point to a margin boundary on the horizontal ruler (left and right margins) or vertical ruler (top and bottom margins) and drag the boundary. Press [Alt] as you drag to display the width of the print area.

- To open the Page Setup dialog box, double-click the shaded part of the ruler that extends over the right margin.

WORD 2002

16. Click **Print Preview** 🔍, click the **Multiple Pages button** ▦, then click the **2 x 3 Pages icon.**

Though the text is not readable, you can see that the line on page 3 is centered vertically and you can see the alignment on the other pages in the document.

17. Click **Normal View** ▤, click **Save** 💾, and close the document.

Formatting Paragraphs

The way that text lines up in relation to the left and right margins is called **horizontal alignment.** In the Word window, text is automatically **left aligned.** Every line begins flush with the left margin, making the left margin perfectly even. You can change this alignment. Text may be **right aligned;** that is, all lines are flush with the right margin. Text may be **justified** or aligned so that it is flush with both margins. Text may be **center aligned,** or centered. With this alignment, short lines of text are placed an equal distance from the left and right margins and neither margin appears perfectly even. The Formatting toolbar provides all four options.

The term **indentation** refers to variations in the left and right side margins of lines in a paragraph and paragraphs on a page. A **first-line indentation** of one-half inch is conventional. **Hanging indentation**—the second and subsequent lines of a paragraph indented under the first line—is also common. In Word, a first-line or hanging indentation may be any width; and whole paragraphs may be indented on the left and/or right any amount of space the user desires.

The amount of white space between text lines is called **line spacing.** Most business documents use single spacing (the default line spacing). Double spacing (a blank line between each line of text) and 1.5 spacing (one-half blank line between each line of text) are also common. You may insert additional space above and below

Did you know?

You can *hyphenate* your text automatically as you type. Word breaks long words at the ends of lines and inserts hyphens at the proper place. To turn on the Hyphenation feature, click the Tools menu, point to Language, and click Hyphenation. Select the desired options.

paragraphs. Adding **paragraph spacing** opens up a page and makes paragraph side headings easy to see. Paragraph spacing is measured in **points.** With Word, you can also adjust the amount of space between characters, called **character spacing.** If you want to affect the spacing between all selected characters, you can expand or condense the space. If you want to affect the spacing of particular letters, choose the kerning option.

In this activity, you will reformat a document by changing the horizontal alignment and indentation options.

Changing Horizontal Alignment

1. Select the text to be aligned.

2. Click the Align Left, Center, Align Right, or Justify button on the Formatting toolbar.

1. Open *Venus Information* in your *Word Data* folder and save it as *Venus Aligned* in your *Tutorial* folder.

2. Click **Normal View** ▤, if necessary. Click the line of text on page 1 and click the **Center button** ▤ on the Formatting toolbar.

3. Click the *Venus* heading at the top of page 2, and click **Repeat Paragraph Alignment** on the Edit menu.

The text appears centered on page 1 and the *Venus* heading appears centered at the top of page 2.

4. Click anywhere in the first paragraph of text on page 2, then click the **Justify button** ▤.

Both the left and right paragraph margins appear even, as shown in Figure 2.5.

Figure 2.5
Centered and justified text

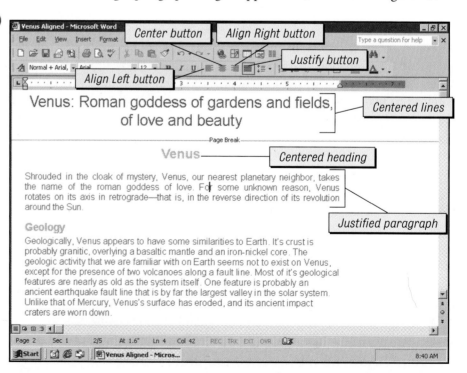

You can use the Reveal Formatting feature to change formatting in a paragraph. Click Reveal Formatting on the Format menu. In the Reveal Formatting task pane, click the blue underlined text and then make the changes in the dialog box that opens.

5. Navigate to the end of page 4 and click after the last character of the last paragraph. Press `Enter⏎` two times, then type the following text, replacing *Your name* and *Current date.*

> *Your name*
> Submitted to Professor Dowdell
> AST 110, Section F3
> *Current date*

6. Select the four lines of text you just typed, and click the **Align Right button** .

The text aligns on the right margin. Now you will begin changing the indentation style of some paragraphs.

7. On page 5, click after the word *Bibliography*, press `Enter⏎` twice, and type the following reference at the left margin: Author, F. M. Venus Overview. [Online] Available: http://www.eps.mcgill.ca/~bud/craters/FaceOfVenus.html [February, 2001].

NOTE *The Web address you typed may be automatically formatted as a hyperlink (underlined and in color). If so, right-click the hyperlink and click Remove Hyperlink on the shortcut menu.*

8. Click anywhere in the text you just typed, then click **Paragraph** on the Format menu.

The Paragraph dialog box appears.

9. Click the **Indents and Spacing tab.** Click the **Special box triangle button** and click **Hanging.** Select the numbers in the *By* box and type *.75.* See the Preview box (Figure 2.6).

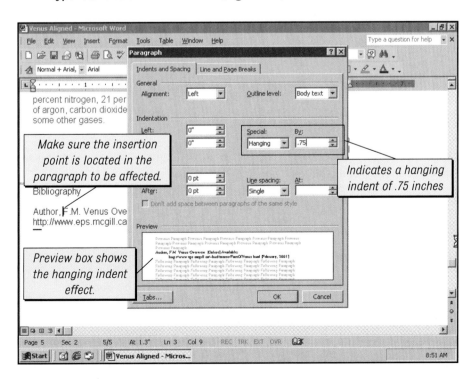

Make sure the insertion point is located in the paragraph to be affected.

Indicates a hanging indent of .75 inches

Preview box shows the hanging indent effect.

Figure 2.6
Paragraph dialog box

The second and third lines are indented three-quarters of an inch under the first line in hanging-indent style.

10. Click within the paragraph under the heading *Atmosphere* on page 4, then click **Paragraph** on the Format menu. Click **First line** in the *Special* box and type *.75* in the *By* box. Check the Preview window and click **OK** to close the dialog box.

The first line of the paragraph is indented three-quarters of an inch from the left margin.

11. Save your changes and close the document.

Setting Spacing Options

In this activity, you will change character, line, and paragraph spacing in a document.

1. Open *Venus Aligned* in the *Tutorial* folder in your *Word Data* folder and save it as *Venus Spacing* in the *Tutorial* folder.

2. Select the *Venus* heading on page 2.

3. Click **Font** on the Format menu, and click the **Character Spacing** tab. In the *Spacing* box, click the **Expanded option**. Verify that the number in the *By* box is 1 pt, and click **OK**.

The spacing between the letters in the heading expands slightly.

4. Select the first paragraph on page 4 (under the *Earth* heading). Click the **Increase Indent button** ⊞ on the Formatting toolbar.

The paragraph is indented one-half inch from the left margin.

5. With the paragraph still selected, click the **Line Spacing triangle button** ⊞⋅ on the Formatting toolbar and click **1.5**. Click to deselect the paragraph.

The line spacing has increased to 1.5, as shown in Figure 2.7. Now you will change line spacing and paragraph spacing.

6. Select the second paragraph on page 4 (under the *Geology* heading) then click **Paragraph** on the Format menu.

The Paragraph dialog box appears.

7. Click the **Indents and Spacing tab**, if necessary. In the *Spacing* section, change the *Before* spacing to **6 pt** and the *After* spacing to **12 pt**. Set the *Line spacing* to **Double**. In the Indentation section, set the Indentation for the right margin at **.5″**. Look at the Preview box and click **OK**.

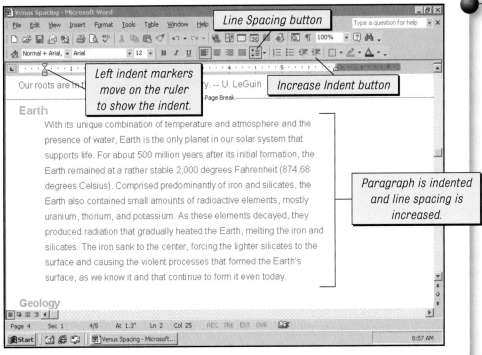

Figure 2.7
Indentation and line spacing changes

The line spacing and indentation appear changed in the selected paragraph.

8. Again select the first paragraph on page 4 under the *Earth* heading, then click **Paragraph** on the Format menu. Change the paragraph spacing to **6 pt** in the *Before* box and **12 pt** in the *After* box and click **OK**.

9. Click the document to deselect the text. Click **Print Layout View** and scroll to view the two reformatted paragraphs.

10. Click **Normal View** then again select the first paragraph on page 4. Click the **Decrease Indent button** on the Formatting toolbar. Click the document to deselect the text.

The indentation is adjusted in the selected paragraph.

11. Click **Save** and close the document.

The abbreviation *pt* stands for *point* which is a unit of measure ($\frac{1}{72}$ of an inch) relating to the height of a printed character.

Tabulating Text

Instead of paragraphs, a columns-and-rows arrangement (a tabular format) makes some text easier to read. This format involves **tab stops** that specify where listed items begin in relation to the left margin as well as the distance between columns of listed items. The default tab stops in Word are *left tabs* at half-inch intervals; they align columns on the left. When you set custom tabs, it is best to clear the default tabs. You may prefer centered tabs for some columns, and columns containing numbers are often best aligned at the right or at decimal points. In addition, the *bar* option will insert a vertical line in the column. All these options are available in the Tabs dialog box (Format menu).

HANDS on

Setting Tab Stops

In this activity, you will set tab stops and type tabulated text on a separate page of the original *Venus Information* document.

1. Open *Venus Information* in your *Word Data* folder.

2. Find the phrase *worn down*, click at the end of the sentence in which it occurs, and press [Enter←] twice.

3. Click **Tabs** on the Format menu.

The Tabs dialog box appears.

4. Click the **Clear All button** to delete the current tabs.

5. In the *Tab stop position* box, type .5; in the *Alignment* section, click **Left**, if necessary. Click the **Set button**.

The Tab setting appears in the *Tab stop position* box as shown in Figure 2.8.

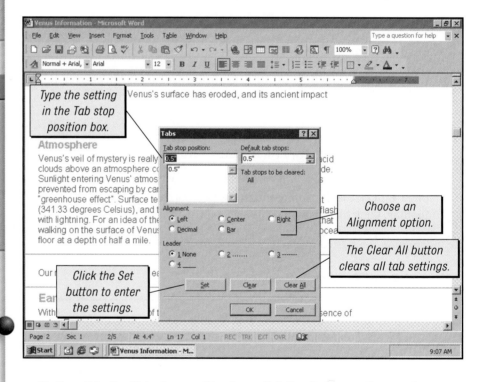

Figure 2.8
Tabs dialog box

6. Type 2 in the *Tab stop position* box, click the **Center option**, and click **Set**. Repeat this procedure to set a left tab at 3″ and a right tab at 5.75″.

All four tab stops appear in the *Tab Stop position* list.

7. Click **OK** to close the dialog box and return to the document.

The tab stops show on the ruler. Distinctive symbols represent the left tab, the center tab, and the right tab.

8. Press ⏫Tab⏫ and type the first word in the table below, watching the screen to see how the text aligns to the left tab. Press ⏫Tab⏫ to move to the next stop (a center tab) and type the column entry. Continue to press ⏫Tab⏫ and type the remaining entries in the first line. At the end of the first line, press ⏫Enter◄┘⏫ to move to the second line.

Mission	Launch Date	Key Event	Key Event Date
Mariner 2	8/27/62	Passed near Venus	12/14/62
Mariner 5			

Your tabulated text should resemble Figure 2.9.

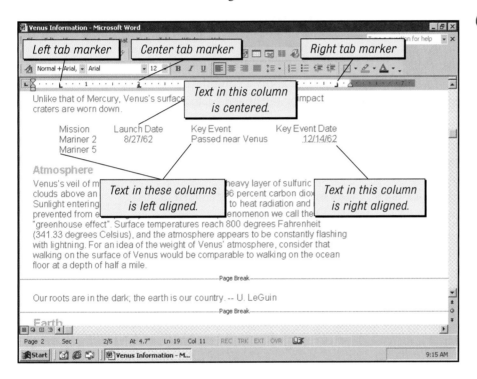

9. Save your changes as *Venus Tabs* in the *Tutorial* folder in your *Word Data* folder, and close the document.

Formatting Newsletter Columns

A multiple-column format is typical in newsletters, newspapers, magazines, brochures, catalogs, directories, flyers, and Web pages. Often certain sections of other documents, including reports, legal documents, and resumes may use a column format. Generally, more text fits attractively on a column-formatted page; and columns are often easier to read than long lines of text.

The Columns button  on the Standard toolbar formats text in one to four columns. The column width is equal and the space between columns is a standard 0.5". Although two- and three-column formats are most common, you can set the number of columns from 1 to 12. You can vary the column widths on a page and specify the amount of space between columns. Preset options include wide columns (6") and narrow columns (under 2"). You can also select an option to draw a vertical line between columns.

Another Way

Click the Tab button at the left end of the ruler repeatedly to find the tab alignment you want, then click the ruler at the desired tab stop position to set the tab. The symbol that appears at the left end of the ruler will correspond to the symbol in the Tab button (Left, Center, Right, Decimal, or Bar tab).

Figure 2.9
Left, centered, and right tab stops

Did you know?

If you double-click the shaded area of the ruler, the Page Setup dialog box will appear.

HINTS & TIPS

In Normal View, multiple-column formats appear as one long column. Switch to Print Layout View to manipulate column formats.

After you insert columns, inspect your document for balance. The basic format is **newsletter columns;** that is, side-by-side columns. Word fills the first column on a page. When that column is full, the text snakes to the next column which may end short of the bottom margin. According to your preference, you can change the vertical balance of columns by inserting a continuous section break into the document.

HANDS on
Creating and Modifying a Column Format

In this activity, you will apply newsletter-style column formatting to a document then you will insert a column break, change the text alignment, and apply a new column format. You will apply a column format to a new blank document then paste text into the document and balance the columns.

1. **Open *Woodsy View News* in your *Word Data* folder and save it as *Columns* in the *Tutorial* folder.**

2. **Click Select All on the Edit menu to select the entire document.**

3. **Click the Columns button ▦ on the Standard toolbar.**

A drop-down panel appears containing four column icons, as shown in Figure 2.10.

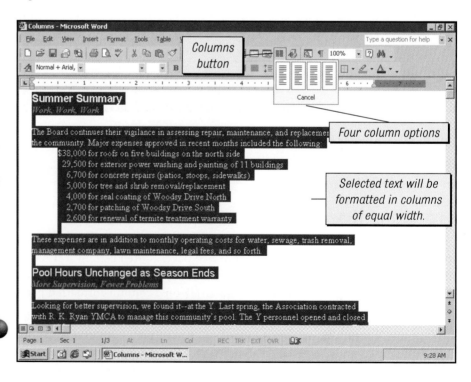

Figure 2.10
Columns menu

4. **Point to the 2 Columns icon then click.**

The document is now arranged in two columns. Also, Word switched to Print Layout View so you could see the results of your action.

5. Click the document to deselect the text, then scroll through the document to observe the two-column format.

6. Click **Select All** on the Edit menu, then click **Columns** on the Format menu.

The Columns dialog box appears, as shown in Figure 2.11, showing five presets and list boxes for specifying the number of columns, width, and spacing.

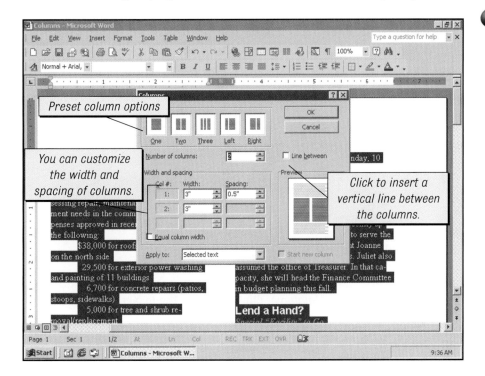

Figure 2.11
Columns dialog box

7. Click the **Three column icon** in the *Presets* section to revise the column layout from two to three columns. Click the **Line between option** to insert a vertical line between columns, then click **OK**.

Your document now appears in a three-column format, and a vertical line extends from the top margin to the bottom margin between the columns.

8. Click the document to deselect the text, then scroll to the bottom of page 1 and click an insertion point before the first character in the heading at the bottom of the first column.

9. Click Break on the Insert menu, select the **Column break option** in the Break dialog box, and click **OK**.

The heading moves to a better location at the top of the next column.

10. Click **Select All** on the Edit menu then click Justify ▤ on the Formatting toolbar. Deselect the text then scroll through the document to observe the modified alignment.

11. Save and close the document.

12. Click the **New Blank Document button** ▯ and click **Print Layout View** ▣, if necessary.

NORTON
ONLINE

Visit **www.glencoe.com/norton/online/**
for more information on creating a
column format.

13. Click **Columns** on the Format menu. In the *Presets* section of the Columns dialog box, click the **Three column icon** and click **OK**.

The default column settings appear on the horizontal ruler.

14. Save the new document as *New Columns* in the *Tutorial* folder in your *Word Data* folder.

15. Open *Ag Ed* in your *Word Data* folder. Select the heading and text from the top of the document through . . . *diffusion of agricultural technology* at the end of the third paragraph.

16. Click the **Copy button**. Close the *Ag Ed* document. Click **Paste**.

The copied text is pasted into the *New Columns* document in the three-column format. A few lines run over to a second page.

17. Click **Select All** on the Edit menu. Click the **Line Spacing triangle button** and click **1.5**.

The line spacing is adjusted so the text fits on page 1, but the columns are not in vertical balance (the third column runs short).

18. Click an insertion point after the last line in the document (next to the period after *technology*). Click **Break** on the Insert menu, click **Continuous** under *Section break types*, and click **OK**.

19. Click **Print Preview** to view the document.

The columns appear balanced vertically.

20. Close the Print Preview window, then save and close the document.

MAINTAINING CONSISTENCY IN A DOCUMENT

Word provides tools to help check for consistency in alignment and formatting of a document. The Show/Hide button ¶ (Standard toolbar) reveals a **paragraph mark** wherever you pressed [Enter←], a dot wherever you pressed [Spacebar], and an arrow wherever you pressed [Tab]. These symbols help you detect inconsistencies in vertical and horizontal spacing and indenting. With the Show/Hide feature you can visually inspect the document to eliminate extra or missing blank lines between paragraphs, spaces between words, or indentations.

The Reveal Formatting task pane shows the current font, paragraph, spacing, image, and table properties for any point in your document and allows you to change any of these properties.

The Find and Go To features, which you learned about in Lesson 1, can also help you check alignment in a document.

HINTS & TIPS

Use the Find and Replace dialog box to find text of similar formatting.

Another Way

To show all formatting marks in a document, click *Show all formatting marks* in the Reveal Formatting task pane.

HANDS on

Checking Consistency in Spacing and Alignment

In this activity, you will check the spacing in headings and between paragraphs; then you will check the tabs (indentations). Finally, you will use Reveal Formatting to change paragraph alignment.

1. Open *Creative Classroom* in your *Word Data* folder and save it as *Quality Assurance* in the *Tutorial* folder.

2. Click the **Show/Hide button** ¶ on the Standard toolbar.

The paragraph and spacing marks are revealed in the document. Notice that two dots appear after the word *Classroom* in the main heading at the top of page 1.

3. Click to the left of one of the dots between *Classroom* and *in* and press ⌨Delete.

4. Click the Find button 🔍 then click the **Go To tab**.

5. Click **Heading** in the *Go to what* box, as shown in Figure 2.12.

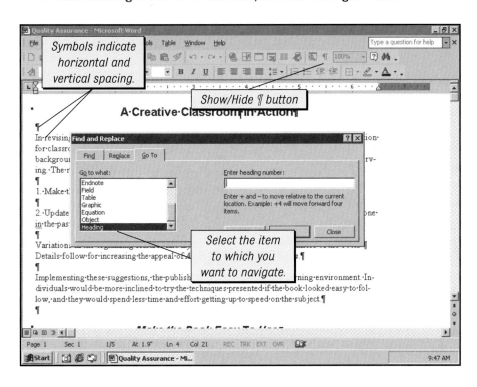

Figure 2.12
Go To tab

6. Click **Next** to advance to the next centered heading.

7. Check the spacing indicated by dots in the heading and edit appropriately. Check all the remaining headings in the document.

8. Click **Page** in the *Go to what* box, and type 1 in the *Enter page number* box. Click the **Go To button**.

Word BASICS

Checking Spacing and Alignment
To check a heading:

1. Click the Show/Hide button (¶) on the Standard toolbar to reveal spacing characters.

2. On the Go To tab in the Find and Replace dialog box, click Heading in the *Go to what* list box.

3. Click Find Next.

To check paragraph marks and tabs:

1. Click the Show/Hide button (¶) on the Standard toolbar to reveal spacing characters.

2. On the Find tab in the Find and Replace dialog box, click More, and then click Special.

3. Click Paragraph Mark or Tab Character.

4. Click Find Next.

Now you will check paragraph marks throughout the document, using the Find feature.

9. On the Find tab, click the **More button** to expand the dialog box. Click the **Special button**.

The Special menu displays, as shown in Figure 2.13.

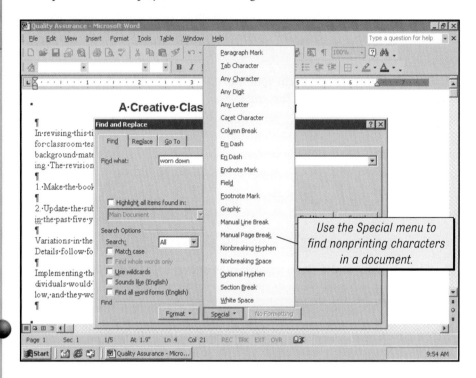

Use the Special menu to find nonprinting characters in a document.

Figure 2.13
Special menu

10. Click **Paragraph Mark** then click the **Less button** to collapse the dialog box.

11. Click the **Find Next button**.

Word jumps to the first paragraph mark at the beginning of the document.

12. Click **Find Next** three times.

The paragraph mark to the right of the main heading is selected.

13. Click **Find Next** again.

Word jumps to the paragraph mark on the next line. This pattern of paragraph marks should appear consistent throughout the document. One paragraph mark should appear at the end of each partial line and one paragraph mark should appear on the next line.

14. Continue checking for extra or missing paragraph marks by clicking **Find Next**. To insert a missing paragraph mark, click the document and press Enter←; to remove an extra paragraph mark, click the document and press Delete. (Do not add extra paragraph marks in the bulleted list in the document.) Stop when Word returns to the top of the document.

Now you will check the consistency of tabs in the document. The document format involves no paragraph indentations; therefore, no tab characters (or arrow symbols) should appear.

15. On the Find tab, click the **More button** and click the **Special button**. In the Special menu, click the **Tab Character option**. Click the **Less button** and then search the document.

No tabs are found; a message appears indicating that the search is complete.

16. Click **OK** in the message box. Close the Find and Replace dialog box and click the **Show/Hide button** ¶.

17. Select the last two paragraphs in the document (under the *Project Management* heading) and click **Reveal Formatting** on the Format menu.

The paragraph alignment is shown as *Left* in the Reveal Formatting task pane (see Figure 2.14).

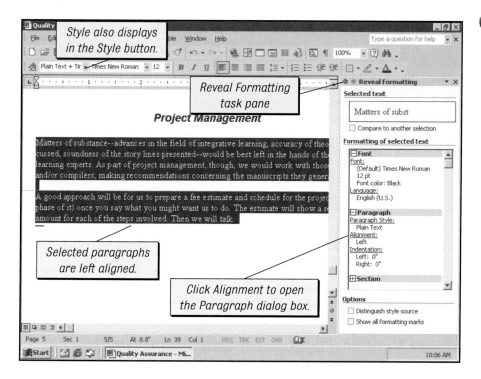

Figure 2.14
Reveal Formatting task pane

18. Click **Alignment** in the Paragraph section of the task pane.

19. The Paragraph dialog box appears.

20. Click the **Indents and Spacing tab** in the Paragraph dialog box. In the General section, click the **Alignment box triangle button**, click **Centered**, and click **OK**.

Both of the selected paragraphs become centered.

21. Close the Reveal Formatting task pane, click **Save** 🖫, and close the document.

ENHANCING THE APPEARANCE OF A DOCUMENT

An effective way to enhance the appearance of a document is to modify some attributes of the characters. For example, you can select a new font or change the font size; add bold, italic, and underline; add color; or even add borders, shading, and highlighting.

These style choices can be attractive additions to edited, reformatted documents. Certain font characteristics can help to set off special copy, such as headings. For example, the characters in a heading may contrast in design, size, darkness, and color. Such contrast makes documents inviting to readers. Setting off text in this way may also provide clues to how document content is organized.

Changing Font Design

A **font** is a set of characters of one design. In Word, a font named **Times New Roman** is the default font. Word offers dozens of other fonts, as you will soon discover. However, the fonts available to you depend upon the printer you are using. A certain printer may convert a fancy Word font to less desirable characters or may not print the font at all. Some fonts are ideal for ordinary copy, while others are best suited for headings. A few special-purpose fonts are designed more for Web pages, posters, and the like rather than memos, letters, and reports. The Times New Roman font is ideal for paragraphs because it is a **serif** font. That is, the characters have *feet* that form a straight line, guiding readers' eyes from left to right. A font without feet—**Arial,** for example—is best for headings. These fonts are called **sans serif.**

Changing Font Size

When you start a new document, all text is the same height and width. All characters are the same **font size** (sometimes called point size). A **point** ($1/72$ of an inch) is a unit of measure applied to fonts. The default size is 12 point. (Files in your *Word Data* folder vary in font size.) The most common font sizes for paragraphs are 10, 11, and 12. Font sizes of 14, 16, and 18 are often used for headings.

Adding Special Effects and Character Effects

Another way to enhance text is to add one or more special effects. You can use the **bold** style attribute to make words stand out from the surrounding copy. Bold is a heavier type style that helps readers see important points or technical terms at a glance. **Italic** is another common style attribute. Italic text has thin, delicate characters that slant to the right. A large block of italic text is hard to read, but italic is an attention-getter when used sparingly. Another way to call attention to certain words is to underline them. Besides the standard solid line, Word offers more than a dozen **underline** styles—solid, dotted, dashed, and wavy. In addition, you can apply **character effects,** such as subscript, superscript, or small caps. There are also a variety of **animations** available that you can apply to text including selections that make text shimmer or sparkle in the document window. The key to using various text effects and style attributes effectively is to avoid using them too much.

Changing Font Color

The default font color is black on a white background. As a Word user, though, you are certainly not limited to black-and-white documents. More than forty basic font colors are provided, along with the tools to create many, many more. (Background colors are equally numerous. Changing the background color, however, switches the document automatically to Web Layout View—not the best view for editing and formatting tasks.)

If your document happens to be a Web page, the use of various colors is critical to attracting and holding the attention of site visitors. Nowadays, too, many offices are equipped with an **intranet**—a Web-like network for communicating within an organization. As a result, many documents never make it to paper; they are published on the intranet instead, and read by company employees from their computer screens. In some schools today, students create documents on the computer and submit them via e-mail or save them to a network drive. These documents, too, never get on paper. Instructors and other students read the documents on their computers. Also, color printers are rapidly becoming standard office equipment. On some black-and-white printers, different font colors appear as various shades of gray.

Adding Borders, Shading, and Highlights

You can make a paragraph or page stand out by adding a border on any or all sides of it or by adding **shading,** a color that will fill the space inside a border. Add a **highlight** if you want a color background to appear over selected text much like a highlighter.

HANDS on

Enhancing Text

In this activity, you will change the font design, size, and color of selected text in a document. You will apply bold, italic, and underline; apply superscript and subscript character effects; add a text animation; and add a border, shading, and highlighting.

1. Open *Venus Information* in your *Word Data* folder, and save the file as *Venus Enhanced* in the *Tutorial* folder in your *Word Data* folder.

2. Select the line of text on page 1 and click the **Font triangle button**
   `Arial` on the Formatting toolbar.

The Font list box displays. The font names are listed in alphabetic order. Recently used fonts form a short list at the top of the Font list box.

3. Scroll down, if necessary, in the Font list box and click **Times New Roman**.

The font style changes.

Figure 2.15

Enhanced text

4. Click the **Bold button** . Click anywhere on the screen to deselect the text.

5. Click **Find** , find the word *roots*, then close the Find and Replace dialog box. Select the entire line of text in which the word *roots* occurs. Click the **Font Size triangle button** , click **14**, and then click the **Italic button** .

Since the italic effect should be applied to the quotation only and not the writer's name, you need to reformat part of the line.

6. Select the name and the dash in front of it, and click the **Italic button** to *remove* the effect. Click the document to deselect the text.

7. After the last character in the author's name, type **1** then select it.

8. Click **Font** on the Format menu. On the Font tab, click to activate **Subscript** in the *Effects* section, then click **OK**.

The number 1 appears in the subscript position, slightly below the line of text.

9. With the number still highlighted, click **Font** on the Format menu, select **Superscript**, and click **OK**.

10. Click anywhere in the document to deselect the text.

Your screen should appear similar to Figure 2.15.

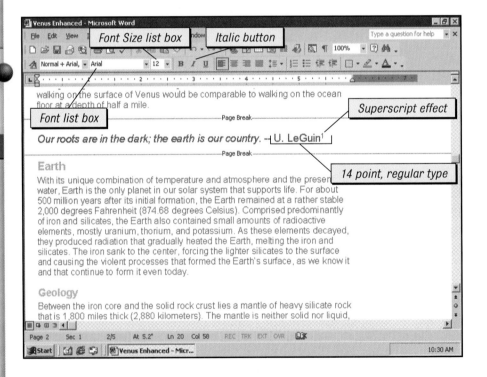

11. Navigate to page 2, select the *Venus* heading at the top of page, and click the **Font Color triangle button** .

The Font Color palette appears. When you point to a color square on the palette, a ScreenTip appears with the color name.

12. Point to the **Sky Blue sample** and click, as shown in Figure 2.16. Click the document to deselect the text.

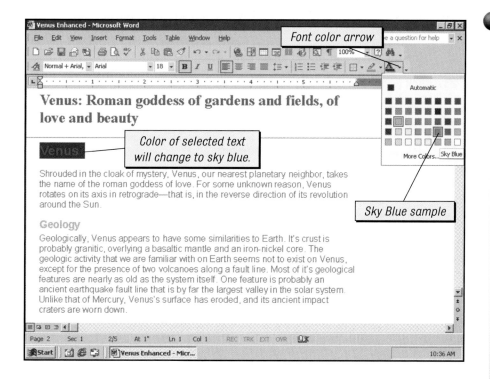

Figure 2.16
Font Color palette

To add shading:

1. Select the text to be shaded.

2. Click Borders and Shading on the Format menu.

3. On the Shading tab, click the shading options and click OK.

To highlight text:

1. Select the text to be highlighted.

2. Click the Highlight triangle button on the Formatting toolbar.

3. Click the desired color sample.

To apply animation:

1. Select the text to be animated.

2. Click Font on the Format menu.

3. On the Text Effects tab, click the desired animation effect and click OK.

13. Scroll through the document, select each additional heading, and click **Repeat Font Color** on the Edit menu to change all heads to sky blue.

14. Select the *Earth* heading on page 4, and click the **Underline button** 🅄.

A solid, single line appears under the selected word.

15. Click Font [Arial ▾] and click **Times New Roman**. Select the number in the Font Size box [16 ▾], type 17 and press [Enter⏎].

NOTE *Because 17 point is not listed in the Font Size list, you must type it in the Font Size box.*

16. Click to deselect the heading, then click **Find** 🔍 and find the word *subduction*. Close the Find and Replace dialog box, then right-click on the word *subduction*, and click **Font**.

17. On the Font tab, click the **Underline style triangle button** and click the single wavy line near the bottom of the list box. Click the **Underline color triangle button** and click a **Gray color sample**. Look at the Preview window and then click **OK**.

18. Select the word *Bibliography* on page 5 and click the **Highlight triangle button** 🖊▾. Select the **Yellow color sample** in the palette.

The word *Bibliography* is highlighted. Now you will add a border and shading to selected text.

19. Select the entire line on page 3, and click **Borders and Shading** on the Format menu.

20. On the Borders tab, click the **Box option**. On the Shading tab, click the **Light Yellow color** in the Fill palette, and click **OK**.

21. Click the document to deselect the text and view the border and shading.

22. Click the selection bar to again select the line on page 3.

23. Click **Font** on the Format menu. On the Text Effects tab, click **Marching Red Ants** in the Animations list box and click **OK**.

24. Deselect the text to view the moving red border.

25. Click **Save** 🖫 and close the document.

HANDS on

Using Format Painter

The Format Painter 🖋 allows you to quickly copy text formats from one part of a document to another. Select the text format you wish to copy, click 🖋, then simply *brush* over the text you want to change with the paintbrush pointer. The new text will assume the same font style, line spacing, indentations, and so on, as the text you copied from.

In this activity, you will use Format Painter to change the plain text in your document to match the text that has already been formatted and enhanced.

Word BASICS

Using Format Painter

1. Select the text that has the formatting you want to copy.

2. Click the Format Painter button on the Standard toolbar. (Double-click the button to apply the copied format repeatedly.)

3. Click the text you want to apply the formatting to.

1. Open *Astronomy 110* in your *Word Data* folder.

2. Click **Find** 🔍 and find the italicized word *subduction*. Close the Find and Replace dialog box and click the **Format Painter button** 🖋 on the Standard toolbar.

A paintbrush appears beside the I-beam pointer.

3. In the same sentence, select the words *sea-floor spreading*.

As you release the mouse button, the selected text becomes italic.

4. Click the bold, red *Geology* heading at the top of page 1; then click the **Format Painter button** 🖋.

5. Click the *Atmosphere* heading that appears in plain text in the next paragraph on the same page.

The 14-point Arial font, bold effect, and red color are copied to this heading. Your screen should now resemble Figure 2.17.

6. Triple-click the paragraph under the *Venus* heading on page 1 to select the paragraph.

7. Click the **Format Painter button** 🖋. Then click anywhere in the paragraph below the *Geology* heading in the next paragraph on page 1.

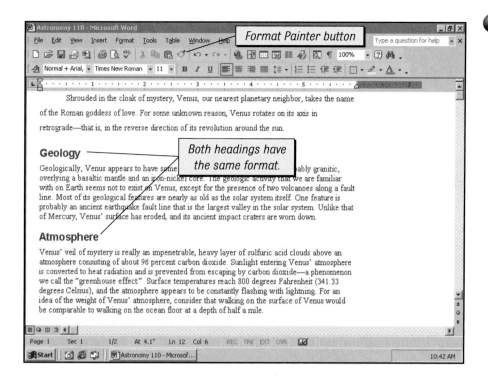

Figure 2.17
Copied text format

WORD 2002

8. Select the *Geology* paragraph you just formatted on page 1, and double-click the **Format Painter button** 🖌.

9. Scroll down to the next single-spaced paragraph (under *Atmosphere*) and click anywhere in it to change the spacing. Scroll down and click each of the remaining single-spaced paragraphs in the document.

10. Click the **Format Painter button** 🖌 to deactivate it or press Esc.

11. Select the *Venus* heading at the top of page 1, and use Format Painter to copy the attributes of the *Venus* heading to the *Earth* heading on page 1.

12. Save the document as *Astronomy Enhanced* in the *Tutorial* folder in your *Word Data* folder, and close the document.

Using the Style Command

Using the Style feature is a quick way to format and enhance documents at the same time. A **style** combines format properties (alignment, indentations, and line spacing) and appearance properties (font and font size and bold, italic, or underline). Thus, when you choose a style, one click takes care of all these factors at once. In a new blank document, the text you type uses the **Normal style**—the base style for the Normal template in Word.

You can apply four different types of styles in a Word document. **Paragraph style** controls all aspects of a paragraph's appearance, such as text alignment, tab stops, line spacing, and so on. **Character style** affects selected text within a paragraph, such as the font and size of text and bold and italic formats. **Table style** provides a consistent look to borders, shading, alignment, and fonts in tables. **List style** applies similar alignment, numbering, or bullet characters and fonts to lists of text. You can also create your own styles.

Word provides more than one style list. One list is *All styles*; another is *Available styles*. A third option, *Custom*, would contain only those styles that a Word user created. Therefore, the Custom list would vary greatly from one computer to another. The *All styles* list is used in the following activity.

Applying and Creating Styles

In this activity, you will apply paragraph styles and character styles to reformat and enhance a document. You will then create a character style.

1. Open *Astronomy Unformatted* in your *Word Data* folder and save it as *Styles* in the *Tutorial* folder.

2. Select the *Venus* heading at the top of the document, and click the **Styles and Formatting button** 🔳.

The Styles and Formatting task pane appears.

3. Click the **Show box triangle button** at the bottom of the task pane and click **All styles**.

In the Styles and Formatting task pane, the name of each style indicates its intended use. For example, *header* indicates a paragraph heading; and *body text* indicates a paragraph itself. Each style also shows how your text will look (font, font color, and alignment or indentation). The symbols in the right column of the list indicate whether a style involves paragraph style (¶), character style (a̲), list style (▤), or table style (⊞). The list also shows the font size and, for paragraph styles, the horizontal alignment. Pointing to a style will display a ScreenTip box containing style and formatting information.

4. Scroll through the *Pick formatting to apply* box and click **Heading 1**.

The style is applied to the *Venus* heading.

5. Select the heading *Geology* that appears a few lines below the *Venus* heading and click **Heading 2**.

6. Select the first paragraph of text (under *Venus*). Scroll through the Style list and click **Body Text Indent 2**, a 12-point body text style.

The style—which includes font size, indentation, line spacing, and paragraph spacing—is applied to the paragraph.

7. Find and select the heading *Earth*. Point to the **Heading 1 style** in the *Pick formatting to apply* box as shown in Figure 2.18.

The ScreenTip box displays the style properties.

8. Click **Heading 1**.

The heading *Earth* is changed to the Heading 1 style.

Word BASICS

Applying and Creating Styles

To apply a style:

1. Select the text to be changed.

2. Click the Styles and Formatting button on the Formatting toolbar.

3. In the Styles and Formatting task pane, scroll and click a style in the *Pick formatting to apply* box.

To create a style:

1. Click the Styles and Formatting button.

2. In the Styles and Formatting task pane, click New Style.

3. In the New Style dialog box, set the style properties and formatting and click OK.

4. Select the text in the document to be changed to the new style and click the new style in the *Pick formatting to apply* box.

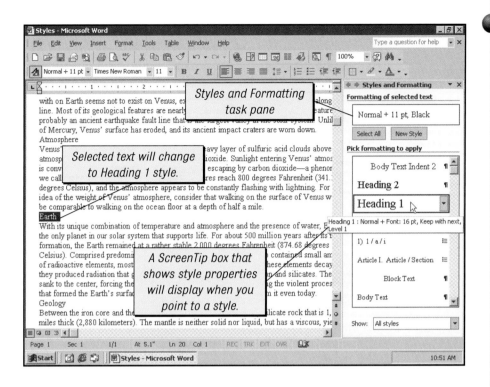

- Styles and Formatting task pane
- Selected text will change to Heading 1 style.
- A ScreenTip box that shows style properties will display when you point to a style.

Figure 2.18
Styles and Formatting task pane

WORD 2002

9. Read the ScreenTip description of the Heading 2 style and change the style of the next heading, *Geology*, to **Heading 2**.

NOTE *You can make additional changes to text after a style is applied—for example, you may add underline or other attributes.*

10. Change the style of the *Geology* paragraph to **Body Text Indent 2**.

11. Find and select the word *subduction* and scroll in the *Pick formatting to apply* box to find and apply the character style **Emphasis**.

Now you will create a new character style.

12. Find and select the words *continental drift*, and click the **New Style button** in the Styles and Formatting task pane.

The New Style dialog box appears.

13. Type Terms in the *Name* box, click the **Style type triangle button** and select **Character**.

14. In the *Formatting* section, click the **triangle buttons** to select **Arial** as the font and **10** as the font size; click the **Bold** button (see Figure 2.19); and then click **OK**.

The *Terms* style appears in the *Pick formatting to apply* box.

15. With *continental drift* still selected, click **Terms** to change the selected text to the new style.

16. Close the Styles and Formatting task pane.

17. Save your changes and close the document.

Figure 2.19
New Style dialog box

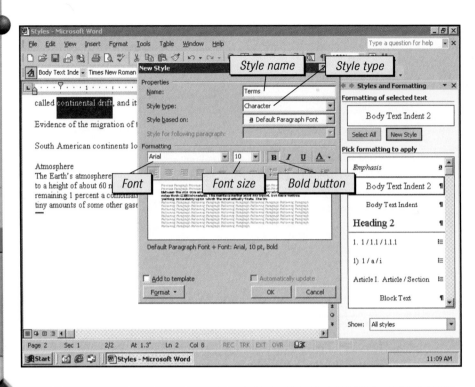

INSERTING AND FORMATTING GRAPHICS

Sometimes it is difficult to get a point across with text alone. In such cases, you can add a **graphic** (also called an **object** or **image**) to a document. A graphic is any element in a document that is not text. Examples include a drawing object made with lines, curves, or decorative text (called **WordArt**) or pictures (clip art or a photograph). Word has an entire folder called the **Clip Organizer** which includes professionally designed objects (pictures, photographs, sound, and video clips) from which you can choose to complement many different subjects in your documents. The graphics in the Clip Organizer are called **clip art,** or clips. The Drawing toolbar has tools that help you draw geometric shapes and other objects, insert WordArt, and access the Clip Organizer.

Browsing the Clip Organizer

The Insert Clip Art button 🖼 on the Drawing toolbar opens the Insert Clip Art task pane. Clips are organized by pictures, sounds, and motion clips and in subject categories identified by keywords such as Animals, Buildings, Character Collections, Food, Healthcare, People, and Travel. You can open the Clip Organizer and browse the categories that fit your subject, or you can search for related clips with keywords. Before you insert a clip into your document, you can preview it.

If the graphic you want to insert into your document is in another location, such as in a program, on the Web, or on a disk, Word will allow you to **import** (or insert) many popular types of graphic files directly into your document. Click the Insert menu, point to Picture, and then click From File or simply click the Insert Picture button 🖼. When you locate the file you want to insert, just double-click it. If you want to import a free image from a Web site, you often must copy and save the image to a local drive.

WARNING *You can use any Clip Organizer image in the documents you create—as long as you are not selling the documents with the image. Before you add any graphic to a document, be sure to verify the legal restrictions for using it. Always secure permission from your instructor before you add a graphic to the Clip Organizer.*

Working With an Image

An inserted clip may be the wrong size and in the wrong place. Therefore, you must be able to resize, move, and align the image on the page. You can perform these tasks with resize handles. To move or resize an image, you must first select the image by clicking it. The **resize handles** surrounding the image allow you to **resize** it. Point to a handle until a two-way arrow appears. To change only the height of an image, drag a vertical two-way arrow until you see the desired image size. To change only the width of an image, drag a horizontal two-way arrow. To maintain the image proportions while you resize it, drag a corner or diagonal resizing handle. To move an image, click the selected object and drag it to the new location.

Tools on the Picture toolbar allow you to handle images more precisely, however, than using sizing handles. When you select a picture, the Picture toolbar appears with editing tools. You can, for example, change the contrast between light and dark colors, **crop** (cut off) unnecessary parts of the picture, and change the size and **layout** (how text aligns and wraps in relation to the picture).

Before you change the height and/or width of an image (in the Format Picture dialog box), you need to guard against distortion. If you make a clip wider, for example, without changing the height an equal amount, you change its height-width relationship, or **aspect ratio.** Before you change either the height or the width, you need to lock the aspect ratio. Thus, when you change either dimension, Word changes the other dimension proportionately. (If you forget to lock the aspect ratio, or otherwise make a mistake in resizing, you can click the Reset Picture button 🖼 to restore the image to original size.)

Graphics almost always share a page with paragraph copy. The **wrapping style,** or text wrapping, refers to the visual relationship of the text and the image. You cannot use the buttons for aligning text (on the Formatting toolbar) to align pictures. Instead, you align objects horizontally by clicking the Format Picture button 🖼 on the Picture toolbar. In a finished document, text and graphics should complement each other. If they compete for readers' attention, you should change the text appearance or the size, wrapping style, and/or alignment of the graphic.

Inserting, Editing, and Formatting an Image

In this activity, you will search for an image, insert the image into a document, and then edit and format the image.

1. **Open *Sandy Reef Island Tour* in your *Word Data* folder and save the file as *Clip Art* in the *Tutorial* folder. Read the document, which describes Sandy Reef Island.**

Another Way 💲

To open the Insert Clip Art task pane, click the Insert menu, point to Picture, and click Clip Art.

2. Point to **Toolbars** on the View menu and click **Drawing**.

The Drawing toolbar appears beneath the document window above the status bar.

3. Position an insertion point two lines below the last line of text in the document, then click the **Insert Clip Art button** [image] on the Drawing toolbar.

The Insert Clip Art task pane displays.

4. In the Search text box, type travel and click the **Search button**.

Travel-related images display in the task pane, as shown in Figure 2.20.

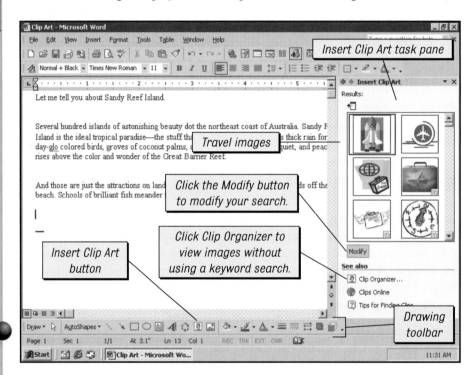

Figure 2.20
Insert Clip Art task pane

NOTE *If you want to view additional images, click Clip Organizer in the* See also *section of the Insert Clip Art task pane. Select a folder in the Collection List box. Available images will display in the right side of the Microsoft Clip Organizer box. The Office clip art images are arranged by category in the Office Collections subfolders.*

5. Click one of the travel images to insert it into your document.

The clip art is inserted at the end of the document.

WARNING *The Clip Organizer graphics must be installed on your computer to view clips from the Clip Organizer. If no pictures, sound files, or motion clips exist in the Clip Organizer, see your instructor. If you have access to the Microsoft Office CD and receive a message that additional clips are on the Microsoft Office CD-ROM, click OK to continue. If you receive a message that Word is indexing clips from previous editions, click Postpone.*

6. Close the Insert Clip Art task pane.

Now you will edit and format the image you just inserted.

NORTON
ONLINE

Visit **www.glencoe.com/norton/online/** for more information on importing graphics.

7. Click anywhere in the clip to select it.

The Picture toolbar floats in the document window. A small box called a *handle* appears at each corner and at the middle of each side of the image. Drag any of the corner handles to resize the image while maintaining its height-to-width proportions (aspect ratio). Resize an image using a center handle to distort the image vertically or horizontally.

8. Click the Format Picture button 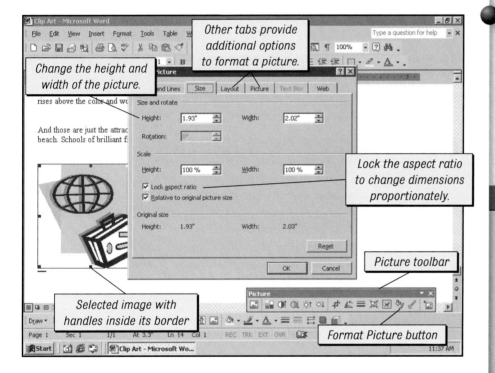 **on the Picture toolbar, and click the Size tab in the Format Picture dialog box. Your document window should look similar to Figure 2.21.**

Figure 2.21
Size tab in the Format Picture dialog box

9. Under Scale, select the Lock aspect ratio check box, if necessary.

10. In the *Size and rotate* section, increase the number in the Height box to approximately 2″.

The number in the Width text box changes automatically because you selected *Lock aspect ratio*.

11. On the Layout tab, click the Square icon under *Wrapping style*. Under *Horizontal alignment*, click Right; then click OK.

The dialog box closes and the image moves to the right below the text. The clip is still selected except now the border is gone and white resize handles surround the image.

12. Point to the center of the clip art image, press and hold the left mouse button, and drag this image to the top of the right side of the document.

Word BASICS

Editing and Formatting a Graphic

To resize a graphic:

1. Select the graphic and click the Format Picture button on the Picture toolbar.

2. On the Size tab of the Format Picture dialog box, click Lock aspect ratio.

3. Change the size in the Height or Width text box.

Or:

• Drag a corner handle to resize the image.

To wrap and align:

1. Select the graphic and click the Format Picture button on the Picture toolbar.

2. On the Layout tab in the Format Picture dialog box, click a wrapping style.

3. Click a horizontal alignment option and click OK.

4. Drag and drop the graphic into the text, if necessary.

To format a picture, click anywhere in the clip to select it, then right-click and click Format Picture. Make the necessary changes in the Format Picture dialog box.

A dotted line indicates where the clip will be located.

13. Release the mouse button to place the image on the right side of the text.

14. Click the document to deselect the image and close the Picture toolbar, then scroll to view the document.

NOTE *If you want to select another wrapping style to improve the overall appearance of your document, select the clip and click the Text Wrapping button* ▨ *on the Picture toolbar. Then click an option.*

15. Move or resize the picture, if desired.

16. Change the text appearance as desired for the text and the picture to complement each other.

17. Point to **Toolbars** on the View menu and click **Drawing** to close the toolbar. Save and close the document.

SORTING WORDS OR NUMBERS

Many documents contain lists—sometimes arranged in alphabetic or numeric order. You can **sort** lists manually by cutting and pasting or dragging and dropping. However, a faster, more accurate way to sort a list is to use the Sort feature on the Table menu. With the Sort feature, you can specify whether you want items sorted in **ascending** or **descending** order. You can sort words, numbers, or dates that appear as text or in tables; the items must be listed vertically, though. Any column in tables can be sorted. If you want to sort all lines in a document, just issue the Sort command. If, however, you want to sort particular lines in a document, select the lines and then sort.

HANDS on
Sorting a List

In this activity, you will sort a list alphabetically in ascending order.

1. Open *Bookmark* in your *Word Data* folder, and save the file as *Sort* in the *Tutorial* folder.

You want to sort a list of software features near the end of this document, so you must select the items to be sorted.

2. Navigate to the top of page 13. Select all the text under the *Word Processing* heading from the words *Block Delete* through *Special characters* (on page 14).

3. Click **Sort** on the Table menu.

The Sort Text dialog box appears. The default options are set to sort text by paragraph in ascending order.

4. Click **OK** to accept the default settings.

Word rearranges the selected items in alphabetic order.

5. Find the phrase *Formula bar* and select the text from *Formula bar* through the last line of text in the document.

6. Click **Sort** on the Table menu. Confirm the options are set to sort the paragraphs of text in ascending order and click **OK**.

7. Save and close the document.

ADDING REFERENCE FEATURES

You can add reference features to long documents to help readers find information and to provide supporting facts or sources. Such reference features include bullets or numbers to highlight listed items, page numbers, headers and footers, footnotes, and a table of contents.

Using Bullets and Numbers

A **bullet** is a character, typographical symbol, or graphic used as a special effect to highlight an item. Word provides bullet characters, including dots, squares, arrows, and check marks; the Clip Organizer also includes images that you can use as a bullet. You can use bullets to distinguish main items from secondary items when the order of items is not critical. You may add bullets to an existing list or add them as you type.

If priority is important in a list of items, use numbers to indicate the order of importance in the list. Also, use numbers when you want the reader to know that the items or steps must be completed in sequence. As with bullets, you may add numbers to an existing list or add them as you type. You may also create an outline numbered list.

HANDS on

Adding Bullets, Numbers, and Outline Numbers to Lists

In this activity, you will add bullets and numbers to a list of items; change existing bullets; create a list while adding bullets as you type; and create a list while adding outline numbers.

1. In your *Word Data* folder, open *Series* and save the document as *Bullets & Numbers* in the *Tutorial* folder.

2. Find *Table of Contents*. Click in the selection bar and drag down to select the text from *Table of Contents* through the end of the paragraph with the *Feedback form* heading (in the middle of the following page).

3. Click the **Bullets button** on the Formatting toolbar and then deselect the text and scroll up to view the formatting.

A bullet appears to the left of each selected item, similar to Figure 2.22. The bullet character in your document may differ, depending upon which bullet character is selected in the Bullets and Numbering dialog box.

Figure 2.22
Bulleted list

Inserting Bullets and Numbers

To insert bullets:

1. Select the items to be bulleted.

2. Click the Bullets button on the Formatting toolbar.

To insert numbers:

1. Select the items to be numbered.

2. Click the Numbering button on the Formatting toolbar.

To insert outline numbers:

1. Select the items to be numbered.

2. Click Bullets and Numbering on the Format menu.

3. Click the Outline Numbered tab in the Bullets and Numbering dialog box.

4. Click the style you want and click OK.

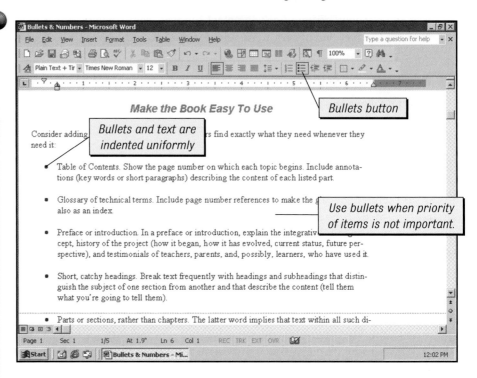

4. **Select the bulleted items again and click Bullets and Numbering on the Format menu. Click the Bulleted tab.**

The Bulleted tab displays seven bullet options.

5. **Click a bullet option that differs from your document and click OK.**

Word changes the bullet in your document to the bullet character you chose.

6. **Find *What WPS Can Do*. Select the bulleted list in this section of the document, and click the Bullets button.**

The bullets disappear and the selected text moves to the left margin.

7. **Click the Bullets button 📄 again.**

Word inserts the bullet design you selected in step 5. The bullets and text are uniformly indented from the left margin, 0.25" and 0.5", respectively.

> **NOTE** *Before proceeding to the next step, click the Tools menu and click AutoCorrect Options. On the AutoFormat As You Type tab, select the* Automatic bulleted lists *check box and click OK.*

8. **Click the New Blank Document button 🗋. In the new document, type an asterisk (*) and press Spacebar. Then type Bookmark and press Enter⏎.**

Your text is automatically changed to a bulleted list.

9. Type the following items. Press ⌈Enter◄┘⌉ after each item: Bullets, Find, Go To, Replace, Sort.

10. After the last item, press ⌈Enter◄┘⌉ twice to turn off the automatic bullets.

11. Click **Bullets and Numbering** on the Format menu and click the **Outline Numbered tab**.

12. Click the option that uses Arabic numbers for first-level items and indents the next level with Arabic numbers, as shown in Figure 2.23. If this option is not available, click any option that does not have the word *Heading* on the sample. Click **OK**.

WORD 2002

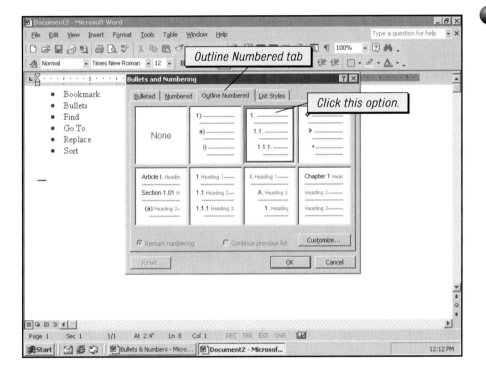

Figure 2.23
Outline Numbered tab

13. Type the following partial outline. Press ⌈Enter◄┘⌉ after each item except the last item. Do not press ⌈Tab⌉. All items will be numbered automatically as first-level items as you type.

Planning Phase
Identifying Potential Employers
Where to Look
Checking and Choosing
Analyzing Jobs and Qualifications
Writing Phase

14. Select the second and third items on the list.

15. Click the **Increase Indent button** 🔳 on the Formatting toolbar.

The indent increases and the selected items become numbered as subordinate (lower-level) items.

16. Select the last two items in the outline; click the **Increase Indent button** 🔳.

Again, the demoted items indent and are renumbered appropriately.

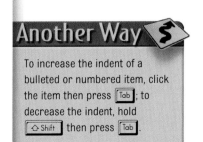

Another Way

To insert numbering automatically as you type, select the *Automatic numbered lists* option on the AutoFormat As You Type tab of the AutoCorrect dialog box (Tools menu).

17. Save the document as *Outline List* in the *Tutorial* folder, and close the document.

18. Go to the top of the *Bullets & Numbers* document. Find the word *Incorporate*. Select this line and the balance of text above the *What WPS Can Do* heading.

19. Click the **Numbering button** ▤ on the Formatting toolbar.

Each selected item is indented and numbered with an Arabic number. The numbering style in your document depends upon which numbering style is selected in the Bullets and Numbering dialog box.

20. Save and close the document.

Numbering Pages

Word adds page numbers to documents automatically. If you should add or delete a page, Word renumbers the pages automatically, too. Page numbers are printed in the margin area at the top or bottom of pages and aligned at the left, center, or right, as you choose. Different types of page numbering are available, including lowercase and uppercase letters and Roman numerals or Arabic numbers. By dividing documents into sections, you can use different numbering in each section.

HANDS on

Adding Page Numbers

In this activity, you will number pages in a document and then modify the original page numbering.

1. Open *Ag Ed* in your *Word Data* folder and save it as *Reference Features* in the *Tutorial* folder.

2. Click **Page Numbers** on the Insert menu.

The Page Numbers dialog box displays, as shown in Figure 2.24.

3. Click the **Position triangle button** then click **Bottom of page (Footer)**. Click the **Alignment triangle button** and click **Center**. Preview the document and then click **OK**.

Word switches to Print Layout View.

4. Scroll down and view the page number at the bottom center of the first page. Navigate to the end of the document and view the page number on the last page.

The page numbers appear dim—they are inactive. The number can only be edited by clicking Header and Footer on the View menu or by double-clicking the number. (You will work with headers and footers in the next activity.) You will now divide the document into three sections and use different numbering for each section.

Word BASICS

Inserting Page Numbers

1. Click Page Numbers on the Insert menu.

2. In the Page Numbers dialog box, click a position and alignment option. If the position is Bottom of page (footer), click *Show number on first page*.

3. Click Format and set the desired options.

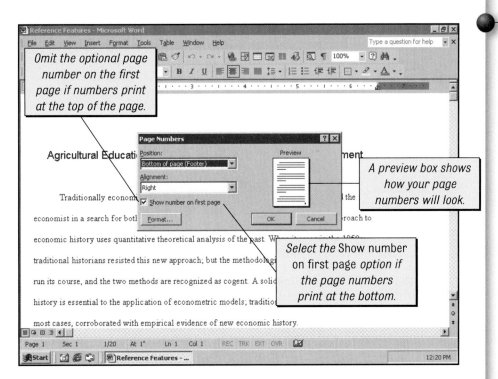

Figure 2.24
Page Numbers dialog box

Omit the optional page number on the first page if numbers print at the top of the page.

A preview box shows how your page numbers will look.

Select the Show number on first page *option if the page numbers print at the bottom.*

5. Navigate to the top of the document. Click before the main heading then click **Break** on the Insert menu. Click **Next Page** under Section break types and click **OK**.

6. Click **Normal View** ▤. Scroll up if necessary.

The section break appears at the end of page 1 above the main heading.

7. Click **Print Layout View** ▣ so you can see the page numbers as you work.

8. Click page 1. Click **Page Numbers** on the Insert menu. Click the **Alignment triangle button** and click **Right**. Then click the **Format button**.

The Page Number Format dialog box appears.

9. Click the **Number format triangle button** and click the **i, ii, iii, ... option**. Click **OK**, preview the page in the Page Numbers dialog box, and click **OK**.

The number *i* appears in the bottom-right corner of the first page. Notice the same style page number on the status bar also. Now you will number pages in the main part of the document with Arabic numbers, starting with 1.

10. Click to the left of the heading at the top of page 2, then click **Page Numbers** on the Insert Menu. Click the **Format button** in the Page Numbers dialog box.

Under Number format, the Arabic numbers format (1, 2, 3 . . .) is already selected; you want to start this numbering at page 1.

You can use the Inside and Outside alignment options to insert page numbers for bound documents. The Inside option aligns the number on the right of even-numbered pages and on the left of odd-numbered pages. The Outside option does just the opposite.

11. In the *Page numbering* section, type 1 in the *Start at* box, and then click **OK**. Click **OK** again to close the Page Numbers dialog box.

The page number in the status bar changes to *Page 1*. Scroll down to verify the number at the bottom of page 1.

12. Go to the *Bibliography* heading. Click at the bottom of the page and insert a *Next page* section break.

13. Click **Normal View** 🔳, click the manual Page Break (after the Section break) and press ⌴Delete⌴. Click **Print Layout View** 🔲.

14. Go to the *Appendix A* heading, click before the heading, and click **Page Numbers** on the Insert Menu. In the Page Numbers dialog box, click the **Format button**.

15. Click the **A, B, C, … option** number format. Type A in the *Start at* box, if necessary; and click **OK**. Click **OK** again to close the Page Numbers dialog box.

The status bar now displays *Page A   Sec 3*.

16. Click the **Print Preview button** 🔍 then the **Multiple Pages button** ⊞ (2 x 2 Pages). Click the page number on the last page twice.

The page enlarges so that you can see the page number *B* clearly.

17. Click the page number again to reduce the page size. Click the top-left page, then click the page number—the Arabic number *18*. Click again to reduce the page size.

18. Scroll to the top of the document in the Preview window. Click the page number on the top-left page—the Roman numeral *i*. Click again to reduce the page. Then, click the **Print Layout View button** 🔲 to close Print Preview.

As you observed, you used a different page numbering style in each of the three sections of your document.

19. Save your changes and close the document.

Creating and Modifying Headers and Footers

In long documents, other pieces of information besides the page number are often printed in the top and/or bottom margin to guide readers who may be looking for a specific topic. For example, on time-sensitive documents, the date and time may appear at the top or bottom of every page. That way readers know they are reading current information. Information repeated in the top margin is called a **header;** information in the bottom margin is called a **footer.** To specify the information, you will work in the Header and Footer view, where you can insert information by using the Click and Type feature, by selecting AutoText items, or by clicking buttons on the Header and Footer toolbar. (In Print Layout View, the **Click and Type** feature automatically applies paragraph formatting when you double-click

certain sections of a document. You can then insert text or an image where the insertion point is located. The pointer shape is a clue to the formatting that Click and Type will apply in any one area of a document.)

Adding Headers and Footers

In this activity, you will insert a header to all pages of a document. The header will contain the file name of the document and the date. Then you will insert a page number in a document footer.

1. Open *Reference Features* in the *Tutorial* folder in your *Word Data* folder and save it as *Header and Footer* in the *Tutorial* folder.

2. Click **Normal View** 📄, if necessary, to view the section breaks. Click anywhere within page 1 of section 2.

3. Click **Header and Footer** on the View menu.

The Header and Footer toolbar appears, as shown in Figure 2.25. Text in the main view of the document is inactive (it appears dim). You must insert header information (text or graphics) in the dotted Header box.

WORD 2002

Word BASICS

Creating a Header or Footer

1. Click Header and Footer on the View menu.

2. Type or insert the desired information (such as the date, time, page number, or other text).

3. Click the Close button.

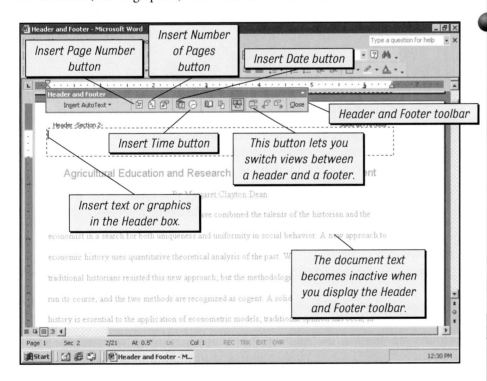

Figure 2.25
Header and Footer toolbar

4. With the insertion point at the left margin in the Header box, click the **Insert AutoText button** [Insert AutoText ▾] on the Header and Footer toolbar. Click **Filename** to automatically insert the document name.

5. Double-click at the right end of the Header box. Click the **Insert Date button** 📅 on the Header and Footer toolbar.

HINTS & TIPS

If your document contains section breaks, you can insert a different header or footer for each section. Click a section where you want the different header or footer, then click the Same as Previous button. Type the new header or footer.

The date is inserted into the header.

6. **Close the Header and Footer toolbar. Click Print Layout View ▣ and scroll through the document.**

The header has been inserted into all pages of the document. The header appears inactive while the main text appears normal.

7. **Navigate to the top of page i and double-click the header.**

The Header and Footer toolbar displays. The header is now active.

8. **Double-click the center of the dotted Header box to place an insertion point at the center of the header. Click the Insert Page Number button ▣ on the Header and Footer toolbar, press ⌷Spacebar⌷, type of, press ⌷Spacebar⌷, then click the Insert Number of Pages button ▣.**

The page number *(i of 21)* appears in the header.

9. **Click the Switch Between Header and Footer button ▣.**

Word displays the Footer box on the same page with the insertion point at the left margin.

10. **Type Author: Margaret C. Dean. Click the Switch Between Header and Footer button ▣ and select the page number (i of 21) in the header. Press ⌷Delete⌷, then again click the Switch Between Header and Footer button ▣.**

11. **Select the letter C. in the footer and type Clayton, then close the Header and Footer toolbar.**

12. **Double-click the page number in the footer on page 1. When the Header and Footer toolbar appears, select the page number and press ⌷Delete⌷. Close the Header and Footer toolbar.**

13. **Scroll the document to examine the header and footer in the three sections. Note that the page number in the footer has been deleted throughout the entire document.**

14. **Save your changes and close the document.**

Using Footnotes

Footnotes may occur at the bottom (or foot) of a page to explain or expand upon key points or provide source information. Footnotes invariably refer to a specific word, sentence, or paragraph. Labeling the footnote and the text it refers to with the same label—a superscripted number or symbol—shows this relationship. A documentation footnote typically has four divisions: author name(s), title, publication date, and page reference. The arrangement and punctuation may vary, depending upon the type of publication noted and the style manual followed.

When you type text that requires a footnote, you must use the Footnote command to insert a footnote. You will then verify that you want the footnotes numbered sequentially with Arabic numbers and type the footnote text in Footnote view. Word will automatically number and place the footnotes below a short horizontal line at the left margin between your main text and the footer.

The footnote text style is based on the Normal style. When you point to a note reference number, the note text displays above the reference number as a ScreenTip. Later, if you want to delete a footnote, you have only to delete the reference number in the main text. If you want to move a footnote to another location, select the reference number and use the Cut and Paste method. Word will renumber automatically and move the footnote to the new location. If you need to edit footnote text, double-click the reference number or click Footnotes on the View menu. (Some writers use **endnotes** instead of footnotes. Endnotes serve the same purpose as footnotes, but they appear together on a separate page at the end of a document. The same Word feature that inserts footnotes also inserts endnotes.)

Inserting Footnotes

In this activity, you will insert footnotes in a multiple-section document.

1. **Open *Header and Footer* in the *Tutorial* folder in your *Word Data* folder, and save it as *Footnote* in the *Tutorial* folder. Click Print Layout View , if necessary.**

2. **Find the second occurrence of the words *economic history*. Click an insertion point after the period that ends the sentence.**

3. **Point to Reference and click Footnote on the Insert menu.**

The Footnote and Endnote dialog box displays, as shown in Figure 2.26.

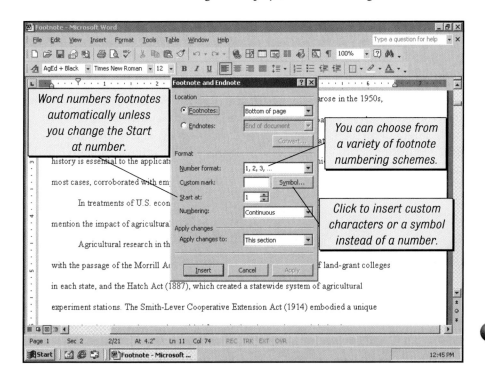

Figure 2.26
Footnote and Endnote dialog box

Word BASICS

Inserting Footnotes

1. Click an insertion point in the document for the footnote number.

2. Point to Reference on the Insert menu, and click Footnote.

3. In the Footnote and Endnote dialog box, click Insert to insert continuously numbered (Arabic) footnotes at the bottom of pages.

4. Type the footnote text.

4. Click **Insert**.

Word places the superscript number 1 at the bottom of the page.

5. Scroll up three paragraphs to view the corresponding superscript number inserted after *economic history*.

6. Scroll back to the bottom of page 1 and type the following footnote text next to the superscript number: Neimi, A. W., U.S. Economic History (1975), pp. 2–3.

NOTE *Do not press* Enter← *after you type the footnote. Word will automatically adjust the spacing if another footnote appears on the same page.*

7. Click the paragraph above the footnote.

8. Find the words *major force* and click an insertion point after the period at the end of this sentence. Click the **Insert menu**, point to **Reference**, and click **Footnote**.

9. Click **Insert** to accept the footnote settings.

Word inserts the footnote number (2) at the bottom of the page and also at the insertion point (after *major force*) in the document.

10. Type the following footnote text: Ibid., p. 230.

Ibid. is an abbreviation of the Latin word *ibidem*, which means *in the same place.* In other words, footnote 2 refers to the same publication as footnote 1.

11. Save your changes and close the document.

Creating a Table of Contents

A **table of contents** (or **TOC**) is a list of the headings and subheadings and the page numbers on which they are found in the document. A table of contents typically appears at the beginning of a document.

Word will create a table of contents on the basis of the heading styles used in your document. Several different arrangements are available. Word automatically inserts a hyperlink for each heading that appears in a table of contents. Thus, you can click headings in the TOC to jump to the corresponding page in your document. If you add text or headings to your document, you can automatically update the table of contents by selecting it and pressing F9.

HANDS on

Inserting a Table of Contents

In this activity, you will create and modify a table of contents for a document.

1. Open *Footnote* in the *Tutorial* folder in your *Word Data* folder and save it as *Contents* in the *Tutorial* folder.

2. Click the heading on page 1 of Section 2; then click the **Styles and Formatting button** to open the Styles and Formatting task pane. Click **All styles** in the *Show* box, if necessary.

Heading 2 displays in the *Formatting of selected text* box at the top of the task pane.

3. Close the Styles and Formatting task pane. Go to the next heading in the document using the Go To tab of the Find and Replace dialog box. Click the *Land-Grant Colleges* heading and verify that Heading 4 appears in the Style button on the Formatting toolbar.

4. Verify the heading styles throughout the document by advancing to each using Go To. Click each head and examine the Style button on the Formatting toolbar.

5. Navigate to the top of the document and click an insertion point on page i.

6. Click the **Insert menu**, point to **Reference**, and click **Index and Tables**. Then click the **Table of Contents tab**.

The Index and Tables dialog box displays with the Table of Contents tab on top, as shown in Figure 2.27.

Word BASICS

Inserting a TOC

1. Apply a Heading style (All styles list) to all headings.

2. Click the insertion point where the table is to appear.

3. Point to Reference and click Index and Tables on the Insert menu to open the Index and Tables dialog box.

4. Click *Show page numbers* and select a Tab header style.

5. On the Table of Contents tab, choose an option in the Formats list box.

6. In the Show levels list box, select the highest heading level to appear in the TOC.

7. Click OK.

WORD 2002

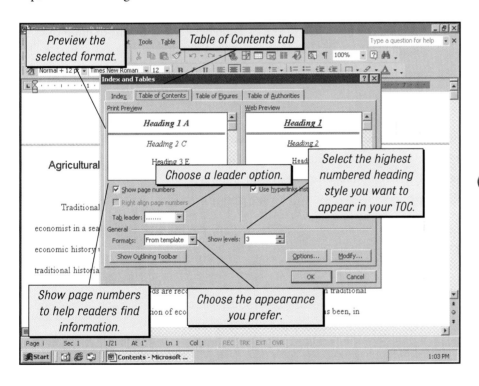

Figure 2.27
Table of Contents tab

7. Click the **Show page numbers option**, if it is not selected. Change the Tab leader to the **solid line option**, if necessary.

8. Click the **Formats triangle button**, and click **Distinctive**.

The tab leader and format display in the Print Preview window. You want to show Heading levels 1–4 in your TOC.

Visit **www.glencoe.com/norton/online/** for more information on creating a table of contents.

WORD 2002

9. Click the **Show levels up triangle button** and change the setting to **4**.

The Heading 4 level appears in the Print Preview window.

10. Click **OK** to create the table of contents.

Word inserts the table of contents at the insertion point.

11. Click an insertion point above the first line of the table of contents and type Table of Contents. Select *Table of Contents*, click the **Style button** `Normal ▾`, and click **Heading 2**.

Now you will update the TOC to include the *Table of Contents* heading you just typed above it.

12. Select the *Table of Contents* heading and the entire TOC. Then press `F9`.

The Update Table of Contents dialog box appears.

13. Click the **Update entire table option** and click **OK**.

Word adds the *Table of Contents* heading and page number to the TOC.

14. Deselect the text, then press `Ctrl` and click *Bibliography* to jump to the page where the heading appears in the document.

15. Save and close the document.

Test your knowledge by matching the terms on the left with the definitions on the right. See Appendix B to check your answers.

TERMS

_d_ **1.** bullet

_e_ **2.** subscript

_c_ **3.** Format Painter

_a_ **4.** indentation

_b_ **5.** font

DEFINITIONS

a. Distance of text from the left or right page margins

b. A set of characters of one design

c. Feature that copies paragraph format and character appearance

d. May be a dot, arrow, square, or check mark

e. Character or symbol that is positioned slightly lower than other text.

E-Mail a Word Document

In this activity, you will explore Help to learn about the features of your e-mail program and how to use Word to send an **e-mail** (electronic mail) message with a document attachment. Before you begin this activity, secure permission from your instructor.

1. **Type** e-mail messages **in the** *Ask a question box* **and press** Enter⏎**. Click the Create a new e-mail message link. Click Show All in the Help window, and read the information. Close the Help window.**

2. **Open the** *Woodsy View News* **document in your** *Word Data* **folder, then click the E-mail button** 🖹 **on the Standard toolbar.**

Word displays an e-mail header. By default, the file name of the open document appears in the *Subject* box of the e-mail header, as shown in Figure 2.28.

3. **In the** *To* **box, type an e-mail address of a friend, a student, or your instructor. (Your instructor may provide the address.) Press** Tab **twice to move to the** *Subject* **box. (Word will include your e-mail address automatically in a** *From* **box that doesn't display in the e-mail header.)**

4. **Select the text in the** *Subject* **box and type** Newsletter **and press** Tab**. In the** *Introduction* **box, type the name of the person to whom you are writing, followed by a comma, then type** the Woodsy View Association newsletter is attached.

5. **To send the e-mail message and the attachment, click the Send a Copy button** ✉Send a Copy**. If you are connected to the Internet, Word will send your message to the address in the** *To* **box and close the e-mail header. If you are not connected, you will receive a message asking you to connect to the Internet.**

6. **Close your document.**

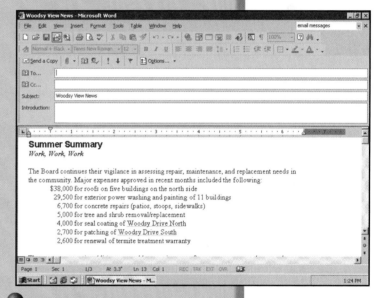

Figure 2.28
E-mail header in the Word window

NAMING FAVORITES

As you probably know, hundreds of thousands of Web sites are available at the click of your mouse. With so many sites available, you may have difficulty keeping track of those that you would like to revisit. Word and Internet Explorer provide an easy way to do just that. You can keep a list of **favorites** or **bookmarks** to which you can return quickly. In this activity, you act as a personal travel consultant for GlenTravel Agency. You will designate a Web page and a document as favorite places.

> **NOTE** *Steps for this activity assume your default Web browser is Internet Explorer. If you are using a different Web browser, the steps may be slightly different. If you are unsure of how to add a favorite (or bookmark) to your particular browser, search your Help menu for information.*

1. Connect to the Internet. Open *Australia Tour Pricing* in your *Word Data* folder. Point to **Toolbars** on the View menu and click **Web**.

2. Click the text in the Address bar of the Web toolbar, type www.travel.com, and press [Enter←].

Your Web browser launches, and the *Travel.com* home page appears.

> **NOTE** *If you have trouble connecting to the* Travel.com *home page, locate an alternative site by clicking Search* [🔍Search] *on the Internet Explorer toolbar and search for Web sites containing the keyword* Travel.

3. Explore the links at this site to find information about Australia that you and other travel agents could use to promote tours of Australia.

4. Return to the *Travel.com* home page by clicking the **Back button** [⇐Back ▼] or by typing the *Travel.com* address in the Address bar.

5. Click **Favorites** [Favorites ▼] on the Explorer toolbar to open the Favorites pane. Click **Add** [📑Add...] and click **OK** in the Add Favorite dialog box to add this site to your list of favorite places.

Travel.com has been added to the list of sites in the Favorites pane. (It has also been added to your Favorites list in Word.) Now at any time you can click the Favorites button [⊛Favorites] in your browser (or Word) to access this link.

6. Click the **Australia Tour Pricing taskbar button** to return to the Word document.

In addition to Web sites, Word also allows you to add documents to your Favorites list. You can use this feature to quickly open documents that you often use.

7. Click the **Favorites button** [Favorites ▼] on the Web toolbar and click **Add to Favorites**.

8. In the Add To Favorites dialog box, type Australia Tour Pricing in the File name box, as shown in Figure 2.29.

9. Click the **Add button**.

Figure 2.29
Add To Favorites dialog box

10. Close the *Australia Tour Pricing* document.

Now you can return easily to the Web site and document designated as favorites.

11. Click the **Favorites button** `Favorites ▾` on the Word Web toolbar, and click the **Open Favorites folder**. Click *Australia Tour Pricing* and click **Open**.

Word remembers where the document is stored and automatically opens the file.

12. Close the document. Click **Favorites** `Favorites ▾` again on the Web toolbar and click the *Travel.com* link.

Your browser launches and loads the *Travel.com* Web site. The Favorites pane appears to the left of the browser window.

13. Right-click the *Travel.com* link in the Favorites pane, click **Delete** on the shortcut menu, then click **Yes** to send the link to the Recycle Bin. Close the browser.

14. Click **Favorites** `Favorites ▾` on the Word Web toolbar and click **Open Favorites**. Right-click *Australia Tour Pricing*, click **Delete** on the shortcut menu, then click **Yes** to delete the link to this file (this will just delete the link; it will not delete the file).

15. Close the Favorites dialog box and the Web toolbar. Close Word. Close your browser and disconnect from the Internet.

> **WARNING** *You may proceed directly to the exercises in this lesson. If, however, you are finished with your computer session, follow the "shut down" procedures for your lab or school environment.*

SUMMARY AND EXERCISES

SUMMARY

Word provides many features for formatting text. Options such as bold, underline, and italic are available for enhancing the appearance of a document. Word enables you to easily format text in newsletter columns. The Format Painter and Style features are handy tools for quickly changing format and appearance. Images add interest to documents; Word equips users with tools to find, insert, and edit images. Word makes short work of page numbering and quickly adds headers and footers, footnotes, or a table of contents. You can send an e-mail right from a Word window and attach a Word document to an e-mail. In addition, Word provides a feature for you to add favorites in both Word and your Web browser so you can quickly return to a document or a Web site.

Now that you have completed this lesson, you should be able to do the following:

- Define a *widow* and an *orphan*. (page 186)
- Insert and modify page and section breaks. (page 187)
- Distinguish between a manual and automatic page break. (page 187)
- Change margins and vertical alignment. (page 189)
- Describe the types of text alignment and indentations involved in page setup. (page 191)
- Modify horizontal alignment and indentation style. (page 192)
- Set character, line, and paragraph spacing and tab stops. (page 194)
- Describe the types of tab stop options and how they align text. (page 195)
- Explain the advantages to formatting text in a newsletter style. (page 197)
- Apply and modify newsletter-style column formats. (page 198)
- Use Reveal Formatting to check paragraph alignment and check for consistency of spacing in headings, between paragraphs, and in tabs. (page 201)
- Explain the purpose of using attributes such as bold or italic or contrasting fonts. (page 204)
- Define *serif* and *sans serif.* (page 204)
- Enhance the appearance of text by applying bold, italic, and underline as well as superscripts and subscripts. (page 205)
- Apply text animation, a border, shading, and highlighting. (page 205)
- Use Format Painter to change text formats. (page 208)
- Define the word *style* and describe the four style types: Paragraph, Character, Table, and List. (page 209)
- Use the Style command to reformat documents. (page 210)
- Search the Clip Organizer for an image, insert the image into a document, and edit the image. (page 213)
- Sort a list alphabetically. (page 216)
- Add and edit bullets, numbers, and outline numbers in a list. (page 217)
- Add and modify page numbers in a document. (page 220)
- Insert and edit headers and footers. (page 222)
- Insert and edit a footnote. (page 224)
- E-mail a Word document as an attachment. (page 229)
- Add favorites in Word and Internet Explorer to a Web site and to a document. (page 230)

SUMMARY AND EXERCISES

CONCEPTS REVIEW

1 TRUE/FALSE

Circle T if the statement is true or F if the statement is false.

T (F) **1.** A footer is the same as a footnote.

(T) F **2.** The font Times New Roman is often used for paragraph text.

T (F) **3.** Character style controls all aspects of a paragraph's appearance. *Paragraph style*

T (F) **4.** For the body text of letters and memos, a font size of 6 to 8 is recommended. *10,11,12*

(T) F **5.** You can use the Reveal Formatting task pane to change formatting in a paragraph.

T (F) **6.** The Align Right button makes text even on both side margins. *Justified*

(T) F **7.** You can add a Web site to Favorites the first time you visit it.

(T) F **8.** Page numbers may be placed at the top or bottom of pages.

(T) F **9.** Open the Paragraph dialog box to choose hanging indentation style.

(T) F **10.** You can use photographs as clip art.

2 MATCHING

Match each of the terms on the left with the definitions on the right.

TERMS	DEFINITIONS
1. serif *a*	**a.** Most common type of font used for paragraph text
2. bold *d*	**b.** Group of characters that share a common design
3. columns *h*	**c.** Vertical measure between lines of text within paragraphs
4. superscript *e*	**d.** Text that looks thick and dark
5. font *b*	**e.** Often used within footnotes
6. clip *f*	**f.** A ready-made image
7. line spacing *c*	**g.** May be a dot, square, arrow, or even a picture
8. widow *j*	**h.** Used to format a newsletter or newspaper
9. styles *i*	**i.** Sets of text characteristics with names like Body or Title
10. bullet *g*	**j.** The last line of a paragraph printed by itself at the top of a page

SUMMARY AND EXERCISES

3 COMPLETION

Fill in the missing word or phrase for each of the following statements.

1. To find the headings in a document, use the ___go to___ tab of the Find and Replace dialog box.

2. Information that repeats at the top or bottom of each page of your document is called a ___header___ or ___footer___ .

3. To change margins or vertical alignment, select ___page setup___ on the File menu.

4. Small boxes called ___handles___ surround a selected clip or drawing.

5. To align all lines of a paragraph so they are flush at both the right and left margins, use the ___justify___ button.

6. If priority is important in a list, use numbers; however, use ___bullets___ when all items have the same priority.

7. Drag a corner handle to resize an image and maintain its height-width proportions, also called ___aspect ratio___ .

8. The ___Tabs___ dialog box has Set, Clear, and Clear All buttons.

9. The ___Break___ command on the Insert menu lets you insert page breaks and section breaks.

10. In a new blank document, the text you type uses the ___Normal___ style—the base style for the Normal template in Word.

4 SHORT ANSWER

Write a brief answer to each of the following questions.

1. Briefly describe how to copy double spacing and italic from one paragraph to another.

2. Explain how to create an outline numbered list.

3. Define paragraph spacing and explain how it differs from line spacing.

4. Describe the four main horizontal alignment options you can apply from the Formatting toolbar.

5. Describe the Insert Clip Art task pane and how it can be used to locate images and insert them into a document.

6. Describe the use and purpose of the Style button on the Formatting toolbar.

7. Explain how to find all formatting marks in a document.

8. Describe the purpose of favorite places.

9. Explain the purpose of section breaks and name two kinds.

10. Besides font and indents, what factors should you consider in creating a paragraph style?

5 IDENTIFICATION

Label each of the elements in Figure 2.30.

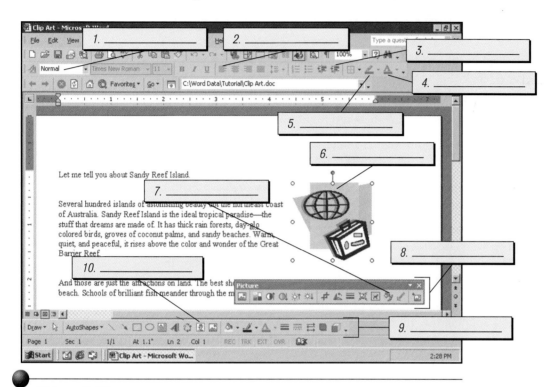

Figure 2.30

SKILLS REVIEW

Complete all of the Skills Review problems in sequential order to review your skills toreformat pages and paragraphs; maintain consistency in a document; enhance the appearance of documents; add tabs and special effects; insert, edit, and format an image; apply styles; work with columns; add a header and footer; sort a list; and add reference features.

1 Reformat Pages and Paragraphs

1. Open *Write this Way* in your *Word Data* folder and save it as *Reformat* in the *Skills Review* folder.

2. Find the word *stopping* and click after the end of this sentence. Click **Break** on the Insert menu, click **Page break**, then click **OK**.

3. Click **Page Setup** on the File menu. Change the margins as follows: Top: 2"; Bottom: 1.25"; Left: 1.25"; Right: 1.25". Click **OK**.

4. Click at the end of the last line on page 1 and press Enter↵. Click **Break** on the Insert menu, click **Next page** under Section break types, and click **OK**.

5. Click **Normal View** 📄 if necessary, click the manual Page Break and press Delete.

6. Click **Show/Hide** ¶ and delete any paragraph marks at the top of page 2. Click page 2 then click **Page Setup** on the File menu and change the top margin to 1.25"; in the Preview section, click **This section** in the *Apply to* box, if necessary, and click **OK**. Click **Show/Hide** ¶, click **Print Layout View** ▣, and scroll to view the document.

7. Click page 1, click **Page Setup** on the File menu, and change the top margin to 1.25". Under *Apply to*, click **This section**. On the Layout tab, change the vertical alignment to **Center**, and click **OK**.

8. Select the main title and subtitle and click the **Align Right button** ▤.

9. Select *Plan* (the paragraph heading on page 1) and click **Align Right** ▤. Select the *Draft* heading on page 1 and click **Align Right** ▤.

10. Select the first paragraph on page 1 below *Five Steps Up and to the Right*, and click **Increase Indent** ▤. Then click the **Line Spacing button** ▤▾ and click **1.5**.

11. Select the first paragraph under the *Plan* heading, right-click, then click **Paragraph**. On the Indents and Spacing tab, click **Justified** in the alignment box. Type 0.5" as the left and right indentation and click **(none)** in the Special list box, if necessary. In the Spacing section, click **12 pt** in the Before and After box and click **OK**.

12. Select the other three paragraphs under *Plan*, right-click, click **Paragraph**, then click the **Indents and Spacing tab**. In the Special section, click **First line by 0.5"**; under Spacing, click **Double** in the Line-spacing box; click **6 pt** before and after. Click **OK**.

13. Save your changes and close the document.

2 Check Spacing and Indentations

1. Open *Creative Classroom* in your *Word Data* folder and save it as *Consistency* in the *Skills Review* folder.

2. Click the **Show/Hide button** ¶ to display the nonprinting characters. Navigate to the end of the document and click an insertion point at the end of the last line.

3. Click the Find button ▨. Click the **More button**. Click the **Special button** then click **Paragraph Mark**. In the Search options list box, click **Up**. Click the **Less button**.

4. Click **Find Next** to advance through the document and verify that each partial line (the end of each paragraph) ends with a paragraph mark and that paragraphs are separated by one blank line (another paragraph mark). Delete extra paragraph marks and insert missing ones. Do not add extra paragraph marks in the bulleted list. Delete extra paragraph marks at the top of the document.

5. When you finish your check of the document, click **More** in the Find and Replace dialog box. Click **All** in the Search Options list then click **Less** to collapse the dialog box.

6. On the Go To tab, click **Heading** in the *Go to what* box (see Figure 2.31). Click **Next** to navigate to each heading and delete extra spaces between the words in the headings. Close the Find and Replace dialog box. Click **Show/Hide** ¶.

7. Save and close the document.

3 Set Tab Stops and Apply Special Effects

1. Click **New Blank Document** [ ] and save the new document as *Decimal Tabs* in the *Skills Review* folder in your *Word Data* folder.

2. Click **Tabs** on the Format menu and click **Clear All** to clear the default tabs. Click **Left** in the Alignment section then type 2 in the Tab stop position box and click **Set**. Continue to set left tabs at each of these positions: 3", 3.75", and 4.75". Click **OK** to close the Tabs dialog box.

3. Press Tab to advance to the first stop. Type the following as column headings pressing Tab after each word: **Actual, Budget, Variance, Total Budget.**

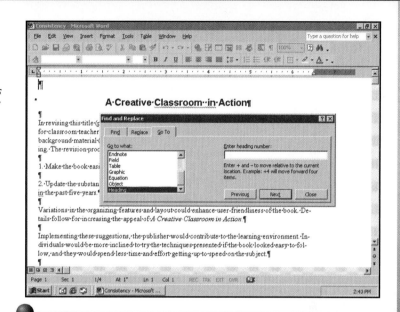

Figure 2.31

4. Press Enter↵, then click **Tabs** on the Format menu. Click **Clear All** and set these new tabs: Left: 1"; Decimal: 2.25"; Decimal: 3.25"; Decimal: 4"; Right: 5.5". Click **OK**.

5. Press Tab then type the entries below. Press Tab after each entry and press Enter↵ at the end of each line.

Income	9,438.00	10,000.00	562.00	120,388.00
Expenses	10,000.00	9,997.00	3.00	196,519.00

6. Select the column headings and click **Bold** [B]. Select each side heading and click **Bold** [B]. Select the *Total Budget* heading and click **Italic** [I]. Select the numbers in the *Expenses* row and click **Underline** [U].

7. Select *Total Budget*, click the **Highlight triangle button** [ ], and click **Turquoise**.

8. Select *Total Budget*, and click **Borders and Shading** on the Format menu. On the Borders tab, click the **Shadow option**, and click **OK**.

9. With *Total Budget* still selected, click **Font** on the Format menu. On the Text Effects tab, click **Sparkle Text** and click **OK**. Deselect the heading to view the effects.

10. Select the *Actual, Budget,* and *Variance* headings, and click **Borders and Shading** on the Format menu.

11. On the Shading tab, click the **Turquoise color** on the Fill palette. Click **Text** in the *Apply to* box, if necessary, and click **OK**.

12. Save your changes and close the file.

SUMMARY AND EXERCISES

4 Enhance Text and Use Format Painter

1. Open *Write this Way* in your *Word Data* folder and save it as *Write Enhanced* in the *Skills Review* folder.

2. Select the title and the subtitle. Click the **Font triangle button** Times New Roman ▾ and click **Arial** or another sans serif font.

3. With the headings still selected, click **Font** on the Format menu. On the Font tab, click **Red** in the Font color box, click to deselect **Outline** in the Effects section, and click **OK**. Deselect the text.

4. Select *Write this Way*, right-click, and click **Font** on the shortcut menu. Click **20** in the Size list box and click **OK**.

5. Select *Five Steps Up and to the Right*, right-click, and change the font size to **16**.

6. Select the opening paragraph, click the **Font color triangle button** ▾, and click **Red**. Click **Font** on the Format menu, type 13 in the Size list box, and click **OK**.

7. Select the *Plan* heading, click the **Font triangle button**, and click the same sans serif font you used for the title. Change the font color to Red and change the Font size to 14.

8. Select the first two paragraphs beneath *Plan* and change the font size to 12.

9. Select the *Plan* heading, double-click the **Format Painter button** ▾, and paint the *Draft* heading.

10. Scroll down and paint the *Revise* heading; then continue to scroll down to paint the *Edit* heading and the *Publish* heading.

11. Click the **Format Painter button** ▾ to deactivate it.

12. Use Format Painter to copy the paragraph formatting of the first paragraph under *Plan* (on page 1) to the first paragraph under *Draft*. Then copy the paragraph formatting of the second paragraph under *Plan* to the second paragraph under *Draft*.

13. Preview the document, save your changes, and close the document.

5 Apply and Create Styles

1. Open *Application Followup* in your *Word Data* folder and save it as *Letter Styles* in your *Skills Review* folder.

2. Select the date. Click the **Styles and Formatting button** ▾. Click **All Styles** in the *Show* box in the Styles and Formatting task pane. (Each time you open this task pane, verify that you are selecting from the *All styles* list.)

3. Scroll in the *Pick formatting to apply* box and click the **Date style**. Close the Styles and Formatting task pane.

4. Select the name and address. Click the **Style triangle button** Normal ▾, then scroll the Styles list and click the **Plain Text style**.

5. Select *Dear Mr. Olivo*, click the **Style triangle button** Normal ▾, then scroll the style list and click **Salutation**.

6. Select *APPLICATION FOLLOWUP* and use the **Style button** [Normal ▾] to apply the **Strong character style**; select the body of the letter and apply the **Body Text style**; select *Sincerely* and apply the **Closing style**.

7. Click an insertion point after *Sincerely*, press [Enter←], and type your name.

8. Click the body text of the letter. Click the **Styles and Formatting button** [A]. (Your document window should appear similar to Figure 2.32.)

9. Click **New Style** in the Styles and Formatting task pane and type **Position** in the *Name* box. Click **Arial, 11 pt**, and **Red** in the Formatting section and click **OK**.

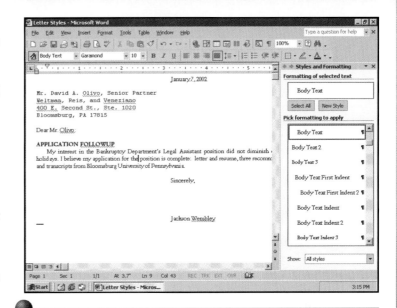

Figure 2.32

10. Select the words *Legal Assistant* in the body of the letter and click the **Position style** in the *Pick formatting to apply* box.

11. Close the Styles and Formatting task pane. Save and close the document.

6 Insert, Edit, and Format an Image

1. Open *Write This Way* in your *Word Data* folder and save it as *Insert Clip* in the *Skills Review* folder. Click **Print Layout View** [▣], if necessary.

2. Click an insertion point after the end of the last line of the first paragraph, and press [Enter←]. Point to **Toolbars** on the View menu and click **Drawing**. Click the **Insert Clip Art button** [▣].

3. Type the keyword business in the *Search text* box in the Insert Clip Art task pane, and click **Search**.

4. Click a clip in the Results box to insert it. Close the Insert Clip Art task pane.

5. Click the image to select it and point to the handle in the lower-right corner. Click when the pointer becomes a diagonal double-headed arrow and drag up and to the left to decrease the image size by about half. (If you make a mistake, click **Undo** [↺▾] and try again.)

6. Click the **Text Wrapping button** [▣] on the Picture toolbar and click **Square**.

7. Drag to place the image on the right margin to the right of the first two paragraphs at the beginning of the document.

8. Click the document to deselect and view the image. Close the Drawing toolbar, then save and close the document.

SUMMARY AND EXERCISES

7 Sort a List and Add Bullets and Numbers

1. Open *Bookmark* in your *Word Data* folder and save it as *Bookmark Sorted* in the *Skills Review* folder.

2. Navigate to the *Master List of Suite Features* heading and scroll down to find the *Spreadsheet* list.

3. Type 5 and press [Spacebar] in front of the following items: AVERAGE function, COUNT function, IF function, MAX function, MIN function, NOW function, SUM function, TODAY function.

4. Select the list items from *Absolute and relative cell references* to *Paste command* at the end of the spreadsheet list.

5. Click **Sort** on the Table menu. Click **Field 1** in the *Sort by* box, click **Number** in the *Type* box, and click **Ascending**. Click **OK**. (The numbered items form a separate alphabetized list at the bottom of the selected text. The other listed items are not alphabetized since you are sorting only items with a number.)

6. Navigate up to the *Word Processing* list. Select all items that end with a 2 and click the **Bullets button** . Click the **Decrease Indent button** to decrease the indentation.

7. Select all items that end with a 4, then click **Bullets and Numbering** on the Format menu. On the Bulleted tab, click a bullet icon that is different than the one you just inserted, and click **OK.**

8. Select all items in the Spreadsheet list excluding the items starting with 5.

9. Click the **Numbering button** . Click **Sort** on the Table menu and accept the defaults by clicking **OK** to sort paragraphs of text in ascending order.

10. Select numbered items 20–29, right-click, and click **Restart Numbering** to number the selected items from 1–10. Right-click again and click **Bullets and Numbering**. On the Outline Numbered tab, click a numbering icon (*do not* click an icon that includes headings). Click **OK**.

11. Deselect the text, click the number *2* (in item 2), and press [Tab]. (Item 2 becomes subordinate and the subsequent items are renumbered.)

12. Click the next item (the new item 2), and click **Increase Indent** twice to make it a subordinate item.

13. Save and close the document.

8 Insert Page Numbers and Add a Header and Footer

1. Open *Bookmark* in your *Word Data* folder and save it as *Bookmark Header* in the *Skills Review* folder.

2. Click **Page Numbers** on the Insert menu.

3. Click **Top of page (Header)** in the Position box. Click **Right** in the Alignment box. Clear the *Show number on first page* check box. Click **OK**.

4. Click **Print Layout View** 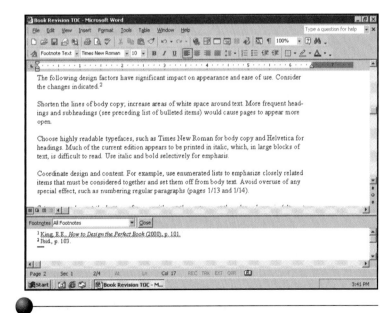, if necessary, and navigate to page 2 to verify the page number. Click at the top of page 2.

5. Click **Header and Footer** on the View menu. Click the **Switch Between Header and Footer button**.

6. Click **Insert AutoText** `Insert AutoText ▾` on the Header and Footer toolbar, and click **Filename** to insert the file name on the left side of the footer. Double-click the center of the footer area and click **Insert Date** on the Header and Footer toolbar.

7. Double-click the right side of the footer area then click **Insert Page Number**. Click after the page number and type `Spacebar` of `Spacebar`. Click **Insert Number of Pages** on the Header and Footer toolbar.

8. Close the Header and Footer toolbar. Scroll through the document to see the footer.

9. Save and close the document.

9 Insert Footnotes and a Table of Contents

1. Open *Book Revision* in your *Word Data* folder, and save it as *Book Revision TOC* in the *Skills Review* folder.

2. Click **Print Layout View**, if necessary. Click after the colon at the end of the last sentence in the first paragraph.

3. Point to **Reference** on the Insert menu and click **Footnote** to open the Footnote and Endnote dialog box. In the Format section, verify that *Continuous* is selected in the Numbering box and click **Insert**.

4. Type the following as the footnote text: King, E. E., *How to Design the Perfect Book* (2000), p. 101.

5. Click **Normal View**. Click at the top of the document and find *The following design factors* in the document. Click at the end of the sentence, point to Reference on the Insert menu, and click **Footnote**. Click **Insert**. Type this footnote text: Ibid., p. 103. (Your document should look like Figure 2.33.) Click **Close** on the Footnote pane.

6. Navigate to the top of the document and click before the main heading. Click **Break** on the Insert menu; click **Page break**, if necessary, and click **OK**.

7. Click **Find** to open the Find and Replace dialog box. On the Go To tab, click **Heading** in the *Go to what* box.

Figure 2.33

8. Click **Next** then click the heading to check the heading levels in the Style button
Normal ▼. Repeat this process to confirm all the heading levels in the document.

9. Go to page 1. Click the **Insert menu**, point to **Reference**, and click **Index and Tables** to open the Index and Tables dialog box. Click the **Table of Contents tab**.

10. In the Formats box, click **Simple**. Select the **Show page numbers check box**, if necessary. Set the *Show levels* box to 2 and click **OK**.

11. Click **Print Preview** 🔍 and navigate to view your TOC. Close Print Preview, then save and close the document.

10 Apply and Modify a Column Format

1. Open *Book Revision* in your *Word Data* folder, and save it as *Book Column* in the *Skills Review* folder. Click **Print Layout View** 🔲, if necessary.

2. Click **Select All** on the Edit menu to select all text in the document.

3. Click **Columns** on the Format menu to open the Columns dialog box.

4. Click the **Two-column icon**, then click the **Line between check box** to insert a vertical line between the columns. Click **OK**.

5. With the columns still selected, click **Justify** ▦. Deselect the text then scroll to view the document.

6. Click **Select All** on the Edit menu. Click **Columns** on the Format menu, click the **Three-column icon**, and click **OK**.

7. Deselect the text and view the document. Save and close the document.

LESSON APPLICATIONS

1 Reformat and Enhance a New Document

Create an announcement for a workshop scheduled in your area by typing columns in a tabular format. Change font size and attributes and apply font effects, borders, shading, highlighting, animation, and color.

1. Open a new, blank document and save it as *Workshop Announcement* in the *Lesson Applications* folder in your *Word Data* folder.

2. Change all the margins to 2"; change the vertical alignment to Center.

3. Set two tabs: Left tab at 1.5"; Center tab at 4".

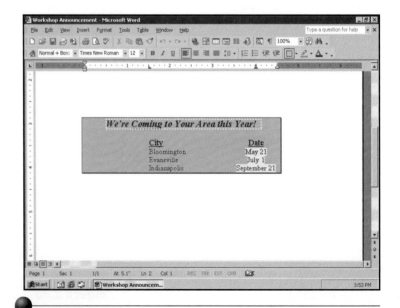

Figure 2.34

4. Type **City** and **Date** at the tabs; underline and change these headings to a larger font.

5. Beneath the headings, type three cities in your state and three dates (omit the year).

6. Above the headings, type: **We're Coming to Your Area this Year!**

7. Add enhancements of your choice, including bold or italic; font effects, such as Outline or Shadow; borders and shading; highlighting; animation; and font color. Your finished document might resemble Figure 2.34, but it will differ somewhat depending on the enhancements you choose.

8. Save and close the document.

2 Insert a Clip and Apply Column Formats

Insert a clip into a document in your *Word Data* folder; format the document in columns.

1. Open *Australian Islands Article* in your *Word Data* folder and save it as *Picture This* in the *Lesson Applications* folder.

2. Open the Insert Clip Art task pane and search for a clip art using the keyword *leisure*. If you don't find a suitable clip, browse the Clip Organizer or insert another clip of your choice.

3. Resize the clip to approximately half its initial size and place it at the very top of the document.

4. Select all the text in the document except the main heading; do not select the graphic.

5. Format the text in two-column format, deselect the text, and view the document. Reformat the columns with a different horizontal text alignment.

6. Select all the text again, excluding the graphic and main heading. Change to a 3-column format with a vertical line between the columns.

7. Save and close the document.

3 A Different Sort

Create and apply styles; apply bullets, numbering, and outline numbering; indent paragraphs; and sort paragraphs alphabetically.

1. Open *Woodsy View News* in your *Word Data* folder and save it as *Woodsy View News Sort* in the *Lesson Applications* folder.

2. Change all of the headings that appear in blue font color as Heading 1 style and change all of the headings that appear in pink font color as Heading 3 style.

3. Under *Memory Joggers*, type a heading, a period, and a space at the beginning of each paragraph as follows: **Water, Carports, Repairs, Gutters, Trash, Trash, Pets, Repairs**. Create a new character style for these headings named *Line Heading*, and apply the new style to each heading.

4. Sort the eight paragraphs in the *Memory Joggers* section alphabetically (in ascending order) then apply a bullet format. Sort the *Thank You* paragraphs (below *Memory Joggers*) in descending order; apply bullets.

5. Number the list under *Summer Summary* at the top of the document. Using the Numbered tab in the Bullets and Numbering dialog box, select the style with a parenthesis after the number. Reduce the list indent so the list begins at the left margin.

6. Insert a page break at the end of the document, and type the following list.

Be sure to attend next month's meeting to learn more about the following:
Swimming Pool
Hiring Lifeguard
Heating Pool
Adding Whirlpool
Winter Contingency Plans
Purchasing New Snow Plow
Salting Roads

7. Select the seven items in the list and apply an outline numbered list format.

8. Make items 2–4 and items 6 and 7 second-level (subordinate) items.

9. Save and close the document.

4 A Contents Set in Style

Number pages and insert a footer. Apply heading styles and insert page and section breaks. Insert a table of contents.

1. Open *Australian Islands Article* in your *Word Data* folder. Save it as *Australian Islands TOC* in the *Lesson Applications* folder.

2. Insert a footnote at the end of the first paragraph. Type **Wilhelm, Gunnar, Visiting Australia (2002), p. 47.** as the footnote text.

3. Apply Heading 1 style to the main heading and Heading 2 style to the other headings.

4. Insert page breaks to put each heading at the top of a new page.

5. Insert a Next page section break at the top of the document.

6. Number the pages at the top center. Change the line spacing in the document to Double.

7. Change the page numbering so Section 1 begins with *i* and Section 2 begins with *1*.

8. Insert a table of contents in Section 1 containing all headings in the document and the corresponding page numbers. Try to use a format and leader character that you have not previously used.

9. Create a footer on all pages of the document showing the file name, today's date, and Page *x* of *y* (where *x* is the page number and *y* is the number of pages).

10. Save and close the document.

PROJECTS

1 My Bio Enhanced

As a legal assistant for a prominent firm, you want your professional biography to be inviting in appearance and stand out from others. Therefore, it is important that you enhance it effectively. Open *My Bio* in your *Word Data* folder and save it in the *Projects* folder as *My Bio Enhanced*. Change the margins and line spacing in the document and indent the first line of each paragraph. Reformat and enhance your bio to project an image in keeping with your personality and apply various font effects and color, as appropriate. Use the Styles and Formatting task pane to create at least one new style and apply it to the document. Check consistency of alignment and formatting in the document, then send it to a classmate as an attachment to an e-mail message.

2 By Design

As a recent graduate seeking a position as a graphic designer, you decide to create your own personalized letterhead to display your abilities. Open a new, blank document and save it as *Personal* in the *Projects* folder in your *Word Data* folder. Design a letterhead for yourself, using fonts, font sizes, font colors, special effects, and character effects of your choice. (Explore Help to learn about other features, such as WordArt.) Remember to use Format Painter to help in copying formats. Before adopting a particular font, verify that the printer you use can print the font. In addition to your name and address, include a telephone number and an e-mail address. Include additional information, such as a favorite quotation, if you wish. (*Hint:* You will want to use a very narrow top margin so that

Figure 2.35

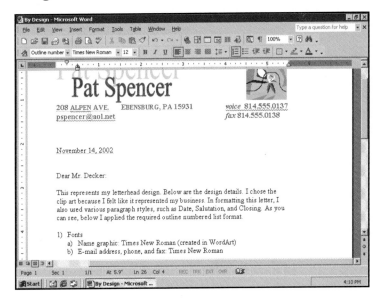

the design is as close to the top edge of the page as possible when the letterhead is printed.) Insert clip art of your choice; size it and position it attractively. Save the file. When finished, write a brief message to your instructor on the letterhead. In the message, name the fonts, font sizes, and effects used in the letterhead. Under each of these categories (fonts, font sizes, and effects) list the information then format this text as an outline numbered list. Describe why you chose the image you inserted. Save the message as *By Design* in the *Projects* folder in your *Word Data* folder. An example is shown in Figure 2.35.

3 Hot Button Sort

In a new, blank document, type a list of five Word toolbar buttons you use most often (type each button name on a separate line). Beneath it, list five additional buttons that you rarely or never use. Add an overall heading (example: *Word Toolbar Buttons*) to introduce your lists. Sort each list in alphabetic order. Increase the font size and add a border and a color fill (shading) to the heading. Apply highlighting and an animation effect to the list of five frequently used buttons and add a footnote explaining their significance. Add one or more font effects (such as Shadow or Outline) to the list of infrequently used buttons. Adjust font sizes as appropriate. Edit, format, and enhance the document according to your preferences. Save the document as *Buttons* in the *Projects* folder in your *Word Data* folder.

4 Tip of the Day

You already knew Microsoft Word features when you started your company Savvy Solutions. You have determined that some employees, though, are still not up to speed. You have decided to encourage employees to teach themselves before investing in formal Word training sessions. To start, you will circulate a how-to sheet to encourage the use of Help (an example appears in Figure 2.36). Soon you will e-mail the information sheet each morning, and eventually such information will be standard fare on Savvy Solutions' intranet (the company's internal network).

In a new document, compile several tips for the information sheet by copying Microsoft Word Help screens for copying, deleting, moving, and renaming files.

Figure 2.36

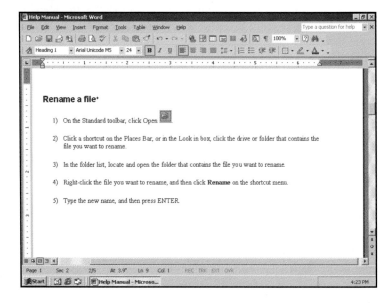

Change the numbered list format in the copied text. Create a table of contents in a separate section at the beginning of the document. Insert a footnote on each page to document the source of the information and encourage users to search Help for more information. Insert page numbers and the file name at the top of each page in the second section—begin the first page of the second section as page 1. Save the document as *Help Manual* in the *Projects* folder in your *Word Data* folder.

5 Travel Brochure

You are one of the three owners of a successful travel agency. The owners have decided it would be a good idea to create a one-page travel advertisement to mail to prospective customers. The owners have already written the text and have decided to meet for the third time to brainstorm about the design of the brochure (the previous two meetings have lacked focus and been unsuccessful). You have decided to create a mock-up of the document with sample illustrations since the other owners are having a hard time imagining the layout. Open *Travel Text* in your *Word Data* folder which contains the text for the advertisement. Save the document as *Travel Ad* in your *Projects* folder. Read the text to get a sense of the theme, then search the Clip Organizer for three representative images you could use in the brochure (search Clips Online, if necessary). Apply styles to the headings and text. Format the document in newsletter-style columns and experiment with different column formats and column text alignment. Place the last line of the document

(Call Kelly Travel right now . . .) in a prominent location in the brochure. Apply a character effect, color, and/or highlighting to this text to make it stand out.

6 My Favorite Cards

Several friends sent you animated greeting cards on your most recent birthday. You enjoyed receiving birthday greetings by e-mail—especially the ones that included a peppy tune—and you also want to be prepared to send e-cards on special occasions. Open your browser and visit each of the following Web sites that offer animated greeting cards: *www.americangreetings.com*, *www.bluemountain.com*, *www.hallmark.com*.

Rate the sites (based on your personal opinion) on the following factors, using a scale of 1 to 10 for each factor: appearance of the home page (color, arrangement, and so on); number of card categories; number and variety of cards in the Birthday category; and clarity of directions for ordering an electronic greeting. Calculate the total rating for each site and add the site(s) with the highest rating(s) to your list of favorites (bookmarks). Set tab stops in a new blank document to display the information in columns in a readable format. Use Styles to create a main heading *(My Favorite Cards)*, a secondary heading *(Online Greetings)*, and column headings *(Company, Ratings)*. Type company names *(American Greetings, Blue Mountain, Hallmark)* in the first column and your ratings in the second. Reformat and enhance the text to make it attractive and easy to read. Add a border, shading, and highlighting to the document. Save the file as *Greeting Cards* in the *Projects* folder in your *Word Data* folder.

Project in Progress

7 Following Through

As the founder-owner of Savvy Solutions, you recently accepted an invitation to present a workshop at Anderson High School. Now it's time to organize the handouts you will take to the workshop. In a new document, list five Word features you learned in Lesson 2 to emphasize at the workshop. For each feature, write a sentence describing what the feature does and give an example of when the students might use it. Include two or three keywords for finding information about the feature in Help. Set up the information in columns using tabs. Use styles attractively. Number the pages. Create a table of contents and add a footnote, giving copyright information for Microsoft Word. *(Hint:* For copyright details, see *About Microsoft Word* on the Help menu.) For the footnote, try inserting a symbol instead of a number. Each feature and the TOC should appear on a separate page. Create an attractive cover sheet for your handouts. Set up the cover sheet as a separate section at the beginning of the file. On the cover sheet, insert clip art that relates in some way to the topic of writing. Size and position the image as desired. Include the title of your presentation, your name, and the date of the presentation on the cover sheet. Reformat and enhance the cover as desired. Check the document for consistency in alignment and formatting, and make any necessary changes. Save the document as *Word Power* in the *Projects* folder of your *Word Data* folder and close the document.

Overview: **Congratulations!** Now that you have completed the Word lessons in this tutorial, you have the opportunity in this capstone project to apply the Word skills you have learned. Your biennial family reunion is set for next August in your hometown. You will be preparing the invitations, sign-up forms, and family newsletter; you also will be creating the family cookbook. As you create the case study documents, try to incorporate the following skills:

- Create and save various kinds of documents.
- Proofread and edit text. Use the Spelling and Grammar and Thesaurus features; use the Undo, Redo, Repeat, and Find and Replace commands.
- Ask the Office Assistant for help as needed.
- Navigate efficiently within and among documents.
- Use templates and wizards as desired to create documents.
- Search the Internet.
- Manage the files you create.
- Use the Office Clipboard to cut, copy, and paste text.
- Change page orientation, page and section breaks, margins, horizontal and vertical alignment, indentations, and character, line, and paragraph spacing; also set tabs.
- Add bullets and numbering to lists.
- Change font styles, sizes, attributes, and color.
- Create headers and footers, footnotes, and a table of contents.
- Add special effects to enhance document appearance, including highlighting, shading, and borders.
- Use the Format Painter and apply styles.
- Create hyperlinks to pages, documents, and Web sites.
- Insert, edit, and format graphics.
- Use Print Preview; print all documents.

Instructions: Read all directions and plan your work before you begin. You will be evaluated on these factors: (1) the number of skills involved in completing the case; (2) creativity; (3) practical applications for the task; (4) appropriate use of word processing features; (5) quality of the documents produced, including mechanical accuracy, format, and writing style; and (6) oral presentation of the case.

1. ***Manage the Files and Research the Data.*** Create a *Reunion* folder in the *Projects* folder in your *Word Data* folder in which to save all your Case Study documents. Search the Web, using keywords such as *reunions, genealogy, family ties,* and *entertaining* for family reunion ideas that you can use.

2. ***Design a Family Graphic.*** Design a family emblem to represent your family or this year's reunion. You may use this emblem on T-shirts, caps, sun visors, and so on. Using the family emblem, design a multi-purpose logo you can use (for example, as part of a letterhead or to incorporate into forms or a newsletter banner). (If necessary, search Help for information on how to draw an object.)

3. ***Prepare the Invitation Letter.*** Develop an invitation letter, incorporating the logo you just designed into your letterhead. Cover what, when, where, and whom to contact; announce the family Web page address; ask to have a sign-up form returned to you by a certain date; request favorite recipes for the family cookbook; request pictures of individuals and families; announce that an all-family picture will be taken at the reunion; announce that a donation will be collected (as usual) to cover expenses.

4. ***Create a Newsletter.*** Create a newsletter sharing family reunion information. Limit the newsletter to two pages. Insert clip art, a poem, and a brainteaser. Secure feedback from others and edit as desired.

5. ***Create the Cookbook.*** Set up the sections of your cookbook. Type section headings on separate pages and apply a Headings style (for example, Desserts; Eggs & Cheese; Meat, Fish, & Poultry; Pasta, Rice, & Other Grains; Salads & Dressings; Soups & Stews; Vegetables). Type a recipe in any two sections, searching the Web for recipes, if necessary. Add a header and/or footer and a table of contents. Create a cover page for the cookbook. Add a border and shading to the cover.

Contents

Artificial Intelligence

What if your home could tell when you arrive and then turn up the heat and play your favorite music? What if your car could tell you that you are turning the wrong way on a trip to the market? (More useful might be a robot that would clean your room!) These things are common in futuristic movies and cartoons; however, the development of artificial intelligence may one day make them an affordable reality.

Artificial intelligence (AI) can be defined as a program or machine that can solve problems or recognize patterns. But a more pure definition of AI might be a computer or program that can fool a human into thinking he or she is dealing with another human. Such a computer could both learn and reason, so yet another definition of artificial intelligence might be a computer that can think like a human being.

Artificial intelligence software is used in many real-world applications, such as determining whether banks should grant loans, in voice recognition software, and in terrain-following missile guidance systems. Even applications like word processors and e-mail make use of AI concepts. Regardless of the actual task, artificial intelligence is used in two basic areas:

- **Problem Solving.** In problem solving, the artificial intelligence program must look at a problem or collection of data and determine what to do next. For example, a bank may use an artificial intelligence system to look at your credit history and life style before deciding whether or not to lend you money. This type of system is called an expert system.

- **Pattern Recognition.** In pattern recognition, the artificial intelligence program looks for repeated or known occurrences of data. Examples include artificial vision and speech recognition.

Of course, many artificial intelligence programs combine elements of both areas to solve a problem. For example, a data compression utility must look for repeated patterns in the data and then decide how to rewrite the data to eliminate the duplications.

Artificial intelligence may be applied in many different ways depending on the problem to be solved and the resources available. Some common techniques include the following:

- **Decision Trees.** These software guides are simply maps that tell the computer what to do next based on each decision it makes. Each decision leads to a new branch with new decisions and consequences.

■ **Rules-Based Systems.** These systems work by following a set of rules given by the programmer. As long as the programmer has anticipated every possible circumstance that the program may encounter, it can solve any problem.

■ **Feedback.** This technique is used to modify programs. Basically, a feedback system monitors the results of a solution to see whether the solution worked or in what areas it failed.

■ **Knowledge-Based Systems.** These systems are similar to a rules-based system, but they use feedback to learn from their mistakes. As a result, knowledge-based systems can actually learn to solve new problems.

To create a true artificial intelligence, scientists could try building an artificial brain called a neural network. The human brain consists of billions and even trillions of neurons, each with as many as one million connections to other neurons. This level of complexity is simply beyond the level of any computer currently in existence, though that won't keep such stuff out of Hollywood fiction. Even the most powerful parallel computers with tens of thousands of processors don't come close to equaling the number or variety of connections in a human brain. Whether artificial intelligence will ever match or surpass the complexity of the human brain is a question for the future.

Excel Basics

CONTENTS

- Introducing Microsoft Excel
- Exploring the Excel Window
- Navigating Within a Worksheet
- Previewing and Printing a Worksheet
- Entering Data
- Editing Cell Contents
- Using Folders and Files
- Using the Spelling Tool and the AutoCorrect Feature
- Finding and Replacing Data and Searching for Files
- Finding and Replacing Cell Formats
- Aligning Data and Merging and Splitting Cells
- Formatting Numbers
- Modifying Font Characteristics and Clearing Cell Formats
- Using AutoFormats
- Using the Comments Feature
- On the Web: Collaborating on the Web

OBJECTIVES

After you complete this lesson, you will be able to do the following:

- ▶ Explain the purpose of worksheets for personal and business use.
- ▶ Identify the unique features of the Excel application window.
- ▶ Navigate within a worksheet.
- ▶ Preview and print a worksheet.
- ▶ Change the page setup options.
- ▶ Enter data, including text and numbers.
- ▶ Edit cell contents.
- ▶ Create a new folder.
- ▶ Save a workbook in a different file format.
- ▶ Spell check a worksheet.
- ▶ Use the AutoCorrect feature to correct common mistakes.
- ▶ Find and replace data.
- ▶ Use the Search command to find files.
- ▶ Align and rotate data.
- ▶ Merge and split cells.
- ▶ Format values using number styles.
- ▶ Modify font characteristics and clear cell formats.
- ▶ Use the AutoFormat feature.
- ▶ Add and edit comments in a workbook and send an Excel workbook via e-mail.
- ▶ Discuss a workbook online using the Web Discussions feature.

INTRODUCING MICROSOFT EXCEL

Microsoft Excel is a powerful **spreadsheet program** that you can use to perform calculations, analyze information, and manage lists of data for both personal and professional use. For example, you can use Excel to track your investments, determine which bank offers the best car loan, set up a personal budget, calculate the future value of an investment, or prepare a profit/loss statement. To help you perform these and other tasks, Excel includes literally hundreds of built-in mathematical formulas—and also allows you to custom-build your own. As you will soon discover, one of Excel's powerful features is its ability to automatically recalculate mathematical equations when you enter new data. Excel's ability to analyze numerical data and quickly perform complex calculations is one reason for the program's popularity.

So that you can easily enter and analyze information, Excel sets up its working area, the **worksheet,** as an electronic grid of columns and rows—sort of a computerized version of an accountant's paper ledger. The intersection of a column and row forms a rectangle called a **cell** into which you can enter information, such as numbers, text, or formulas. As an example, the worksheet in Figure 1.1 contains first quarter sales figures for Super Sports, a fictitious sporting goods store. This worksheet includes the three types of cell entries: text, numbers, and formulas. Text is used to label the months and product categories, numbers are used to indicate the sales figures, and formulas are used to calculate the totals.

Figure 1.1
Worksheets organize and calculate data

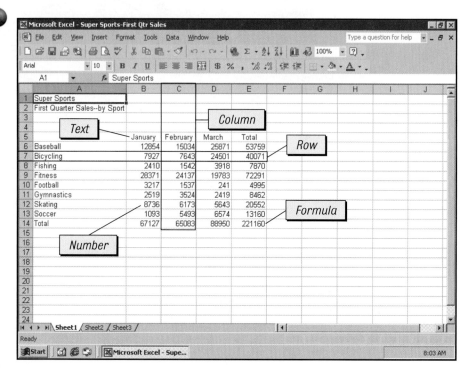

The sales information in Figure 1.1 is arranged in well-marked columns and rows. Row 5 includes the months in which the sales occurred, and column A shows which items were sold. Monthly totals appear in row 14, and first quarter totals are in column E. You can use formulas in Excel to calculate these totals automatically so you don't have to add (and re-add) everything yourself. You can use a simple worksheet such as this to see at a glance how well Super Sports did during the quarter.

After you initially develop a worksheet by entering text, numbers, and formulas, you can make it more interesting and readable by adding enhancements such as italics, shading, and fonts. Arranging and enhancing the appearance of your worksheet is called **formatting.** Compare Figure 1.1 with Figure 1.2. Figure 1.1 is unformatted and plain; Figure 1.2 includes the same information but is formatted for a more professional-looking appearance.

You know you can use Excel to enter and format text and numbers and to perform calculations involving those numbers. However, you can also use Excel to build charts (also called graphs) based on your numerical data. **Charts** display your worksheet data in the form of circles, lines, bars, or other graphical elements.

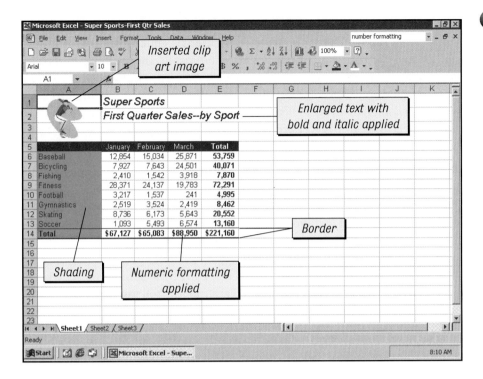

Figure 1.2
Formatting improves a worksheet's appearance

Did you know?

Before the advent of Windows, most PC users had to work with one program and one file at a time. Even experienced users spent a lot of time opening and closing programs.

Charts are not only visually appealing, but they also display statistical or numerical data in an easy-to-understand way. For example, you can create a chart so that your audience can tell at a glance if sales are rising or falling. Figure 1.3 shows a chart of the first quarter sales for the Super Sports organization. As you can see, this chart conveys information more effectively than numbers alone.

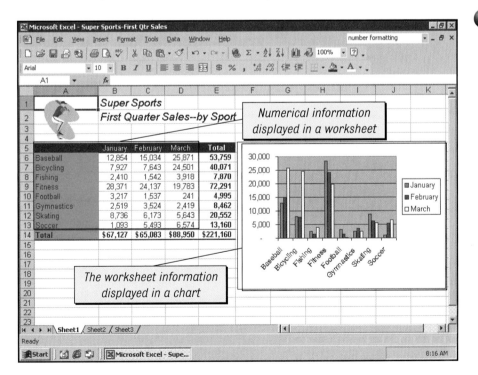

Figure 1.3
Charts graphically present numerical information

NORTON ONLINE

Visit **www.glencoe.com/norton/online/** for more information on Microsoft Excel 2002.

You can also use Excel to organize, filter, and sort large amounts of data in a worksheet using its database capabilities. A **database** is a collection of information organized in a way that you can quickly "mix and match" the data. For example, a phone book is a simple database that's organized alphabetically so that you can locate information. After you initially create a database in Excel, you can sort, search for, and analyze the data. While a mainstay database program such as Access is more powerful than Excel, Excel may have all the database features that you really need.

Excel's main document for setting up your data and charts is called a **workbook.** A workbook is simply a file that contains a group of related worksheets and chart sheets. (In other, similar application programs, these workbook files are called *spreadsheets*.) Think of a workbook as an electronic notebook of related information, and think of each worksheet as a page in the notebook. This arrangement allows you to group related information. For example, you can use a single workbook to set up the yearly revenue for a company by including twelve separate worksheets—one with the sales revenue for each month. You can display the worksheet you want by clicking the **sheet tab** at the bottom of Excel's application window. Using one workbook with separate worksheets to hold related information makes it easy to organize and analyze the data, as illustrated in Figure 1.4.

Figure 1.4
Workbook with several worksheets

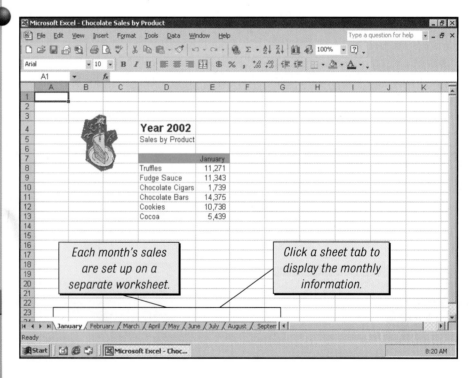

The Internet and the Web are not the same thing, even though many people use the terms interchangeably. The Internet is a worldwide system of linked computer networks. The Web is a hypertext system that uses the Internet as its transport mechanism. You navigate the Web by clicking hyperlinks to jump from one Web document to another.

Excel is also designed to work hand-in-hand with the Web, something commonly referred to as **Web support.** For example, you can include hyperlinks in your workbook that you can click to quickly display a Web page. Additionally, you can save an Excel workbook in **Hypertext Markup Language (HTML)** format so that others can view it on the Web. You can use Excel's Web support features to view and manipulate workbooks using your Web browser, as well as access real-time data using Web queries. For example, you can pull current stock quote information from the Web right into an Excel worksheet. You can also attach comments to your worksheet and send it via a Web-based mail service.

Now that you have an idea of how you can use Excel, grab your mouse and let's get started learning some of the most essential functions of the program.

HANDS on

Launching Microsoft Excel

In this activity, you'll start Microsoft Excel.

> **NOTE** *Before you can start Microsoft Excel, both Microsoft Excel and a current version of Windows (such as Windows Me, Windows 98, or Windows 2000) must be installed on the computer you're using. The figures in this tutorial use Windows 2000; if you are using a different version of Windows, the information appearing on your screen may vary slightly.*

1. Turn on your computer.

After the booting process is complete, the Windows desktop displays.

2. Click the Start button 🏁Start **on the Windows taskbar, point to Programs, and click Microsoft Excel.**

The Excel program starts and its window appears.

EXPLORING THE EXCEL WINDOW

As you already know, the Excel window contains many standard Windows elements, including a title bar, a menu bar, and toolbars. However, the Excel window also contains many items that are unique to the Excel program, as illustrated in Figure 1.5.

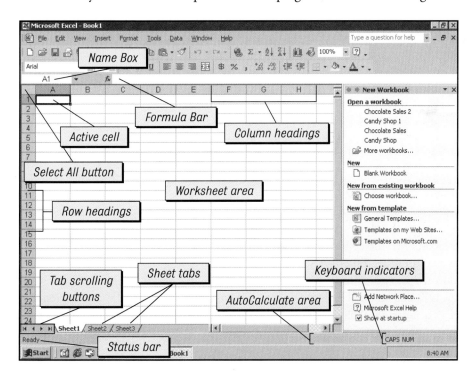

Excel **BASICS**

Launching Microsoft Excel

1. Turn on the computer.

2. Click the Start button and point to Programs.

3. Click Microsoft Excel.

Figure 1.5
Excel window

Just below the toolbars are the Name Box and the Formula Bar. The **Formula Bar** displays the contents of the **active cell**—the cell into which you can currently enter data. A black box called the **cell pointer** surrounds the active cell. You can enter and edit data in the Formula Bar or in the active cell itself. The **Name Box** to the left of the Formula Bar indicates the position of the active cell.

Below the Formula Bar is the worksheet area. The **worksheet area,** which occupies most of the screen, is where your data actually appears. Even though you can enter and edit data in the Formula Bar, many people prefer to do it within the worksheet area instead. The gray area at the top of the worksheet area contains the **column headings,** which are the letters that identify the columns running down the worksheet. The gray area on the left side of the worksheet area contains the **row headings,** which are the numbers that identify the rows running across the worksheet. The gray rectangle in the upper-left corner of the worksheet where the row and column headings meet is the **Select All** button. You can click this button to quickly select all the cells in a worksheet.

As mentioned earlier in this lesson, the worksheet area consists of cells—rectangles formed by the intersection of columns and rows. Of course, the cells are technically separated by **gridlines.** Each cell can hold a single value or a text entry. A cell is identified by its **cell reference,** made up of the column letter and row number. For example, the cell reference of the upper-left cell in a worksheet is called cell A1 because it is located in column A, row 1. The cell directly below cell A1 has a cell address of A2, and so forth. Just as your home address uniquely identifies where you live, so cell references (sometimes called *cell addresses*) indicate where an entry is located.

At the bottom of the worksheet area are the sheet tabs, which you can click to display a different worksheet within a workbook. Additionally, you can use the **tab scrolling buttons** to scroll between sheet tabs if the workbook has more tabs than are currently displayed. The status bar is located at the bottom of the Excel window (right above the Windows taskbar), and is similar to the status bars displayed in other Windows-based applications. The left side of the status bar displays information about a selected command or a current operation, and the right side of the status bar contains keyboard indicators, such as CAPS or NUM. However, one of the unique features of the Excel status bar is the **AutoCalculate area** in the middle of the status bar—you can use it to quickly display the sum, average, or other values of a range of cells.

NAVIGATING WITHIN A WORKSHEET

When you're viewing a worksheet, only a small portion of the entire worksheet is actually shown. In fact, there are 256 columns and more than 65,500 rows in a worksheet! Since letters are used to indicate column headings, and there are only 26 letters in the alphabet, how are columns 27–256 identified? After column Z (the 26th column), the column headings consist of two letters. For example, column 27 has a column heading of AA, column 28 has a heading of AB, and so forth. After column AZ, the column headings become BA–BZ, then CA–CZ, followed by DA–DZ, and so on. The last column in a worksheet is column IV. Always remember that more data may exist in a worksheet than you can see on the screen at the moment, and you are not limited to just entering data in the visible screen area!

Even though a worksheet contains millions of cells, you can enter data into only one cell at a time—the active cell. You can always tell at a glance which cell is the active cell because its cell reference appears in the Name Box, and its contents appear in the Formula Bar. You can make any cell the active cell by clicking it; however, given the fact that an Excel worksheet can be quite large, sometimes the cell you want to make active is quite a distance away! Luckily, the program includes a number of ways that you can quickly navigate within a worksheet. Use the following table to acquaint yourself with some of the keyboard and mouse methods you can use to move around within your worksheet.

Table 1.1	Navigating Within a Worksheet	
To	**Use This Mouse Method**	**Use This Keyboard Shortcut**
Move to an adjacent cell.	Click the cell.	Press the arrow keys.
Move down one screen.	Click in the vertical scroll bar below the scroll box.	Press `PgDn`.
Move up one screen.	Click in the vertical scroll bar above the scroll box.	Press `PgUp`.
Move one screen to the right.	Click in the horizontal scroll bar to the right of the scroll box.	Press `Alt` + `PgDn`.
Move one screen to the left.	Click in the horizontal scroll bar to the left of the scroll box.	Press `Alt` + `PgUp`.
Move to the first worksheet cell (cell A1).	Click the cell.	Press `Ctrl` + `Home`.
Move to a specific cell location.	Click the cell, or issue the Go To command (Edit menu) and enter the cell reference.	Issue the Go To command (press `F5` and enter the cell reference).
Move to the last worksheet cell that contains data.	Click the cell.	Press `Ctrl` + `End`.

HINTS & TIPS

You can split the worksheet screen horizontally or vertically into two panes. To do this, select the column or row where you want to split the worksheet, then choose Split on the Window menu. To redisplay the worksheet in one pane, choose Remove Split (Window menu).

HANDS on

Navigating Within Your Worksheet

To view, enter, and edit data in a worksheet, you need efficient methods of moving the cell pointer to just the location you want. Luckily, you can navigate within a worksheet by using either the keyboard or the mouse. In this activity, you'll open a file in your *Excel Data* folder and practice navigating quickly to various cells.

NOTE *To work through the lessons in this tutorial, you must copy the* Excel Data *folder from the Data CD located on the inside back cover of this tutorial to your hard drive or network drive. If you haven't copied the* Excel Data *folder, ask your instructor for help.*

1. Click the **Open button**  on the Standard toolbar. In the Open dialog box, navigate to your *Excel Data* folder and double-click the *Hickory Hill Horses* workbook to open it.

NOTE *If you need help navigating to a file, ask your instructor for help.*

2. Click **cell D9** (the cell containing *Age*).

Cell D9 becomes the active cell. As illustrated in Figure 1.6, there are several ways in which you can tell that cell D9 is the active cell: the cell pointer (black border) surrounds the active cell; the cell reference appears in the Name Box; and the cell contents are displayed in the Formula Bar. Additionally, column heading D and row heading 9 appear in a contrasting color to indicate that cell D9 is the active cell.

Figure 1.6
Identifying the active cell in a worksheet

Exploring the Worksheet Area

- Click a cell to make it the active cell.

- Press a keyboard arrow key to move the cell pointer.

- Press Ctrl + Home to move the pointer to cell A1.

- Press F5 to display the Go To dialog box.

- Press Ctrl + End to move the pointer to the last cell that contains data.

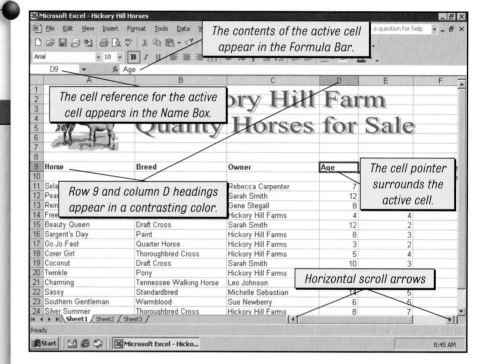

3. Press → four times.

Excel scrolls the display and activates cell H9, displaying the cell reference and contents in the Name Box and Formula Bar, respectively.

4. Press Alt + PgDn.

Excel scrolls one screen to the right, and cell O9 is now the active cell. Notice that the first few columns have scrolled off the screen.

5. Point to the left horizontal scroll arrow and then hold down the mouse button to scroll as far to the left as possible.

When you stop scrolling, column A is redisplayed. However, the Name Box and the Formula Bar show the cell reference and data for cell O9, indicating

The mouse pointer will change shape depending on where it appears on the screen. In the worksheet area, it will appear as a block plus sign. Outside the worksheet area, it will appear as a block arrow.

that it's still the active cell. It is important to note that using the scroll bars to move around the window changes the data you see, but it does not change the active cell. The active cell remains selected until you click another cell.

6. Click cell D21.

Cell D21 becomes the active cell, as indicated by the cell pointer. Now try using the Go To command to quickly locate any worksheet cell—even if you can't see it on your screen.

7. Press F5.

The Go To dialog box is displayed, as shown in Figure 1.7. You can use this dialog box to quickly move the cell pointer to a specific location in your worksheet simply by entering the cell's reference.

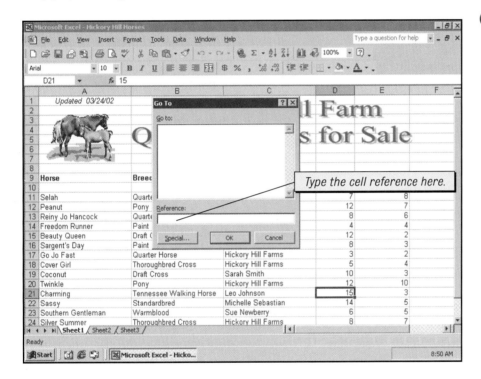

Figure 1.7
Go To dialog box

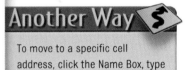

Another Way

To move to a specific cell address, click the Name Box, type the cell address, and press Enter.

8. Type HH650 in the Reference text box, and then press Enter.
(As an alternative to pressing Enter**, you can click OK in the Go To dialog box.)**

The cell pointer moves to cell HH650.

9. Press Ctrl + Home.

Cell A1 becomes the active cell.

10. Press Ctrl + End.

The cell pointer moves to cell I25, the last cell in the worksheet that contains data.

11. Press Ctrl + Home **again to move to cell A1.**

PREVIEWING AND PRINTING A WORKSHEET

Now that you know your way around an Excel worksheet, you're ready to learn more Excel fundamentals such as previewing and printing a worksheet. You'll need printouts for many reasons: to submit assignments to your instructor, to deliver reports to your employer, to mail proposals to clients, and so on. Although Excel offers several advanced printing features, for now you'll just generate a basic print-out of your worksheet.

Before you print a worksheet, it's always a good idea to take a look at it on screen first. A **print preview** provides an accurate on-screen image of your printout. Regularly previewing your worksheets before you print can save valuable time and paper because you can correct mistakes before you generate a hard copy. To use this feature, click the Print Preview button 🔳 on the Standard toolbar (or click Print Preview on the File menu). After you take a look at your worksheet, you can either close the Print Preview window and make additional changes to your file or send the information to the printer by clicking the Print button on the Print Preview toolbar.

If the information in your worksheet is accurate, but you just don't like how your worksheet appears when you view it in Print Preview, you can change the worksheet's layout in the Page Setup dialog box. To access the Page Setup dialog box, click the Page Setup command on the File menu. The dialog box contains four tabs, each of which contains options to change various aspects of your printed worksheet. For example, you can use options on the Page tab of the Page Setup dialog box to make changes to the worksheet's page orientation or to scale it to fit on a specified number of pages.

The **page orientation** refers to how data is printed in relation to the page dimensions. Excel's default way of arranging your worksheet on a printed page is called **portrait orientation.** In portrait orientation, data is printed across the shorter dimension of the page (for example, the 8.5-inch dimension of 8.5 by 11-inch paper). In **landscape orientation,** data is printed across the wider dimension of the page (for example, the 11-inch dimension on 8.5 by 11-inch paper).

When a worksheet does not print attractively in portrait orientation, you can try it in landscape orientation. However, even after you change the page orientation, a worksheet still may not fit on a page attractively. In those cases, you can use **print scaling** to reduce or enlarge the size of printed text without changing the actual font size. To do this, you can use either the *Adjust to* option to specify an exact percentage to which you want to reduce or enlarge text, or you can use the *Fit to* option to automatically "fit" a worksheet onto a specified number of pages.

When you're satisfied that your worksheet data is arranged properly for printing, you're ready to print. To do so, you can click the Print button 🖨 which sends the currently displayed worksheet directly to the printer using Excel's default printing options. Alternately, you can choose Print on the File menu to display the Print dialog box. This gives you a chance to verify printing options before you actually send the job to the printer. Typical print options include identifying the printer you want to use or the number of copies you want to print.

Visit **www.glencoe.com/norton/online/** for more information on Microsoft Excel 2002.

HANDS on

Changing Page Setup Options and Previewing and Printing a Worksheet

In this activity, you'll preview your worksheet, modify page orientation, and print the *Hickory Hill Horses* file.

1. Verify that the *Hickory Hill Horses* workbook is open. Turn on the printer, if necessary.

2. Click the **Print Preview button** .

Excel displays a bird's eye view of the worksheet and shows the Print Preview toolbar at the top of the Print Preview window. Although you can't read the contents of the worksheet in this preview, you can gain a good sense of what the overall printed page(s) will look like.

3. Click the **Zoom button** on the Print Preview toolbar.

Excel enlarges the display so that you can more easily see the worksheet text.

4. Click the **Zoom button** again to return the display to the Full Page View.

Notice that the worksheet appears in portrait orientation, which is the default, and that part of the text is missing from the right side of the page.

5. Click the **Next button** on the Print Preview toolbar.

The remainder of the worksheet appears. If you printed this worksheet now, part of the text would appear on one page and the remainder would appear on another page exactly as shown in Print Preview. Now try changing the page orientation to fit the worksheet on one page.

6. Click the **Close button** on the Print Preview toolbar to close the Print Preview window.

Excel closes the Print Preview window and redisplays the worksheet.

7. Click **Page Setup** on the File menu.

The Page Setup dialog box is displayed, as shown in Figure 1.8.

8. Click the **Page tab** if it is not on top. In the *Orientation* area, click **Landscape**.

Excel BASICS

Working With Printouts

To preview a printout:

1. Click the Print Preview button.

2. Click the Zoom button to zoom in or out.

3. Click the Close button to return to the worksheet area.

To change page setup:

1. Click Page Setup on the File menu.

2. Click the Page tab.

3. Click the desired orientation.

4. Set the Scaling option.

5. Click Print Preview to verify selected options.

6. Click Setup to change page setup or click Print to print the worksheet.

To print a worksheet:

1. Choose Print on the File menu.

2. Verify the printing options.

3. Click OK.

Figure 1.8
Page Setup dialog box

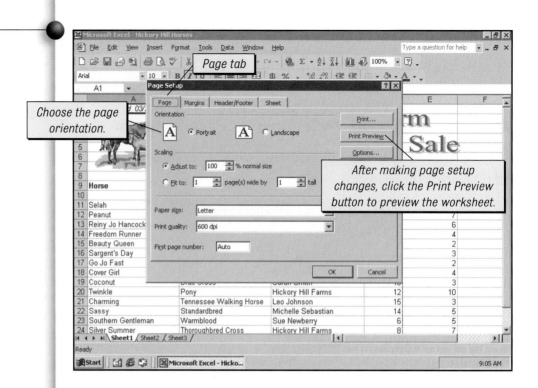

9. Click the **Print Preview button** in the Page Setup dialog box.

A preview of the printout appears in the Print Preview window. You can tell that the printout is still too wide to fit on one page because the Next button on the Print Preview toolbar is active (not dimmed).

10. Click the **Next button** on the Print Preview toolbar to view the next page of the printout.

Even though the worksheet fits better on the pages in landscape orientation than in portrait orientation, it still does not fit on one page.

11. Click the **Setup button** on the Print Preview toolbar to redisplay the Page Setup dialog box.

12. In the *Scaling* area, click the **Fit to option** and verify that this option is set to 1 page(s) wide by 1 tall.

Excel will fit all data in this worksheet onto one page (in landscape orientation).

13. Click **OK** in the Page Setup dialog box.

The worksheet appears on one page in the Print Preview window. Notice that the Next button on the Print Preview toolbar is inactive (dimmed) indicating that all the data is now on one page.

14. Click the **Print button** on the Print Preview toolbar to display the Print dialog box, as shown in Figure 1.9.

Review the print options available in the Print dialog box, and note the default print settings that Excel has preselected.

To change the print scaling option back to 100%, click Page Setup on the File menu and then click the Page tab. Adjust the scaling to 100% normal size and click OK.

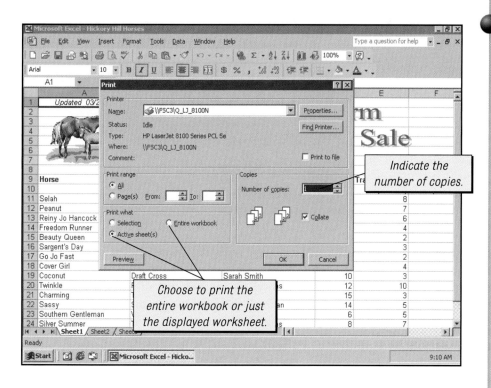

Figure 1.9
Print dialog box

15. Click **OK** in the Print dialog box to print the worksheet using the default print settings.

The worksheet is sent to the printer, reflecting the changes you made in the Page Setup dialog box and the default settings in the Print dialog box.

16. Click the **Print button** 🖨 on the Standard toolbar.

The worksheet prints immediately, without displaying the Print dialog box.

> **NOTE** *Remember, when you click the Print button 🖨 to print a worksheet, the worksheet is sent to the printer immediately; you do not get an opportunity to change options in the Page Setup dialog box or print settings in the Print dialog box. Therefore, to save time, paper, and aggravation, it is a good idea to always click Print Preview 🔍 first!*

17. Click the **Close Window button** ⊠ on the far right side of the menu bar to close the *Hickory Hill Horses* file.

18. Click **No** if Excel asks whether you want to save changes to the file.

Excel closes the workbook file, clearing the Excel window. Since you just closed the only open file, the worksheet area appears blank.

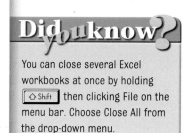

You can close several Excel workbooks at once by holding ⇧ Shift then clicking File on the menu bar. Choose Close All from the drop-down menu.

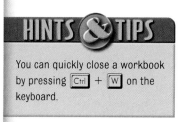

You can quickly close a workbook by pressing Ctrl + W on the keyboard.

ENTERING DATA

You should now be familiar with Excel's window elements and know how to open, navigate, and print a file. You are ready for the next step which involves creating a new, blank workbook and entering data. Creating a new workbook is easy enough—you simply choose New on the File menu and then select Blank Workbook from the New Workbook task pane, or click the New button  on the Standard tool-bar. Entering data requires three steps: (1) select the cell where you want the data to appear; (2) type your data; and (3) finalize the entry. You can finalize or confirm your entry by clicking another cell, pressing [Enter←], or clicking the Enter button ☑ on the Formula Bar.

As you enter information on your worksheet, keep in mind that Excel recognizes three main types of data. First, you can enter **text** (sometimes called *labels*) such as the titles and headings that help others know what the worksheet is all about. You can't perform calculations on text—it is simply there to help others interpret the numerical data. Second, you can enter **values,** such as numbers, dates, and times. Finally, you can create **formulas** to calculate your values in various ways.

Excel determines which type of entry to create based on the first character you type in the cell. If you begin a cell entry with an alphabetic character, Excel realizes you're creating a text entry. When you type only numbers, Excel assumes that you're entering a value. When you type a combination of letters and numbers, Excel treats the data as a text entry. Finally, when you begin an entry with the equal sign, Excel knows that you're creating a formula.

As you enter text, don't worry if your text extends beyond the right border of the active cell. The default column width is only 9 characters, but each cell can include as many as 255. If you enter more than 9 characters in a cell and the adjacent cell to the right is blank, the "extra" characters from the left cell will display in the adjacent cell. On the other hand, if the adjacent cell contains data, the entry in the cell on the left will appear to be truncated (cut off). To confirm that a cell still includes all the data you entered (even though it's not displayed), you can select it and then view its contents in the Formula Bar. To display the full contents of a cell on screen, you can simply widen the column. First, make sure the cell that you want to widen is the active cell. Then point to Column on the Format menu and click AutoFit Selection on the submenu.

HINTS & TIPS

You may include numbers in a text entry. For example, Excel interprets entries such as *Quarter 1, Sales for 2002,* and *2531-IT* as text—and doesn't calculate them.

HANDS on

Adding Data to a Worksheet

In this activity, you'll create a new, blank workbook and then enter text and numbers to show production for a food processing plant that makes cakes and pastries.

1. Click the New button  on the Standard toolbar.

A new, blank worksheet appears and the cell pointer is positioned in cell A1.

2. Press [Caps Lock] to turn on capital letters and type KRISPY KAKE COMPANY.

Notice that the text appears both in cell A1 and in the Formula Bar. The Enter and Cancel buttons for finalizing or canceling your data entry appear in the Formula Bar, as shown in Figure 1.10. The status bar displays messages related to your actions: *Enter* indicates you are entering data; *CAPS* shows that Caps Lock is turned on.

Excel BASICS

Entering Data

1. Click the cell in which you want to enter the data.

2. Type the data.

3. Press [Enter←].

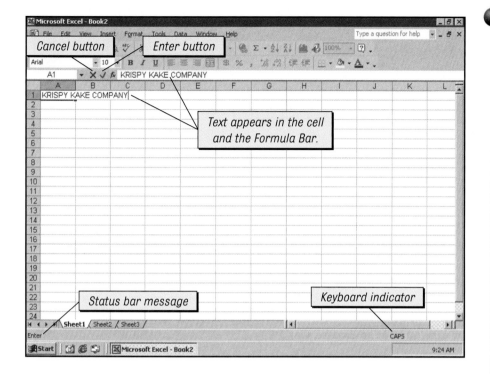

Figure 1.10
Text in the cell and the Formula Bar

EXCEL 2002

3. Press [Enter←].

Excel finalizes the entry and displays the word *Ready* in the status bar, indicating that Excel is ready for you to enter some more data. At the same time, the Cancel and Enter buttons are cleared from the Formula Bar. Finally, the cell pointer moves down one cell to cell A2. (By default, the cell pointer moves down one cell when you press [Enter←].)

4. Type REVENUE **in cell A2.**

5. Press [↓].

Excel finalizes your entry and moves down to cell A3.

6. Press [Caps Lock] **to turn off capital letters.**

7. Type Third Quarter 2002, **and then click the Enter button** ☑ **on the Formula Bar.**

You can finalize data by pressing [Enter←] on the keyboard; by moving the cell pointer to another cell using an arrow key (or by clicking the mouse button); or you can click the Enter button ☑ on the Formula Bar. Notice, however, that the cell pointer did not move to another cell when you clicked the Enter button on the Formula Bar.

8. Click cell A5, type July, **and press** [Enter←].

9. In cell A6, type 122378 **and press** [Enter←].

NOTE *You don't need to type commas or dollar signs or worry about alignment when you enter values. It's more efficient to enter the numbers and then add the formatting later to groups of cells all at once.*

Figure 1.11 shows how Excel arranges each data type in a cell. By default, numbers are aligned on the right side of the cell; the text entries are left-aligned.

HINTS & TIPS

If you leave a blank row between your titles and your data, your worksheet will be easier to read.

Figure 1.11
Default alignment of text
and numbers

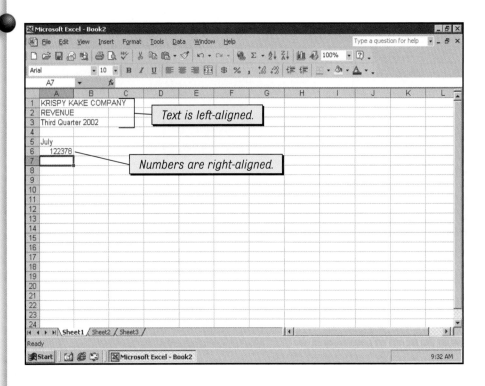

10. Enter the remaining text and numbers from Table 1.2 into the
worksheet to complete data entry of the third quarter sales information. (Do not type any commas within the numbers.)

Table 1.2	Data for Krispy Kake Company		
Cell	**Data to be Typed**	**Cell**	**Data to be Typed**
A7	112751	B9	13425
A8	29013	B10	31245
A9	12834	C5	September
A10	33421	C6	118245
B5	August	C7	115354
B6	114293	C8	36574
B7	116490	C9	12542
B8	30570	C10	35736

Notice that the word *September* does not quite fit within cell C5. To keep it
from intruding into the adjacent cell, you must widen the column.

11. Click **cell C5** then point to **Column** on the Format menu. Click
AutoFit Selection on the submenu.

The column widens and the entire word *September* is visible within cell C5.

12. Press Ctrl + Home. Click the **Save button** 🖫 on the Standard
toolbar.

Because this is the first time you've saved this file, Excel displays the Save As dialog box. This allows you to specify a file name, location, and file format.

13. Type Krispy Kake Company in the *File name* box.

14. Click the **Save in triangle button** and navigate to the *Tutorial* folder in your *Excel Data* folder.

15. Verify that Microsoft Excel Workbook (the default) appears in the *Save as type* box.

16. Click **Save** in the Save As dialog box.

Excel saves your file in the designated folder and displays the new file name in the title bar.

NOTE *Depending on your computer settings, Excel may automatically add an extension of .xls to the end of your file name. This extension identifies the file as an Excel file.*

17. Click **Close** on the File menu.

EDITING CELL CONTENTS

Being able to edit your data entries is almost as important as creating them in the first place. Why? First, it's relatively easy to make mistakes as you enter data. Additionally, you may need to update information in a worksheet to reflect new information such as monthly sales figures. In this section, you'll learn several ways to edit your data efficiently. Before you delve into the hands-on activity, however, it's helpful to know a bit about editing.

When you edit your entries, you'll use either Insert or Overtype mode. In **Insert mode,** which is Excel's default mode, typed text is inserted within existing text, pushing the characters after it to the right. When you're using Insert mode, pressing Delete erases characters to the right of the insertion point, pressing Backspace deletes characters to the left of the insertion point, and pressing ← or → moves the insertion point within the entry. **Overtype mode** is the alternative to Insert mode. In Overtype mode, text replaces existing text as you type.

If you recognize a mistake before you finalize the entry, you can press Backspace to delete one character at a time. Press Esc (or click the Cancel button ✖) to cancel the entire entry and return the cell to its previous state. If you've already finalized your entry, you must select the cell containing the mistake and either edit the contents or overwrite the contents completely. To edit existing text, double-click in the cell you want to edit to place it in **Edit mode.** Drag to select the text you wish to replace and then type your new data. Alternately, you can overwrite the contents of a cell completely without salvaging any existing data by selecting the cell you want to overwrite and then simply typing new data. Finally, if you want to clear the cell of data and leave it blank, press Delete or point to Clear on the Edit menu and click Contents on the submenu.

NORTON ONLINE

Visit **www.glencoe.com/norton/online/** for more information on Microsoft Excel 2002.

HANDS on

Editing Cell Data

In this activity, you'll use various methods to edit the contents of cells in the *Krispy Kake Company* workbook.

1. Open *Krispy Kake Company* in the *Tutorial* folder in your *Excel Data* folder. Click cell D5 and type October**, but do not press** [Enter].

You decide to include a column for quarterly sales after each three-month period (quarter). Since September is the last month of the third quarter, you should enter a column for third quarter sales totals before the October sales column.

2. Press [Esc].

The cell D5 entry is canceled.

3. Type Quarter 3 **and press** [Enter].

4. Click cell A2, *REVENUE*, type Sales**, and press** [Enter].

The newly typed text overwrites the entire contents of the cell. (When an entry is short or you want to replace rather than revise data, it's easier to overwrite the existing text instead of editing it.) Now you will edit (modify) the contents of cell A3 rather than replacing the entire entry as you did with cell A2.

> **WARNING** *Make sure the cell pointer is in cell A3, not cell B3. Even though the text appears to be in both cells, the text is in cell A3. You can confirm this by looking at the Formula Bar. If you select cell B3, no text appears in the Formula Bar.*

5. Double-click cell A3.

An insertion point appears in the cell. The word *Edit* displays on the status bar, indicating that Excel is in Edit mode.

6. Press [End] **to move the insertion point to the right of the last character.**

7. Press [Backspace]**, type** 1**, and press** [Enter].

The edited text appears in cell A3 as shown in Figure 1.12.

8. Click cell E5, type October**, and press** [Enter].

9. Click cell E5 again and press [Delete].

The entry is cleared from the cell.

Excel BASICS

Editing Data

To edit data before pressing [Enter]*:*

- Press [Esc] to cancel the entry and restore the previous cell contents.
- Press [Delete] or [Backspace] to delete characters.

To edit data after pressing [Enter]*:*

- Double-click the cell, drag to select the characters to be replaced, and type new data.

Or

- Click the cell and begin typing new data to overwrite the entire cell contents.

HINTS & TIPS

When a cell is in Edit mode, you must press [Enter] or click the Enter button on the Formula Bar to finalize your entry.

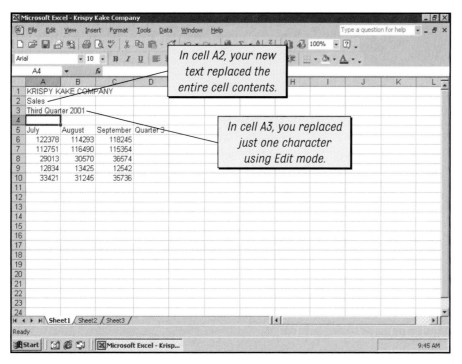

Figure 1.12
Edited text

If you haven't pressed Enter↵, you can cancel a cell entry by clicking the Cancel button on the Formula Bar or pressing Esc.

10. Press Ctrl + Home to move the cell pointer to cell A1, and then click the **Save button** 🔲 to save the changes you made to the *Krispy Kake Company* workbook.

11. Click **Close** on the File menu.

Another Way 💲

You can place an active cell in Edit mode by pressing the F2 key.

USING FOLDERS AND FILES

When you need to open a file, it is important to be able to locate that file quickly. One way to do that is to store related files together in a folder. **Folders** allow you to organize files in a meaningful way by grouping related files together. Creating a new folder is a straightforward process that can be accomplished conveniently in either the Save As or the Open dialog box. Simply click the Create New Folder button 🗁, enter a meaningful name for the new folder, and click OK. However, when creating a folder, you must be aware of *where* you're creating it; whatever drive letter or folder name appears in the *Save in* text box (in the Save As dialog box) or the *Look in* text box (in the Open dialog box) is where your new folder will be located.

Did you know?

If you don't like the name you've given a folder, you can rename it. Right-click the folder in the Open or Save As dialog box, click Rename on the shortcut menu, and type a new folder name.

Sometimes you may need to save an Excel file in a way that allows another program to use it. For example, imagine that you are sharing workbooks with a co-worker who only has access to an older version of Excel. You can save your workbook in a format that both versions of Excel can read so that you can share information seamlessly. Or, perhaps an Excel file contains data that you would like to place in a table in a word processing program. You can save the workbook as a text file that can be read by most word processing applications.

WEB NOTE

You can save a worksheet in HTML format. In the Save As dialog box, choose Web Page from the *Save as type* drop-down list.

Fortunately, with Excel, you can save a workbook using a variety of file formats. **File format** refers to the patterns and standards that a program uses to store data on a disk. But how do you know what file format to use when you save a file? Usually the file format is determined by the type or version of the software that will be used to open the file. So if you decide that, for the most part, your Excel files will be opened using the same version of the Excel application software, you can simply accept the default file format in the Save As dialog box, which is Microsoft Excel Workbook. If, however, you know that the file will be opened in a different application or in an older version of Excel, you can save the file in a different file format. To choose another file format, click Save As on the File menu to open the Save As dialog box. Then click the *Save as type* triangle button and choose a file format from the displayed list.

HANDS on

Creating a New Folder and Saving a Workbook in a Different File Format

In this activity, you'll create a new folder and save the *Krispy Kake Company* workbook in that new folder using a different file format.

1. Open *Krispy Kake Company* in the *Tutorial* folder in your *Excel Data* folder.

2. Click **Save As** on the File menu to display the Save As dialog box.

3. Click the **Create New Folder button** 🗁 on the Save As dialog box toolbar.

As shown in Figure 1.13, the New Folder dialog box appears.

Excel BASICS

Working With Folders and File Formats

To create a new folder:

1. Click the Create New Folder button in the Save As (or Open) dialog box.

2. Type a new folder name in the New Folder dialog box and click OK.

To save a workbook in a different file format:

1. Click the *Save as type* triangle button in the Save As dialog box.

2. Select the appropriate file format from the drop-down list.

3. Change the file name if desired.

4. Click the Save button in the Save As dialog box.

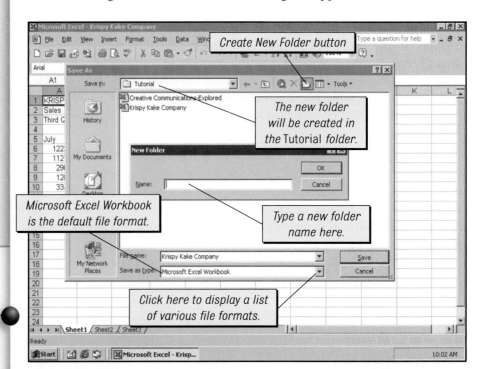

Figure 1.13
New Folder dialog box (within the Save As dialog box)

4. Type Excel 4 Files **in the Name box and click OK.**

The *Excel 4 Files* folder is displayed in the *Save in* box, indicating that this is where the open file will be stored.

5. Click the Save as type triangle button.

A listing of various file formats is displayed.

6. Scroll down the list and click Microsoft Excel 4.0 Worksheet.

You will not overwrite the *Krispy Kake Company* file you saved in the last activity because you've changed the location of this file; however, it is still a good idea to change the file name to avoid any potential confusion.

7. Edit the existing file name to read Krispy Kake Company-Excel 4 Format **in the** *File name* **box and then click Save.**

Excel displays a message box indicating that the older file format doesn't support multiple worksheets in a workbook.

8. Click OK to save only the active sheet and clear the message box.

Your workbook is saved with a new name and file format in a new folder. The new name displays in the title bar.

9. Click Close on the File menu.

The workbook has been removed from memory. You now have two copies of the workbook (one in Microsoft Excel Workbook format and one in Microsoft Excel 4.0 Worksheet format) stored in two separate folders that you can open, view, and modify whenever you'd like.

USING THE SPELLING TOOL AND THE AUTOCORRECT FEATURE

You can rely on Excel's proofing tools—the Spelling tool and the AutoCorrect feature—to identify spelling errors in a worksheet. You can use the Spelling tool to check the spelling of text in a cell, a group of cells (range), a worksheet, or an entire workbook. To activate the feature, click the Spelling button 🗹 on the Standard toolbar or click Spelling on the Tools menu. Words that aren't in Excel's dictionary are highlighted and displayed in the Spelling dialog box. Choose Ignore All in the Spelling dialog box if the word is correct. Change the spelling by selecting or typing the correct entry.

You can also use Excel's AutoCorrect feature to automatically correct typographical errors or misspellings. AutoCorrect can make the following types of corrections:

◆ Correct two initial capital letters by changing the second letter to lowercase.

◆ Capitalize the first letter of a sentence.

◆ Capitalize the names of days.

◆ Correct accidental use of Caps Lock by changing the letters to lowercase except for the first letter of a word that starts a sentence or the names of days.

◆ Replace commonly misspelled or mistyped words with the correct spelling. You can also add commonly misspelled words and their corresponding corrections to the AutoCorrect list.

To confirm that the AutoCorrect feature is turned on (or to change its options), choose AutoCorrect Options on the Tools menu.

HANDS on

Making Corrections to Text

In this activity you'll use both the Spelling tool and the AutoCorrect feature to correct errors in the *Homes Sold* workbook.

1. **Open the *Homes Sold* workbook in your *Excel Data* folder. Cell A1 should be active.**

2. **Click the Spelling button 🧹 on the Standard toolbar.**

The Spelling dialog box appears. The misspelled word *Appalacian* is identified in the *Not in Dictionary* box and two alternate spellings appear in the *Suggestions* box, as shown in Figure 1.14. The cell pointer has identified the location of the error in the worksheet.

NOTE *Move the Spelling dialog box by dragging its title bar to better view the error in the worksheet identified by the cell pointer.*

Excel BASICS

Using the Spelling Checker and AutoCorrect

To use the Spelling tool:

1. Click the Spelling button on the Standard toolbar.

2. Correct highlighted errors.

To use AutoCorrect:

1. Click AutoCorrect Options on the Tools menu.

2. Select the desired features.

3. Click OK and enter data.

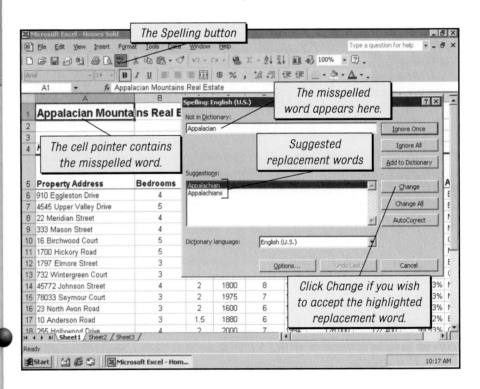

Figure 1.14
Spelling dialog box

3. **With *Appalachian* highlighted in the *Suggestions* box, click the Change button.**

The Spelling tool changes the spelling of *Appalacian* to *Appalachian* and continues to check the spelling in your worksheet. Next, it indicates that *Eto* is not in its dictionary. Since *Eto* is a proper name and is spelled correctly, you can instruct Excel to ignore all occurrences of this word as it continues to check the spelling in the remainder of the worksheet.

4. Click **Ignore All** in the Spelling dialog box.

A message box indicates that Excel has completed the spelling check.

5. Click **OK** to close the message box.

6. Click **AutoCorrect Options** on the Tools menu to open the AutoCorrect dialog box. On the AutoCorrect tab, verify that all check boxes are selected, as shown in Figure 1.15.

If the AutoCorrect Options command does not appear on the Tools short menu, click the double arrow at the bottom of the menu to display the expanded menu.

EXCEL 2002

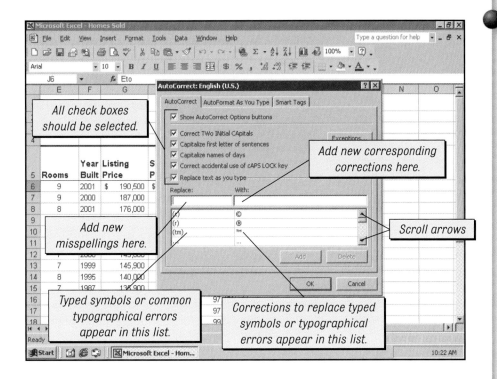

Figure 1.15
AutoCorrect Options dialog box

7. Click the down scroll arrow in the *Replace/With* box until you see *acn* in the *Replace* column and *can* in the *With* column.

8. Click **Cancel** to close the AutoCorrect dialog box. Click in a blank cell in your worksheet, type *acn*, and press ⌷Spacebar⌷.

Excel's AutoCorrect feature recognizes this common typographical error for the word *can* and automatically replaces the word with the correct spelling. (You won't see a change in the word until you press ⌷Spacebar⌷.)

9. Press the **Cancel button** ⊠ to clear the cell.

10. Click **cell A1**. Click **Save As** on the File menu and save the workbook as *Appalachian Mountains* in the *Tutorial* folder in your *Excel Data* folder. Close the file.

To turn off AutoCorrect, click AutoCorrect Options on the Tools menu. Clear the *Replace text as you type* check box and click OK.

FINDING AND REPLACING DATA AND SEARCHING FOR FILES

Occasionally you may want to review or change specific entries without knowing exactly where the data is located within a worksheet. In such instances, you can use Excel's Find command to quickly locate the data. You can then use Excel's Replace command to replace the data with new data.

Both the Find and Replace commands appear on the Edit menu. When you select either of these commands, the Find and Replace dialog box displays. This dialog box contains two tabs—a Find tab and a Replace tab. If you want to locate a specific entry, click Find on the Edit menu to display the Find tab in the Find and Replace dialog box. In the *Find what* text box, type the text, value, or formula you want to locate. Then click Find Next. Excel will move through the worksheet searching for the data and highlighting each occurrence. When you click Find All, Excel displays all occurrences of the data and their exact cell locations in a scrollable list right in the dialog box. Each of the entries in the list appears as a hyperlink that you can click to immediately jump to that location.

If you want to edit or replace several occurrences of data, click Replace on the Edit menu to display the Replace tab in the Find and Replace dialog box. Type the data you want to replace in the *Find what* text box. In the *Replace with* text box, type the replacement data or leave the box blank if you want to delete the data. Click Find Next to find the next occurrence of the data, then click Replace to replace the data; or just click Find Next to leave the data as is and jump to the next occurrence. If you know that you want to replace all occurrences of the data, click Replace All and Excel will globally replace the data throughout the entire worksheet.

Sometimes before you can find data within a file, you need to first find the file itself! Perhaps you know that a file contains a certain word or phrase, but you can't remember the name of the file or where it is stored. Or maybe you would like a list of all the files that contain certain data. You can use Excel's Search command to quickly locate files on your computer, on a network, or even on the Web. You can activate the Search command by clicking the Search button 🔍 on the Standard toolbar or by clicking Search on the File menu. Either of these actions opens the Basic Search task pane where you enter your search criteria and the locations you want to search.

Some computers allow you to save energy by automatically shutting down your monitor after a specified time of inactivity.

Using the Find, Replace, and Search Commands

In this activity, you'll use Find and Replace to locate specific data in the *Appalachian Mountains* workbook. You'll then use Basic Search to locate files on your hard drive.

1. Open the *Appalachian Mountains* workbook in the *Tutorial* folder in your *Excel Data* folder. Click cell **A1**, if necessary, and then click **Find** on the Edit menu.

The Find and Replace dialog box appears.

2. Type Matthews **in the** *Find what* **text box, then click Find Next.**

Excel jumps to the first occurrence of the search text.

3. Click the Replace tab.

4. Double-click *Matthews* **in the** *Find what* **text box, then type** Mayer.

5. Press ⌐Tab⌐ **to move to the** *Replace with* **text box, then type** Bell.

Your dialog box should look like Figure 1.16.

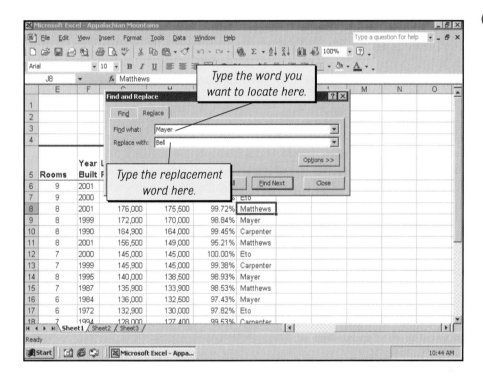

Figure 1.16
Find and Replace dialog box

Excel BASICS

**Finding and Replacing Data
and Searching for Files**

To find data:

1. Click Find on the Edit menu.

2. In the *Find what* box, type the data you want to locate.

3. Click Find Next.

4. Review or edit each occurrence.

5. Close the Find dialog box.

To find and replace data:

1. In the Find dialog box, click the Replace tab or click Replace on the Edit menu.

2. In the *Find what* box, type the data you want to locate.

3. In the *Replace with* box, type the replacement data, then click Find Next.

4. Click Replace to replace each occurrence or click Replace All to replace all occurrences of the data.

To search for a file:

1. Click the Search button on the Standard toolbar.

2. Enter keywords in the *Search text* box of the Search task pane.

3. Click the Search button in the Search task pane.

6. Click the Find Next button.

The cell pointer jumps to Mayer.

7. Click Replace to replace the name *Mayer* **with** *Bell.*

The pointer jumps to the next occurrence of *Mayer.*

8. Click Replace All.

The text is replaced throughout the worksheet. Excel displays a message box to let you know that five additional replacements were made.

9. Click OK to close the message box, and then click Close in the Find and Replace dialog box.

10. Press ⌐Ctrl⌐ + ⌐Home⌐ **to move the cell pointer to cell A1. Save the** *Appalachian Mountains* **workbook as** *Appalachian Mountains Search* **in the** *Tutorial* **folder in your** *Excel Data* **folder. Click the Close Window button** ⌐X⌐ **to close the file.**

NOTE *Whenever you open a workbook, the cell pointer appears in the location it was in when you last saved the file. For that reason, you should develop the habit of moving the cell pointer to cell A1 before saving and closing a workbook.*

Excel's Search feature helps you locate files (rather than the text within a file). In order to change the name *Mayer* to *Bell* in all your Excel workbooks, you must first search for all of the Excel files on your computer that contain the name *Mayer*.

11. Click the Search button 🔍 on the Standard toolbar.

The Basic Search task pane is displayed on the right side of the Excel window. You will enter your search criteria—that is, your search text and the locations you want to search—in this task pane.

NOTE *If the Advanced Search task pane appears instead, click* Basic Search *at the bottom of the task.*

12. Type Mayer **in the *Search text* box.**

Your Basic Search task pane should appear as shown in Figure 1.17. In addition to knowing *what* to search for, Excel needs to know *where* to search. By default, Excel searches all Office files (except Outlook files) and Web pages located on your computer.

Figure 1.17
Basic Search task pane

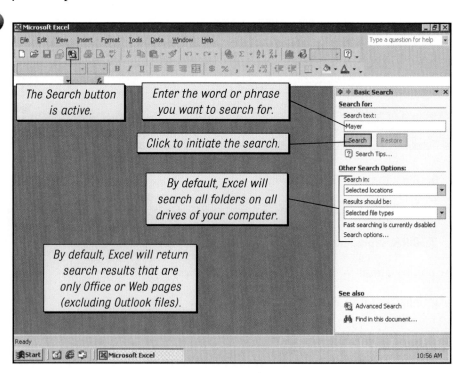

13. Click the Search button in the Basic Search task pane.

After a few moments, a list of files that include the word *Mayer* is displayed in the Search Results task pane.

14. Point to the *Milford Lane Property* workbook on the list.

A ScreenTip appears showing where the file is stored and the date it was last modified. The pointer changes into the shape of a hand (the Hyperlink Select pointer).

15. Click the *Milford Lane Property* workbook to open the file. Click **Replace** on the Edit menu.

The Find and Replace dialog box displays. Notice that *Mayer* still appears in the *Find what* text box and *Bell* appears in the *Replace with* text box.

16. Click **Find Next**, then click **Replace**.

Excel changes the cell entry from *Priscilla Mayer* to *Priscilla Bell.*

17. Close the Find and Replace dialog box. Click **cell A1** and save the revised workbook as *Milford Lane Property-Updated* in the *Tutorial* folder in the *Excel Data* folder. Close the file.

18. Click the **Close button** ☒ in the upper-right corner of the Search Results task pane.

FINDING AND REPLACING CELL FORMATS

You can replace the formatting (appearance) of a cell with another type of formatting. For example, you can replace italic in a cell with bold. Click Options on the Replace tab of the Find and Replace dialog box. Click the Format button to the right of the *Find what* text box. In the Find Format dialog box, click the Font tab. Choose the cell format (such as italic) that you want to find in your worksheet, then click OK. Perform similar steps to set the replacement format: Click the Format button to the right of the *Replace with* text box. In the Replace Format dialog box, click the Font tab and choose the cell format (such as bold) that should replace the existing format. In this example, choose Replace All to quickly replace the italic font style with a bold font style.

Finding and Replacing Formats

In this activity, you will use Find and Replace to replace cell formats within a workbook.

1. Open the *Appalachian Mountains* workbook in the *Tutorial* folder in your *Excel Data* folder. Click **cell A1**, if necessary, and then click **Replace** on the Edit menu.

2. Click the **Options button**, if necessary, to expand the Replace tab.

3. Clear the *Find what* and *Replace with* boxes of data.

4. Click the **Format button** next to the *Find what* text box. On the Font tab of the Find Format dialog box, click **Bold** in the *Font style* box, then click **OK**.

The bold Preview format appears next to the *Find what* text box.

5. Click the **Format button** next to the *Replace with* text box. On the Font tab of the Replace Format dialog box, click **Bold Italic** in the *Font style* box, then click **OK**.

Your dialog box should look like Figure 1.18.

Figure 1.18
Expanded Replace tab

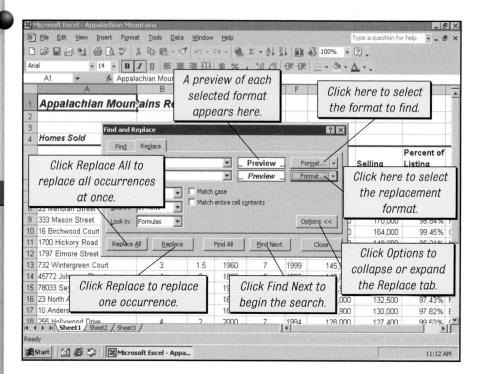

Finding and Replacing Cell Formats

1. Click cell A1, then click Replace on the Edit menu.

2. Click Options, if necessary, to expand the Replace tab.

3. Click the Format button next to the *Find what* box.

4. Click the font, font style, size, or other attribute(s) on the Font tab and click OK.

5. Click the Format button next to the *Replace with* box.

6. Click the replacement font, font style, size, or other attribute(s) on the Font tab and click OK.

7. Click Find Next to begin the search; click Replace or Replace All to apply the new format.

6. Click **Find Next** twice in the Find and Replace dialog box.

The Property Address label is selected.

7. Click **Replace**.

The *Property Address* label becomes bold italic and the adjacent column label *Bedrooms* is selected.

8. Click **Replace All**.

All the text in the worksheet that appears in bold is replaced with the bold italic format; a dialog box informs you of the number of replacements.

9. Click **OK** to close the dialog box. Click **Close** on the Find and Replace dialog box, then scroll to view the changes.

10. Click **cell A1**. Save the *Appalachian Mountains* workbook as *Appalachian Mts Reformatted* in the *Tutorial* folder in your *Excel Data* folder. Close the file.

Conducting Advanced Searches

Have you ever needed to access a file that you *know* you have on your computer, but you just can't remember what you named it? Excel can perform very sophisticated searches to help you locate those elusive files. In this activity, you will use Microsoft Excel Help to learn more about advanced searches.

1. In the Ask a Question box, type find a file, and press `Enter←`. Click **Find a file** in the drop-down list that displays.

2. Click the **Show All hyperlink** in the upper-right corner of the Help window. Read the information.

3. Minimize the Help window and,if necessary, maximize the Excel window.

4. Click the **Search button** 🔍 on the Standard toolbar.

5. Click **Advanced Search** at the bottom of the Basic Search task pane to display the Advanced Search task pane.

6. Applying the information you learned in Microsoft Excel Help, conduct a search for file names that include the word *sports* in your *Excel Data* folder.

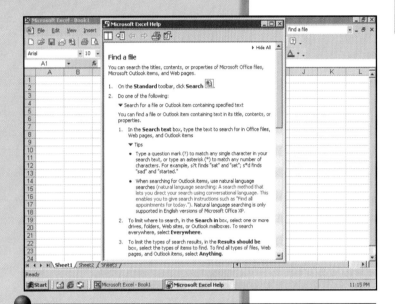

Figure 1.19
Find a file Help topic

Excel should display six files in the Search Results task pane that contain the word *sports* and are stored in the *Excel Data* folder.

7. Close the Search Results task pane.

8. Right-click the **Microsoft Excel Help taskbar** button and click **Close** on the shortcut menu.

ALIGNING DATA AND MERGING AND SPLITTING CELLS

As you know, Excel automatically aligns text on the left side of a cell and aligns numbers on the right side of a cell. You can easily change this default alignment. For example, you can center or right-align a text label to line up better with a column of numbers below. You can also merge cells and center text or numbers across several cells. These features work especially well when you want to center titles above your worksheet data. To add interest to your worksheet, you can also rotate data in a cell or range. Excel allows you to align data quickly with the click of a Formatting toolbar button or by using the Cells command on the Format menu.

You can align data one cell at a time or all at once in a group of cells. First, however, you need to understand a bit about selecting a group, or range, of cells. A **range** is a group of cells in a worksheet. You indicate a range to Excel by providing the first and last cells in the range. For example, the range A1:E5 includes all the cells that make up a rectangular block from cell A1 through cell E5. The most straightforward way to select a range is to hold down the left mouse button and drag over the cells you want to include in the range. Or, if you prefer the keyboard method, click the cell where you want to begin the range to make it the active cell. Then hold down ⇧ Shift and press the appropriate arrow key until the cell pointer is in the last cell of the range. After you select a range, you can execute commands that affect the entire group of cells.

HANDS on

Aligning and Rotating Text and Merging and Splitting Cells

In this activity, you'll select ranges and improve the appearance of the *Sports Shop* workbook by right-aligning and rotating column labels, centering row labels, merging and splitting cells, and centering text across columns.

1. Open the *Sports Shop* workbook in the *Excel Data* folder.

Notice that all the text in this worksheet is left-aligned, and all the numbers are right-aligned.

2. Drag to select the range B5:F5 (the cells containing the column labels).

The cell pointer encompasses cells B5 through F5, and the range is highlighted.

3. Click the Align Right button ▤ on the Formatting toolbar.

Excel right-aligns the selected text so that the labels line up with the numbers below them.

4. With range B5:F5 still selected, click Cells on the Format menu, and then click the Alignment tab.

The Alignment tab of the Format Cells dialog box is divided into four sections, as shown in Figure 1.20. The *Text alignment* section allows you to specify the horizontal and vertical placement of data in cells; the *Orientation* section allows you to specify the degree to which data can be rotated in cells; the *Text control* section allows you to choose more specialized alignment features, such as wrapping text in cells and shrinking text to fit a cell; and the *Right-to-left* section allows you to specify the reading order of the text in the selected cell(s).

Excel BASICS

Aligning and Rotating Data

- To right-align data, select the cell(s) and click the Align Right button.

- To left-align data, select the cell(s) and click the Align Left button.

- To center data in a cell, select the cell(s) and click the Center button.

- To rotate data, select the cell(s), click Cells on the Format menu, and then click the Alignment tab. Click and hold the Degrees up or down arrow until the desired degree of rotation is displayed, and click OK.

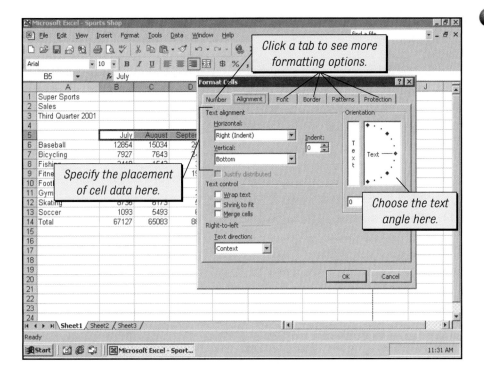

Figure 1.20
Format Cells dialog box
(Alignment tab)

EXCEL 2002

5. Click and hold the **Degrees up arrow** in the *Orientation* section of the dialog box until the angle of rotation reaches **30 degrees**. Release the mouse button and click **OK**.

Excel rotates the text in cells B5:F5 upward at a 30-degree angle.

6. Select **cells A6:A14**.

7. Click the **Center button** ▤ on the Formatting toolbar.

Excel centers the selected text within each cell.

8. Select the **range A1:F1**.

9. Click the **Merge and Center button** ▦ on the Formatting toolbar.

Notice that the cell pointer encompasses the entire range A1:F1. These cells are now **merged** into a single cell. The cell reference for a merged cell is the upper-left cell in the range you selected to merge, and the other cells in the range become inaccessible after the merge is complete. In this case, cell A1 is the cell reference (check the Name Box), and you can't select cells B1:F1. In addition, Excel places only the data in the upper-left cell in the range into the merged cell; if there is data in any other cell in the range, that data will be automatically deleted. Thus, in this instance, if there had been data in cells B1:F1, that data would have been lost.

You can easily reverse the merge operation and **split** a merged cell by selecting the merged cell and clicking the Merge and Center button ▦.

10. Verify that cell A1 is still the active cell, and then click the **Merge and Center button** ▦ again to split the cells. Click **cell A1**.

Now the cell pointer encompasses only cell A1, which contains the data *Super Sports*. Also, you can once again access cells B1:F1. As with many other toolbar buttons, the Merge and Center button is a toggle button—you can turn this command on and off by repeatedly clicking the button.

Excel **BASICS**

Centering Data and Splitting Cells

• To center data over two or more columns and merge the cells together, select the cells that should be merged and click the Merge and Center button.

• To split cells that have been merged, select the cells(s) and click the Merge and Center button.

• To center data over two or more columns without merging the cells together, select the cells over which the data should be centered (including the cell that contains the data), click Cells on the Format menu, click the Horizontal triangle button in the Alignment tab, click Center Across Selection, and click OK.

HINTS & TIPS

To adjust the width of all columns in a worksheet simultaneously, click the Select All button, then drag any column heading boundary. All the columns will be adjusted equally.

11. Once again, select the **range A1:F1** and click the **Merge and Center button** 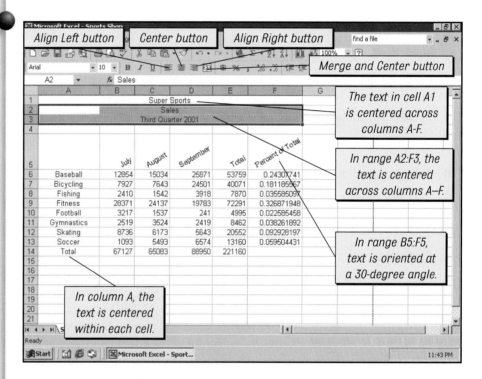.

The range A1:F1 has again been merged into cell A1, and the data is centered in it. Using the Merge and Center button is great when there is data in only one of the cells to be merged, but sometimes you may need to center data across a range when more than one cell contains data.

12. Select the **range A2:F3**.

13. Click **Cells** on the Format menu to display the Format Cells dialog box. If necessary, click the **Alignment tab**.

14. Click the **Horizontal triangle button** and click **Center Across Selection** from the drop-down list. Click **OK**.

Excel centers your text across the selected range, as shown in Figure 1.21. (If you had tried to use the Merge and Center command to center this text, the data in cell A3, *Third Quarter 2001*, would have been deleted.)

Figure 1.21
Text alignment in a worksheet

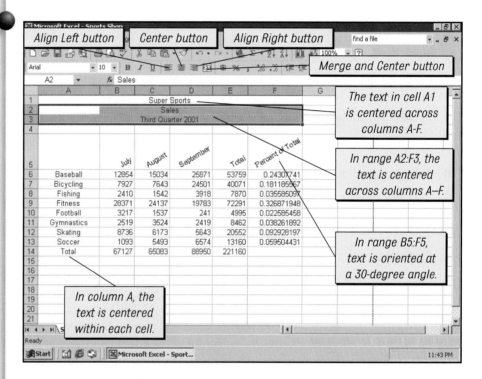

WARNING *When you use the Cells command on the Format menu to center text across a range, the text must be in the leftmost cell of the selected range in order for it to be centered properly in the range. For example, if you have text in cell B1 and center it across the range A1:D1, the text will not center properly.*

15. Click cell **A1**.

The text *Super Sports* appears in the Formula Bar. This text is in cell A1, even though it doesn't appear that way on the screen after you apply the Merge and Center command.

16. Save your revised workbook as *Super Formatting* in the *Tutorial* folder in your *Excel Data* folder, then close the file.

FORMATTING NUMBERS

The numbers you've entered in new worksheets so far have been displayed exactly as you entered them, without commas, dollar signs, or formatting of any type. You can, however, use numeric formats to change the way Excel displays numbers. When you apply a numeric format, you don't modify the way Excel stores the underlying numbers. Formatting changes only the appearance of the data; it does not change the data itself.

Excel has many numeric formats, including formats to add commas, add dollar signs, and display numbers as percentages. Several numeric formats also let you specify exactly how many decimal places are displayed (from 0–15 decimal places).

You can apply numeric formats in two ways. For quick and easy formatting, you can use the buttons on the Formatting toolbar. This toolbar contains several commonly used numeric formats that you can apply with the click of a button. The numeric formats available on the Formatting toolbar are described in Table 1.3. If none of the Formatting toolbar buttons fit your needs, or you want to customize numeric formatting, you can use the options in the Format Cells dialog box.

Table 1.3	Numeric Formats on the Formatting Toolbar	
Name	**Button**	**Function**
Currency Style	$	Displays numbers with fixed dollar signs at the left side of the cell, thousands separators, and two decimal places.
Percent Style	%	Displays numbers as percentages with no decimal places.
Comma Style	,	Displays numbers with thousands separators and two decimal places.
Increase Decimal	.0 .00	Increases the decimal places displayed in the selected cell(s).
Decrease Decimal	.00 .0	Decreases the decimal places displayed in the selected cell(s).

In most cases, when you apply any of these styles, Excel automatically increases the column width to accommodate the extra digits and symbols. However, if Excel cannot display a numeric value completely, it instead shows pound signs (###), to indicate that the number will not fit in the cell. As you may recall, when text is too wide to fit in a cell, it "spills over" into the adjacent cell if that cell is empty, or it is truncated if the adjacent cell contains data. However, this method is not used when displaying numbers, because if a number were truncated, it could easily be misinterpreted. You can widen a column by double-clicking the boundary to the right of the column heading or by dragging the column heading boundary.

HANDS on

Applying Numeric Formats

In this activity, you'll apply numeric formats to the *Super Formatting* workbook to improve its readability and appearance.

1. Open *Super Formatting* in the *Tutorial* folder in your *Excel Data* folder. Select **B6:E13**.

2. Click the **Comma Style button** .

Excel inserts commas as thousands separators and adds two decimal places in the selected range.

3. Click the **Decrease Decimal button** two times.

Each number is displayed with commas but without decimal places.

4. Click cell **B6**.

NOTE *Notice that a comma is displayed in the cell but not in the Formula Bar. The stored number (rather than the displayed number) is shown on the Formula Bar when a cell is active. Formatting only affects the appearance of the data, not the data itself.*

5. Select the **range B14:E14**.

6. Click the **Currency Style button** .

The cells in range B14:E14 now include dollar signs, thousands separators, and two decimal places.

NOTE *If necessary, double-click the boundary to the right of the column heading to widen the column or drag the column heading boundary to adjust the width.*

7. Click the **Decrease Decimal button** two times.

8. Select **cells F6:F13**, then click the **Percent Style button** .

9. Click the **Increase Decimal button** once.

10. Point to the border between column headings A and B. When the pointer becomes a double-headed arrow, drag the border to the left to slightly reduce the size of Column A.

11. Click **cell A1** and save the file as *Super Formatting-1* in the *Tutorial* folder in your *Excel Data* folder. Close the workbook.

Applying Numeric Formats

1. Select the cells to which you want to apply a numeric format.

2. Click the appropriate numeric style button(s).

3. Click the Increase Decimal or Decrease Decimal button to adjust the number of decimal places.

MODIFYING FONT CHARACTERISTICS AND CLEARING CELL FORMATS

So far, you've improved the appearance of your workbook by changing the alignment of text and adding numeric formats. Another easy way to dress up your workbook is to modify the font characteristics of a cell. For example, you can change the typeface, increase or decrease the font size, and add bold, italic, or underline. You can also add borders around cells, change the color of the background of cells, and change the text color. Modifying font characteristics doesn't change the underlying data—it just makes the workbook easier to read and more visually appealing.

The most widely used font-enhancing options are available as buttons on the Formatting toolbar. However, if you want to make several formatting changes at once (or to have more choices available), you can use the Format Cells dialog box. As an example, in the Format Cells dialog box, you can choose a new typeface, a new font size, bold style, and a different color—all in one operation.

If you later decide you want to restore a cell (or range) to its unformatted state, you can clear the cell formatting without affecting the cell contents. To remove all formatting from a range, select the cell(s), point to Clear on the Edit menu, and click Formats on the submenu. If you want to remove only the most recent formatting change that you've made, you can click the Undo button ⟲▾ on the Standard toolbar.

HANDS on

Applying Font Characteristics and Removing Formats

In this activity, you'll improve the appearance of the *Super Formatting* workbook by modifying the font characteristics of selected cells using the Formatting toolbar and the Format Cells dialog box. You will also clear cell formats and then undo the action (restore the formats).

1. Open *Super Formatting-1* in the *Tutorial* folder in your *Excel Data* folder and select the **range B5:F5**.

2. Click the **Bold button** ⓑ on the Formatting toolbar.

Excel changes the text in the selected cells to bold type.

3. Click **cell A1**.

4. Click the **Font Size triangle button** [10 ▾] and click **14**.

Excel changes the font size of the text in the selected cell.

5. Select **cell A2** and click the **Italic button** [*I*], then click **cell A14** and click the **Bold button** ⓑ.

6. Click the **Select All button** above row heading 1 to select all of the cells in the worksheet.

The entire worksheet is highlighted, indicating that all the cells are selected.

7. Click the **Font triangle button** [Arial ▾], scroll the list of fonts, and click **Times New Roman**.

The selected text changes to Times New Roman. (The available fonts may vary depending upon your printer and installed fonts. If Times New Roman is not displayed in your list of available fonts, choose another font.)

8. **Select cells A1:A3 and change the font to Arial.**

The worksheet titles are changed back to the Arial typeface. Since you selected Times New Roman as the font for the rest of the worksheet, any new text you enter will be shown in Times New Roman.

9. **Click any cell in the worksheet to deselect the range. Click cell A3 and then click Cells on the Format menu. Click the Font tab.**

10. **In the Font style section, click Italic. Click the Underline triangle button and click Single.**

Your dialog box should look like Figure 1.22. Notice that the Preview window shows sample text as Arial, italic, 10 point, and underlined.

Figure 1.22
Format Cells dialog box

Applying Font Characteristics and Removing Formats

To apply font characteristics:

1. Select the cell(s).

2. Click the appropriate toolbar button(s) to apply the formatting.

Or

1. Select the cell(s).

2. Click Cells on the Format menu, click the Font tab, and select the desired options.

To remove cell formats:

1. Select the cell(s).

2. Point to Clear on the Edit menu then click Formats.

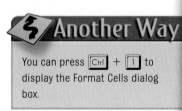

You can press Ctrl + 1 to display the Format Cells dialog box.

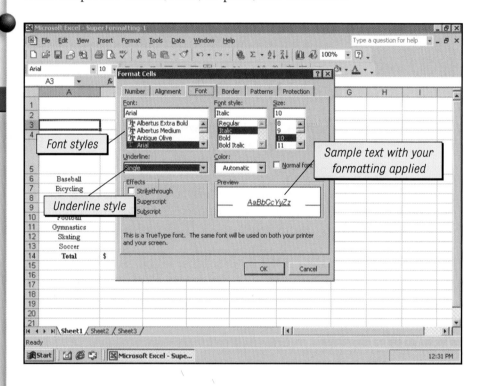

11. **Click OK to close the Format Cells dialog box.**

WARNING *Changing the appearance of text in your worksheet may result in truncation if the column is not wide enough. For example, bold text takes up more horizontal space than regular text. To widen a column, double-click the boundary to the right of the column heading.*

Now you will clear the formatting from cells without affecting the cell contents.

12. **If necessary, click cell A3 to select it. Point to Clear on the Edit menu, then click Formats on the submenu.**

All formatting is removed from the selected cell, but the data remains in place. Notice that even the alignment formatting has been removed.

13. Click the **Undo button**  on the Standard toolbar.

Your last action (removing the formatting) is reversed.

14. Click **cell A1**, then save the workbook as *Super Formatting-2* in the *Tutorial* folder in your *Excel Data* folder. Close the file.

USING AUTOFORMATS

Manually applying font characteristics and numeric formatting to your workbook can be a slow, laborious process. Unless you have a good sense of design and balance, the end result may not be visually pleasing. To make formatting easier and create professional-looking worksheets, Excel provides 16 ready-made worksheet designs called **AutoFormats.** You access these designs by selecting the range you want to format and then choosing AutoFormat on the Format menu. When you apply an AutoFormat, it overrides any existing formatting. For example, if the selected text is bold and you apply an AutoFormat that doesn't include bold text, Excel removes the bold style.

HANDS on

Applying an AutoFormat

In this activity, you'll use the AutoFormat feature to quickly format a worksheet.

1. Open the *Furniture Company* workbook in your *Excel Data* folder and save the file as *Furniture Company with Formatting* in the *Tutorial* folder in your *Excel Data* folder.

2. Select the **range A4:F10**, and then click **AutoFormat** on the Format menu.

Excel displays the AutoFormat dialog box. A sample of each AutoFormat is displayed in the dialog box.

3. Scroll the list to view all the samples. Then click the **Classic 2 sample**.

A dark border surrounds the Classic 2 sample indicating it has been selected, as shown in Figure 1.23.

4. Click **OK** to apply the format, and then click anywhere to deselect the range A4:F10.

> **Excel BASICS**
>
> **Using the AutoFormat Feature**
>
> **1.** Select the range to be formatted.
>
> **2.** Click AutoFormat on the Format menu.
>
> **3.** Click the sample of the format you wish to use.
>
> **4.** Click OK to apply the format.

Figure 1.23
AutoFormat dialog box

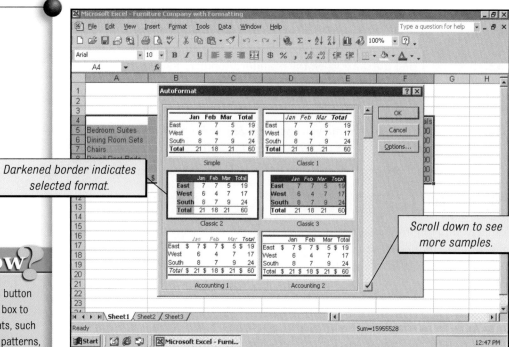

Darkened border indicates selected format.

Scroll down to see more samples.

Excel applies the selected AutoFormat to the range you specified.

5. **Preview and print the worksheet.**

6. **Click cell A1, and save and close the** *Furniture Company with Formatting* **workbook.**

USING THE COMMENTS FEATURE

It is not unusual in business to receive worksheet data sent by others for review. Excel's Comments feature makes it possible to embed comments directly into a worksheet cell while reviewing the worksheet. It's helpful to use the Comments feature when you want to add notes to a cell because comment text won't affect the worksheet contents. A workbook containing comments may be sent as an e-mail attachment in order to request feedback.

HANDS on

Inserting Comments in a Workbook

In this activity you will insert, hide, and display a comment in a workbook; then you will e-mail the file to a recipient of your choice.

1. **Open the** *Surfside Sales* **workbook in your** *Excel Data* **folder.**

Notice that this workbook contains two worksheets, each of which contains data.

2. Click the **Sales sheet tab** to view the first quarter sales data. Then click the **Income Statement sheet tab** to view the first quarter income statement. Click **cell B6** on the *Income Statement* worksheet, then click **Comment** on the Insert menu.

A comment box displays so that you can add notes to the cell. The name of the author of the comment is automatically displayed.

3. Type *Sales are up!* in the Comment box, as shown in Figure 1.24.

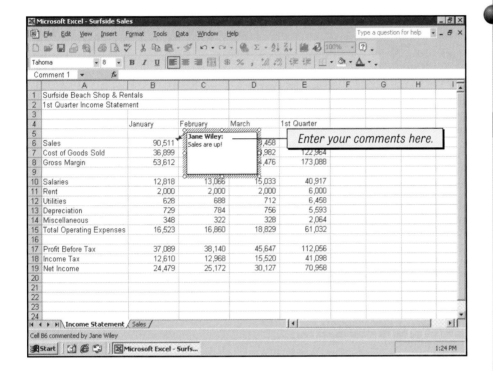

Figure 1.24
Comments feature

Excel **BASICS**

Inserting and Editing Comments

To add or read a comment:

1. Click the cell in which you want to add a comment.

2. Click Comment on the Insert menu.

3. Type the comment text in the comment box.

4. Click a different cell to close the comment box.

5. To read a comment, point to a cell containing a red comment marker.

To edit a comment:

1. Click a cell containing a red comment marker.

2. Click Edit Comment on the Insert menu, then type changes in the comment box.

4. Click outside the box.

A red comment indicator appears in the upper-right corner of the cell.

5. Point to **cell B6** to display the comment. Select **cell B6** to make it the active cell, then choose **Edit Comment** from the Insert menu.

The comment appears selected, as shown by the hatched border and the selection handles. When the comment box is in this state you're able to edit its contents.

6. Select the existing comment text and type *Sales were down in January, but increased overall during the first quarter.*

7. Click outside the cell to hide the comment's display, and click **cell A1**. Click **Save As** on the File menu and save your workbook as *Comments* in the *Tutorial* folder in your *Excel Data* folder. Point to **cell B6**.

Your edited comment should look like Figure 1.25.

Figure 1.25

Edited comment

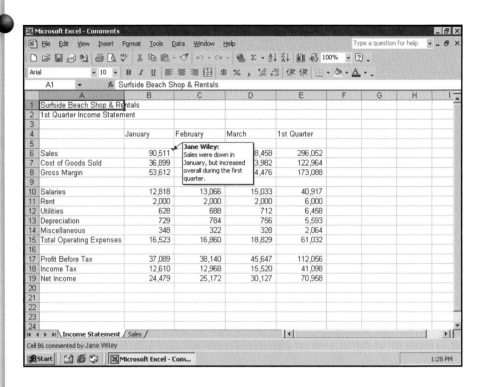

Now try sending your workbook to another user via e-mail.

8. Point to Send To on the File menu, and click Mail Recipient (as Attachment) from the submenu.

NOTE *If the Choose Profile dialog box appears requesting your profile name, check with your instructor.*

Your mail application (such as Outlook Express) automatically launches and creates a new mail message with your *Comments* workbook attached.

9. In your mail application window, enter the e-mail address of your instructor or another student in the *To* text box.

10. Click the Send button (in your mail application window).

Depending on how your messaging software is set up, your message is either placed in the program's Outbox or sent directly to your recipient. If possible, have the recipient add another comment in the worksheet and send the file back to you.

11. Close the *Comments* workbook.

Self Check

Test your knowledge by answering the following questions. See Appendix B to check your answers.

1. To jump quickly to cell A1, press _____ .

2. A darkened border that surrounds a cell is called the _____ and identifies the cell as the _____ .

3. The column letter and row number combination used to identify a specific cell is known as the _____ .

4. When you enter data, pressing _____ finalizes the data you type and moves the cell pointer down one cell.

5. To restore the original contents of a cell in which you've begun to replace the text, press _____ .

COLLABORATING ON THE WEB

In today's business environment, it is often necessary to work together with your colleagues, suppliers, and clients to gather input, solve problems, or provide feedback. In Excel, you can use the Web Discussions feature to participate in an online conversation about an Excel workbook. Every participant with permission to access the server can attach discussion comments to a file for other participants to view and respond to.

> **NOTE** *A server administrator must set up the Web Discussions feature before you can use it. Check with your instructor, lab assistant, or network administrator to verify that your computer can connect to a discussion server and that you have the appropriate permission to view and respond to discussions.*

In a Web discussion, even though the comments are viewed with the file, they may actually be stored separately on a **discussion server**—a computer that stores the discussion comments and information about the location of the file being discussed. (The file itself may be stored on another computer.) The discussion comments are **threaded;** that is, all the responses related to a comment are nested below it in a hierarchical manner so that the discussion is easy to follow. In this activity, you will create a discussion about the *Surfside Sales* workbook in your *Excel Data* folder using the Web Discussions feature.

> **NOTE** *You may complete this activity working as a member of a team consisting of two or three peers; however, you may also complete it individually. If you are working as a member of a team, a different team member should enter each of the comments in the steps below to create the threaded discussion.*

1. Open the *Surfside Sales* workbook in your *Excel Data* folder.

2. Point to **Online Collaboration** on the Tools menu and click **Web Discussions**.

The Web Discussions toolbar appears at the bottom of the Excel window, above the status bar.

3. Click the **Insert Discussion about the Workbook button** 🖻 on the Web Discussions toolbar.

4. In the *Discussion subject* text box, type surfside sales.

5. In the *Discussion text* area, type the following comment and click **OK**:

   In order to achieve our year-end projections, we must increase sales and/or decrease expenses in the upcoming second quarter. Since spring is just around the corner, I suggest we have a "Spring Break" sale of our smaller merchandise, such as sunscreen, sunglasses, and beach toys. Do you have some other ideas?

Your comment appears in the Discussion pane at the bottom of the window. The name and location of the open file are displayed at the top of the discussion pane. The discussion pane also includes the subject line you typed, your name, the message text, and the date and time of the message.

6. Click the **Show a menu of actions triangle button** 🖃 at the end of the comment you just typed.

A shortcut menu appears providing options to Reply, Edit, or Delete the comment.

7. Click Reply.

The Enter Discussion Text dialog box appears for you to enter a reply to the original comment.

8. Type the following, then click OK:

These are all great ideas to improve the bottom line. In addition, it might make sense to examine the new line of swimwear we were contacted about last week. The profit margins on this product would be a great improvement.

NOTE *If you are working as a member of a team, you may need to click the Discussions button* Discussions ▾ *and click Refresh Discussions to download a newly entered comment from the server.*

The reply appears beneath (and subordinate to) the original comment in the discussion pane. Additional comments can be added in the same thread.

9. Click the Show a menu of actions triangle button ▾**, click Reply, type the following, and click OK:** I checked into the feasibility of the new swimwear line. Assuming it is of the same quality, this line is very promising.

If you are working with other team members, your threaded Web discussion may appear similar to Figure 1.26.

10. Click the Close Web Discussions button Close**. Close the** *Surfside Sales* **workbook.**

WARNING *You may proceed directly to the exercises for this lesson. If, however, you are finished with your computer session, follow the "shut down" procedures for your lab or school environment.*

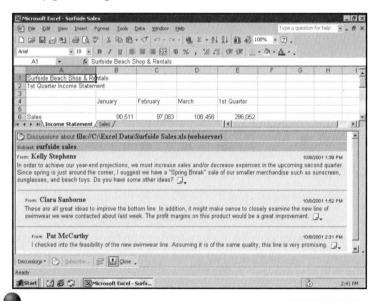

Figure 1.26
Threaded Web Discussion

SUMMARY AND EXERCISES

SUMMARY

Worksheets allow you to present data in an organized form and to perform calculations on that data. In this lesson, you learned basic worksheet terminology, how to navigate within an Excel worksheet, and how to preview and print a worksheet. You also created a new workbook and entered text and values into a worksheet. So that you could modify your data, you learned the basics of editing cells, including the use of the Spelling tool and the AutoCorrect feature. You created a new folder and saved a file in a different file format. You used the Find and Replace commands to locate and replace data within files, and you used the Search command to find files on your hard drive or network drive. To make your worksheets look professional, you applied formatting to cells and ranges using the Formatting toolbar, the Format Cells dialog box, and AutoFormats. Finally, you learned some techniques to collaborate effectively on the Web by using e-mail to send a workbook that contains comments and by creating and participating in a Web discussion.

Now that you have completed this lesson, you should be able to do the following:

- Describe the purpose of worksheets for personal and business use. (page 256)
- Explain the differences between a workbook and a worksheet. (page 258)
- Identify the unique features of the Excel application window. (page 259)
- Navigate within the worksheet area using the mouse, arrow keys, and keyboard combinations. (page 260)
- Preview a worksheet before printing. (page 264)
- Change the page setup options and print a worksheet. (page 265)
- Create a new workbook and enter text and values. (page 267)
- Edit the contents of a cell before finalizing the entry. (page 271)
- Modify existing text. (page 272)
- Overwrite the contents of a cell with new data. (page 272)
- Create a new folder. (page 273)
- Save a workbook using a different file format. (page 274)
- Use the Spelling tool to verify the spelling of text entries. (page 275)
- Use the AutoCorrect feature to correct common mistakes. (page 275)
- Use the Find and Replace commands to locate and replace text. (page 278)
- Use the Search command to locate files. (page 278)
- Use Find and Replace to change cell formats. (page 281)
- Align and rotate data. (page 283)
- Merge and split cells. (page 284)
- Apply various numeric formats. (page 287)
- Modify font characteristics such as sizes, styles, and typefaces. (page 288)
- Clear cell formats. (page 288)
- Apply predefined formatting to your worksheets using the AutoFormat feature. (page 291)
- Add comments to worksheet cells. (page 292)
- Send an Excel workbook as an e-mail attachment. (page 292)
- Discuss a workbook online using the Web Discussions feature. (page 296)

CONCEPTS REVIEW

1 TRUE/FALSE

Circle T if the statement is true or F if the statement is false.

T F **1.** A worksheet is made up of a series of columns and rows that form a grid.

T F **2.** Each worksheet in a workbook is like a page in a notebook.

T F **3.** When you apply an AutoFormat, it overrides existing formatting.

T F **4.** You finalize data that you enter in a cell by pressing the ⇧ Shift key.

T F **5.** Excel interprets text and values the same way in a worksheet, and can perform calculations on both types of entries.

T F **6.** When you click the Print button on the Standard toolbar, the Print dialog box appears, giving you the opportunity to change the printing options before the job is sent to the printer.

T F **7.** You can save Excel workbooks using a variety of file formats.

T F **8.** When you remove formatting from a cell, the cell contents remain unchanged.

T F **9.** You must select a cell to make it the active cell before you can enter text in it.

T F **10.** To move to cell A1, press Ctrl + Home.

2 MATCHING

Match each of the terms on the left with the definitions on the right.

TERMS

1. cell reference
2. cell pointer
3. workbook
4. range
5. landscape orientation
6. Formula Bar
7. values
8. text
9. Overtype mode
10. column headings

DEFINITIONS

a. Specialized name for a group of related Excel worksheets

b. Displays the cell contents of the active cell

c. Data that can be used in calculations

d. Data used for descriptive purposes

e. Text replaces existing text as you type

f. Box surrounding the active cell

g. The letters that identify the columns in a worksheet

h. group of cells

i. Printing across the 11-inch dimension of 8.5 by 11-inch paper

j. Cell identifier formed by a column letter and a row number

3 COMPLETION

Fill in the missing word or phrase for each of the following statements.

1. You can press _____ to quickly display the Go To dialog box.

2. An easy way to determine your position in the worksheet area is to glance at the _____ , which contains the cell reference of the active cell.

3. The intersection of a column and a row is a(n) _____ .

4. You can view how your worksheet will print before actually sending it to a printer by using the _____ feature.

5. To create a new workbook, click the _____ button.

6. To finalize an entry, you can click another cell, press the _____ key on the keyboard, or click the _____ button on the Formula Bar.

7. By default, numbers are aligned on the _____ , and text is aligned on the _____ .

8. You can add _____ , or notes, to a cell.

9. When you _____ a range of cells into a single cell, the cell reference becomes the upper-left cell in the range.

10. A preset group of formatting options is called a(n) _____ .

4 SHORT ANSWER

Write a brief answer to each of the following questions.

1. Suppose you typed *scarlet* in a cell, pressed [Enter←], and then decided to change the text to *red*. What would be an efficient way to change the entry and why?

2. What's the difference between using the Merge and Center button on the Formatting toolbar and using the Center Across Selection option in the Format Cells dialog box? Briefly describe when you would use each.

3. Approximately how large is the worksheet area, in terms of columns and rows?

4. In which two places on the worksheet can you enter and edit data?

5. Why is it important to be able to save an Excel workbook in a different file format?

6. What is the relationship between worksheets and workbooks?

7. Describe when you would manually add formatting features and when you might use an AutoFormat.

8. Describe how you could find the text *ABC Company* and replace it with *XYZ Company* throughout your workbook.

9. What happens when a number is too wide to fit in a cell? Why does this happen?

10. Suppose you have a document that doesn't quite fit on a single page. Describe at least two ways you could try to fit it on a single page.

5 IDENTIFICATION

Label each of the elements in Figure 1.27.

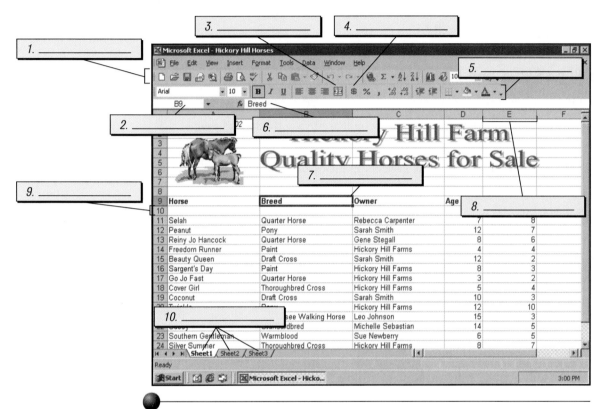

Figure 1.27

SKILLS REVIEW

Complete all of the Skills Review problems in sequential order to review your skills to navigate and print a workbook; enter and edit data and clear cells; save a file in a new folder in a different file format; check spelling and use AutoCorrect; use Find and Replace and Search; format a worksheet; merge and split cells; insert comments; apply an AutoFormat; use the Web Discussions feature; and close a workbook.

1 Launch Excel and Explore a Workbook

1. Click the **Start button** ![Start], point to **Programs**, and click **Microsoft Excel**.

2. Click the **Open button** on the Standard toolbar. In the Open dialog box, navigate to your *Excel Data* folder and double-click the *Personnel Records* workbook to open it.

3. Press Ctrl + End to move to the end of the worksheet.

4. Press PgUp to move up one screen.

5. Click **cell A5**.

6. Press ⟶ four times to navigate to cell E5.

7. Press F5, type BC47 in the Reference text box of the Go To dialog box, and press Enter⏎.

8. Press Ctrl + Home to return to cell A1.

2 Use Page Setup and Preview and Print a Worksheet

1. With the *Personnel Records* workbook open, click the **Print Preview button** 🔍.

2. Click the **Next button** on the Print Preview toolbar to view the second page of the printout.

3. Click the **Setup button** to open the Page Setup dialog box.

4. On the Page tab, change the orientation to Portrait. Click **OK** to close the Page Setup dialog box and redisplay the Print Preview window.

5. Click the **Zoom button** on the Print Preview toolbar to enlarge the display.

6. Scroll in the Print Preview window to view the entire workbook; then click the **Zoom button** again to return to the full-page view.

7. Click the **Print button** 🖨 on the Print Preview toolbar to display the Print dialog box.

8. Verify that the number of copies is set to 1, then click **OK**.

9. Click the **Print Preview button** 🔍. Click **Setup**, then click **Landscape** on the Page tab of the Page Setup dialog box.

10. In the Scaling area, select **Fit to 1 page(s) wide by 1 tall**, and click **OK**. Click **Zoom**, scroll the workbook, and click **Zoom** again.

11. Click **Print**, verify that the number of copies is set to 1, and click **OK**. Close the workbook.

3 Enter and Edit Data in a Worksheet

1. Open *Personnel Records* in your *Excel Data* folder and save it as *Updated Personnel Records* in the *Skills Review* folder in your *Excel Data* folder.

2. Click **cell D10** in the *Updated Personnel Records* workbook and view the cell reference information in the Formula Bar and the Name Box.

3. Press F2 to place cell D10 in Edit mode, and then edit the existing entry to be 3/24/1994. Click the **Enter button** ✓ on the Formula Bar to finalize your entry.

4. Press F5 to display the Go To dialog box. Type A49 in the Reference text box, then click **OK**.

5. Enter the information in Table 1.4 in cells A49 through E49.

6. Click **cell D49**, press Delete, type 3/24/1992, and press Enter⏎.

7. Click **cell C49**, then point to **Clear** on the Edit menu and click **Contents**. Type 42000 and click the **Enter button** ☑.

8. Press `Ctrl` + `Home` to move the cell pointer to cell A1; then click the **Save button** 🖫 to save the *Updated Personnel Records* workbook.

Table 1.4	Workbook Data
Cell	**Data**
A49	Bell
B49	Rebecca
C49	40000
D49	2/24/1995
E49	435-21-1253

4 Create a New Folder and Save a Workbook in a Different File Format

1. Click **Save As** on the File menu to display the Save As dialog box.

2. Click the **Create New Folder button** 📁 on the dialog box toolbar.

3. Type Text Files in the Name text box and click **OK**.

4. Click the **Save as type triangle button**, and click **Text (Tab delimited)**.

5. Edit the existing file name to read **Updated Personnel Records-Text Format** in the *File name* text box and click **Save**.

6. In the Warning dialog box, click **OK** to save only the active sheet.

7. In the message dialog box, click **Yes** to keep this format.

8. Close the workbook. If a message box appears asking if you want to save the changes you made, click **Yes**. (If the Warning and message dialog boxes appear again, repeat steps 6 and 7.)

5 Use the Spelling Tool and the AutoCorrect Feature

1. Open the *Sales Territories* workbook in your *Excel Data* folder.

2. Click the **Spelling button** ☑ on the Standard toolbar. Read the first suggested correction and click **Change**.

3. Correct the remaining misspellings in the worksheet by clicking the appropriate button in the Spelling dialog box to either change or ignore any words that are not in the Excel dictionary. Click **OK** when the spell check is complete.

4. Click **AutoCorrect Options** on the Tools menu.

5. On the AutoCorrect tab, type **regoin** in the *Replace* text box, and type **region** in the *With* text box. Click the **Add button** and click **OK** to close the dialog box.

6. In cells B3, B9, and B15, type the misspelled word **Regoin** and press `Enter↵`. Excel corrects the word automatically.

7. Click **AutoCorrect Options** on the Tools menu. On the AutoCorrect tab, type **reg** in the Replace box. Click the regoin/region entry and click the **Delete button**. Click **OK**.

8. Press `Ctrl` + `Home` to move to cell A1, and save the file as *Spell Check* in the *Skills Review* folder in your *Excel Data* folder. Close the workbook.

SUMMARY AND EXERCISES

6 Use Find, Replace, and Search

1. Open the *Updated Personnel Records* workbook in the *Skills Review* folder in your *Excel Data* folder.

2. Click **Find** on the Edit menu to display the Find and Replace dialog box. Type Lee in the *Find what* text box, and click **Find Next** to highlight the first occurrence of the text. Continue to click **Find Next** to locate all occurrences. Close the Find and Replace dialog box.

3. Select **cells A5:E5** and click the **Bold button** `B`. Press `Ctrl` + `Home` to move the cell pointer to cell A1.

4. Press `Ctrl` + `F` to display the Find and Replace dialog box. Press `Delete` to clear the *Find what* text box. Click the **Replace tab**.

5. Click the **Options button** to expand the Replace tab. Click the **Format button** to the right of the *Find what* text box. In the Find Format dialog box, click the **Font tab**, click **Bold** in the Font style list, and click **OK**.

6. Click the **Format button** to the right of the *Replace with* text box. In the Replace Format dialog box, click **Bold Italic** in the Font style list, and click **OK**.

7. Click the **Find Next button**. Click **Replace** to change the formatting of the column label *Last Name*. Click **Replace** four more times to change the formatting of the remaining column labels.

8. In the Find and Replace dialog box, click the **Format triangle button** to the right of the *Find what* text box and click **Clear Find Format**. Click the **Format triangle button** to the right of the *Replace with* text box and click **Clear Replace Format**. Click the **Options button** to collapse the Find and Replace dialog box to its original size.

9. Type 35000 in the *Find what* text box and type 37500 in the *Replace with* text box. Click **Replace All**.

10. Click **OK** in the message box, and then close the Find and Replace dialog box.

11. Press `Ctrl` + `Home`. Save your *Updated Personnel Records* workbook as *Updated Personnel Records-1* in the *Skills Review* folder in your *Excel Data* folder.

12. Now you want to search for all files related to the Tennessee Furniture Company. Click the **Search button** on the Standard toolbar.

13. In the Basic Search task pane, type Tennessee Furniture Company in the *Search text* box. Use the default settings for all the other options in the Basic Search pane.

14. Click the **Search button** in the Basic Search pane. Click one of the files in the search results. Click the **Close Window button** `X` to close the Search Results task pane. Close all open workbooks.

7 Format a Worksheet

1. Open *Updated Personnel Records-1* in the *Skills Review* folder in your *Excel Data* folder. Verify that cell A1 is the active cell. Click the **Bold button** 🅱, then click the **Italic button** 🅸.

2. Click the **Font Size triangle button** 10 ▾ and click **14** on the list.

3. Point to the gridline between the column A and column B column headings. When the pointer becomes a double-headed arrow, double-click to adjust the width of column A. Click the **Undo button** ↶▾ to restore the original column width.

4. Select **cells A1:E1** and then click the **Merge and Center button** 🀫.

5. Select **cell A2** and click the **Bold button** 🅱.

6. Select **cells A2:D2** and then click the **Merge and Center button** 🀫.

7. Select the **range A5:E5** and click the **Center button** 🀫.

8. Select the **range C5:D5** and click the **Align Right button** 🀫.

9. Select the **range C6:C49** and click **Cells** on the Format menu.

10. On the Number tab, click **Currency** in the Category list, and change the number of decimal places to 0. Click **OK**.

11. Select the **range E5:E49** and click the **Center button** 🀫 twice.

12. Click **cell A2** and click the **Merge and Center button** 🀫 to split the cells. Select **cells A2:E2** and click the **Merge and Center button** 🀫 to properly center the heading over the columns.

13. Press Ctrl + Home and view the changes to the workbook (Figure 1.28).

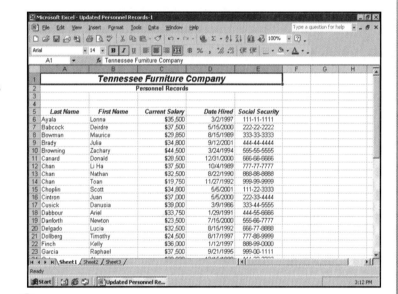

Figure 1.28

14. Save the workbook as *Updated Personnel Records-2* in the *Skills Review* folder in your *Excel Data* folder.

8 Add and Edit Comments

1. In the open *Updated Personnel Records-2* workbook, navigate to cell C25 (the salary for Dorothy Hamilton).

2. Click **Comment** on the Insert menu to display the comment box.

3. In the comment box, type **Dorothy is the highest paid employee.**

4. Click outside the comment to hide the comment box. Then point to the comment indicator and read the comment that displays.

5. Now you will edit the comment. Click **cell C25** to select it, and then click **Edit Comment** on the Insert menu. Add the following text to the comment: She has consistently shown initiative.

6. Click outside the comment to hide the comment box.

7. Press [Ctrl] + [Home]. Save the workbook as *Updated Personnel Records-3* in the *Skills Review* folder in your *Excel Data* folder.

9 Use AutoFormats

1. In the open *Updated Personnel Records-3* workbook, select the **range A5:E49**.

2. Click **AutoFormat** on the Format menu.

3. Click the **Classic 3 AutoFormat**, then click **OK**.

4. Click outside the selected cells to better view the AutoFormat style.

5. Save the workbook as *Updated Personnel Records-AutoFormat* in the *Skills Review* folder in your *Excel Data* folder. Then close the file.

10 Collaborate on a Workbook

NOTE *You may complete this activity individually or exchange discussion comments with a peer.*

1. Open the *Book Store* workbook in your *Excel Data* folder.

2. Point to **Online Collaboration** on the Tools menu and click **Web Discussions**.

3. Click the **Insert Discussion about the Workbook button** 🗔.

4. Type New store sales projections in the *Discussion subject* text box. Press [Tab], type the following in the *Discussion text* box, then click **OK**:

   Projections are that our new store in Boca Raton will have the best first quarter earnings of any of our stores. I think we'll even top Gatlinburg!

5. Click the **Show a menu of actions button** 🗔▾ and click **Reply**.

6. Type the following in the *Discussion text* box: According to my sales figures for Jan-Feb, I think you are right. Keep your fingers crossed that March is strong!

7. Click the **Close Web Discussions button** [Close], then close the *Book Store* workbook.

LESSON APPLICATIONS

1 Navigate a Worksheet and Find Information

Locate and open a workbook. Navigate to specific cells in a worksheet and use Find to locate information. Use Find and Replace to change cell data.

1. Open the *Hickory Hill Horses* workbook in your *Excel Data* folder.

2. Use the methods of your choice to move to the following cells: A25, I25, B9, A1. Use the Find feature to locate all the horses with *Day* as part of their name.

3. Use the Replace feature to increase the price of the horses that are currently for sale at $1,500 to $1,800.

4. Navigate to cell A1 and save the file as *Revised Sales List* in the *Lesson Applications* folder in your *Excel Data* folder. Close the workbook.

2 Create a New Workbook and Enter and Format Data

Create a new workbook, enter and edit data, and adjust column width. Apply an AutoFormat and clear and restore the format. Clear cell contents.

1. Create a new workbook and type **Money Raised by Volunteers** in cell A1.

2. Starting in cell A3, type the information in Table 1.5, including the column labels. Using the techniques you learned in this lesson, correct any data-entry errors you may have made.

3. Format the worksheet title, *Money Raised by Volunteers*, using your choice of font, font size, and font attributes. Adjust the width of column C to accommodate the *Money Raised* label.

4. Format A3:C13 using one of the AutoFormats.

5. If necessary, format the values in your worksheet using Currency Style with no decimal places. If necessary, adjust the width of the *Goal* column.

6. Make the following edits to cells A13:C13: Change *Mincewell* to Minceberg; change *Goal* to 400; change *Money Raised* to 425.

Table 1.5	Data for Worksheet	
Name	**Goal**	**Money Raised**
Alvarez	200	273
Burns, A.	400	481
Burns, D.	400	332
Goldsmith	200	109
Haskell	500	520
Lee	200	227
Mincewell	300	325
Stoll	200	217
Weinmiller	400	375
Yamaguchi	400	399

7. Clear the formatting from your worksheet. Use Undo 🔄 to restore the formatting.

8. Save the file as *Fundraising* in the *Lessons Applications* folder in your *Excel Data* folder. Close the workbook.

3 Change the Page Setup and Preview and Print a Worksheet

Examine a worksheet in Print Preview and change page setup options such as page orientation and scaling. Print the worksheet.

1. Open the *Homes Sold* workbook in your *Excel Data* folder.

2. Use Print Preview to determine what the worksheet will look like when it is printed. In the Page Setup dialog box, change the scaling so that the worksheet will print on one page in Portrait orientation. Use Print Preview to verify that the worksheet will print on one page.

3. Change to Landscape orientation and print one copy of the worksheet.

4. Close the *Homes Sold* workbook without saving your changes.

SUMMARY AND EXERCISES

4 Apply and Modify Cell Formats

Use Excel's formatting features to enhance a worksheet. Use Find and Replace to change cell formats. Merge and split cells.

1. Open the *Mercer Sales* workbook in your *Excel Data* folder.

2. Right-align cells B5:C5, then center cell E5. Merge and center cells A1:F1. Use the Center Across Selection feature to format cells A2:F3.

3. Format cells B6:B16 using the Comma Style. Format cell B17 and cells F7:F9 using the Currency Style. Format cells C6:C16 using the Percent Style, then format these cells to one decimal place.

4. Format cells A5:E5 and A1:A3 as bold. Format cell E5 as underline. Add italic to cell A3. Format cells A17:B17 as bold and italic.

5. Change the font size for cell A1 to 14 points. Format cells E5:F9 using the Times New Roman font.

6. Use Find and Replace to find bold italic data and replace it with regular text. Undo these changes to restore the bold italic.

7. Navigate to cell A1 and save the workbook as *Mercer Sales-Formatted* in the *Lesson Applications* folder in your *Excel Data* folder. Preview, print, and close the workbook.

5 Apply AutoFormats

Apply and remove AutoFormats from a range of cells.

1. Open the *Sales by Department* workbook in your *Excel Data* folder.

2. Format cells A4:E11 using the *Classic 1* AutoFormat. Click outside the range to better view the formatting, then clear the formats (but not the cell contents) for A4:E11. Use Undo to reverse your action.

3. Format cells A4:E11 using the *Accounting 2* AutoFormat.

4. With cell A1 as the active cell, save the revised workbook as *Sales by Department-AutoFormat* in the *Lesson Applications* folder in your *Excel Data* folder.

5. Preview, print, and close the workbook.

6 Check Spelling, Add Comments, and Save a Workbook in a New Folder

Check spelling in a worksheet. Insert and edit comments in a cell. Save a workbook under a new name and in a new folder with a different file format. Navigate to the new folder and open the workbook.

1. Open *Best Times* in your *Excel Data* folder.

2. Check spelling in the worksheet. Make appropriate changes to each misspelled word identified by the spell checker.

3. Add the following comment to cell A7: **Romania is an often-overlooked country.**

4. Add the following comment to cell A4: **Germany is a great trip in early May. There are no crowds, but the weather can be a little cool.**

5. Edit the comment in cell A7 to read as follows: **Romania is often overlooked by crowds.**

6. Save the workbook as *Spell Check* in the *Lesson Applications* folder in your *Excel Data* folder.

7. Create a new folder in the *Lesson Applications* folder named *Excel 4 Format.* Save *Spell Check* in this new folder as *Spell Check-Excel 4* in the Microsoft Excel 4.0 Workbook format. Close the workbook.

8. Navigate to the new *Excel 4 Format* folder in your *Lesson Applications* Folder. Open the *Spell Check-Excel 4* workbook. Close the workbook.

7 Create a Threaded Discussion

Use the Web Discussions feature to create a threaded discussion concerning the contents of a workbook.

NOTE *You may complete this activity individually or exchange discussion comments with a peer.*

1. Open *Building Estimate* in your *Excel Data* folder and activate the Web Discussions toolbar.

2. Type Driveway costs as the subject, then type the following discussion text:

The driveway cost projections at Sandy Valley Road are too high. What do you think about getting another contractor for that excavation?

3. Type the following reply:

We could do that; however, don't forget that the Sandy Valley drive is over three times as long as Hickory Lane. Considering that, the price is very good.

4. As time permits, continue to exchange comments about the *Building Estimate* workbook. When you finish your discussion, close the Web Discussions toolbar and close the *Building Estimate* workbook.

PROJECTS

1 How Can You Use a Worksheet?

Think of something you do in your personal, academic, or business life for which you might use a worksheet. Draw a rough sketch to show how your worksheet might be organized, remembering to arrange the data in columns and rows. Then create a simple, unformatted worksheet based on your sketch. Save your workbook as *Unformatted Worksheet* in the *Projects* folder in your *Excel Data* folder.

2 Make It Look Good!

Describe some ways of formatting a worksheet to make it look more professional. Apply your ideas to *Unformatted Worksheet* in your *Projects* folder that you created in Project 1. (If you did not complete Project 1, use the workbook entitled *Formatting Needed* in your

Excel Data folder.) Apply formatting features individually and then remove the formats from the cells. While formatting your worksheet, practice using these skills: merge and split cells; clear cell content; and change alignment of cell data. Use Find and Replace to locate and change specific cell formats such as bold or italic. Apply each of the AutoFormats to your worksheet. Save your workbook as *Formatted Worksheet* in the *Projects* folder in your *Excel Data* folder.

3 Track Your Monthly Expenses

Use Excel to track your monthly expenditures. Include at least ten spending categories (such as Housing, Auto Expenses, Food, Entertainment, and so on). Enter the amount you spent in each category for the past three months. Adjust the column widths as necessary to accommodate the longest entry in each column. Format the worksheet using an AutoFormat and/or individual formatting features. Identify a repeated value you would like to change and use Find and Replace to change the data. Spell check your worksheet and view it in Print Preview. Modify print settings of your choice in the Page Setup dialog box and then print the worksheet. Save the workbook as *My Expenses* in the *Projects* folder in your *Excel Data* folder. Close the workbook.

4 Explore AutoCorrect Options

Create a new, blank workbook, and then access Help to find out more about the types of corrections that AutoCorrect performs. Verify that the AutoCorrect Options is turned on, and view the words in the AutoCorrect list. Close the AutoCorrect dialog box, and practice entering several erroneous words from the Replace list into the worksheet. (Don't forget to press Enter or Spacebar after each entry to activate the feature.) Reopen the AutoCorrect Options dialog box, add your initials to the AutoCorrect *Replace* list, and add your full name to the AutoCorrect *With* list. Close the dialog box, and then type your initials (followed by Enter or a space) in an empty cell. Open the AutoCorrect dialog box and delete your new entry. Close the workbook without saving it.

5 Compare and Contrast These Worksheets

Open the *Surfside Sales* workbook in the *Excel Data* folder and print it. On the printout, write a sentence or two explaining the use of this worksheet. Open the *Third Quarter Sales* workbook in the *Excel Data* folder and print it. Compare and contrast the two worksheets and write your answers on the *Third Quarter Sales* printout. Additionally, indicate several ways that formatting could enhance each worksheet. Close the workbooks.

ON the WEB   6 Collaborate Online Using E-Mail

Imagine that you want to insert comments into a worksheet and share it with one of your colleagues who is using Excel 97. Open the *Third Quarter Sales* workbook in the *Excel Data* folder and format it attractively. Review the workbook and include comments regarding the categories that have the highest and lowest percentage of sales. Hide the comments, if necessary. Save the workbook as *Q3 Sales with Comments* in the *Projects* folder, using an appropriate file format. Then send it as an e-mail attachment to a classmate, a friend, or your instructor. Close the workbook.

7 Collaborate Online Using Web Discussions

(*Note:* This project is best completed by a two-person team. Each participant should adopt the role of one of the business owners.) You (Pat Wilson) and a friend (Kim Rousch) are partners in a business named Wilson's Fly Shop. In order to determine a sales strategy for the new year, Pat has been analyzing data concerning the three main product lines. Pat needs to communicate important year-end sales numbers to Kim who is out of town for the holidays. Open the *Fly Shop Sales* workbook in your *Excel Data* folder. Activate the Web Discussion toolbar and write a discussion comment regarding the sales data. Writing as Pat, recommend that the store drop the Ackerman line and purchase more Eastwind rods based on the following sales data.

◆ Sales of Ackerman rods are off 27 units ($3,780) from last year.

◆ Sales of Eastwind rods are up 82 units ($38,540) from last year.

Kim receives this information and agrees with the sentiment regarding the Ackerman line. However, Kim has a number of important clients who continue to purchase Ackerman products. Though Ackerman rod sales are declining, that manufacturer will soon be rolling out a new line of rods and even outdoor clothing. Writing as Kim, reply to Pat's comments justifying the retention of the Ackerman line. When your threaded discussion is finished, close *Fly Shop Sales* and close the Web Discussions toolbar.

Project in Progress

8 Check Out These Sales!

Assume you own a small business called Savvy Solutions that provides a variety of writing, editing, and training services to other business owners. You facilitate training seminars; write materials such as brochures, training manuals, annual reports, employee handbooks, and newspaper and magazine articles; and create Web pages for small businesses.

Think of ways you could use worksheets in your business. Then open the *Savvy Solutions* workbook in your *Excel Data* folder (Figure 1.29). Using the navigation methods you learned in this lesson, examine the information in the worksheet.

What other information would you add to this workbook to make it more useful? What would you do to make the workbook look more professional? Format the worksheet using the techniques you learned in this lesson. Preview the worksheet in different orientations and make the necessary adjustments to fit it attractively on one page. Print the workbook and save it as *Savvy Solutions-Lesson 1* in a new folder named *Project in Progress* in the *Projects* folder in your *Excel Data* folder. Close the workbook and exit Excel.

	Jan	Feb	Mar	Apr	May	June	Jul	Aug	Sep
Articles	600	300	250	750	300	0	400	250	250
Employee literature	4580	3000	2575	4200	750	2775	4025	3345	2850
Seminars and training	500	750	1000	775	1000	1200	850	1550	625
Web page creation	780	1200	600	1500	350	200	1250	700	600

Figure 1.29

LESSON 2

Building Simple Workbooks

CONTENTS

OBJECTIVES

After you complete this lesson, you will be able to do the following:

- Use the mouse and keyboard to select single cells, contiguous and noncontiguous ranges, rows, columns, and worksheets.
- Select and print a range.
- Set and clear a print area.
- Clear the contents of one or more cells.
- Undo and redo changes.
- Insert and delete rows and columns.
- Adjust column width and row height.
- Move and copy the contents of one or more cells.
- Create, revise, and copy formulas.
- Understand the order of arithmetic operations.
- Use the AutoSum button.
- Use the SUM, AVERAGE, MINIMUM, and MAXIMUM functions.
- Use AutoCalculate.
- Understand and use relative and absolute cell references.
- Perform a *what if* analysis.
- Identify the elements of a chart.
- Create a chart using the Chart Wizard.
- Move, modify, resize, and print a chart.
- Add hyperlinks to a worksheet.

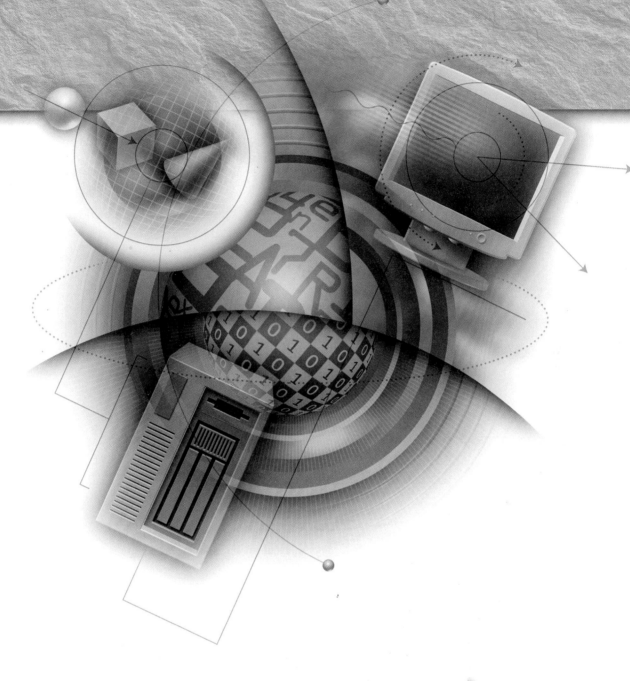

SELECTING GROUPS OF CELLS

It is usually more efficient to work with a group of cells at the same time than to work with them one at a time. Before you apply a command to a group of cells, you should **select** or highlight them. After you select a range of cells, you can perform an action on those cells (such as moving or formatting them). The rule you should remember is to *select before you affect*. That reminder simply means that you must select cells before you can apply a command to them.

As you know, a selected cell or group of cells is called a *range*. Most of the ranges you'll work with in Excel form an adjoining block of cells referred to as a **contiguous** or an **adjacent range.** However, you can also select multiple groups of cells to form a **noncontiguous** or **nonadjacent range.** When you select one cell, it is designated

The ability to work efficiently and effectively are qualities all employers value. In this lesson, you'll learn to perform calculations quickly using various formulas and functions. You will experience the power of performing what-if analysis, an essential skill needed to make sound decisions in today's workplace.

by the cell pointer. When you select multiple cells, they appear highlighted except for the active cell which remains white.

As you already know, each cell has a cell reference to designate its location. Similarly, ranges have **range references** so you can tell where they are in the worksheet. A range reference consists of any two cells in opposite corners of the range separated by a colon (for example, A5:C7). A range can span part of a column, part of a row, or several columns and several rows. Figure 2.1 shows examples of various ranges.

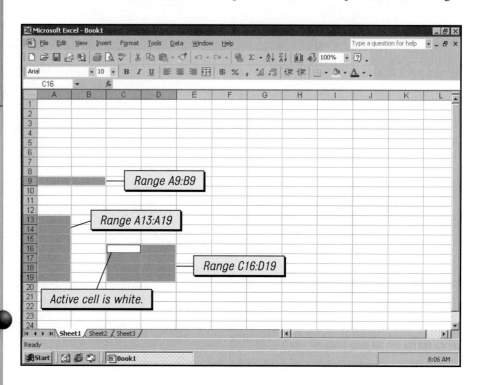

Figure 2.1
Three selected, noncontiguous ranges

Selecting Ranges

Excel provides a number of methods you can use to select cells. For example, you can drag over the cells with the mouse or use keyboard shortcuts. In this activity, you'll learn various methods of selecting groups of cells.

Excel BASICS

Selecting a Range

1. Point to the first cell of the range you want to select.

2. When the pointer becomes the Normal Select pointer, click and drag to the last cell you want to select.

3. Release the mouse button.

1. **Start Excel and open *Sarah's Candy Company* in your *Excel Data* folder.**

2. **Point to cell A13, then hold the left mouse button and drag to select cells A13:D19.**

WARNING *Before you begin to drag, make sure the pointer is the Normal Select pointer ⊕. Since Excel uses different pointer symbols to invoke different actions, you must be certain to use the correct pointer when selecting a range.*

All the cells from A13 through D19 are highlighted.

3. Click any cell.

The range is deselected.

4. Click cell **A13**, press and hold <kbd>⇧ Shift</kbd>, click **A19**, and release the <kbd>⇧ Shift</kbd> key.

The range A13:A19 is selected.

5. Point to the **column C column heading**. When the pointer becomes a down arrow, click the column heading.

The entire column is selected. You can select multiple columns (or rows) by dragging over their headings.

6. Click the **column A heading**, then drag across the **column A–C headings**.

Columns A through C are selected.

7. Point to the **row 14 heading**. When the pointer becomes a horizontal arrow, click the **row 14 heading**.

The entire row is selected.

8. Click the **Select All button**.

NOTE *The Select All button is the blank rectangle located to the left of the column A heading and above the row 1 heading.*

The entire worksheet is selected.

9. Click any cell to cancel the previous selection.

So far you've selected *contiguous* ranges, where the selected cells are adjacent. However, you can also select *noncontiguous* ranges.

10. Drag to select **A11:A19**.

11. Press <kbd>Ctrl</kbd> and then drag to select **C11:C19**.

Both ranges appear selected even though they are not adjacent (see Figure 2.2).

12. Click any cell to deselect the ranges.

Selecting and Printing a Range of Cells

There are two methods for printing a selected range of cells in a worksheet. You can select the range and then choose the Selection option in the Print dialog box. A second method is to set a print area. Set a print area when you want to hold the print settings in order to repeatedly print the same section of your worksheet. This keeps you from having to select the same range every time you want to print.

Excel BASICS

Selecting Entire Rows, Columns, or Worksheets

- To select a row, click the row heading.

- To select a column, click the column heading.

- To select multiple adjacent rows, drag across row headings.

- To select multiple adjacent columns, drag across column headings.

- To select the entire worksheet, click the Select All button.

EXCEL 2002

Another Way

To select multiple columns or rows, click the first column or row heading, press and hold <kbd>⇧ Shift</kbd>, and click the last column or row heading.

Another Way

You can also use mouse and/or keyboard methods to enter the cell references for a range: Click the Name Box, type the range, and press <kbd>Enter ↵</kbd>.

Figure 2.2
Selected noncontiguous ranges

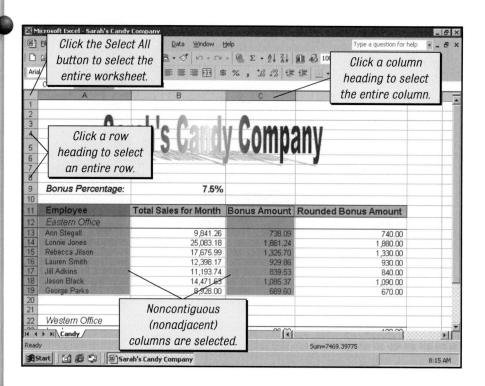

Click the Select All button to select the entire worksheet.

Click a column heading to select the entire column.

Click a row heading to select an entire row.

Noncontiguous (nonadjacent) columns are selected.

Printing a Selected Range

In this activity, you will select and print contiguous and noncontiguous ranges of cells in a worksheet. You will also set and clear a print area.

1. In the open *Sarah's Candy Company* workbook, click in any cell within the range A22:D28 (the Western Office sales) and then press `Ctrl` + `⇧ Shift` + *.

The data area (A22:D28) is selected. The **data area** is a contiguous range that contains data.

2. Click **Print** on the File menu.

The Print dialog box appears as shown in Figure 2.3. Choosing the Selection option in the *Print what* section of this dialog box indicates that you only want to print the selected range—not the entire worksheet.

3. Click **Selection** in the *Print what* section.

4. Click the **Preview button** in the Print dialog box.

5. Click the **Setup button** in the Print Preview window, click **Landscape** in the Page Setup dialog box, and click **OK**.

6. Click **Print** in the Print Preview window.

The data is sent to the printer.

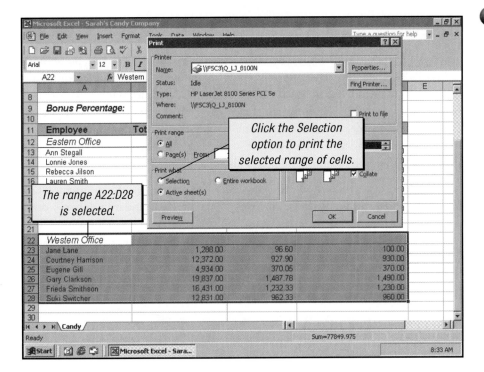

Figure 2.3
Printing a selected range

Setting and Clearing a Print Area

1. Select the range(s) you want to print.

2. Point to Print Area on the File menu, then click Set Print Area.

3. Point to Print Area on the File menu, then click Clear Print Area.

---

7. Drag to select **A11:A19**. Press Ctrl and then drag to select **D11:D19**.

8. Click **Print** on the File menu, click **Selection** in the *Print what* area, and click the **Preview button**.

9. Click **Next** to view the second selection in the Preview window, then click **Print**.

The selected areas print even though they are noncontiguous.

10. Drag to select **A11:C19**, then point to **Print Area** on the File menu and click **Set Print Area**. Click any cell to deselect your range and better view the print area.

A dashed line indicates the perimeter of the print area.

11. Click the **Print Preview button** 🔍.

Only the set print area appears in the Print Preview window.

12. Click the **Print button** 🖨 on the Print Preview toolbar. Click **OK** in the Print dialog box.

The set print area is sent to the printer.

13. Point to **Print Area** on the File menu. Click **Clear Print Area**.

The dashed lines are cleared, indicating that the print area is no longer set.

14. **Close the workbook without saving changes.**

Selecting Noncontiguous Ranges

1. Select the first range.

2. Press and hold Ctrl and select the second range.

3. Repeat step 2 until all desired ranges are selected.

HINTS & TIPS

You can use Page Break Preview to indicate page breaks for a printed workbook. Choose Page Break Preview from the View menu and then drag your worksheet's borders.

DELETING AND RESTORING DATA

An often-repeated step in editing a worksheet is to delete unwanted data. Sometimes you may delete data unintentionally. Luckily, you can use Excel's **Undo** command to reverse your actions. In fact, this command can reverse as many as 16 of your most recent actions. Keep in mind, however, that you can undo *many,* but not *all,* actions. (For example, you can't deselect a range you just selected by issuing the Undo command, and you can't press an arrow key and then move back to your previous location by choosing Undo. You also can't reverse changes you've saved.)

You can use the **Redo** command to reverse the most recent Undo command. The Undo button and the Redo button appear on the Standard toolbar. Notice the triangle buttons that appear to the right of the Undo and Redo buttons. When you click the triangle button, a drop-down list appears displaying the most recent actions you can undo (or redo).

HANDS on

Deleting Cell Contents

In this activity, you'll delete data in a range of cells in the *Sarah's Candy Company* workbook. You'll then update this range with current data and practice using the Undo and Redo commands.

1. **Open the *Sarah's Candy Company* workbook in your *Excel Data* folder.**

2. **Select B13:B19 and press Delete.**

The numbers in the selected range are erased from the worksheet.

> **NOTE** *When you delete B13:B19, data in C13:D19 is replaced by a hyphen since these cells contain formulas relating to the values you deleted.*

3. **Click the Undo button** **.**

Excel reverses your last action and restores the data.

4. **Click the Redo button** **.**

Your Undo command is reversed—and the data is again erased.

5. **Click cell B13 to deselect the range.**

6. **Type the new sales data as shown in Table 2.1.**

> **NOTE** *When you enter new values to cells B13:B19, new data will appear in C13:C19 as the formulas in this range recalculate based on the new values you enter.*

7. **Select cells B13:B19 and click the Bold button** **.**

Table 2.1 — New Sales Data	
Cell	**Data**
B13	9841
B14	25083
B15	15000
B16	10200
B17	9187
B18	15434
B19	7826

Bold is applied to the selected cells.

8. Click the **Undo button** to reverse this formatting change.

9. Click **cell A1** and save the *Sarah's Candy Company* workbook as *Sarah's Candy Company-1* in the *Tutorial* folder in your *Excel Data* folder.

RESTRUCTURING YOUR WORKSHEET

The editing you've done so far involves adding, editing, or deleting the contents of one or more cells. However, you'll often want to completely restructure your worksheet by inserting and deleting cells, rows, and columns. Additionally, you may want to move and copy data. You can perform these actions using menu commands, keyboard shortcuts, or shortcut menus. **Shortcut menus** are context-sensitive menus that you activate by right-clicking an object, such as a cell or a column or row heading.

Inserting and Deleting Columns and Rows

Sometimes you have to insert cells, columns, and rows into your workbook to make room for new data. For example, a manager may give you sales or production figures that need to be inserted into an existing worksheet. When you add new cells, rows, or columns, Excel automatically moves your existing data out of the way. Excel inserts new cells either to the right of or below the cell pointer. Excel inserts new rows above the cell pointer and new columns to the left of the cell pointer.

You can delete cells, rows, or columns you no longer need. Deleting a row, cell, or column is not the same as deleting (or clearing) the *contents* of a row or column. When you delete a row or column, Excel totally removes the row or column, including its contents, and moves up the remaining rows or moves over the remaining columns. In the same way, when you delete a cell the remaining cells move to fill the hole created by the deletion.

HANDS on

Adding and Removing Columns, Rows, and Cells

In this activity you'll insert a new row and a new cell, delete a row, and insert and delete a column in the *Sarah's Candy Company-1* workbook.

1. In the open *Sarah's Candy Company-1* workbook, right-click the **row heading** for row 15.

Right-clicking the row heading selects the entire row and displays a shortcut menu, as shown in Figure 2.4. This shortcut menu includes context-sensitive commands—that is, they are specifically related to the current task (working with rows).

EXCEL 2002

Excel BASICS

Inserting and Deleting Columns

To insert a column:

1. Position the cell pointer anywhere in the column to the right of where you want to insert the new column.

2. Click Columns on the Insert menu.

Or

- Right-click a column heading, then choose Insert from the shortcut menu.

To delete a column:

- Click the column heading, then click Delete on the Edit menu.

Or

- Right-click a column heading, then click Delete on the shortcut menu.

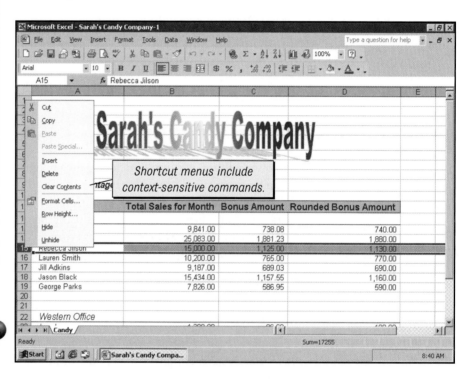

Figure 2.4
Shortcut menu

2. Click **Insert** on the shortcut menu.

A blank row is inserted into your worksheet. The rows below are moved down.

NOTE *The Insert Options button ⬦▾ appears in your worksheet next to the inserted row. Clicking this button provides a list of formatting options.*

3. Click **A15** and type Joyce Johnson. In **B15**, type 12500.

4. Right-click the **row 19 heading**, then click **Delete** on the shortcut menu.

The selected row is deleted from the worksheet. George Park's information that was in row 20 moves up to occupy row 19.

HINTS & TIPS

The best approach to take when creating a new workbook is to plan its structure in advance. Planning decreases the need for major changes in the structure of a workbook.

5. Click any cell in column C and then click **Columns** on the Insert menu.

Excel adds a new column to your workbook, moving the existing columns to the right, as shown in Figure 2.5. Notice that the cell pointer is positioned in the new column.

Inserting and Deleting Rows
To insert a row:

1. Position the cell pointer anywhere in the row below where you want to insert the new row.

2. Click Rows on the Insert menu.

Or

• Right-click a row heading and then click Insert on the shortcut menu.

To delete a row:

• Click the row heading, then click Delete on the Edit menu.

Or

• Right-click a row heading and then click Delete on the shortcut menu.

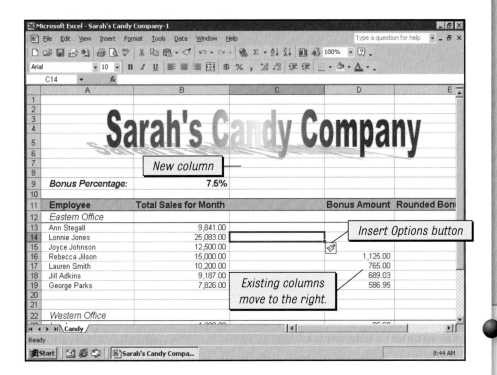

Figure 2.5
Inserted column

6. With the cell pointer positioned in the newly inserted column, click **Delete** on the Edit menu.

The Delete dialog box appears providing options to delete the current row or column.

7. Click **Entire column** and click **OK**.

The column is deleted and the existing columns move over to fill the space.

8. Click **cell B18**, then click **Cells** on the Insert menu.

9. In the Insert dialog box, click the **Shift cells down option**, if necessary, and then click **OK**.

A new, blank cell appears (B18). The data in the cells below shifts down to allow space for the new, blank cell.

10. With the cell pointer still in cell B18, click **Delete** on the Edit menu.

11. In the Delete dialog box, click the **Shift cells up option**, if necessary, and click **OK**.

The blank cell is deleted and the data from the cells below is realigned in its original location.

You can insert multiple rows or columns at once. Select the column or row headings for as many columns or rows as you want to insert, and then choose Columns (or Rows) on the Insert menu.

WARNING *Be very careful when inserting or deleting cells—it is very easy to misalign your data. As a general rule, it is best to insert or delete entire rows or columns, not individual cells.*

12. Click cell **A1** and save the workbook as *Sarah's Candy Company-2* in the *Tutorial* folder in your *Excel Data* folder. Close the workbook.

COPYING AND MOVING DATA

If some of your information is in the wrong location, you don't have to delete it from one place and retype it in another. Instead, you can move or copy the data. Excel provides various methods of moving and copying data. You can use the Cut or Copy commands in conjunction with the Paste command and Clipboard task pane or the drag-and-drop method. Regardless of which method you use, the data you move or copy will replace any existing data in the new location.

The drag-and-drop method of moving cell data is very intuitive. To use this method of moving data, first select the cell(s) you want to move and point to the cell border until the pointer changes to the Move Cell Contents pointer ▣ on top of the Move Object pointer ▣. Click and drag the selection to the new location. To copy data using drag-and-drop, press and hold ⌗Ctrl⌗ while dragging the selection to the new location.

WARNING *The pointer must be the Move Cell Contents pointer ▣ before you begin a move or copy action using drag-and-drop.*

Sometimes as a result of rearranging or reformatting your worksheet you may need to adjust the width of a column or height of a row. You can do this by selecting the row or column, pointing to Row or Column on the Format menu, and clicking Height, Width, or AutoFit.

If you've used other Windows programs, you're probably already familiar with the Cut, Copy, and Paste commands. These commands make use of the **Clipboard,** a temporary storage area for information that is used by all Windows applications. Clicking Cut ▣ moves the selected data from the workbook to the Clipboard; clicking Copy ▣ copies the selected data to the Clipboard (without removing that data from the workbook). The Paste command ▣ places a copy of the Clipboard data in the workbook at the position of the cell pointer. (These commands are also options on the Edit menu.) In Excel, you can copy and paste text, numbers, or formulas. Use the Clipboard task pane when you want to copy and paste multiple selections. The Clipboard allows you to copy up to 24 different items. Access this task pane by clicking Office Clipboard on the Edit menu.

You can also use the Paste Options feature, which allows you to copy not only the cell contents but also the cell's formatting. After you paste a cut or copied selection into your worksheet, the Paste Options button ▣▾ appears next to the pasted data. Click the button to view the options.

You can use Table 2.2 as a reference whenever you need to cut, copy, and paste data in your workbook.

Table 2.2 — Cutting, Copying, and Pasting Data

To	Use this Edit Menu Command	Use this Toolbar Button	Use this Keyboard Shortcut
Copy Data	Copy		Ctrl + C
Cut Data	Cut		Ctrl + X
Paste Data	Paste		Ctrl + V

HANDS on

Copying and Moving Cell Contents

In this activity, you'll copy and paste text from one range to another range and adjust column width and row height. You'll also copy formulas and use the drag-and-drop method of moving cell contents.

1. Open the *Sarah's Candy Company-2* workbook in the *Tutorial* folder in your *Excel Data* folder.

2. Select **range A11:D11** and click the **Copy button** 📋.

The selected range is surrounded by a moving border indicating the range is now copied to the Clipboard. The status bar reads *Select destination and press ENTER or choose Paste.*

3. Click **cell A21**, then click the **Paste button** 📋.

The text you copied to the Clipboard (from cells A11:D11) is copied to A21:D21, as shown in Figure 2.6. The Paste Options button 📋 ▾ appears at the right side of the pasted range. Clicking this button provides various options for formatting and linking cells.

Notice that the moving border still appears around the selected cells A11:D11— they are still copied to the Clipboard. If necessary, you could paste the Clipboard contents repeatedly throughout the worksheet.

4. Press Esc to cancel the Copy command.

5. Click **cell C13**.

This cell includes a formula, as you can see in the Formula Bar. When you copy a formula, you copy the structure only. Excel then calculates information in the new cells and displays the results.

6. Press Ctrl + C, then click **cell C15**.

7. Press Ctrl + V to paste the formula in the new cell. Press Enter to finalize the command.

Using drag-and-drop is a quick method of moving information.

Excel BASICS

Copying Data

1. Select the cell or range you want to copy.

2. Click the Copy button.

3. Click the cell in which you want to paste the data; or, if pasting a range of data, click the upper-left cell in the range.

4. Click the Paste button or press Enter.

Figure 2.6
Copied and pasted range

EXCEL 2002

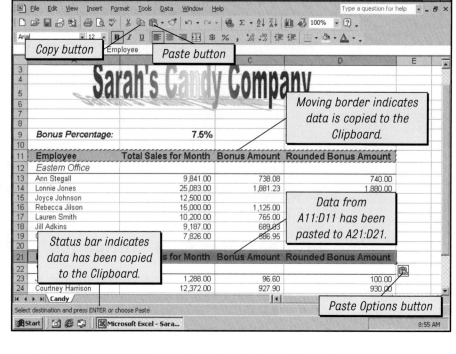

Moving Data

1. Select the cell or range you want to move.

2. Click the Cut button [✄].

3. Click the cell in which you want to move the data; or, if pasting a range of data, click the upper-left cell of the range.

4. Click the Paste button or press [Enter←].

8. Select **A13:D13**, then point to the border of the selected range.

9. When the Move Cell Contents pointer [↖] appears on top of the Move Object pointer [✛], press the mouse button and drag the selected range down to the **range A29:D29**.

As you drag toward the bottom of the window, the worksheet automatically moves up. A ScreenTip appears, as you drag, identifying the current range you would move to if you released the mouse button.

10. Release the mouse button when *A29:D29* appears in the ScreenTip.

Excel moves the selected text into cells A29:D29.

11. Click the **Undo button** [↺▾] to reverse your last action.

12. Click **Office Clipboard** on the Edit menu.

The Clipboard task pane appears at the right side of the Excel window.

13. If the Clipboard is not empty, click the **Clear All button** [Clear All] to clear the Clipboard.

14. Scroll up, select **A11:D11**, and click the **Copy button** [📋].

The cell contents for A11:D11 appear in the Clipboard task pane.

15. Select **A14:D14** and click the **Copy button** [📋]. Select **A17:D17** and click the **Copy button** [📋]. Press [Esc].

The contents of each copied range appear in the Clipboard task pane. The most recent copied data appears at the top.

16. Scroll down and click **cell A30**, then point to *Employee Total Sales* . . . on the Clipboard, and click the triangle button.

A drop-down menu appears, as shown in Figure 2.7.

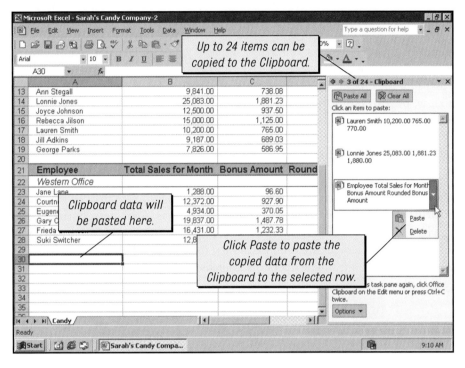

Figure 2.7
Clipboard task pane

EXCEL 2002

17. Click **Paste** on the drop-down menu.

The data is copied to A30:D30.

18. Click **cell A31**, then click *Lonnie Jones* . . . on the Clipboard. Click **A32**, then click *Lauren Smith* . . . on the Clipboard.

The data is pasted into the selected rows.

19. Click the **Clear All button** to clear the Clipboard contents, then click the **Close button** on the Clipboard task pane.

20. Select **cell A9**, click the **Font Size triangle button** and click **9**.

21. Point to **Column** on the Format menu and click **Width**. Type 18 in the Column Width box and click **OK** to reduce the width of column A.

22. Click **Undo**.

The previous column width is restored.

23. Point to **Column** on the Format menu and click **AutoFit Selection** to again reduce the width of column A.

24. Point to the border between row headings 11 and 12. When the pointer becomes a double-headed arrow, drag it down until the ScreenTip reads *Height: 21.00 (28 pixels),* then release the mouse button. Make the same adjustment to rows 21 and 30.

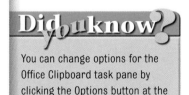

You can change options for the Office Clipboard task pane by clicking the Options button at the bottom of the task pane.

25. Press `Ctrl` + `Home`. Save your workbook as *Sarah's Candy Company-3* in the *Tutorial* folder in your *Excel Data* folder. Close the workbook.

UNDERSTANDING FORMULAS

Excel can calculate values for you. For example, if you have columns listing January, February, and March sales, you can have Excel generate monthly sales totals as well as totals for the quarter. To perform these and other types of calculations, you need to know how to build formulas. You can build formulas from scratch in Excel (sometimes called user-defined formulas) or rely on Excel's built-in functions. In this section we'll concentrate on building formulas; later in this lesson you'll learn how to use the built-in functions.

A **formula** is a group of instructions that tells Excel to perform a calculation and display the results. Formulas consist of values, such as numbers and cell references, and **arithmetic operators,** such as plus and minus signs. Arithmetic operators perform basic mathematical operations such as addition, subtraction, multiplication, and division. These operators tell Excel how to calculate the numbers. Table 2.3 shows some of the arithmetic operators available in Excel.

Table 2.3	Arithmetic Operators	
Symbol	**Function**	**Example**
+	Addition	2+3=5
−	Subtraction	5−2=3
*	Multiplication	2*3=6
/	Division	6/3=2
^	Exponentiation	2^3=8
%	Percent	10*10%=1

In the following activities you'll learn how to create formulas using cell references and logical operators. You'll also see Excel's automatic recalculation feature in action.

Creating User-Defined Formulas

A formula can be as simple as =2+2. In Excel, formulas start with an equal sign (=), which is a signal to Excel that you are entering a formula. If you enter the formula =2+2 in cell A1, Excel displays the result *4* in that cell and shows the formula =2+2 in the Formula Bar.

Based on this example, you may think that entering a formula instead of simply entering the desired result is time-consuming and of little value. However, the power of using formulas becomes apparent when you use cell references instead of numbers in your formulas. **Cell references** are cell addresses in a formula that tell Excel to perform calculations using whatever value is currently contained in the designated cell. For example, if you enter =*B1+B2* in cell B3, cell B3 would display the sum of the values in cells B1 and B2. By using cell references in formulas,

you can perform all sorts of calculations involving data you've already entered in other cells. And, when you revise some or all of the data in those other cells, the formulas will automatically calculate new results based on the changed data.

To edit a formula, select the cell in which the formula appears. Click the Formula Bar, edit as appropriate, and press [Enter←]. You can also double-click the cell in which the formula appears and edit the formula directly in the cell.

You will often use formulas that are very similar. Excel allows you to copy formulas so you don't have to enter them multiple times. In addition, Excel automatically adjusts the cell references in a copied formula to reflect the formula's new location.

Excel interprets cell references (cell or range references) within a formula based on their position *relative* to the cell that contains the formula. Rather than reading a formula literally, Excel reads it as a set of general instructions based upon the position of the cell that contains the formula. For example, Excel would interpret the formula =*D14+D15* within cell D16 as *add together the two cells above this one*. If you were to copy this formula from cell D16 to cell E16, Excel would change the cell references in the formula to correspond to the formula's new location, interpreting those cell references as the two cells above cell E16. Thus, the formula in cell E16 would be =*E14+E15*. Such cell references within formulas are known as **relative references,** since they change to correspond to their new location when copied. By default, Excel interprets all cell references as relative references.

The process of copying and pasting formulas is much like the process of copying and pasting a cell that contains any other type of data. You can use the Copy [icon] and Paste [icon] buttons, the drag-and-drop method, the keyboard shortcuts, or the Fill command (Edit menu).

HANDS on

Creating Formulas

In this activity, you'll open a sample income statement that contains sales and expenses data but no formulas. You will use two methods (typing and pointing) to enter formulas to determine the gross margin for each month.

1. Open the *Income Statement* workbook in your *Excel Data* folder.

This worksheet contains financial data for the first quarter but does not yet include formulas.

2. Select cell B10, type =B8-B9 in the Formula Bar, and press [Tab].

Excel subtracts 135,506 (the cost of goods sold for January) from 318,837 (the sales for January) and displays the result of 183,331 (gross margin) in cell B10.

3. Type =(equal sign) in cell C10.

4. Click cell C8.

Excel enters the cell reference C8 into your formula. As shown in Figure 2.8, a moving border surrounds cell C8, and the status bar reads *Point*.

Figure 2.8
Adding cell references to a formula

Excel BASICS

Creating and Editing a Formula

To create a formula:

1. Click the cell in which you want the result of the formula to appear.

2. Type the formula, beginning with an equal sign. Include values and mathematical operators in the formula.

3. Press `Enter ←`.

To edit a formula:

1. Select the cell in which the formula appears. Press `F2` to place the cell contents in Edit mode. Make revisions and then press `Enter ←`.

Or

2. Double-click the cell in which the formula appears and edit the formula.

Another Way

To copy a formula to adjacent cells, click the cell that contains the formula. Point to the black square in the lower-right corner of the cell, and drag to specify which cells you want to paste the information into.

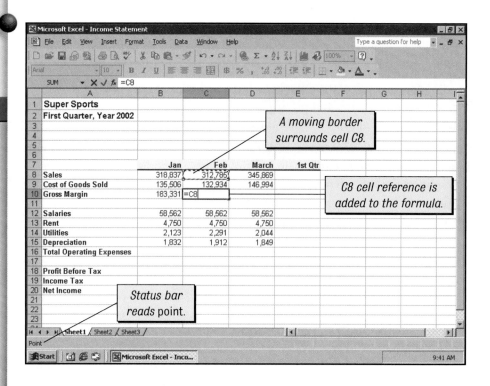

5. Type — (minus sign).

6. Click cell **C9**.

Now cell C9 is surrounded by a moving border, and Excel enters the cell reference for C9 into your formula, which now reads = *C8– C9*.

7. Press `Tab` to finalize the formula.

The result of 179,851 appears in cell C10.

8. Click cell **C10**, right-click, then click **Copy** on the shortcut menu. Click cell **D10**, right-click, and click **Paste** on the shortcut menu.

The result of 198,875 appears in cell D10. Notice that the cell references in cell D10 changed to correspond to their new location. This is known as *relative cell referencing.*

9. Press `Esc`. Click cell **A1** and save your workbook as *Revised Income Statement* in the *Tutorial* folder in your *Excel Data* folder. Close the workbook.

Understanding Operators and Operator Precedence

When formulas have a single operator, such as the plus sign (+), you don't need to worry about how the mathematical expression is evaluated. But when formulas include more than one operator, the various operations are executed in a particular order. Excel doesn't automatically perform operations from left to right. Instead, Excel uses a standard order of **precedence,** a set of rules that determines the order in which mathematical expressions are calculated.

Here is the standard order of operator precedence:

◆ The exponentiation operator (^) has the highest precedence, so two numbers separated by a ^ are evaluated first.

◆ The multiplication (*) and division (/) operators are evaluated next.

◆ The addition (+) and subtraction (−) operators are evaluated last.

NOTE *When operators have the same precedence, they are evaluated from left to right.*

Let's analyze the formula =3+ 4 *5. You might think the result of this formula would be 35 (3+4=7; 7*5=35). Actually, 4 is first multiplied by 5, since multiplication has a higher level of precedence than addition. Then 3 is added to 20 (4*5), for a final result of 23. Similarly, the formula =2* 2^ 3 is equal to 16 (2^3 which is equal to 8, multiplied by 2).

When necessary, you can use parentheses to modify the order in which operators are evaluated. Operations within parentheses are always evaluated first. So, for example, =(3+4)*5 is equal to 35. First 3 is added to 4 and then that result, 7, is multiplied by 5.

You can even use parentheses within parentheses, or **nested parentheses,** to regulate the order in which Excel performs calculations. In such cases, Excel performs the operations in the innermost sets of parentheses first. For example, in the formula =5*((4+4)/2), the first operation is addition (4+4); the second operation is division (8/2); and the last operation is multiplication (5*4).

When entering complicated formulas, carefully check the order in which operations will be calculated. If you're getting strange or unanticipated results, review the operator precedence. To get the results you need, you may have to use parentheses to modify the precedence.

HANDS on

Understanding Arithmetic Operators

In this activity, you will enter and edit formulas to see how the order of operations can affect the result.

1. **Click the New button** 🗋 **on the Standard toolbar to create a blank worksheet.**

2. **Click cell A1, if necessary.**

3. **In the Formula Bar, type =3+4*5, then click the Enter button** ☑ **on the Formula Bar.**

The result, 23, is displayed in the cell. Remember, multiplication takes precedence over addition. Because of this, multiplication (4*5) is performed first and then 3 is added to the result. Now you will edit your formula and change the order of operations.

4. **In the Formula Bar, click an insertion point to the right of the equal sign, then type an opening parenthesis.**

HINTS & TIPS

Type *About calculation operators* in the *Ask a question* box, press ⌈Enter◄─┘⌉ and then click the topic of the same name to find out more about the operators in Excel.

Excel **BASICS**

Editing a Formula

1. Click the cell where you wish to display the result.

2. Enter a formula in the Formula Bar.

3. Edit the formula as necessary using parentheses to change the order of precedence, then click the Enter button.

4. To make further edits, double-click the cell.

5. Click to the right of the number *4*, then type a closing parenthesis.

Your formula should now display as *=(3+4)*5.*

6. Click the **Enter button** ☑ on the Formula Bar.

Excel automatically recalculates based on your revised formula and displays the result (35) in cell A1.

7. Close the worksheet. Click **No** if asked to save changes.

USING FUNCTIONS

You can build highly complex, user-defined formulas using only the operators mentioned earlier (+, −, *, /, ^, and %); however, these formulas can become quite lengthy and time-consuming to enter. Additionally, you can accidentally introduce errors into your formulas if you don't set them up correctly.

Often it is more efficient to use **functions** than to develop formulas from scratch. Functions are predefined formulas that perform specialized calculations. For example, you can use built-in functions that total or average a range. In fact, Excel offers over 360 functions representing categories such as statistical, date and time, financial, logical, and mathematical.

Here's how functions work to speed up entering formulas: Suppose you want to total the values in cells B1 through B10. You can use the addition operator, and your formula will look like this: $=B1+B2+B3+B4+B5+B6+B7+B8+B9+B10$. On the other hand, you can use the SUM function to enter this lengthy calculation quickly. When using functions, you refer to the range reference instead of individual cells. So, to add all the numbers included in range B1:B10, you use the function $=SUM(B1:B10)$. (The cell range can be selected by typing it in the formula, clicking the AutoSum button Σ ▾, or by dragging over the cells.) Additionally, any rows or columns that you insert or delete within or at the bottom of the range reference of the function will be automatically reflected in the result.

Functions consist of three parts. In the example $=SUM(B1:B10)$, the three parts are the equal sign; the name of the function (in this case SUM); and the **arguments** of the function (in this case B1:B10). The arguments of a function include the variable information and must be contained within parentheses. The function operates on the arguments to determine the results. Most functions require at least one argument, and some require more. You can type a function and its arguments in the Formula Bar, or you can build a function using the Insert Function button ƒₓ.

When you click the Insert Function button ƒₓ, Excel displays the Insert Function dialog box. All the Excel functions are listed in the Insert Function dialog box, grouped by category. When you select a category (and a function within the category), Excel displays a description of the function and a Help link to more information on how to use it. After you select the desired function to use in a particular cell, the function's dialog box appears. In the function's dialog box, you can enter or edit cell references or values for each argument in the function.

Statistical functions perform statistical analysis on ranges of data. Excel's statistical functions are some of the most commonly used functions. The AVERAGE function computes the average value for a group of cells. The COUNT function

counts the number of cells in a range that contain data. The MAX function finds the highest or maximum value for a range, and the MIN function determines the lowest or smallest value. Each of these important functions is set up in a similar way: **=SUM(range of cells)** finds the total for the designated range; **=MIN(range of cells)** calculates the smallest value; **=MAX(range of cells)** computes the largest value in the range. You can create these functions by typing them or by using the AutoSum button.

Using the SUM Function

In this activity, you'll use the SUM and AVERAGE functions in the *Revised Income Statement* workbook.

1. Open the *Revised Income Statement* workbook in the *Tutorial* folder in your *Excel Data* folder.

2. Select cell **B16**.

Your first step in entering a function (or a formula) is to position the cell pointer where you want the result to appear. In cell B16, you want to display a total for cells B12 through B15.

3. Type =SUM(B12:B15) and click the **Enter button** ☑ on the Formula Bar.

Excel totals the specified range and displays 67,267 in cell B16. Notice that when the cell pointer is in the cell, the function =SUM(B12:B15) appears in the Formula Bar.

4. Click cell **C16** and type =SUM(, but don't press Enter↵.

5. Drag to select the **range C12:C15** and release the mouse button.

Excel surrounds the designated cells with a moving border and places the range reference in your formula, which should now read *=SUM(C12:C15*. Dragging is an efficient way to indicate a range in formulas.

6. Type a closing parenthesis and then press Enter↵.

Excel totals the specified range, displaying 67,515 in cell C16. As a general rule, you should always include a closing parenthesis ")" after the function arguments. But in this case, even if you forgot to type the closing parenthesis, Excel would understand what you mean and total the designated values.

7. Select the **range D12:D15**.

8. Click the **AutoSum button** Σ▾.

The March operating expense total (67,205) displays in cell D16. When you're totaling values in a range, selecting the range and clicking the AutoSum button Σ▾ is the fastest method because Excel automatically places the total in the cell immediately below the selected range.

Excel **BASICS**

Using the SUM Function

Typing the range address:

1. Type =SUM(

2. Type the address of the range.

3. Type)

4. Press Enter↵.

Dragging to select the range:

1. Type =SUM(

2. Drag to select the range to be summed.

3. Type)

4. Press Enter↵.

Using AutoSum:

1. Select the range to be summed.

2. Click the AutoSum button.

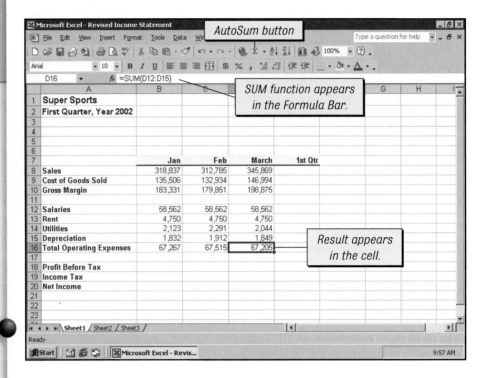
9. Click **cell D16** and look at the Formula Bar.

Notice that Excel has placed the formula =SUM(D12:D15) in this cell, as shown in Figure 2.9.

Figure 2.9
SUM function

10. Click **cell A1** and save your workbook as *Revised Income Statement-1* in the *Tutorial* folder in your *Excel Data* folder. Close the file.

HANDS on

Using the AVERAGE, MIN, and MAX Functions

You can enter statistical functions such as AVERAGE, MIN, and MAX by typing them or by using the drop-down list on the AutoSum button Σ ▾. In this activity, you'll practice using both methods. You'll also perform a *What If* analysis by changing cell data and viewing the calculated results in formula cells.

1. Open the *Personal Expenses* workbook in your *Excel Data* folder.

This workbook includes raw data for figuring the amount you spent on each category in your personal budget. You'll add formulas to help you better analyze spending habits.

2. Click **cell H6**. Click the **AutoSum triangle button** Σ ▾.

The AutoSum drop-down list displays with several commonly used functions, as shown in Figure 2.10. You can choose a function from this list instead of typing it.

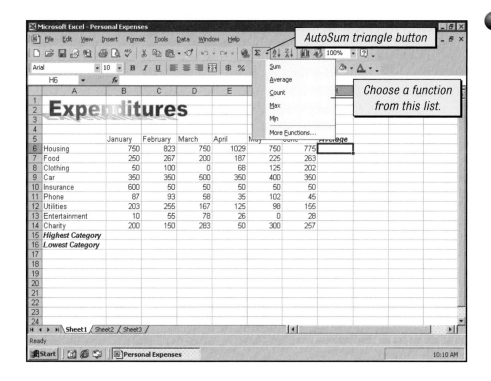

Figure 2.10
AutoSum drop-down list

3. Click **Average** on the drop-down list.

A moving border (a marquee) indicates the range for which Excel will calculate the Average, as shown in Figure 2.11.

> **NOTE** When you use the AutoSum feature, Excel first attempts to calculate the data in the cells above the selected cell. However, if there is no data in those cells, Excel calculates data in the cells to the left of the selected cell.

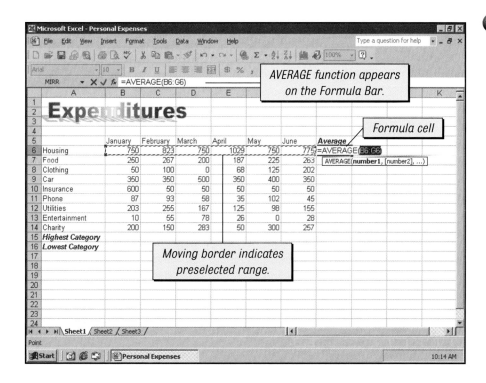

Figure 2.11
Moving border indicates preselected range

4. Verify that the moving border appears around cells B6:G6, then press ⎣Enter⏎⎦.

The average expenditure for housing during the first six months of the year (812.8333) appears in cell H6. Now you will copy this formula to the rest of the cells in column H using the Fill command. This command allows you to copy text, values, or formulas to adjacent cells.

5. Select **H6:H14**.

6. Point to **Fill** on the Edit menu, then click **Down** on the submenu.

The Average formula is copied from cell H6 to cells H7:H14, and the results appear in those cells.

7. Click **cell H7** and look at the Formula Bar which reads *=AVERAGE (B7:G7)*.

The formula *=AVERAGE(B6:G6)* was copied from cell H6, and Excel automatically changed the cell references in the new formulas to reflect the new location. For example, since the formula was copied down one row (from row 6 to row 7), the cell references shift by one row as well.

8. Click **cell B15** and then click the **AutoSum triangle button** Σ ▾. Click **Max** on the drop-down list.

9. Excel displays the moving border around cells B6:B14 to indicate that those cells are automatically included in this function as its arguments.

10. Click the **Enter button** ✓ to accept Excel's preselected range.

The maximum value for January (750) is displayed in cell B15. Now you will type a function to calculate the lowest value for January's expenditures.

11. Click **B16**, type =MIN(B6:B14), and press ⎣Enter⏎⎦.

The lowest value for January (10) is displayed in cell B16.

12. Select cells **B15:G16**.

13. Point to **Fill** on the Edit menu, then choose **Right** on the submenu.

The formulas in B15 and B16 are copied to C15:G16.

14. Click cell **C12**, type 25, and click the **Enter button** ✓ on the Formula Bar.

The calculated amounts in cells C16 and H12 change. When you modify cell data, Excel automatically recalculates to reflect your changes. If you change a cell that contains a value that is included in a formula, the formula recalculates.

NOTE *You can click the Undo button* ↺ ▾ *and then the Redo button* ↻ ▾ *to see the cells recalculate.*

15. Click cell **A1** and save your changes as *Revised Personal Expenses* in the *Tutorial* folder in your *Excel Data* folder.

HANDS on

Using AutoCalculate

When you want to do a quick check of a selected range without entering the formula, you can use Excel's AutoCalculate feature to display the total, average, minimum, or maximum. To do so, select the range for which you want to calculate the total and then view the results in the status bar.

1. In the open *Revised Personal Expenses* workbook, select **cells B7:G7** (the food costs for six months).

The sum for the range (1392) is displayed in the status bar, as shown in Figure 2.12.

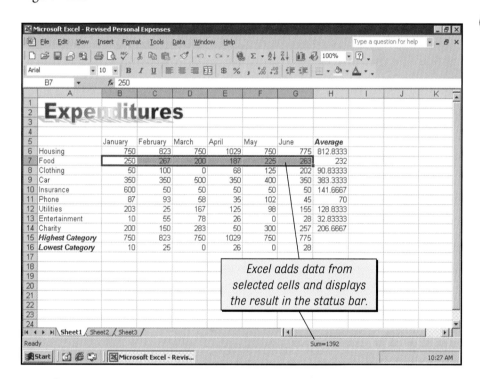

Figure 2.12
AutoCalculate feature

By default Excel totals the selected cells in the AutoCalculate area. However, you can also use AutoCalculate to find the average, minimum, and maximum for a range.

2. Verify that B7:G7 is still selected and then right-click the **AutoCalculate area** on the status bar.

A shortcut menu displays with a list of functions you can use, as shown in Figure 2.13.

3. Click **Min** on the list.

AutoCalculate displays the lowest value in the selected range.

4. Right-click the **AutoCalculate area** on the status bar and then click **Max.**

Using AutoCalculate

1. Select the range you want to calculate.

2. View the total on the status bar.

3. Right-click the status bar and choose another statistical function (such as MAX or MIN) from the shortcut menu.

Figure 2.13
Menu of AutoCalculate functions

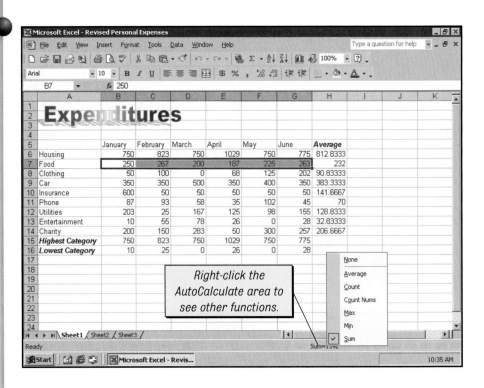

AutoCalculate displays the highest value in the selected range.

5. Right-click the **AutoCalculate area** on the status bar and then click **Sum**.

The total for the selected cells is displayed.

6. Click cell **A1**.

The range B7:G7 is deselected and the AutoCalculate area appears blank.

7. Close the workbook without saving changes.

Using Absolute Cell References

Until now you've used *relative cell references,* in which the references to a cell's contents are adjusted by Excel when you copy the formula to another cell or range. With **absolute cell references,** the reference doesn't adjust or change when you copy or move a formula. Using this type of cell reference is handy when you want to keep a cell reference frozen in place within a formula and don't want it to change if you copy or move the formula to another location. You make a cell reference absolute by typing the dollar sign ($) before both the column letter and row number (such as A1). You can also develop **mixed cell references** by including the dollar sign before only the column letter or the row number.

Here's how it works: Imagine you have a formula that you copy down three rows. If you use a *relative* cell reference, the cell reference in the copied formula will shift to reflect the new location. However, by making the reference absolute, the formula will copy exactly as you entered it, without the cell reference changing automatically to accommodate the new location.

Understanding Automatic Recalculation

Using cell references in your formulas can increase the speed and accuracy of your data entry. But the critical reason to use cell references is that they enable Excel to perform **automatic recalculation**—that is, recalculating the results of formulas when the value in any referenced cell changes. Automatic recalculation allows you to instantly see the impact of changes to your data. Formulas that contain cell references act not on specific numbers but on the numbers currently in the referenced cells. For example, $=A1+A2$ adds the value in A1 to the value in A2, whatever those values happen to be. This seemingly simple feature gives you the power to change values in your worksheet and immediately see the impact on your results. The process of changing values in a worksheet to observe the impact on results is called **what if analysis.**

Working With Absolute Cell References and Performing *What If* Analysis

In the following activity you'll create a formula that uses relative and absolute cell references.

1. Open the *Building Estimate* workbook in your *Excel Data* folder.

This workbook displays estimated building costs for constructing a new home at three different locations. The costs for Land, Electric, Water, Septic, and Driveway are already included in the total costs in cells B15:D15. However, the cost of actually building the home is not entered (see row 14). You'll develop a formula to figure this cost and then manipulate the figures using different estimates for the square footage and the building cost per square foot.

2. Click cell B14, then type =B17*B18. Click the Enter button  **on the Formula Bar.**

This is a formula that estimates the cost of building a 2,300 square foot home at $75 per square foot ($172,500).

3. Select cells B14:D14 and point to Fill on the Edit menu. Click Right on the submenu.

The formula is copied from B14 to cells C14:D14. Cells C14:D14 display zero (or hyphens) as the result. When you pasted the copied formula into cells C14:D14, the relative cell references shifted over to adjust to a new location for the formula. Therefore, they missed the values in cells B17:B18. You can easily fix this problem by using absolute cell references in your formulas.

4. Select cells C14:D14, point to Clear on the Edit menu, and click Contents.

5. Click cell B14. In the Formula Bar, drag over the formula to select it.

Excel BASICS

Creating and Copying a Relative Reference

1. Type a formula in the cell where you want the result to appear.

2. Select the cell that contains the formula.

3. Click the Copy button.

4. Move to the cell to which you want to paste the formula.

5. Press `Enter↵` or click the Paste button.

Excel BASICS

Creating and Copying an Absolute Reference

Creating an absolute reference:

1. Double-click the cell that contains the formula you want to change to include an absolute reference.

2. Select the formula.

3. Press [F4] to insert dollar signs in the cell reference.

4. Press [Enter←] to finalize the formula.

Copying and pasting an absolute reference:

1. Select the cell that contains the formula and click the Copy button.

2. Click the cell into which you want to paste the formula, or drag to select a range.

3. Press [Enter←] or click the Paste button.

Figure 2.14
Absolute cell references

---

6. Press [F4].

The formula is amended with dollar signs so it will use absolute cell references (**=B17*B18**).

7. Click Enter ✓.

The Total Costs amount in cell B15 ($276,700) appears the same as when you used relative cell references. However, the difference becomes apparent when you copy the formula to other cells.

8. Select cells B14:D14. Point to Fill on the Edit menu and click Right on the submenu.

The formula from B14 is copied to C14:D14.

9. Click cell C14 and select the formula in the Formula Bar.

Excel highlights the border of the referenced cells (B17:B18). The formula in cells C14:D14 includes absolute cell references to cells B17 and B18, as shown in Figure 2.14.

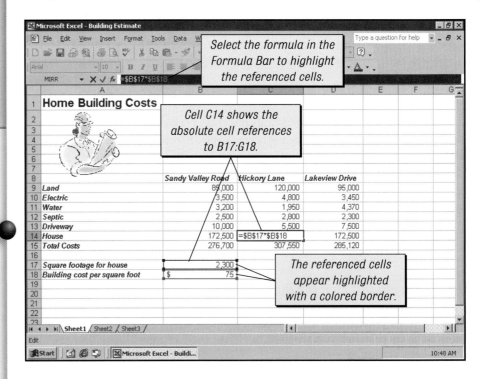

10. Click the Cancel button ✕.

You can use your worksheet as a tool to perform *What If* analysis. For example, you can answer questions such as "What if the cost of building a home rises by $10 per square foot?" or "How much will it cost if I build a smaller home?"

11. Click cell B18, type 85, and press [Enter←] **to reflect an increase in building costs.**

Notice that the cost of building the house increases (as shown in cells B14:D14), which also reflects in the total cost of building (cells B15:D15).

Excel BASICS

Performing *What If* Analysis

1. Edit the contents of a cell that is referred to within a formula.

2. Observe the new result calculated by the changed formula.

12. Click cell **B17**, type 1800, and press [Enter◄─┘] to calculate the cost of building a smaller home.

Excel automatically recalculates formulas in your worksheet so you can better analyze your data. The ability to quickly display the result of various scenarios makes Excel a powerful analytical tool.

13. Click cell **A1** and save the workbook as *Revised Building Estimate* in the *Tutorial* folder in your *Excel Data* folder. Close the workbook.

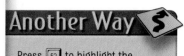

Press [F2] to highlight the referenced cells of a selected formula.

CREATING A CHART FROM YOUR WORKBOOK DATA

Charts are not only visually appealing, but they also provide statistical or numerical data in an easy-to-understand way. You can use charts to quickly communicate comparisons or trends. For example, you can create a graph so your audience can tell at a glance if sales are rising or falling or how productive your company was last quarter. Luckily, Excel includes a number of chart types you can use to display information. The type of chart you choose depends on the numerical data you want to graph. For example, a pie chart, which shows the percentage of a whole, is great for displaying your company's market share. On the other hand, a column chart is better than a pie chart at showing trends over time, such as sales for the past year.

You can create an embedded chart or display the graph on a chart sheet. **Embedded charts** are shown in the same worksheet that contains the numeric data on which the chart is based. Alternately, you can place your charts on a separate worksheet (but still in part of the workbook) on a **chart sheet.** In this lesson, you'll work primarily with embedded charts.

To create an Excel chart, you must first identify the worksheet data on which to base the chart by selecting it. The **data series** is the set of related values you want to chart. A **data point** is one value in a data series.

After you've selected the data for the chart, you can easily create the chart by using the **Chart Wizard.** This interactive tool asks a series of questions about the type of chart you want to create and builds a chart based upon your responses. When using this feature, you simply select the worksheet data to be charted (the data series), start the Chart Wizard, and follow the instructions. You can think of the Chart Wizard as a computerized questionnaire you complete for Excel to create the type of chart you want.

Elements of an Excel Chart

Before you create a chart, however, it's handy to know a bit about typical chart elements or chart objects. Figure 2.15 shows a typical Excel chart. When you create an embedded chart, Excel automatically surrounds the chart with a border. The empty area within this border is referred to as the chart area. An Excel chart usually includes several elements: the chart title; the plot area; the legend; the x-axis (or category axis) and the y-axis (or value axis); and the axis titles. Some of these elements are optional, such as the chart title, the legend, and the axis titles.

When you rest your pointer on an element in a chart, the name of the chart element will appear in a ScreenTip.

You can manipulate each element within a chart independently of the others—that is, you can resize, move, format, or even delete any element. You can select a chart element by clicking it. As an alternative, you can click the Chart Objects triangle button (on the Chart toolbar) and choose a chart element from the list.

Figure 2.15
Elements of a typical Excel chart

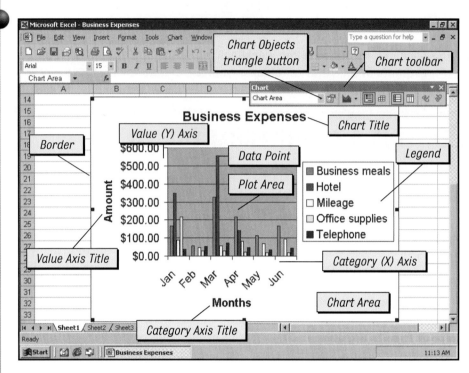

HANDS on

Creating a Chart

In this activity, you'll build a chart to compare the total costs of building a house in three different locations.

1. Open the *Revised Building Estimate* workbook in the *Tutorial* folder in your *Excel Data* folder. Select cells A8:D14 (the data series).

NOTE *When you select the data series to be charted, you should select cells that include descriptive text that you want to display on the chart, as well as cells that contain numbers.*

2. Click the Chart Wizard button ⬛ on the Standard toolbar.

The *Chart Wizard - Step 1 of 4 - Chart Type* dialog box appears as shown in Figure 2.16. This is the first of a series of four pages in the wizard that provides options to create a chart. On this page, you can select the type of chart.

3. In the *Chart type* area, click Bar.

The selections available in the *Chart sub-type* box change so that you can select the exact type of bar chart you want.

Excel BASICS

Using the Chart Wizard

1. Select the cells that contain the data to be charted (the data series).

2. Click the Chart Wizard button.

3. Make choices on each page of the Chart Wizard and then click Next. When you're finished setting options, choose Finish.

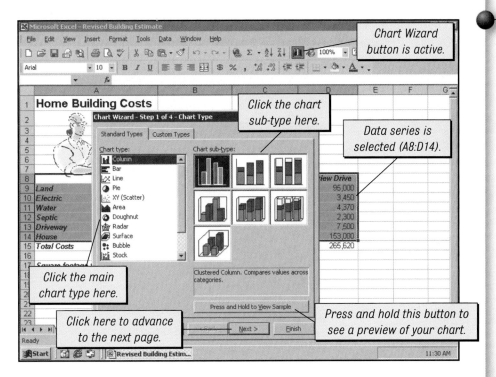

Figure 2.16
Chart Wizard

4. In the *Chart sub-type* area, click the second option in row 1 (Stacked Bar).

5. Click and hold the **Press and Hold to View Sample button** to see a preview of the chart type with data from your worksheet. Then release the mouse button.

6. Click the **Next button** to display the second page of the Wizard (the Chart Source Data page).

You use this page to indicate how you want your data to display (by columns or rows) and the range on which your chart should be based. Notice that a previously selected range is already indicated. For now you'll use these default selections.

7. Click the **Next button** to display the third page of the Wizard (the Chart Options page).

You can use options on this page to add or change several features of the chart, including the title, the data labels, and the placement of the legend. For now you'll use the default settings.

8. Click **Next** to display the fourth page of the Wizard (Chart Location).

This page allows you to insert the chart into the current worksheet or create a new sheet to hold the chart.

9. Click the **As object in option**, if necessary, and then click **Finish**.

Excel generates your chart and places it as an embedded chart object in the worksheet as shown in Figure 2.17. The chart object is selected; that is, a border with black selection handles appears around it. Don't worry that Excel placed

To launch the Chart Wizard, click Chart on the Insert menu.

Visit **www.glencoe.com/norton/online/** for more information on using charts.

the chart object over your worksheet data. You can move or resize this chart object to better display the information.

NOTE *If you click outside the chart, it will be deselected (the border will disappear). Click the chart to select it.*

Figure 2.17
Embedded chart object

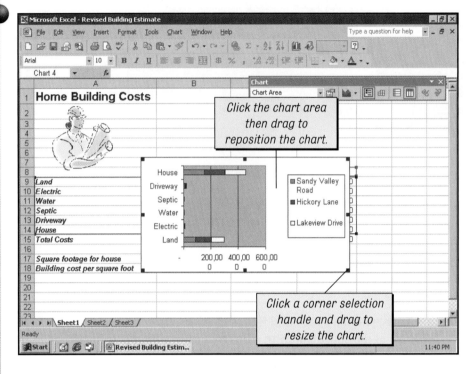

10. Point to the white chart area. When a ScreenTip appears identifying the chart area, drag the chart downward so that the top chart border is in row 20 and the left border is in the middle of column A.

WARNING *To drag the entire chart and not just an object within the chart, be sure to click in the chart area. Do not drag any of the chart elements.*

11. Scroll down until the chart is in the middle of the Excel window. Drag the selection handle in the lower-right corner of the chart down and to the right to increase the size of the chart until it covers column F and row 36.

12. Save your workbook as *Revised Building Estimate-1* in the *Tutorial* folder in your *Excel Data* folder.

It's easy to delete a chart—click in the chart area to select the chart and press [Delete].

Modifying and Printing a Chart

In this activity, you will modify and print the *Revised Building Estimate-1* chart.

1. In the open *Revised Building Estimate-1* workbook, point to the blank area within the chart border. Click when you see the Chart Area ScreenTip to ensure the chart is selected.

Black selection handles appear around the border of the chart.

2. Point to various elements of the chart.

As you point to each chart element, the name of the element (Category Axis, Value Axis, Plot Area, Legend and Chart Area) appears in a ScreenTip.

3. Click each chart element.

When you click each element, selection handles surround the element. When selection handles appear around an object, you can modify that object independently of the other chart objects.

4. Click again within the Chart Area to select the entire chart. Point to Toolbars on the View menu and click Chart.

The Chart toolbar displays in the Excel window, as shown in Figure 2.18. You can use buttons on this toolbar to quickly modify your chart.

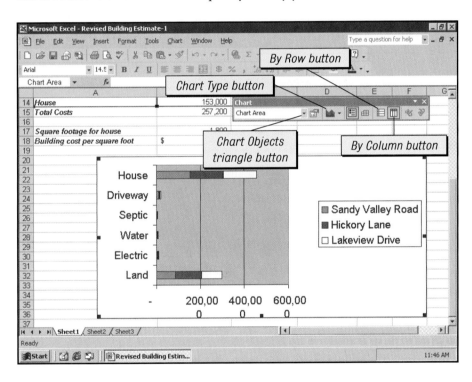

5. Point to each button on the Chart toolbar to read the identifying ScreenTip.

6. With the chart still selected, click the By Row button 📊.

The data displays by location instead of by cost category (see Figure 2.19). You can print just the chart, or you can print both the chart and the data on which it is based.

7. With the chart still selected, click Print on the File menu.

8. In the *Print what* area of the Print dialog box, click the Selected Chart option, if necessary. Click OK to print your chart.

HINTS & TIPS

You can select a chart element by clicking the Chart Objects triangle button on the Chart toolbar.

Figure 2.18
Chart toolbar

Excel **BASICS**

Modifying and Printing a Chart

To modify a chart:

1. Point to Toolbars on the View menu and click Chart.

2. With the chart selected, click the By Row or By Column button on the Chart toolbar to change the appearance of the chart.

To print a chart:

1. To print the chart without the data, select the chart, click Print on the File menu, and click OK.

2. To print the chart with the worksheet data, deselect the chart by clicking the worksheet and click Print on the File menu.

3. Click Active Sheet(s), if necessary, and click OK.

Figure 2.19
Rearranged chart data

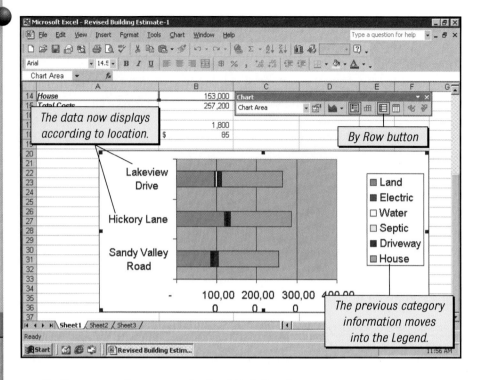

WEB NOTE

Microsoft maintains a
comprehensive Web site
(http://www.microsoft.com
/office/excel/default.htm) that
you can use to find out more
about Excel. For example, you can
find out about features, tips and
tricks for using the software,
pricing information, and updates.

9. Save your changes as *Revised Building Estimate-2* in the *Tutorial*
   folder in your *Excel Data* folder.

Excel saves the chart along with the workbook. (Saving a workbook automatically saves a chart within the workbook.)

10. Close the workbook. Point to **Toolbars** on the View menu and click
    Chart to close the Chart toolbar.

Self Check

Test your knowledge by answering the following questions. See Appendix B to
check your answers.

1. You can use the _____ button to quickly total a column of
   numbers.

2. The formula $=30-5*9+(3+17)$ results in _____ .

3. Functions consist of three parts: the equal sign; the name of the function, such as SUM; and the _____ of the function.

4. Cell references within copied formulas are known as _____
   if they change to correspond to their new location.

5. The _____ is a tool that asks a series of questions about the
   type of chart you want to create and builds a chart based upon your
   responses.

Troubleshooting Charts

Creating and modifying charts in Excel is generally problem-free. However, you might occasionally encounter times when a chart doesn't display data as you'd like. Luckily, you can use Help to find out why.

1. Type troubleshoot charts **in the** *Ask a Question box,* **and press** Enter↵ **.**

2. Click the **Troubleshoot charts topic.**

The *Troubleshoot charts* Help topic appears, as shown in Figure 2.20.

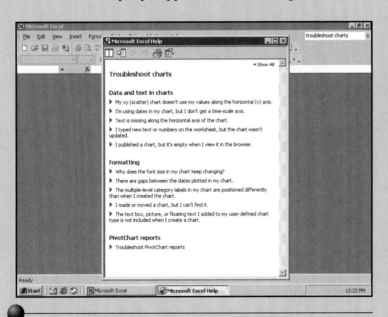

Figure 2.20
Troubleshoot charts Help window

3. Click each of the hyperlinks on troubleshooting charts and read the associated information.

4. When you are finished reading, click the **Close button** ⊠ to close the Help window.

ADDING HYPERLINKS TO A WORKSHEET

Hyperlinks are hot spots you can click to quickly jump to a workbook, a document, or a Web site. Hyperlinks are typically represented by underlined text. Hyperlinks are useful because they allow you to easily locate and display information you need.

In this activity, you will create hyperlinks to jump from one worksheet to another and to an external Web site. You will also edit a hyperlink.

1. **Launch Excel and open the *Surfside Income Statement & Sales* workbook in your *Excel Data* folder.**

2. **Point to Toolbars on the View menu and click Web.**

The Web toolbar displays at the top of the Excel window beneath the Formatting toolbar.

> **NOTE** *If the Web toolbar is floating (unattached) in the Excel window, drag it by the title bar until it docks in position under the Formatting toolbar.*

3. **Click the Sales sheet tab. Notice that the *Sales* worksheet shows how individual items contributed to each month's sales.**

4. **Click the Income Statement sheet tab and then click cell B6.**

This cell contains the sales total for January. You will link this cell to the cells that contain the January sales items on the *Sales* worksheet.

5. **Click the Insert Hyperlink button 🔗 on the Standard toolbar.**

The Insert Hyperlink dialog box displays. You use this dialog box to choose how to link to a worksheet location, file, or Web page.

6. **Click Existing File or Web Page in the *Link to* section, if necessary.**

7. **Click the Look in triangle button and navigate to your *Excel Data* folder, if necessary. Scroll through the *Excel Data* folders and files, then click the *Surfside Income Statement & Sales* workbook.**

The workbook name appears in the *Address* box of the Insert Hyperlink dialog box, and the path to the workbook appears in the Address box of the Web toolbar, as shown in Figure 2.21.

8. **Click the Bookmark button in the Insert Hyperlink dialog box.**

The Select Place in Document dialog box displays.

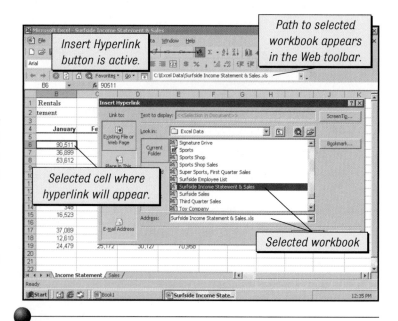

Figure 2.21
Insert Hyperlink dialog box

9. Type B5:B10 in the *Type in the cell reference* box.

10. Click **Sales** in the *Or select a place in this document* box.

Clicking *Sales* tells Excel to create a hyperlink to the worksheet entitled *Sales*. Since the reference is listed as B5:B10, Excel will highlight that range in the *Sales* worksheet (cells B5:B10 contain the January sales figures for individual items sold).

11. Click **OK** to close the Select Place in Document dialog box. Click **OK** in the Insert Hyperlink dialog box.

12. Click **cell A1** so that you can better view the hyperlink in cell B6.

13. Point to **cell B6**.

The pointer becomes the shape of a hand (the Hyperlink Select pointer). A ScreenTip appears showing the path to the designated range in the *Sales* worksheet, as shown in Figure 2.22.

14. Click **cell B6**.

Excel jumps to the *Sales* worksheet and high-lights cells B5:B10, the range you specified when you created the hyperlink.

15. Click the **Back button** ⬅ on the Web toolbar to return to the *Income Statement* worksheet. Create hyperlinks for the February and March sales totals in cells C6 and D6. Link these totals to the corresponding sales data in cells C5:C10 and cells D5:D10 of the Sales sheet, respectively.

16. Click each of the hyperlinks to test them. Click the **Back button** ⬅ on the Web toolbar, when necessary, to return to the *Income Statement* worksheet.

17. Click **cell A1**. Click **Save As** on the File menu and save the revised workbook as *Surfside Income Statement & Sales with Hyperlinks* in the *Tutorial* folder in your *Excel Data* folder.

18. Click **cell A10** in the *Income Statement* worksheet and then click the **Insert Hyperlink button** 🔗.

19. Click the **Existing File or Web Page icon** in the *Link to* section, if necessary.

20. Navigate to your *Excel Data* folder in the *Look in* box, click the *Surfside Employee List* workbook, and click **OK**.

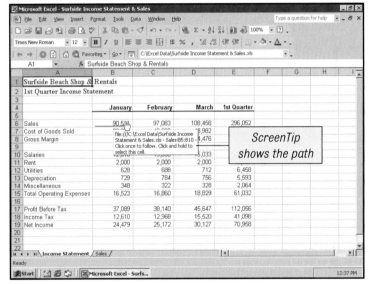

Figure 2.22
Hyperlink path

NOTE *You don't need to set a bookmark in this case since you want to review the entire worksheet instead of highlighting a specific area.*

ON THE WEB

EXCEL 2002

21. Click your newly created hyperlink in cell A10.

Excel opens the *Surfside Employee List* workbook (Figure 2.23) so that you can review the information about the employees.

> **NOTE** *Excel also allows you to create hyperlinks to other types of documents, such as Microsoft Word or PowerPoint files.*

22. Select cell H4 in the *Surfside Employee List* workbook. Click the Insert Hyperlink button.

23. In the *Address* box, type www.usps.gov and click OK. Click your new Zip Code hyperlink.

If your connection to the Internet is already active, Excel will open your browser and jump directly to the Web site for the U.S. Postal Service (Figure 2.24).

> **WARNING** *If your connection to the Internet is not active, either the Sign In or Connect To dialog box will appear so that you can connect to the Internet, or you will receive an error message telling you that no connection is established. Sign in or connect to your Internet service provider and then repeat steps 22 and 23.*

> **NOTE** *Web sites are often updated and their links may change. If the links do not work exactly as specified in this tutorial, click a link that you think will lead you to the appropriate information.*

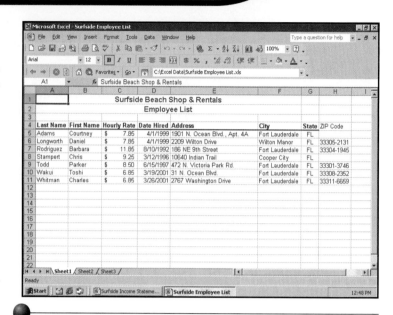

Figure 2.23
Surfside Employee List workbook

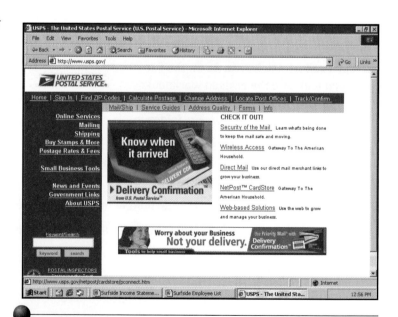

Figure 2.24
U.S. Postal Service Web site

348 Lesson 2

24. Explore the Web page to find the missing ZIP Codes for your *Surfside Employee List* workbook. The addresses for which you are trying to locate ZIP Codes are as follows:

1901 N. Ocean Blvd. Apt. 4A
Fort Lauderdale, FL

10640 Indian Trail
Cooper City, FL

25. After you find the ZIP Codes, navigate to the *Surfside Employee List* worksheet and enter the ZIP codes in the appropriate cells.

26. Point to **cell H4** in the *Surfside Employee List* worksheet. Click and hold for a moment to select the cell. Click the **Insert Hyperlink button** 🔗.

The Edit Hyperlink dialog box appears, displaying the hyperlink (**www.usps.gov**) in the Address box.

27. Click the **Remove Link button**.

28. Click **cell A1** and save the revised workbook as *Revised Surfside Employee List* in the *Tutorial* folder in your *Excel Data* folder. Close the workbook.

29. Save then close the *Surfside Income Statement & Sales with Hyperlinks* workbook. Point to **Toolbars** on the View menu and click **Web** to close the Web toolbar.

30. Close your browser, if necessary, and disconnect from the Internet.

WARNING *You may proceed directly to the exercises for this lesson. If, however, you are finished with your computer session, follow the "shut down" procedures for your lab or school environment.*

SUMMARY AND EXERCISES

SUMMARY

In this lesson you made modifications to worksheets. You selected various sections of the worksheet so that you could work with data more effectively. You rearranged your worksheet by inserting and deleting columns and rows, copied and moved data, and resized columns. When you made mistakes in your worksheet, you reversed the changes with Undo. You also built formulas and functions to perform calculations and studied the order of operations. You saw how Excel automatically recalculates your worksheet to reflect your changes. Additionally, you learned the difference between relative and absolute references. You developed a graph using the Chart Wizard. Finally, you inserted hyperlinks into an Excel workbook.

Now that you have completed this lesson, you should be able to do the following:

- Select single cells and ranges of cells—including rows, columns, and an entire worksheet. (page 313)

- Select two or more noncontiguous ranges. (page 313)

- Define a *data area*. (page 316)

- Select and print a range. (page 316)

- Select, preview, and print noncontiguous ranges. (page 316)

- Set and clear a print area. (page 316)

- Delete the contents of one or more cells. (page 318)

- Cancel and restore changes using Undo. (page 318)

- Clear the contents of a cell. (page 320)

- Insert and delete cells, rows, and columns. (page 320)

- Move and copy cell contents using toolbar buttons, drag-and-drop, and keyboard shortcuts. (page 322)

- Copy and paste multiple items using the Clipboard task pane. (page 322)

- Understand when to use formulas. (page 326)

- Create, revise, and copy formulas. (page 326)

- Use the arithmetic operators in formulas and understand operator precedence. (page 328)

- Describe the three parts of a function. (page 330)

- Use Excel's built-in functions (SUM, AVERAGE, MIN, and MAX). (page 331)

- Use AutoCalculate to quickly check the total, average, minimum, or maximum of a selected range. (page 335)

- Understand and use absolute cell references. (page 336)

- Explain the significance of automatic recalculation. (page 337)

- Perform a *what if* analysis. (page 337)

- Identify the elements of a chart. (page 339)

- Create a chart using the Chart Wizard. (page 340)

- Resize, move, modify, and print a chart. (page 342)

- Insert and edit hyperlinks that jump to other workbooks and to external Web sites. (page 346)

CONCEPTS REVIEW

1 TRUE/FALSE

Circle T if the statement is true or F if the statement is false.

T F **1.** If you issue a command while a group of cells is selected, the command affects the entire group.

T **F** **2.** A range reference contains four cell references, each representing a corner of the range.

T F **3.** You can move data by dragging the cells that contain the data.

T F **4.** If you click a hyperlink to jump to a workbook that is not open, Excel automatically opens the workbook for you.

T **F** **5.** The Undo command can only cancel the most recent action.

T **F** **6.** You can select a range of cells by clicking the first cell, holding *R* (for *Range*), and clicking the last cell.

T F **7.** Addition and subtraction operators have a lower order of precedence than multiplication and division.

T F **8.** You can build your own formulas or use Excel's functions.

T F **9.** Functions include three main parts: the equal sign, the function name, and the arguments.

T F **10.** When you copy a formula from one cell to another, the relative cell references within the formula change to reflect the new position.

2 MATCHING

Match each of the terms on the left with the definitions on the right.

TERMS	DEFINITIONS
1. select	**a.** Cell references within a formula that don't change
2. automatic recalculation	**b.** Cell references within a formula that change when you copy or move them to adjust to the new location
3. absolute cell references	
4. relative cell references	**c.** An interactive tool that takes you step-by-step through the process of creating a chart
5. range reference	
6. range	**d.** To highlight one or more cells
7. hyperlink	**e.** A graphical representation of numerical data
8. Chart Wizard	**f.** Feature that will reverse the last action
9. chart	**g.** An underlined word or phrase that you can click to jump to another worksheet, document, or Web page
10. Undo	**h.** Excel's ability to reflect changes you make to data cells referenced in a formula
	i. A group of cells
	j. Set of two cell references, separated by a colon

SUMMARY AND EXERCISES

3 COMPLETION

Fill in the missing word or phrase for each of the following statements.

1. To select *noncontiguous* ranges, select the first range and then press and hold _____ while dragging to select additional ranges.

2. When operators have the same level of precedence, they are evaluated from _____ to _____ .

3. You can use the _____ command to reverse the effects of your most recent action.

4. A method you can use to move cells with the mouse without using keyboard commands, menu commands, or a toolbar button is called _____ .

5. You can select a range that includes numbers and then use the _____ feature to view the result in the status bar.

6. By default, numbers are aligned on the _____ , and text is aligned on the _____ .

7. To select an adjacent range, click the first cell in the range, press _____ , and then click the last cell in the range.

8. A cell reference in a formula that doesn't change when you copy the formula is called _____ .

9. The process of changing values in a worksheet to observe the impact on the results is called _____ .

10. Predefined formulas that perform specialized calculations are called _____ .

4 SHORT ANSWER

Write a brief answer to each of the following questions.

1. What type of chart would best show market share? Why?

2. What is one primary difference between text and values?

3. How can you reverse your most recent action?

4. What is Excel's automatic recalculation feature?

5. What is the order of operations?

6. How can you change the order of operations for a formula?

7. Name two techniques you could use to select the range A5:B10.

8. How could you select columns A through D?

9. How could you select rows 3 and 7?

10. Briefly describe the Copy, Cut, and Paste commands.

5 IDENTIFICATION

Label each of the elements in Figure 2.25.

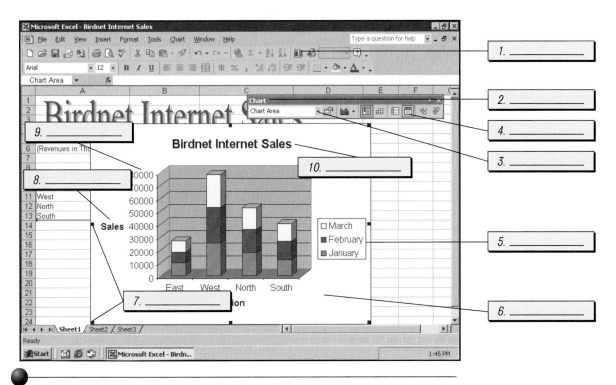

Figure 2.25

SKILLS REVIEW

Complete all of the Skills Review problems in sequential order to review your skills to select ranges of cells, erase data, undo and redo changes, insert and delete columns and rows, create and copy formulas and functions, use automatic recalculation, and create a chart.

1 Select Ranges

1. Open the *Home Builders Employee List* workbook in your *Excel Data* folder.

2. Click **cell A5** to select it. Drag to select **A5:C11**.

3. Click **cell A5** again, press and hold [⇧ Shift], then click **cell D11** to select the range containing the employees' names, pay rates, and hire dates.

4. Click **row heading 6** to highlight the entire row containing Sarah Johnson's information.

5. Click **column heading F** to select the list of cities.

6. To select the entire worksheet, click the **Select All button** (located to the left of the column A heading).

7. Click any cell to remove the highlighting from the worksheet.

8. Select **range A7:D7**. Press and hold [Ctrl] and drag to select **A10:D11**.

9. Click any cell to remove the highlighting.

2 Erasing Data and Reversing Changes

1. Click **cell A5** in the *Home Builders Employee List* workbook.

2. Press [Delete] to erase the data in the cell. Type **Putnam** and press [Enter←].

3. Click **cell C8**, select the value in the Formula Bar, type **9.45**, and click the **Enter button** [Enter←].

4. Click the **Undo button** [↰▾] to change the pay rate back to 9.25.

5. Click the **Redo button** [↱▾].

6. Add the information as indicated in Table 2.4.

7. Click the **Undo triangle button** [↰▾]. Click at the top of the list and drag down to highlight all entries up to and including *Typing 'Birch' in A12* (8 actions). Release the mouse button.

8. Click **cell A1** and save your changes as *Updated Employee List* in the *Skills Review* folder in your *Excel Data* folder.

Table 2.4	Data for Input
Cell	**Data**
A12	Birch
B12	Owen
C12	7.85
D12	10/16/2001
E12	172 Second Avenue
F12	Jackson
G12	OH
H12	45694

3 Insert and Delete Rows, Columns, and Cells

1. Click **row heading 9** in the *Updated Employee List* workbook to select the row that contains data for Todd Adkins.

2. Click **Delete** on the Edit menu.

3. Right-click **row heading 7** (Ann Sanders) and click **Insert** on the shortcut menu to insert a blank row.

4. Click **row heading 9** (Lee Parks). Click **Rows** on the Insert menu to insert another blank row.

5. Click **column heading A** to select the column, then click **Columns** on the Insert menu to insert a blank column.

6. Click **cell B12** and click **Delete** on the Edit menu. Click **Shift Cells left** in the Delete dialog box, if necessary, and click **OK**.

7. Click **Cells** on the Insert menu. Click **Shift cells right** in the Insert dialog box and click **OK**.

8. Type White in cell B12, and press
   [Enter←]. (Your worksheet should look
   like Figure 2.26.)

9. Click **cell A1** and save the workbook as
   Updated Employee List-1 in the *Skills
   Review* folder in your *Excel Data* folder.

4 Copy and Move Data and Resize a Column and Row

1. Select the range **B8:I8** in the *Updated
   Employee List-1* workbook and click the
   Copy button 📋.

2. Click **cell B9** and press [Enter←] to copy
   the selected row.

3. Click **cell C9**, type Mary, and press [Tab].

4. Type 7.85 in the Hourly Rate column
   and press [Tab]. Type 4/16/2001 in the
   Date Hired column and press [Enter←].

5. Select **range B1:B2** (the worksheet title), and click the **Cut button** ✂. Click
   cell A1 and press [Enter←] to move the title.

6. Select range **B5:I5**, point to the border of the selected range, and drag the selection
   to range **B7:I7**. Release the mouse button.

7. Click **row heading 5** and click **Delete** on the Edit menu to delete the blank row.

8. Click the **column F heading**, then point to **Column** on the Format menu and
   click **AutoFit Selection** to adjust the column width.

9. Click **cell A4**. Point to the border between row headings 4 and 5. Drag down to
   increase the row height to 18.00 (watch the ScreenTip).

10. Click **cell A1** and save the workbook as *Updated Employee List-2* in the *Skills
    Review* folder in your *Excel Data* folder. Close the workbook.

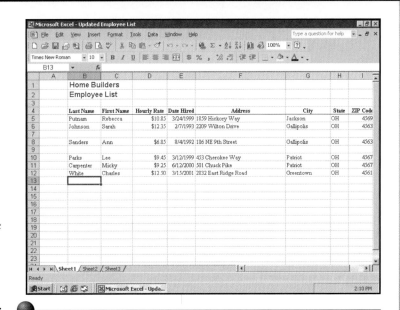

Figure 2.26

5 Use Formulas and Automatic Recalculation

1. Open the *Petty Cash* workbook in your *Excel Data* folder.

2. Click **cell E4**, type =D4 in the Formula Bar, and press the **Enter button** [Enter←].

3. In **cell E5**, type =E4-C5+D5 and press [Enter←].

4. Click **cells E4** and **E5** to verify that you typed the formulas correctly. Edit these
   cells, if necessary.

5. Click **cell E5** and click the **Copy button** 📋.

6. Select the **range E6:E17** and press [Enter←] to paste the formula.

7. Click **cell C5**, type 11.50, and press [Enter←] to observe the recalculation in range
   E5:E17.

EXCEL 2002

8. Click **cell A1** and save the workbook as *Petty Cash Register* in the *Skills Review* folder in your *Excel Data* folder. Close the workbook.

6 Enter a Formula Without Values and Use the SUM Function

1. Open the *Personal Budget* workbook in your *Excel Data* folder.

2. Click **cell B22**, type the formula =B6-E20, and press Enter↵.

3. Click **cell B6**, type =SUM(B4:B5), and press Enter↵ to calculate the total monthly income.

4. Click **cell E20**. Select **cells E4:E19** and click the **AutoSum button** Σ▾ to total the monthly expenses. Click **cell B22**. Observe that the formula you entered in cell B22 calculates the difference between income and expenses.

5. Click **cell E21**, type =MAX(, and drag to select **E4:E19**.

6. When the range appears in the formula, type a closing parenthesis and press Enter↵.

7. Select **cells E4:E19**. View the total for this range ($3,134) in the AutoCalculate area of the status bar to verify the total in cell E20.

8. Right-click the **AutoCalculate area** of the status bar and click **MAX**.

9. Right-click the **AutoCalculate area** of the status bar and click **MIN**.

10. Right-click the **AutoCalculate area** of the status bar and click **SUM**.

11. Click **cell A1** and save the revised workbook as *Sample Personal Budget* in the *Skills Review* folder in your *Excel Data* folder. Close the workbook.

7 Create and Copy a Relative Reference and Insert a New Row

1. Open the *June Payroll* workbook in your *Excel Data* folder.

2. In the June 9 worksheet, click **cell E5** and type =C5*D5. Click the **Enter button** ✓ on the Formula Bar.

3. With cell E5 still selected, press Ctrl + C to copy the formula to the Clipboard.

4. Select cells **E6:E11** and press Ctrl + V to paste the formula from cell E5. Press Esc.

5. Click each cell in E6:E11 and observe that the formulas contain relative cell references.

6. Right-click **row heading 10** to select the row, and click **Insert** on the shortcut menu.

7. Enter the following information for a new employee:

Cell A10: **Johnson**
Cell B10: **Kenneth**
Cell C10: **7.85**
Cell D10: **5**

8. Press Tab or → after typing the data in cell D10. Observe that Excel automatically adds a formula (in cell E10) to calculate the gross pay.

9. Click **cell A1** and save your workbook as *Revised June Payroll* in the *Skills Review* folder in your *Excel Data* folder.

8 Create an Absolute Cell Reference

1. Click **cell H2** in the *June 9* worksheet in the *Revised June Payroll* workbook. Type Bonus, and press Enter←.

2. Type .05 in cell H3, and press Enter←.

3. In cell F5, type =E5+E5*H3 and press Enter← to calculate the first employee's gross pay including the 5 percent bonus.

4. Click **cell F5** and click **Copy** on the Edit menu. Select **cells F6:F12** and click **Paste** on the Edit menu.

5. Click **cell F6** to view the formula (=E6+E6*H4) which is incorrect. (The reference H4 doesn't point to the bonus value in H3.) Observe that the bonus is not calculated correctly because Excel copied the formula using relative cell references.

6. Double-click **cell F5** in the *June Payroll* workbook and click an insertion point before the reference to cell H3.

7. Press F4 to insert dollar signs in the cell reference and press Enter←.

8. Click **cell F5** and then copy and paste the edited formula to cells F6:F12.

9. Click **cell A1** and save your workbook as *Revised June Payroll-1* in the *Skills Review* folder in your *Excel Data* folder.

9 Perform *What If* Analysis Using Absolute Cell References

1. In the *Revised June Payroll-1* workbook, click **cell H3** (the cell that contains the bonus percentage).

2. Type .07 and press Enter←. Click **Undo** then click **Redo** to observe the increase from 5 to 7 percent.

3. Click **cell D11**, type 20, and press Enter← to recalculate the gross pay and bonus.

4. Click **cell A1** and save your workbook as *Revised June Payroll-2* in the *Skills Review* folder in your *Excel Data* folder.

10 Calculate Averages, Counts, Minimums, and Maximums

1. Click **cell A15** in the *Revised June Payroll-2* workbook.

2. Type the following labels:

   Cell A15: **Number of Employees**
   Cell A16: **Average Hours Worked**
   Cell A17: **Fewest Hours Worked**
   Cell A18: **Greatest Hours Worked**

3. In cell C15, type =COUNT(D5:D12) and press Enter← to calculate the number of employees.

4. In cell C16, type =AVERAGE(D5:D12) and press Enter← to calculate the average number of hours worked.

5. In cell C17, type =MIN(D5:D12) and press [Enter◄┘] to calculate the fewest number of hours worked by an employee.

6. In cell C18, type =MAX(D5:D12) and press [Enter◄┘] to calculate the greatest number of hours worked by an employee.

7. Click cell A1 and save your workbook as *Revised June Payroll-3* in the *Skills Review* folder in your *Excel Data* folder.

11 Use the Chart Wizard

1. Open the *Business Expenses* workbook in your *Excel Data* folder.

2. Select **cells A5:A9**. Press and hold [Ctrl] and select **cells H5:H9**.

3. Click the **Chart Wizard button** 📊 to display the first page of the Chart Wizard.

4. In the *Chart type* box, click **Pie**. In the *Chart sub-type* box, click **Pie with a 3-D visual effect** (the second option in row 1).

5. Click the **Press and Hold to View Sample button** to see a preview of your chart. Release the mouse button.

6. Click **Next** to view the Chart Source Data (Step 2 of 4). Accept the defaults by clicking **Next**.

7. In the Chart Options box (Step 3 of 4), click the **Titles tab**, if necessary. Type Business Expenses for January through June in the *Chart title* box.

8. Click the **Data Labels tab** and select the **Percentage box**.

9. Click the **Legend tab** and click **Bottom** in the Placement box.

10. Click **Next** to display the last page of the Chart Wizard (Chart Location, Step 4 of 4).

11. Click the **As object in option**, if necessary, and click **Finish**.

12. Point to the chart's bottom-right corner selection handle and drag it down and to the right to enlarge the chart.

13. Drag the middle-right selection handle to the right to widen the chart so that the chart title fits on one line.

14. Drag the chart to center it below the worksheet data. Your chart should look similar to Figure 2.27.

15. Click **cell A1** and save the workbook as *Expenses Pie Chart* in the *Skills Review* folder in your *Excel Data* folder. Close the workbook.

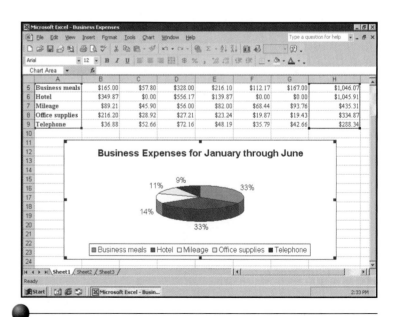

Figure 2.27

LESSON APPLICATIONS

1 Change the Data and Rearrange the Worksheet

Correct errors in a worksheet; insert a new row and column; resize a column; select ranges; create and copy formulas; and insert the SUM, AVERAGE, MINIMUM, and MAXIMUM functions.

1. Open the *Signature Drive* workbook in your *Excel Data* folder.

2. Change the Goldsmith signatures to 112 and the hours to 12.

3. Insert a new row above the row that contains the data for Stoll. In the new blank row, type data for a participant named *Siegel* (187 signatures; 12 hours).

4. Add a new column with the heading *Days* between the Signatures and Hours columns. In the Days column, type 8, 15, 11, 6, 17, 7, 12, 5, 8, 13, and 14 to represent the total number of days each person has worked.

5. In cell A1, make the text bold and the font size 14.

6. Use the AutoFit feature to increase the width of column A.

7. Enter the following data: cell A15: **Total**; cell A16: **Average**; cell A17: **Best**; cell A18: **Lowest**.

8. In cell B15, use the SUM function to total the Signatures column. Copy the formula in cell B15 to cell C15.

9. Total cells D4:D14 using AutoSum (place the result in cell D15).

10. In cell B16, enter a function that determines the average for cells B4:B14, then copy the formula to cells C16 and D16.

11. In cell B17, enter a function that determines the highest value in the Signatures column, then copy the formula from cell B17 to cells C17:D17.

12. Using the Formula Bar, enter a function that determines the lowest value for the Signatures column. Place the result in cell B18. Copy the formula to cells C18:D18.

13. Change the following values as indicated: Alvarez signatures: 305; Goldsmith signatures: 250. Observe the changes in the formula cells.

14. Save the workbook as *Revised Signature Drive* in the *Lesson Applications* folder in your *Excel Data* folder. Close the workbook.

2 Use AutoCalculate and Print Selected Areas of a Worksheet

Use AutoCalculate to quickly find the total, average, maximum, and minimum values for a range of cells. Select, preview, and print noncontiguous areas of a worksheet. Set a print area.

1. Open the *Real Estate* workbook in your *Excel Data* folder.

2. Determine the total sales for the properties in B4:B10 using AutoCalculate.

3. Use AutoCalculate to determine the average and the maximum and minimum values of cells B4:B10, then again determine the total.

4. Simultaneously select A4:A7; C4:C7; A12:A14; and C12:C14. Preview then print these selected ranges.

5. Set A2:A9 as a print area, then preview and print this range. Clear the print area.

6. Close the *Real Estate* workbook without saving changes.

3 Create a Bar Chart With the Chart Wizard

Use the Chart Wizard to create a 3-D bar chart from the sales data in a workbook.

1. Open the *Chocolate Sales* workbook *(Sheet 1)* in your *Excel Data* folder.

2. Use the Chart Wizard to create a clustered column bar chart with a 3-D visual effect. Enter **First Quarter Sales** as the chart title.

3. Create the chart as an embedded object in the *Chocolate Sales* worksheet. Position the chart so that it displays below the worksheet data and enlarge it to an appropriate size.

4. Change data in your worksheet as follows: cell B5: **8,000**; cell C5: **12,000**. View the corresponding changes in the chart.

5. Using the Chart toolbar, display the chart data by row so that the items appear in the Legend and the months appear in the Category Axis (Figure 2.28).

6. Click cell A1 and save the revised workbook as *Chocolate Sales Bar Chart* in the *Lesson Applications* folder in your *Excel Data* folder. Close the workbook.

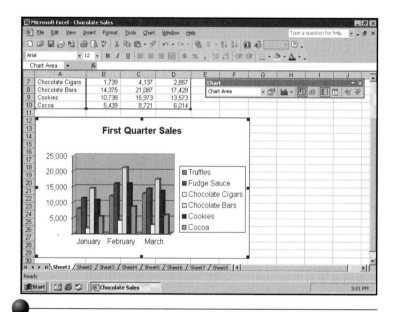

Figure 2.28

4 Use the SUM Function and Perform *What If* Analysis

Total a range using the SUM function. Increase the sales of a product to observe the impact on total sales. Create and copy an absolute reference.

1. Open the *A Sporting Time* workbook in your *Excel Data* folder.

2. Type **Totals** in cell A14 and create a SUM function in cell B14 that totals April sales. Copy the formula in cell B14 to cells C14:E14.

3. Create a SUM function in cell E6 that totals quarterly sales for baseball equipment. Copy the formula in cell E6 to cells E7:E13.

4. Perform *what if* analysis to determine how total sales would be affected if gymnastic equipment sales were doubled in April–June. (*Hint:* You can double the sales figures by creating a formula such as =2890*2.) Observe how the sales totals change.

5. Type **Percent of Total** as a column label in cell F5. In cell F6, enter a formula that divides second quarter baseball equipment sales by the total quarterly sales.

6. Copy the formula in cell F6 to cells F7:F13 and observe the relative cell reference error in those cells.

7. In F6, change the appropriate cell reference to an absolute reference and recopy the formula to F7:F13.

8. Format the data in column F using Percent Style and one decimal place (Figure 2.29).

9. Save the revised workbook as *Second Quarter Sales* in the *Lesson Applications* folder in your *Excel Data* folder. Close the workbook.

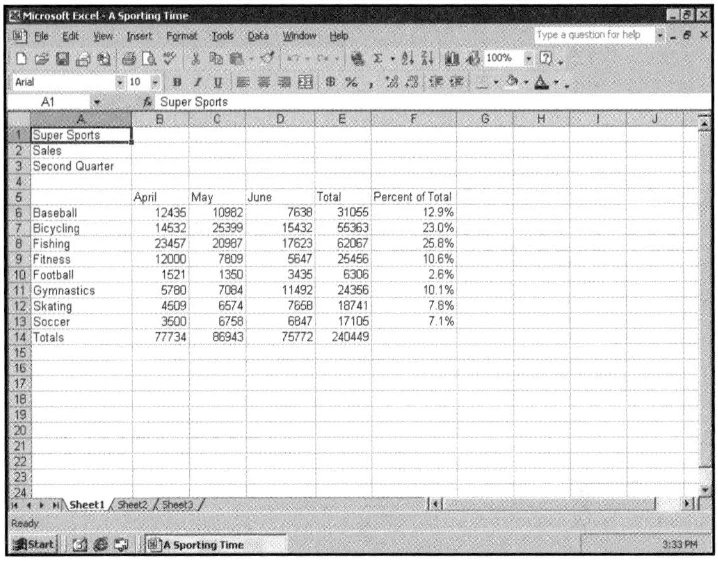

Figure 2.29

PROJECTS

1 A Burst of Sales

You would like to track sales of your home-based business—selling and decorating with balloons. Create a new workbook. Type the title **BALLOON SALES** in cell A1 of your worksheet.

Skip a row and enter the data shown in Table 2.5 beginning in row A3. Check the spelling of text entries in the worksheet. Print one copy of the worksheet. Save the file as *Balloon Sales* in the *Projects* folder in your *Excel Data* folder. Send the workbook in an e-mail to your instructor or another student in your class.

Table 2.5	Balloon Sales					
Jan	**Feb**	**Mar**	**Apr**	**May**	**Jun**	**Jul**
202	212	222	232	242	252	262
204	214	224	234	244	254	264
206	216	226	236	246	256	266
208	218	228	238	248	258	268
210	220	230	240	250	260	270

2 Identify the Colors

Open the *Balloon Sales* workbook in the *Projects* folder in your *Excel Data* folder that you saved in Project 1. (If you did not complete Project 1, use the file named *Balloons* in your *Excel Data* folder.) Insert a new column to the left of the Jan column. Type the following text into the new column, beginning in cell A4: **Red, Green, Blue, Yellow, Purple**.

Change the number of red balloons sold in June to 253, and change the number of purple balloons sold in January to 347. Below the row for red balloons, add new rows for Orange and Polka-Dotted balloons. Fill the Orange row with the values 123, 234, 345, 456, 567, 678, and 789 from left to right. Since the same number of yellow balloons and polka-dotted balloons were sold, copy the numbers from the Yellow row to the Polka-Dotted row. Widen column A to better accommodate the Polka-Dotted label. Increase the height of row 3. Drag to move the BALLOON SALES heading in cell B1 to cell A1.

Since you've decided to show only sales of balloons for the first half of the year, delete the *Jul* column. Lastly, move the Polka-Dotted balloons row to appear as the last row, immediately following the data for the purple balloons. Delete the blank row. Check the spelling of all text entries in the worksheet. Set a print area including only the range of cells containing data. Preview and print one copy of the worksheet. Clear the print area. Save the workbook as *Balloon Sales Revised* in the *Projects* folder in your *Excel Data* folder. Close the workbook.

3 Setting Goals

You are the national sales manager for Good Life Insurance Company. Your manager has asked you to analyze the sales made over the past year and set realistic goals for each region for the coming year. Create a new workbook that contains the information provided in Table 2.6, beginning with *Region* in cell A4. Enter an appropriate title for the worksheet. (Do not enter commas in the values.)

Table 2.6	Year 2001 Good Life Insurance Company Sales		
Region	**No. of Agents**	**No. of Sales**	**Amount of Sales**
East	15	1500	750000
Southeast	12	1650	891000
Midwest	33	3600	1674000
Central	12	1300	517400
West	37	3900	1786200
Southwest	24	2400	1231200

Adjust the width of columns B, C, and D to fit the data in them. Copy the data in range A4:A10 and paste it below the worksheet data, starting in cell A14. In cell B14, type the label **2001 Sales** and copy the sales amounts for each region into cells B15:B20.

In cell C14, enter the label **2002 Goals**. Enter formulas that calculate the 2002 sales goals for each region based on the goal of increasing sales by 5% in 2002. Type **Good Life Insurance Company** in cell A1 and type **Annual Sales, 2001** in cell A2, then add a blank row below this heading.

Select cells A5:A10 and D5:D10 and use the Chart Wizard to create a 3-D pie chart. Accept all defaults and place the chart as an embedded object in the worksheet. Move and resize the chart below the worksheet data. Save the revised file as *Good Life Sales* in the *Projects* folder in your *Excel Data* folder. Close the workbook.

4 Tracking Inventory

You work as the office manager at USA Computer Center. You have been asked to create a worksheet to track inventory of the computers, printers, and monitors in stock. Create a new workbook. Type the company name in cell A1; type **Inventory** in cell A2. Starting in cell A4, enter the information in Table 2.7. Edit the cells as necessary for accuracy.

Table 2.7	Types of Products Sold			
Type	**Stock No.**	**Quantity**	**Cost**	**Price**
Computer	C250	22	800	999
Computer	C350	13	1040	1299
Computer	C450	15	1520	1899
Computer	C550	19	2070	2599
Monitor	M100	20	210	259
Monitor	M200	6	385	479
Monitor	M300	18	425	529
Printer	P60	10	320	399
Printer	P70	12	560	699
Printer	P80	17	720	899
Printer	P90	3	1120	1399

In the column to the right of the Price column, type a new column label—**Profit Per Item**. In the first cell in the Profit column, enter a formula that subtracts the cost of each item from its price, then copy the formula to all appropriate cells.

Type **Total Profit** in cell A16. Using the Formula Bar, type a SUM function that totals the profit of all of the products (the result should appear in F16). Widen columns as necessary to accommodate the data. Click cell A1 and save the workbook as *USA Computer Inventory* in the *Projects* folder in your *Excel Data* folder.

5 How Many Items Did You Sell?

Create a new workbook. In cell A1, type **Bead Bag Sales** and in cell A2, type **Sales by Product**. Using the data in Table 2.8, enter the column labels in row 4 and enter the first product beginning in cell A5.

Adjust the column widths to accommodate all the data. Create a formula in the first cell in the Sales by Product column to calculate how much money was made for necklaces. Copy the formula to other cells in the Sales by Product column. Format the cells with a comma and two decimal places.

In cell D11, enter a function into a formula to calculate total sales for all products (place the relevant range into the formula by dragging). Format the cell using Currency Style and two decimal places. Enter a formula in E5 to calculate how much each product contributed to the total sales (as a percentage). (*Hint:* Use an absolute cell reference.) Copy the formula to the other cells in column E. Format the numbers in the Quantity Sold column with commas and no decimal places.

Table 2.8	Bead Bag Sales Data			
Product	**Quantity Sold**	**Price per Item**	**Sales by Product**	**Percent of Sales**
Necklaces	1587	78.99		
Earrings	2302	25.75		
Bracelets	644	10.99		
Anklets	310	5.99		
Pins	299	15.99		
Watches	79	35.99		
Total Sales				

Format the numbers in the Percent of Sales column as percentages with one decimal place. Center the numbers in the Percent of Sales column.

Use bold type for the worksheet titles and column labels, adjusting column widths as necessary. Use italic type for each product name. Select cells A4:B10. Create an exploded 3-D pie chart to display the quantity of each product sold. Place the chart as an object in the worksheet and position the chart to avoid obscuring the worksheet data. Click cell A1 and save the workbook as *Bead Bag Sales* in the *Projects* folder in your *Excel Data* folder (see Figure 2.30).

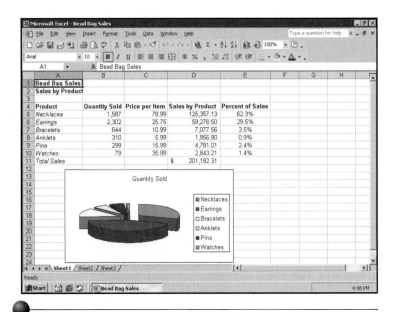

Figure 2.30

 6 Link to the Web

You own a small travel agency and you use Excel to keep track of your business. You have started a list of the most commonly requested travel locations. Now you decide to create a hyperlink for each location in your list to jump to a related Web site with travel information. Open *Travel Agency* in your *Excel Data* folder. Create a hyperlink in cell A4 to **www.germany -travel.net/**. Create a hyperlink in A5 to **www.travelalaska.com/homepage.html**. Create a hyperlink from A6 to **www.initaly.com/**. Connect to the Web and test the hyperlinks. If the Web pages are no longer available, use your search engine to locate other appropriate Web sites. Edit your hyperlinks to include the new links, if necessary. Save the workbook as *Revised Travel Agency* in the *Projects* folder in your *Excel Data* folder and then close the file.

Project in Progress

7 Adding Sales Data and Formulas to Your Workbook

EXCEL 2002

As the owner of a small business that provides writing, editing, and training services, you track your sales in a workbook. Open the *Savvy Solutions-2* workbook in your *Excel Data* folder. Insert a row above *Seminars and Training*. In the new row, type the data provided in Table 2.9.

Change the text in cell A5 to **News articles** and change the amount in cell G9 to **250**. Check the spelling of all text entries in the worksheet. Type **Totals** in cell A10. Create a formula to calculate total sales for each month and copy and paste it to the Totals row. Type **Totals** in cell N4 and calculate total sales for each category of sales (across each row). Be sure to calculate the total of all the monthly sales as well. In cells A13:A15, type the labels **Average Monthly Sales**, **Highest Monthly Sales**, and **Lowest Monthly Sales**. In cells B13:B15, enter the appropriate formula to calculate average, highest, and lowest sales for January. Copy the Average formula from B13 to C13:M13. Copy the formula for the highest and lowest monthly sales for January to the appropriate cells for Feb–Dec. Verify that your formulas are correct and that the results are logical.

Format the worksheet as desired to improve its appearance. Align column labels and the title as desired. Change column widths, if necessary, and make any other formatting adjustments to improve the appearance of the worksheet. Use the Chart Wizard to create an embedded clustered column chart to show the sales totals for each category for all 12 months. Resize and position the chart as desired. Save the workbook as *Revised Savvy Solutions-Lesson 2* in the *Project in Progress* folder in your *Projects* folder.

Table 2.9	Sales Data
Cell	**Data**
A7	Promotional materials
B7	3500
C7	2405
D7	1760
E7	3190
F7	2580
G7	1600
H7	2000
I7	2450
J7	3040
K7	1780
L7	2075
M7	1700

Overview: **Congratulations!** Now that you have completed the Excel lessons in this tutorial, you have the opportunity in this capstone project to apply the Excel skills you have learned. You will plan and create a workbook to track costs for a small home building business. As you create the workbook, you'll incorporate the following skills:

- Create and save a workbook.
- Enter and edit data.
- Fill ranges with values.
- Insert a row.
- Adjust column widths.
- Create and copy formulas.
- Format numbers.
- Use functions.
- Chart data.
- Insert a comment.
- Apply an AutoFormat.
- Preview and print a workbook.

Instructions: Follow these instructions to create your workbook for this case study.

1. Create a new workbook and save it as *Excel Case Study* in the *Projects* folder in your *Excel Data* folder.

2. On *Sheet1,* enter the information provided in Table CS.1. Adjust the column widths as necessary. Format the numbers with commas and no decimal places.

3. At the bottom of each column, enter functions that total the estimated and actual costs for the house. Type a row label identifying the totals. Insert a blank row above the Totals row.

Table CS.1	Workbook Data	
Construction Phase	**Estimated**	**Actual**
Land	75000	72000
Improvements	25000	30000
Foundation	5000	5000
Footer	1200	1200
Framing	45000	46000
Plumbing	5000	4800
Electric/Fixtures	8000	7800
HVAC	7500	8200
Insulation	1500	1400
Drywall	4500	4200
Painting	1500	2000
Cabinets	10000	9600
Flooring	10000	8000
Trim	5000	3000
Appliances	2000	1500
Windows	6000	5500
Stairs	1500	1600
Porch	8000	8000
Fireplace	10000	10000

4. Create a column chart (as an embedded object in the worksheet) that compares the estimated and actual costs. Resize the chart and move it to the right of your data so that you can better view the data and chart together. Analyze which phases of construction ran over budget and which ones were under budget. (Hint: Point to each column to see the charted values in a ScreenTip.)

5. Create a doughnut chart that shows the estimated costs for construction. Resize the doughnut chart and position it below the column chart. Select the legend and then delete it from the chart. Point to each segment to view the charted values.

6. Below the cell containing the total for the Estimated column, enter a formula calculating the maximum value of that column. Copy and paste the formula into the corresponding cell of the Actual column. Add a row label identifying the formula results in these cells. Following the same procedure, calculate the minimum costs in the next row and label the row.

7. In the cell to the right of the actual value in the Land row, enter a formula to subtract the actual value from the estimated value. Copy the formula, and then in one action paste it into the appropriate cells to perform the same calculation for all Construction Phase items. Add the column heading *Difference* to the column, and then total it in the Totals row. Manually verify that the total of the Difference column is the same as the Estimated column total minus the Actual column total.

8. Apply an AutoFormat of your choice to the worksheet data.

9. Insert a comment into a selected cell regarding one of the costs in your worksheet.

10. Use the Page Setup dialog box to change the orientation of the worksheet to Landscape so that you can see all the information when you print.

11. Save your work. Preview and then print the worksheet.

Contents

Managing the "Infoglut"

Data warehousing and data mining offer a new approach

For many corporations, data is their lifeblood. For years, companies have collected, sorted, stored, and spit out vast amounts of data about their customers, products, inventories, employees, sales, and stores. They also store external data about their competitors and their industry. This data is crucial for managers, employees, and executives to better understand their organization and industry.

All this collected data—this **infoglut**—raises two major issues that affect companies all around the world: Where's the best place to store all this data? And once we have it stored, how can we access it efficiently? The usual approach to managing infoglut is to maintain well-designed databases. At some point, however, the law of diminishing returns comes into play—there is just too much information, and it simply is not practical to create a new database or a new database management system (DBMS) for each new situation that comes along.

One approach to solving the problem of infoglut is to store data in *data warehouses* and then *data mine* the warehouse for critical information. A data warehouse is a massive collection of related databases, and often contains gigabytes, terabytes (1,000 gigabytes) or even petabytes (1,000 terabytes) of data. A data warehouse can include any and all data that is relevant to running a company.

All this data is stored in databases spread among many storage devices on computers running tens or even hundreds of central processing units.

However, setting up a data warehouse is much more complicated than simply dumping all kinds of data into one storage place. The following factors must be considered when setting up a data warehouse:

What type of processing scheme will be used?
Generally, two types of technologies—symmetric multiprocessing (SMP) or massively parallel processing (MPP)—are used. For smaller storage needs, such as between 50 GB to 300 GB, companies use SMP. For data warehouses larger than 300 GB, many companies opt for MPP because of the ability to scale (or add) additional processors as their storage needs grow.

How much storage space is needed and what type of backup plan is needed? One of the most popular storage schemes is RAID (Redundant Array of Independent Disks). RAID is a storage system that links any number of disk drives to act as a single disk. In this system, information is written to two or more disks simultaneously to improve speed and reliability and to ensure that data is available to users at all times. RAID's capabilities are based on three techniques: (1) mirroring, (2) striping, and (3) striping-with-parity:

■ In a *mirrored* system, data is written to two or more disks simultaneously, providing a complete copy of all the information on a drive, should one drive fail.

■ *Striping* provides the user with speedy response by spreading data across several disks. Striping alone, however, does not provide backup if one of the disks in an array fails.

■ *Striping-with-parity* provides the speed of striping with the reliability of parity. Should a drive in such an array fail, the system administrator can use the disk that stores the parity information to reconstruct the data from the damaged drive. Some arrays using the striping-with-parity technique also offer a technique known as *hot swapping,* which enables a system administrator to remove a damaged drive while the array remains in operation.

What type of data scrubbing will be set up? Whenever a lot of data is collected, it will, no doubt, contain some errors. *Data scrubbing* means sifting through data and performing such tedious tasks as eliminating duplications and incomplete records and making sure that similar fields in different tables are defined in exactly the same ways.

After a data warehouse has been set up, a company can perform targeted data mining to solve complex business problems, such as determining better ways to serve the needs of customers, outsmarting the competition, discovering trends in the market, and developing new products. To be successful, a company must mine its vast storehouse of information effectively to find out exactly what it knows, how to get to it, and what to do with it. By understanding and using the full capability of the Microsoft® Access 2002 program, you will be well on your way to building effective databases to manage the infoglut!

Access Basics

CONTENTS

- Introducing Microsoft Access
- Understanding the Database Window
- Objects: The Components of Access
- Planning Ahead
- Creating a Database
- Creating Tables
- Saving a Table
- Modifying Tables in Design View
- Entering Records Using a Datasheet
- Retrieving Data From Other Sources
- Navigating the Datasheet and Editing Records
- Defining Relationships Between Tables
- On the Web: Searching the Internet From Access

OBJECTIVES

After you complete this lesson, you will be able to do the following:

- ► Understand databases and how they work.
- ► Name the main features of the Database window.
- ► Identify the different types of objects an Access database can contain.
- ► Select an object using the Objects bar and switch between object views.
- ► Navigate a table and edit a record in a table.
- ► Enter a record using a form.
- ► Find specific records using a query.
- ► Preview and print a report.
- ► Plan a database.
- ► Create a database.
- ► Create tables using the Table Wizard or Design view.
- ► Understand data types.
- ► Set primary keys.
- ► Modify field properties.
- ► Modify tables in Design view.
- ► Create an input mask.
- ► Enter records using a datasheet.
- ► Retrieve data from other sources.
- ► Navigate a datasheet and edit records.
- ► Define table relationships and understand referential integrity.
- ► Search the Internet from the Access program.

INTRODUCING MICROSOFT ACCESS

Microsoft Access is a powerful database management program that you can use to organize, track, and retrieve data in a database. A **database** is an organized collection of data from which specific information can be easily extracted. A database does not have to be stored on a computer; a Rolodex of contact names, a paper filing system of customer orders, or a telephone book are all examples of databases. You can use an electronic database such as Access to store massive amounts of data in a very small space, to manipulate data with ease, and to quickly extract required information.

Access Basics   **373**

In an Access database, data is stored in **tables,** and each table contains data that pertains to only one particular subject, such as employees, customers, or inventory items. Most Access databases contain multiple tables that you can use together when the need arises. For example, assume a database contains two tables—one for general customer information, such as name and address, and one for specific customer orders. To create a customer invoice, you would need to retrieve data that is related to both of these tables. You can do this easily in Access because it is a **relational database management system (RDBMS).** In an RDBMS, you can establish relationships between multiple tables, provided the tables have one field in common. In Figure 1.1, both the Customers and Orders tables include a field that contains customer ID numbers; Access can find each customer's orders by scanning the Orders table for records that match a customer ID number in the Customers table. Because of this powerful feature, you do not have to store copies of data, such as the customer name and address, in several places. This not only streamlines your database (because it doesn't contain multiple copies of the same data), it also reduces the risk of data entry error (because you are only entering data one time).

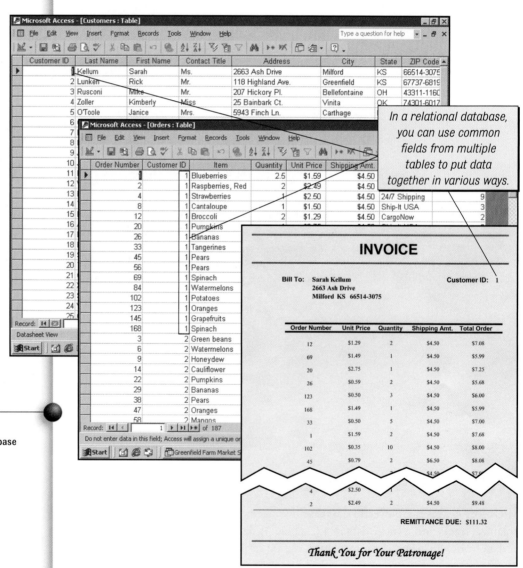

> In a relational database, you can use common fields from multiple tables to put data together in various ways.

Figure 1.1
Example of a relational database management system

Now that you have a general idea of what Access is, let's start the Access program, open a database, and learn more about the fundamentals of Access.

HANDS on

Launching Microsoft Access and Opening a Database

In this activity, you will start Microsoft Access and open the *Greenfield Farm Market Sample* database. The *Greenfield Farm Market Sample* database stores operational information for a fictitious family-owned business in Greenfield, Kansas. Greenfield Farm Market sells fresh fruits and vegetables on the premises, by catalog, and online.

> **NOTE** *Before you can start Microsoft Access, both Microsoft Access and Windows 98 (or higher version) must be installed on the computer you're using. The figures in this tutorial were created using Windows 2000; if you are using a different version of Windows, the information appearing on your screen may vary slightly.*

1. Turn on your computer.

After the booting process is complete, the Windows desktop appears.

2. Click the Start button 🔲Start **on the Windows taskbar, point to Programs, and click Microsoft Access.**

The Access program starts and its application window appears. The menu bar and the Database toolbar appear at the top of the application window; however, many commands are not yet available because you haven't opened a database. For example, note that if you click Insert on the menu bar, all the options beneath are grayed (meaning that they're currently disabled). As you will soon find out, the available Access options change depending on what you're doing at the moment.

> **NOTE** *To work through the lessons in this tutorial, you must copy the* Access Data *folder from the Data CD located in the back of this tutorial to your hard drive or network drive. If you haven't copied the* Access Data *folder, ask your instructor for help.*

3. Click the Open button 📂 **on the Database toolbar. In the Open dialog box, navigate to your** *Access Data* **folder and double-click the** *Greenfield Farm Market Sample* **database to open it. (If you need help navigating to a file, ask your instructor for help.)**

Access opens the *Greenfield Farm Market Sample* database and displays the Database window, as shown in Figure 1.2. As you study the Access application window, notice that many more menu and toolbar commands become available.

Access BASICS

Launching Microsoft Access and Opening a Database

1. Turn on the computer.

2. Click the Start button and point to Programs.

3. Click Microsoft Access.

4. Click the Open button on the Database toolbar.

5. In the Open dialog box, navigate to the appropriate folder.

6. Double-click the file name.

Another Way

You can also open a database from the New File task pane.

Figure 1.2
Database window

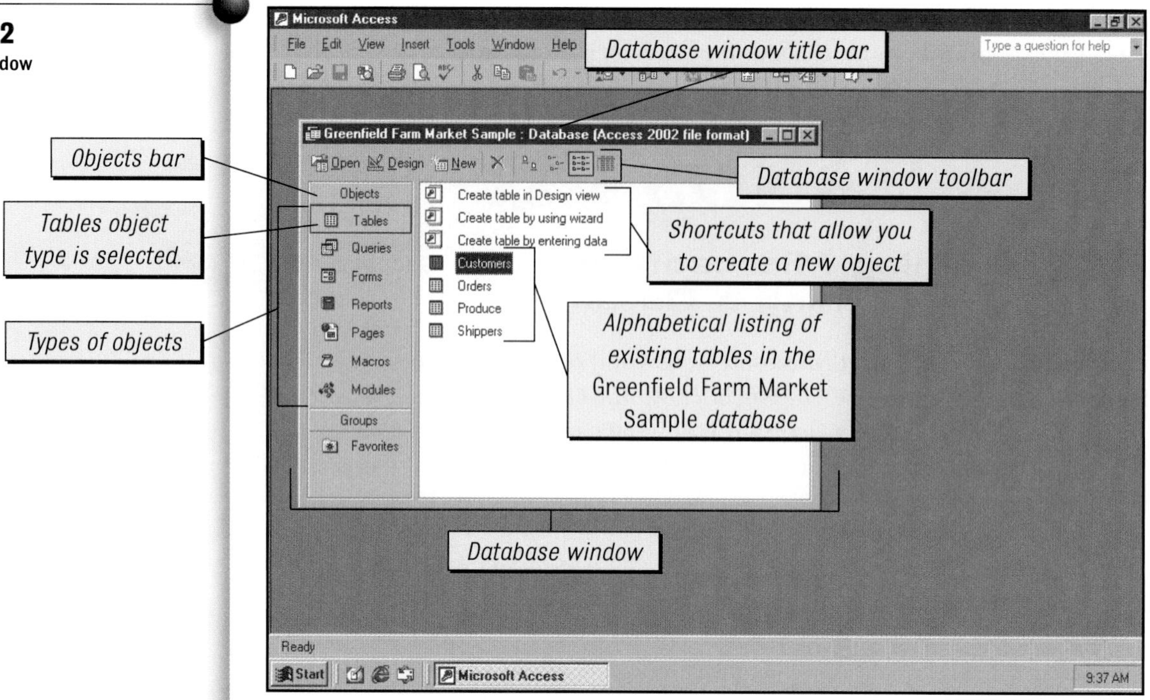

Objects bar

Tables object type is selected.

Types of objects

Database window title bar

Database window toolbar

Shortcuts that allow you to create a new object

Alphabetical listing of existing tables in the Greenfield Farm Market Sample *database*

Database window

UNDERSTANDING THE DATABASE WINDOW

The **Database window** allows you to gain access to all the data and objects stored in your database. (We'll talk more about objects in just a moment.) The title bar of the Database window displays the name and file format of the database. The Database window toolbar, which appears directly below the title bar, provides shortcuts to open or modify existing objects, create new objects, delete objects, and change the view of the list of objects (Large Icons, Small Icons, List, and Details). The **Objects bar** that appears along the left side of the Database window represents the types of objects available in Access.

When you click an object type in the Objects bar, a list of the objects of that type appears in the right pane of the Database window. The first two or three items in the list are shortcuts that allow you to create a new object. The remaining items are an alphabetical listing of existing objects in the database. For example, in Figure 1.2, the Tables object in the Objects bar is selected, and the first three items in the right pane are shortcuts that allow you to create new tables. The remaining items represent existing tables in the *Greenfield Farm Market Sample* database. The list of objects in the right pane of the Database window changes depending upon which object type you select in the Objects bar. For example, clicking Reports in the Objects bar would display shortcuts for creating a new report and any existing reports in the database, clicking Forms in the Objects bar would display shortcuts for creating a new form and any existing forms in the database, and so on.

OBJECTS: THE COMPONENTS OF ACCESS

In Access, the term *database* means not just the raw data stored in the database, but also a collection of database objects. These **objects** provide the **structure** of an Access database, and you use these objects to enter, manipulate, and extract data. Objects can be tailored to fit the data that will be stored in the database, and they can be modified as a database grows and changes over time. An Access database can contain seven types of objects—tables, queries, forms, reports, pages, macros, and modules. In this section, you will open and briefly examine several of these objects in the *Greenfield Farm Market Sample* database.

Views and Toolbars

You can work with an Access database using many different **views** and many different toolbars, depending upon the type of object you open and whether you want to work with the object's content (the data) or the object's design (the structure). Two of the more common views are **Datasheet view** and **Design view.** The data in a database is arranged in a column-and-row format called a **datasheet.** (If you're familiar with Excel, you may see some similarity between an Access datasheet and an Excel worksheet.) In Datasheet view, data in a table, query, or form is displayed in a column-and-row format. (There is no Datasheet view for reports, data access pages, macros, or modules.) You use Datasheet view to view, add, delete, and edit the actual information in a database. In Design view, you work with the structure of an object, not the data. You use Design view to create new database objects and modify the design of existing objects. Just as each object has its own views, each object also has its own set of toolbars. While the toolbars for each object may seem very similar, each serves a specific purpose, depending upon the type of object with which you're working and the view in which you're working.

Tables

You've already learned a little about one Access object: the table, which is the basic structure that holds all of the data in an Access database. A table organizes information into a series of **fields** (columns) that contain categories of data and **records** (rows) that contain the set of fields for one particular entity. For example, a customer address table may include fields for the customer's last name, first name, address, city, state, and ZIP Code categories. In this case, a record would consist of all the fields that apply to a single customer.

Navigating a Table and Viewing Table Design

In this activity, you will move among the records in one of the tables in the *Greenfield Farm Market Sample* database. Then you will view the table design.

1. In the Database window of the *Greenfield Farm Market Sample* database, click **Tables** in the Objects bar, if it is not already selected.

In the right pane of the Database window, the names of the tables in the *Greenfield Farm Market Sample* database are displayed in alphabetical order as the last four items in the list of table objects.

2. If it is not already selected, click the **Customers table** in the right pane, and then click the **Open button**  on the *Database window* toolbar. (Be sure to click the Open button  on the

WEB NOTE

The Internet connects your computer to millions of other computers all over the world. You can exchange messages, programs, and data files with every one of them.

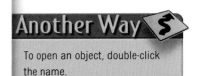

Another Way

To open an object, double-click the name.

Opening a Table in
Datasheet View

1. Open the database that
   contains the table you want to
   open.

2. Click the Tables option in the
   Objects bar.

3. Click the name of the table
   you want to open.

4. Click the Open button on the
   Database window toolbar.

Database window toolbar, not the Open button 🖻 on the *Database* toolbar. The Open button 🗁 Open on the Database window toolbar is used to open an object in a database, while the Open button 🖻 on the Database toolbar is used to open another database.)

The Customers table appears in Datasheet view, with data arranged in a grid of columns (fields) and rows (records), as shown in Figure 1.3. Now that you have opened a table, the Database toolbar has been replaced with the Table Datasheet toolbar. These two toolbars are very similar; however, the Table Datasheet toolbar contains buttons that are used specifically for working with tables. Also, a set of navigation buttons appears at the bottom of the window to help you move efficiently among records in the table.

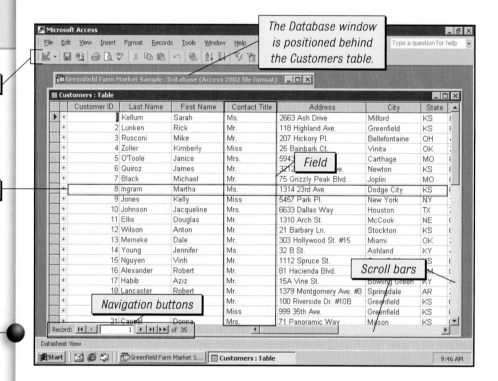

Figure 1.3
Customers table in Datasheet view

As you can see, the Customers table initially displays at a reduced size, and is actually positioned in front of the Database window. If you drag the table downward, you can see the Database window. Since it is easier to work with the table at full size, let's maximize the window.

> **3.** Click the **Maximize button** 🗖 on the right side of the Customers:Table title bar.

The table is displayed at full size.

> **4.** Use the vertical and horizontal scroll bars—the shaded bars along the bottom and right side of a window—to view portions of the table not visible on the screen.
>
> **5.** Press [Ctrl] + [End] to move to the end of the table.
>
> **6.** Press [Ctrl] + [Home] to move to the beginning of the table.
>
> **7.** Press [Tab] twice.

This action selects the word *Sarah*. Pressing ⎡Tab⎤ moves the insertion point to the next column (field).

8. Press ⎡⇧ Shift⎤ + ⎡Tab⎤ twice.

This action returns the insertion point to the first field. Pressing ⎡⇧ Shift⎤ + ⎡Tab⎤ moves the insertion point to the previous field.

9. Press ⎡↓⎤.

Pressing ⎡↓⎤ moves the insertion point down one row (record) at a time. Now let's use the navigation toolbar at the bottom of the window to move to various records in the table.

10. Click the Next Record button ▶ on the navigation toolbar to move to the third record in the table.

Notice that the number *3* is displayed in the Specific Record box on the navigation toolbar.

11. Click the Last Record button ▶| to move to the last record in the table.

12. Click the Previous Record button ◀ to move to the previous record.

13. Double-click in the Specific Record box on the navigation toolbar to select the current record number (34), type 15, and press ⎡Enter⏎⎤.

The insertion point moves to record 15 in the table.

14. Click the First Record button |◀ to move to the first record in the table.

Now let's switch to Design view to examine the structure of the table.

15. Click the View button 🗠▾ on the Table Datasheet toolbar.

You now see the Customers table in Design view, as shown in Figure 1.4. Notice that the Table Datasheet toolbar has been replaced with the Table Design toolbar. The Design view is split into two panes. The upper pane shows the names of the fields (columns) in the table, along with other information about the fields. The lower pane further defines the properties of the field that is currently selected. Later in this lesson, you will use Design view to set up and modify the layout of a table. For now, though, let's just explore the Design view of the Customers table.

16. Press ⎡↓⎤ to move to the ContactLastName field in the upper pane.

Notice that the field properties displayed in the lower pane change also.

17. Press ⎡F6⎤.

The insertion point moves to the lower pane.

Access BASICS

Viewing Table Design

If the table is open in Datasheet view, click the View button on the Table Datasheet toolbar.

If the table is closed, select the table name and then click the Design button in the Database window.

NORTON ONLINE

Visit **www.glencoe.com/norton/online/** for more information on Access 2002.

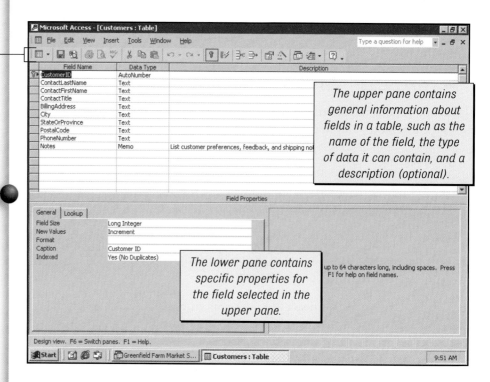

Table Design toolbar

The upper pane contains general information about fields in a table, such as the name of the field, the type of data it can contain, and a description (optional).

The lower pane contains specific properties for the field selected in the upper pane.

Figure 1.4
Design view of the Customers table

18. Press 🔲 again.

The insertion point moves back to the upper pane.

19. Click the View button 🔲 **on the Table Design toolbar.**

You are once again viewing the table in Datasheet view.

NOTE *The View button is a toggle button that allows you to switch between Datasheet view and Design view. Notice that the icon on the button changes depending upon the view you are currently using.*

20. Click File on the menu bar and then click Close.

Access closes the Customers table, and returns to the Database window for the *Greenfield Farm Market Sample* database. Since you maximized the table in step 3, the Database window is now maximized as well.

Queries

A **query** is just what the name implies: a question to the database, generally asking for a set of records from one or more tables that meets specific criteria. For example, you might ask the database to display all the customers from a specific state or any customers whose bills are past due. Queries are particularly valuable because they enable you to both view and manipulate selected subsets of your data. It is important to note that a query is a stored *question,* rather than the stored *answer* to a question—when a query is run, the results of the query will change if the underlying data in the database changes. Thus, you can ask the same question over and over again, and the query result will always reflect any changes in the underlying data. There are several different types of queries, as shown in Table 1.1.

Table 1.1 — Types of Queries

Query Type	Description
Select query	A select query is the most common type of query. It is used to retrieve data from one or more tables and display results in a datasheet. You can update the records in a database by modifying the results of a select query.
Parameter query	When a parameter query is run, it displays a dialog box prompting you for the information it needs to retrieve records.
Crosstab query	Crosstab queries are used to perform calculations on records and then group the results by two types of information—one down the left side of the datasheet and the other across the top.
Action query	An action query is used to make changes to several records in just one operation. There are four different types of action queries: delete queries, update queries, append queries, and make-table queries.
SQL query	A SQL query is created from SQL statements that can be used with Access and other relational databases.

Just as with tables, you can view a query using different views. You use Datasheet view to display the results of a query and Design view to display and modify the underlying structure of a query. (Access also provides other views for queries, such as SQL view, PivotTable view, and PivotChart view; however, these views are beyond the scope of this tutorial.)

Running a Select Query and Viewing Query Design

In this activity, you will run a select query that asks for a list of all the Greenfield Farm Market customers who reside in Kansas. Then you will view the query design.

1. **In the Database window, click Queries in the Objects bar.**

In the right pane of the Database window, you will see two options that allow you to create new queries, followed by the name of an existing query in the *Greenfield Farm Market Sample* database.

2. **Click the Kansas Customers query, if it is not already selected, and then click the Open button  on the Database window toolbar.**

When you open a select query, Access automatically runs (executes) the query and displays the results in Datasheet view. The results of the Kansas Customers

ACCESS 2002

query are shown in Figure 1.5. Notice that this query displays only selected records from the Customers table—that is, it only displays the customers who reside in Kansas. The name of the query (Kansas Customers) and the type of query (Select Query) are identified in the title bar, and the Query Datasheet toolbar appears below the menu bar.

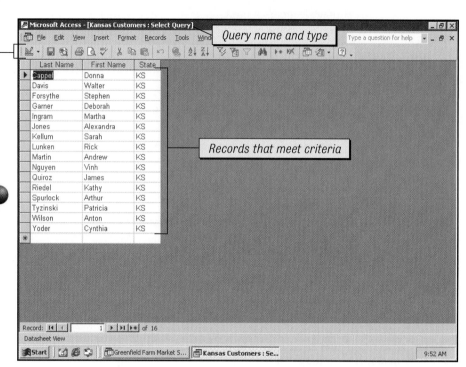

Figure 1.5
Query results in Datasheet view

Access BASICS

Viewing Query Design

If the query results are displayed in Datasheet view, click the View button on the Query Datasheet toolbar.

If the query is closed, select the query name and then click the Design button in the Database window.

3. Click the **Close Window button** ⊠ at the right end of the menu bar.

Access closes the query results, and returns to the Database window.

4. With the Kansas Customers query still selected, click the **Design button** 📐 Design on the Database window toolbar.

Access opens the query in Design view, as shown in Figure 1.6. In Design view, you can see the structure of the query, and you can choose the fields to be displayed, the order in which the fields will appear, and the criteria to be used to select records.

5. Click the **Close Window button** ⊠ at the right end of the menu bar.

Once again, you return to the Database window.

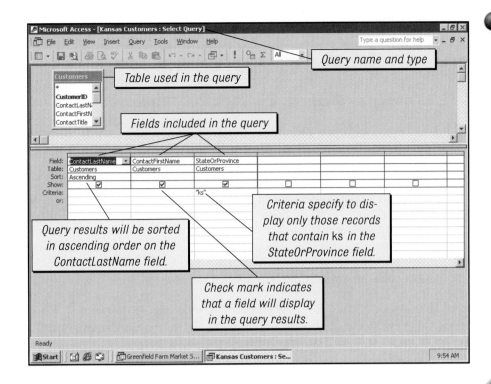

Figure 1.6
Design view of a query

Forms

If you only have a few records to enter or edit, this can easily be accomplished directly in a table, where all the data is laid out in a grid of rows and columns. However, if you need to enter or edit a lot of records, it is more efficient to use a form. Access **forms** are the electronic equivalent of paper forms, and they enable you to create a custom layout for your data—determining how, and what, data from your tables is presented. For example, you could create a form that displays a single record at a time for data entry or editing, or one that displays only certain fields from a particular table. Forms are especially useful when you want to create a more friendly or visually manageable environment for data entry or when you need to control which data is displayed.

Forms have three views: Datasheet view, Design view, and Form view. As you may have guessed, you use Design view to create a new form or change the structure of an existing form. To view, enter, and edit data in forms, you can use either Datasheet view or Form view. When a form is displayed in Datasheet view, you see several records at one time, and it is very similar to viewing a table in Datasheet view. In **Form view,** however, you can view one record at a time, if you wish, and display only pertinent fields in a record. Thus, Form view is often used as a means to enter records into a database.

NORTON
ONLINE

Visit **www.glencoe.com/norton/online/** for more information on Access 2002.

HANDS on

Using a Form to Add a Record

In this activity, you will open a form that displays all of the fields for one record in the Customers table. You will use the form to add a new record to the table, and then view the structure of the form in Design view.

1. Click Forms in the Objects bar in the Database window.

You will see two options that you can use to create new forms and one form that has already been created.

2. Double-click the Columnar Form with All Fields form.

Access displays the Columnar Form with All Fields form in Form view. By default, this form shows the first record from the Customers table you saw earlier. Take a moment to examine the application window. Notice that new toolbars appear—the Formatting toolbar and the Form View toolbar. As you may have guessed, these toolbars are used specifically for working with forms. In addition, navigation buttons appear at the bottom of the window, and the status bar indicates that you are using Form view to display the record.

3. Click the New Record button ▶* on the Form View toolbar.

A new blank record is displayed.

4. Press `Tab`.

The insertion point moves to the text box for the second field, Last Name.

> **NOTE** *When you start typing data in the Last Name field, Access will automatically insert a number in the Customer ID field.*

5. Type each of the following entries into the form, pressing `Tab` after each item. The new record should look like the one in Figure 1.7.

Last Name:	Wells
First Name:	Jason
Contact Title:	Mr.
Address:	228 Riverdale Way
City:	Milford
State:	KS
ZIP Code:	665142061
Phone Number:	6205553658
Notes:	Mr. Wells said his neighbor, Mr. Martin, recommended that he visit Greenfield Farm Market.

6. Click the View button ⬚▾ on the Form View toolbar.

You can now view the design of the form.

Sidebar (left column)

Access **BASICS**

Working With Forms

To display a form and add data:

1. Click the Forms option in the Objects bar of the Database window.

2. Double-click the form you want to view.

3. Click the New Record button to add a record.

4. Type data into each field of the new record.

To view form design:

If the form is open, click the View button on the Form View toolbar.

If the form is closed, select the form name and then click the Design button in the Database window.

HINTS & TIPS

When you enter the ZIP code and phone number, Access fills in the punctuation marks normally used in these items. Also, a new blank form appears when you press `Tab` after entering data in the last field of the form.

ACCESS 2002

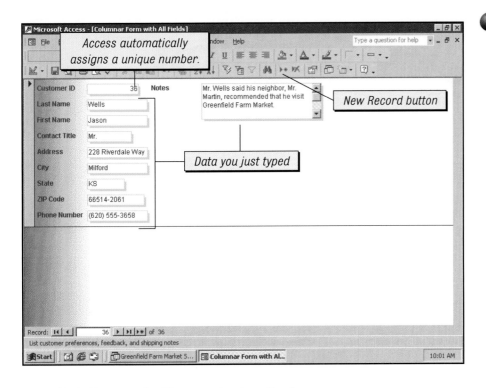

Figure 1.7
Entering a new record using a form

7. Click **Close** on the File menu to close the form.

Access closes the form, and returns to the Database window. Now let's check to see if the new record was added to the Customers table.

8. Click **Tables** in the Objects bar in the Database window, double-click **Customers**, and click the Last Record button  on the navigation toolbar.

The data you entered appears in the fields of the last record.

9. Click the **Close Window button** ☒ to close the table.

Another Way 💲

To create a new record, you can also click the New Record button on the navigation toolbar.

Reports

Often you will want to not only display a set of data on the screen, but also print some type of output as well. You may need printouts to submit assignments to your instructor, to deliver reports to your boss, to mail information to a client, or for some other purpose. You can print forms, as well as tables and queries, but **reports** enable you to control the size and appearance of data in order to produce presentation-quality output. Reports are based on data from tables or queries, and they can contain totals and grand totals of the values in a particular field, such as salary or sales.

You can use three different views to work with reports: Design view, Print Preview, and Layout Preview. You use Design view to create a new report or change the structure of an existing report. You use Print Preview to display a **WYSIWYG** (**w**hat **y**ou **s**ee **i**s **w**hat **y**ou **g**et) preview of all the data in a report, which gives you a good idea of what an entire report will look like when it's actually printed. You use Layout Preview to view the layout of a report, which contains only a portion of the data contained in the report.

HANDS on

Previewing and Printing a Report

Before you print a database report, you should preview the report on the screen. In this activity, you will display a database report using Print Preview, view the design of the report, and then print the report.

1. Click Reports in the Objects bar in the Database window.

Access displays two options that help you create reports, and also displays one report in the *Greenfield Farm Market Sample* database.

2. Click the Produce Pricing Sheet report, if it is not already selected, and then click the Preview button 🔍 Preview **on the Database window toolbar.**

Access displays the Produce Pricing Sheet report, as shown in Figure 1.8. Notice that a new toolbar—the Print Preview toolbar—appears below the menu bar in the application window, and navigation buttons appear above the status bar.

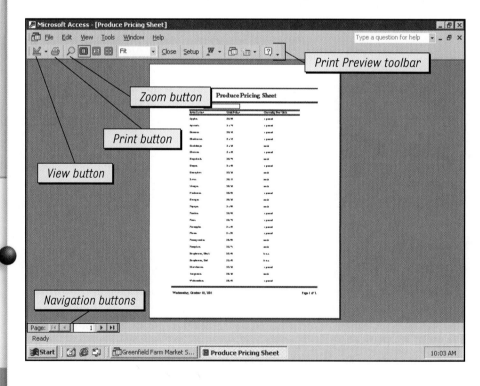

Access **BASICS**

Working With Reports

To preview and print a report:

1. Click the Reports option in the Objects bar of the Database window.

2. Double-click the report you want to preview.

3. Click the Print button on the Print Preview toolbar to print the report.

To view report design:

If the report is open, click the View button on the Print Preview toolbar.

If the report is closed, select the report name and then click the Design button in the Database window.

Figure 1.8
Previewing a report

Did you know?

You can print tables, queries, forms, and reports directly from the Database window by clicking the object name to select it and then clicking the Print button on the Database toolbar.

3. Click the Zoom button 🔍 **on the Print Preview toolbar to enlarge the report.**

4. Click the Zoom button 🔍 **again to fit one page of the report in the window.**

5. Click the Next Page navigation button ▶ **to preview the next page in the report.**

6. Click the **First Page navigation button** ⏮ to move back to the first page in the report.

7. Click the **View button** 🔍▾ on the Print Preview toolbar to view the design of the report.

Notice once again that different toolbars appear in the application window (the Formatting toolbar and the Report Design toolbar).

8. Click the **View button** 🔍▾ on the Report Design toolbar to return to Print Preview.

9. Turn on your printer, if necessary.

10. Click the **Print button** 🖶 on the Print Preview toolbar.

One copy of the Produce Pricing Sheet report is printed.

11. Click **Close** on the File menu.

Access closes the report, and returns to the Database window.

Data Access Pages

Businesses are finding, more and more, that it is a necessity to be able to publish current, real-time information on the Web. With Access, you can create data access pages to publish live data on the Web. A **data access page** (often simply called a **page**) is a Web page that is connected to an Access database. Using data access pages, you can view and edit records stored in an Access database from a remote location via the Internet or an **intranet.** You can also use data access pages to distribute database information via e-mail.

You can work with data access pages in three different views: Page view, Design view, and Web Page Preview. When you open a data access page, it displays in Page view by default. You can switch to Design view to change the structure of the page, or you can switch to Web Page Preview to see how the page will look when viewed through a Web browser.

HANDS on

Exploring a Data Access Page

1. In the Database window, click **Pages** in the Objects bar, and double-click **GFM Product Selections**.

The GFM Product Selections data access page opens in Page view, as shown in Figure 1.9.

2. Continuously click the **Next button** ▶ on the record navigation toolbar to scroll through the records.

3. Click the **First button** ⏮ on the record navigation toolbar to return to the first record.

Another Way

To print a report, you can also click Print on the File menu. This method allows you to customize your printing by choosing the number of copies and choosing which printer is used if your computer is networked to more than one printer.

ACCESS 2002

Access **BASICS**

Opening a Data Access Page

1. Click the Pages option in the Objects bar of the Database window.

2. Double-click the data access page you want to open.

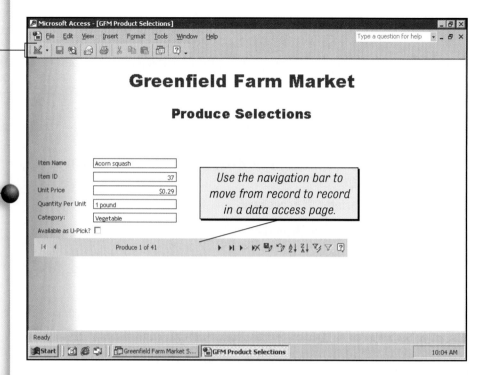

Page View toolbar

Figure 1.9
A data access page in Page view

Viewing Page Design

If the data access page is open, click the View button on the Page View toolbar.

If the data access page is closed, select the page name and then click the Design button in the Database window.

4. Click the **View button** to display the page in Design view.

You could now modify the design of the data access page using the various toolbars that appear.

5. Click the **View triangle button** and click **Web Page Preview** from the drop-down list.

Now you are viewing the data access page through your Web browser window.

6. Click the **Close button** on the title bar to close your browser window.

You are now viewing the data access page in Design view.

7. Click the **Close Window button** to close the data access page.

Once again, you return to the Database window.

8. Click the **Close button** in the Database window.

The *Greenfield Farm Market Sample* database closes. Access closes the file, clearing the screen completely. Since you just closed the only open file, the Access application window is now blank and does not contain a Database window.

Macros and Modules

Strictly speaking, macros and modules are database objects; however, their main purpose is to automate tasks that you perform over and over again. A **macro** is a set of commands called **actions** that you can create to automate a task that you repeat frequently. Instead of issuing several separate actions manually, you can run a macro and the set of actions will be performed automatically. Macros are designed to save time and effort. Macros are best used for relatively simple tasks, such as opening forms or running reports. For more complex tasks, a module can be programmed. A **module** is a set of Microsoft Visual Basic program statements, declarations, and procedures that are stored together as a unit.

PLANNING AHEAD

Now that you are familiar with the various objects that comprise a database, you are ready to create a new database. Creating a database requires careful thought. Although you can certainly make changes to a database, making those changes is a bit more complex than when using another type of program, such as a word processor. Advanced planning alleviates the problems you can experience from quickly creating a database without preparation. After you plan your database, actually creating it and building a few tables will be remarkably easy. Before beginning to build a database, you should answer several questions:

◆ What is the database for and what should the database do?

◆ What categories of information (or fields) are needed to achieve the desired results?

◆ How should these fields be divided into separate tables?

◆ How might these tables relate to each other to use information from two or more of them simultaneously?

Determining the Purpose of the Database

The first step in determining how to configure your database is to decide how you will use the database. If you have an existing manual database system, investigate that system; review any reports and forms that you'll need to duplicate and note the items of information they must include. Also be sure to talk to people who actually use the database; check to see what they use the system for and what they need.

If you're not working with an existing system, think very carefully about what you want the new system to do; jot down the items of information the system should track and sketch any forms and reports you think you'll need. Throughout the planning process, remember that as you determine what you want your database to do, you are learning what data you must have in your database. For example, if you need to be able to print salary reports according to department, your database must list the department for each employee. Also, consider how you want to sort or extract data. For instance, if you'll want to sort customers by last name, you'll need to include separate fields for a first name and a last name, rather than a single field that contains both names. At this stage in planning, you can make just one large list of all the information you need. You'll then learn how to organize this information into more manageable subsets.

In the planning stage, you can ask users of the current system to supply you with a wish list of things they'd like to be able to do. Remember that you aren't confined to duplicating a current manual system; often you can improve on the existing system while computerizing.

Did you know?

Access will retrieve data and update more slowly when tables contain redundant data. You can use the Table Analyzer Wizard to split the data into related tables so you can store the data more efficiently.

Determining the Categories of Information You Need

The second step in creating a database is to determine all of the categories of information you need. At this point, you do not need to list the categories in any particular order. For instance, the sample application in this tutorial is the database for Greenfield Farm Market. Some of the information categories needed in this database include:

◆ The name, address, and phone number of each customer, as well as notes about customer remarks, preferences, and shipping information.

◆ The types of produce offered, their unit prices, and the quantity per unit.

◆ The customer order information, such as the items and quantities ordered, the date an order was placed, the employee who took the order, and shipping information.

Determining How Many Tables You Need

Each table in an Access database should contain information on a single subject. Thus, you must not only determine what categories of information (or fields) your database should contain, but also how that information should be broken down logically into several tables. In the database for Greenfield Farm Market, there is one table that contains customer information, a second table that contains information about items available for sale, and a third one that contains order information. This way of breaking down a database avoids duplication of data, or **redundancy.** For example, you wouldn't include customer names and addresses in an Orders table, because these fields describe the customer, not the order. You want to avoid entering the customer's name and address in each order, because this wastes storage space, requires extra typing, and increases the likelihood of data-entry errors. If you store a customer's name and address information in a single customer record rather than in multiple order records, you can more easily update that data later. At first, you may think that dividing the data among multiple tables is inefficient—for example, you may want to use information about both customers and orders in an invoice form—but remember that Access is a relational database program, and thus enables you to combine data from many sources as you create forms and reports.

Tables also should not contain multiple instances of the same field or a similar set of fields. For example, suppose you had a mail-order business and your customers often ordered multiple items at once. To record all of those orders in the Orders table, you could have one long record with similar fields for each item ordered. A better solution would be to have a separate Items table where each item being ordered is in a separate record.

Finally, as a general rule, do not include fields in your table that will contain data that you can calculate from other fields. For instance, if you have one field for price and one for quantity, you can calculate the total by multiplying these two values together—you don't need to create a separate field for the total. Figure 1.10 shows a tentative list of fields for the three tables in Greenfield Farm Market's database.

WEB NOTE

Although many people use the terms *Internet* and *World Wide Web* synonymously, they are separate entities. The World Wide Web (or Web) is just one tool used to access the Internet. The Web organizes information into easy-to-use pages, called Web pages.

Figure 1.10
Lists of fields in each table

ACCESS 2002

GREENFIELD FARM MARKET FIELDS

Customers	Orders	Produce
Customer ID	Order Number	Item ID
Last Name	Customer ID	Item Name
First Name	Order Date	Unit Price
Contact Title	Item	Quantity Per Unit
Address	Quantity	Category
City	Unit Price	Available as U-Pick
State	Shipping Amount	
ZIP Code	Shipper	
Phone Number	Employee ID	
Notes		

Determining How Tables Will Work Together

After you've decided how to divide the database information into multiple tables, you have a corresponding task—to determine how to set up those tables to combine the information they contain into single forms or reports. For instance, if you have separate tables for orders and customers, you clearly need a way to pull the data from both tables to create an invoice that includes corresponding customer and order information.

For you to be able to use two or more tables in combination, they must include a **common field.** For example, to ensure that you can relate the Greenfield Farm Market's Customers and Orders tables, you can include a Customer ID field in both tables. This field enables Access to match the order with the customer who placed the order. When determining the **relationship** (the association between common fields in two tables) between tables, you must also consider the concept of primary keys: A **primary key** is a field or set of fields that uniquely identifies each record in a table. Assigning a primary key is particularly important if you must link data in two tables. In the Greenfield Farm Market database, for instance, you need a primary key in the Customers table—some way to uniquely identify each customer so that you can tell which orders belong to which customers. A Customer ID field can serve this purpose. (You wouldn't want to use the name fields as the primary key, in case there are two customers with the same name.) When you set a primary key, Access automatically sorts records in order according to the values in that key. Because the primary key must uniquely identify each record, Access won't permit you to enter duplicate values in the primary key field(s).

Later in this lesson, you'll learn more about establishing relationships between tables. For right now, however, you'll just include common fields in the tables you plan to use together, and set some primary keys. Then in Lesson 2, you'll learn how to create queries that pull data from multiple tables.

CREATING A DATABASE

As you know, tables are the basic structures that hold all of the data in an Access database. However, before you begin to create tables in which to store your data,

NORTON
ONLINE

Visit **www.glencoe.com/norton/online/** for more information on creating a database.

you must first create a database. A database will contain not only tables (filled with data), but also other objects, such as queries, forms, and reports. There are two ways to create an Access database: (1) you can use the Database Wizard, which helps you create both a database and its objects based on a template, or (2) you can create a blank database and then create each database object individually as you need it.

In some respects, it is easier to create a database using the Database Wizard than to create a blank database, because the wizard automatically creates several database objects (tables, forms, reports) in one operation. However, a database created in this manner may contain tables (and fields) and other objects that you don't necessarily want, and thus is not as flexible as creating a blank database and then creating each object as you need it. In either case, however, you can always modify the database at any time after it's been created.

HANDS on

Creating and Naming a Blank Database

In this activity, you will create a blank database to hold your tables. Then you'll assign a name to identify the database.

1. Click the New button 🗋 on the Database toolbar.

The New File task pane appears on the right side of the application window.

2. In the New File task pane, click Blank Database.

The File New Database dialog box appears, as shown in Figure 1.11. Notice that this dialog box is very similar to the Open dialog box you saw earlier in this lesson.

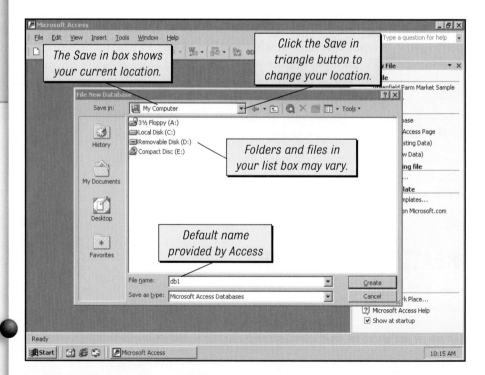

Access **BASICS**

Creating a Blank Database

1. Click New on the Database toolbar.

2. In the New File task pane, click Blank Database.

3. In the File New Database dialog box, navigate to the drive and folder in which you want to save the database.

4. Type a name in the File name text box and click Create.

Figure 1.11
File New Database dialog box

Lesson 1

3. Click the **Save in triangle button**, and navigate to your *Access Data* folder.

4. Click the *Tutorial* folder in the window below the Save in box, and click the **Open button** in the File New Database dialog box.

The *Tutorial* folder opens and its contents appear in the window.

5. Double-click the default file name *db1* in the File name text box.

6. Type Greenfield Farm Market-Lesson 1 to replace the default file name and click the **Create button**.

Access displays the Database window for the *Greenfield Farm Market-Lesson 1* database. When you create a blank database, it doesn't contain any objects—you must create the objects that will be stored in the database. Notice that the Tables option in the Objects bar is selected. Three options appear to help you create tables, but no actual tables exist yet. If you selected any of the other object options, you would see that they also contain no queries, forms, reports, or other objects—only options to create new objects.

To create a database, you can click New on the File menu. Then click Blank Database in the New File task pane.

ACCESS 2002

CREATING TABLES

Now that you've created a database, the next step is to create some tables to hold your data. A table provides the structure for your data, so to create a table, you must design its structure by identifying the fields in the table and defining the properties for those fields. Later in this lesson, you'll enter and edit data in the tables you've created. Creating tables and populating those tables with data are the first two essential steps for building a database.

There are three ways in which you can create tables in Access: (1) by using the Table Wizard; (2) by using Design view; or (3) by entering data into a blank datasheet. In this section, you will create one table using the Table Wizard and another table using Design view.

You can click the New button on the Database window toolbar and select the method by which you want to create a table.

Creating a Table With the Table Wizard

In the following three activities, you'll use the Table Wizard to design Greenfield Farm Market's Customers table, which will include the names and addresses of the Greenfield Farm Market customers. When you use a **wizard,** Access displays a series of dialog boxes that prompts you for the information it needs to perform a multi-step operation. There are several different wizards available in Access; the Table Wizard is used specifically to create tables. You'll use the wizard to select fields to be included in the table, remove and rename fields, name the table, and select a primary key.

HANDS on
Selecting Fields

The first step in creating a table is to select the fields to be included. In this activity, you'll start the Table Wizard and select fields from the samples provided.

1. In the *Greenfield Farm Market-Lesson 1* Database window, click **Tables** in the Objects bar, if it is not already selected.

2. Double-click the **Create table by using wizard option** in the Database window.

The first Table Wizard dialog box appears. Don't be overwhelmed by the number of options. This is simply a long selection of sample tables—and their accompanying fields—from which you can choose.

3. Verify that the **Business category** is selected, and then click **Customers** in the *Sample Tables* list box.

Notice that the list of field names in the *Sample Fields* list box changes; this list box now includes sample fields appropriate for a table that contains customer data. (If you want to see a list of sample tables that are targeted to personal use, click the Personal option button.)

4. Click the **CustomerID field name**, if it is not selected.

5. Click the **Add Field button** $\boxed{>}$.

This button permits you to add one field at a time to your new table. As shown in Figure 1.12, Access lists the CustomerID field in the *Fields in my new table* list box on the right side of the Table Wizard dialog box. The CustomerID field will be used to link customers and orders.

6. Click the **ContactFirstName sample field** and click the **Add Field button** $\boxed{>}$.

The ContactFirstName field appears directly beneath the CustomerID field in the *Fields in my new table* list box. The order in which the fields are listed here is the order in which the fields will appear in the table. Note that the ContactLastName field in the *Sample Fields* list box is now selected.

7. Click the **Add Field button** $\boxed{>}$.

Access adds the ContactLastName field to the *Fields in my new table* list box.

8. Double-click the **BillingAddress field** in the *Sample Fields* list box.

Access adds the BillingAddress field to the list on the right; double-clicking one of the sample fields is a shortcut for adding a field name to a table.

9. Add the fields **City, StateOrProvince, PostalCode, PhoneNumber, FaxNumber**, and **Notes**, in that order.

You may have to scroll down in the *Sample Fields* list box to find all of these fields. Access lists all the selected fields in the *Fields in my new table* list box.

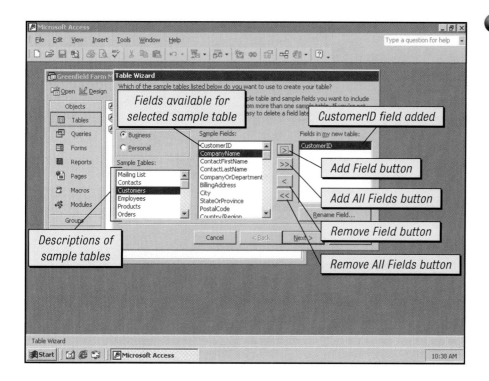

Figure 1.12
Adding a field using the Table Wizard

HANDS on

Changing Fields in the Field List

At times, you may decide against including a particular field in your table. Fortunately, this kind of change to the field list is very simple to make. In this activity, you will remove a field from the field list and rename another field.

1. Click **FaxNumber** in the *Fields in my new table* list box.

2. Click the **Remove Field button** <.

Access promptly removes the FaxNumber field from the list. You can change field names with ease, too.

3. Click the **PostalCode field** in the *Fields in my new table* list box.

4. Click the **Rename Field button**.

The Rename field dialog box appears with the current field name selected.

5. Type ZIPCode, as shown in Figure 1.13.

6. Click **OK**.

ZIPCode appears in the *Fields in my new table* list box.

Access BASICS

Removing and Renaming Fields

1. Click the field you wish to remove and click the Remove Field button.

2. Click the field you wish to rename, click the Rename Field button, type the new name, and click OK.

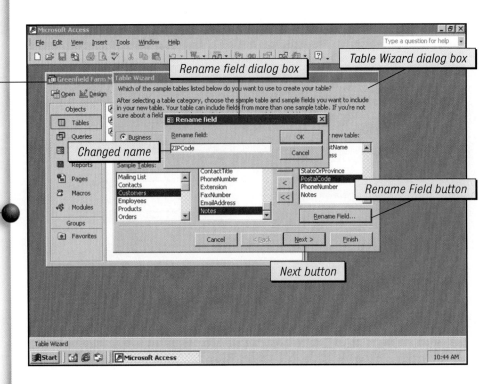

Database window

Rename field dialog box

Table Wizard dialog box

Changed name

Rename Field button

Next button

Figure 1.13
Rename field dialog box

HANDS on

Naming the Table and Selecting a Primary Key

You have now selected the desired fields for your table and are ready to choose a name for the table. In this activity, you provide a name when the Table Wizard prompts you to enter one. Then you will choose a field to act as the primary key.

Access **BASICS**

Naming the Table and Selecting a Primary Key

1. Type a name for the table.

2. Click the *No, I'll set the primary key.* option and click Next.

3. Select the field to be used as the primary key and click Next.

1. **Click the Next button near the lower-right corner of the Table Wizard dialog box.**

The next Table Wizard dialog box appears, in which you name your table and set the primary key.

Access suggests the name *Customers*—the name of the sample table you selected—for your new table. At this point, you can change the table name or keep the suggested name. Object names such as table names, as well as field names, can be up to 64 characters long. Access allows any combination of letters, numbers, spaces, and many punctuation characters. Access does not permit any of the following: period, exclamation mark, grave accent, square brackets, or double quotation marks. Also, object names cannot begin with a space or an equal sign. Let's keep the suggested table name *Customers*.

2. Click the **No, I'll set the primary key.** option and then click **Next**.

Access displays the next Table Wizard dialog box, as shown in Figure 1.14.

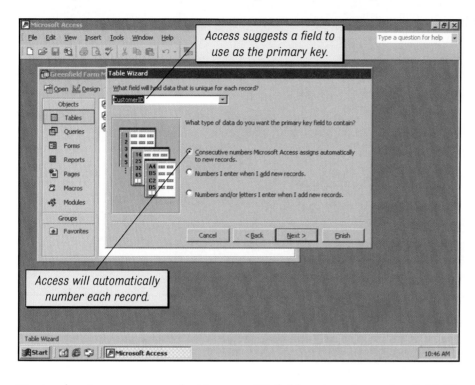

Figure 1.14
Selecting a primary key

Notice that Access suggests the CustomerID field as the primary key field. You could change this by selecting another field from the drop-down list; however, since each customer will have a unique ID number, this field is an appropriate one to set as the primary key.

Also notice that the *Consecutive numbers Microsoft Access assigns automatically to new records.* option is selected. When you choose this option, Access automatically provides the CustomerID numbers, ensuring that you don't enter duplicate values in any CustomerID field.

3. Click the **Next button** to accept the selections.

Access displays the final Table Wizard dialog box.

4. Choose the **Modify the table design.** option and click the **Finish button**.

Access displays the Customers table in Design view, as shown in Figure 1.15.

5. Click the **Customers: Table Close button** ✕.

You return to the *Greenfield Farm Market-Lesson 1* Database window, which now includes the Customers table.

Many Internet sites allow you to look up postal addresses, phone numbers, and e-mail addresses of companies and individuals.

Visit **www.glencoe.com/norton/online/** for more information on Access 2002.

Figure 1.15
Design view of Customers table

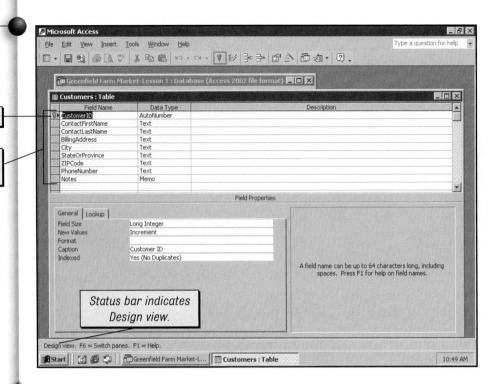

Primary key indicator

Fields you selected
using the Table Wizard

Status bar indicates
Design view.

Creating Tables in Design View

The Table Wizard makes creating a table a straightforward process, but allows you little flexibility. Fortunately, you can also create tables in Design view, which gives you much more control over field characteristics, including their size and the type of data they'll contain. You can use Design view to both create new tables and modify existing tables—whether you created them in Design view or with the Table Wizard.

HANDS on

Using Design View to Create a Table

In this activity, you'll create a new table in Design view, which is a bit more involved than using the Table Wizard. You'll create two fields in the Orders table for the Greenfield Farm Market database to get a feel for the process. After that, you'll learn more about the various aspects of fields before you complete the table.

1. Click Tables in the Objects bar in the Database window, if it is not already selected. Double-click the Create table in Design view option.

Access opens an empty table in Design view. Notice that the **insertion point**—the flashing vertical line—is in the Field Name column. Read the information in the lower-right corner of the window, which describes field names.

2. Click the Maximize button ▢ to enlarge the table.

ACCESS 2002

3. Enter the field name OrderNumber in the Field Name column.

4. Press `Tab` to move to the Data Type column.

Access displays the default data type (Text), as well as a triangle button that provides you with access to other choices. The **data type** controls the kind of data that can be entered into a field. A brief description of data types is displayed in the lower-right corner of the window.

5. Click the **Data Type triangle button**.

Access reveals a drop-down list box displaying the available data types, as shown in Figure 1.16.

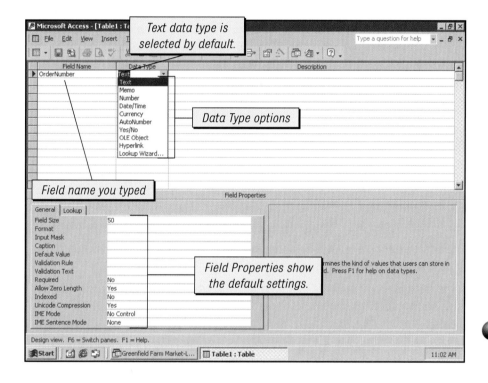

Figure 1.16
Selecting a data type

6. Click the **AutoNumber data type**. Then press `Tab`.

Your insertion point moves to the Description field, which is an optional field. You can enter a description of up to 255 characters for each field. Access provides information about field descriptions in the lower-right corner of the window.

7. In the Description field, type the text Do not enter data in this field; Access will assign a unique order number automatically.

8. Press `Tab` to move to the second row in the Field Name column.

9. Type CustomerID and press `Tab`.

The insertion point moves to the Data Type column.

10. Click the **Data Type triangle button** and click the **Number data type**. Then press `Tab`.

Access BASICS

Creating a Table in Design View

1. Double-click the Create table in Design view option in the Database window.

2. Type the first field name and press `Tab`.

3. Click the desired data type and press `Tab`.

4. If desired, type a description for the field and press `Tab`.

5. Repeat steps 2–4 for each field.

ACCESS 2002

Another Way

To select the data type more quickly, type the first letter while the insertion point is in the Data Type column. For example, type **n** to choose number, **c** to choose currency, and so on.

11. In the Description field, type the text Enter same Customer ID used in the Customers table.

12. Press `Tab`.

Access moves the insertion point down to the next row, ready for you to enter the specifications for another field. You'll enter additional fields later, after you learn more about some of the field characteristics you've just encountered.

More About Data Types

When you create a table using the Table Wizard, Access automatically assigns a data type to each field. However, when you create a table using Design view, you are responsible for assigning the data types. Before you assign a data type to a field, you must determine what types of values you want users to enter in the field. For example, if you want users to enter only numbers in a field, you should assign either the Number or Currency data type to the field; if you want users to enter a combination of letters, numbers, and punctuation, such as a street address, you should assign the Text data type. The ten data types available in Access are described in Table 1.2.

Table 1.2	Data Types

Data Type	Description
Text	Holds up to 255 characters, including letters, numbers, and punctuation marks. Use this data type for fields with (1) numbers that won't be used to perform calculations and (2) both numbers and some type of punctuation characters (such as phone numbers or Social Security numbers).
Memo	Holds up to 65,535 letters, numbers, and punctuation marks. Use this data type for fields with large amounts of text (such as free-form comments or fairly lengthy descriptions).
Number	Holds only digits, the decimal point, and the minus (negative) sign. Use this data type for fields with numbers only and for numbers to be used to perform calculations—for example, quantity or discount fields.
Date/Time	Holds dates and times. When you use this data type, Access prevents you from entering invalid dates or times (such as 2/31/02 or 34:35). Access provides different display formats for dates and times and lets you sort dates and times in chronological order. You can also perform date arithmetic—subtracting one date from another to determine the number of days between them, or adding or subtracting a specified number of days to or from a date to calculate a later or an earlier date.
Currency	Holds numeric values (such as salaries or prices) that you want to display with a currency symbol, a decimal point, and separators (usually commas) for every three digits.
AutoNumber	Holds numbers that Access increments by 1 automatically as each new record is added to the table. You cannot edit the values in an AutoNumber field. AutoNumber fields can be used as primary keys because a unique value for each record will be created automatically.
Yes/No	Can accept only one of two logical values. Usually the responses are shown as either Yes or No, but they can also be displayed as True or False or as On or Off.
OLE Object	Holds objects—such as Microsoft Word documents, pictures, graphs, and sounds—that have been created in other programs using the OLE protocol.
Hyperlink	Allows you to store text or graphics that link to a file or an Internet site.
Lookup Wizard	Lets you choose values from another table or create a list of values to be used. Choosing this option starts the Lookup Wizard.

HANDS on

Adding Field Names and Data Types

In this activity, you will add more field names and data types to the Orders table you are creating in the *Greenfield Farm Market-Lesson 1* database.

1. **If necessary, click in the row below the CustomerID field name.**

The insertion point is positioned in the third row in the Field Name column.

2. **Type OrderDate and press** [Tab].

The insertion point moves to the Data Type column, automatically selecting Text as the data type.

3. **Click the Data Type triangle button and click Date/Time.**

4. **Click directly below the OrderDate field.**

5. **Type Item as the field name and press** [Tab]**. Press** [Tab] **two more times to accept Text as the data type and move to the next row.**

6. **Enter the remaining field names and data types as shown in Table 1.3.**

NOTE *You can enter the data types more quickly if you use the keyboard instead of the mouse. Simply type the first letter of the data type and Access will complete it for you.*

ACCESS 2002

Table 1.3	Fields and Data Types for Orders Table
Field Name	**Data Type**
Quantity	Number
UnitPrice	Currency
ShippingAmount	Currency
Shipper	Text
EmployeeID	Number

Setting Field Properties

After assigning a data type to a field, you may have noticed that Access automatically sets default (preset) values in the property boxes in the Field Properties pane (lower pane) of the Design view window. These property boxes vary depending on the data type of the selected field, and they enable you to change a range of properties, or characteristics, associated with the current field. These **field properties** control the way a field looks and behaves.

Even though Access assigns default values to field properties, you can modify the field property settings. For example, fields specified as Text data types can be anywhere from 0 to 255 characters, and Access automatically sets the default field size to 50 characters. However, you can determine the size of the field simply by clicking the Field Size property box in the Field Properties pane and entering the desired value. The number you enter determines the maximum number of characters permitted in the field.

You'll usually want to decrease the sizes of Text and Memo fields by setting the Field Size property to the number of characters you think you'll need. Among other reasons, decreasing field sizes helps ensure that correct values are entered. As an example, you would set the field size of a field designated to hold state abbreviations to two characters. Limiting this field size will prevent users from entering more than two characters in the field.

For Number fields, you modify the field size by specifying the *type* of number the field will contain—the number type restricts the size of the number, usually by limiting the number of digits to the right and the left of the decimal point. There are seven number types; however, in this lesson you will only work with the more common number types.

HANDS on

Modifying Field Properties

Now that you have additional knowledge of some of the basic field properties, you're ready to complete the *Greenfield Farm Market-Lesson 1* Orders table in Design view. In this activity, you'll change the properties of some of the fields.

1. Click the Item field name. Press F6.

Access moves to the Field Size property box in the Field Properties pane. Note the default size for the Item field is 50.

2. Type 30 in the Field Size property box.

The value you type replaces the default, as shown in Figure 1.17.

3. Click the CustomerID field name, press F6, and read the description for Field Size in the lower-right corner of the Field Properties pane.

To establish a relationship between this Orders table and the Customers table you created earlier, the field size for the CustomerID field in the Orders table must be set to Long Integer in order to be compatible with the field size for the CustomerID field in the Customers table, which is set to AutoNumber.

4. Click the Quantity field name and press F6.

The Field Size is displayed as *Long Integer.* You can save storage space by making this field smaller.

5. Click the Field Size triangle button.

The list of number type options appears.

6. Click Integer. With the Quantity field still selected, double-click the Default Value property box.

The 0 in the box is highlighted.

7. Type 1 in the Default Value property box.

Now when an order is completed, Access will assume the quantity ordered is one. The default settings set by Access have now been modified to meet your needs.

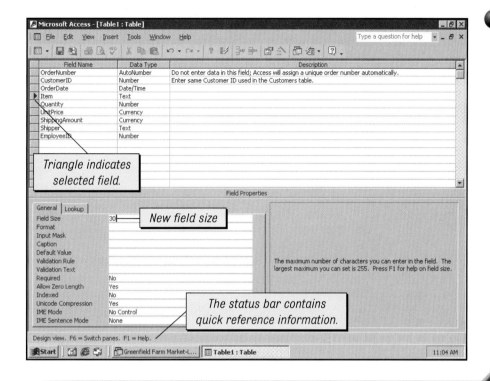

Figure 1.17
Changing the field size
of the Item field

Choosing a Primary Key

When you create a table with the Table Wizard, you set the primary key in the Table Wizard dialog box or you allow Access to set one. When you create a table in Design view, you must set the primary key yourself. To set the primary key, you must first select the appropriate field by either clicking anywhere in the field row (Field Name, Data Type, or Description columns), or by using the row selector. The **row selector** is the small box to the left of a field. Then you click the Primary Key button on the Table Design toolbar.

HANDS on

Setting the Primary Key

In this activity, you will designate the OrderNumber field as the primary key.

1. Click the row selector to the left of the OrderNumber field.

The entire OrderNumber row is highlighted.

2. Click the Primary Key button 🔑 on the Table Design toolbar.

NOTE *To assign the primary key, you can also click Primary Key on the Edit menu or right-click the highlighted row and click Primary Key on the shortcut menu that appears.*

Access places a small key-shaped icon in the row selector for the OrderNumber field, as shown in Figure 1.18.

Figure 1.18
Setting the primary key

Key icon indicates that this field is set as the primary key.

The small, gray boxes to the left of the field names are called row selectors.

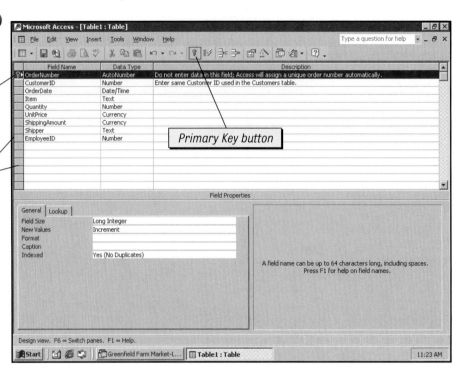

For some tables, you need to set a combination of two or more fields as the primary key. For instance, if the Orders table didn't contain the OrderNumber field, no other single field could be used as a primary key since none uniquely identifies each record. For instance, if you picked the CustomerID field as the primary key, you would not be able to distinguish between different orders made by the same customer. In this case, you could select the CustomerID, OrderDate, and Item fields and then issue the Primary Key command. The combination of these three fields would be considered the primary key.

You've completed the structure for the Orders table, but you need to complete one more step; you need to save this table for future use.

SAVING A TABLE

As you know, in computer terminology, *saving* is the process of taking information from your computer's memory and storing it on a more permanent medium—usually a hard drive or a removable disk. When you create tables with the Table Wizard, Access automatically saves them, using the table name you supply. In contrast, when you create or modify tables in Design view, you need to tell Access to save the table, much as you need to save documents you create with a word processing program.

When you use the Save command to save a table for the first time, Access requests a table name. When you update your table design and save again, the modified table is simply saved under the same name, so Access has no need to prompt you for a new name. If, for some reason, you want to save a copy of the table under a new name, you can do so by clicking Save As on the File menu.

When you save a table, the table is stored in the file of the associated database. For example, both the Customers table you created earlier and the Orders table you just created will be stored in the *Greenfield Farm Market-Lesson 1* database.

HANDS **on**

Saving the Orders Table

In this activity, you'll save the *Greenfield Farm Market-Lesson 1* Orders table so you can change the design later if necessary, and, equally important, so you can enter data into the table.

1. Click the Save button 📅 **on the Table Design toolbar.**

Access displays the Save As dialog box, as shown in Figure 1.19. You will enter a name for your table in this dialog box.

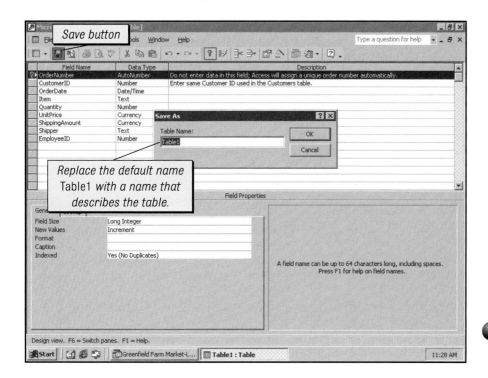

Save button

Replace the default name Table1 with a name that describes the table.

Figure 1.19
Save As dialog box

2. Type Orders **in the Table Name text box to replace the default name** *Table1* **and click** OK**.**

The Save As dialog box closes, and the table name *Orders* now appears in the title bar.

3. Click the Close Window button ☒ **at the right end of the menu bar.**

Access closes the Orders table and returns to the Database window for the *Greenfield Farm Market-Lesson 1* database.

If you were to attempt to close a table that included unsaved design changes, Access would display a dialog box asking whether you wanted to save your changes. You would choose Yes to save the changes, No to discard them, or Cancel to cancel the operation and return to Design view.

Another Way

To save a table, click Save on the File menu.

Understanding Field Size Settings for the Number Data Type

Now that you've created two tables, use Help to learn more about the various field size settings you can use with the Number data type.

1. **Type** field size property **in the Ask a Question box and press** `Enter←`.

2. **Click the FieldSize Property option to open the associated Help window. Maximize the Help window, if necessary (Figure 1.20).**

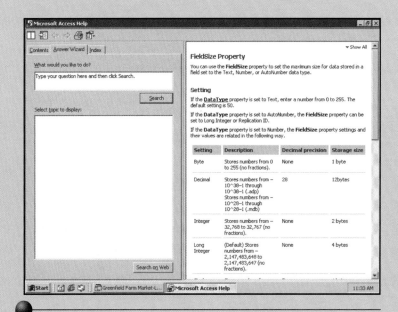

Figure 1.20
Using Help to research the field size property for the Number data type

3. **Find and click the glossary term *Number* to view the definition for Number data type.**

4. **Read the information in the Help window regarding the seven different field size property settings for the Number data type.**

5. **Scroll down in the Help window and read the Remarks section.**

6. **When you are finished exploring, click the Close button [X] to close the Help window.**

MODIFYING TABLES IN DESIGN VIEW

Whether you've created a table with the Table Wizard or in Design view, at some point you may need to make changes to the structure of your table. You might need to change field names or data types, add a field you left out, eliminate a field you no longer need, or reorder the fields to better suit your needs or your sense of order. All of these changes can be made in Design view.

> **WARNING** *You can change the table structure after you've entered data into the table, but proceed with caution if you do. You run the risk of losing or unintentionally modifying your data.*

Adding Captions to Fields

It is a good practice to enter a field name as one word with no spaces, such as OrderNumber or CustomerID, to avoid potential conflicts with any Microsoft Visual Basic for Applications (VBA) programming that may be executing in the background. However, these field names are not always easy to read, and in fact, seem incorrect when a table is displayed in Datasheet view. You can use the **Caption** field property to change the field name that displays when you view a table in Datasheet view. Captions are also used as labels in forms, reports, and other objects. When you create a table using the Table Wizard, captions are automatically created for field names that contain two or more words. However, when you create a table in Design view, captions are not automatically created; you must create them.

HANDS on

Modifying the Caption Field Property

In this activity, you will create captions for fields in the Orders table in the *Greenfield Farm Market-Lesson 1* database.

1. In the *Greenfield Farm Market-Lesson 1* Database window, double-click the **Orders table** to open it in Datasheet view.

Notice that the two-word field names are displayed with no spaces. Now let's switch to Design view and add captions to these fields.

2. Click the **View button** on the Table Datasheet toolbar.

The Orders table appears in Design view, and the OrderNumber field is selected.

3. Press [F6] to switch to the Field Properties pane.

4. Navigate to the Caption property box and type Order Number.

5. Press [F6] to return to the upper pane.

6. Create captions for each of the following fields:

CustomerID	Customer ID
OrderDate	Order Date
UnitPrice	Unit Price
ShippingAmount	Shipping Amt.
EmployeeID	Employee ID

7. Click the **Save button** 🖫 on the Table Design toolbar to save the changes you just made.

Since you named and saved this table earlier, Access saves the updated table without first prompting you for a table name.

8. Click the **View button** 🔲▾ on the Table Design toolbar.

As you can see, the captions now display as the field names in Datasheet view.

9. Click the **Close Window button** ⊠ to close the Orders table.

Adding and Removing Fields

Although you should always plan ahead regarding fields to be included in your database, sometimes you'll discover that you need to make changes. Access allows you to add and remove fields in Design view. You can easily add a field after the last field, as you already know. You can also insert fields between other fields and delete fields that become unnecessary. There are several ways to insert a field (row): click Rows on the Insert menu; right-click the field and click Insert Rows on the shortcut menu; or click the Insert Rows button 彐ᶜ on the Table Design toolbar. There are also several ways to delete a field: click Delete Rows on the Edit menu; right-click the field and click Delete Rows on the shortcut menu; or click the Delete Rows button 彐ᵡ on the Table Design toolbar.

HANDS on

Inserting and Deleting Fields

In this activity, you will insert some new fields between existing fields and delete a field in the Customers table of the *Greenfield Farm Market-Lesson 1* database.

1. In the *Greenfield Farm Market-Lesson 1* Database window, click the **Customers table** and click the **Design button** 🔍 Design on the Database window toolbar.

The Customers table appears in Design view.

2. Click anywhere in the PhoneNumber row in the top pane of the Design view window.

3. Click the **Insert Rows button** 彐ᶜ on the Table Design toolbar.

As shown in Figure 1.21, Access adds a blank row above the PhoneNumber field and places the insertion point within this row.

4. Type Country in the Field Name column and press ⎆Tab.

Access automatically inserts *Text* in the Data Type column, which is the data type you want to assign to this field.

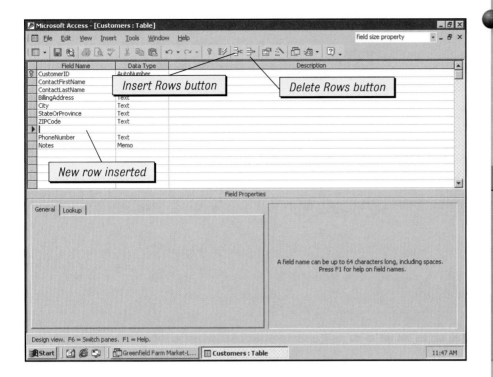

Figure 1.21
Inserting a row

Did you know?

Clicking the row selector highlights the entire field. You can select multiple adjacent fields by dragging over their row selectors. You can select nonadjacent fields by pressing Ctrl and clicking the row selector of each field to be selected.

5. Click anywhere in the Notes row in the top pane.

6. Click the **Insert Rows button** 3← on the Table Design toolbar.

7. Type ContactTitle in the Field Name column and press F6.

Access automatically inserts *Text* in the Data Type column and jumps to the Field Size property box in the Field Properties pane.

8. Type 10 in the Field Size property box.

9. Type Contact Title in the Caption property box.

Since Greenfield Farm Market is not an international company, you decide to delete the Country field from the table design.

10. Click anywhere in the Country row in the upper pane.

11. Click the **Delete Rows button** →* on the Table Design toolbar.

Access deletes the active row—in this case, the Country field.

Another Way

- To insert a row, you can click Rows on the Insert menu or right-click and click Insert Rows on the shortcut menu.

- To delete a row, you can click Delete Rows on the Edit menu or right-click and click Delete Rows on the shortcut menu.

Moving Fields

The order in which fields are listed in Design view (top to bottom) is the same order in which they appear in Datasheet view (left to right). After reviewing all of the fields in a table, you may decide that the order in which they appear could be improved. Access allows you to easily change the order of fields by dragging them to their new locations in Design view.

HANDS on

Reorganizing Fields and Improving Table Design

After reviewing your table design, you decide to display each customer's last name before the customer's first name and display the customer's personal title after the customer's first name. In this activity, you will rearrange the order of these fields. Then you will make additional modifications to the table to improve its appearance and efficiency.

Access **BASICS**

Moving a Field

1. Click the row selector of the field you wish to move.

2. Drag the field to the new position.

1. **Click the row selector for the ContactFirstName field.**

Access highlights the entire row.

2. **Point to the row selector for the selected row; click and hold the mouse button and drag downward until the dark horizontal line appears just below the ContactLastName field, as shown in Figure 1.22.**

Access attaches a small gray rectangle to the bottom of the pointer and also displays a dark horizontal line; the selected field will move to just below the horizontal line when you release the mouse button.

Figure 1.22
Moving a field

Select the field you want to move.

As you drag, a small, gray rectangle appears at the bottom of the pointer.

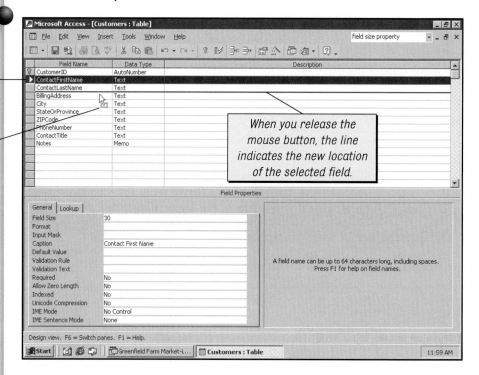

When you release the mouse button, the line indicates the new location of the selected field.

3. **Release the mouse button.**

Access moves the field to the new location in the table, below the ContactLastName field.

4. **Click the row selector for the ContactTitle field to select the entire row.**

5. Point to the **row selector** for the selected ContactTitle field, and click and drag the ContactTitle field below the ContactFirstName field.

The first four fields in the Customers table should now be CustomerID, ContactLastName, ContactFirstName, and ContactTitle. Now let's modify some field properties to improve the efficiency and appearance of the table.

6. Change the field size of the ContactLastName field to 30.

7. Change the size of the BillingAddress field to 50.

8. Change the size of the City field to 30.

9. Change the size of the StateOrProvince field to 2.

Notice that the Caption property box for the StateOrProvince field contains the text *State/Province*. When a table is created using the Table Wizard—as this one was—a caption is automatically assigned to a field name. However, when you add or modify fields in Design view, captions are not automatically created. It is a good practice to create or modify captions for all fields that you add or modify in Design view.

10. Since Greenfield Farm Market's products are not sold internationally, change the caption for the StateOrProvince field to State.

11. Click the **ZIPCode field** in the top pane of the window.

Earlier in this lesson, you created this field using the Table Wizard. So why didn't Access automatically create a caption? If you'll recall, you changed the name of the field from PostalCode to ZIPCode. When you change a field name, Access does not automatically create a caption.

12. Type ZIP Code in the Caption property box for the ZIPCode field.

13. Type List customer comments and shipping notes in the Description column for the Notes field.

Since you have made several changes to the design of the Customers table, you should save the table.

14. Click the **Save button** 🖫 on the Table Design toolbar.

Since you named and saved this table earlier, Access saves the updated table without first prompting you for a table name.

Creating an Input Mask

A database is only as good as the information it contains. You can create well-designed tables with pertinent fields arranged in a logical order, but if a user enters information incorrectly into the fields, the database is not useful. Fortunately, Access provides several ways to help you control how information is entered. You already used one of these methods when you specified data types for the fields in the Customers and Orders tables. As you may recall, the data type determines what kind of data can be entered into a field. You further restricted the information that could be entered into the database when you limited the field size property of certain fields, such as the StateOrProvince field in the Customers table.

Did you know?

If you make a change and then immediately realize that you didn't want to make that change, you can click the Undo button to reverse the last action you completed. Conversely, if you undo a change and then realize that you do indeed want that change, you can click the Redo button to reverse the undo action.

Another way to control how data is entered is by creating an input mask. An **input mask** is a pattern that you create that specifies what kind of data to enter and the number of characters allowed in a field. It is easier to enter data into fields that contain input masks because the input mask shows you exactly how to enter the data. As with most multi-step operations, Access provides a wizard—aptly named the Input Mask Wizard—to guide you through the process of creating an input mask.

HANDS on

Using the Input Mask Wizard

In this activity, you will use the Input Mask Wizard to create input masks for two of the fields in the Customers table of the *Greenfield Farm Market-Lesson 1* database.

Access BASICS

Creating an Input Mask

1. In Design view, click in the field in which you want to add an input mask.

2. Press F6 to jump to the Field Properties pane and navigate to the Input Mask property box.

3. Click the Build button to activate the Input Mask Wizard.

4. Select the appropriate input mask from the sample list.

5. If desired, change the input mask and the placeholder characters.

6. Select the appropriate option to store the data with or without symbols.

7. Click Finish.

1. With the Customers table open in Design view, click the **ZipCode field** and press F6 to jump to the Field Properties pane.

2. Navigate to the Input Mask property box and click the **Build button** .... at the right end of the property box.

NOTE *If Access displays a message indicating that the Input Mask Wizard is not installed on your system, install the feature from your application program CD or check with your instructor.*

The Input Mask Wizard dialog box appears, as shown in Figure 1.23.

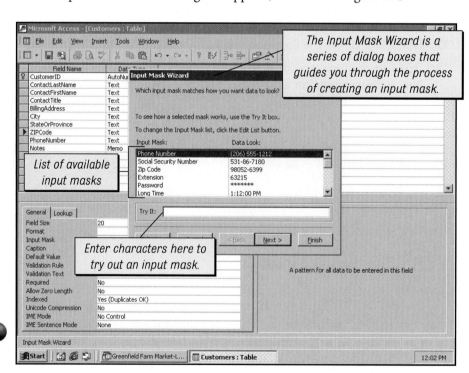

The Input Mask Wizard is a series of dialog boxes that guides you through the process of creating an input mask.

List of available input masks

Enter characters here to try out an input mask.

Figure 1.23
Input Mask Wizard dialog box

3. Scroll through the Input Mask list in the dialog box to see the different masks that are available.

4. Click **Zip Code** in the Input Mask list, and then click at the left edge of the Try It text box.

The input mask appears in the Try It text box with the insertion point positioned at the beginning of the input mask.

5. Try typing letters or special characters into the input mask.

Since letters and special characters are not valid in a ZIP Code, the input mask does not allow you to enter them.

6. Type any nine numbers into the input mask.

The input mask accepts the numbers. Notice that you did not have to type the hyphen separator; it is included as part of the input mask.

7. Click **Next** in the Input Mask Wizard dialog box.

In this dialog box, you can change the input mask (for example, from nine digits to five digits) and the placeholder character that will display in the field.

8. Click **Next** to accept the default placeholder character.

The next dialog box asks if you want to store the data with or without the symbol (hyphen separator). It is more efficient to store the data without the symbol, and even if the data is stored without the symbol, it will still be displayed with the symbol. However, if at some point in the future you want to create mailing labels, you should store the data with the symbol.

9. Click to select the option to store the data with the symbols in the mask, and click **Next**.

10. Click **Finish** in the final dialog box.

Access creates the input mask for the ZIPCode field and closes the Input Mask Wizard. After you create an input mask with the Input Mask Wizard, you must save it.

11. Click the **Save button** 🖫 on the Table Design toolbar.

Now let's create an input mask for the PhoneNumber field.

12. Click the **PhoneNumber field** in the upper pane, press 🔳 to jump to the Field Properties pane, and navigate to the Input Mask property box.

13. Click the **Build button** to activate the Input Mask Wizard.

The Input Mask Wizard dialog box appears with the Phone Number input mask selected.

14. Click at the left edge of the Try It text box and experiment with the kinds of characters you can enter in the input mask.

15. Since the default settings in the remainder of the dialog boxes are acceptable, simply click **Finish** to create the input mask and close the Input Mask Wizard.

At any time while using a wizard to perform a multi-step operation, you can click the Back button to back up one step.

Visit **www.glencoe.com/norton/online/** for more information on Input Mask Wizard.

16. Click **Save** 🖫 on the Table Design toolbar to save the input mask.

17. Click the **Close Window button** ☒ to close the Customers table.

The Customers table closes and you return to the Database window.

ENTERING RECORDS USING A DATASHEET

Now that you have designed some tables—by creating the fields to be included in the tables and assigning properties to those fields—you're ready to actually enter data into them. Usually forms are the most often used object for data entry, especially if you are entering a large number of records; however, sometimes it is more efficient to use the datasheet to add, delete, or make minor modifications to only a few records. As you may have guessed, you use Datasheet view to work with a datasheet.

HANDS on

Adding Data to a Table in Datasheet View

In this activity, you'll type the information for several records into the Customers table.

1. If necessary, open the *Greenfield Farm Market-Lesson 1* database and maximize the Database window. Click **Tables** in the Objects bar and click the **Customers table**, if it is not already selected.

2. Click the **Open button** 📑 Open on the Database window toolbar.

When you click the Open button 📑 Open, Access opens the table in Datasheet view by default. Your Customers table should resemble Figure 1.24. You can see some of the **field selectors** (the gray boxes at the top of each column that contain the captions), but the table is empty; that is, it contains no data. The blank row that appears directly below the field selectors is a new record into which you can enter data. The gray box to the left of the record is called the **record selector,** and the triangle within the record selector indicates the **current record,** or the record with the **focus.**

3. Press ⌨Tab to move to the Contact Last Name field.

Access moves the insertion point to the Contact Last Name field. (Since the Customer ID field is an AutoNumber field, Access will enter data in that field automatically.)

4. Type Kellum in the Contact Last Name field and press ⌨Tab.

As soon as you start typing, Access automatically enters a value into the Customer ID field for this customer. When you press ⌨Tab, the insertion point moves into the Contact First Name field. Note that Access has created a second blank record with an asterisk (*) in the record selector. An asterisk indicates a new record in which you can type data. The record in which you are typing has a pencil icon in the record selector. The pencil icon indicates that you are currently editing the record and the edits have not yet been saved.

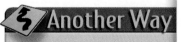

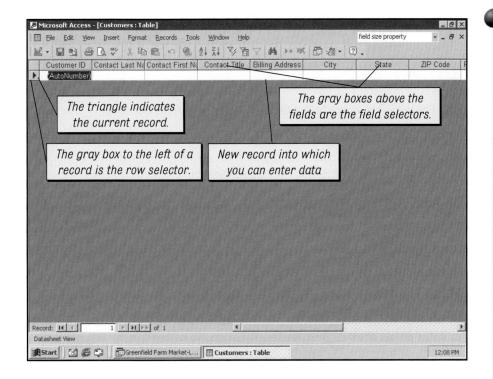

Figure 1.24
An empty table in Datasheet view

5. Type Sarah **in the Contact First Name field and press** [Tab].

Access moves the insertion point to the Contact Title field.

6. Type Ms. **in the Contact Title field and press** [Tab].

Access moves the insertion point to the Billing Address field.

7. Type 2663 Ash Drive **in the Billing Address field and press** [Tab].

8. Type Milford **in the City field and press** [Tab].

9. Type KS **in the State field and press** [Tab].

10. In the ZIP Code field, type 66514 **and then type** 3075.

Note that you didn't have to enter the hyphen; because of the input mask, Access automatically formats the ZIP Code with the hyphen in its proper place.

11. Press [Tab] **to move to the Phone Number field.**

Access scrolls the display so you can see the Phone Number field in full. Only some of the fields of a large table show in Datasheet view at once. Pressing [Tab] automatically scrolls the display to bring additional fields into view.

12. In the Phone Number field, type 620, **type** 555, **and finally type** 7331 **and press** [Tab].

Access once again enters the punctuation because of the input mask associated with the Phone Number field. Notice that a description of the Notes field appears on the status bar. As you may recall, you entered this description when you modified the table design earlier.

HINTS & TIPS

If you want to move back to a previous field, you can click the field or press [←].

13. Press ⌷Tab⌷ to leave the Notes field blank.

Since Notes is the last field in the record, the insertion point jumps to the first field in a new record.

14. Press ⌷Tab⌷ to move to the Contact Last Name field and type Lunken. Then press ⌷Tab⌷ again.

As before, Access automatically increments the value in the Customer ID field and creates a new blank record at the end of the table.

15. Type Rick in the Contact First Name field and press ⌷Tab⌷.

16. Type Mr. in the Contact Title field and press ⌷Tab⌷.

17. Type 118 Highland Ave. in the Billing Address field and press ⌷Tab⌷.

As you typed, some of the address scrolled out of view. When you pressed ⌷Tab⌷ to move to the next field, only the beginning of the address displays. The information is still there, even though you cannot see everything in the field.

18. Point to the right boundary of the field selector for the Billing Address field.

The pointer changes into a vertical bar with a horizontal double-headed arrow attached, as shown in Figure 1.25. This pointer indicates that you can drag to the left to narrow the column or drag to the right to widen the column.

HINTS & TIPS

To quickly resize a column so you can see all of the data in the field (or the entire field name if it's longer than the data), double-click the right boundary of the field selector.

A pencil icon indicates that this is the record into which you are currently entering or editing data.

An asterisk indicates that this is a new record into which you can enter data.

Access will automatically enter a number in this field.

Using this pointer, you can change the column width by dragging or double-clicking.

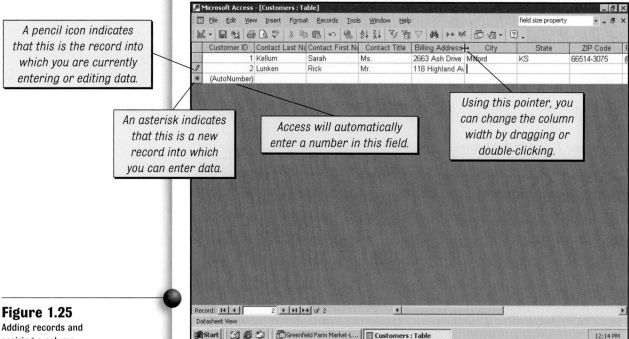

Figure 1.25
Adding records and resizing a column

19. Drag to the right to widen the Billing Address field until the entire address for Rick Lunken is visible.

20. Type Greenfield in the City field and press `Tab`, then type KS in the State field and press `Tab`.

21. Type 67737-6819 in the ZIP Code field, press `Tab`, and type (620) 555-5008 in the Phone Number field. (Remember, you do not need to type the punctuation.)

22. Press `Tab` and type the following information in the Notes field. (Do not press `Tab` after typing the data.)

Mr. Lunken asked how far in advance he could place an order for sweet corn.

You have now entered all of the data for the second record.

23. Click the **New Record button** ⏭ on the Table Datasheet toolbar.

Access moves down to the next row (the new blank record), ready for you to enter data.

24. Enter the names and addresses listed in Table 1.4. Leave all the Notes fields blank.

Table 1.4	Names and Addresses to Enter		
Field	**Record 3**	**Record 4**	**Record 5**
Contact Last Name	Rusconi	Zoller	O'Toole
Contact First Name	Mike	Kimberly	Janice
Contact Title	Mr.	Miss	Mrs.
Billing Address	207 Hickory Pl.	25 Bainbark Ct.	5943 Finch Ln.
City	Bellefontaine	Vinita	Carthage
State	OH	OK	MO
ZIP Code	43311-1160	74301-6017	64836-9834
Phone Number	(419) 555-1425	(918) 555-6701	(417) 555-1337

If you're used to word processing and spreadsheet programs, you may be wondering when to save your data. Access automatically saves your data when you move to a new record. If you want to save before that point, however—perhaps you're entering a long memo field—you can click Records on the menu bar and then click Save Record or press `⇧ Shift` + `Enter⏎`.

25. Close the table. Click **Yes** in response to the message to save changes to the layout of the Customers table.

HINTS & TIPS

The New Record button creates a new record at the bottom of the table. You can use this button to complete your entry of a record. As you saw with the entry of the first record, pressing `Tab` in the last field also moves you to a new blank record.

NOTE *Even though Access automatically saves changes to data (when you move to a new record), you must still instruct Access to save changes to the table design. By changing the width of the Billing Address field in step 19, you changed the design of the table.*

RETRIEVING DATA FROM OTHER SOURCES

Sometimes you'll find that some of the data you need in your database is already stored in another database or in another application file, such as Excel or dBase. There are various ways that you can populate your database with data from other sources to avoid rekeying large amounts of data. You can copy records from a table in another database and **append** (paste append) them to a table in your database, provided the order of the fields in the two databases is the same. Unfortunately, you can't simply open two databases and copy data from one to another; Access does not permit you to have two databases open at once (unless you have two instances of Access running). However, you can copy the data to the **Office Clipboard**—a temporary place to store items that you copy from a variety of places (such as another database, other Office programs, Web pages, etc.)—and then append it to a table in another database.

In addition to copying data using the Clipboard, you can also **import** data from another Office application, such as Microsoft Excel; from a non-Office application, such as dBase; or from another Access database. When you import data, you actually copy an entire object into your database, which includes both the records (data) and the structure (design) of the object. While there are many advantages to importing data from other applications, you will often need to make modifications to the table design afterwards.

HANDS on

Appending Records to Tables

In this activity, you will append records to two tables. First, you will open the Clipboard task pane, copy records from a table in the *Greenfield Farm Market Sample* database to the Office Clipboard, and append the records to the Customers table in the *Greenfield Farm Market-Lesson 1* database. Then, you will copy records from another table in the sample database into the Orders table, using the same technique.

1. **Click Office Clipboard on the Edit menu.**

The Clipboard task pane appears on the right side of the application window and the Office Clipboard icon displays on the Windows taskbar (in the system tray to the left of the clock).

2. **Click Open on the File menu, and navigate to your *Access Data* folder.**

3. Double-click the *Greenfield Farm Market Sample* database. Click **Tables** in the Objects bar, if necessary.

You should see the *Greenfield Farm Market Sample* Database window. The Customers, Orders, Produce, and Shippers tables appear in the list of table objects.

4. Open the **Customers table** in Datasheet view.

5. Click the **record selector** in front of record 6, scroll down to record 36, press [⇧ Shift], and click the **record selector** for record 36.

Access highlights records 6 through 36 in the table.

6. Click the **Copy button** 🖹 on the Table Datasheet toolbar.

Access copies all of these records to the Office Clipboard, and they are displayed in the Clipboard task pane, as shown in Figure 1.26.

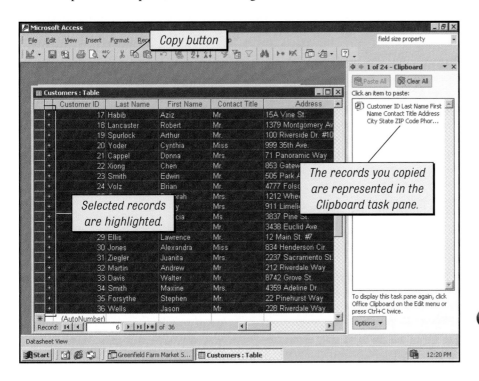

7. Click the **Close button** ☒ to close the Customers table.

Access displays a warning message about the large amount of data on the Clipboard.

8. Read the text in the warning box and click **Yes** to save the data on the Clipboard.

Access closes the Customers table and returns to the *Greenfield Farm Market Sample* Database window.

Figure 1.26
Copying records to the Office Clipboard

Another Way

To copy, click Edit on the menu bar and click Copy.

9. Click the **Open button** 🗁 on the Database toolbar. Navigate to and open the *Greenfield Farm Market-Lesson 1* database in the *Tutorial* folder in your *Access Data* folder.

10. Double-click the **Customers table** in the Database window.

You will see the Customers table with the records that you entered earlier.

11. Click **Paste Append** on the Edit menu.

NOTE *If the Paste Append command doesn't appear, click the double arrow at the bottom of the Edit menu to display the expanded menu.*

The Paste Append option lets you add records to the end of your table. Before adding the records, however, Access displays a message asking if you're sure you want to paste the records. In this box, you can click Yes to add the records or No to cancel the operation.

NOTE *You can't use the normal Paste button 🖹 on the Table Datasheet toolbar to paste these records from the Clipboard; you must use the Paste Append command on the Edit menu.*

12. Read the text in the dialog box and click **Yes** to add the records from the Clipboard to the Customers table.

13. Click anywhere within the table to remove the highlighting. Then click the **Maximize button** ▢.

The navigation button bar at the bottom of the table window indicates that the table now contains 36 records.

14. Close the **Customers table.**

Now you will copy the records from another table into your Orders table.

15. Open the *Greenfield Farm Market Sample* database in your *Access Data* folder, and open the **Orders table** in Datasheet view.

NOTE *Remember, the names of the most recently used databases appear at the bottom of the File menu. You can click File on the menu bar and then click the* Greenfield Farm Market Sample *file name to open the database.*

16. Press ⌨Ctrl + ⌨A to select all records.

All of the records in the Orders table are selected (or highlighted).

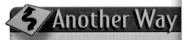

Another Way

To highlight all records, click Select All Records on the Edit menu.

17. Click the **Copy button** 🖹.

Notice that a second item now appears in the Clipboard task pane above the item you copied in the last activity, as shown in Figure 1.27.

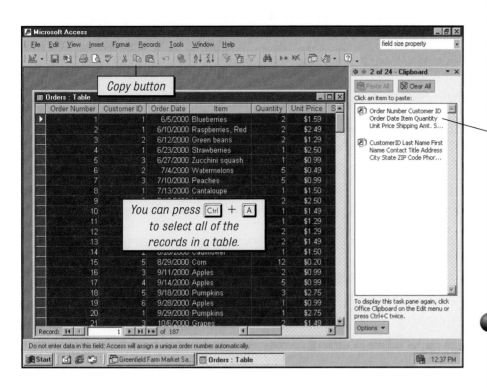

Figure 1.27
Selecting all records and copying to the Clipboard

18. Close the Orders table. When the warning message asks if you want to save the data you copied on the Clipboard, click **Yes**.

19. Open the *Greenfield Farm Market-Lesson 1* database in the *Tutorial* folder in your *Access Data* folder. Open the Orders table.

Notice that no data has been entered into the table yet.

20. Click **Paste Append** on the Edit menu.

A dialog box asks if you want to paste 187 records into the table.

21. Click **Yes**.

Your table now contains 187 records. Imagine how much time you saved by copying and pasting the data rather than entering each record one at a time!

22. Close the Orders table, and close the Clipboard task pane.

Importing Data From Another Application

In this activity, you will use the Import feature to create a new table with data from an Excel worksheet. Then you will modify the table design.

Using the Import Spreadsheet Wizard

1. Click File on the menu bar, point to Get External Data, and click Import.

2. In the Import dialog box, change the Files of type to the application file type you wish to import, such as Microsoft Excel, and double-click the file you want to import.

3. Respond to the prompts in the Import Spreadsheet Wizard dialog boxes.

1. With the *Greenfield Farm Market-Lesson 1* Database window open, click **File** on the menu bar, point to **Get External Data** on the expanded menu, and then click **Import** on the submenu.

The Import dialog box appears.

2. In the Files of type list box, click **Microsoft Excel**. Navigate to your *Access Data* folder and double-click the Excel file *GFM Employees*.

The Import Spreadsheet Wizard dialog box appears, as shown in Figure 1.28. This dialog box lets you select the worksheet that you want to import from the *GFM Employees* workbook into the *Greenfield Farm Market-Lesson 1* database.

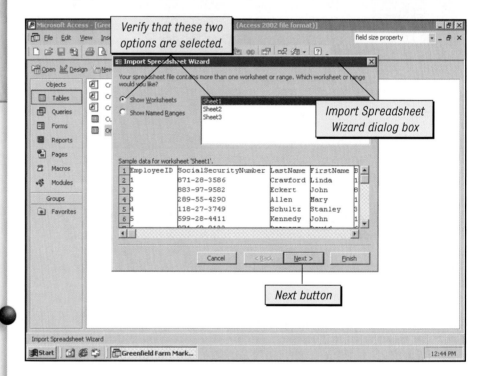

Figure 1.28
Import Spreadsheet Wizard dialog box

3. Click **Show Worksheets** and **Sheet1**, if they are not already selected. Then click **Next**.

4. Verify that a check mark appears before First Row Contains Column Headings and click **Next**.

The Import Spreadsheet Wizard now asks where you want to store your data.

5. Click **In a New Table** if it is not already selected, and click **Next**. In the Field Options section, verify that *EmployeeID* appears in the Field Name text box. Then click **Next**.

6. Click **Choose my own primary key**. If necessary, click the **triangle button** to the right of the text box and click **EmployeeID** from the drop-down list. Then click **Next**.

The wizard now requests the name of the table. A suggested name appears in the Import to Table text box.

7. Change the name to Employees and click **Finish**.

After importing, the Import Spreadsheet Wizard displays a message indicating the name of the file that was imported and the name of the table to which it was imported.

8. Click **OK**.

Access returns to the Database window, and you should see the new Employees table in the table list.

9. Open the **Employees table** in Datasheet view and review the data you imported.

10. Switch to Design view and review the table design.

As you can see, many of the fields are extremely large and do not contain captions or input masks.

11. Make the modifications as shown in Table 1.5 to the field properties of the Employees table.

WARNING *Before you can create the input masks as indicated in Table 1.5, Access will require you to save the table. When you attempt to save the table, a warning message will appear indicating that some data may be lost because some of the fields have been changed to a shorter size. Click Yes to continue.*

12. Save and close the table.

ACCESS 2002

Table 1.5	Employees Table Design Modifications		
Field Name	**Field Size**	**Caption**	**Other**
EmployeeID	Long Integer	Employee ID	
SocialSecurityNumber	25	Social Security Number	Create input mask using Input Mask Wizard.
LastName	30	Last Name	
FirstName	20	First Name	
BirthDate		Birth Date	
HireDate		Hire Date	
Address	50		
City	30		
State	2		
ZIPCode	15	ZIP Code	Create input mask using Input Mask Wizard.
HomePhone	15	Home Phone	Create input mask using Input Mask Wizard.

NAVIGATING THE DATASHEET AND EDITING RECORDS

After you've entered a substantial amount of data in your table, you need to know how to move around in the datasheet. When you have only a few records, you can always move the focus to another record just by clicking. When you have larger amounts of data, you need a few additional strategies to find the records you want and select specific fields. You'll learn both keyboard and mouse techniques for navigating the datasheet while you move through the records that you recently entered into the Customers table. Remember, the record with the focus is simply the one you're editing at the moment. This record usually has a triangle in the record selector, but will have a pencil if you've made any changes that you haven't yet saved.

After you've located the records in which you're interested, you're ready to begin editing. You can delete or replace the contents of a particular field, and you can add to or change the contents of a field easily. You can delete one or more entire records as well. The Undo feature is useful when you need to reverse a previous editing action, and, if you act quickly enough, you can even undo changes you've made to a record that's already been saved.

To make data entry and editing easier, you can use the Zoom window. Move to the field in which you wish to enter or edit text and press ⬦Shift + F2 to open the Zoom window. Type or edit the text and click OK.

HANDS on

Moving Among Records and Editing Data

In this activity, you will navigate the datasheet and edit records.

1. **With the *Greenfield Farm Market-Lesson 1* database in the *Tutorial* folder open, double-click the Customers table. Click the Maximize button ▢.**

Notice the navigation buttons at the bottom of the window, as shown in Figure 1.29. You use these buttons to move from record to record. Note that the Specific Record box reads "1" and the gray area to the right reads "of 36." This tells you that the table has 36 records and the focus is on the first record.

Figure 1.29
Navigation buttons

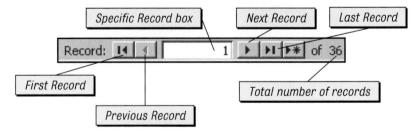

2. **Click the Last Record button ▐▶Ⅰ.**

Access moves the focus to the last record in the table, placing a triangle in the record selector and highlighting the data in the Customer ID field. Record 36 is now displayed in the Specific Record box.

NOTE *When you use any of the navigation buttons, Access moves the focus to a new record but leaves the same field highlighted. For instance, if the Contact First Name field is selected, clicking the Last Record button [▶|] moves the focus to the last record in the table and highlights that record's Contact First Name field.*

3. Click the First Record button [|◀].

Access moves the focus to the first record in the table—the record for Sarah Kellum. Once again, the data in the Customer ID field is selected.

4. Click the Next Record button [▶] two times.

Access moves the focus to the record for Mike Rusconi, the third record.

5. Click the Previous Record button [◀].

The focus moves to the record for Rick Lunken, the second record.

6. Double-click the current record number in the Specific Record box on the navigation buttons bar.

7. Type 25 and press [Enter←].

The focus moves to record 25—that of Deborah Garner.

8. Press [F5], type 5, and press [Enter←] to move to the record for Janice O'Toole.

9. Press [Tab] until you get to the Contact First Name field for Janice O'Toole.

Access selects the first name *Janice.* Note that the entire field is highlighted. **Select** means to choose an item to indicate to Access that you want to operate on that particular item. You now see the field in **reverse video,** with white text against a dark background.

WARNING *If you press [Delete] when any field is selected, you will delete the contents of the field, and anything you type will replace that content.*

10. Click after the *e* in Janice or press [F2].

Notice that the highlighting disappears and is replaced by a blinking insertion point immediately after the *e* in Janice. As you probably know, the insertion point indicates where the text you type will appear, as well as where any deletions will occur.

11. Press [Backspace] three times and type et to change the name to Janet.

12. Press [←].

This action does not move you to the previous field, but instead moves the insertion point one character to the left.

Access **BASICS**

Navigating a Table
To navigate records:

- Use the navigation buttons to move to the first, last, previous, or next record.

- To move to a specific record, type the number of the record to which you want to move in the text box at the bottom of the datasheet, and press [Enter←].

- Press [↓] or [↑] to move to an adjacent record.

To navigate fields:

- Press [Tab] to move one field to the right.

- Press [⇧ Shift] + [Tab] to move one field to the left.

- Press [End] to move to the last field of a record.

- Press [Home] to move to the first field of a record.

- Press [Ctrl] + [Home] to move to the first field of the first record.

- Press [Ctrl] + [End] to move to the last field of the last record.

Access **BASICS**

Editing Data in a Table

1. Move to the record you wish to edit.

2. Press [F2] or click the text you wish to edit.

3. Type to change the text.

ACCESS 2002

13. Press `F2` to select the contents of the Contact First Name field.

14. Press `←` again.

This time, pressing `←` selects the Contact Last Name field for Janet O'Toole's record.

15. Type Harmon.

Access automatically deletes the last name *O'Toole*, replacing it with the name *Harmon*.

HANDS on

Undoing Editing Mistakes and Deleting Records

When you're making changes to a table, you can make changes to the wrong field or the wrong record. Fortunately, you can use the Undo feature to reverse changes. In this activity, you'll use the Undo feature and also delete a record from the Customers table.

1. Navigate to record 28 and select the last name *Sullivan* in the Contact Last Name field.

2. Press `Delete` to delete the name.

3. Click the **Undo button** 🔄.

Access reverses the change, bringing back the name you just deleted.

4. Select the last name *Ingram* in record 8.

5. Type Martinez and press `Tab` to move to the Contact First Name field.

Access replaces the old name with the new one.

6. Type Juanita and press `Tab` two times.

7. Type 427 Kemper Ln. in the Billing Address field, but do not press `Tab` or `Enter←`.

8. Press `Esc` or click the **Undo button** 🔄.

The address changes from *427 Kemper Ln.* back to *1314 23rd Ave.*

9. Press `Esc` again or click the **Undo button** 🔄 two more times, and watch the Contact First Name and Contact Last Name fields.

Access reverses the rest of the changes to the current record all at once, restoring the name *Martha Ingram*.

NOTE *Depending on the last action you performed, the Undo button's name changes. For instance, if you just typed text and want to undo it, the ToolTip for the Undo button reads Undo Typing. If you want to undo a deletion you just made, the name changes to Undo Delete.*

Thus far, you have learned how to undo changes to the current field or undo multiple changes to the current record. When you complete the edits in a record and move to another record, your changes are saved automatically. You might think that the regular Undo keys will not reverse these changes. Fortunately, the Undo option will reverse the changes if you catch them in time.

10. **Move the insertion point to the Notes field for record number 4, Kimberly Zoller.**

11. **Type** Wants to receive a catalog **and press** Tab .

Access automatically saves the changes to Kimberly Zoller's record when you move to the next record.

12. **Click Undo Saved Record on the Edit menu.**

Access reverses the changes to the Zoller record, even though the record has been saved. This Undo command reverses only the most recent action; if you've done anything else since then, you can't undo the changes to a saved record in this way.

13. **Click the record selector for Douglas Ellis's record (record number 11).**

The entire record is selected.

14. **Click the Delete Record button**  **on the Table Datasheet toolbar.**

Access displays the warning box shown in Figure 1.30, warning you that you're about to delete a record and giving you a chance to stop the change. (If you have the Office Assistant displayed, the warning will appear in the Office Assistant balloon.)

WARNING *When you delete one or more records, you cannot undo the operation with the Undo command. Your only way out is to click No to cancel the operation when Access displays the warning box.*

15. **Read the text in the box and click Yes.**

Access deletes the selected record and moves the subsequent records up. Note, however, that the values in the Customer ID field have not changed. As you'd expect, customers retain the same ID numbers even if other customers are removed from the database.

NOTE *You can also delete entire fields in Datasheet view by clicking Delete Column on the Edit menu. However, be extremely sure that you want to delete a field and all of its contents before issuing this command. This action cannot be reversed with the Undo command, so if you change your mind, you must add the field and retype all of the data in it.*

As a new feature in Access 2002, you can now perform multiple undo and redo actions in Design view.

To delete a record, select the record and press Delete .

The F2 function key is a toggle key. Use F2 to switch between Selection mode and Edit mode.

Figure 1.30
Deleting a record

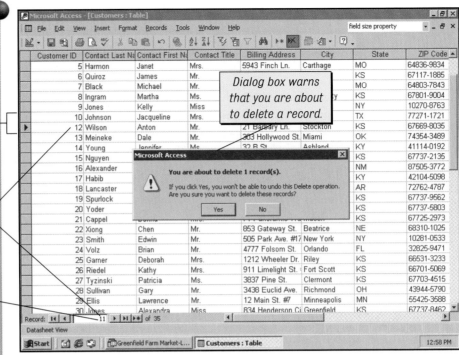

Record 11 has been deleted.

In this instance, record number 11 identifies the record for Customer ID 12.

The record number represents a record's physical location in a table.

16. Click the **Close Window button** ☒ to close the Customers table. If asked if you want to save changes to the design of the table, click **Yes**.

DEFINING RELATIONSHIPS BETWEEN TABLES

Now that you've created some tables in your database, you should establish relationships between them. This way, Access will always be certain which records match up and also will understand precisely the type of relationship the tables have. Defining a relationship allows you to create queries, reports, and other objects that combine data from two or more tables. Defining relationships between tables involves only a few simple steps. After you've established the relationships, you can print this information for your reference.

Understanding Relationship Types and Referential Integrity

Any two tables can have one of three types of relationships: one-to-one, one-to-many, and many-to-many. If two tables have a **one-to-one relationship,** every record in one table can have either no matching records or only a single matching record in the other table. This situation might arise, for example, if you want to keep track of mailing addresses as well as regular addresses. You could include the mailing addresses in a separate table; each person would have at most one mailing address in this table, and many people would have none, because their mailing addresses would be the same as their regular addresses.

When you have a **one-to-many relationship,** one of the tables is called the primary table, while the other is called the related table. The **primary table** holds a primary key that is unique. In your Customers table, the CustomerID field is the primary key. You ensured that the CustomerID field would be unique by defining it as an AutoNumber field. In that way, no two customer records have the same Customer ID.

The second table in a one-to-many relationship is called the **related table.** The related table has a field that links it to the primary table. This field is called the **foreign key.** It need not be unique. In the Orders table, the foreign key is the CustomerID field. This field was not defined as an AutoNumber field, because one customer can place many orders. Two tables have a one-to-many relationship when each record in the primary table can have no records, one record, or many matching records in the other table, but every record in the related table has exactly one associated record in the primary table—no more and no less.

In a **many-to-many relationship,** a record in either table can relate to many records in another table. While you will not create such a relationship in the *Greenfield Farm Market-Lesson 1* database, they are fairly common.

Referential integrity refers to certain rules that Access enforces to safeguard your data, ensuring that you don't accidentally modify or delete data that is related to another table. For instance, suppose you've established a one-to-many relationship between the Customers and Orders tables in the *Greenfield Farm Market-Lesson 1* database. When referential integrity is enforced, Access won't let you delete a record in the primary table (the Customers table) if there are matching records in the related table (the Orders table), because to do so would damage the integrity of the information in the related table.

HANDS on

Creating and Printing Database Relationships

In this activity, you will create a one-to-many relationship between the Customers table (the primary table) and the Orders table (the related table); you will also create a one-to-many relationship between the Employees table (the primary table) and the Orders table (the related table). Then you will print these database relationships.

1. **Make sure there are no open tables in the *Greenfield Farm Market-Lesson 1* database. (You cannot create relationships between open tables.) Then click the Relationships button ⊞ on the Database toolbar.**

The Show Table dialog box appears, which lets you choose the tables you want to relate.

> **NOTE** *If the Show Table dialog box does not automatically appear, click the Show Table button ⊞ on the Relationship toolbar.*

NORTON ONLINE

Visit **www.glencoe.com/norton/online/** for more information on Access 2002.

Working With Relationships

To create a relationship:

1. Click the Relationships button on the Database toolbar.

2. Double-click the tables you wish to work with in the Show Table dialog box and then close the dialog box.

3. Drag a field name from one Field list to the same field name on another Field list.

4. If desired, click the Enforce Referential Integrity option and click the Create button.

5. Close the Relationships window.

To print database relationships:

1. Click Relationships on the Tools menu.

2. Click Print Relationships on the File menu.

3. Click the Print button on the Database toolbar.

---

2. Click **Customers** in the Show Table dialog box, if it is not already selected, and click **Add**.

A Field list appears for the Customers table in the Relationships window. Just as its name implies, the Field list is a list of all the fields in the table.

3. In the Show Table dialog box, double-click **Orders** and then double-click **Employees**, in that order.

4. Click the **Close button** in the Show Table dialog box.

The Customers, Orders, and Employees Field lists are displayed in the Relationships window.

5. Click the **CustomerID field** in the Customers Field list to select it.

6. Drag and drop the CustomerID field from the Customers Field list onto the CustomerID field in the Orders Field list.

The Edit Relationships dialog box appears, as shown in Figure 1.31.

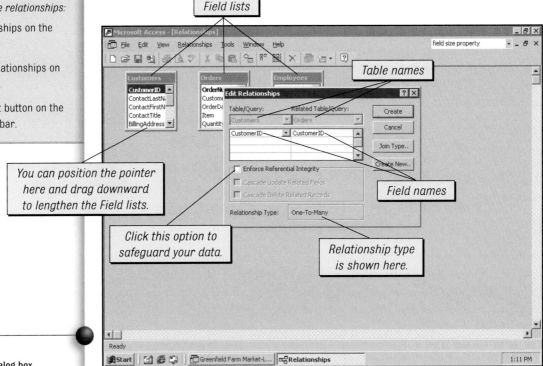

Figure 1.31
Edit Relationships dialog box

7. In the Edit Relationships dialog box, click to select the **Enforce Referential Integrity option**, and then click **Create**.

Access creates the relationship, the dialog box closes, and a relationship line now appears between the CustomerID fields in the two tables.

8. Scroll down the Orders Field list until the EmployeeID field is visible. Then drag and drop the EmployeeID field from the Employees Field list to the EmployeeID field in the Orders Field list.

9. When the Edit Relationships dialog box appears, click to select the **Enforce Referential Integrity option**, and click **Create**.

Relationship lines connect the related fields, as shown in Figure 1.32. (The Field lists in Figure 1.32 have been lengthened to show the relationship lines in their entirety.) The small 1 on a line indicates the "one" side of a relationship, while the ∞ on a line shows the "many" side of a relationship.

ACCESS 2002

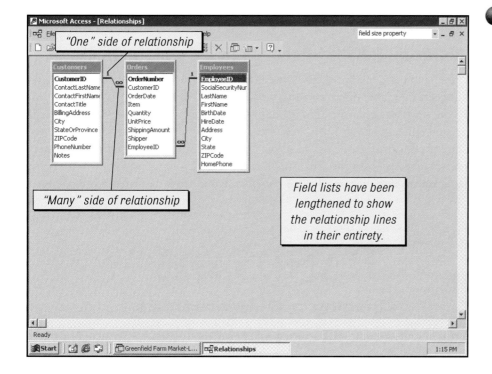

Figure 1.32
Assigning relationships

To lengthen the Field lists, position the pointer on the bottom of the Field list frame and drag downward when the pointer changes to a vertical, double-headed arrow.

10. Click the **Close Window button** ✕ in the Relationships window.

A warning box asks if you want to save changes to the layout of the relationships.

11. Click **Yes**.

The changes are saved and you return to the Database window.

12. Click **Relationships** on the Tools menu.

The Relationships window reappears, displaying the assigned relationships between the tables.

13. Click **Print Relationships** on the File menu.

A database relationships report opens in Print Preview.

14. Click the **Print button**  on the Print Preview toolbar to print the report.

15. Close the Print Preview window.

A warning box appears and asks if you want to save changes to the design of the report.

16. Click **No** and then close the Relationships window.

Access closes the window and returns to the *Greenfield Farm Market-Lesson 1* Database window.

Displaying Related Records in a Subdatasheet

When you create relationships between tables, Access automatically creates sub-datasheets in a table that has either a one-to-one relationship or is the "one" side of a one-to-many relationship. **Subdatasheets** allow you to view and edit data in a related table, query, or form. For instance, since the Customers table has a one-to-many relationship with the Orders table, you can view and edit a customer's order(s) directly from the Customers table using a subdatasheet. You can bring subdatasheets into view by clicking the plus sign in front of any record in a table.

HANDS on

Opening a Subdatasheet

In this activity, you'll open a subdatasheet for the first customer listed in the Customers table.

1. Open the **Customers table** in Datasheet view.

Notice that a plus sign now appears before each record in the Customers table.

2. Click the **plus sign** in front of the record for Sarah Kellum.

A subdatasheet from the Orders table appears, as shown in Figure 1.33, showing all of the orders for Sarah Kellum. If desired, you can enter and edit data directly in the subdatasheet.

3. Click the **minus sign** in front of the record for Sarah Kellum.

Access closes the subdatasheet.

4. Close the Customers table, and close the *Greenfield Farm Market-Lesson 1* database.

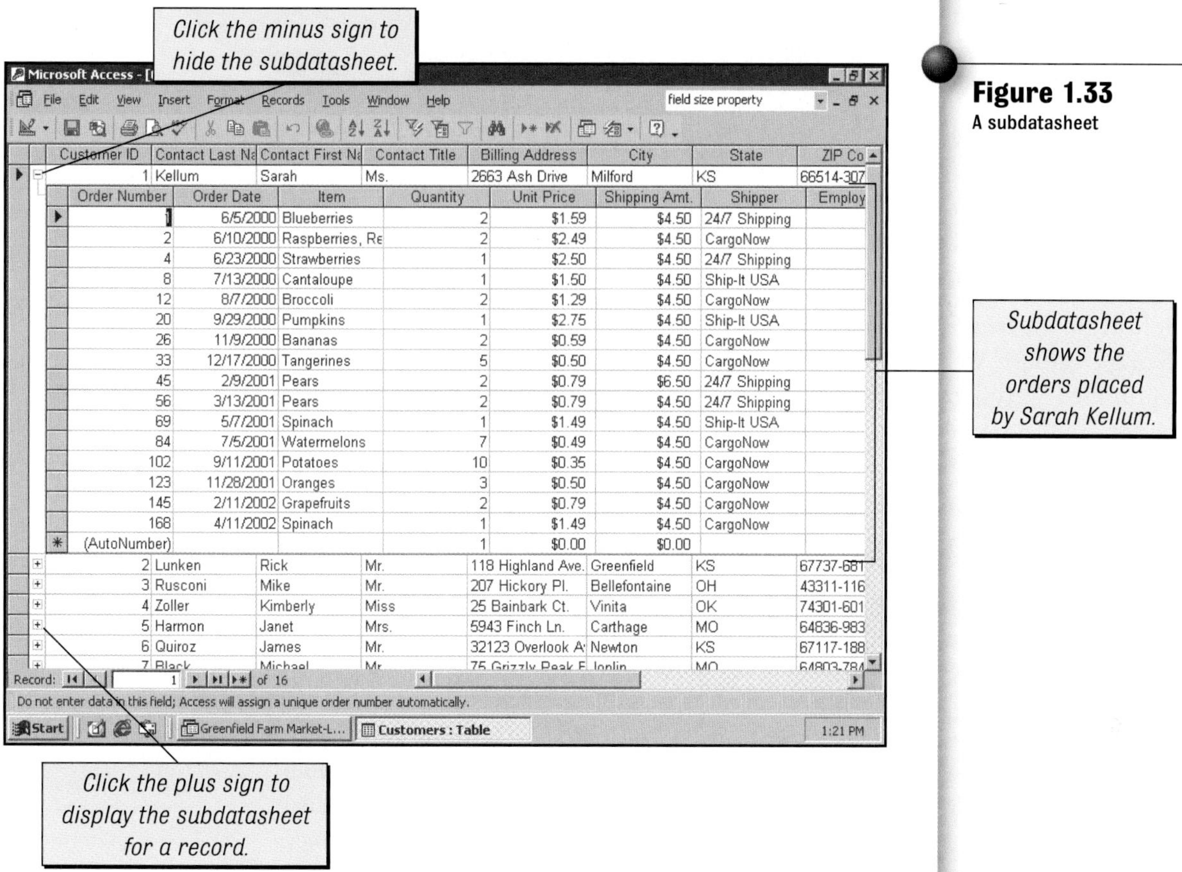

Figure 1.33
A subdatasheet

Click the minus sign to hide the subdatasheet.

Subdatasheet shows the orders placed by Sarah Kellum.

Click the plus sign to display the subdatasheet for a record.

Self Check

Test your knowledge by answering the following questions. See Appendix B to check your answers.

1. In an Access database, information is organized in a series of columns called _____ that contain categories of data and rows called _____ that contain all the categories for one particular entity.

2. _____ are the various components of Access that you use to enter, display, print, and manipulate the information in a database.

3. To create or modify the structure of a table, you must use _____ view.

4. A _____ is a field or set of fields that uniquely identifies each record in a table.

5. To ensure that you don't accidentally modify or delete data that is related to another table, Access enforces _____ to safeguard your data.

SEARCHING THE INTERNET FROM ACCESS

Often you'll want to use the Internet to find information on a specific topic, but you don't know the address of specific sites that have the information. In these cases, you can search the Internet directly from the Access program.

Assume you are the marketing manager for Greenfield Farm Market, and you've been considering creating a Web site for the company in hopes of increasing sales. One link on the proposed Web site would provide customers with general health and nutrition information. In this activity, you will use the Web toolbar in Access to search for Web sites that contain information on health and nutrition. After you locate an appropriate Web site, you will save it so you can return to it easily.

1. **Connect to the Internet and, if necessary, start Access.**

2. **Click the Search the Web button** 🔍 **on the Web toolbar.**

> **NOTE** *To display the Web toolbar, right-click the Database toolbar and click Web on the list that appears.*

Access launches your browser, and the home page of the default search engine of your browser appears. A **search engine** allows you to search for information on a particular topic. Some search engines search every word of every document they find on the Internet; others search only portions of documents they find.

3. **Type nutrition in the Search text box (Figure 1.34), and click the button to process your search request.**

The button that processes your search request is often labeled *Search* or *Find*.

> **NOTE** *The exact names and appearance of the browser buttons used in this activity will vary depending upon the browser you are using.*

4. **When the results of your search appear, scroll down to see the numerous sites to which you can connect.**

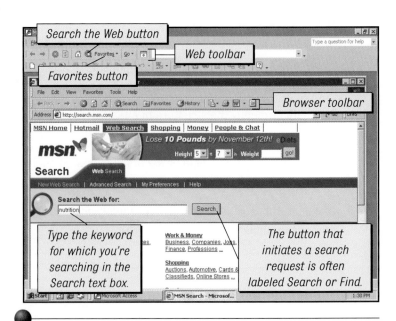

Figure 1.34
A sample search engine

The results of your search appear in the form of links that you can click to navigate to the page described. The results that you get from typing the keyword *nutrition* will vary depending on the search engine you use. The top (or bottom) of the page may tell you how many results were found. For a search as general as this one, you are likely to find thousands of Web sites pertaining to nutrition. Instead of muddling through thousands of results, many of which don't pertain to your situation, you can use more specific keywords to narrow your search.

5. Type the keywords food pyramid in the Search text box, and click the button to process your search request.

When the results appear, scroll down to see them. As you can see, when you use more specific keywords, the resulting sites are more targeted to the information you are seeking.

6. Click one of the links that you think will lead to a Web page that contains information about the food pyramid. Explore the site.

7. Click the Back button ⟸ Back ▾ on your browser toolbar to return to the list of results. If time allows, explore a link to another site.

8. In the list of search results, click the link to a Web site that you think would be appropriate to include on the future Greenfield Farm Market Web site.

9. Click Favorites ⊡ Favorites on the browser toolbar, click the Add button ⊞ Add... to add this Web address to your list of Favorites, and then click OK in the Add Favorite dialog box.

10. Close the browser window.

You return to the Access window. Now let's return to the Web site you just saved in your Favorites list.

11. Click the Favorites button Favorites ▾ on the Web toolbar. Scroll down the list and click the link you added to your Favorites list in step 9.

The Web site reappears.

12. Close your browser and disconnect from the Internet (unless your instructor tells you to remain connected). Hide the Web toolbar and exit Access.

> **WARNING** *You may proceed directly to the exercises for this lesson. If, however, you are finished with your computer session, follow the "shut down" procedures for your lab or school environment.*

SUMMARY AND EXERCISES

SUMMARY

Access is a relational database management system that allows you to organize, maintain, and retrieve information electronically. In Lesson 1, you learned basic database terms, opened an existing database, and used the Database window to access the objects and data in a database. An Access database can contain seven different types of objects, and you worked briefly with four of those objects—a table, a query, a form, and a report. To build an effective database, you must plan ahead to avoid redundancy. In the latter part of Lesson 1, you created a new database, and then you created two tables—one using the Table Wizard and one using Design view. You modified the tables by changing the field properties, including creating input masks. You entered records into a datasheet, appended records to existing tables, and imported data from another Office application. You defined relationships between tables and gained an understanding of referential integrity. Finally, you searched the Internet for information directly from Access.

Now that you have completed this lesson, you should be able to do the following:

■ Describe a relational database management system and explain its use. (page 374)

■ Start Microsoft Access, open a database, and identify the parts of the Database window. (page 375)

■ Explain the purpose of the database objects in Access—tables, queries, forms, reports, pages, macros, and modules. (page 376)

■ Understand the various views and toolbars associated with each database object. (page 377)

■ Describe the difference between a record and a field. (page 378)

■ Navigate a table in Datasheet view; examine table structure in Design view. (page 378)

■ Run a select query and view the design of a query. (page 381)

■ Use forms and reports. (page 383)

■ Explore a data access page in Page view, Design view, and Web Page Preview. (page 387)

■ Plan and create a database. (page 389)

■ Create a table using the Table Wizard and using Design view. (page 393)

■ Understand data types. (page 399)

■ Set and modify field properties. (page 401)

■ Choose a primary key. (page 403)

■ Add captions to fields; insert, delete, and rearrange fields. (page 407)

■ Create an input mask. (page 411)

■ Add data to a table in Datasheet view and append records to a table. (page 414)

■ Import data from another application. (page 418)

■ Navigate a datasheet and edit records. (page 424)

■ Undo editing mistakes and delete records. (page 424)

■ Define relationships between tables; understand referential integrity; open a subdatasheet. (page 428)

■ Search the Internet from Access and add a Web site to the Favorites list. (page 434)

CONCEPTS REVIEW

1 TRUE/FALSE

Circle T if the statement is true or F if the statement is false.

T F **1.** You can modify the structure of an object in Design view.

T F **2.** In an RDMS, you can establish relationships between multiple tables provided the tables have at least two fields in common.

T F **3.** A telephone book is an example of a database.

T F **4.** You can move to the beginning of a table by pressing [⇧ Shift] + [Home].

T F **5.** A field in a database contains the set of data for one entity, such as the name, address, and phone number for one customer.

T F **6.** Creating a table in Design view allows you more flexibility than when you create one with the Table Wizard.

T F **7.** Text, Number, and Currency are examples of data types.

T F **8.** You should always create at least two tables that contain redundant data to help you check for data-entry errors.

T F **9.** In Design view, the row selector is the box to the left of each field.

T F **10.** Access creates captions when you type field names in Design view.

2 MATCHING

Match each of the terms on the left with the definitions on the right.

TERMS

1. query
2. objects
3. record
4. relational database management systems
5. WYSIWYG
6. referential integrity
7. AutoNumber
8. Date/Time
9. Office Clipboard
10. input mask

DEFINITIONS

a. Database programs that allow you to link tables

b. Screen display that reflects how data will appear when it is printed

c. Question requesting database records that meet specific criteria

d. Name for various components of Access

e. Group of fields related to a particular entity

f. A field with this data type can be used as a primary key because Access enters unique values in this field that cannot be edited

g. A pattern that specifies what kind of data to enter and the number of characters allowed in a field

h. Data type that enables you to perform date arithmetic

i. Rules that safeguard your data and ensure that data in a related table is not accidentally modified or deleted

j. Temporary place to store items that you copy from a variety of places

SUMMARY AND EXERCISES

3 COMPLETION

Fill in the missing word or phrase for each of the following statements.

1. You can use a(n) _____ to view and edit records stored in an Access database from a remote location via the Internet or an intranet.

2. When you want presentation-quality hard copy, you should print a(n) _____ .

3. A(n) _____ is a field or set of fields that uniquely identifies each record in a table.

4. If you want to view an object's content, use _____ view; if you want to view an object's structure, use _____ view.

5. When you _____ data into a database, you actually copy the entire object, including both the data and the design of the object.

6. The _____ guides you through each step of creating a table, prompting you for the needed information.

7. To change a field name that appears in a datasheet without actually renaming the field, you would use the _____ field property in Design view.

8. In the top pane of the Design view window, you specify the _____ , _____ , and _____ for each field in a table.

9. You should use a _____ if you want to display a single record at a time for data entry or editing.

10. A plus sign before a record in a datasheet indicates that a _____ exists for that record.

4 SHORT ANSWER

Write a brief answer to each of the following questions.

1. What is a datasheet and how is it related to tables, queries, and forms?

2. What are the seven types of Access objects, and what is the purpose of each?

3. Identify the three types of relationships and explain the differences between them.

4. From within a Database window, how would you open a table to change the layout?

5. What is the difference between a field and a record?

6. Why is it important that each table in a database contains information on only one subject?

7. Identify one advantage and one disadvantage of creating tables using the Table Wizard.

8. Explain why you can't enter duplicate values in primary key fields.

9. Explain the difference between (1) copying data from another source and appending it to a table, and (2) importing data from another source into a database.

10. Describe various ways in which you can control how data is entered into a database and provide examples of each.

5 IDENTIFICATION

Label each of the elements of the Access window in Figure 1.35.

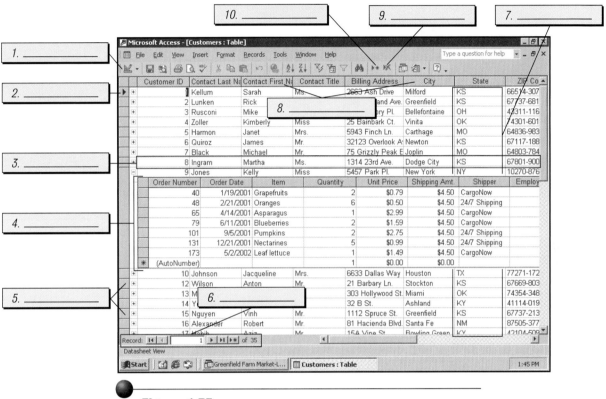

Figure 1.35

SKILLS REVIEW

Complete all of the Skills Review problems in sequential order to review your Access skills to open an existing database; display various views of database objects; create a blank database; create tables using the Table Wizard and Design view; modify field properties; retrieve data from other sources; navigate a datasheet; enter and edit records in a datasheet; and define relationships between tables.

1 Launch Access, Open a Database, and Open a Table

1. Click the **Start button** ![Start] on the Windows taskbar, point to **Programs**, and click **Microsoft Access**.

2. Click **More files** in the New File task pane.

3. In the Open dialog box, navigate to your *Access Data* folder and double-click *Coburne College Sample*. Click **Tables** in the Object bar, if necessary (see Figure 1.36 on the following page).

4. Click the **Student Information table** if it is not already selected, and then click the **Open button** 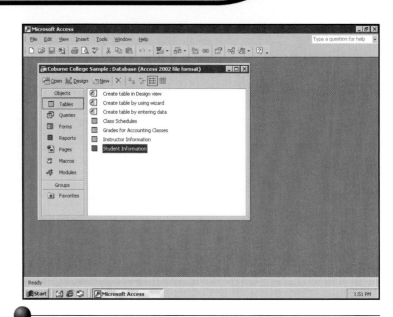 on the Database window toolbar.

5. Click **Maximize** ▢ in the table window.

2 Edit a Record and View Table Design

1. Press [Tab] three times to move to the Address field for George Robinson.

2. Type **1765 Lyle Ave.** and press [Tab].

3. In the City field, type **Atlanta** and press [Tab] twice.

4. In the ZIP Code field, type **303371202** and press [Tab].

Figure 1.36

5. In the Phone Number field, type **4045552969** and press [Enter←].

6. Click the **View button** on the Table Datasheet toolbar.

7. Press [F6] to jump to the Field Properties pane.

8. Click the **View button** on the Table Design toolbar to display the table in Datasheet view.

9. Click the **Close Window button** ✕ on the menu bar to close the table.

3 Work with More Objects and Views

1. Click **Queries** in the Object bar in the Database window and double-click the **Student Grades for Basic Accounting Classes query.**

2. Click the **View button** on the Query Datasheet toolbar to view the query in Design view.

3. Click the **Close Window button** ✕ on the menu bar to close the query.

4. Click **Forms** in the Object bar in the Database window and double-click the **Student Information form.**

5. Click the **New Record button** on the Form View toolbar (or on the navigation toolbar) and press [Tab].

6. Type each of the following entries into the form, pressing [Tab] after each item:

Last Name:	Pittinger
First Name:	Rose
Address:	2575 Delk Rd.
City:	Marietta
State:	GA
ZIP Code:	300676584
Phone Number:	7705550737
GPA:	3.4
Major:	Management
Full Time:	(press [Spacebar] to insert a check mark)
Expected Graduation:	5/15/2004

7. Click the **Close Window button** ☒ on the menu bar to close the form.

8. Click **Reports** in the Objects bar in the Database window, and select the **Students Listed by Major report**, if it is not already selected.

9. Click the **Preview button** 🔍Preview on the Database window toolbar.

10. Click the **Next Page button** ▶ on the navigation toolbar.

11. Click the **Print button** 🖨 on the Print Preview toolbar.

12. Click **Close** on the File menu.

13. Click **Pages** in the Object bar in the Database window, and double-click the **Coburne College Class Schedules data access page**.

14. Continuously click the **Next button** ▶ on the record navigation toolbar to scroll through the records.

15. Click the **View button** 📝▾ on the Page View toolbar to view the page in Design view.

16. Click the **View triangle button** 📄▾ and click **Web Page Preview** from the drop-down list to view the page through your Web browser window.

17. Click the **Close button** ☒ on the browser title bar.

18. Click the **Close Window button** ☒ on the menu bar to close the data access page.

4 Create a Blank Database and Use the Table Wizard

1. Click the **New button** ☐ on the Database toolbar. In the New File task pane, click **Blank Database**.

2. In the File New Database dialog box, navigate to the *Skills Review* folder in the *Access Data* folder.

3. Type Coburne College-Lesson 1 in the File name box. Click the **Create button**.

4. In the Database window, double-click the **Create table by using wizard option**.

5. Verify that the **Business option** is selected, and then click **Students** in the *Sample Tables* box.

6. Click the **StudentID field name** and click the **Add Field button** [>].

7. Double-click the **FirstName field** to add it to the *Fields in my new table* box.

8. Add the following fields to the *Fields in my new table* box: **MiddleName, LastName, ParentsNames, Address, City, StateOrProvince, PostalCode, PhoneNumber**, and **Major**.

9. Click the **ParentsNames field** in the *Fields in my new table* box and click the **Remove Field button** [<].

10. Click the **StateOrProvince field** in the *Fields in my new table* box. Click the **Rename Field button** and type **State** in the Rename field dialog box. Then click **OK**.

11. Click **Next** in the Table Wizard dialog box.

12. Edit the suggested name *Students* to **Student Information**.

13. Click the **No, I'll set the primary key. option** and click **Next**.

14. Select the **StudentID field** from the drop-down list, if it is not already selected.

15. Click the **Consecutive numbers Microsoft Access assigns automatically to new records. option**, if it is not already selected. Then, click **Next**.

16. Click **Modify the table design. option** and click **Finish**.

17. Review the field names, data types, and field properties in Design view. Then click the Close button [X] to close the table.

5 Create a Table in Design View, Change Field Properties, and Save a Table

1. In the *Coburne College-Lesson 1* Database window, double-click the **Create table in Design view option**. Type StudentID in the first row of the Field Name column; then press [Tab].

2. Click the **Data type triangle button**, click **Number**, and press [Tab].

3. Type Enter same Student ID used in the Student Information table in the Description column. Then press [F6] to jump to the Field Properties pane.

4. Navigate to the Caption property box and type Student ID.

5. Press [F6] to return to the upper pane and type ClassCode as the second field name. Press [Tab] twice to accept Text as the data type and to move to the Description column.

6. Type Enter Class Code used in the Class Information table in the Description column and press [F6].

7. Type 7 in the Field Size property box. Then navigate to the Caption property box and type Class Code.

8. Press F6 to return to the upper pane, type **Grade** as the third field name, and press Tab.

9. Click the **Data type triangle button** and click **Number**. Then press F6 to jump to the Field Properties pane.

10. In the Field Size box, click the **triangle button** and click **Byte**.

11. Press F6 to return to the upper pane. Then click and hold the mouse button on the row selector to the left of the StudentID field to select the entire field and drag to include the ClassCode field. Both rows will be highlighted.

12. Click the **Primary Key button** (Figure 1.37).

13. Click the **Save** button on the Table Design toolbar, type **Grades for Accounting Classes** in the Table Name text box, and click **OK**.

14. Click the **Close button** in the Design window.

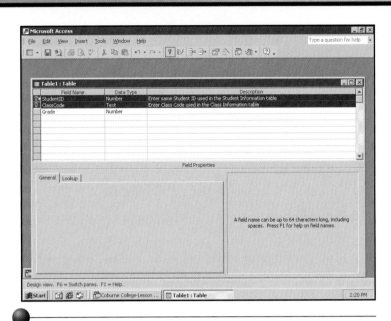

Figure 1.37

6 Modify Tables and Use the Input Mask Wizard

1. In the *Coburne College-Lesson 1* Database window, click the **Student Information table** and click the **Design button** on the Database window toolbar.

2. Click the **PostalCode field**, press F6, click the **Caption property box**, double-click the word *Postal*, and type ZIP.

3. Press F6 and click in the blank row below the Major field. (Scroll down if necessary.) Type **FullTime** in the Field Name column and press Tab.

4. Type **y** in the Data Type column to assign the Yes/No data type.

5. Press F6, navigate to the Caption property box, and type **Full Time** in the Caption text box.

6. Add the following field below the FullTime field: Field Name: EstimatedGraduationDate; Data Type: Date/Time; Caption: Expected Graduation. (If necessary, refer to the steps you followed to add the FullTime field.)

7. Click anywhere within the Major field in the top pane of the Design window.

8. Click the **Insert Rows button** on the Table Design toolbar.

9. Type **GradePointAverage** in the Field Name column, press Tab, and type **n** to select the Number data type.

10. Press F6, and make the following modifications to the field properties: select **Single** in the Field Size property box, select **Fixed** in the Format property box,

select **1** in the Decimal Places property box, and type **GPA** in the Caption property box.

11. Click anywhere in the FirstName field.

12. Click the **Delete Rows button** 📑 on the Table Design toolbar.

13. Since you realize you meant to delete the MiddleName field instead, click the **Undo button** 🔄.

14. Click the **MiddleName field** and click the **Delete Rows button** 📑.

15. Click the row selector in front of the FirstName field.

16. Drag downward until the dark horizontal line appears directly below the LastName field and release.

17. Make the following modifications to the Field Size property: change the field size of the LastName field to **30**, the FirstName field to **30**, the Address field to **50**, the City field to **30**, the State field to **2**, and the Major field to **20**.

18. Navigate to the Input Mask property box for the PostalCode field and click the **Build button** ⏹. When asked if you want to save the table, click **Yes**.

19. In the Input Mask Wizard dialog box, click **Zip Code** and click **Next**.

20. Click **Next** to accept the default input mask (00000-9999) and the default place-holder character (_).

21. Choose the **With the symbols in the mask option**, click **Next**, and then click **Finish**.

22. Use the Input Mask Wizard to create an input mask for the PhoneNumber field. (If necessary, refer to the steps you followed to create an input mask for the PostalCode field.)

23. Click the **Save button** 💾 on the Table Design toolbar, and then close the Student Information table.

24. Close the *Coburne College-Lesson 1* database.

7 Append Records to a Table

1. Click **Office Clipboard** on the Edit menu.

2. Open the *Coburne College Sample* database, and open the **Student Information table** in Datasheet view.

3. Press ⌃Ctrl + ⒶA to select all records.

4. Click the **Copy button** 📋 on the Table Datasheet toolbar.

5. Close the table and click **Yes** when the warning box asks you if you want to save the data to the Clipboard.

6. Reopen the *Coburne College-Lesson 1* database in the *Skills Review* folder and open the **Student Information table** in Datasheet view.

7. Click **Paste Append** on the Edit menu.

8. When the message appears asking if you want to paste the records, click **Yes**.

9. Click the **Close button** ☒ in the Clipboard task pane to close the Office Clipboard.

10. Click anywhere in the table to remove the highlighting and click the **Maximize button** ▢.

8 Add a New Record to a Table

1. If necessary, open the **Student Information table** in the *Coburne College-Lesson 1* database in Datasheet view.

2. Click the **New Record button** ▸* on the Table Datasheet toolbar.

3. Press `Tab` to jump to the Last Name field, type **Chaney**, and press `Tab`.

4. Type **Roger** in the First Name field and press `Tab`.

5. Type **5975 Enterprise Dr.** in the Address field and press `Tab`.

6. Type **Canton** in the City field and press `Tab`.

7. Type **GA** in the State field and press `Tab`.

8. Type **301148969** in the ZIP Code field and press `Tab`.

9. Type **7705554729** in the Phone Number field and press `Tab`.

10. Type **3.2** in the GPA field and press `Tab`.

11. Type **Accounting** in the Major field and press `Tab`.

12. Press `Spacebar` to insert a check mark in the Full Time field and press `Tab`.

13. Type **5/15/2005** in the Expected Graduation field and press `Tab`.

14. Close the Student Information table.

9 Import Data

1. With the *Coburne College-Lesson 1* Database window open, click **File** on the menu bar, point to **Get External Data**, and click **Import** on the submenu.

2. Click **Microsoft Excel** as the Files of type.

3. Navigate to the *Accounting Grades* file in your *Access Data* folder, and double-click the file name.

4. In the Import Spreadsheet Wizard dialog box, click **Show Worksheets** and **Sheet 1**, if they are not already selected. Then click **Next**.

5. Verify that a check mark appears before **First Row Contains Column Headings** and click **Next**.

6. Click to select the **In an Existing Table** option; then click the **triangle button** at the right end of the text box and select **Grades for Accounting Classes** from the drop-down list. Click **Next**.

7. Click **Finish**, and click **OK**.

8. Open the **Grades for Accounting Classes table** in Datasheet view and review the data you just imported.

9. Close the table.

10. Click **File** on the menu bar, point to **Get External Data**, and click **Import** on the submenu.

11. Click **Microsoft Access** as the Files of type.

12. Navigate to the *Coburne College Sample* database in your *Access Data* folder, and double-click the file name.

13. In the Import Objects dialog box, click the **Tables tab** if it is not already selected, click **Class Schedules** in the list of tables, and click **OK**.

14. Double-click the **Class Schedules table** in the Database window and review the table you just imported.

15. Close the table.

10 Navigate a Datasheet

1. Open the **Student Information table** in the *Coburne College-Lesson 1* database and maximize your view, if necessary.

2. Click the **Next Record navigation button** ▶ five times. Note which record is current.

3. Click the **Last Record button** ▶❙.

4. Click the **Previous Record button** two times ◀.

5. Click the **First Record button** ❙◀.

6. Double-click the current record number in the Specific Record box on the navigation buttons bar.

7. Type 40 and press Enter↵. The focus moves to the record for Rebecca Flemming.

8. Press ↑ four times. The focus moves to the record for Francis Ruff.

9. Press ↓ twice. The focus moves to the record for Carla Carson.

10. Press Tab four times.

11. Press ⇧Shift + Tab to move back one column.

12. Press Ctrl + End to move to the last field of the last record.

13. Press Ctrl + Home to move to the first field of the first record.

11 Edit and Delete Records and Undo Changes

1. Press F5, type 19, and press Enter↵ to move to the record for Karen Hale.

2. Press Tab nine times to move to the Major field. Type **Economics** and press Tab.

3. Navigate to the Address field for record number 15 (Victoria Ramos). Double-click the abbreviation *Pky* and type **Ridge Rd** so that the address reads *5716 Treecrest Ridge Rd.* (*Hint:* If you wish, you can press ⇧Shift + F2 to use the Zoom window to edit the address.)

4. Navigate to the City field for Manuel Figueroa (record 45), press $\boxed{\text{Delete}}$, and press $\boxed{\text{Enter} \leftarrow}$.

5. Click the **Undo button** 🔄 to reverse the change.

6. Move to the first record (for George Robinson) and change the Phone Number field to (770) 555-1508, and change the major to **Accounting**. Click the **Undo button** 🔄 to change the major back to Finance.

7. Click the **Undo button** 🔄 two more times to change the phone number back to (404) 555-2969.

8. Click the record selector for James Wilson (record 51). Click the **Delete Record button** ❌. When the warning box appears asking if you want to delete the record, click **Yes**.

9. Move to the Address field for Marietta Jolly (record 2).

10. Change the apartment number to #310. (*Hint:* If you wish, you can press $\boxed{\text{Shift}}$ + $\boxed{\text{F2}}$ to use the Zoom window to edit the address.)

11. Close the Student Information table. When asked if you want to save changes to the design of the table, click **Yes**.

12 Create and Print Relationships

1. Make sure there are no open tables in the *Coburne College-Lesson 1* database. Then click the **Relationships button** 🔲 on the Database toolbar.

2. In the Show Table dialog box, double-click the **Student Information table**, the **Class Schedules table**, and the **Grades for Accounting Classes table**. Close the Show Table dialog box.

3. Click the **StudentID field** in the Student Information Field list and drag it to the StudentID field in the Grades for Accounting Classes Field list.

4. When the Edit Relationships dialog box appears, click the **Create button**.

5. Click the **ClassCode field** in the Class Schedules Field list and drag it to the ClassCode field in the Grades for Accounting Classes Field list.

6. When the Edit Relationships dialog box appears, click the **Enforce Referential Integrity option** and click the **Create button**.

7. Close the **Relationships window**.

8. When the warning box asks if you want to save changes to the layout of the relationships, click **Yes**.

9. Click **Relationships** on the Tools menu.

10. Click **Print Relationships** on the File menu. Then, click the **Print button** 🖨 on the Print Preview toolbar.

11. Close the Print Preview window. When asked if you want to save changes to the design of the report, click **No**.

12. Close the Relationships window.

13 Open a Subdatasheet

1. Open the **Class Schedules table** in Datasheet view.

2. Click the **plus sign** in front of the record for AC203.

3. Look at the subdatasheet that appears, listing the grades earned by students enrolled in this class.

4. Close the subdatasheet by clicking the minus sign in front of the record for AC203.

5. Close the Class Schedules table.

6. Close the *Coburne College-Lesson 1* database and exit Access.

LESSON APPLICATIONS

1 View and Edit Tables

As a new employee of Star Realty, Inc., you need to familiarize yourself with the database that the agency uses to track employee information and data on homes available for sale. Start by opening and editing some tables.

1. Start Access and open the *Star Realty Sample* database in your *Access Data* folder. Maximize the window.

2. Open the Employees table in Design view. Review the table design.

3. Switch to Datasheet view and review the data. Change Julia Whitaker's phone number to (541) 555-2706, and then close the Employees table.

4. Open the New Listings table in Design view and review the table design. Change the caption for the EmployeeID field to Agent ID (Figure 1.38).

5. Save the table design, and then switch to Datasheet view and review the change.

6. Close the New Listings table.

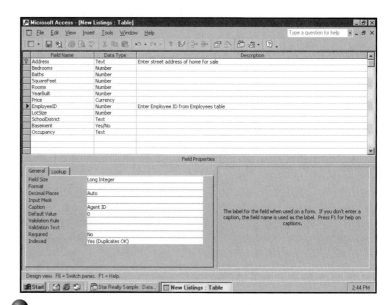

Figure 1.38

2 Work With a Query

One of Star Realty's clients is looking for a home in the Landale school district. Display the results of a query that meets the criteria. Then view the design of the query.

1. Open (run) the Homes in Landale School District query in the *Star Realty Sample* database.

2. Review the data in all of the fields of the query.

3. Switch to Design view to examine the design of the Homes in Landale School District query. Note especially the criteria listed in the SchoolDistrict field and the table used in the LastName field.

4. Close the query.

3 Add a Record Using a Form

As an employee of Star Realty, you also need to know how to add records to their database. First, add a new listing using a form. Then, examine the design of the form.

1. Open the New Listings form in the *Star Realty Sample* database.

2. Add the following new record:

Address:	8450 Hopewell Rd.
Bedrooms:	5
Baths:	3.5
Square Feet:	3690
Rooms:	12
Year Built:	2001
Price:	245000
Agent ID:	3
Lot Size (Acres):	2.0
School District:	Taft Local
Basement:	Yes
Occupancy:	Immediate

3. Switch to Design view and examine the design of the form.

4. Close the New Listings form.

4 Preview and Print a Report and Close a Database

Your manager has asked you to print a report that shows the basic facts of newly listed homes. Preview a report that provides this information, and then print a copy for your manager.

1. Open the New Listings by Agent report in the *Star Realty Sample* database in Print Preview.

2. Use the navigation buttons to review the report.

3. Print the report and then close it.

4. Close the *Star Realty Sample* database.

5 Create a Database and Use the Table Wizard

Create a blank database and use the Table Wizard to create a table, add fields, remove and rename fields, name the table, and assign a primary key.

1. Create a new, blank database named **Star Realty-Lesson 1** and save it in the *Lesson Applications* folder.

2. Create a table using the Table Wizard. Use the Employees sample table and add the following fields: DepartmentName, EmployeeID, FirstName, LastName, Address, City, StateOrProvince, PostalCode, HomePhone, Birthdate, and DateHired.

3. While using the Wizard, remove the Birthdate field from the *Fields in my new table* box.

4. Rename the EmployeeID field to AgentID.

5. Name the table **Agents** and select the AgentID field as the primary key. Indicate that you want the primary key field to contain numbers that you enter when you add new records. Also indicate that you want to modify the table design after the wizard creates the table.

6. Review the table design and then close the table.

6 Create a Table in Design View

Create a table in Design view and add field names, data types, and descriptions.

1. Open the *Star Realty-Lesson 1* database in the *Lesson Applications* folder, if it is not already open. In the Database window, select the option to create a table in Design view.

2. Enter the field names, data types, and descriptions found in Table 1.6.

Table 1.6	Information to Add	
Field Name	**Data Type**	**Description**
Address	Text	Enter street address of home for sale.
Bedrooms	Number	
Baths	Number	
Rooms	Number	
YearBuilt	Number	
Price	Currency	
SellingPrice	Currency	
AgentID	Number	Enter Agent ID from Agents table.
LotSize	Number	
SchoolDistrict	Text	
Basement	Yes/No	
Occupancy	Text	

3. Assign the Address field as the primary key.

4. Save the table as New Listings.

7 Change Field Properties, Add Captions, and Insert and Remove Fields

Change field sizes and other properties in the New Listings table and add captions to a few of the fields. Then add and delete fields and undo a change.

1. In the *Star Realty-Lesson 1* database in the *Lesson Applications* folder, open the New Listings table in Design view, if necessary.

2. Change the field size of the Address field to 40.

3. In the Field Properties pane for the Price field, change the Decimal Places property to **0** (zero).

4. In the Field Properties pane for the SellingPrice field, change the Decimal Places property to **0** (zero).

5. Make the following changes to the Baths field properties: change the Field Size to **Decimal**, change the Format to **General Number**, change the Precision to 4, and change the Scale to 1.

6. Add appropriate captions to the YearBuilt, SellingPrice, AgentID, and SchoolDistrict fields.

7. Use the Insert Rows button to add a field between the Baths and Rooms fields. In the new field, type **SquareFeet** as the field name and assign **Number** as the data type.

8. In the Field Properties pane for the SquareFeet field, type **Sq. Feet** as the caption, assign a format of **Standard**, and enter **0** (zero) as the Decimal Places property.

9. Insert another field between the Rooms and YearBuilt fields.

10. Since you decide that you don't want to add another field, use the Undo command to reverse the change.

11. Make the following changes to the LotSize field properties: change the Field Size to **Decimal**, assign **Standard** as the Format, 4 as the Precision, 2 as the Scale, and 2 as the Decimal Places. Type **Lot Size (Acres)** as the caption.

12. Delete the SellingPrice field, since this table will only list homes currently for sale.

13. Save and close the table.

8 Move Fields and Change Field Properties

Modify the field properties of the Agents table and rearrange the order of some of the fields.

1. In the *Star Realty-Lesson 1* database in the *Lesson Applications* folder, open the Agents table in Design view.

2. Create a caption for the AgentID field.

3. Change the field size of the DepartmentName field to **20** and type **Sales** in the Default Value property box.

4. Change the field size of the FirstName field to **20**, the LastName field to **30**, the Address field to **50**, the City field to **30**, and the StateOrProvince field to **2**.

5. Change the caption of the State/Province field to **State**, and change the caption of the PostalCode field to **ZIP Code**.

6. Use the Input Mask Wizard to create an input mask for the PostalCode field and the HomePhone field. Use the Input Mask Wizard to change the input mask for the DateHired field (use the Short Date input mask).

7. Reverse the order of the FirstName and LastName fields.

8. Move the DepartmentName field to appear as the last field (Figure 1.39).

9. Save and close the table.

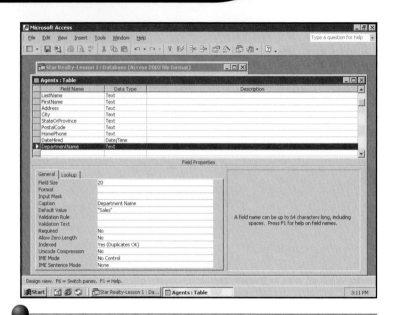

Figure 1.39

9 Enter and Edit Records

As an employee of Star Realty, Inc., you need to add records to the tables in the *Star Realty-Lesson 1* database by keying the data and by copying and pasting records from another table.

1. Open the New Listings table in the *Star Realty-Lesson 1* database in the *Lesson Applications* folder.

2. Type the data in Table 1.7 into records 1 through 4.

Table 1.7	Data For the New Listings Table			
Field	**Record 1**	**Record 2**	**Record 3**	**Record 4**
Address	129 Kenton Ave.	5328 Fox Run Rd.	826 Oak Ridge Ct.	79 Roselawn Ave.
Bedrooms	4	2	4	3
Baths	2.5	1	3	1.5
Sq. Feet	2400	1560	2600	2000
Rooms	8	6	9	7
Year Built	2000	1964	2002	1988
Price	$192900	$84900	$225000	$115000
Agent ID	2	3	4	1
Lot Size	.75	.25	1.5	.50
School District	Jackson	East Princeton	Landale	East Princeton
Basement	No	Yes	Yes	No
Occupancy	Immediate	30 days	Immediate	60 days

3. Open the *Star Realty Sample* database in the *Access Data* folder.

4. Open the New Listings table, and then open the Office Clipboard.

5. Copy all the records to the Clipboard and close the table.

6. Reopen the New Listings table in the *Star Realty-Lesson 1* database in the *Lesson Applications* folder. Append the records to the table, and then close the Clipboard.

7. Maximize the table window, and adjust the width of each column in the table to better fit the data contained in it.

8. Change the price of the house at 121 Pleasant Ridge Ave. (record 7) to $127,900.

9. You realize that you changed the price of the wrong home; reverse the change and then change the price of the house at 117 Pinehurst Dr. (record 6) to $127,900.

10. The house at 47 Lakeview Dr. (record 16) has just sold. Delete the record for this house.

11. Close the table. When prompted to save changes to the table layout, click Yes.

12. Reopen the *Star Realty Sample* database in the *Access Data* folder, and open the Employees table.

13. Copy all the records and append them to the Agents table in the *Star Realty-Lesson 1* database in the *Lesson Applications* folder.

14. Review the records and close the Agents table.

10 Import Data From Another Application and Modify the Table Design

Use the Import command to create a new table in the *Star Realty-Lesson 1* database.

1. In the *Star Realty-Lesson 1* database in the *Lesson Applications* folder, click File on the menu bar, point to Get External Data, and click Import.

2. Navigate to the *Access Data* folder in the Import dialog box, and import the Excel worksheet named *Agent Statistics* into the *Star Realty-Lesson 1* database. Set the Indexed option to Yes (No Duplicates), and set the AgentID field as the primary key. Name the table **Agent Statistics**.

3. Open the Agent Statistics table in Design view and review the table layout. Add appropriate captions for each of the fields, change the Field Size property for the AgentID field to Long Integer, and change the Data Type for the YTDCommissions field to Currency.

4. Save the table. Click **Yes** in response to the dialog box that appears, warning about changing the Field Size property to a shorter size.

5. Switch to Datasheet view and review the data. Adjust the width of each column in the table to better fit the data.

6. Save and close the table.

SUMMARY AND EXERCISES

11 Create a New Record and Undo Changes to a Saved Record

Enter data for a new record. Then when you discover the sellers have changed their minds, undo the changes to the saved record.

1. Open the New Listings table in the *Star Realty-Lesson 1* database in the *Lesson Applications* folder, and click the New Record button.

2. Enter the following data, pressing [Tab] to move from field to field: Address, 1206 Parkway Ave.; Bedrooms, 4; Baths, 2.5; Sq. Feet, 1950; Rooms, 8; Year Built, 1967; Price, 166,900; Agent ID, 1; Lot Size, 1; School District, **Jackson;** Basement, Yes; Occupancy, **60 days.**

3. Press [Tab] to save the record.

4. You just found out that the sellers have decided to wait to sell their home. Use the Undo Saved Record command to remove the entire record you just created.

5. Close the table.

12 Define Relationships and View Subdatasheets

Create relationships between the tables in the *Star Realty-Lesson 1* database. Then view two subdatasheets in two of the tables.

1. In the *Star Realty-Lesson 1* database in the *Lesson Applications* folder, click the Relationships button on the Database toolbar to display the Relationships window.

2. In the Show Tables dialog box, double-click each table to display it and then close the dialog box.

3. Create a relationship between the AgentID fields in the Agent Statistics and Agents tables. Do not choose the option to enforce referential integrity.

4. Create a relationship between the AgentID fields in the Agents and New Listings tables. Choose the option to enforce referential integrity.

5. Close the Relationships window, saving the changes to the layout.

6. Open the Agent Statistics table and view the subdatasheet for the first record. Close the subdatasheet, and then close the table.

7. Open the Agents table and click the plus sign in front of the record for Frank Rebelo (record 3).

8. Click the **minus sign** in front of Frank Rebelo's record to collapse the subdatasheet, and then close the table.

9. Close the *Star Realty-Lesson 1* database.

PROJECTS

1 Making Sense of a Lot of Data

You have recently been hired as the store manager for Everything Electronic, a retail store that sells computers, televisions, stereos, and other electronics. One of your first tasks is to design a database to organize, track, and retrieve store data. After interviewing several sales associates and office employees, you determine that the database should include information in three general categories—products, sales, and employees.

Create and name a blank database *Everything Electronic-Lesson 1* in the *Projects* folder in the *Access Data* folder. Use the information provided in Table 1.8 to design the tables. Assign appropriate captions, input masks, and other field properties to the fields. Set a primary key for each table. After saving and closing each table, close the *Everything Electronic-Lesson 1* database.

WARNING *It is important to use the exact field names, data types, and field sizes provided in Table 1.8 in order to successfully import data later in Projects 2 and 3.*

Table 1.8	Everything Electronic Table Designs	

Products Table

Field Name	Data Type	Field Size
ProductID	AutoNumber	Long Integer
ProductCategory	Text	50
Brand	Text	50
Model	Text	50
Price	Currency	not applicable
Notes	Text	255

Sales Table

Field Name	Data Type	Field Size
SalesID	AutoNumber	Long Integer
ProductID	Number	Long Integer
QuantitySold	Number	Long Integer
SalesDate	Date/Time	not applicable
EmployeeID	Number	Long Integer

Employees Table

Field Name	Data Type	Field Size
EmployeeID	AutoNumber	Long Integer
LastName	Text	30
FirstName	Text	20
SocialSecurityNumber	Text	30
HourlyRate	Currency	not applicable
Status	Text	10
Position	Text	30
DateHired	Date/Time	not applicable

2 In With the New . . . and In With the Old

Now that you've created the tables for Everything Electronic, you're ready to enter data into them. You decide to enter the data for the Products table first. The store has just received a shipment of new DVD players, so you'll start by typing the data for these new items. Open the *Everything Electronic-Lesson 1* database in the *Projects* folder and type the information in Table 1.9 as the first five records of the Products table. (If you wish, you can press ⇧Shift + F2 to use the Zoom window to enter the information in the Notes field.) Then close the table.

Table 1.9	Data For Products Table				
Product ID*	**Product Category**	**Brand**	**Model**	**Price**	**Notes**
1	DVD Player	Gemini	GE220	$199.99	Includes a multi-brand remote.
2	DVD Player	Gemini	GE440	$249.99	Includes optical/coaxial digital audio outputs for enhanced sound.
3	DVD Player	Technica	TE3000	$179.99	Features MP3 decoder for playing up to 10 hours of recorded music.
4	DVD Player	Technica	TE6000	$469.99	Portable DVD player weighs only 2 lbs. and features a 5" LCD monitor.
5	DVD Player	Yamachi	YA300	$279.99	Features a multidisc changer.

* Since the data type for the ProductID field is AutoNumber, Access will automatically enter the Product ID number.

Now you need to add the records for the products that are currently in inventory. The previous store manager had created an Excel worksheet to store product information. You decide to import that worksheet into your database. Import the Excel worksheet named *Everything Electronic Products* located in the *Access Data* folder and append it to the Products table. Review the datasheet and adjust column widths as necessary. Save and close the table.

3 Our Employees Are the Best!

At your request, PayRite, the payroll service that handles the payroll for Everything Electronic, has provided an Excel worksheet that contains the pertinent employee infor-mation that you need to populate the Employees table. Import the *Everything Electronic Employees* worksheet located in the *Access Data* folder to the Employees table. Review the datasheet and adjust column widths as necessary. Save and close the table.

4 'Tis the Shopping Season

The previous store manager had tracked sales for November and the first week of December on an Excel worksheet named *Everything Electronic Sales* in the *Access Data* folder. Import that sales data into your Sales table. Then enter the sales data shown in Table 1.10 for the second week of December. After you've entered all the data, review the datasheet and adjust the column widths as necessary. Save and close the table.

Table 1.10	Sales Data For Second Week of December			
Sales ID*	**Product ID**	**Quantity Sold**	**Sales Date**	**Employee ID**
81	10	1	12/7/2001	5
82	7	1	12/7/2001	4
83	17	2	12/7/2001	8
84	18	1	12/8/2001	4
85	11	1	12/8/2001	8
86	4	1	12/8/2001	7
87	17	1	12/8/2001	7
88	10	1	12/9/2001	5
89	15	1	12/9/2001	4
90	12	2	12/9/2001	8
91	4	1	12/9/2001	3
92	17	1	12/9/2001	9
93	30	1	12/10/2001	25
94	14	1	12/10/2001	10
95	20	1	12/10/2001	16
96	26	1	12/11/2001	20
97	10	2	12/11/2001	22
98	9	2	12/11/2001	24
99	6	2	12/11/2001	11
100	15	1	12/12/2001	14
101	27	1	12/12/2001	16
102	16	1	12/12/2001	19
103	7	2	12/13/2001	21
104	1	2	12/13/2001	25
105	5	1	12/13/2001	24

* Since the data type for the SalesID field is AutoNumber, Access will automatically enter the Sales ID number.

5 More Product Changes

A few prices and features of some of your products have changed, so you need to edit the table that contains them. Open the Products table in the *Everything Electronic-Lesson 1* database in the *Projects* folder. Change the price of the Keiko KE650 television (record 15) to $1,199.95 and change the price of the UltraAudio UA2500 stereo (record 18) to $269.95. Reverse the last change (the price change to record 18) and change the price of the JLG JL700 stereo (record 19) to $269.95 instead. Type **Manufacturer is offering a**

$100 rebate on video cameras sold between 12/15/2001 and 12/24/2001 in the Notes field of the Wilkenson WI233 video camera (record 30). (If you wish, you can press ⇧Shift + F2 to use the Zoom window.) Close the table.

6 Everything's Related

Since you'd like to view subdatasheets, you decide to assign relationships between the tables in the *Everything Electronic-Lesson 1* database in the *Projects* folder in the *Access Data* folder. Create a one-to-many relationship between the EmployeeID fields of the Employees and Sales tables, enforcing referential integrity.

Then create a one-to-many relationship between the ProductID fields of the Products and Sales tables, enforcing referential integrity. Save the changes to the Relationships layout. Open the Products table, and open the subdatasheet for record 18 to see how many UltraAudio stereos have been sold. Then open the Employees table and use a subdatasheet to view the sales by Jason Wilson (record 4). Close all open tables.

> **NOTE** *If you receive an error message when you try to create a relationship between the Employees and Sales tables, close the Relationship window, open the Sales table, and compare the Employee ID and Product ID data you entered for records 81-105 with the Employee ID and Product ID data provided in Table 1.10. Correct any keying errors, close the Sales table, and try to create the relationships again.*

7 More Sales Coming In

Marta Fuentes (Employee ID 7) sold one ClearPict CPX27 television (Product ID 14) on 12/14/2001. Add this record to the Sales table. (*Challenge*: Use the subdatasheet in the Products table to enter the record.) Then add another record showing that Gregory Caldwell (Employee ID 21) sold one ClearPict CPX27 television on the same date. Move to the next record and then undo the change to the saved record, since the customer immediately returned the television. Close the table.

ON the WEB 8 Do Some Research on the Web

The regional manager for Everything Electronic is considering adding a line of televisions that use cutting-edge technology, such as high definition TV (HDTV), digital TV (DTV), and flat screen/plasma TVs to all the retail stores in the region. She has asked you to do some preliminary research on these types of televisions. Connect to the Internet and use a search engine to find appropriate information. Save one of the Web sites to your Favorites list so you can show it to the regional manager. Disconnect from the Internet, and close the *Everything Electronic-Lesson 1* database.

SUMMARY AND EXERCISES

Project in Progress

9 Building a Database for a Communications Business

You own a growing business called Savvy Solutions that provides a variety of writing, editing, and training services to other business owners. You facilitate training seminars; write materials such as brochures, training manuals, annual reports, employee handbooks, and newspaper and magazine articles; and create Web pages for small businesses. Up to this point, you have been using Excel worksheets to organize and track the data for your business; however, you now decide that it would be more efficient to create an Access database. Create and name a blank database *Savvy Solutions* in a new folder called *Project in Progress* in the *Projects* folder in the *Access Data* folder. (To create a new folder, navigate to the *Projects* folder in the File New Database dialog box, click the Create New Folder button on the toolbar, and enter the name of the new folder in the dialog box that appears.) Use the Table Wizard and/or Design view to create three tables named Customers, Projects, and Employees, respectively. Create and modify the tables so that they contain the fields and field properties listed in Table 1.11.

Table 1.11	Information For Savvy Solutions Tables			
Field Name	**Data Type**	**Field Size**	**Caption**	**Other**
Table Name: Customers				
*CustomerID	AutoNumber	Long Integer	Customer ID	
CompanyName	Text	50	Company Name	
ContactLastName	Text	30	Contact Last Name	
ContactFirstName	Text	20	Contact First Name	
ContactTitle	Text	30	Contact Title	
BillingAddress	Text	50	Billing Address	
City	Text	30		
State	Text	2		
ZIPCode	Text	20	ZIP Code	Create an input mask.
PhoneNumber	Text	20	Phone Number	Create an input mask.
Table Name: Projects				
*ProjectID	AutoNumber	Long Integer	Project ID	
CustomerID	Number	Long Integer	Customer ID	
ItemDeveloped	Text	30	Item Developed	
ServicesPerformed	Memo		Services Performed	
ProjectManager	Number	Long Integer	Project Manager	
TotalHours	Number	Long Integer	Total Hours	
Fee	Currency			Use zero decimal places.

ACCESS 2002

SUMMARY AND EXERCISES

Table 1.11	Information For Savvy Solutions Tables—cont.

Field Name	Data Type	Field Size	Caption	Other
Table Name: Employees				
*EmployeeID	AutoNumber	Long Integer	Employee ID	
LastName	Text	30	Last Name	
FirstName	Text	20	First Name	
Address	Text	50		
City	Text	30		
State	Text	2		
ZIPCode	Text	20	ZIP Code	Create an input mask.
HomePhone	Text	20	Home Phone	Create an input mask.
Position	Text	30		
Salary	Currency			

* Set as primary key.

Import the data from the *SS Customers* worksheet in the *Access Data* folder to the Customers table. Adjust the column widths appropriately, and then add the records listed in Table 1.12 to the Customers table.

Table 1.12	Records to Add to Customers Table

Fields	Record 1	Record 2	Record 3
Customer ID	(AutoNumber)	(AutoNumber)	(AutoNumber)
Company Name	Jacobsen Heating & Cooling Co.	Father Tyme Vintage Clocks	Targeted Temporaries
Contact Last Name	Jacobsen	Schwartz	Gaston
Contact First Name	Ronald	Leo	Allison
Contact Title	Owner	Proprietor	Manager
Billing Address	801 Harrison Ave.	224 Main St.	580 Prentice Ln.
City	Chicago	Crown Point	Oak Lawn
State	IL	IN	IL
ZIP Code	60603-3811	46308-3813	60454-3810
Phone Number	(312) 555-9382	(219) 555-2569	(708) 555-2367

Import the data in the *SS Projects* worksheet in the *Access Data* folder to the Projects table. Also import the data in the *SS Employees* worksheet in the *Access Data* folder to the Employees table. Adjust the column widths of each of the tables appropriately. Make changes to your tables as indicated in Table 1.13.

Table 1.13	Revisions to Tables
Table Name	**Revision**
Projects	In record 17, change the total hours to **47**, and change the fee to **$2,350**.
Projects	In record 30, add **writing** and **editing** to the services performed, change the hours to **56**, and change the fee to **$2,800**.
Customers	In record 36, change the phone number to **(708) 555-7500**.
Customers	In record 16, change the contact's name to **Teresa King**.
Employees	In record 7, change the address to **417 West St.**, change the ZIP Code to **60651-3243**, and change the phone number to **(773) 555-9016**.
Employees	In record 21, change the position to **Writer**, and change the salary to **$37,200**.

Create a one-to-many relationship between the CustomerID fields in the Customers and Projects tables and enforce referential integrity. Then create a one-to-many relationship between the EmployeeID field in the Employees table and the ProjectManager field in the Projects table, and enforce referential integrity. Save the changes to the relationship layout, and print the database relationships. (Do not save the changes to the design of the relationships report.) Close the *Savvy Solutions* database and exit Access.

Creating Forms, Queries, and Reports

CONTENTS

- Creating and Using Simple Forms
- Designing Basic Queries
- Querying Multiple Tables
- Building Complex Queries
- Formatting and Printing a Datasheet
- Creating, Previewing, and Printing Simple Reports
- On the Web: Creating Hyperlinks in an Access Database

OBJECTIVES

After you complete this lesson, you will be able to do the following:

- ► Create an AutoForm.
- ► Add and delete records using forms and subforms.
- ► Use the Form Wizard to create a form based on multiple tables.
- ► Create a query using the Simple Query Wizard.
- ► Sort records in a query.
- ► Specify criteria in a query.
- ► Add, delete, and move fields in a query.
- ► Edit the data in the results of a query.
- ► Create and modify a multi-table query.
- ► Use the Expression Builder to create calculated fields in a query.
- ► Use aggregate functions and grouping in a query.
- ► Format and print a datasheet.
- ► Create various types of AutoReports.
- ► Use the Report Wizard to create a report based on a table and a query.
- ► Group and sort records in a report and include summary information.
- ► Preview and print reports.
- ► Use Microsoft Access Help to understand spacing and alignment of controls on forms and reports.
- ► Create a hyperlink to another object in a database and to a Web site.

CREATING AND USING SIMPLE FORMS

One of the most tedious and exacting tasks that you must perform when working with a database is getting accurate information into the database in the first place. As you learned in Lesson 1, you can populate a database by importing or copying data from another application or database. This is an excellent strategy to follow when the data you need has already been captured electronically. Oftentimes, however, the data has not been captured electronically—perhaps it exists only in written form, such as a completed order form received via e-mail, fax, or regular mail, or it originates as a result of a telephone conversation. In those cases, the data must be entered using the keyboard.

In Lesson 1, you entered data directly into the datasheet, and—while this is certainly an acceptable way to enter a few records or make minor modifications to existing records—you may have noticed that it is sometimes difficult to keep track of your location within the datasheet. Due to the nature of the datasheet's row-and-column format, you usually can't see all the fields for a record at one time; thus you often spend a lot of time scrolling the display to navigate to a particular field. Fortunately, there is a more effective way to enter data. You can create forms to provide an efficient, user-friendly interface. You can build forms that display a single record at a time, as well as forms that reveal only selected fields from one or more tables. Forms are particularly helpful when you want to streamline data entry by providing only those fields the users need in a format that is easy to navigate.

The quickest way to create a basic form is by using the **AutoForm** command. To create an AutoForm, you simply select the table (or query) on which you want to base the form and then click a single button. The AutoForm command creates a form that displays all the fields in the underlying table (or query) for every record, one record at a time. In an AutoForm, the field names (or captions) are displayed on the left, and text boxes into which you enter data are displayed on the right. The sizes of the text boxes depend on the data type of the underlying field—most of the text boxes are the same size; however, a field with a Memo data type is larger, whereas a field designated as a Yes/No data type is displayed as a check box. If the table upon which you base a form has a related table (subdatasheet), the AutoForm will also contain a **subform,** a form within the main form that contains fields from the subdatasheet.

You can also use the Form Wizard to create a form. Using the Form Wizard is much like using the Table Wizard; the Form Wizard prompts you for information, and Access builds a form based on your responses. When you use the Form Wizard, you have more control over the fields contained in the form and the appearance of the form than when you use the AutoForm command. For maximum control over what a form contains and how it appears, you can use Design view to create a form. However, it is usually more efficient to create an AutoForm or a form using the Form Wizard and then use Design view to modify it.

Sometimes you may want to use forms to browse your data. The real purpose of forms, however, is to facilitate the entering and editing of data. With forms, as with datasheets, you need to know how to find the records that you want to edit. Fortunately, the techniques for navigating a form are basically the same as those for moving around in a datasheet. You navigate fields and records in a form by using movement keys on the keyboard ([Tab], [←], [→], etc.) to move from field to field, and navigation buttons at the bottom of the window to move from record to record. One advantage of using forms is that you can view all of the fields for a single record at one time. If you wish, however, you can switch to the form's Datasheet view to see multiple records at once.

After you've navigated to the appropriate record, you can modify it. When you add, edit, or delete records in a main form or subform, the change is automatically reflected in the appropriate table. The changes you make to the main form affect one table, while the changes you make to the subform affect the related table. As you will soon discover, the techniques you learned in Lesson 1 to add, edit, delete, and select data in a datasheet are much the same as those used for forms.

Did you know?

In addition to the basic AutoForm, there are also five other types of AutoForms: Columnar, Tabular, Datasheet, PivotTable, and PivotChart. Click the New Object triangle button on the Database toolbar, click Form, and double-click the AutoForm of your choice in the New Form dialog box.

HANDS on

Creating and Using an AutoForm

In this activity, you'll create an AutoForm based on the Customers table. Since the records in the Customers table contain subdatasheets, Access will automatically create a subform for each record. You will then navigate from record to record using the navigation buttons, view the data contained in the form in both Form view and Datasheet view, and modify records using the form and subform.

1. **If necessary, turn on your computer and start Access.**

2. **Navigate to the *Tutorial* folder in your *Access Data* folder and open the database named *Greenfield Farm Market-Lesson 2.***

   NOTE *The* Greenfield Farm Market-Lesson 2 *database is based on the* Greenfield Farm Market-Lesson 1 *database you created in the previous lesson. It reflects all the modifications detailed in the Lesson 1 Hands On activities, and also includes some new objects and data.*

3. **Maximize the Database window. Click Tables in the Objects bar of the Database window and select the Customers table, if it's not already selected. Click the New Object triangle button 钷▾ on the Database toolbar and click AutoForm.**

Access automatically creates a form based on the Customers table, as shown in Figure 2.1. The form displays the data for the first record in the Customers table and includes all of the fields for the record. Notice that the Notes field has a larger text box than the other fields because it has a data type of Memo. Because a one-to-many relationship exists between the Customers table and the Orders

ACCESS 2002

Access **BASICS**

Creating and Navigating an AutoForm

1. Select the table on which you want to base the form, click the New Object triangle button, and click AutoForm.

2. Click the navigation buttons to move from record to record.

3. Click the View triangle button and click the appropriate option to change views.

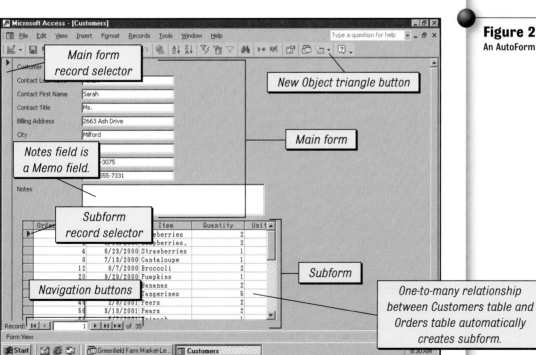

Figure 2.1
An AutoForm

table, a subform that contains the orders for this customer is created automatically and is displayed below the last field of the main form.

4. Click the Last Record navigation button ▶❙.

Access displays the information for the last record in the table. All the navigation buttons at the bottom of the form work as they do in the datasheet.

5. Click the Previous Record button ◀ two times.

Access moves back two records in the table.

6. Click the View triangle button 🖉▾ and click Datasheet View.

Access displays the form in Datasheet view. In Datasheet view, the data appears in columns and rows. If you like, you can scroll up and down (and left and right), just as you can when working with a table in Datasheet view.

7. Click the View triangle button 🖉▾ and click Form View.

Access returns to Form view. In Form view, the data appears like a paper form.

8. Click the Save button 🖫 on the Form View toolbar.

9. In the Save As dialog box, type Customers AutoForm as the form name and click OK. Click the Close Window button ☒ at the right end of the menu bar.

Access closes the form and returns to the Database window.

10. Click Forms in the Objects bar in the Database window.

Notice that the Customers AutoForm you just created is listed in the Database window.

11. Double-click Customers AutoForm.

Access opens the form and displays the first record from the underlying table.

12. Click the New Record button ▶❊ on the Form View toolbar or in the set of navigation buttons at the bottom of the form.

Access displays a new blank record.

13. Press ⟦Tab⟧ to move to the Contact Last Name field. Type Reinhart and press ⟦Tab⟧.

Notice that Access automatically enters a customer ID number in the Customer ID field.

14. Type Carl in the Contact First Name field. Pressing ⟦Tab⟧ to move from field to field, type Mr. in the Contact Title field, 5850 Whitegate Ct. #32 in the Billing Address field, Greenfield in the City field, KS in the State field, 67737-1122 in the ZIP Code field, and (620) 555-7182 in the Phone Number field. Leave the Notes field blank for now.

You have now entered all the data for this new customer in the Customers table. Let's assume that this customer also places an order. Rather than entering the order data in the Orders table, you can enter it in the subform that is currently displayed. Access will automatically update the Orders table to reflect the new order.

A form can contain more than one subform.

15. Press [Tab] until you get to the Order Date field of the subform.

16. Type 6/17/2002 and press [Tab].

As shown in Figure 2.2, once you start typing in the Order Date field, the order number is automatically assigned. Notice that another set of navigation buttons appears immediately above and to the right of the original set of navigation buttons. The top set of buttons is used to navigate among the records in the subform (Orders table), while the bottom set of buttons is used to navigate among the records in the main form (Customers table).

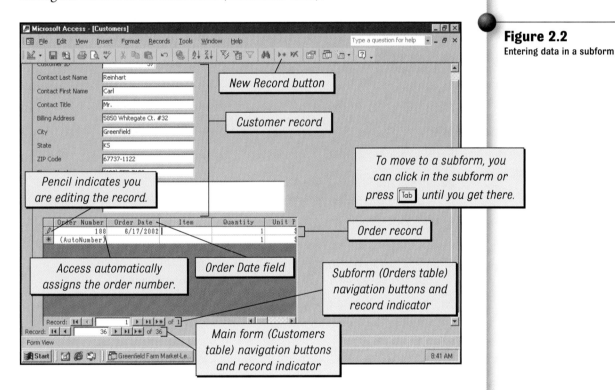

Figure 2.2
Entering data in a subform

17. Pressing [Tab] to move among fields, type Blueberries in the Item field, 2 in the Quantity field, 1.59 in the Unit Price field, 4.50 in the Shipping Amt. field, 24/7 Shipping in the Shipper field, and 10 in the Employee ID field.

At this point, you have entered two records—a customer record using the main form and an order record using the subform. Now you will delete a customer record and its related order record.

18. Use the navigation buttons on the main form to move to record number 34—the record for Stephen Forsythe. (Remember, record numbers and Customer ID numbers are not necessarily the same.)

The insertion point is positioned in the Employee ID field of the subform for record number 34. (As you may recall, when you use the navigation buttons, Access moves the focus to a new record but leaves the same field highlighted.)

NORTON
ONLINE

Visit **www.glencoe.com/norton/online/** for more information on using an AutoForm.

19. Click the **record selector** for the main form—the long vertical bar on the left side of the window (see Figure 2.1 on page 129).

The record selector turns a darker shade of gray, which indicates that the entire record is selected.

20. Press the **Delete Record button** ☒ on the Form View toolbar to remove the record.

Why do you think Access displays a warning message? As you may recall, in Lesson 1, you asked Access to enforce referential integrity when you defined the relationship between the Customers and Orders tables. As a result, Access will not permit you to delete a customer record when there are order records associated with that customer. If you did, there would be order records floating around in the database and you wouldn't know to whom they belonged, which would compromise the integrity of the database. Therefore, to delete Mr. Forsythe's customer record from the database, you must first delete his order record. Let's assume that Mr. Forsythe canceled his order and requested that his name be removed from the company's records.

21. Click **OK** to remove the warning message and click the **record selector** for Mr. Forsythe's order in the Orders subform.

The entire record is highlighted.

22. Press the **Delete Record button** ☒ on the Form View toolbar to remove the order record.

Access displays a warning to verify that you want to delete the record.

23. Click **Yes** in the warning dialog box and click the **record selector** for Mr. Forsythe's customer record in the main form.

24. Press the **Delete Record button** ☒ on the Form View toolbar to remove the customer record.

Once again, Access displays a warning to verify that you want to delete the record.

25. Click **Yes** to delete the record. Then close the form.

Access closes the Customers AutoForm and returns to the Database window.

HANDS on

Creating a Form With the Form Wizard

If you have uncomplicated needs, AutoForms might do the job. Often, however, you'll want more control over your forms—you might want to choose their layout and decide the fields to include. If so, you can use the Form Wizard. In this activity, you'll use the Form Wizard to create a form that incorporates fields from the Orders, Customers, and Employees tables.

1. **Click Forms in the Objects bar in the *Greenfield Farm Market-Lesson 2* Database window.**

2. **Double-click the Create form by using wizard option in the Database window.**

The first Form Wizard dialog box appears. Notice how similar it looks to the Table Wizard you used in Lesson 1.

3. **Click the triangle button in the Tables/Queries text box and click Table: Orders.**

The list of available fields changes to reflect the fields in the Orders table. You can choose the fields to include in the form, as well as the order in which to display them.

4. **Click the OrderNumber field, if it is not already selected, and click the Add Field button ⟩.**

The OrderNumber field is added to the Selected Fields list.

5. **Double-click the CustomerID field.**

The CustomerID field is added to the Selected Fields list.

6. **Click the triangle button in the Tables/Queries text box and click Table: Customers.**

Now the fields from the Customers table are displayed in the Available Fields list.

7. **In the Available Fields list, double-click the ContactLastName and ContactFirstName fields.**

Both fields are added to the Selected Fields list.

8. **Click the triangle button in the Tables/Queries text box and click Table: Orders.**

9. **Click the Add All Fields button ⟩⟩.**

All of the remaining fields in the Orders table are added to the Selected Fields list.

10. **Click the triangle button in the Tables/Queries text box and click Table: Employees.**

11. **In the Available Fields list, double-click the LastName and FirstName fields.**

Both fields are added to the Selected Fields list.

Creating a Form With the Form Wizard

1. Click Forms in the Objects bar.

2. Double-click *Create form by using wizard*.

3. Select the Table/Query in the Tables/Queries text box.

4. Double-click the fields to include in the form and click Next.

5. Click the layout and click Next.

6. Click the style and click Next.

7. Type a name for the form and click Finish.

ACCESS 2002

To change the existing order of fields, remove the fields and then add the fields one by one in the desired order.

12. Click the **Next button** near the lower-right corner of the Form Wizard dialog box.

The next Form Wizard dialog box appears and asks how you want to view your data.

13. Click **by Orders**, if it is not already selected, and click **Next**.

Access displays the next Form Wizard dialog box in which you must choose the type of layout you want for the form.

14. Click each of the layout options and examine the previews. Then click **Justified** and click **Next**.

The next Form Wizard dialog box lets you choose a style for your form. Styles include pictures, shading, and colors to give a special look to the form. When you select an option, a preview of the style appears in the dialog box.

15. Click each of the style options and examine the previews. Then click **Blends** and click **Next**.

Access displays the final Form Wizard dialog box.

16. Name the form Orders for Existing Customers **and choose Open the form to view or enter information. Then click the Finish button.**

The form opens in Form view, as shown in Figure 2.3.

17. Click the **Close Window button** ⊠ on the right end of the menu bar.

Access closes the form and returns to the Database window.

Figure 2.3
Form created using the Form Wizard

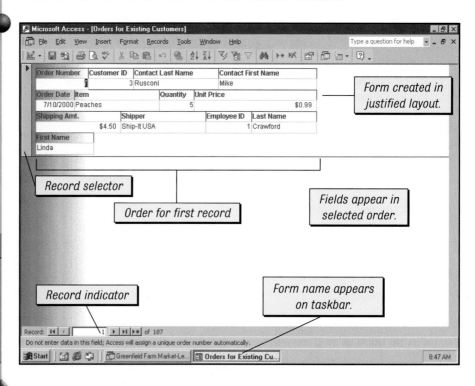

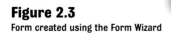

DESIGNING BASIC QUERIES

Thus far, you've concentrated on getting data *into* a database—by building tables in which to organize and store data, creating forms by which to enter data, and then copying, importing, and entering data either directly into datasheets or by using forms. While storing data in an organized manner is an important function of an Access database, it is of little use if you cannot get useful information *out of* the database quickly and reliably. Fortunately, queries allow you to do just that. Using queries, you can sort your data in a variety of ways and extract the data you need based on criteria that you define. You can use queries to perform calculations and to work with data from multiple tables. You can also use the results of queries in forms and reports. You can even save your queries so you can use them in the future—getting up-to-the-minute responses to questions about the data in your database.

Access allows you to create several different kinds of queries. This lesson concentrates on the most often-used query type—select queries. You can use **select queries** to sort, select, and view specific records from one or more tables. When you run a query, the results are displayed in Datasheet view. These query results represent only the portion of the data that meets the requirements you defined in the query. When the underlying data upon which a query is based changes, the query results also change; thus, you always get up-to-date results each time you run a query. In most instances, you can make changes to the records in the query result, and those changes will be automatically reflected in the underlying table(s).

It probably comes as no surprise that there is more than one way to create a query. In fact, there are two ways—by using a wizard or by using Design view. Using a wizard is easier, but using Design view gives you more flexibility and control over the process. A good strategy to follow is to first create a basic query using a wizard, and then modify it in Design view.

HANDS on

Creating a Query Using the Simple Query Wizard

In this activity, you'll use the Simple Query Wizard to create a list of names and addresses of Greenfield Farm Market's customers.

1. **In the *Greenfield Farm Market-Lesson 2* Database window, click Queries in the Objects bar.**

No queries exist in the *Greenfield Farm Market-Lesson 2* database.

2. **Double-click Create query by using wizard.**

The first Simple Query Wizard dialog box appears, as shown in Figure 2.4.

Figure 2.4
Using the Simple Query Wizard

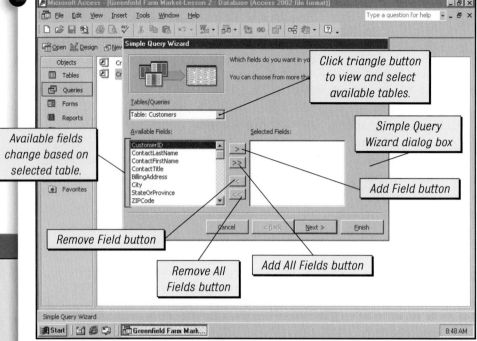

Access BASICS

Creating a Query Using the Simple Query Wizard

1. Click Queries in the Objects bar of the Database window.

2. Double-click *Create query by using wizard.*

3. Choose the table(s) you wish to use in the Tables/Queries text box.

4. Double-click the available fields you wish to add to your query and click Next.

5. Choose Detail or Summary and click Next.

6. Enter a name for your query and click Finish.

3. Verify that Table: Customers appears in the Table/Queries text box.

4. Double-click the **ContactLastName field** in the Available Fields list.

Access adds the field name to the Selected Fields list.

5. In the Available Fields list, double-click the following fields in the order presented to add them to the Selected Fields list: **ContactFirstName, BillingAddress, City, StateOrProvince,** and **ZIPCode.** Then click **Next.**

6. In the next dialog box, enter the title Customer Names and Addresses **and verify that the option Open the query to view information is selected. Then click Finish.**

Access runs (executes) the query and displays the results in Datasheet view. Notice that only the fields you specified appear in the query results.

HANDS on

Modifying a Query Using Design View

Creating a query using the Simple Query Wizard is, indeed, simple; however, the results are not particularly useful. Even though the query you just created contains all the customers' names and addresses, they are not in any particular order, making it very difficult to find a specific address. In this activity, you'll modify the Customer Names and Addresses query in Design view to make it more useful. Then you'll create a new query based on an existing query.

1. If necessary, open the Customer Names and Addresses query in Datasheet view (in other words, run the query) in the *Greenfield Farm Market-Lesson 2* database.

2. Click the **View button**  on the Query Datasheet toolbar.

You now see the Customer Names and Addresses query in Design view. The Design view is split into two panes. The upper pane contains the Field list from the Customers table—the table on which the query is based. (If the query had been based on multiple tables, multiple Field lists would be displayed in the upper pane.) The lower pane contains a **design grid,** which consists of columns and rows. Each column contains information about one field in the query. You use the design grid to determine what fields to include in a query, how to sort the query results, what fields to display in the query results, and what conditions must be met in order to be included in the query results. Take a moment to examine the design grid more closely:

◆ The *Field* row contains the names of the fields used in the query.

◆ The *Table* row contains the name(s) of the table(s) where the fields are located. When a query is based on fields from multiple tables, the *Tables* row helps you identify which fields belong to which tables.

◆ You use the *Sort* row to indicate that you want the query results to be sorted on a particular field in either ascending or descending order. If the *Sort* row is empty, the query results will not be sorted in any particular order.

◆ A check mark in a *Show* check box indicates that a field will be displayed in the query results. If you clear the *Show* check box for a particular field, that field will not be displayed in the query results. This feature is most useful when used in conjunction with the *Criteria* row; you can specify a condition in the *Criteria* row for a particular field, but not display the field in the query results.

◆ You use the *Criteria* and *Or* rows to specify conditions that limit the scope of the query. If necessary, you can add more conditions in the empty rows below the *Or* row.

3. Click in the *Sort* row under the ContactLastName field. Click the **triangle button** that appears and select **Ascending** from the drop-down list.

When you run the query, the query results will be displayed in alphabetic order by last name.

4. Click in the *Sort* row under the ContactFirstName field. Click the **triangle button** and select **Ascending** from the drop-down list.

If two or more records in the query results have the same last name, the records will be alphabetized by the first names.

5. Click the **Run button** ▮ on the Query Design toolbar.

As you can see, the results are sorted alphabetically by last name and then first name (see the records for Edwin Smith and Maxine Smith).

6. Click the **Save button** 🖫 on the Query Datasheet toolbar to save the changes you just made to the Customer Names and Addresses query.

Now suppose you want to identify all the customers who live in Kansas. You can use the existing query to create a new query.

7. Click the **View button** 🔍▾ on the Query Datasheet toolbar to switch to Design view.

8. Type KS in the *Criteria* row under the StateOrProvince field. Then press ⎆Tab to move to another field.

Notice that Access automatically inserts quotation marks around the letters *KS*. When you run the query, only those records that contain *KS* in the StateOrProvince field will be included in the query results. Your query window should look like the one shown in Figure 2.5.

Figure 2.5
Completed query window

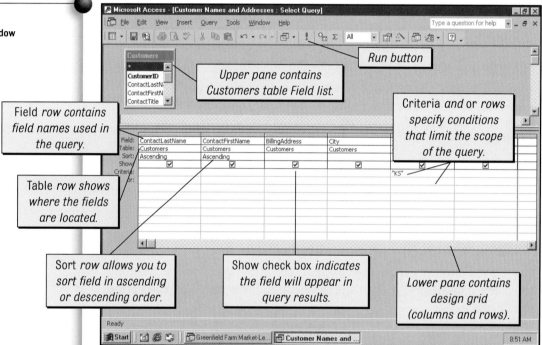

Run button

Upper pane contains Customers table Field list.

Field *row contains field names used in the query.*

Criteria *and or rows specify conditions that limit the scope of the query.*

Table *row shows where the fields are located.*

Sort *row allows you to sort field in ascending or descending order.*

Show check box *indicates the field will appear in query results.*

Lower pane contains design grid (columns and rows).

9. Click the **Run button** 🛚 on the Query Design toolbar and examine the query results.

10. Click **Save As** on the File menu.

WARNING *Do not click the Save button or you will immediately overwrite the Customer Names and Addresses query.*

Saving a query doesn't save the data you currently see in the query results, but instead saves the query design—the set of instructions for sorting and extracting a particular set of data. Access displays a Save As dialog box much like the one that is displayed when you save a table. This time, however, Access requests a query name rather than a table name.

11. Type Kansas Customers as the query name and click **OK**.

The new query name appears in the title bar and in the taskbar button.

You can use the Simple Query Wizard to create queries based on more than one table.

12. Click the **Close Window button** ☒ at the right end of the menu bar.

Access closes the query and returns to the Database window. Notice that there are two queries listed in the Database window—the Customer Names and Addresses query and the Kansas Customers query.

Adding, Deleting, and Moving Fields in a Query

You can easily add, delete, and move fields in query Design view. In this activity, you will modify the Customer Names and Addresses query to create a customer telephone list by adding, deleting, and moving fields.

1. In the *Greenfield Farm Market-Lesson 2* Database window, click the **Customer Names and Addresses query** and click the **Design button** 📐 Design.

2. In the design grid, point to the **BillingAddress column selector**— the small blank gray box above the *Field* row. The pointer will change to a down arrow. Hold down the mouse button and drag to select the **BillingAddress**, **City**, **StateOrProvince**, and **ZIPCode column selectors**. All four columns should be highlighted, as shown in Figure 2.6.

ACCESS 2002

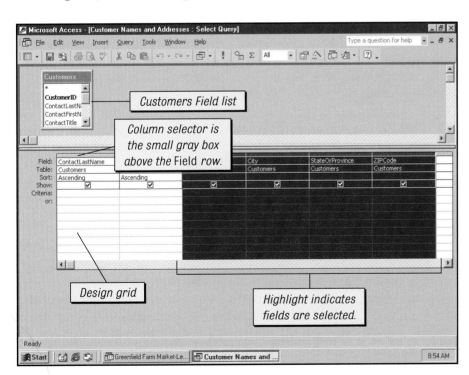

Customers Field list

Column selector is the small gray box above the *Field* row.

Design grid

Highlight indicates fields are selected.

Figure 2.6
Selecting fields in the query design grid

3. Release the mouse button and press Delete.

Access deletes the fields from the design grid. The insertion point is now positioned in the *Field* row of the third column.

ACCESS 2002

4. Click the **triangle button** in the *Field* row of the third column. Scroll down in the drop-down list that appears and click **PhoneNumber**.

The PhoneNumber field is added to the *Field* row. In addition, the Customers table automatically displays in the *Table* row, and a check mark appears in the *Show* check box.

5. Double-click the **ContactTitle field** in the Customers Field list in the upper pane of the design grid.

The ContactTitle field is added in the next available column of the design grid.

6. Click **Save As** on the File menu and type Customer Phone List in the Save As dialog box. Then click **OK**.

7. Click the **Run button** [ ] to execute the query.

While this query is useful, suppose you decide that the ContactTitle field should appear after the ContactFirstName field.

8. Click the **View button** [ ] to return to Design view. Then click the **ContactTitle column selector**.

The entire ContactTitle column is highlighted.

9. Point to the **column selector** of the ContactTitle column; click and hold the mouse button and drag to the left until the dark vertical line is positioned between the ContactFirstName field and the PhoneNumber field. Then release the mouse button.

The ContactTitle field is now positioned between the ContactFirstName and PhoneNumber fields. As you may have noticed, the procedure for moving a field in query Design view is very similar to the procedure for moving a field in table Design view.

10. Click the **Run button** [ ] to view the revised query results. Then save and close the query.

HANDS on

Editing Query Results

Usually, to update data in a database, you would use either a form (Form view or Datasheet view) or a table (Datasheet view). However, in some instances, you can edit query results (Datasheet view) to change the data in the underlying table. In this activity, you will run a query and edit some of the data contained in the query results.

1. Double-click the **Customer Phone List query** in the *Greenfield Farm Market-Lesson 2* Database window.

Access displays the results of the Customer Phone List query in Datasheet view. (You can run queries from the Database window by either double-clicking the name or selecting the query name and clicking the Open button ![Open].) Now you'll change data in the query results, noting that your changes are reflected in the underlying table.

2. Navigate to the record for Deborah Garner (record 6) and change her phone number to (785) 555-1287. Then close the query.

3. In the Database window, click **Tables** in the Objects bar and open the Customers table.

4. Navigate to the record for Deborah Garner (record 24) and scroll to the right until you can see the phone number field.

Notice that the new number you entered in the query results is reflected in the Customers table.

5. Close the table.

QUERYING MULTIPLE TABLES

As you've just learned, queries that extract subsets of data from a single table are very useful. However, that only scratches the surface of what you can accomplish with queries. You can create queries that extract data from multiple tables (or even other queries) to put diverse, yet related, information together in new, meaningful ways. When you include more than one table in a query, you must establish a **join** between the tables—that is, you must tell Access how the data in one table is related to the data in the other table. Establishing a join between tables in a query is very similar to establishing a relationship between tables. In fact, if you have already established a relationship between the tables in a database, Access automatically establishes a join between the tables when you use them in a query. In some cases, Access will establish a join even if you haven't created a relationship between tables— if the tables contain a common field, and the common field in one of the tables is a primary key, Access will create a join.

HANDS on

Creating a Multi-Table Query

Just as with single-table queries, you can either use a wizard to create a multi-table query or create one "from scratch" in Design view. In this activity, you will create and modify a multi-table query in Design view that extracts data from both the Customers and Orders tables in the *Greenfield Farm Market-Lesson 2* database.

1. Select the **Customers table** in the *Greenfield Farm Market-Lesson 2* Database window, if it is not already selected, and click the **New Object triangle button** ![button] on the far right side of the Database toolbar.

2. Click **Query** from the drop-down list.

Access displays the New Query dialog box, as shown in Figure 2.7.

Figure 2.7
New Query dialog box

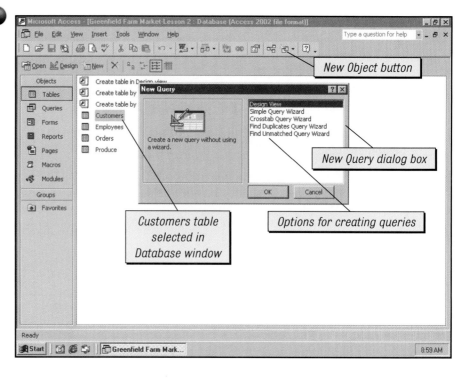

3. Click the **Design View option** and click **OK**.

Access opens a new query in Design view. Since the Customers table was selected when you chose to create the query, its Field list is already displayed; you must add the Field list from the Orders table.

4. Click the **Show Table button** 🔁 on the Query Design toolbar.

The Show Table dialog box appears.

5. Double-click the **Orders table** and then close the Show Table dialog box.

The Field list for the Orders table is added to the upper pane of the query window. Since a one-to-many relationship was previously assigned to these tables, Access automatically inserts a join line showing the joined fields.

6. In the Customers Field list, double-click the **ContactLastName field** and then double-click the **ContactFirstName field**.

Access adds both of these fields to the design grid.

7. Choose a sort order of **Ascending** for the ContactLastName field and for the ContactFirstName field.

8. Drag the **Item field** in the Orders Field list to the design grid, and type Pears in the *Criteria* row for the Item field.

9. Click the **Run button** 🔘.

Access displays the query results, which list records for customers who have ordered pears. Notice that customers who ordered pears more than once are listed more than once.

Creating a Multi-Table Query in Design View

1. In the Database window, click the name of one of the tables you wish to use in the query.

2. Click the New Object triangle button and click Query.

3. Click the Design View option and click OK.

4. Click the Show Table button, double-click the names of the tables you wish to use in the query, and close the Show Table dialog box.

5. Drag the desired fields from the Field lists to the design grid.

6. Set the sort and criteria options for the fields.

7. Run and save the query.

---

10. Click the **View button**  to return to Design view.

11. Click anywhere in the query window outside the design grid and the Field lists. Then click **Properties** 🖻 on the Query Design toolbar.

The Query Properties window opens, as shown in Figure 2.8.

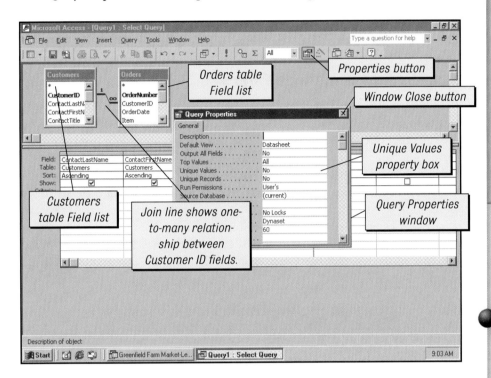

Figure 2.8
Query Properties window

12. Click in the Unique Values property box; then click the **triangle button** and click **Yes** in the drop-down list.

When the Unique Values property is set to Yes, only unique values—that is, no duplicates—will appear in the query results.

13. Click the **Close button** ⊠ in the Query Properties window.

14. Click the **Run button** 🏮.

Access displays the query results. As you can see, each customer who ordered pears is listed only once.

15. Click **Save As** on the File menu. Type Pear Orders as the query name. Then click **OK** and close the query.

You are back to the *Greenfield Farm Market-Lesson 2* Database window. Even though you created the new query from the Tables option, you do not see the new query in the Tables list. The query is listed under the Queries option.

16. Click **Queries** in the Objects bar to see the Pear Orders query listed in the Database window.

BUILDING COMPLEX QUERIES

In Access, you can easily build complex queries to extract specific information from a database by using expressions, calculated fields, and statistical functions. The criteria specified in a query can range from simple text or numeric data to complex calculations and expressions. For example, in the Kansas Customers query you created earlier, you entered a simple text criterion *(KS)* in the *Criteria* row of the StateOrProvince field to narrow the information to include only those records for customers who reside in Kansas.

Using Expressions in a Query

Oftentimes you may need to extract information from a database that falls between a range of values—for example, you might need to identify all the customers who placed an order during a specific time frame. In contrast, you might need to extract information from a database by excluding particular records, such as when you want to display all records except those of customers who reside in-state. You can use expressions in queries to extract these types of information. An **expression** is a combination of field names, values, and comparison operators that Access can evaluate. An essential part of most expressions is the comparison operator. A **comparison operator** is a symbol that is used to compare a value or text in the database to characters that you enter. Table 2.1 describes the common comparison operators used in Access.

Table 2.1	Comparison Operators
Operator	**Description**
=	Equal to
<>	Not equal to
>	Greater than
<	Less than
> =	Greater than or equal to
< =	Less than or equal to
Between…And	Between two specified values

You can also create expressions using *AND* or *OR*. In an *AND* expression, all conditions in the expression must be met in order for the expression to be true. For example, to display the records for customers who placed orders between 9/1/2000 and 9/1/2001, you could enter the expression *>8/31/2000 and < = 8/31/2001* in the *Criteria* row of an Order Date field. In order for a record to meet the conditions required by this *AND* expression, it must contain a date in the Order Date field that is both greater than 8/31/2000 and less than 8/31/2001. When you create an *AND* expression for a single field, you must place the entire expression on the same line in the *Criteria* row in the design grid.

When you enter values in the *Criteria* row for multiple fields, Access treats those criteria as an *AND* expression—that is, when you run the query, Access will display only those records that meet all of the criteria specified. For example, if you enter *Blueberries* in the *Criteria* row of an Item field, and you enter *KS* in the

To enter numeric data as criteria in a query, type the number without any formatting, such as dollar signs or commas.

Criteria row of a State field, Access will return only those records that contain both *Blueberries* in the Item field and *KS* in the State field.

In an *OR* expression, if just one condition is met, the expression is true. For example, to display the records for customers who live in Kansas, Missouri, or Oklahoma, you could enter the expression *KS or MO or OK* in a State field. In order for a record to meet the conditions required by this *OR* expression, it must contain only one of the conditions—either KS, or MO, or OK—in its State field. When you create an *OR* expression for a single field, you can either place the entire expression in the *Criteria* row or place each *OR* condition in a separate *or* row in the design grid.

Perhaps you want to create an *OR* expression that involves multiple fields. In that case, you would enter one value in the *Criteria* row of one field and another value in the *or* row in another field. For example, suppose you enter *Blueberries* in the *Criteria* row of an Item field, and you enter *KS* in the *or* row of a State field. Access would return records that meet either of these two conditions—records with Blueberries in the Item field (with no regard as to what data is listed in the State field) and records with KS in the State field (with no regard as to what data is listed in the Item field).

Using Calculated Fields in a Query

As you may recall from the discussion on planning a database in Lesson 1, you should not include fields in your database that contain data you can calculate from other fields. For instance, if you have one field for unit price and one for quantity, you can calculate the total cost by entering an expression to multiply the values in these two fields together in a **calculated field.** You can create a calculated field in a query by typing the name of the calculated field, followed by a colon and then the expression, directly into the *Field* row of the design grid. Any field names used in the expression must be enclosed in square brackets ([ ]). For example, to calculate the total mentioned above, you could enter the expression *Total:[UnitPrice]*[Quantity]*. However, instead of entering an expression manually, you can use the **Expression Builder** to choose the fields on which you want to perform calculations and the operators you want to use in those calculations.

Creating a Calculated Field

In this activity, you will create a query that contains a calculated field to determine the total price of a customer order, including shipping charges.

1. In the *Greenfield Farm Market-Lesson 2* Database window, double-click **Create query in Design view**.

2. In the Show Table dialog box, double-click the **Customers** and the **Orders tables** to display their Field lists. Then close the Show Table dialog box.

The Customers and Orders Field lists appear in the upper pane of the query window. As before, Access displays a join line between the two CustomerID fields.

Creating a Calculated Field

1. Open an existing query in Design view or create a new query.

2. Scroll to the first blank field in the design grid, click in the *Field* row, and click the Build button on the Query Design toolbar.

3. In the Expression Builder dialog box, select the fields and operators you wish to include in the expression. Then click OK to close the dialog box.

4. Right-click anywhere in the calculated field column in the design grid, and select Properties from the shortcut menu.

5. Type a caption for the calculated field, and close the Field Properties window.

6. Run and save the query.

3. From the Customers Field list, double-click the **ContactLastName** and **ContactFirstName fields** to add them to the design grid.

4. Click **Ascending** from the drop-down lists in the *Sort* row of the ContactLastName field and the ContactFirstName field.

5. Add the **OrderNumber**, **OrderDate**, **UnitPrice**, **Quantity**, and **ShippingAmount** fields from the Orders Field list to the design grid, in that order.

6. Click the **Run button** 🔳 and view the query results.

7. Save the query as Customer Orders.

8. Click the **View button** 🖾 to return to Design view.

9. Scroll to the first empty column (after ShippingAmount) in the design grid and click in the *Field* row.

10. Click the **Build button** 🔲 on the Query Design toolbar.

The Expression Builder dialog box opens with the *Customer Orders* folder open in the first column and the fields available displayed in the second column, as shown in Figure 2.9.

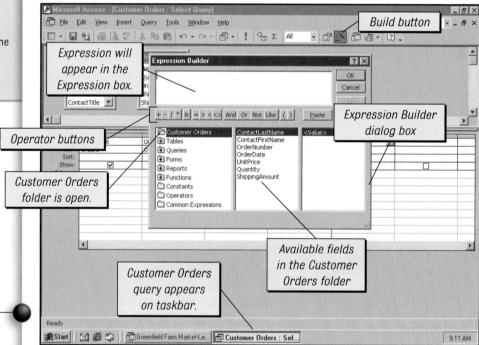

Figure 2.9
Expression Builder dialog box

11. Double-click the **UnitPrice field** in the second column.

Access inserts the UnitPrice field, enclosed in brackets, in the Expression box at the top of the Expression Builder dialog box.

12. Click the **asterisk button** in the row of operator buttons directly beneath the Expression box.

An asterisk (multiplication symbol) appears in the Expression box.

13. Double-click the Quantity field in the second column.

Access inserts the Quantity field in the Expression box, enclosed in brackets.

14. Click the plus sign button in the row of operator buttons.

A plus sign (addition symbol) appears in the Expression box.

15. Double-click the ShippingAmount field in the second column.

This calculation will allow you to obtain the total cost (unit price × quantity + shipping amount = total cost).

16. Click OK in the Expression Builder dialog box.

The Expression Builder dialog box closes, and the expression you just created is inserted in the field. (You can press ⇧Shift + F2 to view the entire expression in the Zoom window.)

17. Click anywhere in the design grid to finalize the entry.

Notice that Access has assigned the field name *Expr1* to this calculation, which is not very descriptive.

18. Double-click Expr1 in the calculation to select it. Then type TotalOrder.

WARNING *When substituting a more descriptive field name for the default name of an expression, be sure not to delete the colon that separates the name from the actual expression.*

The name *TotalOrder* replaces the name *Expr1* as the name of the expression. When you run the query, *TotalOrder* will appear as the field name instead of the default name *Expr1*.

19. Click the Run button .

The last column of the query datasheet displays the total for each customer order (unit price * quantity + shipping amount). The field name you assigned is also displayed; however, the datasheet would look more professional if you used a caption in place of the field name. As you may recall from Lesson 1, a caption is a field property. Just as you changed the properties of fields in tables in Lesson 1, you can also change the properties of fields in queries.

20. Return to Design view. Right-click anywhere in the calculated field column of the design grid, and click Properties on the shortcut menu.

The Field Properties window opens.

NOTE *If the Query Properties window opens instead of the Field Properties window, close the Query Properties window, click in the field, then right-click again, and select Properties from the shortcut menu.*

21. Type Total Order in the Caption property box of the Field Properties window. Then close the Field Properties window.

HINTS & TIPS

To rename a field in a query, right-click anywhere in the column of the field whose name you want to change and click Properties on the shortcut menu that appears. In the Caption text box of the Field Properties window, type the new caption for the field.

NORTON ONLINE

Visit **www.glencoe.com/norton/online/** for more information on complex queries.

22. Run the query again to view the change.

23. Save and close the Customer Orders query.

Using Aggregate Functions and Grouping in a Query

With Access, you can use predefined calculations, called **aggregate functions,** to calculate totals and perform other types of common computations. The aggregate functions available in Access are AVG (average), COUNT, MAX (largest value), MIN (smallest value), SUM, STDEV (standard deviation), and VAR (variance). To use these functions in a query, you click the Totals button Σ on the Query Design toolbar. Access then adds a *Total* row to the design grid. For each field in the design grid, you specify the function to be performed on that field. When you apply a function to a field, Access displays a new field name in the query results by combining the function and the field name. For example, if you apply the SUM function to a Quantity field, Access would display the field name *SumOfQuantity.*

Oftentimes you may want to group certain records together and then use an aggregate function to calculate a total or an average for the group. You can use Group By in the *Total* row to indicate the fields on which you want to group records. Group By is the default entry in the *Total* row of the design grid. Group By doesn't perform any calculations; instead you use Group By to define a grouping of data on which you want to perform an aggregate function.

HANDS on

Creating a Query That Includes Aggregate Functions

In this activity, you will create a query that calculates a total and an average for all the Greenfield Farm Market customer orders.

1. Double-click **Create query in Design view** in the *Greenfield Farm Market-Lesson 2* Database window.

2. In the Show Table dialog box, click the **Queries tab,** and double-click **Customer Orders** to display its Field list. Then close the Show Table dialog box.

3. From the Field list, double-click **TotalOrder** to add it to the design grid.

The TotalOrder field is the calculated field you created in the previous activity that displays the total amount of each customer order. You want to use this field to perform two calculations—one calculation to determine the total of all the customer orders and another calculation to determine the average of all the customer orders. In order to use this field twice, you must add it to the design grid again.

4. Double-click **TotalOrder** in the Field list again to add another copy of it to the design grid.

5. Click the **Totals button** Σ on the Query Design toolbar.

Access inserts the *Total* row in the design grid and the Group By entry (default) appears in both fields in the *Total* row.

6. Click in the *Total* row of the first column and click the **triangle button** that appears.

The list of available functions appears.

7. Click **Sum** in the drop-down list, as shown in Figure 2.10.

ACCESS 2002

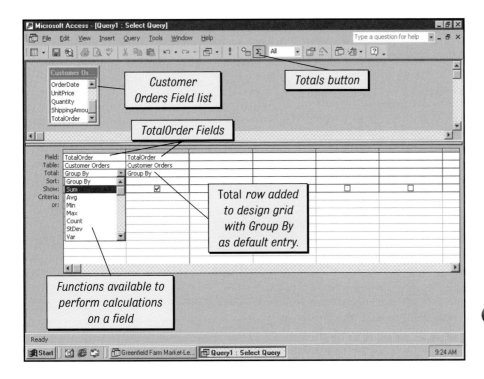

Figure 2.10
Entering an aggregate function in the query design grid

8. Click in the *Total* row of the second column, click the **triangle button** that appears, and click **Avg** in the drop-down list.

9. Run the query.

Access runs the query, displaying the sum and the average of all the order totals.

10. Double-click the right boundary of each field selector to widen the columns.

Notice that Access renamed the TotalOrder fields in the query datasheet as *SumOfTotalOrder* and *AvgOfTotalOrder*, respectively.

11. Save the query as Order Statistics, and then close the query.

Using Grouping in a Query

While the Order Statistics query you just created provides useful, overall information about Greenfield Farm Market's orders, perhaps you would like to review this total and average data broken down by customer. In this activity, you will

Using Grouping and Aggregate Functions in a Query

1. Open an existing query in Design view or create a new query.

2. Click the Totals button on the Query Design toolbar.

3. In the design grid, verify that *Group By* appears in the row of the field(s) you wish to be grouped.

4. Click in the *Total* row of the field(s) on which you wish to apply an aggregate function.

5. Click the triangle button and click the desired aggregate function from the drop-down list.

6. Run and save the query.

create a new query based on the Order Statistics query that displays the total order amount and average order amount for each customer.

1. **Open the Order Statistics query in Design view and save it as** Customer Orders Summary.

2. **Double-click the ContactLastName and ContactFirstName fields in the Customer Orders Field list.**

The fields are added in the next two available columns in the design grid (columns 3 and 4). Notice that Group By appears in the *Total* row for these two fields by default.

3. **Click the column selector for the ContactLastName field, press and hold** 〈Shift〉**, and click the column selector for the ContactFirstName field.**

Both fields are highlighted.

4. **Drag one of the highlighted column selectors to the left until the dark vertical line is positioned before the first column; then release the mouse button.**

The ContactLastName and ContactFirstName fields are now positioned in the first two columns, respectively.

5. **Run the query. Scroll the query datasheet to view the results.**

Now let's sort the query results in order to identify the top customers.

6. **Return to Design view. Click the *Sort* row for the TotalOrder field in column 3 and click Descending from the drop-down list.**

Your query window should resemble the one shown in Figure 2.11.

Figure 2.11
Query design that contains grouping and aggregate functions

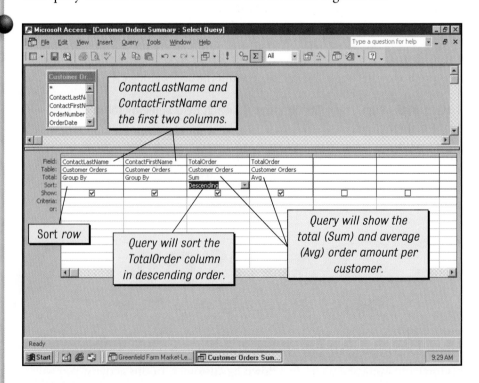

7. Run the query again.

The query results are now sorted on the SumOfTotalOrder field in descending order.

8. Save and close the query.

FORMATTING AND PRINTING A DATASHEET

Perhaps you've noticed as you've worked with tables and queries that, while the datasheet contains useful information, it is not very attractive, and—in the case of large datasheets—it is difficult to navigate. Usually the columns are too narrow or too wide, or fields that you need to reference scroll out of view. Sometimes you may want to hide columns and redisplay them only when you need them. Access offers formatting options that allow you to adjust column widths, hide columns, and freeze columns. With the click of a few buttons, you can also change the type-face, type size, type and background colors, and a host of other effects to enhance the look of a datasheet.

Oftentimes, you may need a printout of the information contained in a datasheet, but you don't want to create a report. In those cases, you can easily print a datasheet.

Modifying the Appearance of a Datasheet and Printing a Datasheet

In this activity, you will format the Customer Orders query datasheet in the *Greenfield Farm Market-Lesson 2* database by changing the typeface, type size, and type and background color; adjusting column widths; and hiding and freezing columns. Then you will print the datasheet.

1. Open (run) the Customer Orders query in the *Greenfield Farm Market-Lesson 2* Database window.

2. Click the Font triangle button `Arial ▾` **on the Formatting (Datasheet) toolbar. Scroll down the font list and click Times New Roman.**

NOTE *If the Formatting toolbar is not displayed, right-click the Query Datasheet toolbar and click Formatting (Datasheet) in the toolbar submenu that appears.*

If Times New Roman is not available for your system configuration, select another font.

The typeface for the data in all the fields, including the captions in the field selectors, changes to Times New Roman.

When you close a datasheet, Access does not save any changes you make in the Page Setup dialog box. Thus, you must reset Page Setup options (such as landscape orientation) every time you print a datasheet.

Modifying the Appearance of a Datasheet

1. Open a datasheet.

2. Click the Font triangle button, scroll the list of available fonts, and click to choose a font.

3. Click the Font Size triangle button, and click to choose a font size.

4. Click the Fill/Back Color triangle button, and select the desired color.

5. Click the Font/Fore Color triangle button, and select the desired color.

BASICS

Changing Multiple Column Widths

1. Click the field selector for the first column.

2. Press and hold ⇧Shift and click the field selector for the last column.

3. Click Column Width on the Format menu.

4. In the Column Width dialog box, enter an appropriate number in the Column Width text box or click Best Fit.

3. Click the **Font Size triangle button** 10 ▾ on the Formatting toolbar, and click **12** from the drop-down list.

The type size for the data and the captions changes to 12 point.

4. Click the **Fill/Back Color triangle button** ▾ on the Formatting toolbar, and select the **pale yellow color (column 3, row 5)** from the color palette.

5. Click the **Font/Fore Color triangle button** ▾ on the Formatting toolbar, and select the **royal blue color (column 6, row 2)**.

The background of the datasheet is now pale yellow, and the type is royal blue.

6. Click the **field selector** for the **Contact Last Name field** (first column) and, while continuing to press the mouse button, drag to select the **Contact First Name field**. Then release the mouse button.

7. Click **Freeze Columns** on the Format menu. (You may need to expand the menu.)

8. Click anywhere in the datasheet to remove the highlighting.

A thin black vertical line appears to the right of the Contact First Name field, indicating that the columns to the left of the line are frozen in place.

9. Scroll to the right.

The Contact Last Name and Contact First Name fields remain on the screen.

10. Click the **field selector** for the **Contact Last Name field** (first column). Press and hold ⇧Shift and click the **field selector** for the **Total Order field**.

The entire datasheet, including the captions, is selected.

11. Click **Column Width** on the Format menu. In the Column Width dialog box, click **Best Fit**. Then click anywhere in the datasheet to remove the highlight.

All of the columns are resized to best fit the data (or captions).

12. Click the **Unit Price field selector** and drag to select the **Quantity** and **Shipping Amt. fields**.

All three fields are highlighted (selected), as shown in Figure 2.12.

13. Click **Hide Columns** on the Format menu.

The Unit Price, Quantity, and Shipping Amt. fields are hidden.

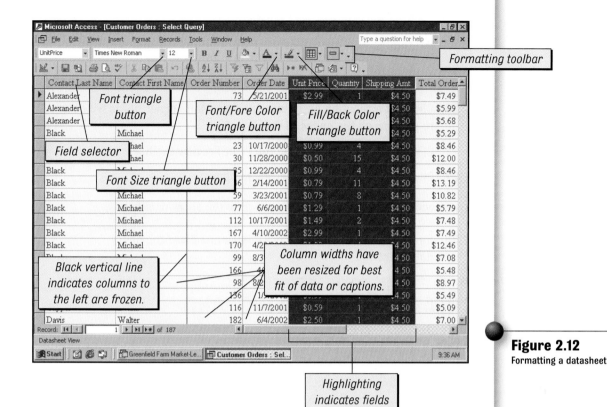

Figure 2.12
Formatting a datasheet

Labels on figure:
- Formatting toolbar
- Font triangle button
- Font/Fore Color triangle button
- Fill/Back Color triangle button
- Field selector
- Font Size triangle button
- Black vertical line indicates columns to the left are frozen.
- Column widths have been resized for best fit of data or captions.
- Highlighting indicates fields are selected.

---

14. Click **Unhide Columns** on the Format menu.

15. In the Unhide Columns dialog box, click to select **Unit Price**, **Quantity**, and **Shipping Amt**.

Each hidden field is redisplayed as soon as you select its option in the Unhide Columns dialog box.

16. Close the Unhide Columns dialog box.

Assume that you need to provide a printout of all the customer orders to the general manager. Before printing any type of document, it is a good idea to preview it.

17. Click **Print Preview** 📄 on the Query Datasheet toolbar.

A preview of the datasheet is displayed in **portrait orientation**—the default printing layout where the height of the page is greater than its width. Notice that some of the fields are missing from the right side of the preview. The printout will probably look better if the datasheet is printed using **landscape orientation**—where the width of the page is greater than its height.

> **NOTE** *If your datasheet is already displayed in landscape orientation, go to step 20.*

18. Click **Setup** on the Print Preview toolbar.

19. In the Page Setup dialog box, click the **Page tab**, and click to select the **Landscape option**. Then click **OK** to close the dialog box.

All of the fields are now displayed in the preview.

20. Click the navigation buttons in the lower-left corner of the window to preview all the pages of the datasheet.

21. Click the **Print button** 🖨 on the Print Preview toolbar.

22. Click **Close** on the Print Preview toolbar.

The preview window closes and you return to the query datasheet.

23. Save the changes to the query design and close the query datasheet.

CREATING, PREVIEWING, AND PRINTING SIMPLE REPORTS

Being able to print a datasheet is handy, especially when you need just a simple printout of information quickly, without too much concern about appearance. However, many times you may need to prepare professional-looking printed output. For example, you may need to provide handouts for a presentation, or perhaps you need to provide a report on sales activity every month. You can create professional-looking documents in Access by creating reports. Unlike datasheet printouts, reports look more polished and provide more control over how your data is presented. In addition, you can group and sort records in reports and calculate summary data, such as totals and grand totals.

Just as with forms, you can create a report in three ways—by using the AutoReport command, the Report Wizard, or Design view. An **AutoReport** can be generated by Access with little input from you, and is based on a single table or query. When you issue the AutoReport command, Access creates a "no-frills" report that contains all the fields and records in the underlying table (or query) arranged in columns. You can also create two other types of AutoReports that require an extra keystroke or two—a columnar AutoReport and a tabular AutoReport. These two AutoReports contain a report header and a page header and/or page footer. A **report header** appears at the top of the first page only and contains the name of the table or query on which the report is based. A **page header** is text information printed at the top of every page of a report. A **page footer** appears at the bottom of every page and includes the date on which the report is printed, the page number, and the number of pages in the entire report. In a columnar report, each field in a record is printed on a separate line, with its label (field name or caption) immediately to its left. In a tabular report, the labels are printed across the top of a page, with the corresponding fields below. If the fields in a record contain a lot of text, such as a Memo field or a large Text field, it is usually better to use a columnar report layout. If there are several fields in a record and/or the fields are relatively small, it is usually better to use a tabular report layout.

If you need a standard report based on a single table or query, an AutoReport might do the job. If, however, you want to base a report on more than one table or query, decide the fields to include and their order, determine the text layout on the page (columnar, tabular, or justified), choose a style for the report, group the detail

records into categories, and perform calculations, such as totals and averages, then you should use the Report Wizard. Using the Report Wizard is similar to using the other wizards you've encountered thus far: Access prompts you for information and then constructs a report based on your replies.

You can also use Design view to create a report from scratch; however, it is usually more efficient to create an AutoReport or a report using the Report Wizard and then use Design view to customize it. After you've created (and saved) a report, you can preview it on screen or print it at any time. An Access report is a dynamic document—the information contained in a report changes each time you preview or print the report if the data in the underlying tables or queries changes.

HANDS on

Creating AutoReports

In this activity, you will create three different AutoReports based on the same query, and observe the differences between them.

1. In the *Greenfield Farm Market-Lesson 2* Database window, click the **Customer Phone List query** to select it, but do not open it.

2. Click the **New Object triangle button** 🔽 on the Database toolbar and click **AutoReport** from the drop-down list that appears.

Access displays a preview of a basic "no frills" report based on the Customer Phone List query.

3. Click the **Zoom triangle button** `100%  ▾` on the Print Preview toolbar and click **Fit** from the drop-down list, if it is not already selected.

One page of the report now fits in the preview window.

4. Use the navigation buttons to scroll the pages of the report.

5. Click the **Close Window button** ☒ on the menu bar to close the report. When asked if you want to save changes, click **Yes** and name the report Basic AutoReport Phone List. Then click **OK**.

Access saves the report and returns to the Database window.

6. With the Customer Phone List query still selected in the Database window, click the **New Object triangle button** 🔽 on the Database toolbar and click **Report** from the drop-down list.

NOTE *The icon on the New Object button changes to reflect the last object that was created.*

The New Report dialog box appears, as shown in Figure 2.13. This dialog box lists the various methods you can use to create reports. The Customer Phone List query is listed as the query on which to base the report because you had already selected it in the Database window.

Figure 2.13
New Report dialog box

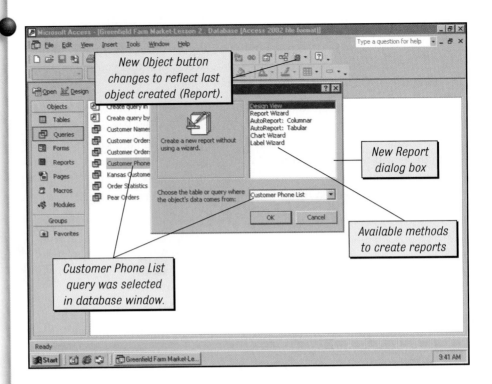

7. Click AutoReport: Columnar in the New Report dialog box and click OK.

Access displays a preview of the columnar AutoReport.

8. If the preview is displayed at 100% of size, click the preview to fit one page in the preview window. Then use the navigation buttons to preview all the pages in the report.

Notice that the columnar AutoReport contains a report title (Customer Phone List) at the top of the first page and a page footer on every page.

9. Save the report as Columnar AutoReport Phone List and close the report.

Access saves the report and returns to the Database window.

10. With the Customer Phone List query still selected in the Database window, click the New Object button  **on the Database toolbar.**

NOTE *If the icon on the New Object button reflects the type of object you wish to create, you can simply click the button instead of selecting an object from the drop-down list.*

11. In the New Report dialog box, click AutoReport: Tabular and click OK.

12. If necessary, click the preview to fit one page of the report in the preview window. Then use the navigation buttons to preview all the pages in the report.

The tabular AutoReport contains a report title on the first page and both a page header and page footer on every page. Notice that this tabular report consists of

Another Way

To create a report, click Report on the Insert menu in the Database window, and select the report type in the New Report dialog box.

two pages, whereas the columnar AutoReport you created in step 7 consists of six pages, and the basic AutoReport you created in step 2 consists of five pages.

13. Save the report as Tabular AutoReport Phone List and close the report.

14. Click Reports in the Objects bar in the Database window.

The three reports you just created are listed in the right pane of the Database window.

HANDS on

Creating a Report With the Report Wizard

In this activity, you will use the Report Wizard to create a report based on fields from the Employees table and the Customer Orders query in the *Greenfield Farm Market-Lesson 2* database. In this report, you will group the customer orders by employee, calculate a total of all customer orders taken by each employee, and calculate a grand total of all orders taken by all employees.

1. If necessary, click Reports in the Objects bar of the *Greenfield Farm Market-Lesson 2* Database window. Then click the New button ⊞New on the Database window toolbar.

2. In the New Report dialog box, double-click Report Wizard.

Access displays the first Report Wizard dialog box.

3. Click the Tables/Queries triangle button and select Table: Employees from the drop-down list.

4. Double-click LastName and FirstName, respectively, in the *Available Fields* list.

The two field names are added to the *Selected Fields* list.

5. Click the Tables/Queries triangle button and select Query: Customer Orders from the drop-down list.

6. Click the Add All Fields button ⏵⏵.

Access moves all of the field names to the *Selected Fields* list.

7. Click ContactLastName in the *Selected Fields* list and click the Remove Field button ⏴.

Access removes the ContactLastName field from the *Selected Fields* list.

8. Click ContactFirstName in the *Selected Fields* list and click the Remove Field button ⏴.

Access removes the ContactFirstName field from the *Selected Fields* list.

Access **BASICS**

Creating a Report With Report Wizard

1. In the Database window, click the New Object triangle button and click Report.

2. Double-click Report Wizard.

3. Select the table or query name in the Tables/Queries box.

4. Select the fields to include in the report and click Next.

5. Double-click the field on which you want to group, if desired, and click Next.

6. Click the first field's triangle button and click the field on which you want to sort. Click the Sort button beside the field name to change the sort order, if desired.

7. Click the Summary Options button, select the summary values you would like Access to calculate, and click Next.

8. Click the desired layout and orientation options and click Next.

9. Click the style and click Next.

10. Type a name for the report and click Finish.

9. Click **Next**.

Access now asks you to provide information on grouping levels within the report. When you group records, you arrange them into categories. You can group records by any field in a report. In this case, you want to group the records by employee last name.

10. Click **LastName** in the dialog box, if it is not already selected, and click the **Add Field button** $\boxed{>}$.

The LastName field appears in blue and is listed first in the sample area on the right side of the dialog box, indicating that the order records will be grouped according to employee last name.

11. Click **Next**.

Thus far, you've determined that the customer orders (the detail records) will be grouped by employee last name. In addition to grouping the records, you must also determine the sort order of the detail records. You can sort the records on up to four fields. The order of these four fields is important—the field designated as the first sort field will appear first in the report, the second sort field will appear as the second field in the report, and so on. For this report, you want Access to sort the detail records in chronological order by order date; however, you want the employee's first name to appear as the first field. Thus, the FirstName field will be the first sort field, and OrderDate will be the second sort field.

12. In the dialog box, click the **triangle button** beside the number 1 field and click **FirstName** from the drop-down list.

The button to the right of the field is a toggle button that allows you to sort in ascending or descending order. Ascending order is the default.

13. In the dialog box, click the **triangle button** beside the number 2 field and click **OrderDate** from the drop-down list.

One of the goals of this report is to show a total of all the orders taken by each employee. In addition, you would also like the report to show the grand total of all the orders taken by all the employees.

14. Click the **Summary Options button** in the dialog box.

A Summary Options dialog box appears in which you can select four different types of summary information—totals (Sum), average (Avg), minimum value (Min), and maximum value (Max)—for each numeric field in the report. The option buttons on the right allow you to choose between *Detail and Summary* or *Summary Only*. If you choose *Detail and Summary,* you will see the data for each record as well as summary information for each group of records and a grand total for all the records. If you choose *Summary Only,* you will see the summary information for each group and a grand total for all the records, but you will not see the data for individual records.

15. Click to select the **Sum check box** for the **TotalOrder** field. Verify that the *Detail and Summary* option is selected. Then click **OK** and click **Next**.

This dialog box allows you to choose the report layout and the orientation. You can choose from six different layout options and either portrait or landscape orientation.

16. **Click each layout option and preview the corresponding samples in the preview window. Then select Align Left 1 for the layout, select Landscape for the orientation, and click Next.**

In this dialog box, you can choose from six preformatted report styles.

17. **Click each report style and preview the corresponding samples in the preview window. Then click Corporate and click Next.**

18. **In the final Report Wizard dialog box, type** Customer Orders by Employee **as the title for the report. Verify that the option to preview the report is selected, and then click Finish.**

The report is displayed in the preview window, as shown in Figure 2.14. Access has grouped the records by employee last name and sorted the detail records in each group by employee first name and order date.

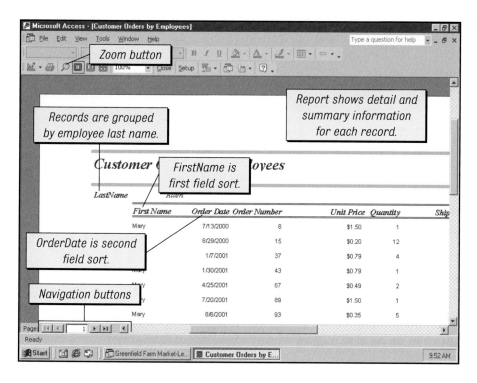

ACCESS 2002

Figure 2.14
Preview of a report that contains grouping, sorting, and summary information

19. **Click the Zoom button ⌕ to fit the report in the preview window, and use the navigation buttons to preview the report.**

20. **Navigate to the last page of the report to see the grand total for all the records.**

21. **Click Print on the File menu.**

The Print dialog box appears. Since this report is fairly lengthy, you will only print the first three pages.

Access BASICS

Printing a Report

1. Open the report you wish to print.

2. Click Print on the File menu.

3. Change the settings in the Print dialog box, if desired, and then click OK.

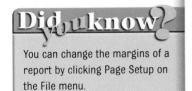

Did you know?

You can change the margins of a report by clicking Page Setup on the File menu.

22. In the Print Range section of the Print dialog box, click to select **Pages**, type 1 in the From text box, press `Tab`, and type 3 in the To text box. Then click **OK**.

Access prints the first three pages of the report.

23. Click the **Close Window button** ☒ on the menu bar.

Access closes the report and returns to the Database window.

Modifying Reports and Forms

When you create a form or a report using a wizard, the spacing and alignment of the controls—the labels, text boxes, decorative lines, and other elements—don't always look perfect. In some cases, the entire text of a label may not be visible, or a label is not properly aligned with the data beneath it. Use Help to learn how you can modify a report or form in Design view.

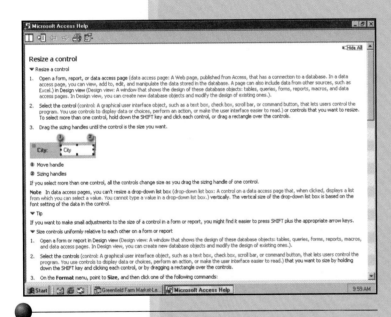

Figure 2.15
Learning about resizing controls

1. Type **resize a control** in the Ask a Question box and press `Enter`.

2. Click **Resize a control** in the list of options that appears.

3. Maximize the Help window, expand the topics, and read the Help information on resizing a control (Figure 2.15).

4. Explore for answers to these questions: What is a control? What view do you use to resize a control? How do you resize a control to fit its contents?

5. Click the **Show button** 🔲 on the Help window, if necessary, and then click the **Contents tab**.

6. Click the **plus sign** before the Microsoft Access Help topic.

7. Click the **plus sign** before the Controls and Charts topic.

8. Click the **plus sign** before the Customizing Controls topic.

9. Open the **Align controls to each other** topic. Expand the topics and explore for information on aligning controls.

10. Close the Help window.

Self Check

Test your knowledge by answering the following questions. See Appendix B to check your answers.

1. A(n) _____ is a form within a main form that contains fields from a subdatasheet.

2. In the query design grid, you use the _____ or _____ rows to specify conditions that limit the scope of a query.

3. When you include more than one table in a query, you must establish a(n) _____ between the tables so that Access knows how the data in one table is related to the data in the other table.

4. A(n) _____ is a combination of field names, values, and comparison operators that Access can evaluate.

5. When you use the _____ , you can create a report that groups and sorts records, and includes summary information.

CREATING HYPERLINKS IN AN ACCESS DATABASE

You can create **hyperlinks** in Access to navigate quickly and easily to another object in the same database, to an object in a different database, or to a Web site. In a form, you can create hyperlinks that appear as text, graphics, buttons, or other shapes. In a datasheet, text that contains hyperlinks usually appears in a different color than other items (often blue) and is underlined. Typically, after you click a hyperlink, the text changes color—generally turning purple—to remind you that you followed the link. In this activity, you will create and test hyperlinks to another object in the same database and to a Web site.

1. If necessary, open the *Greenfield Farm Market-Lesson 2* database in the *Tutorial* folder in your *Access Data* folder. Open the Orders for Existing Customers form in Design view. Maximize the view, if necessary, and display the Web toolbar.

   NOTE *If the Toolbox is in the way, place the pointer on the Toolbox title bar and drag it to the bottom of the window.*

2. Click the **Insert Hyperlink button** on the Form Design toolbar.

The Insert Hyperlink dialog box appears, as shown in Figure 2.16.

3. Click **Object in This Database** under *Link to* on the left side of the dialog box.

4. Click the **plus sign** in front of Queries under *Select an object in this database*, and click **Customer Phone List** from the list that appears.

As soon as you select the Customer Phone List query, the query name appears in the *Text to display* text box. (If you wish, you can edit this text; however, for this activity, we will use the default query name.)

5. Click the **ScreenTip button** in the upper-right corner of the dialog box. In the Set Hyperlink ScreenTip dialog box, type the text Click to jump to customer phone list and click **OK**.

6. Click **OK** to close the Insert Hyperlink dialog box.

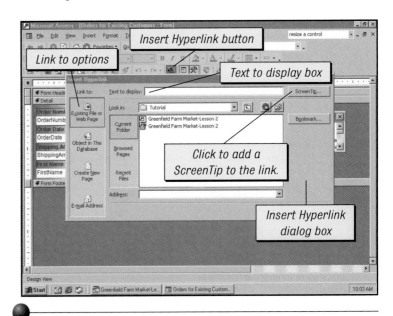

Figure 2.16
Insert Hyperlink dialog box

Access inserts the hyperlink at the top left corner of the form, but it is not in a very good location. Notice that selection handles appear around the hyperlink.

7. Move the pointer over the hyperlink until the pointer changes into the shape of a hand. (Do not position the pointer on a selection handle.) When the pointer takes the shape of a hand, click and drag the hyperlink to the lower-right corner of the form (under LastName). Then release the mouse button.

8. Click the **View button** to switch to Form view.

The Customer Phone List hyperlink appears on the form.

9. Point to the hyperlink and notice that the pointer changes to the shape of a hand and the ScreenTip you created earlier appears. Click the hyperlink.

Access opens the Customer Phone List query. Notice that three buttons appear on the taskbar: one for the *Greenfield Farm Market-Lesson 2* database, one for the Orders for Existing Customers form, and one for the Customer Phone List query.

10. Click the **Back button** ⬅ on the Web toolbar to return to the Orders for Existing Customers form.

To return to a previously viewed object, you can click the Back button ⬅ on the Web toolbar or you can click the object's taskbar button.

11. Save the changes to the Orders for Existing Customers form and close the form. Then close the Customer Phone List query.

Now you will create a hyperlink to a Web site in the Customers table.

12. Open the Customers table in Design view. Insert a row above the ZIPCode field.

13. Type ZIPCodeLookup as the field name for the new field, and select **Hyperlink** as the data type. Type ZIP Code Lookup in the Caption property text box.

14. Save the table, switch to Datasheet view, and widen the new column you just created.

15. Click in the ZIP Code Lookup field for the first record, and click the **Insert Hyperlink button** 🔗 on the Table Datasheet toolbar.

The Insert Hyperlink dialog box appears.

16. Click **Existing File or Web Page** under *Link to* in the dialog box. Then type the following URL in the Address text box:
www.usps.com/ncsc/lookups/lookup_ctystzip.html

A **URL (Uniform Resource Locator)** is the address of a Web site. A URL can be made up of letters, numbers, and special symbols that are understood by the Internet. As you type the URL in the Address text box, it also appears in the *Text to display* text box.

17. Click the **ScreenTip button**, type Click to jump to USPS ZIP Code Lookup in the Set Hyperlink ScreenTip dialog box, and click **OK**. Then click **OK** to close the Insert Hyperlink dialog box.

18. Connect to the Internet, if necessary. Then test your new hyperlink.

19. When the Web page for the USPS City/State/ZIP Code Associations appears, explore the link by looking up the ZIP Code for your own city and state. Also explore the link to the list of USPS 2-letter state abbreviations.

20. Close your Web browser and disconnect from the Internet unless your instructor tells you to remain connected. Hide the Web toolbar and close the database, saving all changes. Then exit Access.

WARNING *You may proceed directly to the exercises for this lesson. If, however, you are finished with your computer session, follow the "shut down" procedures for your lab or school environment.*

SUMMARY AND EXERCISES

SUMMARY

While typing data directly into datasheets is an acceptable way to get information into a database, it is usually more efficient to use a form. In this lesson you created a simple AutoForm with the push of a button and you created a form using the Form Wizard. You then used a form and a subform to enter records into and delete records from a database. Getting data into a database is very important, but it is just as important to get meaningful data out of a database. In this lesson you also designed a query based on a single table using the Simple Query Wizard. You modified a query using the design grid to sort the query results and add criteria to limit the scope of the query. In addition, you created a query from an existing query by adding, deleting, and moving fields. You then created complex multi-table queries in Design view that included calculated fields, aggregate functions, and grouping. Oftentimes you need to format a datasheet to make it more useful and attractive. In this lesson you learned to adjust column widths, hide columns, and freeze columns. You also changed the typeface, type size, and type and background colors to enhance the appearance of a datasheet. While you can quickly and easily print a datasheet, many times you need to generate a professional-looking report. In this lesson you created three different types of AutoReports based on a single query. You then used the Report Wizard to create a report that contained grouped and sorted records and summary information. Finally, you added hyperlinks to a form and a table to quickly navigate to another object in the same database and to a Web site.

Now that you have completed this lesson, you should be able to do the following:

- Create an AutoForm. (page 465)
- Add and delete records using forms and subforms. (page 465)
- Use the Form Wizard to create a form based on multiple tables. (page 468)
- Create a query using the Simple Query Wizard. (page 471)
- Sort records in a query. (page 473)
- Specify criteria in a query. (page 474)
- Add, delete, and move fields in a query. (page 475)
- Edit the data in the results of a query. (page 476)
- Create and modify a multi-table query. (page 477)
- Use the Expression Builder to create calculated fields in a query. (page 481)
- Use aggregate functions and grouping in a query. (page 484)
- Format and print a datasheet. (page 487)
- Create various types of AutoReports. (page 491)
- Use the Report Wizard to create a report based on a table and a query. (page 493)
- Group and sort records in a report and include summary information. (page 494)
- Preview and print reports. (page 495)
- Use Microsoft Access Help to understand spacing and alignment of controls on forms and reports. (page 496)
- Create a hyperlink to another object in a database and to a Web site. (page 498)

CONCEPTS REVIEW

1 TRUE/FALSE

Circle T if the statement is true or F if the statement is false.

T   F   **1.** A page header is text information printed at the top of only the first page of a report.

T   F   **2.** The $>=$ comparison operator can be translated as greater than or equal to.

T   F   **3.** You use the Field Properties pane in query Design view to modify a query.

T   F   **4.** When you click the Totals button on the Query Design toolbar, Access adds a *Total* row to the design grid.

T   F   **5.** The main purpose of forms is to facilitate the entering and editing of data.

T   F   **6.** When you run a query, the results are displayed in Query Results view.

T   F   **7.** If you print a datasheet in portrait orientation, the width of the page will be greater than its height.

T   F   **8.** You must use Design view to modify a table, form, query, or report.

T   F   **9.** When you apply an aggregate function to a field in a query, Access creates a new field name in the query results by combining the function with the field name.

T   F   **10.** You can create a form using the AutoForm command, the Form Wizard, or the Expression Builder.

2 MATCHING

Match each of the terms on the left with the definitions on the right.

TERMS	DEFINITIONS
1. comparison operator	**a.** Lower pane of query Design view window in which you enter information such as sorting and selection criteria
2. aggregate function	**b.** An Access tool that creates a database object based on your responses to a series of questions
3. portrait orientation	
4. page footer	**c.** A form within a main form
5. subform	**d.** The default layout for printed output
6. design grid	**e.** A symbol used to compare a value or text in a database to characters that you enter
7. AutoForm	**f.** A field that contains the results of calculations performed on other fields
8. Freeze Columns	**g.** A predefined calculation that performs common computations, such as totaling or averaging
9. wizard	
10. calculated field	**h.** If you want a column to remain visible when you scroll in a datasheet, you should use this command
	i. Text that appears at the bottom of every page in a report
	j. Use this to quickly create a basic form

SUMMARY AND EXERCISES

3 COMPLETION

Fill in the missing word or phrase for each of the following statements.

1. Before you print a hard copy of a report, you should _____ it on screen.

2. When you want to extract specific records from a database and sort them into some order that you can use again in the future, you should create a(n) _____ .

3. To quickly navigate to another object in the same database, to an object in a different database, or to a Web site, you must create a(n) _____ .

4. The comparison operator that means less than or equal to is _____ .

5. Clicking the _____ buttons in the Print Preview window will move you from page to page in a report.

6. A(n) _____ appears only at the top of the first page of a report.

7. When you _____ records in a report, you arrange them into categories.

8. When you _____ data, you arrange it in either ascending or descending order.

9. When you run a query, the results are displayed in _____ view.

10. In query Design view, the upper pane contains the _____ of the tables or queries upon which you want to base your query.

4 SHORT ANSWER

Write a brief answer to each of the following questions.

1. In what circumstances will Access not allow you to delete a record?

2. Describe the difference between an *AND* expression and an *OR* expression.

3. Describe how you would create a query to display the last names, first names, and ZIP Codes of customers who have a ZIP Code lower than 45000.

4. Describe the benefit of creating a form for data entry. What are the advantages of using a form to enter data, as opposed to entering data directly into a table in Datasheet view?

5. What must you do to display summary information in a report? What option would you choose if you want individual records displayed as well?

6. Describe briefly what Access does when you click the AutoForm button. What are the characteristics of a form created in this manner?

7. Describe how you would create a query using both the Customers and Orders tables to show all customers who ordered either pears or apples. The query results should contain the First Name, Last Name, and Items fields.

8. Describe the difference between hidden and frozen columns in a datasheet.

9. Describe the difference between a columnar report and a tabular report.

10. What are the advantages and disadvantages of AutoForms and AutoReports?

5 IDENTIFICATION

Label each of the elements of the query design window in Figure 2.17.

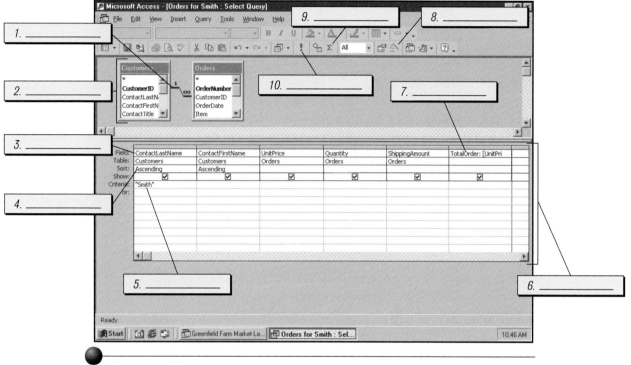

Figure 2.17

SKILLS REVIEW

Complete all of the Skills Review problems in sequential order to review your Access skills to create and use forms, create and use queries, format and print datasheets, and create, preview, and print reports.

1 Create an AutoForm and Add and Edit Data

1. Start Access and open the *Coburne College-Lesson 2* database in the *Skills Review* folder in your *Access Data* folder.

2. Click **Tables** in the Objects bar in the Database window and click the **Instructor Information table**.

3. Click the **New Object triangle button** 🔁 on the Database toolbar and click **AutoForm**. Maximize the form, if necessary.

4. Click the **Next Record button** ▶ several times to move through the records. (Be sure to use the navigation buttons for the main form, not the subform.)

5. Click the **View triangle button** 🔛 and click **Datasheet view**.

6. Return to Form view.

7. Click the **Save button** 🔲 on the Form View toolbar. In the Save As dialog box, type **Instructor Information AutoForm** as the form name and click **OK**. Then close the form.

8. Click **Forms** in the Object bar in the Database window, open the Instructor Information AutoForm, and click the **New Record button** ⏭ on the Form View toolbar.

9. Type **Morrison** in the Instructor Name field.

10. Pressing Tab to move through the remaining fields, type **General Business** in the Department field, **8/15/2002** in the Start Date field, **General Business** in the Undergraduate Degree field, **Education** in the Graduate Degree field, and **PT** in the FT/PT field.

11. In the Class Code field of the subform, type **BU202**; type **Business Ethics** in the Class Name field; type **TR** in the Days field; and type **10:00-11:30 am** in the Time field. Access will automatically add the new class data to the Class Schedules table.

12. With the Instructor Information AutoForm still open, navigate to the record for the instructor named Kellinghaus in the main form.

13. Since the time for the economics class taught by Kellinghaus has been changed, replace the 8:00-8:50 am time currently indicated for the EC101 class with **10:00-10:50 am.**

14. Navigate to the record for the instructor named Alfonso. Mr. Alfonso is retiring and his Public Relations class will no longer be offered at Coburne College. Click the **record selector** for the Public Relations class in the subform and press Delete. Then click **Yes** to confirm that you want to delete this record.

15. Click the **record selector** for Mr. Alfonso's record in the main form and press the **Delete Record button** ⏮ on the Form View toolbar. Click **Yes** to confirm that you want to delete the record.

16. Click **Close** on the File menu to close the form.

2 Create a Form With the Form Wizard

1. If necessary, click **Forms** in the Objects bar in the *Coburne College-Lesson 2* Database window.

2. Double-click the **Create form by using wizard option** in the Database window.

3. Click the **triangle button** in the Tables/Queries text box and click **Table: Student Information.**

4. Click the **StudentID field**, if it is not already selected, and click the **Add Field button** >.

5. Double-click the following fields in the Available Fields list to add them to the Selected Fields list: **LastName, FirstName, GradePointAverage, Major,** and **FullTime.**

6. Click the **triangle button** in the Tables/Queries text box and click **Table: Class Schedules.**

7. Click the **Add All Fields button** >>, and click **Next.**

8. In the next dialog box, verify that **by Student Information** and **Form with subform(s)** are selected. Then click **Next**.

9. In the next dialog box, click **Datasheet** as the layout for the subform if it is not already selected, and click **Next**.

10. Click **International** as the style for the form and click **Next**.

11. Accept the name **Student Information** for the form and **Class Schedules Subform** for the subform. Choose **Open the form to view or enter information**. Then click the **Finish button** (Figure 2.18).

12. Click the **Close Window button** on the right end of the menu bar to close the form.

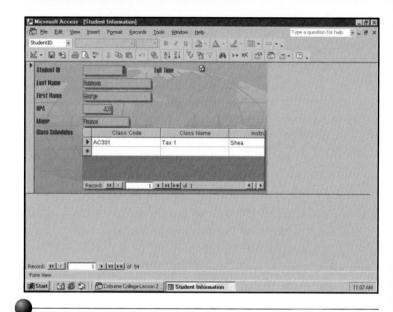

Figure 2.18

3 Create a Query With the Simple Query Wizard and Modify Query Design

1. In the *Coburne College-Lesson 2* Database window, click **Queries** in the Objects bar.

2. Double-click **Create query by using wizard**.

3. Click the **Table/Queries triangle button** and click **Table: Instructor Information**.

4. Click the **Add All Fields button** [>>], and click **Next**.

5. In the next dialog box, enter the title **Full Time Instructors** and click to select the option **Modify the query design**. Then click **Finish**.

6. In the *Sort* row of the InstructorName field, select **Ascending**.

7. Type **FT** in the *Criteria* row of the FullTime/PartTime field, and click to clear the **Show check box** to hide the field.

8. Click the **Run button** [!] on the Query Design toolbar.

9. Save and close the query.

4 Create a Query Using Design View and Edit Query Results

1. Click **Queries** in the Objects bar in the *Coburne College-Lesson 2* Database window and double-click **Create query in Design view**.

2. In the Show Table dialog box, double-click **Class Schedules** and close the Show Table dialog box.

3. Double-click **ClassName** in the Class Schedules Field list to add the field to the design grid.

4. Add the **Instructor**, **Days**, and **Time** fields to the design grid.

5. Choose **Ascending** in the *Sort* row for ClassName, and type **Kellinghaus** in the *Criteria* row under Instructor.

6. Click the **Run button** ⏻ on the Query Design toolbar to view the classes taught by Kellinghaus.

7. Click the **Save button** 🖫, and type Classes Taught by Kellinghaus as the query name. Then click **OK**.

8. In the query datasheet, change the name of the Advertising class to **Principles of Advertising**. Then close the query.

9. Open the Class Schedules table and verify that the class name change is reflected in the table (record 23). Then close the Class Schedules table.

5 Add, Delete, and Move Fields in a Query

1. Open the Classes Taught by Kellinghaus query in Design view.

2. Click **Save As** on the File menu, type Accounting Classes as the query name, and click **OK**.

3. Drag across the Days and Time column selectors and press ⌦ to delete the fields from the query.

4. Click the **triangle button** in the *Field* row of the third column. Click **ClassCode** in the drop-down list that appears.

5. Click the **ClassCode column selector** to highlight the entire ClassCode column.

6. Point to the ClassCode column selector; then drag the column to the left of the ClassName column.

7. In the *Sort* row of the ClassCode field, click **Ascending**.

8. Type AC* in the *Criteria* row for the ClassCode field. (*Hint:* The asterisk is a wild-card character that is used to represent any number of unknown characters.)

9. Delete "Kellinghaus" in the *Criteria* row of the Instructor field.

10. Click the **Run button** ⏻.

11. Save and close the query.

6 Create a Multi-Table Query

1. Select the **Class Schedules table** in the *Coburne College-Lesson 2* Database window, click the **New Object triangle button** 🔲, and click **Query** from the drop-down list.

2. Click **Design View** in the New Query dialog box and click **OK**.

3. Click the **Show Table button** 🔲 on the Query Design toolbar.

4. Add the **Student Information** table and then add the **Grades for Accounting Classes** table. Close the Show Table dialog box.

5. In the Class Schedules Field list, double-click **ClassName**.

6. In the Student Information Field list, double-click **LastName**.

7. In the Grades for Accounting Classes Field list, double-click **Grade**.

8. Type Accounting 1 in the *Criteria* row under ClassName.

9. Click **Descending** in the *Sort* row under Grade.

10. Click the **Run button** .

11. Save the query as **Grades for Accounting 1**. Then close the query.

7 Use an Aggregate Function in a Query

1. Click **Queries** in the Objects bar in the *Coburne College-Lesson 2* Database window and double-click **Create query in Design view**.

2. In the Show Tables dialog box, click the **Queries tab**, click **Grades for Accounting 1**, and click **Add**. Close the Show Table dialog box.

3. Double-click the **Grade** field in the Grades for Accounting 1 Field list three times to add three occurrences of the field to the design grid.

4. Click the **Totals button** Σ on the Query Design toolbar.

5. Click in the *Total* row in the first column, and click **Min** on the drop-down list.

6. Click in the *Total* row in the second column, and click **Max** on the drop-down list.

7. Click in the *Total* row in the third column, and click **Avg** on the drop-down list.

8. Click the **Run button** on the Query Design toolbar to view the query results.

9. Save the query as **Class Statistics for Accounting 1** and close the query.

8 Format and Print a Datasheet

1. Click **Tables** in the Objects bar in the *Coburne College-Lesson 2* Database window, and open the Student Information table.

2. If necessary, right-click the Table Datasheet toolbar and click **Formatting (Datasheet)** on the Toolbars submenu to display the Formatting toolbar.

3. Click the **Font triangle button** Arial on the Formatting toolbar. Scroll down the font list and click **Comic Sans MS**. (If Comic Sans MS is not available on your computer system, choose another font.)

4. Click the **Font Size triangle button** 10 on the Formatting toolbar and click **11** on the drop-down list.

5. Click the **Fill/Back Color triangle button** on the Formatting toolbar, and select the **pale blue color (column 5, row 5)**.

6. Click the **Font/Fore Color triangle button** , and select the **dark blue color (column 7, row 1)**.

7. Click the **Student ID field selector**, scroll to the last field (Expected Graduation), press ⇧ Shift , and click the **Expected Graduation field selector** to select the entire datasheet.

8. Click **Column Width** on the Format menu. In the Column Width dialog box, click **Best Fit**. Press `Ctrl` + `Home` to move to the beginning of the datasheet.

9. Click the **Student ID field selector** and drag to select the **Last Name** and **First Name fields**. Then click **Freeze Columns** on the Format menu.

10. Click anywhere in the datasheet to remove the highlight (Figure 2.19).

11. Scroll to the right, click the **GPA field selector**, and drag to select the **Major, Full Time**, and **Expected Graduation** fields.

12. Click **Hide Columns** on the Format menu.

13. Click **Print Preview** 🔍 on the Table Datasheet toolbar.

14. Click **Setup** on the Print Preview toolbar. In the Page Setup dialog box, click the **Page tab**, click **Landscape**, and click **OK**.

15. Click the navigation buttons to preview all the pages of the datasheet.

16. Click the **Print button** 🖨 on the Print Preview toolbar.

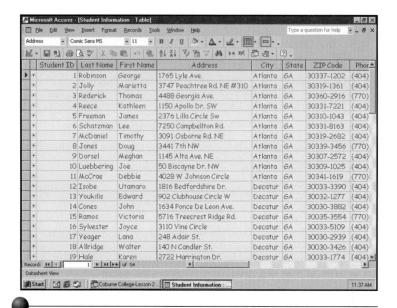

Figure 2.19

17. Click **Close** on the Print Preview toolbar.

18. Click **Unhide Columns** on the Format menu. In the Unhide Columns dialog box, click to select **GPA, Major, Full Time**, and **Expected Graduation**. Then close the dialog box.

19. Save and close the datasheet.

9 Create Three AutoReports

1. In the *Coburne College-Lesson 2* Database window, click the **Class Schedules table** to select it, but do not open it. Then click the **New Object triangle button** 🔳 on the Database toolbar, and click **AutoReport**.

2. Preview the report, save it as **Basic AutoReport Class Schedules**, and close it.

3. Click the **New Object triangle button** 🔳 on the Database toolbar, click **Report**, and click **AutoReport: Columnar**. Click **OK**.

4. Preview the report, save it as **Columnar AutoReport Class Schedules**, and close it.

5. Click the **New Object triangle button** 🔳 on the Database toolbar, click **Report**, click **AutoReport: Tabular**, and click **OK**.

6. Preview the report, save it as **Tabular AutoReport Class Schedules**, and close it.

10 Create a Report With the Report Wizard

1. Click **Reports** in the Objects bar in the *Coburne College-Lesson 2* Database window, and double-click **Create report by using wizard**.

2. Click **Query: Full Time Instructors** in the Tables/Queries box.

3. Add the **InstructorName**, **Department**, **UndergraduateDegree**, **GraduateDegree**, and **StartDate** fields, in that order. Then click **Next**.

4. In the dialog box that requests a grouping field, click **Department** and click the **Add Field button** $\boxed{>}$. Then click **Next**.

5. Click the **triangle button** beside the first field in the Sorting dialog box and click **InstructorName**. Click **Next**.

6. Click the **Align Left 1 option** and then click **Portrait** (if necessary) as the report layout. Click **Next**.

7. Click **Bold** as the style and click **Next**.

8. Type Full Time Instructors by Department as the report title, verify that the option to preview the report is selected, and click **Finish**.

9. Scroll the first page of the report.

10. Click anywhere on the page to zoom out.

11. Close the report.

11 Build and Print a Report With Summary Information

1. Double-click **Create report by using wizard** in the *Coburne College-Lesson 2* Database window.

2. Click **Table: Student Information** in the Tables/Queries box and add the **LastName**, **FirstName**, **Major**, **GradePointAverage**, and **EstimatedGraduationDate** fields to the Selected Fields list, in that order. Then click **Next**.

3. Select **Major** as the grouping field.

4. Click **Next** and click **GradePointAverage** in the first field in the Sorting dialog box.

5. Click the **Summary Options button** and click to select the **Avg check box** for the GradePointAverage field. Verify that the *Detail and Summary* option is selected. Then click **OK** and click **Next**.

6. Click the **Outline 1 layout** and **Portrait orientation**. Then click **Next**.

7. Click the **Formal style** and click **Next**.

8. Type GPAs of Students by Major and click **Finish**.

9. Navigate the report to see the summary information for each major.

10. Click **Print** on the File menu. In the Print Range section of the Print dialog box, click to select **Pages**, type 1 in the From text box, press $\boxed{\text{Tab}}$, and type 1 in the To text box to print only the first page of the report. Then click **OK**.

11. Close the report.

12. Close the *Coburne College-Lesson 2* database.

LESSON APPLICATIONS

1 Create Forms

As an employee at Star Realty, Inc., you decide to create some Access forms to make data entry easier for yourself and other employees. You will create an AutoForm that displays agent addresses and other information.

1. Open the *Star Realty-Lesson 2* database in the *Lesson Applications* folder in your *Access Data* folder.

2. Click the Agents table in the Database window, and use the New Object button ▤▾ to create an AutoForm. Maximize the form and navigate all of the records.

3. View the form in Datasheet view; then return to Form view and close the form, saving the form as **Agents AutoForm**.

4. Open the Agents AutoForm and add two new records that contain the data in Table 2.2.

Table 2.2	Agents Autoform Data	
Field	**1st New Record**	**2nd New Record**
Agent ID	5	6
Last Name	Grafton	Martin
First Name	Robin	Lance
Address	2463 Rainbow Ct.	1188 Far Hills Dr.
City	Salem	Salem
State	OR	OR
ZIP Code	97301-1872	97301-4993
Home Phone	(541) 555-1334	(541) 555-2567
Date Hired	06/01/2002	09/01/2002

5. In the subform for Robin Grafton, add the following new listings, as shown in Table 2.3.

Table 2.3	Robin Grafton Subform Data	
Field	**Listing 1**	**Listing 2**
Address	5275 Fieldstone Ct.	6101 Delcrest Dr.
Bedrooms	5	3
Baths	3	2.5
Sq. Feet	2,095	1,800
Rooms	10	7
Year Built	2001	1989

Table 2.3	Robin Grafton Subform Data (continued)	
Field	**Listing 1**	**Listing 2**
Price	$227,000	$105,500
Lot Size (Acres)	1.3	.5
School District	East Princeton	Landale
Basement	Yes	No
Occupancy	Immediate	30 days

6. Lance Martin has decided to take a job with a different company. Delete his record while in Form view.

7. Move to the record for Frank Rebelo and change his telephone number to (541) 555-0503.

8. Close the form.

2 Create, Modify, and Run a Query

Your manager would like you to generate some facts about properties that have been sold by Frank Rebelo, one of the Star Realty agents.

1. Open the *Star Realty-Lesson 2* database in the *Lesson Applications* folder in your *Access Data* folder, if necessary.

2. Click Queries in the Database window, and choose the option to create a query using a wizard.

3. Base your query on the Properties Sold table, and add the following fields in the order shown to the design grid: AgentID, PropertyAddress, ListingPrice, SellingPrice, and YearBuilt.

4. Save the query as **Properties Sold by Rebelo** and choose the option to modify the query design.

5. Type appropriate criteria in the AgentID field to show only those properties listed by Frank Rebelo, agent 3.

6. Sort the records in descending order by SellingPrice and run the query.

7. Return to Design view and choose the option to hide the AgentID field.

8. Delete the YearBuilt field from the query.

9. Position the insertion point in the *Field* row of the first available column in the design grid (column 5), click the Build button ![Build button], and use the Expression Builder to calculate the percentage of the difference between the listing price and the selling price (SellingPrice / ListingPrice).

10. Change the name *Expr1* in the calculated field to **PercentofListingPrice**.

11. Run the query.

12. Return to Design view, right-click anywhere in the calculated field column of the design grid, and click Properties to open the Field Properties window. Select Percent as the Format property and type **Percent of Listing Price** as the Caption property. Close the Field Properties window.

13. Run the query.

14. Display the Formatting toolbar and make the following changes to the appearance of the query datasheet: change the font to Comic Sans MS, apply the Bold attribute, change the font size to 11, adjust the column widths to best fit the data, and change the type color to dark blue.

15. Hide the Formatting toolbar and close the query, saving the design changes.

3 Query Two Tables

Your manager has asked you to generate a list of 3- or 4-bedroom homes available for sale that are priced under $180,000 and have basements. Your list should include the agents' last names and be sorted in descending order by price.

1. Open the *Star Realty-Lesson 2* database in the *Lesson Applications* folder in your *Access Data* folder, if necessary.

2. Create a new query in Design view using Field lists from the New Listings and Agents tables.

3. Add the following fields to the design grid: LastName, Address (from the New Listings Field list), Bedrooms, Baths, Price, and Basement.

4. Enter criteria that will limit the number of bedrooms to either 3 or 4. (*Hint:* Enter the expression *3 or 4* in the *Criteria* row of the Bedrooms field.)

5. Sort the query results by Price in descending order.

6. Enter criteria that will limit the query to homes priced under $180,000. (*Hint:* Do not enter the dollar sign or the comma separator in the expression.)

7. Type **Yes** in the Basement *Criteria* row to include only those properties with basements. Then run the query.

8. Return to Design view and move the LastName field so that it appears as the last field in the query. Run the query again (Figure 2.20).

9. Save the query as **Homes under $180K with 3-4 Bedrooms and Basement** and close the query.

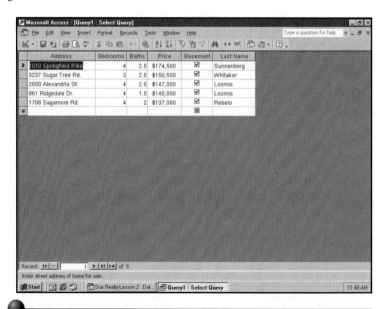

Figure 2.20

SUMMARY AND EXERCISES

4 Calculate Sales Totals and Commissions

Your manager has requested a list of sales agents and a total, by agent, of the actual selling price of the homes each has sold. In addition, your manager asks you to calculate a 3 percent commission on the total for each agent.

1. In the *Star Realty-Lesson 2* database, create a new query in Design view and add Field lists for the Agents and Properties Sold tables.

2. Add the LastName and SellingPrice fields to the design grid and sort the records alphabetically by LastName. Run the query.

3. Return to Design view, click the Totals button, and select Sum in the *Total* row for the SellingPrice field. Run the query.

4. Return to Design view, right-click anywhere in the SellingPrice field, click Properties on the shortcut menu, and type **Total Sales** as the Caption property. Close the Field Properties window.

5. Save the query as **Agent Totals and Commissions**.

6. In Design view, position the insertion point in the *Field* row of the first empty column in the design grid, click the Build button ![Build button], and use the Expression Builder to create the expression *SumOfSellingPrice*0.03*.

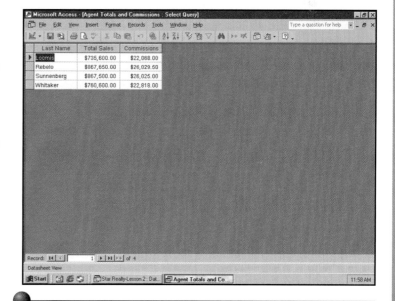

7. Right-click anywhere in the calculated field column and click Properties on the shortcut menu.

8. In the Field Properties window, select Currency as the Format property and type **Commissions** as the Caption property. Close the Field Properties window.

9. In the design grid, select Expression from the drop-down list in the *Total* row for the calculated field.

10. Run the query and review the results (Figure 2.21). Then save and close the query.

Figure 2.21

5 Create and Navigate Reports

The agents with whom you work have asked you to generate some reports. You'll create a columnar AutoReport based on the Properties Sold table and a grouped report based on the New Listings table.

1. Open the *Star Realty-Lesson 2* database in the *Lesson Applications* folder in your *Access Data* folder, if necessary.

2. Create a columnar AutoReport based on the Properties Sold table.

3. Preview the report.

4. Save the report as **Properties Sold AutoReport**, and then close it.

5. Use the Report Wizard to create a tabular report based on the New Listings table. Include the Address, SquareFeet, Bedrooms, Baths, LotSize, Price, and SchoolDistrict fields, in that order.

6. Group the records in the report by school district. Within each group, sort the records in ascending order by price.

7. Assign the Align Left 2 layout, landscape orientation, and the Casual style. Save the report as **New Listings Grouped by School District**.

8. Preview the report. Then print the report and close it.

6 Create and Print a Report That Calculates Totals

You'd like to create a report that shows how the agents are doing as a team. Create a report that sums the total listings, properties sold, and commissions earned by the Star Realty agents.

1. In the *Star Realty-Lesson 2* database in the *Lesson Applications* folder, use the Report Wizard to create a report based on the Agent Statistics table. Include all of the fields in the table in the report.

2. Group the records by Agent ID.

3. In the Summary Options dialog box, choose to sum the YTDHomesSold, YTDNewListings, and YTDCommissions fields. Choose the *Summary Only* and the *Calculate percent of total for sums* options.

4. Choose the Stepped layout, portrait orientation, and the Bold style.

5. Save the report as **Combined Sales, Listings, and Commissions**.

6. Preview, print, and close the report.

7 Create and Print a Report That Calculates Averages

Your last activity for the day requires you to generate a report about the properties that have been sold through Star Realty. Your report should list all of the properties that were sold, grouping them by the number of bedrooms in each. Within each group, the records should be sorted by selling price, and the list and selling prices should be averaged within each group.

1. In the *Star Realty-Lesson 2* database in the *Lesson Applications* folder, use the Report Wizard to create a columnar report based on the Properties Sold table. Include the PropertyAddress, Bedrooms, Baths, ListingPrice, SellingPrice, and AgentID fields in the report.

2. Group the records by the number of bedrooms in each home. Sort the records in each group in descending order by selling price.

3. In the Summary Options dialog box, choose to average the ListingPrice and SellingPrice fields. Choose the *Detail and Summary* option.

4. Choose the Align Left 1 layout, landscape orientation, and the Corporate style.

5. Save the report as **Average Listing and Selling Prices** and view the report.

6. Print and then close the report.

7. Close the *Star Realty-Lesson 2* database.

PROJECTS

1 Should We Keep This Product?

As the store manager at Everything Electronic, you like to track sales of each product sold to analyze whether you should continue stocking. In the past few months, two products—Product ID numbers 11 and 19—have not been selling well. Open the *Everything Electronic-Lesson 2* database in the *Projects* folder in your *Access Data* folder. Create a query using the Sales table that lists the sales for the Keiko 36" television (Product ID 11). Include the ProductID, SalesID, EmployeeID, and SalesDate fields, in that order. Sort the records in ascending order by SalesDate. Run the query and save it as **Keiko KE450 Televisions Sold**. Create another query with the same information except use this query to analyze the JLG stereo, model JL700 (Product ID 19). Run the second query and save it as **JLG JL700 Stereos Sold**.

Open each of the queries you just created and add the QuantitySold field. Remove the EmployeeID field from each, and hide the ProductID field. In the Keiko KE450 Televisions Sold query, edit the quantity sold to 2 for sale number 85. Run each query again. How many of each product were sold? Close the queries, saving the changes, and open the Sales table. Was your edit incorporated? Close the Sales table.

2 Recognizing the Best

Create a new query that uses the Sales, Products, and Employees tables in the *Everything Electronic-Lesson 2* database in the *Projects* folder in your *Access Data* folder. Include the following fields in the order given: SalesDate, LastName, ProductCategory, Brand, Model, Price, and QuantitySold. Sort the records in ascending order by SalesDate. Set the criteria to show only the sales made by Marta Fuentes, one of your past sales leaders, and hide the LastName field. Run the query. Format the datasheet attractively using some of the techniques you learned in this lesson, and then print it. Save the query as **Sales by Fuentes** and then close it.

3 New Products and New Sales

As the store manager at Everything Electronic, you want to create a form in Access and use it to add, change, or delete records in the Products table. Create an AutoForm based on the Products table, and save it as **Products AutoForm**. Then use the form to add the two new product records shown in Table 2.4.

Table 2.4	Record Data	
Field	**1st New Record**	**2nd New Record**
Product ID	(AutoNumber)	(AutoNumber)
Product Category	MP3-CD Player	CD Recorder/Player
Brand	Yamachi	Keiko
Model	YA500	KE7500
Price	$139.95	$429.95
Notes	Portable; includes earphones and AC adaptor	$20 manufacturer instant rebate

So far, your sales associates have sold two of the new MP3-CD Players and three of the new CD Recorder/Players. Record the data in Table 2.5 in the subform for each of the products. Then close the Products AutoForm.

Table 2.5	Subform Data	
Yamachi YA500 MP3-CD Player		
Sale ID	(AutoNumber)	(AutoNumber)
Quantity Sold	1	1
Sales Date	12/19/2001	12/20/2001
Employee ID	3	22
Keiko KE7500 CD Recorder/Player		
Sale ID	(AutoNumber)	(AutoNumber)
Quantity Sold	2	1
Sales Date	12/20/2001	12/20/2001
Employee ID	7	16

4 Submitting a Printout of Employee Updates

You need to submit a copy of selected employee information to PayRite, the payroll service that handles the payroll for Everything Electronic. In the *Everything Electronic-Lesson 2* database in the *Projects* folder, use the Report Wizard to create a columnar report that contains the DateHired, FirstName, LastName, HourlyRate, and Position fields from the Employees table, in that order. Sort the report in descending order by hire date. Choose portrait orientation and a style of your choice. Save the report as **Employees by Hire Date**. Preview, print, and close the report.

5 Analyzing Big Ticket Items

You want to analyze the prices of some of the products available at Everything Electronic, specifically those priced over $500. To generate a list of products that meet the criteria, first create a query based on the Products table in the *Everything Electronic-Lesson 2* database in the *Projects* folder. Include all of the fields in the query and sort the records in the query in ascending order by price; include only those that sell for more than $500. Name the query **Products Priced Over $500**.

Create a tabular report based on the query you just created. In the report, include only the ProductCategory, Brand, Model, and Price fields. Group the records by product category and sort the records within each group in ascending order by price. Choose landscape orientation, Align Left 2 layout, and a style of your choice. Name the report **Products Over $500 Grouped by Product Category**. Preview, print, and close the report.

6 Totaling the Sales

Your district manager wants you to generate a report that lists and totals sales by product for the month of November, 2001. In the *Everything Electronic-Lesson 2* database in the *Projects* folder, create a query based on fields from the Sales and Products table, arranged in the following order: SalesDate, ProductCategory, Brand, Model, Price, and QuantitySold. Restrict the data so that only sales made during the month of November will display in the query results. Sort the query results in ascending order by product category and do not show the SalesDate field in the query results. Name the query **November Sales**. Create a calculated field that multiplies price by quantity sold and change the name of the calculated field to *Total*. Then create a report based on all of the fields in the November Sales query except the SalesDate field. Group the records by product category and sort the records within each group in ascending order by brand. Calculate totals for the Total field as well as a grand total for the month. Choose the Align Left 1 layout, landscape orientation, and Corporate style. Name the report **November Sales by Product Category**. Preview, print, and then close the report.

7 Linking Your Data

ON the WEB Use the Form Wizard to create a sales form that includes all of the fields in the Sales table in the *Everything Electronic-Lesson 2* database located in the *Projects* folder. Apply the Columnar layout and the International style. Save the form as **Sales Transactions**. Some of the new employees at Everything Electronic haven't yet memorized all of the product IDs, making it difficult for them to use the form. They find themselves switching back and forth between the Sales Transactions form and the Products table to look up product IDs. To help them out, add a hyperlink next to the Product ID field on the Sales Transactions form that links to the Products table. Include a ScreenTip that contains the text **Click to jump to the Products table**. Test the hyperlink to verify that it opens the Products table.

Also, you've been talking with a representative from Zenith, a manufacturer of electronics, about selling their products. To learn more about Zenith, you decide to add a hyperlink field to the Products table between the ProductCategory and Brand fields that links to Zenith's Web site at **www.zenith.com**. Name the new field **ZenithCompare** and type **Zenith Product Comparison** as the caption. Include a ScreenTip that contains the text **Click to compare with Zenith's products**. Test the hyperlink. Close the Sales Transactions form and the Products table, saving changes when prompted. Then close the *Everything Electronic-Lesson 2* database. Close your browser and disconnect from the Internet unless your instructor tells you to remain connected.

SUMMARY AND EXERCISES

WARNING *Between the time that Web site information is gathered and published, it is not unusual for some sites to have closed or moved. If the Web address provided above is no longer valid, perform a search on the keywords* electronics companies *to locate a comparable site.*

Project in Progress

8 Creating Forms, Queries, and Reports in the *Savvy Solutions* Database

As the owner of Savvy Solutions, you would like to create a form that can be used to enter and edit customer and project data. Open the *Savvy Solutions* database that you created for Lesson 1, Project 9, located in the *Project in Progress* folder in the *Projects* folder. (*Note:* Check with your instructor if you did not complete Lesson 1, Project 9.) Create an AutoForm named **Customers and Projects** based on the Customers table. Then use the new form to add the new customer and projects data shown in Table 2.6.

Table 2.6	Customer and Project Data
Main Form	
Customer ID	(AutoNumber)
Company Name	The Ad Specialists
Contact Last Name	Tucker
Contact First Name	Veronica
Contact Title	Owner
Billing Address	3710 Sherman Ave.
City	Chicago
State	IL
ZIP Code	60677-3811
Phone Number	(312) 555-1093
Subform	
Project ID	(AutoNumber)
Item Developed	Web site
Services Performed	Web page creation
Project Manager	14
Total Hours	120
Fee	$7,200

Table 2.6	Customer and Project Data (continued)

Lock-All Security Systems Subform (customer record 19)

Project ID	(AutoNumber)
Item Developed	brochure
Services Performed	editing
Project Manager	8
Total Hours	24
Fee	$1,440

Create a query that uses all three tables. Include the CompanyName (Customers table), ItemDeveloped (Projects table), ServicesPerformed (Projects table), ProjectManager (Projects table), and LastName (Employees table) fields. In your query, include only brochures, advertisements, and Web sites developed, and sort the query results in ascending order by the item developed. Format the query datasheet attractively and print it on onc page. Save the query as **Brochures, Ads, and Web Sites**. Close the query.

Now you would like to generate a report that summarizes all of the projects completed for each customer. Generate a tabular report using the following fields: CompanyName (Customers table), ItemDeveloped (Projects table), ServicesPerformed (Projects table), ProjectManager (Projects table), TotalHours (Projects table), and Fee (Projects table). Group the records by the company name, sorted alphabetically by the items developed, and sum the hours and fees for each group. Use landscape orientation and a layout and style of your choice. Save the report as **Customer Projects Summary**. Preview and print the report. Close the *Savvy Solutions* database and exit Access.

Overview: **Congratulations!** Now that you have completed the Access lessons in this tutorial, you have the opportunity in this capstone project to apply the Access skills you have learned. You have opened a daycare and want to use a database to track employees, students, and classes. As you create and use the database, try to incorporate the following skills:

- Plan and create a new database.
- Create tables and add data to them.
- Import data from another Office application.
- Assign appropriate data types to fields.
- Determine the primary keys.
- Establish relationships between tables and enforce referential integrity.
- Create input masks.
- Format a datasheet.
- Use subdatasheets to view data.
- Create a multi-table query.
- Create a query that contains calculated fields.
- Create a form.
- Add data to a form.
- Create a report with groups and totals.
- Preview and print a report.

Instructions: Follow these instructions to create and use a database for this case study.

1. **Create a blank database and save it as *Tiny Tots Daycare* in the *Projects* folder in your *Access Data* folder.**

2. **Create a table named Employees. The Employees table must contain the following fields: EmployeeID, LastName, FirstName, SocialSecurityNumber, Position, HourlyRate,**

and FT/PTStatus (full-time or part-time status). Assign appropriate data types, field sizes, captions, and other field properties. Create an input mask for the SocialSecurityNumber field. Designate an appropriate field as the primary key. Then enter the data in Table CS.1 in the Employees table.

Table CS.1	Data for Employees Table					
Employee ID	**Last Name**	**First Name**	**Social Security Number**	**Position**	**Hourly Rate**	**FT/PT Status**
1	Strickley	Betty	111-11-1111	Asst. Teacher	$8.00	FT
2	McVey	Robert	222-22-2222	Asst. Teacher	$8.00	FT
3	Williams	Lorna	333-33-3333	Asst. Teacher	$7.25	PT
4	Delgado	Mario	444-44-4444	Head Teacher	$9.50	FT
5	Huffman	Eric	555-55-5555	Asst. Teacher	$8.00	FT
6	Hughes	Arthur	666-66-6666	Head Teacher	$9.50	FT
7	Dugan	Maria	777-77-7777	Head Teacher	$9.50	FT
8	Renning	Stacey	888-88-8888	Head Teacher	$9.25	FT
9	Iwasaki	Tatsu	999-99-9999	Asst. Teacher	$7.25	PT
10	Milton	Matthew	101-01-0101	Asst. Teacher	$7.75	FT
11	Wolfe	Donna	110-11-0011	Head Teacher	$9.25	FT
12	Levine	Mary	121-21-2121	Asst. Teacher	$7.50	FT
13	Shepherd	Dale	131-31-3131	Head Teacher	$9.25	FT
14	Crofts	Gordon	141-41-4141	Head Teacher	$9.00	FT
15	Gregg	Chris	151-51-5151	Asst. Teacher	$7.25	FT

3. Create a second table named **Classes** that contains the following fields: ClassID, ClassName, RoomNumber, HeadTeacher, AgeRange, Ratio, and WeeklyFee. Once again, assign appropriate data types, field sizes, captions, and other field properties. Designate an appropriate field as the primary key. Then enter the data in Table CS.2 in the Classes table on the following page.

4. Import the Excel worksheet *Daycare Students* (stored in the *Projects* folder in your *Access Data* folder) into a new table named **Students** in your *Tiny Tots Daycare* database. Designate an appropriate field as the primary key. Modify the data types, field sizes, captions, and other field properties, as appropriate. Create input masks for the BirthDate field and the GuardianPhoneNumber field.

NOTE *You must change the Field Size property of the ClassID field to Long Integer in order to establish a relationship between the Classes table and the Students table in the next step. When you save the design changes to the Students table, Access will warn you that some data may be lost because you changed the Field Size property. Click Yes in response to the warning.*

Table CS.2 — Data for Classes Table

Class ID	Class Name	Room Number	Head Teacher	Age Range	Ratio	Weekly Fee
1	Infants	1	13	2 to 18 months	1:4	$165
2	Toddler 1	2	11	19 to 28 months	1:6	$155
3	Toddler 2	5	6	29 to 36 months	1:7	$150
4	Young Threes	7	8	37 to 42 months	1:7	$145
5	Old Threes	8	14	43 to 48 months	1:7	$135
6	Four Year Olds	4	4	49 to 60 months	1:7	$130
7	Five Year Olds	9	7	61 to 72 months	1:7	$125

5. Create a one-to-many relationship between the Employees table and the Classes table by relating the EmployeeID field and the HeadTeacher field; do not enforce referential integrity. Then create a one-to-many relationship between the Classes and Students tables by relating the Class ID fields, and enforce referential integrity.

6. Format the three datasheets as desired to enhance their usefulness and appearance.

7. Open the Classes table and use the subdatasheets to view the names of the students enrolled in each class. How many students are enrolled in the Toddler 2 class? How many students are enrolled in the Five-Year-Olds class?

8. Your supervisor would like to identify the full-time assistant teachers who earn $7.25 per hour and the full-time head teachers who earn $9.25 an hour. Create a query to display a list of employees who meet these criteria. Save the query as **Full-Time Employee Pay Rates**.

9. Two new students have just enrolled in the daycare. Create a columnar form named **Student Information** that includes all of the fields in the Students table. Make sure the student's first name field appears before the last name field and that the guardian's first name field appears before the last name field. Use the form to enter the data shown in Table CS.3.

Table CS.3 — Data for Student Information Form

Student ID	Student Name	Birth Date	Class	Guardian	Guardian Phone	Allergies/ Special Needs
29	Nicholas Carson	09/30/1999	Toddler 2	Angela Carson	(402) 555-4023	Nicholas has a mild case of asthma.
30	Karen Feingold	06/02/2002	Infants	Kenneth Feingold	(402) 555-1902	

10. The daycare is considering implementing a field trip program for some of the older students. Create a query that lists students born between 12/31/95 and 1/1/98, sorted in descending order by class name. For each student, include the student's full name, birth date, class name, room number, and teacher's last name. Save the query as **Students Eligible for Field Trips**.

11. The daycare director is considering increasing the weekly fees by either 2% or 5%. Create a query that calculates a 2% increase and a 5% increase. Include the class ID, class name, current weekly fee, and proposed 2% and 5% increases in the query results. Modify the properties of the calculated fields to reflect appropriate captions and formats. Name the query **Proposed Fee Increases**.

12. The daycare director would like a report that lists all of the student records, grouped by the classes in which the students are enrolled. Generate a report that includes each student's name, birth date, class name, and weekly fee. Group the report by class name, and sort it by student last name. Save the report as **Class Lists**, and preview it.

13. Search the Web for information on early childhood and preschool education. Insert a hyperlink in the Classes table to one of the Web sites you find.

Contents

Graphics Piracy on the Internet

Ignorance is no excuse!

One reason the World Wide Web has become so popular is its support of graphics in Web pages. By adding all sorts of images to HTML documents, Web designers make their sites more attractive and appealing to visitors. Similarly, Internet services such as FTP and newsgroups enable users to find, download, and exchange files of all types quickly, including graphics.

This easy access to images, however, has also created a cottage industry of graphics piracy because some Internet users gather large quantities of images and distribute them online. The primary purpose of hundreds of Web sites and Usenet newsgroups is to provide users with a place to find, exchange—and sometimes even purchase—illegally obtained graphics.

The Internet provides a seemingly limitless number of pirated images, including clip art, electronic photographs, scanned artwork and photographs, video clips, and more. As you might imagine, the subject matter of these images runs the gamut from family-oriented cartoons, to celebrity images, to pornography.

Although a small percentage of these online graphics are homemade (created by the person distributing them), the vast majority is illegally acquired by scanning or copying from digital sources. You can easily find images scanned directly from popular magazines,

clips pirated from videotapes, and still images captured from television shows and movies.

The real problem is that pirates distribute these copyrighted graphics freely, ignoring the rights of the images' actual owners. The most daring pirates scan images from popular magazines, and then attempt to sell them over Web sites, through newsgroups, or on CD-ROM as though this were perfectly legal.

Undoubtedly you will occasionally want to jazz up your PowerPoint presentations with graphic images. Make sure you are handling electronic graphics properly by following these steps:

- **Consider the Source.** If you find images of any kind on a Web site or newsgroup, consider them suspect. If you need electronic images for a document of your own, especially if you want to sell the document, look for sources of license-free images (you do not need to pay a license fee to use them) or be ready to pay a fee for an image from a legitimate source.

- **Get Proof and Permission.** Regardless of where you obtain an image, the distributor should be willing and able to provide proof of ownership of the image and to grant or deny permission to use it, regardless of whether a fee is involved. If you cannot obtain this type of documentation in writing (not over e-mail or on a Web page), then do not use the image in your presentation.

- **Never Upload Images to Newsgroups or the Web.** Whether you illegally scan published images or acquire images from a legitimate source, resist the urge to put them on the Internet. Even if you own an image or have the right to use it commercially, you can assume that once it is on the Internet, it will be copied and distributed in ways you never intended.

- **Know What You Are Doing.** If you get involved in using electronic graphics, become acquainted with copyright laws and the protections in place to safeguard the rights of copyright holders. Ignorance is no excuse!

LESSON 1

PowerPoint Basics

CONTENTS

OBJECTIVES

After you complete this lesson, you will be able to do the following:

▶ Describe the purpose of presentations and presentation software.

▶ Identify the unique features of the PowerPoint window.

▶ Switch among the three PowerPoint views.

▶ Navigate a presentation using PowerPoint's scrolling tools or your keyboard.

▶ Add text to a slide, and edit or delete text in various ways.

▶ Promote and demote titles, subtitles, and bullets.

▶ Check the spelling of a single word or an entire presentation.

▶ Use the Undo, Redo, and Repeat commands.

▶ Use the Find and Replace features to locate and replace text in a presentation.

▶ Use PowerPoint's search tools to find files on your computer or network disks.

▶ Select, move, and delete slides in either Normal View or Slide Sorter View.

▶ Review a presentation in slide show view.

▶ Change the Page Setup options.

▶ Preview and print slides, notes, outlines, and handouts.

▶ Create a new folder.

▶ Save a presentation in a different file format.

▶ Add hyperlinks to another slide within a presentation and to a Web page.

INTRODUCING MICROSOFT POWERPOINT

Microsoft PowerPoint is a powerful presentation program that enables you to create slide show presentations, speaker notes, and audience handouts. A presentation is a series of images, or **slides,** shown on a computer, projector, or paper. Slides are an effective way to present information. Research shows that people retain information better if they see and hear it simultaneously, instead of just reading it. A well-produced presentation has more impact than printed text alone because a presentation communicates through two channels. The audience hears the material as spoken by the presenter and sees the material as it appears on the slides.

PowerPoint in the workplace

Successful companies strive to present a high-quality image of themselves and their products. Businesses either have specialized departments to generate presentations, hire consultants to create presentations for them, or expect employees to use presentation programs to develop presentations. Whatever your career choice, becoming proficient with PowerPoint will increase your potential for success in the workplace.

A **presentation program,** such as PowerPoint, enables you to deliver information with a variety of media elements—and this can keep an audience listening and watching. For example, PowerPoint presentations can include text, bullets, illustrations, charts, photos, shapes, animations, sounds, and even movie clips. As a result, an effective presentation requires fewer words than a text document.

Suppose you work for PermaDry, a company that makes waterproofing products. You are presenting a newly developed wood sealant to a group of retailers who sell hardware and deck-building supplies. You want the retailers to buy your sealant, and then resell it to their customers. A description of the product and key selling points could fill several sheets of paper, but you can effectively convey the information in just three slides, as shown in Figures 1.1, 1.2, and 1.3.

The **title slide,** the first slide in a presentation, introduces the presentation to the audience. Each of the remaining slides focuses on a specific point or topic. Note that these slides all have a consistent appearance; this increases the presentation's effectiveness. If all the elements are uniformly designed, the message is easier to follow and remember. Every slide contains a title; most contain a title and several subtitles. A **title** is the main topic of a slide and usually appears at the top of the slide, like a headline. A **subtitle** is a point that expands on the slide's main topic. In PowerPoint, a subtitle is any text below the title (except text appearing in a chart, picture, or drawing). A slide can also contain one or more bulleted lists, and each bulleted item is considered to be a subtitle also.

PowerPoint is also designed to work hand in hand with the Web, something commonly referred to as **Web support.** For example, you can include hyperlinks in your presentation that you can click to quickly display a Web page. Additionally, you can save a PowerPoint presentation as a set of Web pages so that others can view your slides on the Web. You can use PowerPoint's Web support features to view and manipulate presentations using your Web browser. You can also attach comments to your presentation and send it via a Web-based mail service.

Figure 1.1
Title slide

NORTON ONLINE

Visit **www.glencoe.com/norton/online/** for more information on PowerPoint 2002.

A title slide introduces your presentation to the audience.

$H_2Go!$

Water Repellant for Wood Siding and Decking

Figure 1.2
Expanding on a specific point

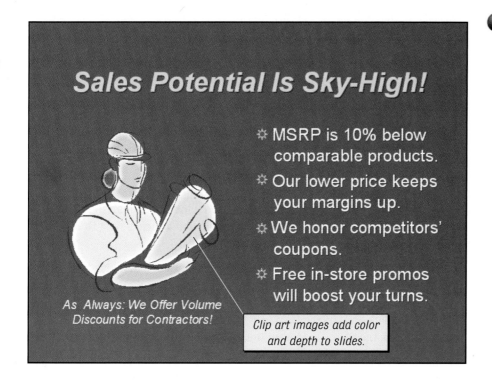

Figure 1.3
Showing a product's sales potential

Now that you have an idea of how you can use PowerPoint, grab your mouse and let's get started learning some of the most essential functions of the program.

Did you know?

You have many options for presenting slide shows directly from a PC, using either a large monitor or a digital light projector. You can even broadcast slide shows over the Internet.

HANDS on

Launching Microsoft PowerPoint

In this activity, you'll start Microsoft PowerPoint.

> **NOTE** *Before you can start Microsoft PowerPoint, both Microsoft PowerPoint and a current version of Windows (such as Windows Me, Windows 98, or Windows 2000) must be installed on the computer you are using. The figures in this tutorial use Windows 2000; if you are using a different version of Windows, the information appearing on your screen may vary slightly.*

1. **Turn on your computer.**

After the booting process is complete, the Windows desktop appears.

2. **Click the Start button** 🏁 Start **on the Windows taskbar, point to Programs, and click Microsoft PowerPoint.**

The PowerPoint program starts and its window appears. Let's confirm that the PowerPoint window is set up to match the figures in this tutorial.

3. **Point to Toolbars on the View menu and verify that check marks appear before *only* these options on the Toolbars submenu: Standard, Formatting, and Task Pane. If check marks appear before only these three options, go on to step 4. If a check mark does not appear next to each of these options, click to select the toolbar. If a check mark appears next to other toolbars, click to clear these toolbars. (You must redisplay the Toolbars submenu each time you select or clear a toolbar on the Toolbars submenu. If necessary, click a blank area of the application window to close the Toolbars submenu and the View menu.)**

4. **Click the View menu. If a check mark does not appear next to Ruler, click a blank area of the application window to close the View menu and go on to step 5. If a check mark appears next to Ruler, click Ruler to clear or hide the ruler.**

5. **Verify that the Standard and Formatting toolbars are displayed as separate rows. If the toolbars are on the same row, click Customize on the Tools menu, click the Options tab if it is not on top, and click Show Standard and Formatting toolbars on two rows. Click the Close button in the Customize dialog box.**

EXPLORING THE UNIQUE FEATURES OF THE POWERPOINT WINDOW

As you already know, the PowerPoint window contains many standard Windows elements, including a title bar, a menu bar, and one or more toolbars. However, the PowerPoint window also contains many items that are unique to the PowerPoint program, as discussed here and illustrated in Figure 1.4.

PowerPoint BASICS

Launching PowerPoint

1. Turn on the computer.

2. Click the Start button and point to Programs.

3. Click Microsoft PowerPoint.

POWERPOINT 2002

Figure 1.4 shows PowerPoint in Normal View, which is the view you will probably use most often. You can switch from one view to another by using the View toolbar at the lower-left corner of the window. (You will practice switching views in a later activity.)

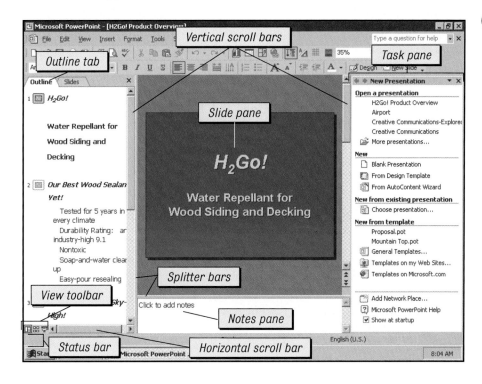

Figure 1.4
Various elements of the PowerPoint window

POWERPOINT 2002

Normal View gives you quick access to the program's essential tools and lets you look at various parts of a presentation at one time. In Normal View, the PowerPoint window is divided into three panes:

◆ Slide pane. This pane displays the slide you are currently editing. You can zoom in or out on the slide in this pane, to make more or less of it visible. You can also display horizontal and vertical rulers that let you size and position objects precisely on the slide. You can work directly on a slide in this pane, typing text, inserting objects, changing colors, and performing many other tasks.

◆ Notes pane. This pane appears directly below the slide pane. You can create a set of notes for each slide in a presentation. You can use these notes as reminders to yourself during a presentation, or print them to give to your audience as handouts. You can enter and edit notes directly in this pane.

◆ Left pane. The left pane includes two tabs: the Outline tab and the Slides tab. The Outline tab displays the text for each slide; you can add and edit text on this tab. The Slides tab displays miniature versions of the slides (called **thumbnails**) and allows you to quickly jump to a different slide or rearrange the slides by dragging them.

If a pane cannot display all of its contents, horizontal and/or vertical scroll bars appear. All three panes can display scroll bars, if needed. You can use a scroll bar to bring hidden portions of the presentation into view.

The slide, notes, and left panes are separated from one another by narrow bars, called **splitter bars.** When all three panes are open, PowerPoint displays horizontal and vertical splitter bars. To resize one of the panes in Normal View, point to

HINTS & TIPS

If the left pane or notes pane gets in your way while you are working in Normal View, you can use a splitter bar to hide it. To hide the left pane, drag the vertical splitter bar to the left until the pane is no longer visible. To hide the notes pane, drag the horizontal splitter bar down until the pane disappears. To see a pane again, drag its splitter bar back.

PowerPoint Basics   **533**

the appropriate splitter bar; when the pointer changes to a double-headed arrow, drag the bar in the desired direction.

Depending on the type of tasks you are performing, a task pane may appear along the right edge of the PowerPoint window. The task pane is a special kind of menu that provides fast access to sets of related commands or features. PowerPoint offers ten different task panes, each designed to help with a specific kind of operation such as creating a new presentation, choosing different types of slides, and others.

A task pane may appear when you choose a certain menu command. (When you click New on the File menu, for example, the New Presentation task pane appears.) You can also open the task pane by clicking Task Pane on the View menu. You can select one of the task panes by clicking the Other Task Panes triangle button. To resize the task pane, point to its left edge; when the pointer changes to a double-headed arrow, drag right or left. To close the task pane, click its Close button ⊠.

NOTE *The figures in this tutorial show the task pane only if it is being used or discussed. If you do not need to use the task pane, close it. You can easily reopen it by clicking Task Pane on the View menu.*

At the bottom of the PowerPoint window, the status bar appears. The status bar contains boxes that display information about the current presentation. The left-hand box tells you which slide you are working on and how many slides the presentation includes, such as *slide 1 of 3*. The status bar's center box displays the name of the design template currently in use. (You'll learn about design templates in a later lesson.) The right-hand box tells you which language is currently selected for PowerPoint's language tools, such as the spelling checker.

NAVIGATING AMONG DIFFERENT POWERPOINT VIEWS

PowerPoint lets you view presentations in various ways to assist with editing and formatting. Using the View toolbar shown in Figure 1.4, you can switch between three viewing options. Table 1.1 describes the views and the best uses for each. Learn to examine your slides in different views as you create them; doing so will give you a more complete picture of your work.

Table 1.1	The View Toolbar

Button	View Name	Action
	Normal View	Displays the slide, notes, and left panes, enabling you to edit various parts of a presentation in a single view. Use Normal View to design your presentation and add text, graphics, and other objects to your slides.
	Slide Sorter View	Displays multiple slides in miniature (thumbnail) format. Use Slide Sorter View to quickly reorganize a presentation by moving, copying, or deleting slides and to preview animations or transition effects.
	Slide Show	Displays each slide in full-screen mode. Use Slide Show View to see your slides as they would appear in a presentation.

HANDS on

Switching Views

In this activity, you will open the *Agenda* presentation, and then use the View toolbar to view the presentation in different ways.

NOTE *To work through the lessons in this tutorial, you must copy the* PowerPoint Data *folder from the Data CD, located on the inside back cover of this tutorial, to your hard drive or network drive. If you haven't copied the* PowerPoint Data *folder, ask your instructor for help.*

1. Click the **Open button** 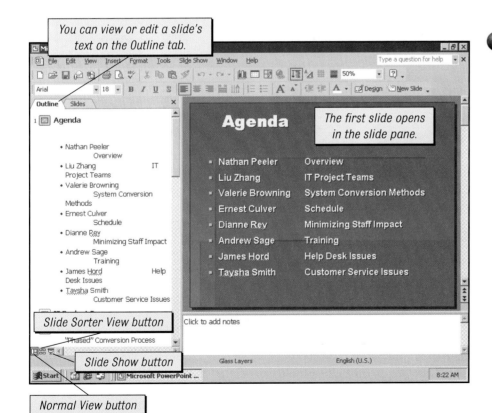 on the Standard toolbar.

2. In the Open dialog box, navigate to your *PowerPoint Data* folder.

3. Click the *Agenda* presentation if it is not already selected, and click **Open**.

NOTE *If you need help navigating to a file, ask your instructor for assistance.*

4. If necessary, click the **Normal View button** on the View toolbar.

PowerPoint switches to Normal View, as shown in Figure 1.5. By default, Normal View limits your view of the current slide, but enables you to see the outline and notes for each slide in your presentation.

PowerPoint BASICS

Switching Views

1. To change to a different view, click a View toolbar button.

2. Adjust pane sizes, if necessary, by dragging the vertical or horizontal splitter bar.

Figure 1.5
Agenda presentation in Normal View

5. **Point to the splitter bar that divides the screen vertically into panes, and notice the two-way arrow that appears. Notice also where the splitter bar aligns with the Formatting toolbar.**

6. **Drag the vertical splitter bar to the left to enlarge the slide pane.**

As you drag the splitter bar, the pane borders move and the panes resize to fill the screen.

7. **Drag the vertical splitter bar back to its original position.**

8. **Point to the splitter bar that divides the screen horizontally into panes, and again notice the two-way arrow that appears. Notice also where the splitter bar aligns with the Outline tab.**

9. **Drag the horizontal splitter bar down to enlarge the slide pane.**

The slide pane enlarges, hiding part of the notes pane.

10. **Drag the horizontal splitter bar back to its original position.**

11. **Click the Slide Sorter View button ▦ on the View toolbar.**

PowerPoint switches to Slide Sorter View, as shown in Figure 1.6. The view's name appears in the status bar, and the Slide Sorter toolbar is displayed above the application window.

You can also switch views by clicking the Normal, Slide Sorter, and Slide Show commands on the View menu.

Figure 1.6
Slide Sorter View

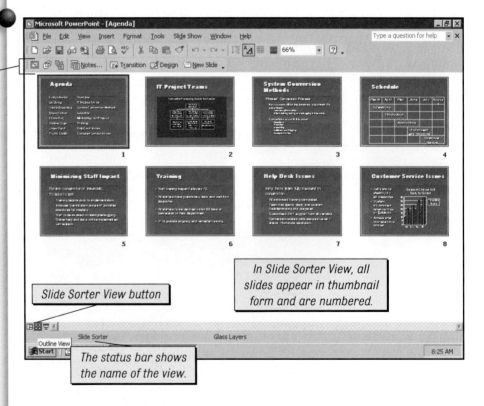

Slide Sorter toolbar

Slide Sorter View button

In Slide Sorter View, all slides appear in thumbnail form and are numbered.

The status bar shows the name of the view.

12. **Click the Slide Show button 🖳 on the View toolbar.**

PowerPoint switches to Slide Show View and only the current slide is displayed. The taskbar and all menus and toolbars are hidden.

13. **Press Esc.**

PowerPoint returns to Slide Sorter View.

14. **Click the Normal View button**  **on the View toolbar.**

PowerPoint returns to Normal View. Because Normal View displays more tools than the other views, you can do most of your work in Normal View. You can enlarge or reduce the size of each pane by moving the splitter bars as needed to perform tasks as you develop a presentation.

NAVIGATING YOUR SLIDE SHOWS

PowerPoint provides several tools that let you navigate slides quickly and easily: scrolling tools, magnification tools, and keyboard shortcuts. (See Figure 1.7 on page 49 for an illustration of the scrolling and magnification tools.)

Scrolling Tools

The scrolling tools consist of scroll bars, scroll boxes, and scroll arrows. Vertical scroll bars let you jump from one slide to another. Horizontal scroll bars allow you to scroll across a pane to see all areas, if necessary. You can also move through a presentation at varying speeds by clicking the scroll arrows at each end of the bar, dragging the scroll box inside the bar, or clicking between the scroll box and a scroll arrow.

In Normal View, if there is more than one slide in the presentation, vertical scroll bars are found on the Outline and Slides tabs and in the slide pane. In Slide Sorter View, if a presentation has too many slides to fit in a single screen, a vertical scroll bar appears at the right edge of the PowerPoint window.

In the left pane of Normal View, you can use the vertical scroll bar to move to a different part of the outline or to a different thumbnail, depending on whether the Outline or Slides tab is visible. In the slide pane of Normal View, the vertical scroll bar provides more options. When you drag the scroll box, for example, a Slide Indicator box displays the slide number and title that will appear if you release the mouse button at that point. The slide pane's vertical scroll bar lets you move to the previous or next slide by clicking the scroll bar, a scroll arrow, or the Previous Slide ⬆ or Next Slide ⬇ button.

Keyboard Shortcuts

If you prefer to keep your hands on the keyboard as much as possible, you can use special keys or key combinations (commonly referred to as keyboard shortcuts) to navigate a presentation. In Normal View, for example, you can press the [PgUp] or [PgDn] key to move through the presentation one slide at a time. To quickly jump to the first slide, press [Ctrl] + [Home]; to jump to the last slide, press [Ctrl] + [End].

In Slide Sorter View, you can use the same keystrokes to navigate a presentation if there are more slides than can fit into the window. You can also use your keyboard's arrow keys to move from one slide to another in Slide Sorter View.

Magnification Tools

Choosing a magnification level for your view goes hand in hand with navigation. Depending on the view you use, the size of the panes, and your display settings, you may want to adjust the zoom level (magnification) so you can see more clearly and edit slides more accurately.

NORTON ONLINE

Visit **www.glencoe.com/norton/online/** for more information on PowerPoint 2002.

POWERPOINT 2002

The Zoom box `100% ▾` controls the magnification levels used in Normal and Slide Sorter Views. In Normal View, each pane can have a different zoom setting. Magnification measurements are in percentages. In the left pane, the magnification options range from 25% to 100% for the Outline and Slides tabs. To adjust the magnification in the left pane, first click a slide button on the Outline tab or click a slide on the Slides tab, click the Zoom box triangle button, and then click a new percentage.

In the slide and notes panes, magnification options range from 25% to 400%. To adjust the magnification in the slide or notes pane, click the pane, click the Zoom box triangle button, and then click a new percentage. The slide pane also provides a Fit option, which fits the entire slide exactly into the slide pane, no matter what the pane size is.

In Slide Sorter View, the Zoom box provides magnification options ranging from 25% to 100%. To adjust the magnification in Slide Sorter View, just click the Zoom box triangle button and click a new percentage.

When you select a low magnification, you zoom out. You will see more of the outline, text, or slide, but the information may be too small to read. When you select a high magnification, you zoom in. You will see only a small portion of the outline, text, or slide.

HANDS on

Scrolling a Presentation

In this activity, you will navigate the Agenda presentation using the scroll bars, keyboard, and zoom levels.

PowerPoint BASICS

Scrolling a Presentation

1. To see a specific slide, click one of the scroll arrows.

2. To jump to the previous or next slide, click the Previous Slide or Next Slide button.

1. In Normal View, adjust the pane sizes, as shown in Figure 1.7.

2. In the left pane, click the **Outline tab**, if it is not on top. Then, click the **down scroll arrow** until you can see the title for slide 8.

3. Click the **slide button** next to the title for slide 8.

Slide 8 appears in the slide pane. Because the size of the slide pane is so small, however, you can see only a small portion of the slide.

4. In the slide pane, drag the vertical scroll box to the top of the scroll bar.

The Slide Indicator box, as shown in Figure 1.7, shows that the *Agenda* slide is the first of eight slides in this presentation. The slide number also appears in the status bar.

5. In the slide pane, click the **down scroll arrow** until the status bar shows that you are viewing slide 2.

6. At the bottom of the vertical scroll bar in the slide pane, click the **Next Slide button** ⬇.

PowerPoint navigates directly to slide 3.

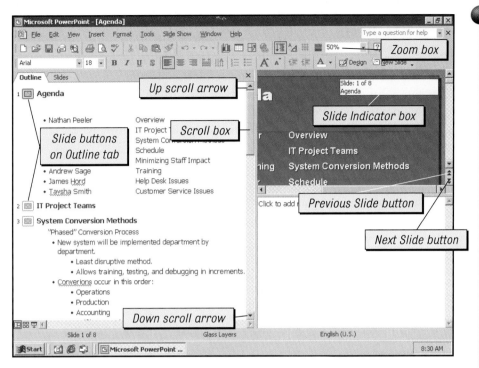

Figure 1.7
Navigation and magnification tools

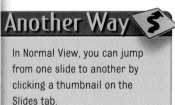

Another Way

In Normal View, you can jump from one slide to another by clicking a thumbnail on the Slides tab.

7. Click the **Zoom box** [100% ▾] triangle button on the Standard toolbar and click **Fit**.

PowerPoint adjusts the magnification so the entire slide appears in the small slide pane.

8. Click the **Previous Slide button** [▲] in the slide pane.

PowerPoint moves back to slide 2.

9. Press [Ctrl] + [End].

PowerPoint jumps to the last slide in the presentation.

10. Press [Ctrl] + [Home].

PowerPoint jumps to the beginning of the presentation.

11. Scroll to slide 2.

12. On the Outline tab, click the **slide button** next to the title for slide 2. Click the **Zoom box** triangle button [100% ▾], and then click **75%**.

The text on the Outline tab becomes larger.

13. Use the scrolling tools on the Outline tab to view the contents while it is at the greater magnification level. Then drag the Outline tab's vertical scroll box to the top of the scroll bar.

14. Click the **Zoom box triangle button** [100% ▾] and click **33%**.

The Outline tab returns to its original magnification level.

15. Enlarge the slide pane by dragging the vertical splitter bar to the left and the horizontal splitter bar down.

WEB NOTE

You can often guess a company's Web site address. Many companies use the format **www.companyname.com** to identify their home pages. What company do you think of when you think of chocolate? Hershey's? Godiva? And what do you think these companies would use as their Web page addresses? If you guessed **www.hersheys.com** and **www.godiva.com**, you guessed right!

ADDING AND EDITING TEXT

When you are creating slides, one of the first things you must do is add text. In a blank slide, adding text is as simple as placing the insertion point and typing. When you point to the text area of a slide or an outline, the pointer changes to the I-beam pointer. If you click when the pointer is shaped like an I-beam, a blinking vertical line, called the **insertion point,** appears, indicating where text will appear when you type.

When you edit slides, sometimes you will need to insert a character, word, or phrase within existing text. You can do this by placing the insertion point and typing new text. As you edit slides, you may want to delete characters, words, or phrases. You can delete text in several ways:

◆ You can place the insertion point directly in front of the characters you want to delete and then press Delete to delete the characters one at a time.

◆ To delete multiple characters, words, or phrases, first select them and then delete them. Dragging across a single letter selects the letter, and dragging over words or phrases selects them. You can select a word by double-clicking it. After you select text, you can press Delete to remove it.

◆ You can also delete text as you type. If you make a mistake while you are typing, press Backspace to delete characters to the left of the insertion point. Then, retype the text.

You can also replace text as you are deleting it. To do this, select one or more characters, words, or phrases, and then start typing the replacement text. PowerPoint overwrites the selected text with the new characters.

HANDS on
Inserting and Editing Text

In this activity, you will insert new text in the *Agenda* presentation, and then edit existing text on the Outline tab and in the slide pane.

1. On the Outline tab, click the up or down scroll arrow until all the text for slide 3 is visible.

2. Click at the end of the bulleted item *Allows training, testing, and debugging in increments.*

The insertion point appears at the end of the bulleted item.

3. Press Enter←.

A new bullet appears at the bottom of the list, ready for you to add text.

4. Type this sentence: Phases may overlap to ensure smooth workflow.

As you type on the Outline tab, notice that the text appears on the slide in the slide pane. Whenever you make changes to the left pane or slide pane, the other pane updates automatically to reflect your changes.

5. On the Outline tab, click the **slide button** for slide 5.

Slide 5 appears in the slide pane.

6. In the slide pane, click before the word *System* in the first sub-title. To select the subtitle, drag the pointer over the sentence *System conversion is traumatic.*

The slide's first subtitle should be selected, as shown in Figure 1.8.

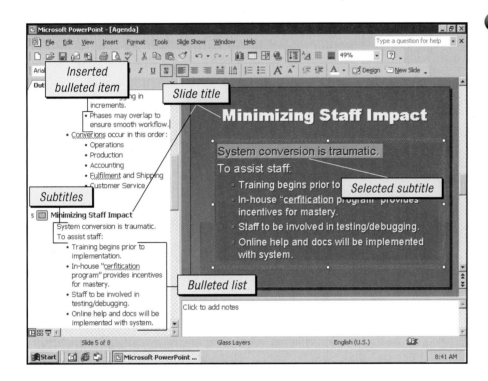

Figure 1.8
Editing text in a slide

7. Type Goal #1 is to preserve revenue. **without pressing** Spacebar **or** Enter↵ .

The new text replaces the selected subtitle.

8. Press Backspace **eight times until the subtitle's period and the word** *revenue* **have been deleted.**

9. Type productivity. **without pressing** Spacebar **or** Enter↵ . **(Be sure to include the period at the end of the subtitle.)**

10. Scroll down to slide 6.

11. In the last bulleted item in the slide pane, place the insertion point immediately before the word *to.*

12. Press Delete **twice to delete the word** *to.* **Then, type** will **to replace the word** *to.*

13. Scroll to slide 1 and select the name *Valerie Browning.*

14. Type your name.

Your name replaces *Valerie Browning.*

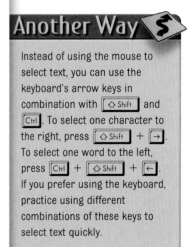

Another Way

Instead of using the mouse to select text, you can use the keyboard's arrow keys in combination with ⇧Shift and Ctrl. To select one character to the right, press ⇧Shift + →. To select one word to the left, press Ctrl + ⇧Shift + ←. If you prefer using the keyboard, practice using different combinations of these keys to select text quickly.

Promoting and Demoting Subtitles and Bullets

Each subtitle has an **indent level**—a number that describes the position of the subtitle in relation to the title. A level 1 subtitle conveys a more important point than a level 2 subtitle; therefore, the level 1 subtitle has larger text and a larger bullet than a level 2 subtitle.

You can assign a different indent level to any subtitle. When you move a subtitle to the next higher indent level, you **promote** it: A level 2 subtitle becomes a level 1, and so on. You **demote** a subtitle when you move it to the next lower indent level: A level 1 subtitle becomes a level 2, and so on.

Just as subtitles have indent levels, each bullet in a bulleted list is also assigned a level, a number that describes the position of the bullet. You can promote and demote bullets in the same way that you promote and demote subtitles.

HANDS on

Changing the Indent Level of a Subtitle

In this activity, you will promote and demote subtitles on the Outline tab and in the slide pane of the *Agenda* presentation.

> **PowerPoint BASICS**
>
> **Promoting and Demoting Subtitles**
>
> 1. Select the subtitle to promote or demote.
> 2. Click the Decrease Indent or Increase Indent button.

1. Display the text for slide 7 on the Outline tab.

Slide 7 has a title *(Help Desk Issues)*, one level 1 subtitle *(Help Desk team fully involved in conversion)*, and a bulleted list.

2. On the Outline tab, select the level 1 subtitle.

3. On the Formatting toolbar, click the Decrease Indent button ⊞.

As shown in Figure 1.9, the level 1 subtitle is promoted to a title and the number of slides increases to nine.

4. With the text still selected, click the Increase Indent button ⊞ once.

The selected title is demoted back to a level 1 subtitle, and the text is added back to slide 7.

5. Press Ctrl + Home.

This keyboard shortcut takes you to the beginning of the first slide in the presentation. At this point, it is a good idea to save the presentation just in case something goes wrong; for example, your computer malfunctions, lightning strikes, or the electricity suddenly goes out.

6. Click Save As on the File menu.

PowerPoint displays the Save As dialog box. This allows you to specify a file name, location, and file format.

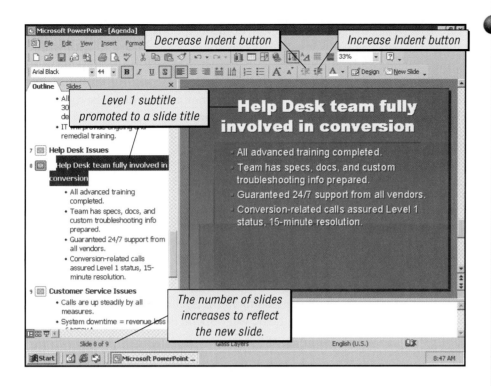

Figure 1.9
Promoting a subtitle to a title

POWERPOINT 2002

7. Type Agenda Revised in the File name box.

After naming the file, you must tell PowerPoint where you want to store the file. You will save this file in the *Tutorial* folder in your *PowerPoint Data* folder.

8. Navigate to the *Tutorial* folder and click twice to open it.

9. Verify that the *Save as type* box is set to Presentation (the default).

10. Click the **Save button** in the lower-right corner of the Save As dialog box.

PowerPoint saves your file in the designated folder and displays the new file name in the title bar and on the taskbar button. (Depending on your computer settings, PowerPoint may automatically add an extension of *.ppt* to the end of your file name. This extension identifies the file as a PowerPoint file.) Your open file remains in the window.

> **WARNING** *You should save your files often—especially after making any changes. As a rule, you should save your work at least once every five minutes, or even more frequently if you make numerous changes to a file. Even if you have saved a file, changes you haven't saved will be lost if your computer malfunctions or a power outage occurs.*

Checking Spelling in a Presentation

An effective presentation not only presents information in the best possible way, but also is error-free. Always carefully proofread your slides just as you would any other document, such as a letter or report. PowerPoint flags potential spelling errors by placing a red, wavy line under questionably spelled words, indicating that these questionable words do not match any of the words in PowerPoint's spelling dictionary.

Always use short sentences or sentence fragments in your slides for better readability. As a rule of thumb, slide titles should never contain more than four or five words. (One- to three-word titles are best.) Subtitles should never be more than two full lines in length, and bulleted items should never be more than 1–1.5 lines long.

If you right-click a flagged word, a shortcut menu appears that may provide a list of suggested replacement words, but always contains the Ignore All and Add to Dictionary commands. You can eliminate the wavy lines by correcting the word or by telling PowerPoint to ignore the word. PowerPoint also allows you to add words to the dictionary. (However, you should not add words to the dictionary unless you own the computer or you have your instructor's permission.) You can also spell-check an entire presentation without looking for red, wavy lines by clicking the Spelling and Grammar button on the Standard toolbar.

HANDS on
Checking Spelling

In this activity, you will check the spelling in the *Agenda Revised* presentation, starting with the name *Rey* on slide 1. You will work on the Outline tab, although you can check spelling in the slide pane as well.

Checking Spelling

To check spelling as you type:

1. Right-click words that have a red, wavy underline.

2. Click an option to correct the error or to ignore the word.

To check spelling in an entire presentation:

1. Click the Spelling and Grammar button on the Standard toolbar.

2. Click an option to correct the error or to ignore the word.

1. **On slide 1 on the Outline tab, right-click the name *Rey* to see various spelling options.**

NOTE *If* Rey *does not have a red, wavy underline on your screen, the Spelling feature may not be active. To turn on the Spelling feature, click Options on the Tools menu. Then, on the Spelling and Style tab of the Options dialog box, click to select the* Check spelling as you type *check box. If the* Hide all spelling errors *check box contains a check mark, click to clear the check box. Then, click OK to close the Options dialog box.*

The shortcut menu suggests five words to replace *Rey* along with the Ignore All and Add to Dictionary commands. In this case, however, *R-e-y* is the correct spelling of Dianne's last name.

2. **On the shortcut menu, click Ignore All.**

By selecting Ignore All, you erase the flag from this word and any other occurrences of *Rey* in the entire presentation.

3. **Right-click the name *Hord.* Because this name should be spelled *Horde,* click the appropriate suggested word in the shortcut menu.**

The name changes to *Horde,* and the red, wavy underline disappears.

4. **If any other name on slide 1 is flagged, right-click it and click Ignore All.**

Now let's use the Spelling and Grammar dialog box to check the spelling throughout the entire presentation.

5. **On the Standard toolbar, click the Spelling and Grammar button.**

You can spell-check a presentation by pressing [F7].

PowerPoint immediately jumps to and selects the next potential spelling error on the Outline tab: *Converions.* The Spelling and Grammar dialog box appears, as shown in Figure 1.10. The misspelled word *Converions* appears in the *Not in Dictionary* box. The *Change to* box and the *Suggestions* list box show the proper spelling, *Conversions.* If other suggested spellings were to appear in the *Suggestions* list box, you could select an appropriate one.

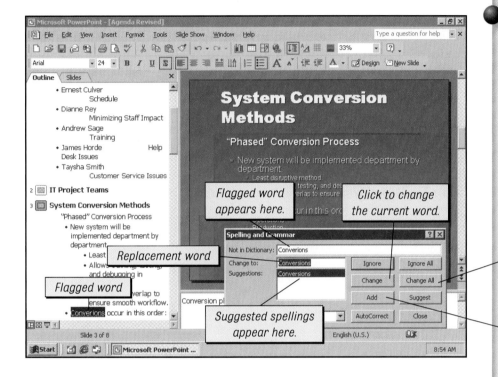

Figure 1.10
Spelling and Grammar dialog box

6. In the Spelling and Grammar dialog box, click **Change**.

PowerPoint replaces the misspelled word with the correct spelling, and then goes to the next questionable word, *Fulfilment.*

7. In the Suggestions list box of the Spelling and Grammar dialog box, select *Fulfillments,* and then click **Change All**.

PowerPoint makes this change throughout the entire presentation and proceeds to the next questionable word.

8. Review the remaining flagged words in the *Agenda Revised* presentation. If the appropriate correction for each flagged instance appears in the Suggestions list box, select the correction and then click **Change**. On slide 5, change *cerfitication* to *certification.* On slide 6, change *worklfow* to *workflow.* On slide 2, change *Tye* to *Dye*; change *Merla* to *Marla*; ignore *Trane*; ignore *Zhung*; and ignore *Viv.* On slide 7, ignore *CyTech.*

PowerPoint announces that the spelling check is complete.

9. Click **OK**, and click the **Save button** 📇 on the Standard toolbar.

Having trouble finding just the right word? Get help on the Web. You can find an online version of the classic *Roget's Thesaurus* at **www.thesaurus.com**; find the Merriam-Webster dictionary, thesaurus, and other reference materials at **www.dictionary.com**.

HANDS on

Editing Text With the Undo, Redo, and Repeat Commands

As you add or delete text or change a presentation in any other way, you may be indecisive about a particular word choice, the position of a chart, or whether a deleted slide should be returned to the sequence. These moments of indecision call for the Undo button ⟲▾ and the Redo button ⟳▾. As the name implies, the Undo button reverses mouse and keyboard actions. (The Undo button's ScreenTip changes to Can't Undo if you cannot reverse the last action.) The Redo button reverses the result of an Undo command. For example, after you select and delete a slide, you can restore the slide by clicking the Undo button. However, after restoring, you can click the Redo button to delete the slide again. (The ScreenTip changes to Can't Redo if you cannot reverse the previous undone action.) The Repeat command is another important timesaving editing tool; it repeats your last action in a single step. In this activity, you will select and delete text and use the Undo, Redo, and Repeat commands in the *Agenda Revised* presentation.

1. On the Outline tab, scroll to slide 5.

2. In the second level 1 subtitle, double-click the word *staff* and type workers.

3. Point to the bullet in front of *Staff to be involved in testing/debugging*.

The pointer changes to a four-way arrow.

4. Click the bullet to select the line and then press ⌦Delete.

PowerPoint deletes the bulleted item.

5. On the Standard toolbar, click the **Undo triangle button** ⟲▾ and move the pointer down to highlight the top two actions (*Clear* and *Typing*), as shown in Figure 1.11. Then, click to undo your last two actions.

PowerPoint restores the deleted bulleted item and changes the word *workers* back to *staff.*

6. On the Standard toolbar, click the **Redo button** ⟳▾ twice.

The word *staff* changes back to *workers,* and the bulleted item is deleted again.

7. On the Outline tab, scroll up until the title for slide 2 is visible. Click at the beginning of the slide 2 title (*IT Project Teams*) to place the insertion point before the first word.

8. Type Initial and press ⎵Spacebar to change the slide's title to *Initial IT Project Teams.*

9. Scroll down, if necessary, until the title for slide 4 is visible.

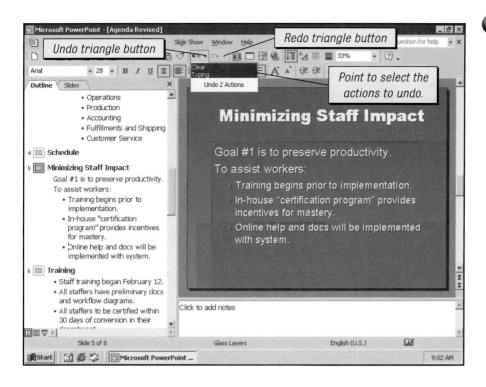

Figure 1.11
Undoing the last two actions

10. Click at the beginning of the slide 4 title (*Schedule*). Click **Repeat Typing** on the Edit menu.

PowerPoint repeats your last action, which was to type the word *Initial* and a blank space. The title of slide 4 is now *Initial Schedule*.

11. As you watch the Outline tab, click the **Undo button** 🔄 twice.

The word *Initial* and the extra space are removed from the titles of slides 2 and 4.

12. Save your work.

HANDS on

Using Find and Replace

Even if a presentation is not very long, it can be difficult to find every occurrence of a word or phrase. For example, suppose that throughout a presentation you have incorrectly used the word *demolish* instead of the word *repair*. You need to change every instance of *demolish*. The Find and Replace features handle this task quickly and accurately. In this activity, you will find each occurrence of the informal abbreviation *docs* (whether capitalized or not) and decide whether to replace it with the complete word, *documentation*. Because the *Agenda Revised* presentation contains an organization chart and a table that do not appear on the Outline tab, you will complete this activity in the slide pane.

1. On the Outline tab, press Ctrl + Home. Enlarge the slide pane. In the slide pane, click directly in front of the slide 1 title (*Agenda*) to place the insertion point there. Click **Replace** on the Edit menu.

2. Type docs in the *Find what* box of the Replace dialog box. In the *Replace with* box, type documentation, as shown in Figure 1.12.

Another Way

- To undo your most recent action, press Ctrl + Z.

- To redo the last undone action, press Ctrl + Y.

- To repeat your most recent action, press F4.

Another Way

To find text without replacing it, click Find on the Edit menu. In the Find dialog box, type the text in the *Find what* box and click Find Next. Keep clicking Find Next until you reach the occurrence you are looking for. If you decide to replace the text, click Replace. The Replace dialog box appears to provide text-replacement tools.

Figure 1.12

Replace dialog box

Start at the beginning of the first slide.

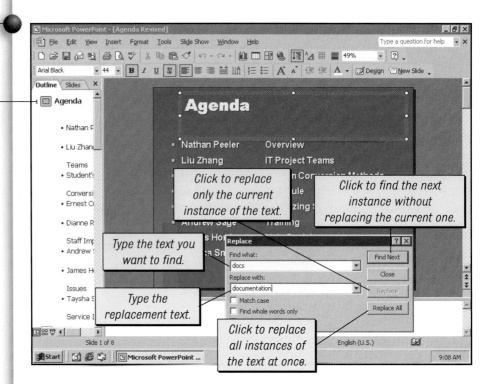

3. Click **Find Next** in the Replace dialog box.

PowerPoint finds the first instance of the word in the organization chart on slide 2. Replacing the abbreviation with the longer word will force the chart's boxes to resize; so it's best not to replace it in this instance.

> **NOTE** *You may need to drag the Replace dialog box out of the way to uncover text on the slide pane.*

4. Click **Find Next** in the Replace dialog box.

Without replacing the first occurrence of *docs,* PowerPoint looks for the next instance of the word. The word *docs* appears again on slide 5.

5. Click **Replace** in the Replace dialog box.

PowerPoint replaces *docs* with *documentation* on slide 5, and then jumps immediately to the next instance of the word on slide 6.

6. Click **Replace** in the Replace dialog box.

PowerPoint again replaces *docs* with *documentation* on slide 6 and jumps to the next instance of *docs* in the presentation.

7. Replace each instance of the abbreviation *docs* in the remainder of the presentation.

PowerPoint displays a message when the operation is finished.

8. Click **OK** to close the message box, click **Close** to close the Replace dialog box, and save your work. Click **Close** on the File menu to close the file.

Using Find and Replace

1. Click in front of the title of a slide.

2. Click Replace on the Edit menu.

3. Specify the text you want to find and the text to replace it with.

4. Click Find Next.

5. When PowerPoint finds an occurrence of the text, do one of the following:

• Click Replace to replace the text and find the next occurrence.

• Click Find Next to find the next occurrence without replacing the current one.

• Click Replace All to replace all occurrences of the text.

Finding Files With PowerPoint's Search Tools

In this activity, you will search Microsoft PowerPoint Help to learn how to find files on your computer or network disks. Then you will use the Help information to locate a file on a disk.

1. **Click the Ask a Question box, type** find a file, **and press** Enter↵**. In the list of Help topics, click** *Find a file*. **Then, read the Help information that appears.**

2. **Click the Search button 📇 on the Standard toolbar.**

The Basic Search task pane appears. This task pane provides tools that enable you to search for a file if you forget its name or where it is stored. Suppose you want to locate a presentation that contains a reference to a dam.

3. **In the** *Search text* **box, type** dam.

4. **Click the Search in triangle button, and then click the My Computer option, if necessary, so that a check mark appears next to it. If a check mark appears next to any of the other options, click to clear the check mark. Click outside the drop-down list to close it.**

5. **Click the Results should be triangle button, and then click the PowerPoint Files option, if necessary, so that a check mark appears next to it. Make sure that none of the other options has a check mark. Click outside the drop-down list to close it.**

6. **Click Search.**

The Search Results task pane displays a list of files that contain the search word *dam*. As it turns out, the files are located in your *PowerPoint Data* folder.

7. **Point to the file named** *Rainfall,* **click the triangle button, and click Edit with Microsoft PowerPoint.**

The presentation opens in the PowerPoint window, as shown in Figure 1.13.

8. **Review the presentation. Close the task pane by clicking its Close button ✕, and close the presentation without making any changes to it. Close the Help window.**

Figure 1.13
Results of a file search

SELECTING, MOVING, AND DELETING SLIDES

You can move slides in several ways. The two most common methods for moving slides are the drag-and-drop method and the cut-and-paste method. Both methods work in Normal View and in Slide Sorter View, and both require you to select a slide before moving it. To select a slide in Normal View, click its button on the Outline tab or click its slide miniature on the Slides tab. To select a slide in Slide Sorter View, click the slide. On the Outline tab, a selected slide's button and all of its text is highlighted; on the Slides tab and in Slide Sorter View, a border surrounds a selected slide.

You can use other methods to select slides. In Slide Sorter View and on the Slides tab, for example, you can select a slide by pressing an arrow key until you reach the slide you want or by clicking the slide. In the slide pane of Normal View, you can drag the scroll box until the Slide Indicator box shows the slide you want, and then release the mouse button. You can also select multiple slides at the same time: You can select multiple adjacent slides by selecting the first slide with the mouse, and then pressing and holding down ⇧ Shift as you select the last slide. You can select multiple nonadjacent slides by pressing and holding down Ctrl as you select the slides with the mouse.

To move a slide by *cutting and pasting,* select the slide in Slide Sorter View or on the Outline tab or Slides tab and click the Cut button ✂ on the Standard toolbar. This stores the slide on the Office Clipboard. After placing the insertion point in the slide's new position, you can insert the slide back into the presentation or into a different presentation by clicking the Paste button 📋 on the Standard toolbar.

To move a slide by *dragging and dropping,* select the slide in Slide Sorter View or on the Outline tab or Slides tab, and then click it and hold the mouse button. While holding the mouse button, move the pointer to the slide's new location. The slide is "dragged" along with the pointer. When the pointer reaches the slide's new location, release the mouse button to "drop" the slide. When you drag a slide, the pointer displays a small box icon and PowerPoint displays a thin line that shows you where the slide will be dropped.

You can delete a selected slide by pressing Delete. Note that deleting is not the same as cutting. When you cut a slide by clicking the Cut button ✂, the slide is just moved to the Office Clipboard for relocation later; but when you delete a slide by pressing Delete, the slide is removed from the presentation.

HANDS on

Rearranging and Removing Slides

In this activity, you will change the order of slides and delete two slides in the *Agenda Revised* presentation.

1. Open *Agenda Revised* in your *Tutorial* folder. Resize the panes to enlarge the Outline tab, as shown in Figure 1.14. Click the slide pane, click the **Zoom box triangle button** 100% ▾, and click **Fit** to make sure that the slide fits in the resized slide pane. Then, return to the Outline tab and click the slide 5 button.

As shown on the Outline tab of Figure 1.14, the slide button and text are highlighted. Slide 5 appears in the slide pane.

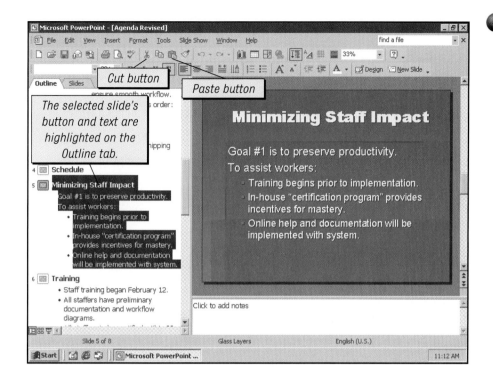

Figure 1.14
Selecting a slide on the Outline tab

POWERPOINT 2002

2. On the Standard toolbar, click the Cut button 📋.

The original slide 5 disappears from the screen, and PowerPoint automatically renumbers all the remaining slides in the presentation. The original slide 6 (*Training*) becomes the new slide 5.

3. Scroll to the bottom of the Outline tab, and click after the text for the last slide.

4. On the Standard toolbar, click the Paste button 📋.

The cut slide reappears at the end of the presentation, and now becomes slide 8.

5. Click the Slides tab.

A black border appears around the selected slide, and slide 8 appears in the slide pane.

6. Click the slide 8 miniature again, hold the mouse button, and slowly drag upward.

As you drag, the pointer displays a small box icon indicating that you are dragging the slide. As you move upward, a horizontal line appears between the slide miniatures, showing where the selected slide will be dropped if you release the mouse button.

7. Drop the selected slide between slides 4 and 5.

The selected slide becomes slide 5 once more. PowerPoint again automatically renumbers the slides that follow slide 5.

PowerPoint **BASICS**

Moving and Deleting a Slide
To cut and paste:

1. Select the slide and click the Cut button on the Standard toolbar.

2. Click the new location and click the Paste button on the Standard toolbar.

To drag and drop:

1. Select the slide.

2. Drag and drop the slide into the new location.

To delete a slide:

1. Select the slide.

2. Press `Delete`.

NORTON ONLINE

Visit **www.glencoe.com/norton/online/** for more information on PowerPoint 2002.

POWERPOINT 2002

8. On the View toolbar, click the **Slide Sorter View button** ⊞.

PowerPoint switches to Slide Sorter View with your slides arranged in rows across the screen. Notice that slide 5 is still selected.

9. Click slide 2 to select it, and then drag it around the screen without dropping it.

The pointer again displays an icon, indicating that you are dragging an object. As you move around, a vertical line appears between the slide miniatures, showing where the selected slide will be dropped if you release the mouse button.

10. Drop the selected slide between slides 3 and 4.

The moved slide now becomes slide 3; PowerPoint renumbers the former slide 3 as slide 2.

11. Select slide 4. Press and hold [△ Shift] while you select slide 8, and then release both [△ Shift] and the mouse.

Slides 4, 5, 6, 7, and 8 are all selected.

12. Press [←].

Now only slide 3 is selected; the black border has disappeared from slides 4 through 8.

13. Select slide 2. Press and hold [Ctrl] while you select slide 4, and then release both [Ctrl] and the mouse.

Slides 2 and 4 are both selected, as shown in Figure 1.15.

Figure 1.15

Selecting multiple slides in Slide Sorter View

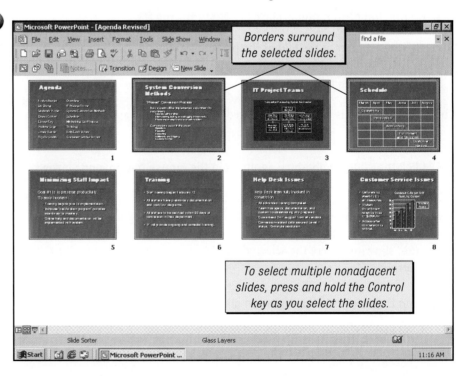

14. Press Delete.

Both of the selected slides are deleted from the presentation.

15. Save your work.

REVIEWING PRESENTATIONS IN SLIDE SHOW VIEW

Whenever you develop a presentation, you will want to make sure that your slides work together to create an effective presentation to convey the right message to your audience. One way to judge the effectiveness of a slide show is to preview it—that is, view the slides on screen just as they would appear to your audience. PowerPoint's Slide Show View lets you preview your presentation from beginning to end, allowing you to look for missing or overlapping information and to verify the readability of each slide. Previewing is the best way to make sure your slides are complete, correctly worded, consistent in appearance and tone, and visually appealing.

In Slide Show View, you can navigate your slides in three ways. You can click the mouse button once to move to the next slide; you can right-click and use the shortcut menu to select navigation options; or you can use the Slide Navigator dialog box, which lets you quickly jump to any slide. You can also use the keyboard to navigate a slide show. For example, you can press Spacebar or PgDn to advance to the next slide, or press Backspace or PgUp to return to the previous slide.

Using Slide Show View

In this activity, you will review the *Agenda Revised* presentation in Slide Show View.

1. While in Slide Sorter View, click slide 1.

2. On the View toolbar, click the Slide Show button 🖵.

The presentation's first slide fills the screen.

3. Click anywhere on the screen to move to the next slide.

Slide 2 appears on the screen.

4. Press Spacebar.

Slide 3 appears on the screen.

5. Press Backspace.

Slide 2 reappears.

6. Right-click the screen to display the shortcut menu, and click Previous, as shown in Figure 1.16, to return to slide 1.

PowerPoint **BASICS**

Previewing a Slide Show

1. Click slide 1 to start from the beginning.

2. Click the Slide Show button on the View toolbar.

3. Click the screen to advance to the next slide.

4. To exit a show, right-click the last slide and click End Show on the shortcut menu.

Or

When the *End of slide show, click to exit* message appears, click to exit the show.

Figure 1.16
Shortcut menu

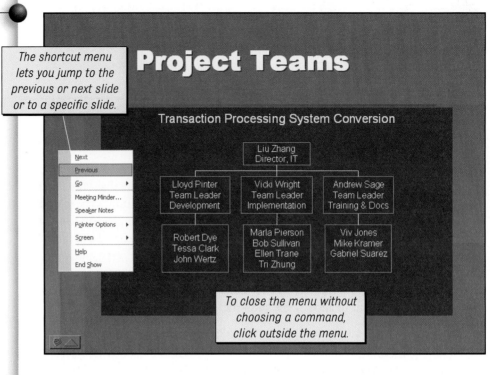

The shortcut menu lets you jump to the previous or next slide or to a specific slide.

To close the menu without choosing a command, click outside the menu.

7. Click the screen five more times, pausing briefly to view each slide.

8. Click the screen one more time.

The *End of slide show, click to exit* message appears on the screen.

9. Click once more to end the slide show preview.

PowerPoint returns to Slide Sorter View.

> **NOTE** *If your presentation did not end in a black screen (the* End of slide show *screen), click Options on the Tools menu. On the View tab of the Options dialog box, click to select the* End with black slide *box. Click OK to close the Options dialog box.*

10. With slide 1 selected, click the **Slide Show button** 🖳 again.

11. Right-click, point to **Go**, and then click **Slide Navigator**.

The Slide Navigator dialog box lists each slide in the presentation by number and slide title.

12. In the Slide Navigator dialog box, double-click **Help Desk Issues**.

Slide 5 appears.

13. Right-click, and click **End Show**.

PowerPoint returns to Slide Sorter View.

When your slides are just the way you want them, preview them repeatedly and practice your speech as the slides appear on the screen. Time yourself to determine how long each slide should be visible. This can help you determine whether you have too many or too few slides for the discussion.

PREVIEWING AND PRINTING PRESENTATION COMPONENTS

Now that you know your way around in a PowerPoint presentation, you're ready to learn more PowerPoint fundamentals—such as previewing and printing a presentation. You'll need printouts for many reasons: to submit assignments to your instructor; to deliver a written report to your boss; to distribute handouts to an audience before, during, or after a presentation; or to mail information to a client. At times, therefore, you may want to print some or all of the components in a presentation. These components can include one or more of the slides, your presentation notes, or the presentation's outline. You can print these components individually. You can also create handouts of your presentation by printing one or more slides on a page.

Before you print any handouts or individual components from your presentation, get into the habit of looking at the presentation on-screen first. A **print preview** provides an accurate on-screen image of your printout. Regularly previewing your presentations before you print can save valuable time and paper because you can correct mistakes before you generate a hard copy. To use the Print Preview feature, click the Print Preview button 🔍 on the Standard toolbar (or click Print Preview on the File menu). After you look at the presentation, you can either make changes to the presentation's layout, close the Print Preview window and make additional changes to your file, or send the information to the printer by clicking the Print button 🖨 Print... on the Print Preview toolbar. This toolbar's buttons let you navigate from page to page as you preview your print jobs, select which part of the presentation you want to print, and set a variety of printing options.

If the information in your presentation is accurate, but you want to change the presentation's layout before you print the presentation, you can do so in the Page Setup dialog box. To access the Page Setup dialog box, click Page Setup on the File menu. The Page Setup dialog box contains six options which change various aspects of your printed presentation. For example, you can use the orientation options to change the way the components are printed on the page, or you can print a component on various sizes of paper.

Orientation refers to whether you print a component vertically or horizontally on the page. PowerPoint's default way of arranging slides on a printed page is called **landscape orientation** (information is horizontally oriented, or printed across the long edge of the paper). In **portrait orientation,** information is vertically oriented, or printed across the short edge of the paper. You can print slides using one orientation and other components using the other orientation, if you like. If you are printing slides as overhead transparencies, open the Page Setup dialog box again, click the *Slides sized for* triangle button, click Overhead, and then click OK to save your settings.

When you're satisfied that your presentation is arranged properly for printing, you're ready to print. When you click the Print button 🖨 on the Standard toolbar, PowerPoint prints one copy of each slide in the default **Grayscale** mode. PowerPoint adjusts the color scheme and uses different shades of gray to suggest contrasting colors. When you click Print on the File menu, the Print dialog box appears. The

HINTS & TIPS

- To see your slides in Grayscale mode without using the Print Preview feature, click the Color/Grayscale button on the Standard toolbar; then click Grayscale.

- To see your slides in Pure Black and White mode without using the Print Preview feature, click the Color/Grayscale button on the Standard toolbar; then click Pure Black and White.

Print dialog box offers several printing options, including a more efficient mode called **Pure Black and White.** Pure Black and White mode saves printer memory and time by ignoring colors, printing all slides in black and white only.

> **NOTE** *If you have a color printer and use Windows 2000, PowerPoint will print your slides in color by default. You can use PowerPoint's Print dialog box to print individual print jobs in Grayscale mode, or you can use the settings in Windows' Control Panel to set your printer to print in Grayscale mode by default.*

In the Print dialog box, you can choose to print only the current slide (the slide holding the insertion point), the currently selected slides, several slides, or all slides. To print a few slides of a presentation, type slide numbers with a hyphen or comma between two numbers to tell PowerPoint which slides to print. For example, typing 1,3,5-8 would result in printing slides 1, 3, and 5 through 8. Whenever you print parts of a slide show, be sure to check the setting for the number of copies to be printed. You can control this setting in the *Number of copies* box in the Print dialog box.

HANDS on

Changing Page Setup Options, Previewing, and Printing

In this activity, you will modify the page setup options, use the Print Preview feature to check the appearance of the components, and print various components in the *Agenda Revised* presentation.

1. With slide 1 selected in Slide Sorter View, click Page Setup on the File menu.

The Page Setup dialog box opens.

2. In the *Slides sized for* box, verify that Letter Paper is selected. In the *Orientation* area, verify that *Slides* is set to the Landscape option and that *Notes, handouts & outline* is set to the Portrait option. Then, click OK.

3. On the Standard toolbar, click the Print Preview button [icon].

PowerPoint switches to Print Preview mode. A grayscale version of the first slide appears on the screen, and the Print Preview toolbar appears.

> **NOTE** *If presentation components are too small to read in Print Preview mode, you can select a higher magnification level by clicking the Zoom box triangle button and clicking a higher number. The image should then appear larger on your screen.*

4. Press [PgDn] to advance through the slides, pausing to review each one. When you are finished, press [Ctrl] + [Home] to return to the beginning of the presentation.

5. Click the **Close Preview button**  on the Print Preview toolbar.

PowerPoint returns to Slide Sorter View with slide 1 selected.

6. Click **Print** on the File menu.

The Print dialog box opens, as shown in Figure 1.17. Note the print options available and the default print settings that PowerPoint has preselected.

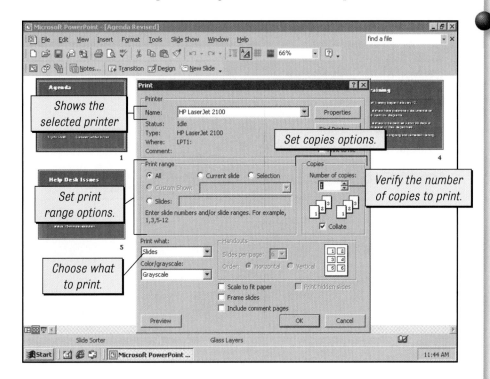

Figure 1.17
Print dialog box

7. In the *Print range* area of the Print dialog box, click the **Current slide option**. In the *Copies* area, verify that the *Number of copies* is set to **1**. In the *Print what* area, verify that **Slides** is selected. Under Color/grayscale, verify that **Grayscale** is selected. Then, click **OK**.

PowerPoint will print the slide you selected. While you wait for that slide to print, let's send slides 3 and 6 to the printer.

8. Click **Print** on the File menu. In the *Print range* area of the Print dialog box, click the **Slides option** and type 3,6 in the text box (with no space after the comma). Verify that the *Number of copies* is set to **1** and that *Print* what is set to **Slides**. Click the **Color/grayscale triangle button**, and click **Pure Black and White**. Then, click **OK** to print one copy of slides 3 and 6.

PowerPoint will print slides 3 and 6 in black and white.

9. Click **Print** on the File menu. In the *Print range* area of the Print dialog box, click the **All option**, if it's not already selected. Verify that the *Number of copies* is set to **1** and that *Print what* is set to **Slides**. Click the **Color/grayscale triangle button**, and click **Grayscale**. Then, click **OK** to print the entire presentation.

HINTS & TIPS

If you have Internet access and an e-mail account, you can send a presentation to someone else. First, connect to the Internet. With the presentation open in PowerPoint, click Send To on the File menu and click mail Recipient (as Attachment). Your e-mail program will open a new message window, and the presentation file will be attached to the message. Address and send the message as usual.

Working With Printouts

To print all slides in grayscale (one copy):

In Normal or Slide Sorter View, click the Print button to print an entire presentation in grayscale.

To print other presentation components:

1. Click Print on the File menu or click Print on the Print Preview toolbar.

2. In the Print dialog box, verify the printing options.

3. Click OK.

PowerPoint will print all the slides.

10. Click the **Print Preview button** 📷 on the Standard toolbar.

11. On the Print Preview toolbar, click the **Print What triangle button** and click **Notes Pages**.

The preview window changes to show the first notes page of the presentation. The top half of the notes page contains a miniature slide, and the bottom half contains any notes that appeared in the notes pane for that slide. (Notice that there are no notes on this slide.)

12. Click the **Next Page button** 📷 on the Print Preview toolbar until you advance to page 4.

13. Click the **Zoom box triangle button**, and click **66%** to resize the notes pages as shown in Figure 1.18.

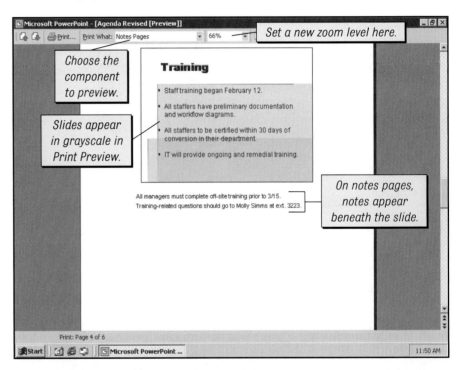

Figure 1.18
Notes page in Print Preview mode

14. Advance through the notes pages by clicking the **Next Page button** 📷. Then, click the **Previous Page button** 📷 until you return to the beginning of the presentation.

15. Click **Print** on the Print Preview toolbar. In the *Print range* area of the Print dialog box, verify that **All** is selected. In the *Copies* area, verify that the *Number of copies* is set to **1**. In the *Print What* box, verify that **Notes Pages** is selected. Finally, verify that **Grayscale** is selected in the Color/grayscale box. Then, click **OK**.

Notice that on some of the printed pages, the notes section is blank because some slides have no notes.

16. On the Print Preview toolbar, click the **Print What triangle button**, and click **Outline View**.

The contents from the Outline tab now appear in the Print Preview window.

17. Click the **Print button**  on the Print Preview toolbar. In the *Print range* area of the Print dialog box, verify that **All** is selected. In the *Print what* area, verify that **Outline View** is selected. Click the **Color/grayscale triangle button** and click **Pure Black and White**. Verify that the *Number of copies* is set to **1**. Then, click **OK** to print the outline.

The printout contains no slides, graphics, layouts, or notes; only the text is printed as it appears on the Outline tab of the *Agenda Revised* presentation.

18. Click the **Print What triangle button** and click **Handouts (6 slides per page)**.

All six slides in the presentation appear in miniature in the Print Preview window.

19. Open the Print dialog box. Verify that you will print one copy of all handouts in Grayscale mode. In the *Handouts* area, verify that the *Slides per page* option is set to **6** and that the Order is set to **Horizontal**. Then, click **OK** to print the handouts.

PowerPoint prints one page containing six miniature images of the slides in the *Agenda Revised* presentation.

20. Close the Print Preview window and save your work.

MORE ABOUT FOLDERS AND FILES

As you may have noticed, when you need to open a presentation file, it is important to be able to locate that file easily. One way to do that is to store related files together. Folders allow you to organize files in a meaningful way by grouping related files together. Creating a new folder is a straightforward process that you can do conveniently in either the Save As or the Open dialog box; simply click the Create New Folder button , enter a meaningful name for the new folder, and click OK. However, when creating a folder, you must be aware of *where* you're creating it; whatever drive letter or folder name appears in the Save in text box (Save As dialog box) or the Look in text box (Open dialog box) is the drive where your new folder will be located.

At times you may need to save a PowerPoint presentation in a way that allows another program to use it. For example, imagine that you are sharing presentations with a coworker who only has access to an older version of PowerPoint. You can save your presentation in a format that both versions of PowerPoint can read so that you can share information seamlessly. Fortunately, with PowerPoint you can save a presentation by using a variety of file formats. A **file format** is the patterns and standards that a program uses to store data on a disk. But how do you know what file format to use when you save a file? Usually the file format is determined by the

WEB NOTE

A virus is a program that copies itself into files and can damage a computer by causing crashes or erasing data. To avoid viruses, always use antivirus software to check files, especially files you receive from an outside source via a disk or the Internet. For reliable information about viruses and antivirus software, visit the Computer Security Resource Center's Web site at **http://csrc.ncsl.nist.gov/virus**.

type or version of the software that will be used to open the file. So, if you decide that, for the most part, your PowerPoint files will be opened using the PowerPoint application, you can simply accept the default file format in the Save As dialog box, which is Presentation. If, however, you know that the file will be opened in a different application or in an older version of PowerPoint, you can save the file in a different file format. To choose another file format, click Save As on the File menu to open the Save As dialog box. Then, click the *Save as type* triangle button, and choose a file format from the displayed list.

HANDS on

Creating a New Folder and Saving a Presentation in a Different File Format

In this activity, you'll create a new folder and save the *Agenda Revised* presentation in the new folder using a different file format.

1. Click **Save As** on the File menu to display the Save As dialog box.

2. Click the **Create New Folder button** on the toolbar near the top of the Save As dialog box.

As shown in Figure 1.19, the New Folder dialog box appears, requesting a name for the new folder. Note that the *Tutorial* folder is displayed in the Save in box of the Save As dialog box; this is where your new folder will be stored.

Figure 1.19
Creating a new folder in the Save As dialog box

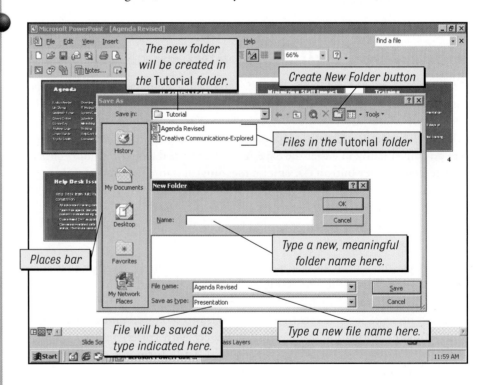

3. Type PowerPoint 97 Files in the Name text box and click **OK**.

Now the *PowerPoint 97 Files* folder is displayed in the Save in box, indicating that this is where the file will be stored.

4. Click the **Save as type triangle button** in the Save As dialog box to see a listing of various file formats.

5. Scroll down the list and click **PowerPoint 97-2002 & 95 Presentation**.

You will not overwrite the *Agenda Revised* presentation you saved in the last activity because you've changed the location of this file; however, it is still a good idea to change the file name to avoid any potential confusion.

6. Change the existing file name to Agenda Revised-PowerPoint 97 **in the File name text box, and then click Save**.

PowerPoint displays a message box indicating that the older file format may not be compatible with the newer format.

7. Click **Yes** to save the presentation and clear the message box.

Your presentation is saved with a new name in a different file format and in a new folder. The new name appears in the title bar.

8. Click **Close** on the File menu.

The presentation has been removed from memory. You now have two copies of the presentation (one in Presentation format and one in PowerPoint 97-2002 & 95 Presentation format) stored in two separate folders that you can open, view, and modify whenever you'd like.

9. Click **Exit** on the File menu.

PowerPoint disappears from the screen, and you return to the Windows desktop.

Working With Folders and File Formats

To create a new folder:

1. Click the Create New Folder button in the Save As (or Open) dialog box.

2. Type a new folder name in the New Folder dialog box and click OK.

To save a presentation in a different file format:

1. Click the Save as type triangle button in the Save As dialog box.

2. Select the appropriate file format from the list that appears.

3. Change the file name if desired.

4. Click the Save button in the Save As dialog box.

Self Check

Test your knowledge by answering the following questions. See Appendix B to check your answers.

T F **1.** PowerPoint presentations can include text, bullets, illustrations, charts, photos, shapes, animations, sounds, and even movie clips.

T F **2.** Using the View toolbar, you can switch between seven viewing options.

T F **3.** When you select a low magnification, you zoom out.

T F **4.** A title is the main topic of a slide.

T F **5.** Because slide shows are meant to be shown to an audience, they are never printed.

ADDING HYPERLINKS TO A PRESENTATION

As you have learned, a hyperlink is text or a graphic that serves as a shortcut, or jump, to another slide, presentation, or Web page. You create hyperlinks in Normal View, but they work only in Slide Show View. When showing large presentations, you may want to use a hyperlink to jump quickly from one slide to another slide in the same presentation or in another presentation, or to jump to a Web address. In this activity, you will open a presentation and link an item on one slide to another slide in the presentation and to a Web site.

1. Connect to the Internet using your Internet service provider (ISP). If necessary, type your user name and password. If you are not sure how to connect to the Internet or you do not know your user name and password, ask your instructor for assistance.

2. Open *Benefits* in your *PowerPoint Data* folder and save the file as *Benefits with Hyperlinks* in the *Tutorial* folder.

3. In Normal View, go to slide 2. Then, on the Outline tab, select the first bulleted item *Health care.*

4. On the Standard toolbar, click the **Insert Hyperlink button** 🔗.

5. In the *Link* to panel of the Insert Hyperlink dialog box, click **Place in This Document**.

A list of all the slides appears in the *Select a place in this document* list box.

6. Click slide 3 as the place for the hyperlink, as shown in Figure 1.20.

7. Click **OK** to insert the hyperlink and close the Insert Hyperlink dialog box.

8. Deselect the text by clicking the slide pane.

In the slide pane, the words *Health care* are now underlined, colored text, indicating a hyperlink.

9. Switch to Slide Show View and point to *Health care.*

In Slide Show View, the pointer changes to the shape of a hand when you point to a hyperlink. (This only happens in Slide Show View.)

10. Click the hyperlink and notice that the *Health Care* slide from the same presentation appears on the screen.

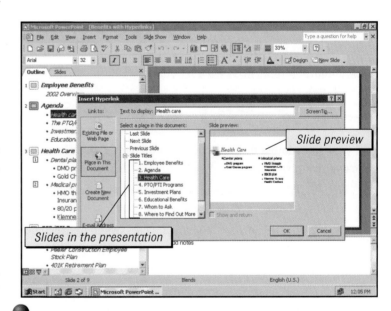

Figure 1.20
The Insert Hyperlink dialog box

11. Press ⎋, navigate to slide 2, and note that the hyperlink *(Health care)* has changed color in the slide pane, indicating that you followed the link. Save the updated file.

12. Navigate to slide 8. On the Outline tab, select the slide title *(Where to Find Out More)*, and click the **Insert Hyperlink button** .

13. In the *Link to* panel of the Insert Hyperlink dialog box, click **Existing File or Web Page**.

Another option now appears in the Insert Hyperlink dialog box—the Address box.

14. In the Address box, type http://www.prufn.com, as shown in Figure 1.21, to add a link to the Prudential Financial Web site.

> **NOTE** *To insert a link to another presentation, in the Insert Hyperlink dialog box, click the Browse for File button to open the Link to File dialog box. Navigate to the file you want to link to, click its name, and click OK to close the Link to File dialog box and to insert the file name in the Address box of the Insert Hyperlink dialog box.*

In the Insert Hyperlink dialog box, you should specify an easy-to-read ScreenTip. Otherwise, the Web address will appear as the ScreenTip when you point to the hyperlink.

15. Click the **ScreenTip button**. In the Set Hyperlink ScreenTip dialog box, type Prudential Financial in the text box and then click **OK**.

16. Click **OK** to close the Insert Hyperlink dialog box.

17. On slide 8, deselect the title and click the **Slide Show button** .

Slide 8 appears in Slide Show View with the title text as a hyperlink.

18. Point to the hyperlink and read the ScreenTip. Then, click the hyperlink.

PowerPoint will jump directly to the Prudential Financial site. (When you click a Web page hyperlink, you may have to manually switch to your browser or manually connect to the Internet, depending on your computer setup.)

19. When the home page appears, navigate the Web site. Then, minimize your browser's window and return to your presentation. Press [Esc] to end the slide show and return PowerPoint to Normal View.

20. Save your changes, close the file, and exit PowerPoint. Close your browser and disconnect from the Internet unless your instructor tells you to remain connected.

> **WARNING** *You may proceed directly to the exercises for this lesson. If, however, you are finished with your computer session, follow the "shut down" procedures for your lab or school environment.*

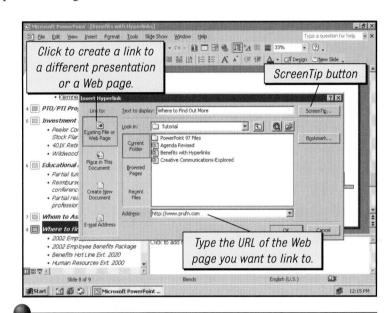

Figure 1.21
Adding a link to a Web page

SUMMARY AND EXERCISES

SUMMARY

Using PowerPoint, you can create a presentation and relay information to an audience in an efficient, effective way. The PowerPoint window contains tools that make it easy to work with and navigate presentations. The View toolbar contains buttons for PowerPoint's three views, each of which is suited for specific tasks. Working with slides can involve a variety of PowerPoint features, such as Find and Replace for locating and replacing text in a presentation; Undo and Redo for reversing mouse and keyboard actions; Slide Show View for previewing a presentation; and Print Preview for viewing the components of a slide show before printing them. Frequently, you will want to print slides, notes, and outlines to review. You can print the different parts of a presentation in different color modes, depending on your printer's capabilities. If you have a black-and-white printer, you can print presentations in Grayscale mode or in Pure Black and White mode; if you have a color printer, you can print presentations in color. The Save As command enables you to save an existing presentation with a different file name and/or in a different folder. By adding hyperlinks to your presentations, you can link to another slide in the same presentation, link to a different presentation, or link to a Web site.

Now that you have completed this lesson, you should be able to do the following:

- Describe the purpose of presentations and presentation software. (page 529)
- Identify the unique features of the PowerPoint window. (page 532)
- Switch among the three PowerPoint views. (page 534)
- Navigate a presentation using PowerPoint's scrolling tools or your keyboard. (page 537)
- Add text to a slide, and edit or delete text in various ways. (page 540)
- Promote and demote titles, subtitles, and bullets. (page 542)
- Check the spelling of a single word or an entire presentation. (page 543)
- Use the Undo, Redo, and Repeat commands. (page 546)
- Use the Find and Replace features to locate and replace text in a presentation. (page 547)
- Use PowerPoint's search tools to find files on your computer or network disks. (page 548)
- Select, move, and delete slides in either Normal View or Slide Sorter View. (page 549)
- Review a presentation in Slide Show View. (page 553)
- Change the Page Setup options. (page 555)
- Preview and print slides, notes, outlines, and handouts. (page 555)
- Create a new folder. (page 559)
- Save a presentation in a different file format. (page 559)
- Add hyperlinks to another slide within a presentation and to a Web page. (page 562)

CONCEPTS REVIEW

POWERPOINT 2002

1 TRUE/FALSE

Circle T if the statement is true or F if the statement is false.

T F **1.** Normal View enables you to view a slide along with its outline and notes.

T F **2.** Changing the Zoom level in Normal View changes the size of text in all panes.

T F **3.** Changing the Zoom level on the Outline tab from 25% to 33% enables you to see more text.

T F **4.** In Slide Sorter View, a border around a slide indicates that the slide is selected.

T F **5.** Hyperlinks work only in Slide Show View.

T F **6.** Grayscale is a more efficient print mode than Pure Black and White.

T F **7.** The best way to review a presentation is to see it in Slide Show View.

T F **8.** A PowerPoint presentation can enable you to make the same points as a written report, but in far fewer words.

T F **9.** Vertical scroll bars appear in certain PowerPoint views, but horizontal scroll bars never appear.

T F **10.** If you want to delete a slide, you must first select it.

2 MATCHING

Match each of the terms on the left with a definition on the right.

TERMS	DEFINITIONS
1. Normal View	**a.** Lets you jump from a slide to a Web site
2. insertion point	**b.** Indented text on a slide
3. promote	**c.** First line of text on a slide
4. Slide Navigator dialog box	**d.** Shows where text will appear when you type
5. Slide Show View	**e.** Allows you to move to any slide in a presentation
6. Slide Sorter View	**f.** The best view for copying, deleting, and moving slides
7. Print Preview	**g.** A means of reviewing a presentation on-screen as an audience would see it
8. subtitle	**h.** Decrease a subtitle's indent level
9. title	**i.** The best place to work on text, graphics, and speaker notes at the same time
10. hyperlink	**j.** An on-screen view that shows how a presentation's components will look when printed

SUMMARY AND EXERCISES

3 COMPLETION

Fill in the missing word or phrase for each of the following statements.

1. Use the _____ command to save an existing file with a different name or to a different location.

2. If you want to see how a slide will look during an actual presentation, click the _____ button.

3. If you don't want to change the spelling of a questionably spelled word, you can tell PowerPoint to _____ it.

4. To change the size of text on the Outline tab, adjust the _____ .

5. On the Outline tab, you can click a(n) _____ button to see a slide in the slide pane.

6. To exit PowerPoint, click the _____ button on the title bar or click _____ on the File menu.

7. You can move a slide without using the Office Clipboard by _____ it.

8. If you want to locate a word in a presentation and put a different word in its place, you can use the _____ command.

9. Hyperlinks can be attached to text or _____ .

10. The _____ button will change a level 2 subtitle to a level 1 subtitle.

4 SHORT ANSWER

Write a brief answer to each of the following questions.

1. What is a presentation?

2. If you make a mistake as you type, how can you immediately fix it?

3. How do you display the next slide in Slide Show View?

4. In Normal View, where can you always see the number of the current slide?

5. If the magnification of outline text is too small to read, how do you enlarge it?

6. How can you make sure that your slide show ends with a black slide?

7. Assume you have just moved slide 3 to follow slide 9. How do you renumber slide 3?

8. What is a subtitle?

9. Describe the procedure for printing all slides for an entire presentation in Grayscale mode.

10. What is the advantage of using Slide Sorter View?

POWERPOINT 2002

5 IDENTIFICATION

Label each of the items of the PowerPoint window in Figure 1.22.

Figure 1.22

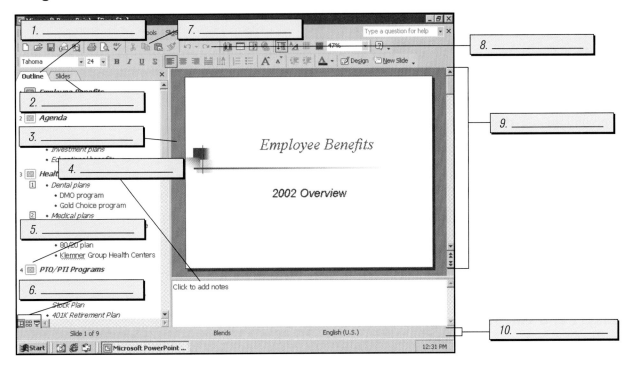

SKILLS REVIEW

Complete all of the Skills Review problems in sequential order to review your skills to switch views and navigate a slide show; add and edit text; promote and demote subtitles and bullets; check spelling; use the Undo, Redo, and Repeat commands; use Find and Replace; move and delete slides; use Slide Show View; preview and print presentation components; save and close a file; and save a presentation in a new file folder and with a different file format.

1 Launch PowerPoint and Navigate a Presentation

1. Click the **Start button** ![Start], point to **Programs**, and click **Microsoft PowerPoint**.

2. Click **Open** 📂 on the Standard toolbar. In the Open dialog box, navigate to the *PowerPoint Data* folder.

3. Click the *Moving* presentation and click **Open**.

4. Click the **Slides tab**, and then click the **Outline tab**.

5. Drag the horizontal splitter bar upward until the notes pane is about two inches high.

6. Click the **Slide Sorter View button** ![icon], scroll to the end of the presentation, and then select slide 13.

7. Click the **Slide Show button** 🖳. Click the screen to advance to the *End of slide show, click to exit* message. Then, click to end the slide show.

8. Click the **Normal View button** 🔲. Drag the slide pane's vertical scroll box to the top of the scroll bar.

9. On the Slides tab, click the scroll arrow until you reach the end of the presentation. Click slide 14.

10. In the slide pane, click the **Previous Slide button** 🔺 until slide 7 is visible.

11. Click the **Next Slide button** 🔽 until you see slide 10.

12. On the Standard toolbar, click the **Zoom box triangle button** 100% ▾ and set a magnification level of 100%.

13. Click the **Zoom box triangle button** again and select **Fit**.

14. Click the **Outline tab**, scroll to the beginning of the presentation, select slide 1, and change the magnification level to 25%.

15. Switch to Slide Show View. Right-click and point to **Go**. Then, click **Slide Navigator** on the shortcut menu.

16. In the Slide Navigator dialog box, double-click **Location**. Then, right-click and click **End Show**.

2 Insert and Edit Text

1. With slide 4 visible in the slide pane, place the insertion point at the beginning of the slide's title.

2. Type **Our New** and press ⌴Spacebar once.

3. On the Outline tab, go to slide 14 and click after the last bulleted item.

4. Change the Zoom setting for the Outline tab to 33%.

5. Press ⌨Enter⏎ to add a new bulleted item, and then type SAC, Hold, and Conference features without pressing ⌴Spacebar or adding a period.

6. On slide 11, in the slide pane, select the text *Box everything*. Then, replace it by typing Pack items in approved containers only!

7. On the Outline tab, go to the third bullet on slide 7. Select the text *installed and*. Press ⌨Delete.

3 Promote and Demote Subtitles and Bullets

1. On the Outline tab, navigate to slide 14.

2. Select the two subtitles that begin with *Same*. Demote the subtitles one indent level by clicking the **Increase Indent button** 🔧 one time.

3. Still working on the Outline tab, go to slide 7. Select the four bulleted items and promote them one indent level by clicking the **Decrease Indent button** 🔧 one time.

4. In the slide pane, select the same four bulleted items again and demote them one level by clicking the **Increase Indent button** 🔧 one time.

4 Check Spelling

1. Return to slide 1. In the slide pane, place the insertion point at the beginning of the slide's title.

2. On the Standard toolbar, click the **Spelling and Grammar button** .

3. For each highlighted word in the presentation, take the appropriate action: Select or type the correct word in the *Change to* box and click the **Change button**, or click the **Ignore All button**. Assume that all names have been spelled correctly (see Figure 1.23). Do not add words to the PowerPoint dictionary.

4. When the spell check is complete, close all open dialog boxes.

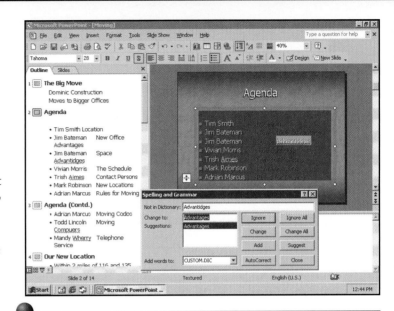

Figure 1.23

5 Use the Undo, Redo, and Repeat Commands

1. On the Outline tab, go to slide 4 and insert two words so that the second bulleted item reads as follows: **Within 3 miles of Greater Radley International Airport.**

2. Look at the slide pane. Since the subtitle is too close to the map, undo your typing of the two words by clicking the **Undo button** twice.

3. In the first bulleted item, type **I-** (for Interstate) in front of *116* and *135*. Check the slide pane and undo the changes by clicking the **Undo button** twice.

4. Click the **Redo button** twice to restore *I-116* and *I-135*. Then select *Freeways* and press Delete.

6 Use Find and Replace

1. Return to slide 1. In the slide pane, place the insertion point at the beginning of the slide's title.

2. Click **Replace** on the Edit menu.

3. In the *Find what* box of the Replace dialog box, type **Schedule**. In the *Replace with* box, type **Timetable**.

4. Click **Find Next**.

5. Click **Replace** to replace each occurrence of the word *Schedule* with the word *Timetable* on slides 2, 7, and 8.

6. When you are finished, close all open dialog boxes.

7 Rearrange and Remove Slides

1. On the Outline tab, select slide 5 by clicking its slide button, and click the **Cut button** [✂] on the Standard toolbar. Click **OK** in the box which asks if you want to continue.

2. Select slide 10, and then click the **Paste button** [📋] on the Standard toolbar.

3. Switch to Slide Sorter View. Select slide 8 and click **Cut** [✂]. Click at the end of the presentation and then click **Paste** [📋].

4. Drag slide 12 and drop it between slides 9 and 10.

5. Switch to Normal View and click the **Slides tab**. Select slides 1 and 13 and delete them.

8 Review a Presentation in Slide Show View

1. In Normal View, go to slide 1.

2. Click the **Slide Show button** [🖥].

3. Click until you reach slide 5.

4. Press [Backspace] to go back to slide 4.

5. Right-click, point to **Go**, and then click **Slide Navigator**. In the Slide Navigator dialog box, double-click slide 8.

6. Press [Spacebar] once to go to slide 9.

7. Right-click, and click **End Show** on the shortcut menu.

9 Preview and Print a Presentation

1. In Normal View, go to slide 1. Click **Page Setup** on the File menu.

2. In the Page Setup dialog box, click the **Slides sized for triangle button** and click **Letter Paper (8.5x11 in)**. Verify that the orientation for slides is set to **Landscape** and the orientation for Notes, handouts & outline is set to **Portrait**. Click **OK**. Switch to Slide Sorter View.

3. On the Standard toolbar, click the **Print Preview button** [🔍]. Change the magnification level to **Fit** if you can't see all the copy on the slide.

4. Scroll through the slides in Print Preview mode.

5. On the Print Preview toolbar, click the **Print What triangle button** and click **Handouts (6 slides per page)**.

6. Scroll through the handout pages.

7. Click **Print** 🖨️Print... on the Print Preview toolbar. In the Print dialog box, change the settings as necessary to print a set of handouts in Pure Black and White mode with six slides per page. Click **OK**.

8. Click the **Print What triangle button**, and select **Outline View**. Increase the zoom level, if necessary, so you can read the outline.

9. Click the **Print button** 🖨️Print... on the Print Preview toolbar. In the Print dialog box, change the settings to print the entire presentation in Grayscale mode. Click **OK**.

10. On the Print Preview toolbar, click the **Print What triangle button** and click **Slides**. In the Print dialog box, print all the slides for your presentation in Grayscale mode.

11. Close the Print Preview window.

12. Click **Save As** on the File menu. In the Save in list box, navigate to the *Skills Review* folder in your *PowerPoint Data* folder.

13. Name the file *Moving Revised* and click **Save** (see Figure 1.24).

Figure 1.24

10 Create a New Folder and Save a Presentation in a Different File Format

1. Click **Save As** on the File menu to display the Save As dialog box.

2. Click the **Create New Folder button** 📁 on the toolbar near the top of the Save As dialog box.

3. Type RTF Files in the Name text box and click **OK**.

4. Click the **Save as type triangle button**, and click **Outline/RTF**.

5. Change the existing file name to **Moving Revised-RTF Format** in the File name text box and then click **Save**.

6. Close the presentation.

SUMMARY AND EXERCISES

LESSON APPLICATIONS

1 Counting Raindrops

Open a presentation, make changes, and check spelling. Review the presentation in Slide Show View, save the changes, and close the file.

1. Open *Rainfall* in your *PowerPoint Data* folder. Save the file as *Rainfall Revised* in the *Lesson Applications* folder.

2. Switch to Normal View, and click the Outline tab. Scroll to slide 4.

3. Change the title of slide 4 to **2001 Rainfall in Perspective**. In the first subtitle, change *5* to *five*. Undo both changes; then redo them.

4. Scroll to slide 6. Demote the second, fourth, and fifth bulleted subtitles by one indent level (see Figure 1.25).

5. Go to the beginning of the presentation, and check the spelling in the entire presentation. (Note that the name *Torborg* is correctly spelled. In *aquaduct*, the second *a* should be an *e*.)

6. Review the presentation in Slide Show View. After the slide show ends, switch to Slide Sorter View.

7. Save your changes and close the file.

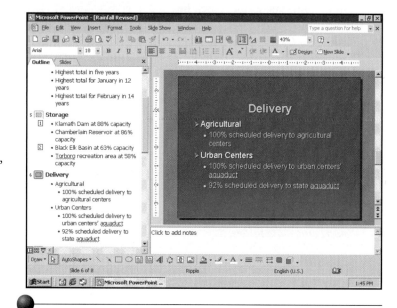

Figure 1.25

2 At the Library

Move and delete slides, find and replace text, and view the slides in Print Preview mode. Print one slide from the presentation, and then print a handout.

1. Open the *Library* presentation in your *PowerPoint Data* folder. Save the file as *Library Revised* in the *Lesson Applications* folder.

2. Move slide 7 up so it becomes slide 3. Select slide 6 and delete it.

3. Use the Find and Replace features to find all occurrences of the abbreviation *Misc.* (including the period) and replace them with *Miscellaneous* (without a period).

4. View the entire presentation in Print Preview mode.

5. Print a single handout sheet (in Pure Black and White mode) containing all six slides.

6. Print one copy of slide 6 in Grayscale mode.

7. Close the Print Preview window. Save your changes and close the file.

3 The Game Is Ping Pong

Edit text, promote and demote subtitles, and then rearrange the slides. Preview the presentation; print the slide show and notes pages.

1. Open *Ping Pong* in your *PowerPoint Data* folder. Save the file as *Ping Pong Revised* in the *Lesson Applications* folder.

2. On slide 2, change *20 percent* to *20%*.

3. On slide 5, promote all level 2 subtitles, and then undo this change. In each level 2 subtitle, delete *the* and add *s* to *player*.

4. Change the order of slides as shown in Table 1.2.

Table 1.2	Order of Ping Pong Slides	
Current Slide Number	**Slide Title**	**Revised Slide Number**
4	2002 Model Line	1
5	Three Winning Model Lines	2
3	Sales Potential	3
1	New X20 Ping Pong Table	4
2	The X20 Is Clearly Superior	5

5. View the presentation in Print Preview mode, and then return to Normal View.

6. Print the entire presentation, without using the Print dialog box.

7. Print all of the presentation's notes pages in Pure Black and White mode, using the Print dialog box.

8. Save your changes and close the file.

PROJECTS

1 In-Depth Analysis

Your job title at Stand and Deliver is presentation specialist. Your employer offers a range of services related to creating and presenting slide shows. After working with Dominic Construction's *Moving* presentation, you realize that this presentation would be useful in training sessions. The presentation includes slides with a variety of features and methods to present information. However, before you can use it for training, you must first analyze the entire presentation. Open *Moving* in your *PowerPoint Data* folder. As you review the slides, look for these features in the presentation: subtitles of different levels, text in two columns, a table, a chart, a shape (such as a circle), and a picture. Close the presentation without making any changes or saving it.

2 Rainfall Revisited

A few Fortune 500 companies are among your clients, though most clients are local businesses, such as Dominic Construction Inc. and the Liberty County Environmental Services Department (ESD). Right now, you have a presentation *(2001 Rainfall Totals)* from Liberty County ESD on your desk. Open *Rainfall* in your *PowerPoint Data* folder.

Yesterday you noted that slide 8 is too wordy. Now you will rewrite it. On a separate sheet of paper, write new, shorter subtitles to replace the client's paragraphs. Notice that the slide contains three bulleted subtitles, each of which is several lines long. Focus on creating more subtitles, each containing only a few words. (*Hint:* Consider creating three new level 1 subtitles and placing one or two bulleted level 2 subtitles under each one, as a series of points and subpoints. See Figure 1.26.) Working on the Outline tab, edit the slide's text using your newly written text. Review the presentation in Slide Show View to ensure smooth flow. Make other changes to the presentation as desired. Explore Help for information on features you want to use but have not yet learned in this tutorial, such as changing a font size. Save your file as *Edited Rainfall* in the *Projects* folder in your *PowerPoint Data* folder.

Analysis

➢ 2001 rainfall higher than expected.
  ○ Drought-ravaged reserves replenished.
  ○ Deliveries now at or near 100%.
➢ Culver reporting station damaged.
  ○ State and Fed to share repair costs.
  ○ Access road repairs starting now.
➢ NWS predicts more rain this season.

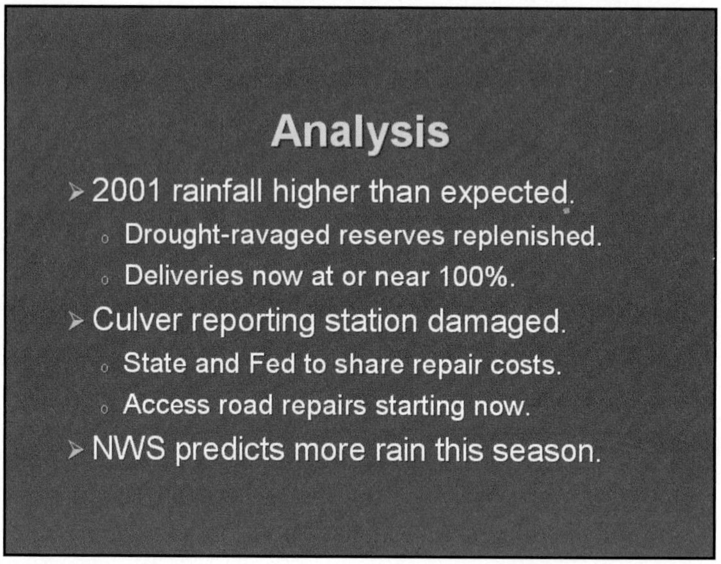

Figure 1.26

3 Designer Backgrounds

As designers of many varied presentations for Stand and Deliver clients, you and your coworkers are interested in the different looks available in PowerPoint and other presentation programs. For example, the *Rainfall* presentation had a design that truly matched its content and was pleasing to look at. You have decided to prepare a catalog of presentation designs, containing the information shown in Table 1.3.

Table 1.3	Catalog of Presentation Designs				
File Name	**Design Name**	**Main Color**	**Other Colors**	**Objects**	**Description**
Agenda	Glass Layers				
Library	Radial				
Rainfall	Ripple				
Ping Pong	Edge				
Moving	Textured				

To begin, you first explore Help to learn about designs. (*Hint:* In the Ask a Question box, type **design** and explore the About design templates option.) Re-create Table 1.3 on a sheet of paper. Open each file in the File Name column and verify its design. (You can see the name of a presentation's design in PowerPoint's status bar.) In the color columns, list the primary color used in the design and any complementing colors that consistently appear in the slides. In the Objects column, list any objects you find in the presentation, such as tables, charts, clip art, and so on. In the Description column, write one to four words to describe the mood of the design, such as Lively, Somber, or Relaxing. Close the files.

4 Making a Model

Presentation specialists like to show models (sample presentations) when they interview clients about new presentations. Showing other clients' presentations to a new client is not a good idea, however, because the slides may contain confidential information. Ideally, each specialist has a model that lists the advantages of using presentations.

Open *Congratulations* in your *PowerPoint Data* folder and save the file as *Advantages* in the *Projects* folder. This blank presentation contains five slides: a title slide and four slides with placeholders for a title and subtitles. Type a title and subtitles on the slides, as shown in Table 1.4. Type either in the slide pane or on the Outline tab. As appropriate, use material from Lesson 1 for the subtitles in your presentation.

Table 1.4	Text for the *Advantages* Presentation	
Slide	**Slide Title**	**Subtitles**
1	Stand & Deliver Presentations	Your Name, Presentation Specialist
2	What Is a Presentation?	Supply two or more subtitles to complement the slide's title.
3	Uses for Presentations	Supply two or more subtitles to complement the slide's title.
4	Features of Presentations	Supply two or more subtitles to complement the slide's title.
5	Advantages of Presentations	Supply two or more subtitles to complement the slide's title.

For at least three of the slides, type a sentence in the notes pane—a comment you would make while showing that slide to your client. Run the slide show, and make desired changes. Preview and print the presentation's slides and notes pages in Grayscale mode. Save your changes and close the file.

5 Notes and Handouts

In some cases, your clients ask you to present the slide shows you have created for them. One such client is the Park County Library Board, which has asked you to prepare and give a presentation that reviews a number of improvement projects undertaken at the library. You need to present the slides to the Board tonight, and they require some finishing touches.

Open *Library* in your *PowerPoint Data* folder and save the presentation as *Notes and Handouts* in the *Projects* folder. Before you give your presentation, you want to add a few notes to it. Then you need to print a set of handouts to give to the audience.

Working in Normal View, add two notes each to at least three of the slides. These notes can be reminders to yourself about specific points or facts to help you explain the slides better (see Figure 1.27 for an example). Next, switch to Print Preview mode. Print one complete set of notes pages in Pure Black and White mode, and then print a complete set of handout pages (with three slides on each page) in Grayscale mode. Return to Normal View. Save your changes and close the file.

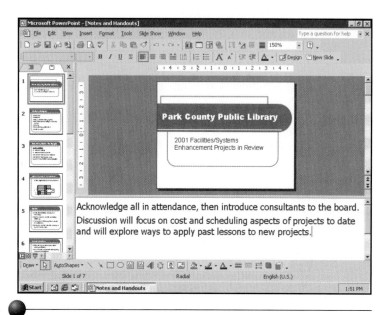

Figure 1.27

6 Links

You're busy—job, college courses, home, family. You're always looking for ways to get organized. A little trick you read about recently is to have a PowerPoint file that contains links to files you use often and Web sites you especially like or need to visit frequently. Open *Links* in your *PowerPoint Data* folder and save the presentation as *My Links* in the *Projects* folder. This presentation contains only two slides. On the first slide, add hyperlinks to any two or more presentations in the *Projects* folder—the ones that show your best work. On the other slide, add links to two or more of your favorite Web sites. Use the name of the Web site, not the URL, as the ScreenTip. Test all hyperlinks. Save your changes and close the file.

Project in Progress

7 Now You're in Business

You have received state approval to start a business named Savvy Solutions. Your company will provide a variety of writing and editing services for small- and medium-sized organizations in your area. Open *Title* in your *PowerPoint Data* folder and save the file as *Savvy Solutions-Lesson 1* in a new folder named *Project in Progress* in the *Projects* folder in your *PowerPoint Data* folder. Use the first slide in this presentation as a title slide for your company. For the slide's title, use a short slogan that you want to use to promote your business—one that you think reflects the company's goals or attitude. Use your name, the company's name, and your (real or fictional) e-mail address as subtitles (see Figure 1.28 for an example). Add some notes to the title slide, which you can use to help introduce yourself as you deliver this presentation to prospective clients. Next, print one copy of the title slide in Grayscale mode. Save your changes. Close the presentation and exit PowerPoint.

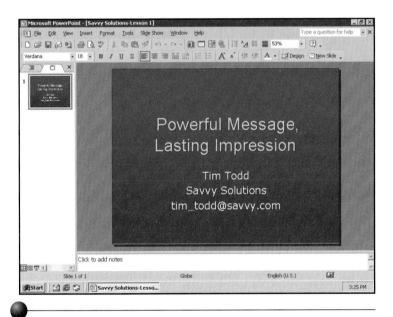

Figure 1.28

LESSON 2

Designing a Presentation

CONTENTS

OBJECTIVES

After you complete this lesson, you will be able to do the following:

▶ Create a presentation from a design template or from a blank slide.

▶ Add new slides and text to a presentation.

▶ Apply a different design template and layout to a slide.

▶ Customize a design template.

▶ Import a Word outline and export a presentation as an outline.

▶ Format and align text on a slide.

▶ Add and adjust clip art and image files on a slide.

▶ Add a sound effect and a movie to a slide.

▶ Draw and edit shapes on a slide.

▶ Create and enhance a chart and import an Excel chart into a slide.

▶ Create and enhance a table and import a Word table into a slide.

▶ Use Help to add an action button to a slide.

▶ Use the slide master to change formatting throughout a presentation.

▶ Add headers and footers to slides, notes pages, and handouts.

▶ Create and apply slide transitions and animate text and objects.

▶ Publish a slide show for viewing on the World Wide Web.

WORKING WITH DESIGN TEMPLATES

A **design template** (sometimes called just a **template**) is a collection of formatting options—including fonts, bullets, alignments, colors, and a background—that you can apply to a presentation. Templates give you a head start in developing a presentation because much of the design work is already done. The template provides everything you need for a professional-looking slide show; all you have to do is add the text and any objects you want to use, such as tables or clip art.

PowerPoint offers dozens of design templates. Before selecting a template, however, you should carefully plan your presentation. Think about the material you are presenting, your audience, and the style in which you want to deliver the information. Try to determine the number of slides you will need, and then decide which ones will include a picture, graph, or table.

When you start a new presentation from scratch, you can choose a design template as your first step. You can select a design template in several ways, but the easiest way is to use PowerPoint's task pane. When you launch PowerPoint (or click the New command on the File menu), the New Presentation task pane appears. This task pane provides the From Design Template option, which lets you create a presentation based on a template. If you select this option, the Slide Design task pane appears, displaying all the available design templates.

You can also open the Slide Design task pane by clicking the Slide Design command on the Format menu, or by clicking the Slide Design button [Design] on the Formatting toolbar. When the Slide Design task pane opens, you can view all the available design templates on your computer or network disks and select one for your presentation.

When you create a new presentation from a design template, PowerPoint assumes you want to use a title slide as the first slide in the presentation, and applies the Title slide layout. You can quickly begin building a presentation by adding text and inserting new slides. To add a new slide to a presentation, you choose a slide layout. As you work on your presentation, you can choose a different template for all the slides or for any individual slide, or choose a different layout for any of the slides.

HANDS on

Creating a Presentation From a Design Template

In this activity, you will start a new presentation using a design template. The presentation will contain a title slide. Later, you will add more slides to the presentation.

1. Start PowerPoint.

PowerPoint launches and the New Presentation task pane appears on the right side of the screen. (If PowerPoint is already open, click the Normal View button 🔲 to switch to Normal View, if necessary. If the task pane is not visible, click New on the File menu.)

> **NOTE** *If the New Presentation task pane does not appear whenever you start PowerPoint, click Options on the Tools menu. In the Options dialog box, click the View tab, and then click the Startup Task Pane check box until a check mark appears. Click OK.*

2. In the New section of the task pane, click **From Design Template**.

The Slide Design task pane opens and displays small graphical samples (called thumbnails) of the available templates.

3. Point to one of the thumbnail images. When the triangle button appears on the thumbnail's right edge, click it to open a menu. When the menu appears, make sure that the **Show Large Previews command** has a check mark. If no check mark is visible, click the option.

The thumbnails now appear larger, making them easier to view, as shown in Figure 2.1.

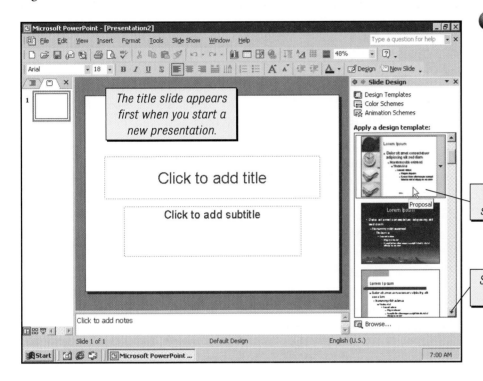

Figure 2.1
Viewing design templates in the task pane

Point to a thumbnail to see the template's name.

Scroll to see available templates.

4. Scroll slowly through the list of design templates, pointing to each of the thumbnails.

When you hold your pointer over a thumbnail, a ScreenTip appears and shows the template's name.

5. Click the **Proposal template triangle button**, and when the menu opens, click **Apply to All Slides**.

PowerPoint applies the Proposal design template to the new presentation. Notice that the title slide, which was already visible in the document window, has changed from a simple text-only, black-and-white design to a colorful design with different fonts, boxed areas for text, and graphics in the background.

NOTE *If the Proposal design template is not available and you do not have the Microsoft Office compact disc to install the template, select another design template.*

6. Click the **Save button** . In the Save As dialog box, save the file as *Staffing Proposal* in the *Tutorial* folder in your *PowerPoint Data* folder.

WEB NOTE

In addition to the templates on your computer, you can find PowerPoint design templates on Microsoft's Web site. To view the templates, first connect to the Internet, and then click Templates on Microsoft.com in the New Presentation task pane. Internet Explorer launches and opens the Microsoft Office Template Gallery page. Click the *Search for* box, type PowerPoint, and click Go. A new page appears, listing all the available templates.

Adding Text and Slides to a Presentation

Adding a new slide requires you to select a slide layout. A **slide layout** is a blank slide that is designed to store one or more specific types of content, such as text or graphics. PowerPoint offers more than 20 layouts for slides; the Title Slide layout is one example. To add a new slide to a presentation, click the New Slide button [New Slide] on the Formatting toolbar. The Slide Layout task pane appears, displaying all the available layouts. You can select a slide layout the same way you selected a design template in the previous activity.

PowerPoint provides different layouts to hold different kinds of information—text, pictures, charts, and tables. Each of PowerPoint's slide layouts is named according to the type of material it is designed to hold. Some layouts—such as the Title and 2-Column Text layout—are designed to hold only text, arranged in a specific way. Other layouts hold only **objects,** which are items such as pictures, tables, or charts. A third category of layouts can hold text and objects in various combinations.

Within a slide layout, boxed areas—called **placeholders**—reserve space for the slide's contents. At the top of most slide layouts, you will see a placeholder labeled *Click to add title.* This placeholder is called the **title area,** and holds the slide's main title. Below the title area, most slide layouts contain one or more text areas or object areas. A **text area** is a placeholder that is designed to store only text, such as a set of subtitles or a bulleted list. An **object area** is a special type of placeholder which is designed to store an object, such as a table, chart, or graphic.

If you enter more text than will fit in a placeholder, PowerPoint automatically uses its AutoFit feature to reduce the text's point size when you reach the bottom of the placeholder. To deactivate this feature, click AutoCorrect Options on the Tools menu. In the AutoCorrect dialog box, click the AutoFormat As You Type tab. Click the *AutoFit title text to placeholder* and *AutoFit body text to placeholder* boxes to remove their check marks and click OK.

Typing Text and Inserting New Slides

In this activity, you will add a slide to the *Staffing Proposal* presentation. You will replace the text placeholders on the two slides by typing titles, subtitles, and a bulleted list. Then you will add a third slide with a different layout.

1. On the Formatting toolbar, click the New Slide button [New Slide].

Two things happen when you click this button. First, the Slide Layout task pane appears, as shown in Figure 2.2. Second, PowerPoint automatically adds a new slide to the presentation, containing placeholders for a title and a bulleted list. This layout is commonly used for the second slide in a presentation. You could replace this new slide, selecting a different layout from the task pane. Because it is exactly the layout you need for the new slide, however, keep it.

> **NOTE** *If the Slide Layout task pane does not appear, click Options on the Tools menu. When the Options dialog box opens, click the View tab,*

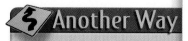

if necessary. Click the Slide Layout task pane when inserting new slides
box *to place a check mark in it. Click OK.*

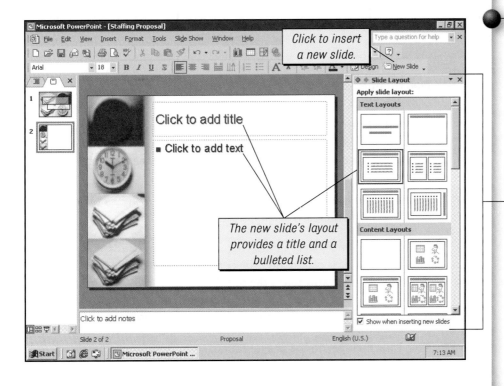

Figure 2.2
Inserting a new slide

Click to insert a new slide.

The new slide's layout provides a title and a bulleted list.

You can select any available slide layout from the Slide Layout task pane.

2. In the slide pane, scroll to slide 1 and click the title area to select it.

A hatched box surrounds the title area, and eight small circles appear around its edges. These circles are called **handles** (they are also called *selection handles, sizing handles, resize handles,* or *move handles*), and you can use them to change the placeholder's size and shape, if you need to. The sample text disappears and the insertion point blinks inside the box, where you will add text.

**3. Type ARM Distribution as the slide title. Click the subtitle place-
holder and type Holiday Staffing Proposal in this box.**

**4. Scroll to slide 2, click the slide's title area, and type The Holiday
Crunch.**

**5. Click the placeholder for the bulleted list. Type Package processing
demand rises 30% October - January. and press** Enter◄┘.

The insertion point drops to a new line, and a new bullet appears.

6. Type Special staffing needs include: and press Enter◄┘.

Another new bullet appears.

7. Click the Increase Indent button ▦ **on the Formatting toolbar.**

The bullet changes and is indented one level. This is a level 2 bullet.

8. Type 25 dock laborers and press Enter◄┘. **Type 12 drivers and press**
Enter◄┘. **Type 5 order-entry clerks and press** Enter◄┘. **Type 2 AR
clerks and press** Enter◄┘.

PowerPoint **BASICS**

Adding Slides and Text
To add slides:

- To add a slide with the Title
  and Text layout, click the
  New Slide button.

- To add a slide with a
  different layout, in the Slide
  Layout task pane, click a
  layout's triangle button and
  click Insert New Slide.

To add text:

1. Click the placeholder and
   type the text.

2. Click outside the
   placeholder to deselect it.

Designing a Presentation   **583**

9. Click the **Decrease Indent button** ⬚ on the Formatting toolbar, and then click the **Bullets button** ⬚.

Clicking the Decrease Indent button promoted the last line to a level 1 bullet. By clicking the Bullets button, you removed the bullet from this line. This line is now a level 1 subtitle.

10. Type All hires must be made by Oct. 1!, **but do not press** Enter↵. Click the blank area outside the slide to deselect the placeholder.

11. In the Slide Layout task pane, scroll down to the category of layouts named Text and Content Layouts. Point to each of the thumbnails in turn, and note each layout's name in a ScreenTip and a triangle button at the right edge of the thumbnail.

12. Find and click the **Title, Text, and Content layout triangle button**. When the menu appears, click **Insert New Slide**.

PowerPoint inserts a new slide using the Title, Text, and Content layout. (When you insert a new slide, it is placed after the currently selected slide.) Notice that this layout includes a title area across the top, and two placeholders arranged in columns. One of the placeholders is a text area for a bulleted list; the other is an object area for a table, chart, or some other kind of object.

13. Save your changes to the presentation.

HANDS on

Changing Designs and Layouts

PowerPoint offers flexibility as you create your presentations. After you select a design template, for example, you can select a different one whenever you like. You can apply a different template to an entire presentation or to a single slide. If you see that a different layout would work better for a particular slide, you can change that, too. The task pane makes it easy to change many aspects of a presentation quickly. In this activity, you will choose a new design template for the *Staffing Proposal* presentation and select a different layout for one slide. You will then modify the slide's contents to better fit the new layout.

1. On the Formatting toolbar, click the **Slide Design button** 🖺 Design.

2. In the Slide Design task pane, click the **Capsules design template triangle button**. When the menu appears, click **Apply to All Slides**.

NOTE *You can apply different design templates to individual slides. To do this, select the slide or slides that will use the different template. In the Slide Design task pane, point to the desired template, click the triangle button, and click Apply to Selected Slides. You can use a different template for every slide, if you wish.*

3. Switch to Slide Sorter View to see how the entire presentation's appearance has changed; then switch back to Normal View.

4. Go to slide 2. Click **Slide Layout** on the Format menu.

The Slide Layout task pane appears. Note, however, that when you use the menu command to open this task pane, PowerPoint does not automatically insert a new slide into the presentation.

5. In the Slide Layout task pane, find and click the Title and 2-Column Text layout triangle button, and click Apply to Selected Slides.

Slide 2 changes to a two-column text layout. The bottom portion of the slide is set up to hold two bulleted lists, arranged side by side. The original text appears in the first column, while the second column is empty.

6. Click immediately in front of the second level 1 bullet (beginning with *Special*), and drag to select it and the four level 2 bullets beneath it. Do not select the last sentence in the column (beginning with *All hires*).

7. Drag the selected text into the second column, and release the mouse button.

The selected text is moved from the first column to the second column, balancing the slide's appearance.

8. Click the last subtitle in the first column (beginning with *All hires*). On the Formatting toolbar, click the Bullets button ▤.

The unbulleted subtitle becomes bulleted. Your slide should now look like Figure 2.3.

9. Close the task pane by clicking the Close button ☒ **in its upper-right corner. Save and close the presentation.**

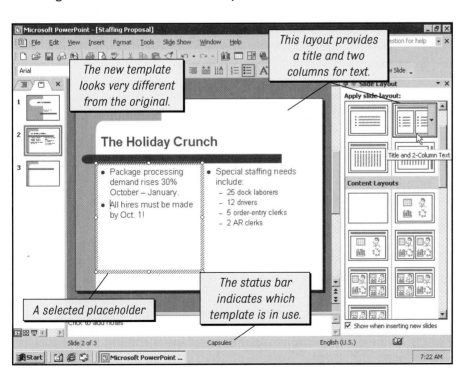

Figure 2.3
Slide 2 with a different template and layout

HANDS on
Customizing a Design Template

You don't have to use PowerPoint's design templates exactly as they are. You can make many different kinds of changes to a design template, and the changes will be reflected throughout your presentation. The easiest way to customize a design template is to change its color scheme. You can choose one of nine preset color schemes, or you can apply specific color settings to various parts of your slides. After you customize a design template, you can save it under a new name, and then reuse it in the future. In this activity, you will open the *Results* presentation, which uses a design template; then you will customize the template by applying a new color scheme. You will then edit the color scheme.

> **NOTE** *PowerPoint's slide master gives you fine control over the appearance of your slides, including font sizes, bullet styles, and much more. You'll learn about the slide master later in this lesson.*

1. Open *Results* in your *PowerPoint Data* folder and save the file as *Color Changes* in the *Tutorial* folder. Review the entire presentation; then return to slide 1.

This presentation uses the Curtain Call design template. This is an attractive template, but uses a dark background. You decide that you like the theme, but you want to use a lighter background color. This change will make it easier for a large audience to pick up the template's theme if the presentation is displayed on a large screen.

2. On the Formatting toolbar, click the Slide Design button ☑ Design.
When the Slide Design task pane appears, click the Color
Schemes link.

The task pane changes to display a set of preset color schemes. Each scheme provides a color for the template's background, title, bulleted lists, charts, and other elements.

3. In the task pane, scroll to the color scheme with the teal background. Point to its thumbnail, click its triangle button, and then click Apply to All Slides.

4. Review the presentation again, and save your changes.

After reviewing the slides, you decide that the basic color scheme is good, but you would like the slide titles to be a lighter color so that they stand out more.

5. At the bottom of the task pane, click the Edit Color Schemes link.

PowerPoint BASICS

Changing and Editing Color Schemes

To apply a different color scheme:

1. In the Slide Design task pane, click Color Schemes.

2. Point to a color scheme in the task pane.

3. Click the color scheme's triangle button, and click Apply to All Slides.

To edit a color scheme:

1. In the Slide Design task pane, click Color Schemes, and then click Edit Color Schemes.

2. In the Edit Color Scheme dialog box, click the Custom tab.

3. Click the slide element you want to recolor.

4. Click Change Color, and then click the Standard or Custom tab.

5. Select a new color for the element and click OK. Click Apply.

The Edit Color Scheme dialog box appears, as shown in Figure 2.4. You can use this dialog box to select one of the standard color schemes for a presentation or to make changes to a standard color scheme.

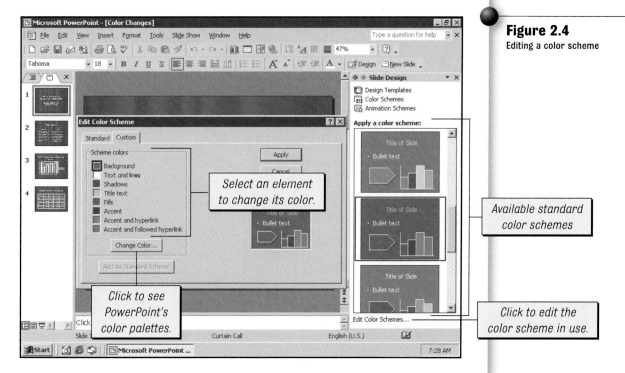

Figure 2.4
Editing a color scheme

POWERPOINT 2002

Available standard color schemes

Click to edit the color scheme in use.

6. Click the **Custom tab**, if it is not already selected.

On this tab, you can specify a different color for each of the eight standard slide elements.

7. Click the *Title text* color box, and click **Change Color**.

The Title Text Color dialog box appears. You can use either the Standard or Custom tab to specify a new color for the title text on your slides.

8. Click the **Standard tab**; then click a yellow dot in the hexagonal color palette.

In the New/Current area, the new selected color is shown above the current color for title text. Based on this comparison, you may decide to select a different color.

9. When you have selected the color that looks best, click **OK** to close the Title Text Color dialog box. Then, click **Apply** to close the Edit Color Scheme dialog box.

The titles in your slides change to a yellow color.

10. Save the changes to your presentation once again; then close the file.

PowerPoint saves statistical information about each presentation you create. This information includes the presentation's title, author, date and time created, and more. To view and modify these statistics for a particular file, first open the file, and then click Properties on the File menu.

NOTE *You can save a customized design template so that you can apply it to future presentations. Do not save the template, however, unless you have permission from the computer's owner or from your instructor. To save a customized template, click Save As on the File menu. Click the* Save as type *triangle button and click Design Template. The Save in box automatically changes to the folder where other PowerPoint templates are stored, so you don't need to navigate to the folder. Click the File name box, type a name for the new template, and click Save. The new template will appear with other templates in the Slide Design task pane.*

Did you know?

A printout is often referred to as a *hard copy*. Because you can actually touch the printout, it's considered "hard." Similarly, monitors, keyboards, printers, and other parts of the computer that you can touch are called *hardware*.

CREATING A PRESENTATION FROM A BLANK SLIDE

The fastest way to start a presentation is simply to launch PowerPoint and begin adding text to the blank slide that appears in the document window. This process is called *starting from a blank slide* or *starting from a blank presentation*. (If another presentation is open on your screen, you can click the New button 🗋 on the Standard toolbar to start a new presentation from a blank slide.) The slides will simply have black text on a white background; they will have no background, colors, or special fonts. You can add those elements later.

HANDS on

Starting a Presentation From a Blank Slide

In this activity, you will create a simple presentation from a blank slide. Later, you will return to this presentation and customize it by adding some design elements.

1. On the File menu, click New.

The New Presentation task pane appears.

2. In the task pane, click Blank Presentation.

A blank title slide appears in the document window, and the Slide Layout task pane appears. To start your new presentation, all you need to do is type text and add slides. Because nearly all professional presentations begin with a title slide, you can start with the one on your screen.

3. Click the title area and type DCM Planning Meeting without pressing Enter←. Click the subtitle area and type April 10, 2002.

4. In the Slide Layout task pane, find and click the Title and Text layout triangle button. When the layout's menu appears, click Insert New Slide.

5. In the new slide, click the title area and type Agenda. Click the text placeholder below the title, type 10:00 and press Tab; then type Bill Jones - 2001 Results and press Enter←.

PowerPoint BASICS

Starting From a Blank Slide

1. Click New on the File menu.

2. In the New Presentation task pane, click Blank Presentation.

3. Type text in the blank title slide's placeholders.

4. Add new slides by choosing layouts from the Slide Layout task pane.

6. Type 11:00 and press [Tab]; then type Mary Smith - New Policies and press [Enter←]. Type Noon and press [Tab]; then type Lunch Break and press [Enter←]. Type 1:30 and press [Tab]; then type Sandra Kay - Facilities Plan and press [Enter←]. Type 3:00 and press [Tab]; then type Sam Elliot - Hiring Plan and press [Enter←]. Type 4:00 and press [Tab]; then type Walt King - Technology Initiative. Click outside the text area.

Your screen should look like Figure 2.5.

Figure 2.5
Starting a presentation from a blank slide

7. Click the **Save button** 🖫. In the Save As dialog box, save the file as *Plain Agenda* in the *Tutorial* folder in your *PowerPoint Data* folder.

Another Way

You can also open the Save As dialog box by pressing [F12].

8. Close the task pane by clicking the **Close button** ⊠; close the file.

WORKING WITH OUTLINES

PowerPoint enables you to create a new presentation using data from a Microsoft Word file. You can also add slides to a presentation by inserting a Word document or an outline. Text created in Word's Outline View works best because this text automatically contains **styles,** or sets of character and paragraph attributes. (Of course, a Word user can add styles to ordinary text.) When you import a Word document, PowerPoint uses the outline structure from the styles in the document. A Heading 1 style becomes a slide title; a Heading 2 style becomes a level 1 subtitle, and so on. If the Word document contains no styles, PowerPoint uses the paragraph indentations or tabs at the beginning of paragraphs to create an outline.

Suppose you want to create a presentation from a report. Instead of importing or inserting the entire document to PowerPoint, you should edit the report in Word, condensing the paragraphs into outline form and making sure that each paragraph has an appropriate style. This approach gives you ready-made titles and subtitles for your slides.

Did you know?

It's a good idea to begin a presentation by creating an outline, just as you would for any other document that is divided into sections. It may seem like extra work, but an outline can make presentation design easier by giving you a plan to follow.

PowerPoint lets you export a presentation's outline in two ways: (1) use PowerPoint's Send To feature to send a presentation directly to Microsoft Word and (2) save the outline as a new file in **Rich Text Format** (RTF), which can then be used in many other programs. Microsoft Word, for example, can open an RTF-format document, so you can edit it, add text to it, and format it any way you like. Both of these procedures save only the text you can see in PowerPoint's Outline tab; the Word file or RTF file won't contain any tables, charts, or other objects from the presentation.

HANDS on

Creating Slides From a Word Outline

In this activity, you will open the *Write This Way* presentation, and then insert a Word outline into the presentation.

Using a Word Outline in PowerPoint

1. Open the presentation that will use the outline.

2. On the Insert menu, click Slides from Outline.

3. Select the outline file and click the Insert button.

1. **Open *Write This Way* in your *PowerPoint Data* folder. Save the presentation as *Import Word Outline* in the *Tutorial* folder.**

The Outline tab and the status bar indicate that this presentation contains only one slide—a title slide.

2. **On the Insert menu, click Slides from Outline.**

3. **In the Insert Outline dialog box, navigate to your *PowerPoint Data* folder, if necessary.**

The Word outline, also named *Write This Way,* appears in the list of available files, as shown in Figure 2.6. Your presentation files do not appear in this dialog

Figure 2.6
Insert Outline dialog box

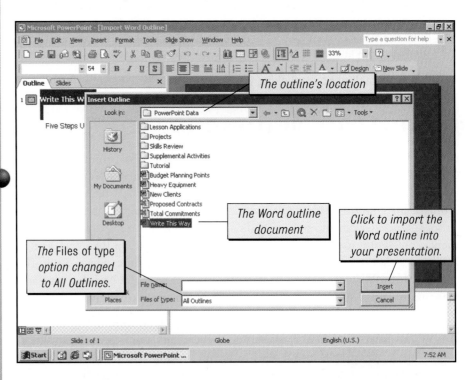

box because the *Files of type* option was automatically set to All Outlines when you clicked Slides from Outline on the Insert menu.

4. Select the *Write This Way* file, and click the **Insert button**.

The Word file opens into PowerPoint, adding five slides to your presentation.

WARNING *If PowerPoint does not provide the tools for inserting an outline, as described here, see your instructor.*

5. Navigate the presentation in Normal View, beginning with slide 1. Save the changes to your presentation; then close the file.

HANDS on

Sending a Presentation to Word

In this activity, you will open the *Construction* presentation and send it to Microsoft Word.

WARNING *If Microsoft Word is not installed on your computer, see your instructor.*

1. Open *Construction* in your *PowerPoint Data* folder. Save the presentation as *Send* in the *Tutorial* folder.

2. Review the presentation from beginning to end in Normal View. Look at the contents of the Outline tab as well as the slides themselves. Notice that the presentation includes titles, subtitles, and bulleted text items, as well as objects such as a table, a chart, and two graphic elements. Return to slide 1.

3. On the File menu, click **Send To**.

4. When the submenu appears, click **Microsoft Word**.

5. In the Send To Microsoft Word dialog box, click the **Outline only** option.

6. Click **OK**.

The *Outline only* option tells PowerPoint to send only the presentation's outline to Word. No slides, notes, or other elements of the presentation will be sent. Microsoft Word launches and opens a new document, which contains the outline from your presentation. The titles, subtitles, and bulleted items are formatted in a way that resembles their appearance in the slides, making it easy to distinguish them. However, no tables, charts, or other objects have been imported with the outline.

7. Save the new Word document as *Sent Outline* in the *Tutorial* folder, and close it without making any changes. Close Word and return to PowerPoint, where the *Send* presentation remains open.

PowerPoint **BASICS**

Sending a Presentation's Outline to Word

1. Open the presentation.

2. Click Send To on the File menu, and then click Microsoft Word.

3. Click *Outline only*, and then click OK.

NORTON

ONLINE

Visit **www.glencoe.com/norton/online/** for more information on using Word with PowerPoint.

Designing a Presentation **591**

HANDS on

Saving and Printing a Presentation's Outline

In this activity, you will save the *Send* presentation's outline as a new file and open it in another program. Then you will print the outline.

1. With the *Send* presentation still open in Normal View, click **Save As** on the File menu.

The Save As dialog box appears.

2. In the Save in box, navigate to the *Tutorial* folder of your *PowerPoint Data* folder, if necessary. In the File name box, type **Construction Outline**. **Click the Save as type triangle button** and click **Outline/RTF**.

The *PowerPoint 97 Files* folder appears in the window, but no files are listed, because the *Tutorial* folder contains no other RTF-format files.

3. Click **Save**.

4. Launch Microsoft Word or another word processing program that can open an RTF file. Open *Construction Outline* in the *Tutorial* folder in your *PowerPoint Data* folder.

5. Review the outline; then close it. Close your word processing program and return to PowerPoint, where the *Send* presentation remains open.

6. In **Normal View**, click **Print** on the File menu. In the *Print range* section, click the **All option**, if necessary. In the *Copies* section, verify that the number of copies is set to **1**. Click the **Print what triangle button** and click **Outline View**. Click the **Color/grayscale triangle button** and click **Pure Black and White**. Click **OK**.

The outline is sent to your printer. Your hard copy should look just like the contents of the Outline tab, with slide numbers and slide buttons, as well as the outline's text.

7. Close the file without saving it.

FORMATTING TEXT

PowerPoint offers many special text formatting features. Text format involves the appearance of the characters (design, size, and color) and special effects that are used to emphasize certain words. Formatting also includes **alignment,** the position of text in relation to the left and right edges of its placeholder. Subtitle text is usually aligned at the left side. Slide titles are commonly aligned in the center of

---

their placeholder, but they may also be aligned at the right or left side. Once you format a piece of text—a subtitle, for example—you can copy its formatting to other text by using the Format Painter button .

There are three main attributes in text formats: the font, the font size, and the font color. A **font** is a set of named characters of one design. PowerPoint offers dozens of fonts. (The fonts available to you, however, depend on the printer you are using.) Some fonts—like Times New Roman—are ideal for subtitles. Times New Roman is also ideal for paragraphs because it is a **serif** font. That is, the characters have "feet" that form a straight line, guiding readers' eyes from left to right. A **sans serif** font (a font without feet) is better for titles and labels. Arial is an example of a sans serif font.

In PowerPoint, the **font size** (the size of a piece of text—sometimes called *point size*) varies depending on its level in the outline. Titles are largest; 44 points is a common title size. Level 1 subtitles are larger than level 2 subtitles, and so on. If level 1 subtitles are 32 points, for example, level 2 subtitles may be 28 points, and level 3 subtitles may be 24 points. As a general rule, no subtitles should be smaller than 18 points. (Special text, such as footers and labels on pictures and charts, may be much smaller.)

Font colors depend on the design template that is used. PowerPoint's templates use font colors that contrast with the background color, but you can easily vary from the template by using a different font color on one or more slides. When you create a blank presentation, the automatic font color is black on a white background. If you start with a blank slide and then apply a background color, you may need to change the font color for adequate contrast.

After formatting some text in a presentation, you can use the Format Painter button to change other text to match. Select the formatted text, click the Format Painter button, and drag your pointer over other text. PowerPoint instantly copies the formats to any text your pointer touches.

Formatting also includes special effects used for emphasis, such as bold, italic, underline, and text shadow. **Bold** is a thick, heavy effect; **italic** is a thin, right-slanted effect; and **underline** is a line below an occasional word or phrase or below a hyperlink. Text **shadow,** a shading effect slightly to the right of each character of the text, is decorative—a way to add appeal. The key to using bold, italic, and underline is in not using them too much so that they continue to be special. Use the text shadow only on slide titles with very large characters.

HANDS on

Changing the Font, Size, and Color of Text

In this activity, you will open the *Plain Agenda* presentation (that you created earlier in the *Starting a Presentation From a Blank Slide* Hands On activity in this lesson), which is unformatted. Then you will apply a color scheme and format the text by selecting different fonts, font sizes, and font colors.

1. **Open *Plain Agenda* in the *Tutorial* folder in your *PowerPoint Data* folder, and save it as *Formatted Agenda* in the same folder.**

Changing Text Formatting

To choose a color scheme:

1. Click the Slide Design button. Click Color Schemes.

2. Choose a color scheme, click its triangle button, and click Apply to All Slides.

To change font size:

1. Select the text you want to change.

2. Click the Font Size triangle button and select the desired size.

To use the Format Painter:

1. Select some text with a format you want to copy.

2. Click the Format Painter button.

3. Select the text you want to change.

4. Deselect the changed text.

To change font:

1. Select the text you want to change.

2. Click the Font triangle button and select the desired font.

To change font color:

1. Select the text you want to change.

2. Click the Font Color triangle button and select the desired color.

This is the presentation you created earlier in this lesson. The slides are still unformatted. Start by choosing a color scheme.

2. Click the **Slide Design** button 🔲 Design on the Formatting toolbar. When the Slide Design task pane appears, click **Color Schemes**.

3. Point at the dark blue color scheme, click its triangle button, and then click **Apply to All Slides**. Close the task pane.

The slides now have a dark blue background, with light blue titles and white subtitles and bullets.

4. Go to slide 1 and select its title by dragging the pointer across it. Notice that the font size is 44 points.

5. Click the **Font Size triangle button** 12 ▾ on the Formatting toolbar, and click **54**.

The title enlarges from 44 points to 54 points, nearly filling its placeholder.

6. With the title still selected, click the **Format Painter button** 🖌.

The pointer changes and now displays a small brush icon. This indicates that you can apply the title's formatting to other text.

7. Scroll down to slide 2, and drag the pointer across the slide's title.

Notice that the pointer remains a formatting pointer until you click and release the mouse button. This means you can scroll to another slide without disabling the tool. After you drag across the title of slide 2 and release the mouse button, notice that the Format Painter button is deactivated. The two slide titles are now formatted identically.

8. Select all the bulleted text on slide 2—that is, all the text below the slide's title.

9. Click the **Font triangle button** [Times New Roman ▾] on the Formatting toolbar.

The Font drop-down list opens, listing all the available fonts on your system, as shown in Figure 2.7. Notice that the text is formatted as Arial.

10. Scroll down the Font list, and click **Times New Roman**.

The selected text is reformatted as Times New Roman.

11. In the first line of the bulleted list, select *10:00*.

12. Click the **Font Color triangle button** 🔺▾ on the Formatting toolbar. In the small palette of colors, click the **bright yellow color box**. Then click the gray area outside the slide to deselect the text.

The selected text and the bullet become bright yellow.

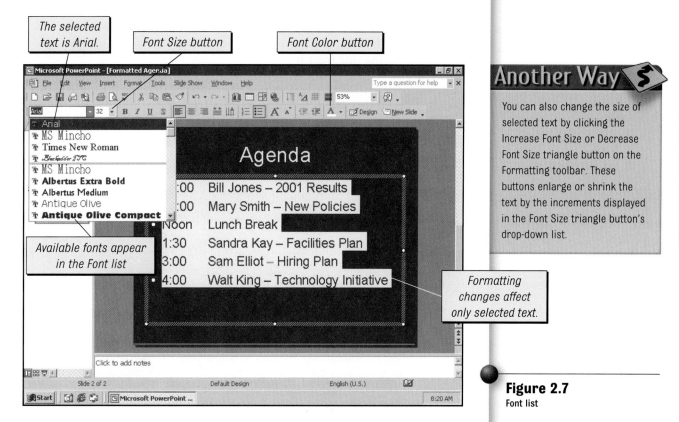

Figure 2.7
Font list

The selected text is Arial.

Font Size button

Font Color button

Available fonts appear in the Font list

Formatting changes affect only selected text.

Another Way

You can also change the size of selected text by clicking the Increase Font Size or Decrease Font Size triangle button on the Formatting toolbar. These buttons enlarge or shrink the text by the increments displayed in the Font Size triangle button's drop-down list.

POWERPOINT 2002

13. Reselect the yellow text, and double-click the **Format Painter button**. Drag the pointer across each of the times in the bulleted list, one at a time.

Because you double-clicked the Format Painter button, it remains active while you copy the formatting to multiple pieces of text.

14. When all the times are yellow, click the **Format Painter button** to deactivate it. Deselect any selected text on the slide. Save your changes to the presentation.

HANDS on

Adding Special Text Effects and Changing Alignment

In this activity, you will add special text effects and change alignments in the open presentation, *Formatted Agenda*.

1. Go to slide 1 and select the slide's title. Click the **Bold button** on the Formatting toolbar.

2. Go to slide 2 and select the slide's title. Click the **Underline button** on the Formatting toolbar.

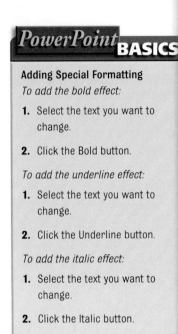
Adding Special Formatting

To add the bold effect:

1. Select the text you want to change.

2. Click the Bold button.

To add the underline effect:

1. Select the text you want to change.

2. Click the Underline button.

To add the italic effect:

1. Select the text you want to change.

2. Click the Italic button.

3. Go through each line in the bulleted list one at a time. In each line, select any text that follows a dash; then click the **Italic button** *I* on the Formatting toolbar.

The subject of each person's presentation should appear in italic, as shown in Figure 2.8.

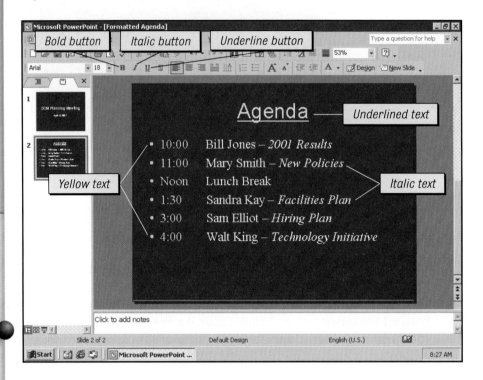

Figure 2.8
Slide with formatted text

4. Go to slide 1 and click at the end of the slide's subtitle (after the date). Press [Enter←] to add a new line of text to the subtitle, and type Conference Room 1.

You can use alignments to create a minor theme within a presentation. For example, you may like to left-align or right-align all level 1 subtitles.

5. Click anywhere in the new line of text, and then click the **Align Right button** [≡] on the Formatting toolbar.

The new line of text, which was originally centered in the placeholder, moves to the right.

> **NOTE** *You don't have to select an entire line of text to change its alignment. Just click anywhere inside the line to position the insertion point within it, and then click the desired alignment tool.*

6. Click the line above the new line, and press [F4].

Pressing [F4] issues the Repeat command, which repeats the last action you took. Now both subtitles are right-aligned, as shown in Figure 2.9.

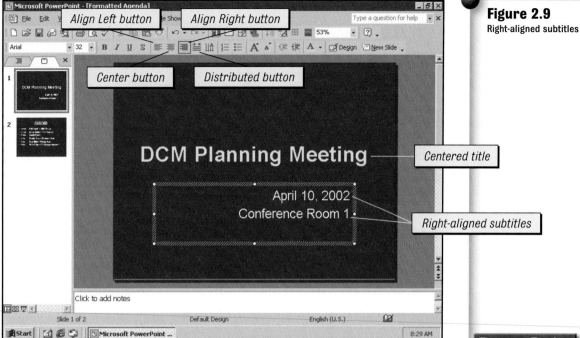

Figure 2.9
Right-aligned subtitles

7. Go to slide 2 and click the title area. Click the **Align Left button** 📄 on the Formatting toolbar.

The slide title, which originally was centered, moves to the left.

8. Click the **Center button** 📄 on the Formatting toolbar.

The word *Agenda* looks rather small by itself at the top of the slide, so you will change the title to give more weight to the title area. Then you will distribute the text across the title area's width.

9. Select the title and type Our Speakers for Today to replace the original title. Click the **Distributed button** 📄 on the Formatting toolbar.

The slide's title is now evenly distributed across the title area.

NOTE *Be careful about using the Distributed button. If there is too little text in the placeholder, PowerPoint will spread the characters apart to fill the placeholder, and this can make the text hard to read. Conversely, if your text already fills the placeholder, distributing it probably will not make a noticeable difference.*

10. Save your changes and close the file.

WORKING WITH CLIP ART AND IMAGES

To maintain your audience's attention, you should design your presentations so they include more than just text. A quick way to emphasize a slide and add variety

PowerPoint **BASICS**

Adding Alignments
To right-align text:

1. Click the line of text you want to change.

2. Click the Align Right button.

To left-align text:

1. Click the line of text you want to change.

2. Click the Align Left button.

To center text:

1. Click the line of text you want to change.

2. Click the Center button.

To distribute text evenly:

1. Click the line of text you want to change.

2. Click the Distributed button.

to a presentation is to use clip art. **Clip art** (sometimes called just **clips**) is a collection of ready-to-use graphic images that is installed with PowerPoint. The clips—which include simple line art, colorful drawings, and photographs—are stored in a special folder called the Clip Organizer. After you insert a clip, you can adjust its size, scale, and placement on the slide.

The fastest way to insert clip art is to select a slide layout that features a placeholder for an object, such as a piece of clip art, a chart, a table, or some other type of non-text object. When you select a slide layout that contains an object placeholder, you can click one of six icons to choose the exact type of object you want to insert.

If a slide has adequate space for clip art, you can add clip art to any slide—with or without a placeholder—by clicking the Insert menu, pointing to the Picture command, and then clicking the Clip Art command. You can also import any graphic into a slide from another source, such as a bitmap image file that is on a disk or your computer's hard drive. If you import an image this way, you treat it just like a clip art image.

HANDS on

Adding Clip Art to a Slide With or Without a Placeholder

In this activity, you will open the *Transportation Projects* presentation, and then add a slide using a slide layout that contains an object placeholder. You will then add a clip to the title slide, which does not contain an object placeholder.

1. Open *Transportation Projects* in your *PowerPoint Data* folder and save the file as *Transportation Projects with Clips* in the *Tutorial* folder.

2. On the Slides tab, select **slide 3**.

3. Click **Slide Layout** on the Format menu.

4. In the Slide Layout task pane, scroll down to the section named **Text and Content Layouts**. Point to the **Title, Text, and Content slide layout**, click its **triangle button**, and click **Insert New Slide**.

PowerPoint inserts the new slide immediately following slide 3.

5. Click the title area and type Our Strengths as the slide's title.

6. Click the text area on the lower-left side of the slide. Type Industry leader in civil engineering projects **and press** [Enter←]. **Type** Computer-based design and project management **and press** [Enter←]. **Type** Experience in every type of civil construction **without pressing** [Enter←].

7. Point to each of the six small icons in the object placeholder on the right side of the slide.

When you hold the pointer over each of the icons, a ScreenTip appears, telling you what type of object you can insert by clicking that icon.

8. Click the **Insert Clip Art icon** in the object placeholder.

The Select Picture dialog box appears, as shown in Figure 2.10, and displays all the clips that are currently installed on your system. Clips are categorized by subject, such as *business, people, concepts,* and others. Most pictures belong to more than one category. If you hold your pointer over any of the pictures, a ScreenTip appears and shows you which categories the clip belongs to, as well as its size in pixels, its size in bytes, and its file format.

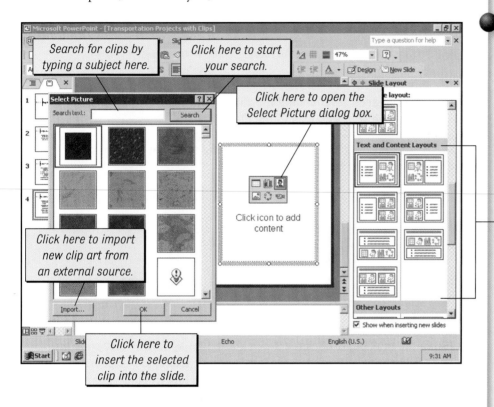

POWERPOINT 2002

Figure 2.10
Select Picture dialog box

NOTE *On your computer, the pictures in the Select Picture dialog box may vary from those shown in Figure 2.10, depending on what has been imported or deleted by other users of the computer.*

9. Scroll the collection of pictures and point to a few of them to see their information.

Instead of scrolling through the clips and selecting one visually, you can search for clips by typing search text that describes the type of image you need. If PowerPoint has a category of clips that matches your search text, it displays the clips in the dialog box.

10. Click the *Search text* box and type **construction**. Then click the **Search button**.

A group of clips with a construction theme appears in the dialog box.

11. Click the drawing that shows a construction worker using a jackhammer.

Did you know?

In the United States, *all* graphic images are protected by copyright. Even though PowerPoint lets you import graphic files from virtually any source, remember that you may be violating someone's copyright if you use an illustration or photograph without getting permission. Instead of taking graphics from Web sites or scanning images from magazines, look for sources of clip art files that you can freely use.

NOTE *If you do not find this clip in the dialog box, click another clip that you think symbolizes* Our Strengths.

12. Click **OK**.

The Select Picture dialog box disappears and the selected picture replaces the clip art placeholder on the slide. The clip art is surrounded by eight small circles, sizing handles, which you can use to move the clip or to change its size or shape. Just above the clip is a small green circle, which you can use to rotate the clip on the slide.

NOTE *When you insert a clip, the Picture toolbar may appear on your screen. If so, leave the toolbar in place.*

13. Click the area surrounding the slide to deselect the placeholder. Then, save your changes to the file.

14. Go to slide 1. Click the area surrounding the slide to make sure that no part of the slide is selected.

15. Point to **Picture** on the Insert menu, and then click **Clip Art**.

The Insert Clip Art task pane appears. You can use this task pane to find and insert clips on a slide without using a placeholder.

WARNING *PowerPoint may display the Add Clips to Organizer dialog box, which allows you to catalog all the media files on your computer. If this dialog box appears, click Later.*

16. In the task pane, click the **Search in triangle button**, and click the **Everywhere option**, if necessary, until a check mark appears in front of it. (The other three options in this box will have check marks also.) Click outside the box to close it. Click the **Results should be triangle button** and click the **Clip Art option** until a check mark appears in front of it. The other options in this box should not be selected.

17. Click the **Search text box**, type transportation, and click the **Search button**.

The task pane changes to display available clips that have a transportation-related theme.

18. Scroll through the clips and point to the picture of an airport symbol. Click the clip's triangle button, and click **Insert**. (If you cannot find a picture of an airport symbol, select a different clip to insert.)

The clip appears in the middle of the slide along with the Picture toolbar, as shown in Figure 2.11. (If the Picture toolbar does not appear on your screen, right-click the clip. When the shortcut menu appears, click Show Picture Toolbar.)

19. Save your changes to the presentation.

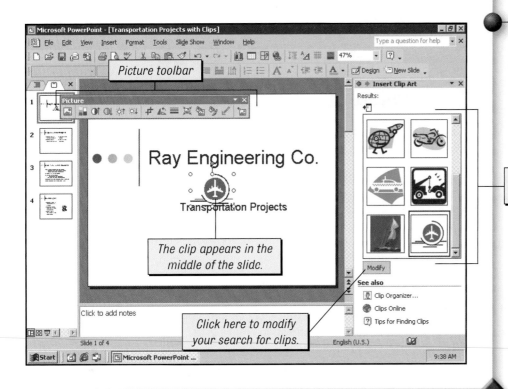

Figure 2.11
Clip art inserted without
a clip art placeholder

Select a clip from
the task pane.

The clip appears in the
middle of the slide.

Click here to modify
your search for clips.

Moving, Sizing, and Reshaping Clip Art

After you insert a piece of clip art, you may need to move it around on the slide to place it in the best position. You can move clips by dragging or by using the Cut and Paste commands. However, using Cut and Paste is not the most effective way to move clip art because precision pasting is not always possible. No matter how you move a clip, be sure to place it at least 0.25 inches from the slide's edges.

You may also need to change the size of a clip. Select the clip and then drag one of the corner handles (small white circles) away from the clip's center to enlarge it or toward the clip's center to shrink it. In this process, the pointer first becomes a two-way arrow; then it changes to the crosshair pointer. When you drag a corner handle diagonally—either toward or away from the clip's center—you change the clip's height and width proportionally, preventing distortion of the image.

You can also use the middle sizing handles to resize clips. If you drag the middle handle on any side of the clip, you stretch the clip in the direction you drag. For example, if you click the middle handle on the clip's right side and drag it away from the clip's center, you stretch the clip horizontally to the right. This distorts the clip, but it may give you the effect you want. If you accidentally stretch a clip by dragging a handle, immediately click the Undo button ◀ on the Standard toolbar. This returns the clip to its former shape.

You can reposition and resize clip art by using the Format Picture dialog box. Using the dialog box's Size tab, you can change height and width separately. You can also change height and width of an image proportionally by locking the **aspect ratio,** the relationship between the height and the width. You lock the aspect ratio by select-ing a check box. With the aspect ratio locked, you specify either the height or the width; the other dimension will be changed accordingly. If the aspect ratio is not locked when you change height or width, the image may be distorted. Using the Position tab, you can set the clip's distance from the slide's top left corner or center.

HINTS & TIPS

You can issue the Cut, Copy, and Paste commands in several ways:

To issue the Cut command, you can do one of the following:

- Click Cut on the Edit menu.

- Click the Cut button on the Standard toolbar.

- Press ⌈Ctrl⌋ + ⌈X⌋.

To issue the Copy command, you can do one of the following:

- Click Copy on the Edit menu.

- Click the Copy icon on the Standard toolbar.

- Press ⌈Ctrl⌋ + ⌈C⌋.

To issue the Paste command, you can do one of the following:

- Click Paste on the Edit menu.

- Click the Paste icon on the Standard toolbar.

- Press ⌈Ctrl⌋ + ⌈V⌋.

HANDS on

Resizing and Moving a Clip

In this activity, you will resize the clip on slide 1 of your *Transportation Projects with Clips* presentation. Then you will move the clip into a better position.

1. Verify that the clip art on slide 1 is selected.

Handles appear around the clip art. The Picture toolbar should be visible.

2. Right-click the clip; then click Format Picture on the shortcut menu that appears.

The Format Picture dialog box appears.

3. Click the Size tab. Verify that a check mark appears before the *Lock aspect ratio* option, as shown in Figure 2.12.

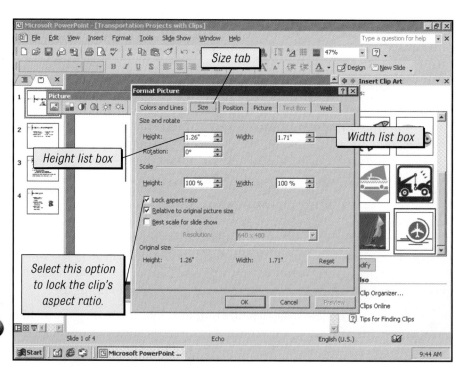

Figure 2.12
Format Picture dialog box

4. In the *Size and rotate* section, click the Height list box, select the number that appears there, and type 2. Also in the *Size and rotate* section click the Width list box.

PowerPoint changes the image size according to the height in the Height list box and adjusts the width proportionately.

5. Click OK.

The Format Picture dialog box closes. The clip, now resized, remains at the center of the slide.

NORTON
ONLINE

Visit **www.glencoe.com/norton/online/** for more information on using clip art.

POWERPOINT 2002

NOTE *If you want to resize the clip, repeat steps 2–5, changing the height in step 4.*

6. **Point to the center of the clip until the pointer changes to a four-way arrow.**

7. **Drag the clip to the lower-left corner of the slide and drop it there. (If the Picture toolbar is in your way, click its title bar and drag it out of the way.)**

If you make a mistake, remember to click the Undo button 🔄▾. Then repeat steps 6 and 7 to place the clip art properly.

8. **Go to slide 4 and select the clip. Point to the sizing handle in the clip's lower-left corner. When the two-way pointer appears, click and drag the handle until the bottom of the clip is even with the bottom of the last line of text in the bulleted list. Then, drag the upper-right handle until the top of the clip is even with the top of the first line of text in the bulleted list. Deselect the clip.**

9. **Close the task pane, if it is still visible. Save your changes and close the file.**

Inserting an Image From a File

You can obtain graphics from all kinds of sources, such as photographs you take or drawings you create in a draw program. The process of bringing in an image from a separate file, bypassing the clips that are provided by PowerPoint, is called **inserting** or **importing.** PowerPoint requires an inserted image to be in a standard bitmap file format, which means the image is stored as a grid of dots with varying colors and brightness. PowerPoint supports many bitmap file formats, including Windows Metafile (WMF), Graphics Interchange Format (GIF), Joint Photographic Experts Group (JPEG or JPG), and many others.

To insert an image from a file, click Picture on the Insert menu and then click From File. The Insert Picture dialog box appears, allowing you to find and select a picture file. After you insert an image this way, you can move and resize it just as you move and resize a clip art graphic.

Importing a Bitmap Image Into a Slide

In this activity, you will open the *Speaker* presentation and insert a photographic image that is stored as a bitmap file in your *PowerPoint Data* folder.

1. **Open *Speaker* in your *PowerPoint Data* folder, and save the file as *Speaker with Photo* in the *Tutorial* folder.**

Inserting an Image From a File

1. Click Picture on the Insert menu; then click From File.

2. In the Insert Picture dialog box, navigate to the file you want to use, select it, and click Insert.

3. Resize and move the picture as desired.

Figure 2.13
Picture inserted from a file

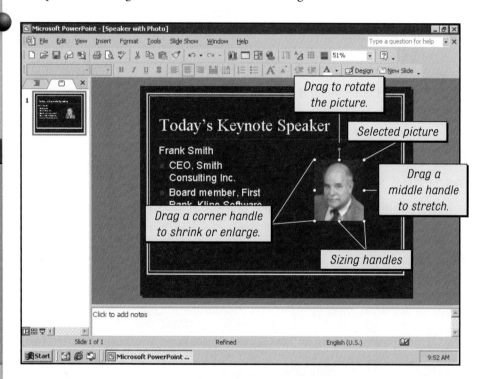

2. Click **Picture** on the Insert menu, and then click **From File**.

3. In the Look in box of the Insert Picture dialog box, navigate to your *PowerPoint Data* folder. Click the *Smith* file and click **Insert**.

A black and white photo appears on the slide, surrounded by sizing handles.

4. Right-click the picture, and click **Format Picture** on the shortcut menu.

5. On the Size tab of the Format Picture dialog box, make sure the *Lock aspect ratio* check box has a check mark in it. Click the **Height list box**, select the number that appears there, and type 2.2. Click the **Width list box**, and click **OK**.

The picture is enlarged on the slide, as shown in Figure 2.13.

HINTS & TIPS

If a color graphic doesn't look right on your slide, try changing it to grayscale or black and white. Right-click the image and click Show Picture Toolbar. When the Picture toolbar appears, click the Color button, and then click either Grayscale or Black & White. If you don't like the results, use the Undo command to reverse your action.

6. Drag the picture, if necessary, so that it is roughly centered in the blank right-hand area of the slide. Click outside the slide to deselect the picture. Then, save and close the file.

ADDING SOUND EFFECTS AND MOVIES TO A SLIDE

You can add all types of sounds and movies to your slides. If you present your slides directly from your computer's disk, you can play the sounds and movies, too. Your slides can include music tracks played from a compact disc, recorded messages stored on your hard disk, or one of the many sound effect clips provided by PowerPoint. Of course, your PC must include the appropriate multimedia capabilities (such as a sound card and speakers) to play sounds. You simply click Movies and Sounds on the Insert menu, and click the appropriate movie or sound option on the submenu. Browse to find the appropriate clip and click Insert.

HANDS on

Inserting a Sound Into a Slide

In this activity, you will use the *Teamwork Award* presentation to add a sound effect to a slide.

1. Open *Teamwork Award* in your *PowerPoint Data* folder and save the file as *Sound Effect* in the *Tutorial* folder.

2. Point to **Movies and Sounds** on the Insert menu, and then click **Sound** from Clip Organizer.

The Insert Clip Art task pane appears, displaying a collection of sound clips stored on your system.

3. Pause the pointer over each of the clips and note the ScreenTip, which displays the clip's name, size, and file format.

4. Find and click the **Claps Cheers clip triangle button**, and then click **Insert** on the menu that appears.

5. When a message box appears, asking if you want the sound to play automatically when the slide is opened in a presentation, click **No**.

PowerPoint inserts a sound icon on the slide. The sound will play only when you click the sound icon in Slide Show View.

6. Click the sound icon and drag it to the bottom of the slide, below the text *Give the team a big hand!*, as shown in Figure 2.14. Drag the icon's sizing handles to resize the icon, if you want.

PowerPoint BASICS

Adding Sound to a Slide

1. Click the Insert menu, click Movies and Sounds, and then click Sound from Clip Organizer.

2. Find the desired clip, click its triangle button, and then click Insert on the menu that appears.

3. Choose whether you want the sound to play automatically or not.

4. Drag the sound icon into position on the slide.

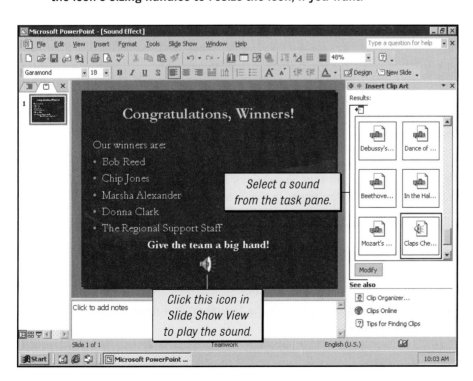

Figure 2.14
Sound effect on a slide

7. Click the **Slide Show button** 🖳.

8. When the slide appears in Slide Show View on your screen, click the sound icon and listen to the sound of clapping and cheering (if your computer has speakers). Press Esc to return to Normal View. Close the Insert Clip Art task pane, and then save and close the presentation.

WORKING WITH DRAWING OBJECTS

Besides using clip art, you can enhance slides by drawing shapes on them, such as an arrow or a circle. You can use a drawn object to emphasize a line of text, for example, or to serve as the background for text. The Drawing toolbar contains tools for drawing simple geometric shapes, such as lines, rectangles, and ovals. You click the desired toolbar button and drag the crosshair pointer diagonally in the slide pane. As you drag the pointer, the shape appears on the screen. The farther you drag the pointer, the larger the shape becomes.

In addition to the geometric shapes, the Drawing toolbar offers a collection of pre-drawn, geometrically shaped objects, called **AutoShapes.** AutoShapes are grouped in categories, including lines, connectors, basic shapes, and others. You create an AutoShape the same way you create a geometric shape: Select the desired AutoShape from the Drawing toolbar, and then drag the pointer across the slide. You can move, resize, and scale a shape or an AutoShape using the same methods you applied to clip art earlier in this lesson.

You can use several tools on the Drawing toolbar to enhance a shape or an AutoShape. If you draw a rectangle, for example, you can change its interior color—called the **fill color**—using the Fill Color button 🖍▾. You can change the color or thickness of a shape's outline; for example, you can change a circle's outline from black to red, or change its line type from solid to dotted. The line style is the weight, or thickness, of the line, which is measured in points, like fonts.

HANDS on

Adding an AutoShape to a Slide

In this activity, you will open the *Marketing* presentation, add an AutoShape to one slide, and then move the object.

1. Open *Marketing* in your *PowerPoint Data* folder and save the file as *Marketing with Shapes* in the *Tutorial* folder.

2. Click **Toolbars** on the View menu, and then click **Drawing**.

The Drawing toolbar appears on your screen.

3. Go to slide 3.

4. On the Drawing toolbar, click the **AutoShapes button** AutoShapes ▾ and click **Block Arrows**.

The Block Arrows palette opens, as shown in Figure 2.15.

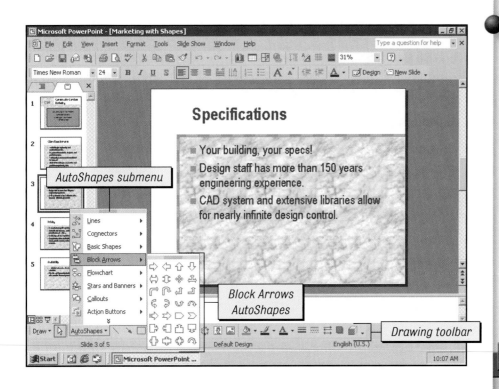

Figure 2.15
Selecting a block arrow AutoShape

POWERPOINT 2002

5. In the Block Arrows palette, click the **Left Arrow**. Click just above the bullet next to the first subtitle on the slide, and drag down and to the right, creating an arrow that is about twice as wide as the bullet. When the arrow is complete, release the mouse button.

As you drag, the arrow forms on the screen. If you drag too much in one direction, the shape can become distorted. In that case, click the object; then click one of the sizing handles and drag until the object resumes its original shape. Otherwise, you can select the object, press Delete to delete it from the slide, and repeat steps 4 and 5.

6. Drag the object to the right end of the first bulleted subtitle and drop it there, so it points back to the line of text.

7. Click the area outside the slide to view your work. Save your changes.

HANDS on

Drawing and Enhancing a Geometric Shape

In this activity, you will draw a basic geometric shape on a slide in the *Marketing with Shapes* presentation. Then you will change the shape's fill and line colors, change the line width, and apply a shadow effect.

1. In the *Marketing with Shapes* presentation, go to slide 5. On the View menu, click **Ruler**.

The horizontal and vertical rulers appear in the slide pane.

Designing a Presentation   **607**

Working With Geometric Shapes

To draw a basic shape:

1. Select the slide that will contain the shape.

2. Open the Drawing toolbar, if necessary.

3. On the Drawing toolbar, click the shape you want to draw.

4. Click the slide, drag to create the shape, and then release the mouse button.

5. Resize and move the shape on the slide, as needed.

To change a shape's fill color:

1. Select the shape to be changed.

2. On the Drawing toolbar, click the Fill Color triangle button, and then click the desired color.

To change a shape's line color:

1. Select the shape to be changed.

2. On the Drawing toolbar, click the Line Color triangle button, and then click the desired color.

To change a shape's line style:

1. Select the shape to be changed.

2. On the Drawing toolbar, click the Line Style button, and then click the desired line style.

2. On the Drawing toolbar, click the **Rectangle button** .

3. Click the slide just below the last subtitle. Drag to the right and downward, until your rectangle is about 1.5″ tall and 6.5″ wide; then release the mouse button.

As you draw the rectangle, watch the rulers and use them as a guide.

4. With the rectangle still selected, click the **Fill Color triangle button** on the Drawing toolbar.

The Fill Color palette displays a group of neutral colors which complement the color scheme used by this presentation's design template. Additional colors are available by clicking More Fill Colors.

5. On the color palette, click the taupe color that matches the slide's bullets.

The rectangle's fill color changes.

6. On the Drawing toolbar, click the **Line Color triangle button** . When the color palette appears, click the brown color that matches the brown dashes surrounding the slide's text area.

7. Click the **Line Style button** . Click the **4½ pt solid line style**.

8. With the rectangle still selected, click the **Shadow Style button** on the Drawing toolbar. When the palette of shadow options appears, click **Shadow Style 4**.

9. Click outside the slide to deselect the rectangle, as shown in Figure 2.16. Then, clear the check mark next to **Ruler** on the View menu. Save and close the presentation. Close the Drawing toolbar.

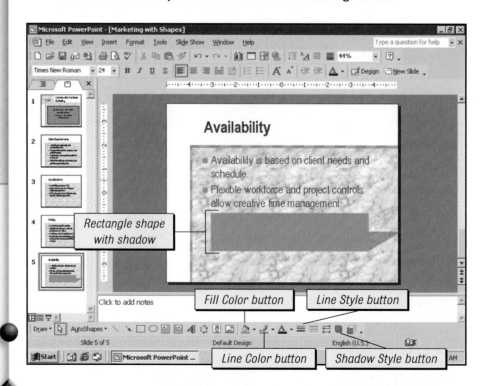

Figure 2.16
Rectangle with a shadow

WORKING WITH CHARTS

Charts are useful tools for relaying numeric information to an audience. A **chart** (also called a **graph**) is a graphical representation of numerical data; examples include the familiar column chart and the pie chart. Several slide layouts include object placeholders that can hold a chart. Simply double-click the chart icon in the placeholder to display the chart-building tools. You can also insert a graph without a placeholder by clicking the Insert Chart button 📊 on the Standard toolbar, or if a chart exists in one of your Excel worksheets, you can import it into a PowerPoint slide.

To help you create a chart, PowerPoint displays a special window called a **datasheet.** A datasheet is a table which resembles a small Excel worksheet, divided into rows and columns. The intersection of each row and column is called a **cell.** To create a table, type numerical data into the cells, and PowerPoint translates the data into a graphical chart.

After you add a chart to a slide, you can resize and move it just as you resize and move other objects, such as clip art or shapes. If you need to edit the chart, reopen its datasheet by double-clicking the chart. You can also make other modifications to a chart, such as changing the type of chart.

WEB NOTE

If you have some favorite Web sites that you visit often, you can add them to your Favorites list and access them with a couple of clicks. In Internet Explorer, visit a favorite site. To add it to the list, click Add to Favorites on the Favorites menu, and click OK. Later, when you use PowerPoint (or any other Office application), you can open the Web toolbar and choose a site from the Favorites list. Internet Explorer will launch and immediately go to that Web site.

HANDS on
Using the Datasheet

In this activity, you will insert a chart into a slide in the *Commitments* presentation by using the datasheet.

1. Open *Commitments* in your *PowerPoint Data* folder and save the file as *Commitments with Chart* in the *Tutorial* folder.

2. Close the left pane by clicking its **Close button** ☒. Also close the task pane, if necessary.

The slide pane now fills the document window.

> **NOTE** *To bring the left pane and notes pane back into view, you can click Normal (Restore Panes) on the View menu.*

3. Scroll to slide 3 and double-click the chart placeholder.

The PowerPoint window changes in several ways when you create a chart. The datasheet appears in a small window of its own, as shown in Figure 2.17. The Standard toolbar now includes tools for working with charts, and the Formatting toolbar changes to include tools for formatting charts. The Data and Chart menus are added to PowerPoint's menu bar.

4. In the datasheet, click the cell that contains the word *East* and type Wesley. Then replace the word *West* with Oak Woods and replace *North* with Bradley. Click the empty cell under *Bradley* and type Old Farley.

As you type in the datasheet, the chart displays the new related data.

PowerPoint **BASICS**

Creating a Chart From a Datasheet

1. Double-click a chart placeholder in a slide.

2. Delete the sample data from the datasheet.

3. Type your data into the datasheet, and then close it.

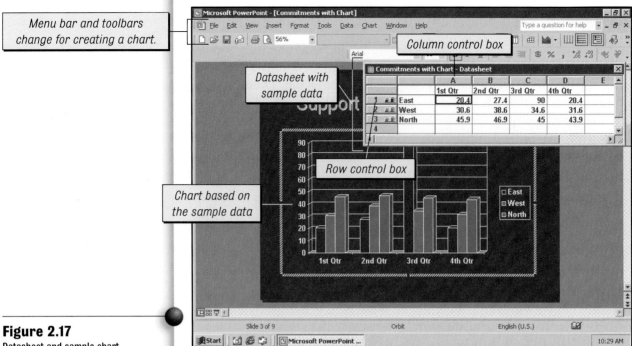

Figure 2.17
Datasheet and sample chart

Callouts in figure:
- Menu bar and toolbars change for creating a chart.
- Column control box
- Datasheet with sample data
- Row control box
- Chart based on the sample data

5. Click the first cell in column A and type OCT, press ⌧Tab to move one cell to the right and type NOV, and then press ⌧Tab to move one more cell to the right and type DEC.

6. Starting in cell A1 and ending in cell C4, type the data shown in Table 2.1.

Table 2.1	Chart Data		
Rows	**Columns**		
	A	B	C
1	5	4	2
2	3	5	4
3	6	6	6
4	2	2	1

7. Click the **Column D Control box**, press ⌧Delete, and click a cell in column E.

8. Close the datasheet window by clicking its **Close button** ⌧.

The new chart appears on slide 3, and remains selected so you can continue working on it.

9. Save your changes to the file.

HANDS on

Changing a Chart's Type

By default, PowerPoint always creates a column chart. However, you can change the type of chart to a more appropriate one, such as a bar chart or an area chart, depending on the type of data you need to present. To change a chart's type, click the Chart Type triangle button ▦▾, which appears on the Standard toolbar when the chart's datasheet is open. In this activity, you will use the *Commitments with Chart* presentation to explore the Chart Type options.

1. In the *Commitments with Chart* presentation, verify that the chart is selected. (If the chart is not selected, double-click the chart you just created on slide 3.) On the Standard toolbar, click the **Chart Type triangle button** ▦▾. In the palette of chart types, click the **3-D Bar Chart option**.

PowerPoint reformats the chart.

2. Click the blank area surrounding the slide two times. Save the reformatted chart, which should look like Figure 2.18.

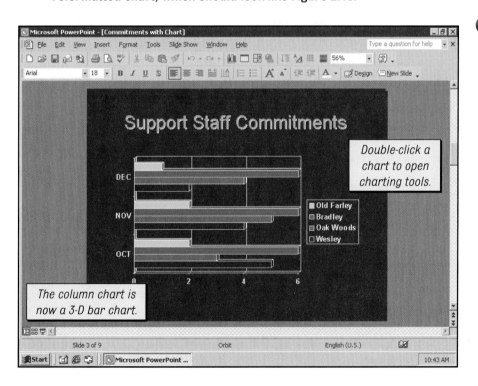

The column chart is now a 3-D bar chart.

Double-click a chart to open charting tools.

Figure 2.18
3-D bar chart

HINTS & TIPS

There are many kinds of charts. Column charts are good for comparing amounts of different items, while pie charts show how different items add up to create a whole. Be sure to choose a chart type that best conveys your meaning.

Importing a Chart From Excel

If you have created a chart in Excel, you can insert the chart into a PowerPoint slide in several ways. The easiest way to import an Excel chart is to use Windows' **Object Linking and Embedding (OLE)** capabilities. With OLE, you can easily re-use data from one application in another application.

Did you know?

When you use the Cut or Copy command, the cut or copied data is moved to a temporary storage space in your computer's memory called the Office Clipboard. When you use the Paste command, data is copied from the Office Clipboard into the open application. The Office Clipboard can hold up to 24 different pieces of data. To view the Office Clipboard's contents, click Office Clipboard on the Edit menu.

When you use OLE, PowerPoint treats the Excel chart as an object, embeds it in the slide, and creates a link back to the original slide in the Excel worksheet. Because this link exists, any changes made to the original chart are automatically reflected in the PowerPoint slide. For this reason, linking and embedding are much more powerful and flexible than simply copying the chart in Excel and pasting it into the slide.

To link or embed an Excel chart into a slide, open the Excel worksheet and select the chart. On the Edit menu, click Copy. Open PowerPoint and go to the slide that will contain the chart; then click the Paste Special command on the Edit menu. This opens the Paste Special dialog box, where you select the Excel chart object. If you want to create a linked object, click Paste link and click OK. If you want to create an embedded object, click Paste. In the As box, click the desired file format and then click OK. PowerPoint links or embeds the chart into the slide.

In PowerPoint, if you decide to make changes to the chart or its source data, double-click the chart to open it in Excel. This feature enables you to edit the chart in its native application. The changes will appear in the original chart and also in the embedded copy in PowerPoint.

HANDS on

Linking an Excel Chart Into a Slide

In this activity, you will open an Excel worksheet named *Total Commitments,* which contains a chart, and then link the chart into the *Commitments with Chart* PowerPoint presentation.

1. Go to slide 9 in the *Commitments with Chart* presentation.

2. Launch Microsoft Excel and open the workbook file named *Total Commitments* in your *PowerPoint Data* folder. Save the workbook file as *Revised Total Commitments* in the *Tutorial* folder.

NOTE *If Microsoft Excel is not installed on your computer, ask your instructor for directions.*

3. Click the **Chart worksheet tab** to view this worksheet, if the tab isn't already selected.

The Chart worksheet contains the chart you will link to the current PowerPoint slide.

4. In the worksheet, click the thin border that surrounds the chart to select it.

Black sizing handles appear around the chart.

5. Click **Copy** on the Edit menu. Then, switch to PowerPoint and click **Paste Special** on the Edit menu.

PowerPoint BASICS

Linking an Excel Chart Into a Slide

1. Select the slide that will hold the chart.

2. Launch Excel and select the chart.

3. Click Copy on the Edit menu.

4. Return to PowerPoint, and click Paste Special on the Edit menu.

5. Click the *Paste* or *Paste link* option, click Microsoft Excel Chart Object, and clear the *Display as icon* check box.

6. Click OK.

6. In the Paste Special dialog box, click the **Paste link option**, as shown in Figure 2.19. In the *As* list box verify that Microsoft Excel Chart Object is selected. Verify that the *Display as icon* check box is not selected. Click **OK**.

The Excel chart appears in the slide.

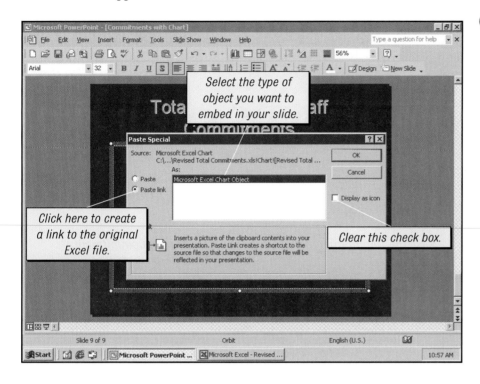

Figure 2.19
Linking an Excel chart into a slide

7. **Double-click the chart in the slide**.

The Excel worksheet opens again, with the chart displayed. Notice that the height of the last column is 8. You can edit the chart here, and when you save the worksheet, the changes will be reflected in PowerPoint.

8. Click the **Total Commitments worksheet tab** to open that sheet. Click **cell B8**, type 3, and press . Save and close the Excel worksheet and close Excel. Return to slide 9 in the PowerPoint presentation, and save your presentation.

Notice that the chart's last column has changed height, from 8 to 3.

> **NOTE** *If your chart's last column still has a height of 8, you need to update the chart to reflect the change you just made to the worksheet. To do this, right-click the chart; when the shortcut menu appears, click Update Link.*

HINTS & TIPS

When you have multiple programs open at the same time, you can quickly switch between them by pressing [Alt] + [Tab]. This frees you from minimizing application windows or using the taskbar.

WORKING WITH TABLES

Because charts present information in a visual way, they attract attention. Sometimes, however, seeing data in columns and rows—like a table—is also effective. In fact, a table can renew the audience's attention, especially when it follows several charts or text-only slides. With a colorful border and fill color on the whole table or only in certain cells, a table is information and a graphic rolled into one. You can size and move tables just like other graphic objects.

The simplest way to create a table in PowerPoint is to use a slide layout that contains a table placeholder. When you double-click the placeholder, PowerPoint instantly provides all the tools you need to create a new table. You can then specify the number of columns and rows for the table. A PowerPoint table should be simple and small, fitting comfortably on the slide, with cell entries no smaller than 18 points. Ideally, a table has three or four rows and only two or three columns. No table should exceed five rows and four columns.

If a slide doesn't have a table placeholder, you can click the Insert Table button 📖 on the Standard toolbar to add a table.

HANDS on

Creating and Filling in a Table

In this activity, you will rename the *Commitments with Chart* presentation and add a table to one slide.

1. Save the *Commitments with Chart* presentation as *Commitments with Table* in the *Tutorial* folder in your *PowerPoint Data* folder.

2. Go to slide 7 and double-click the table placeholder.

3. In the Insert Table dialog box, select or type 4 in the *Number of columns* box. Select or type 5 in the *Number of rows* box. Click **OK**.

PowerPoint inserts a table into the slide.

4. Click the first cell of the table, if necessary.

The table is selected. The Tables and Borders toolbar appears whenever you select a table.

5. Press [Tab] to move the insertion point to the second cell in the first row. Type Site Prep and press [Tab]. In the first row's third cell, type Paving and press [Tab]. In the last cell, type Power.

6. Click the first cell in row 2, type Wesley, and press [↓] to move to the first cell in row 3. Type Oak Woods and press [↓]. Type Bradley and press [↓]. Type Old Farley.

7. In the remaining cells, type the numbers shown in Table 2.2.

8. Click outside the table to deselect it, then save your changes to the file.

Table 2.2	Table Data	
Site Prep	**Paving**	**Power**
2	4	2
7	4	4
2	3	6
2	2	1

Using Borders, Fill Colors, and Alignments in a Table

You use the buttons on the Tables and Borders toolbar to enhance the appearance of tables. In your table, for example, you can add a colored border to any or all of the cells. The borders can match or be different colors in different parts of the table. You can vary the border style (using solid, dashed, or dotted lines) and width (creating very narrow or wide lines). In addition, you can emphasize information by applying a fill color to any or all cells, using the same color for all or a pattern of different colors. To add a border or fill color, you must first select the affected cells.

To select a cell before adding a border or fill color to it, you simply click the cell. If you want to add borders or fill colors to a column or row, however, you need to drag the pointer over those cells or use the Select commands on the Tables and Borders toolbar.

Changing the horizontal and vertical alignment of text in cells is another way to enhance a table. By default, text is top-aligned and left-aligned within its cell. Just as you learned with regular text earlier in this lesson, you change horizontal alignment of text in cells with the four alignment buttons on the Formatting toolbar. You use the buttons on the Tables and Borders toolbar (Align Top ▣, Center Vertically ▣, and Align Bottom ▣) to arrange text vertically in cells.

Enhancing a Table

In this activity, you will enhance the table on slide 7 in the *Commitments with Table* presentation, using the Tables and Borders toolbar buttons.

1. In the *Commitments with Table* presentation, click the *Site Prep* cell. Drag across the row and down to the last cell in the *Power* column to select the three columns.

The three columns are selected.

2. On the Formatting toolbar, click the **Center button** ▤. On the Tables and Borders toolbar, click the **Center Vertically button** ▣.

The data is now centered vertically and horizontally in the selected cells.

3. Select the table's first column by clicking the first cell and dragging downward to the bottom cell in the column. Center the contents of the cells vertically by clicking the **Center Vertically button** ▣.

4. Deselect the table by clicking the blank area surrounding the slide.

5. Select the entire table by clicking the top left cell and dragging to the bottom right cell. Click the **Border Color button** 🖉 on the Tables and Borders toolbar. When the color palette appears, click **More Border Colors**.

6. In the Colors dialog box, click the **Standard tab**, if necessary. Click a light orange color near the center of the color chart, as shown in Figure 2.20. Then click **OK**.

Figure 2.20
Colors dialog box with a new color selected

POWERPOINT 2002

PowerPoint BASICS

Changing a Table's Appearance

To align text in cells:

1. Select the cell(s) containing text to be aligned.

2. Click one vertical and one horizontal alignment button.

To add borders:

1. Select the cell(s) to be bordered.

2. Select the border style, width, and color on the Tables and Borders toolbar.

3. Click the Outside Borders button, and click the desired option.

To add fill color:

1. Select the cell(s) to be filled with color.

2. Click the Fill Color button, and click the desired color.

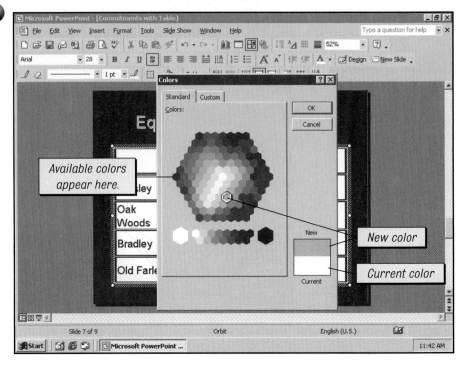

7. Click the **Border Width triangle button** `¼ pt` and click 1½ pt.

8. Click the **Outside Borders triangle button**, and click the **All Borders option**.

An orange border surrounds the table, and the lines between the cells remain.

9. Click the empty cell in the table's top left corner and drag across the top row to select the entire row. Click the **Fill Color triangle button**. When the color palette appears, click the **lighter gray square**.

10. Click any cell to deselect the top row, and drag to select the first column in the table. Click the **Fill Color button** to reapply the gray color. Deselect the table, and save your changes.

Importing a Table From Word

If you have created a table in Word, you can import the table into a PowerPoint slide. As you learned when you imported an Excel chart into a slide, the easiest way to import a Word table is by using the Copy and Paste Special commands, which take advantage of PowerPoint's OLE capabilities. When you use OLE, PowerPoint treats the Word table as an object, embeds it in the slide, and creates a link back to the original table in the Word document. Because this link exists, any changes made to the original table are automatically reflected in the PowerPoint slide.

To link or embed a Word table into a slide, open the Word document and select the table. On the Edit menu, click Copy. Open PowerPoint and go to the slide

NORTON ONLINE

Visit **www.glencoe.com/norton/online/** for more information on the use of tables.

that will contain the table; then, click the Paste Special command on the Edit menu. This opens the Paste Special dialog box, where you select the Word table. If you want to create a linked table, click Paste link and click OK. If you want to create an embedded table, click Paste; and in the As box, click the desired format. Then, click OK. PowerPoint then links or embeds the table into the slide.

In PowerPoint, if you decide to make changes to the table or its source data, double-click the table to open it in Word. This feature enables you to edit the table in its native application. The changes will appear in the original table and in the embedded copy in PowerPoint.

HANDS on

Linking a Word Table Into a Slide

In this activity, you will open *Heavy Equipment*, a Word document that contains a table, and link the table into the *Commitments with Table* PowerPoint presentation.

1. Go to slide 8 in the *Commitments with Table* presentation.

You want to insert a small table that already exists in a Word document in the blank space at the bottom of this slide.

2. Launch Microsoft Word and open *Heavy Equipment* in your *PowerPoint Data* folder. Save the file as *Revised Heavy Equipment* in the *Tutorial* folder.

NOTE *If Microsoft Word is not installed on your computer, ask your instructor for directions.*

3. Click the **Table menu**, point to **Select**, and click **Table** to select the entire table.

4. Click **Copy** on the Edit menu. Switch to PowerPoint; then click **Paste Special** on the Edit menu.

5. In the Paste Special dialog box, click the **Paste link option**. In the *As* list box, click **Microsoft Word Document Object**. Verify that the *Display as icon* check box is not selected. Then, click **OK**.

The table appears in the slide. Notice, however, that you can see the selection handles that appear around the table, but not the table itself. This is because the table's text is black and it has no background. You can fix this by applying a background color.

6. If necessary, activate the Tables and Borders toolbar by pointing to **Toolbars** on the View menu and clicking **Tables and Borders**. On the Tables and Borders toolbar, click the **Fill Color triangle button** and click the white square.

The table's cells fill with white; the black text is now visible.

PowerPoint BASICS

Linking a Word Table Into a Slide

1. Select the slide that will hold the table.

2. Launch Word and open a file containing a table.

3. Click Table, point to Select, and click Table to select the table.

4. Click Copy on the Edit menu.

5. Return to PowerPoint, and click Paste Special on the Edit menu.

6. Click the *Paste* or *Paste link* option, select Microsoft Word Document Object, and clear the *Display as icon* check box.

7. Click OK.

NOTE *If the slide layout changes from the one-column layout called Title and Text to a Title and 2-Column Text layout, click Slide Layout on the Format menu. In the Slide Layout task pane, click the Title and Text triangle button, and click Apply to Selected Slides. Close the Slide Layout task pane.*

7. Drag the table to the bottom half of the slide. Drag the sizing handles to enlarge it, so the text can be easily read. Reposition the table on the slide, as needed, so that the slide is balanced, as shown in Figure 2.21.

Figure 2.21
Embedded Word table

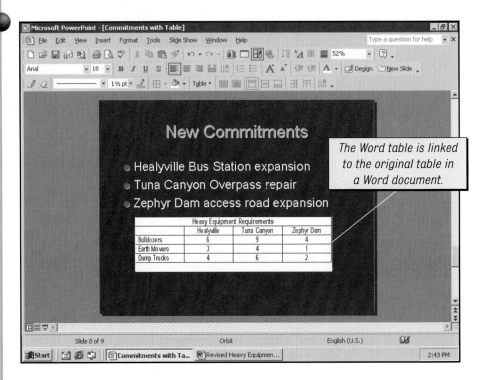

The Word table is linked to the original table in a Word document.

WEB NOTE

To learn more about PowerPoint, learn more professional-grade techniques, and subscribe to online newsletters about PowerPoint and other Microsoft products, visit Microsoft's PowerPoint home page at **http://www.microsoft.com/office /powerpoint/default.htm**.

8. Double-click the table in the slide.

The Word document opens again, with the table displayed. You can edit the table here, and when you save the document, the changes will be reflected in PowerPoint.

9. Click the table's last cell, delete the number *2*, and type *3*. Save and close the Word file, and close Word. Return to slide 8 in the PowerPoint presentation.

Notice that the table has already been updated to reflect the change you just made to the Word document.

10. Save your changes and close the file. Close the Tables and Borders toolbar.

Adding Action Buttons to Slides

An action button is an icon you can add to a slide. In Slide Show View, you can click the button to perform an action, such as jumping to another slide, playing a sound or movie file, or launching another program. In this activity, you'll search Help for information about adding an action button to a slide. Then you will apply the information to the *Employee Benefits* presentation.

1. In the Ask a Question box, type action button and press Enter↵.

2. Click the About action buttons option. Read the information. Expand the Help window, if necessary. On the Contents tab, explore additional information about action buttons and how to insert an action button. When you are finished, close the Help window.

3. Open *Employee Benefits* in your *PowerPoint Data* folder and save the presentation as *Employee Benefits with Action Button* in the *Tutorial* folder. Scroll to slide 8.

When you give the presentation, you want to be prepared to provide information from the company's annual report. An easy way to do this is to open another presentation, which features that information. You can do this with an action button.

4. Point to Action Buttons on the Slide Show menu and click the Information button.

5. In the lower-right corner of the slide, click and hold the mouse button. Drag diagonally about an inch to create a button, and then release the mouse button.

6. In the Action Settings dialog box, click the Mouse Click tab, if necessary. Click the Hyperlink to option button, and then click the Hyperlink to box's triangle button. Scroll down through the list of options, and click Other PowerPoint Presentation.

7. In the Hyperlink to Other PowerPoint Presentation dialog box, click the Look in box triangle button, navigate to the *PowerPoint Data* folder, and click the *Annual Report* file. Then, click OK.

8. In the Hyperlink to Slide dialog box, verify that the title of slide 1 is selected, and click OK. Then in the Action Settings dialog box, click OK. When the dialog box closes, click the blank area outside the slide to deselect the action button. Save the presentation.

9. Switch to Slide Show View. When slide 8 appears on your screen, click the action button.

10. Press Esc twice to return to Normal View. Save and close the *Employee Benefits with Action Button* presentation.

USING THE SLIDE MASTER TO CHANGE FORMATTING

As you have seen, you can easily customize the individual slides in a presentation. By using PowerPoint's slide master feature, however, you can customize an entire presentation in one easy step. A **slide master** is a special form that belongs to a design template and defines many of the template's attributes, such as font sizes and styles, bullets, size and placement of placeholders, the background and colors, and more. If you make a change to a slide master, the change is **global;** that is, the change is reflected throughout the presentation.

You can also use a slide master to incorporate custom repeating elements in a presentation. For example, you can place a logo on the slide master and that logo will appear in the same place on every slide.

Every presentation that uses a design template has a slide master, a title master, a handout master, and a notes master. The slide, handout, and notes masters actually appear in their own views. (You can view a presentation's title master along with its slide master.) To switch to Slide Master View and open the presentation's title and slide masters, press ⬆Shift while you click the Normal View button 🔲. The slide and title masters display text placeholders and sample text, even if the actual slides contain real text.

Changing Fonts and Bullets for an Entire Presentation

You may like the design template you are using, but prefer a slightly different style for certain elements. Using the slide master, you can change a font style, size, and/or color for all slides at once, instead of changing each slide individually.

Even though design templates include bullets for each subtitle level, you may want to use a different type of bullet. In addition to the styles available in the Bullets and Numbering dialog box (on the Format menu), you can select bullet characters from a large collection of symbols and icons. The Clip Organizer also contains a number of tiny pictures that you can use as bullets.

Using the slide master, you can globally change the color and size of all bullets to enhance your presentation. You can select a color from PowerPoint's template colors in the Bullets and Numbering dialog box, or you can select a color from the standard color chart. Bullet size is measured as a percentage of text size. The percentage may range from 25 percent (one-fourth the size of text) to 400 percent (four times the size of text). Bullet sizes of 50 percent and 100 percent are common.

Sometimes the text appears too close to the bullets, especially if you enlarge the bullets. Using the slide master, you can increase (or decrease) the distance between the bullets and text for all subtitle levels at one time.

The slide master shows the effect of your work, but you cannot scroll an entire presentation while in Slide Master View. To review changes made in the Slide Master, you must switch back to Normal View.

HANDS on

Using the Slide Master to Change Fonts

In this activity, you will open the *Benefits* presentation and display its slide master. Then you will make font and bullet changes to the entire presentation.

1. Open *Benefits* in your *PowerPoint Data* folder and save the presentation as *Benefits Customized* in the *Tutorial* folder.

2. Make sure the presentation appears in Normal View by clicking the **Normal View button** 🖽, if necessary. Close the left pane by clicking its **Close button** ☒; then scroll to slide 2.

The slide pane enlarges to fill the document window.

3. Click the title area of slide 2 and look at the font shown in the Font list box `Times New Roman ▾`. **Then check the first subtitle's font.**

The title font is Times New Roman; the subtitle font is Arial.

4. Hold `⇧ Shift` and point to the **Normal View button** 🖽.

The ScreenTip reveals a new name for the button, Slide Master View.

5. While still holding `⇧ Shift`, click the **Slide Master View button** 🖽. Release `⇧ Shift`.

The presentation's slide master appears, as shown in Figure 2.22. Even though the slides themselves contain real text for a presentation, the slide master contains sample text and displays all the different subtitle styles that are available for use in the presentation. The master also has a three-part area for a footer. On the left side of the window, a new pane appears, displaying thumbnail versions of the slide and title masters for this template.

6. Click the title placeholder text on slide 1 (the slide master). On the Formatting toolbar, click the **Font triangle button** `Times New Roman ▾`, and then click **Arial Narrow**. With the title area still selected, click the **Italic button** 𝐼 to eliminate the italic effect. Now, click the area surrounding the slide.

The title placeholder text, *Click to edit Master title style,* displays the style changes you made.

7. Click the bullet at the level 1 subtitle to select all five subtitle levels.

8. Click the **Font triangle button** `Times New Roman ▾` and change the font to **Times New Roman**. Then remove the italic effect and click the area surrounding the slide.

All the subtitles appear in the new font. The text in the title area does not change.

Figure 2.22

Slide master

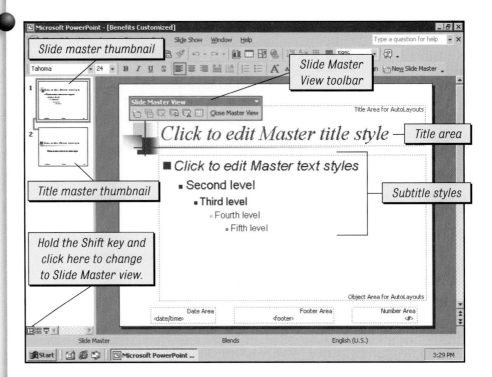

Be careful not to use too many different fonts, sizes, and colors in a presentation. This kind of inconsistency can distract your audience, and some may consider it unattractive. As a rule, limit a slide to two or three fonts, colors, and sizes.

NOTE *You should use the same font for all subtitle levels. Different font sizes and indents distinguish the levels.*

   9. Click the bullet at the level 1 subtitle once more, selecting all sub-title levels. On the Format menu, click **Bullets and Numbering**.

The Bullets and Numbering dialog box appears.

   10. Click the **shadow box bullet style** (a large white box with a black outline, with a narrow shadow along its right and bottom edges). (If the shadow box bullet style is not available, click a different style.) Then, click **OK**.

All the bullets are replaced by the new style. Notice that the new bullets remain sized appropriately for each subtitle's indent level.

   11. Click the blank area surrounding the slide to deselect the text, and click the **Normal View button** 🔲 to close the slide master.

NOTE *If the left pane reappears when you return to Normal View, close it once again.*

   12. Scroll the presentation and click each title; then read the name of the font. (Every slide's title now uses the Arial Narrow font.) In each slide that has subtitles, click one subtitle and read the name of the font, which should be Times New Roman.

All slides reflect the changes made in the slide master.

   13. Go to slide 1. Save the changes to the file.

ADDING HEADERS AND FOOTERS

A slide master includes placeholders below the object area that can hold a footer. A **footer** is text that appears at the bottom of every slide (although you can omit the footer from the title slide, if you want). By default, the footer includes three parts: a date area, a footer area, and a slide number area. To add or change the information in any of these areas, use the View menu to open the Header and Footer dialog box.

In addition to footers, you can add **headers** to your notes pages and printed handouts. Header text appears at the top of each page. To create headers, open the Header and Footer dialog box and click the Notes and Handouts tab. The header and footer information you enter there does not appear on the slides themselves.

HANDS on

Setting Up Headers and Footers

In this activity, you will use the *Benefits Customized* presentation to add a footer to your slides. Then you will add a header and footer to your notes pages and handouts.

1. With the *Benefits Customized* presentation still open, save the file as *Benefits with Headers and Footers* in the *Tutorial* folder.

2. Click **Header and Footer** on the View menu.

The Header and Footer dialog box appears, as shown in Figure 2.23.

3. On the Slide tab, click the **Date and time check box**, and then click the **Update automatically option**.

NOTE *If you prefer, you can enter a fixed date that will not update automatically each time you open the presentation. On the Slide tab in the Header and Footer dialog box, simply click Fixed and enter a date.*

The current date will be displayed each time you show the presentation.

4. Click the **Update automatically triangle button** and select this date style: August 9, 2002.

5. Click the **Slide number check box**.

6. Click the **Footer check box** and type Peeler Construction in the Footer text box.

7. Click the **Don't show on title slide check box**. Click the **Apply to All button** to add the footer to all slides.

NOTE *Click Apply to add the information to the current slide only.*

8. Scroll through the presentation, noting the footer on all but the title slide.

Figure 2.23
Header and Footer dialog box

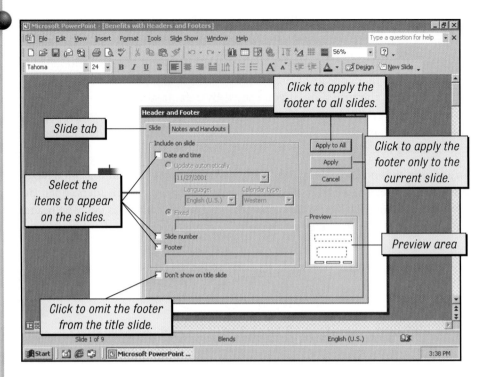

Slide tab

Select the items to appear on the slides.

Click to apply the footer to all slides.

Click to apply the footer only to the current slide.

Preview area

Click to omit the footer from the title slide.

9. Go to slide 1; click **Notes Page** on the View menu.

PowerPoint opens slide 1 in Notes Page View. The slide appears at the top of the page, and a blank area for notes appears at the bottom of the page.

10. Click **Header and Footer** on the View menu.

11. In the Header and Footer dialog box, click the **Notes and Handouts tab**, if necessary. Click the **Date and time check box** and the **Update automatically option**. Leave the date style unchanged.

12. Click the **Header check box**. In the Header text box, type Employee Benefits Plan. Click the **Page number check box**.

The date and page number will appear in the footer area of each notes page. The header text will appear in the header area of each notes page.

13. Click **Apply to All**. Scroll through your notes pages to check your header and footer.

NOTE *In this activity, you added headers and footers while working in Normal View. You can also add and edit headers and footers while working with the slide master. To do this, switch to Slide Master View, select the slide master, open the Header and Footer dialog box, and set up your header and/or footer. Click Apply to All. When you return to Normal View or Notes Page View, you will see the header and/or footer.*

14. Return to Normal View. Save your changes and close the presentation.

ANIMATING PRESENTATIONS

As computer projection continues to replace traditional slide shows, presenters increasingly add special effects to their presentations. For example, PowerPoint lets you add **animation**—or motion effects—to your slide shows, by making text and objects move on the screen and by adding motion to the transition from one slide to the next.

A **transition,** an eye-catching way to move from slide to slide, determines how one slide replaces another during a slide show. PowerPoint has dozens of different slide transitions. Transition effects have descriptive names such as *Fade Smoothly, Checkerboard Across, Push Down, Uncover Right, Wipe Up,* and *Random Transition.*

Slide Sorter View is a good place to apply and review transition effects. A transition symbol appears below a slide when an effect is applied to it. If you click the symbol, PowerPoint shows how the slide's transition will look. Of course, you can see the full effect in Slide Show View, too. When you run a slide show that contains transition effects, PowerPoint displays the transition effect when you move from one slide to the next.

In developing a presentation, you may apply a transition to a slide, a group of slides, or the entire presentation or you may use a different transition effect for each slide. Like any other special effect, however, transitions lose their ability to grab attention if they are overused. Therefore, you should identify only a few transitions to a slide show.

POWERPOINT 2002

HANDS on

Applying Slide Transitions

In this activity, you will open the *Moving* presentation and enhance it by adding transition effects.

1. **Open *Moving* in your *PowerPoint Data* folder and save the file as *Transition* in the *Tutorial* folder. Switch to Slide Sorter View.**

The Slide Sorter toolbar appears.

2. **Click slide 3 and click the Slide Transition button** [Transition].

The Slide Transition task pane opens.

3. **In the *Apply to selected slides* list box in the Slide Transition task pane, click the Blinds Horizontal transition.**

A transition symbol appears below slide 3, as shown in Figure 2.24.

4. **Click the transition symbol to preview the Blinds Horizontal effect.**

NORTON
ONLINE

Visit **www.glencoe.com/norton/online/** for more information on animating your presentation.

Figure 2.24

Applying a transition effect to a slide

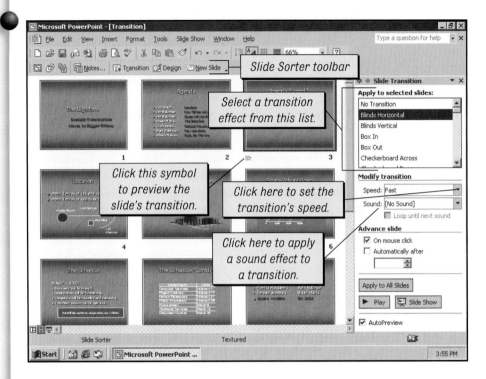

PowerPoint BASICS

Setting Slide Transitions

1. Switch to Slide Sorter View.

2. Select a slide that will have a transition.

3. Click the Slide Transition button.

4. In the task pane, select a transition.

5. Change the Speed and Sound options, if desired.

6. If you want to apply the transition to all slides, click the Apply to All Slides button after selecting the transition options.

---

5. Click **slide 8**. In the *Apply to selected slides* list box, click **Checkerboard Across**.

6. In the *Modify transition* area, click the **Speed triangle button** and click **Medium**. Preview the transition by clicking the **transition symbol**.

7. With slide 8 still selected, select the **Cover Right-Down transition**, and change the transition speed to **Slow**. Click the **Apply to All Slides button** in the Slide Transition task pane.

The effect is now applied to all slides. A transition symbol appears below every slide.

8. Click **slide 1**; then press and hold Ctrl while you click **slides 4, 9, 10, and 14**. Release Ctrl.

9. With slides 1, 4, 9, 10, and 14 selected, click **Fade Smoothly** in the *Apply to selected slides* list box. Then, click **No Transition** in the *Apply to selected slides* list box.

The transition symbol disappears from the selected slides.

10. Click between any two slides to deselect all the selected slides. Close the Slide Transition task pane by clicking its **Close button** ☒. Save your changes and close the file.

Applying Text and Object Animations

You can animate text and objects on a slide, a group of slides, or in the entire presentation. Animation allows you to focus on important information and add interest to presentations. **Animated text** appears on a slide one subtitle at a time. Besides animating text, you can create interesting effects using **animated objects**. As you might guess, animated objects are graphics that appear progressively, rather than all at once.

On the Slides tab and in Slide Sorter View, an animated icon appears next to the slides that contain animated text or objects. You can preview these animation effects by clicking the icon. Of course, you can change or remove the animation effects on any slide at any time.

When you look at a presentation in Slide Show View, the animation effects require extra clicks. A slide containing three subtitles with animated text, for example, takes four clicks: one to advance to the slide and one to display each animated subtitle. Likewise, you need to click the screen to display each animated object. PowerPoint provides a timer option for displaying animations automatically during an actual slide show.

HANDS on

Animating Text and Objects

In this activity, you will open the *Photo* presentation and add animation effects to text and objects.

1. Open *Photo* in your *PowerPoint Data* folder and save the file as *Builds* in the *Tutorial* folder. On the Slides tab, select **slides 3**, **4**, **5**, and **6**.

2. On the Slide Show menu, click **Animation Schemes**.

The Slide Design task pane appears. The task pane displays a list of preset animation schemes that you can apply to any or all slides in a presentation. These preset animations are grouped into four categories: *No Animation*, *Subtle*, *Moderate*, and *Exciting*.

> **NOTE** *PowerPoint's preset animations behave in different ways. Some apply to everything on the slide, some apply only to titles, and some apply only to subtitles and bulleted items. For this reason, it's a good idea to preview all the different schemes to determine which ones will suit your needs best.*

3. In the *Apply to selected slides* list box, scroll down to the Moderate category and click **Ascend**, as shown in Figure 2.25.

This effect causes each line of body text on the selected slides to float up from the bottom of the slide. Watch the preview of the animated effect on slide 3. When all subtitles appear, an animation icon appears next to slides 3–6.

Figure 2.25
Adding animation effects to slides

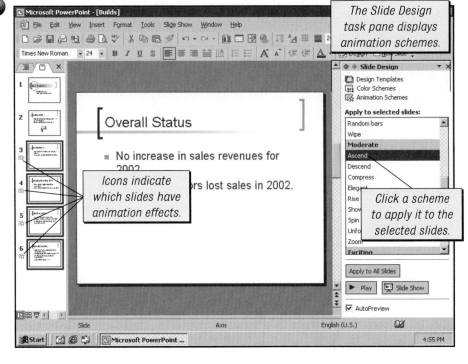

The Slide Design task pane displays animation schemes.

Icons indicate which slides have animation effects.

Click a scheme to apply it to the selected slides.

PowerPoint BASICS

Animating Text and Objects

To apply text animations:

1. Select the slide(s) that will be animated.

2. On the Slide Show menu, click Animation Schemes.

3. In the task pane, click an animation scheme.

To apply object animations:

1. In Normal View, go to the slide that will be animated.

2. Click the object.

3. On the Slide Show menu, click Custom Animation.

4. In the task pane, click the Add Effect button, and then click an animated effect.

5. Set other animations, if desired.

4. Go to slide 1. In the *Apply to selected slides* list box, scroll to the Subtitle category and click **Brush on underline**. Watch the preview of this animation effect on slide 1.

5. Click **Apply to All Slides** to add the *Brush on underline* animation effect to the entire presentation.

6. Go to slide 2, and click the clip art image at the bottom of the slide.

Sizing handles appear around the clip, indicating that it is selected. To animate a single object on a slide, you can use a custom animation.

7. On the Slide Show menu, click **Custom Animation**.

The Custom Animation task pane appears. You can use this task pane to create a custom animation effect for an element on a slide.

8. In the task pane, click the **Add Effect button** . When the submenu appears, click **Entrance**, and click **Fly In**.

PowerPoint immediately demonstrates the effect, and you can see the clip fly into position from the bottom edge of the slide.

9. In the task pane, click the **Direction triangle button** and click **From Right**. Next, click the **Speed triangle button** and click **Medium**.

When you make each selection, PowerPoint demonstrates how the animation effect works.

10. Go to slide 1, switch to Slide Show View, and review the presentation. Close the task pane, save your changes, and close the file.

Test your knowledge by matching the terms on the left with the definitions on the right. See Appendix B to check your answers.

TERMS	DEFINITIONS
_____ **1.** design template	**a.** Graphics that appear progressively
_____ **2.** title master	**b.** Space on a slide reserved for text or an object
_____ **3.** animated objects	**c.** Collection of formatting options that can be applied to a presentation
_____ **4.** placeholder	**d.** Form that controls the appearance of the title slide
_____ **5.** handles	**e.** Tools that allow you to resize an object in a slide

ON THE WEB

PUBLISHING PRESENTATIONS ON THE WEB

You can share your PowerPoint presentations by publishing them on the World Wide Web or to a local intranet. An **intranet** is a local area network that is set up to operate like the Web, enabling users to navigate and open files by using a Web browser. **Publishing** a presentation means saving your PowerPoint file as a set of Web pages on a Web or an intranet server. A **Web server** is a computer that has a permanent connection to the Web or to an organization's intranet, and which stores Web pages and responds to requests from Web browsers, such as Microsoft Internet Explorer or Netscape Navigator.

PowerPoint lets you convert a presentation into Web pages in two ways. One is simply to save the presentation by clicking the Save as Web Page command on the File menu, and storing the Web pages on your computer's hard drive or to a network drive. If others have access to the location where you stored the file, they can open the presentation in their Web browsers. Another way is to click the Save as Web Page command; then click the Publish button to select special options for optimizing your presentation for viewing in a Web browser. This method lets you specify support for certain browsers, allow the viewer to see speaker notes, include specific slides in the presentation, and do many other tasks.

In this activity, you will open the *Moving* presentation and preview it as a set of Web pages by using the Internet Explorer Web browser. Then you will save the presentation on your computer in the form of a Web document. This will enable you to open the file in your browser whenever you like. (Your instructor may ask you to save the presentation in a specific drive and folder on the school's network or Web server so that others can open it.)

1. Open *Moving* in your *PowerPoint Data* folder. Click **Web Page Preview** on the File menu.

After a few seconds, Microsoft Internet Explorer opens.

2. Maximize the browser window, if necessary.

Your screen should resemble Figure 2.26. The slide titles appear automatically as hyperlinks in the outline frame at the left.

Figure 2.26
Moving presentation displayed in Internet Explorer

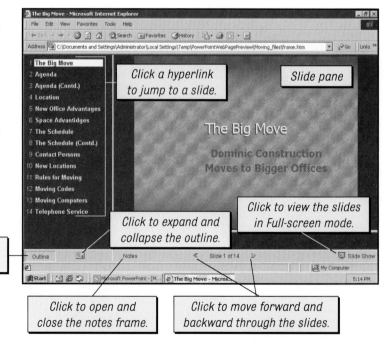

3. Click the hyperlink named **The Schedule** in the outline frame. Click the **Next Slide button** ⏩ (the right arrow below the browser window) to jump to slide 8. Click the **Previous Slide button** ⏪. Advance to the *Moving Codes* slide.

4. Click the **Slide Show button** 🖳 Slide Show (in the bottom right corner of the screen). The show begins with the current slide. Click the screen twice to advance two slides. Press Esc to exit the full-screen show.

5. Click the **Notes button** Notes to hide the notes pane. Click the **Expand/Collapse Outline button** 🗐 to see subtitles along with slide titles in the outline frame. Next, click the **Outline button** Outline to hide the outline altogether. Close your browser.

6. In PowerPoint, click **Save as Web Page** on the File menu.

The Save As dialog box opens. Notice that the dialog box contains more tools than usual. These tools are designed specifically for publishing a presentation as a Web page.

7. In the *File name* box, type Moving Web Page as the file name. Verify that the *Save as type* box is set to Web Page. In the *Save in* box, specify the *Tutorial* folder of your *PowerPoint Data* folder. Do not click the Save button yet; you need to set some other options first. (If you wanted to save your Web page as an HTML document, you would click the Save button now.)

> **NOTE** *Your instructor may ask you to save the presentation to a different drive and folder, or to use a different file name or publishing options.*

8. Click the **Change Title button** to open the Set Page Title dialog box. Type Moving Plans for the title; then click **OK**.

This title will appear in the title bar of the browser when someone views your presentation online. The presentation's title slide will not be changed.

9. Click the **Publish button** to open the Publish as Web Page dialog box. In the *Publish what?* section, click the **Complete presentation option**, if it is not already selected. Deselect the **Display speaker notes check box**. Under *Browser support*, click the **All browsers listed above (creates larger files) option**. Select the **Open published Web page in browser check box**, if it is not already selected, and then click the **Publish button**.

PowerPoint saves your presentation as a collection of Web pages, and then displays the title slide in your Web browser. The process can take several seconds, so be patient.

10. Navigate the slides in your browser, and then close the browser. In PowerPoint, close the *Moving* presentation without saving it.

> **WARNING** *You may proceed directly to the exercises for this lesson. If, however, you are finished with your computer session, follow the "shut down" procedures for your lab or school environment.*

SUMMARY AND EXERCISES

SUMMARY

When you start PowerPoint, you can begin a presentation with a design template, or start with a blank slide. Each additional slide requires you to select a slide layout. You can insert text simply by clicking a text area and typing, or by importing an outline from Microsoft Word. Conversely, you can send a presentation's outline to Word. You can apply a new design template to a presentation at any time, or customize the current template. You can also apply a different layout to a slide. You can enhance a presentation by formatting the text. You can insert a graphic by selecting one of PowerPoint's clip art images or by inserting one from a separate graphics file. Just as you can add graphics to a slide, you also can add sounds and movies that play during a presentation. You can draw geometric shapes and AutoShapes on a slide by using the Drawing toolbar, and then enhance those shapes. Slides can hold charts and tables, as well; you can create them directly on a slide or import Excel charts or Word tables. A slide master allows you to make global formatting changes to your slides. You can apply finishing touches to your presentation by adding slide transitions or by animating text and objects. You can also publish your PowerPoint presentation on the Web and save the file as a set of Web pages.

Now that you have completed this lesson, you should be able to do the following:

- Create a presentation from a design template or from a blank slide. (page 579)
- Add new slides and text to a presentation. (page 582)
- Apply a different design template and layout to a slide. (page 584)
- Customize a design template. (page 586)
- Import a Word outline and export a presentation as an outline. (page 589)
- Format and align text on a slide. (page 592)
- Add and modify clip art and image files on a slide. (page 597)
- Add a sound effect or a movie to a slide. (page 604)
- Draw and edit shapes on a slide. (page 606)
- Create and enhance a chart and import an Excel chart into a slide. (page 609)
- Create and enhance a table and import a Word table into a slide. (page 613)
- Use Help to add an action button to a slide. (page 619)
- Use the slide master to change formatting throughout a presentation. (page 620)
- Add headers and footers to slides, notes pages, and handouts. (page 623)
- Create and apply slide transitions and animate text and objects. (page 625)
- Publish a slide show for viewing on the World Wide Web. (page 630)

CONCEPTS REVIEW

1 TRUE/FALSE

Circle T if the statement is true or F if the statement is false.

T **(F)** **1.** A slide layout is the same thing as a design template.

T **(F)** **2.** Clicking the New Slide button [New Slide] opens the Slide Design task pane.

(T) F **3.** Clip art can be inserted with or without a placeholder.

(T) F **4.** The AutoShapes button [AutoShapes ▾] is on the Drawing toolbar.

T **(F)** **5.** When you select an object, such as a clip, it is surrounded by crosshairs. *handles*

(T) F **6.** You can use a presentation's slide master to change bullet styles on all of the slides in the presentation.

T **(F)** **7.** You can add headers to your slides, but not to notes pages.

(T) F **8.** A transition is the way a slide is replaced by another slide during a presentation.

(T) F **9.** A sentence that appears on the screen one word at a time is an example of animated text.

T **(F)** **10.** On a slide, text is an example of an object.

2 MATCHING

Match each of the terms on the left with the definitions on the right.

TERMS	DEFINITIONS
1. slide layouts	**a.** Represents a place where a graphic or text will be inserted
2. object	**b.** Blank slides with placeholders for text and/or objects
3. animation	
4. Header and Footer dialog box	**c.** Controls how one slide replaces another
5. transition	**d.** A clip art image is an example
6. OLE	**e.** Lets you use data from one application in another application
7. datasheet	
8. placeholder	**f.** Motion effects
9. AutoShapes	**g.** Predrawn, geometrically shaped objects
10. transition symbol	**h.** A table that holds data for a chart
	i. Indicates that a slide has an effect applied to it
	j. The place to add slide numbers

SUMMARY AND EXERCISES

3 COMPLETION

Fill in the missing word or phrase for each of the following statements.

1. You can select a design template from the _____ task pane.

2. Slide layouts contain one or more blank _____ , where you can insert text or objects.

3. If you want to use a Microsoft Word document as an outline for a presentation, the document's paragraphs should have _____ applied.

4. To make a global change to a presentation's fonts, you can make the change in the presentation's _____ .

5. The Select Picture dialog box provides access to small drawings and photographs, called _____ , which you can add to a slide.

6. You can click the _____ button on the Formatting toolbar to distribute text evenly across its placeholder.

7. The Header and Footer command is located on the _____ menu.

8. After copying a chart from Microsoft Excel, you can embed it into a PowerPoint slide (and maintain a link to the Excel worksheet) by using the _____ command.

9. When viewing a presentation in Slide Show View, you can go back one slide by pressing the _____ key.

10. You can make a clip "fly" onto the slide by applying a(n) _____ effect to it.

4 SHORT ANSWER

Write a brief answer to each of the following questions.

1. Explain how to add slide numbers to your slides, while leaving out the date and other footer information.

2. What is a design template?

3. Describe how the pointer changes in the process of resizing an object, such as clip art.

4. How can you switch to Slide Master View?

5. What does the term *OLE* stand for, and what does it enable you to do?

6. Where can you find transition effects to apply to slides?

7. Which command can you use to convert a presentation into a set of Web pages, for viewing in a Web browser such as Internet Explorer?

8. You have just applied a transition to all the slides in your presentation. How do you remove the transition from the slides?

9. How can you insert a clip art image into a slide that does not have a placeholder for clip art?

10. You have a presentation open in PowerPoint and want to start a new presentation from a blank slide. How can you start the second presentation?

5 IDENTIFICATION

Label each of the items of the PowerPoint window in Figure 2.27.

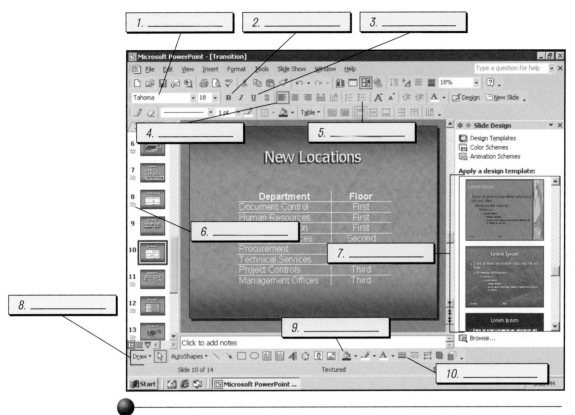

Figure 2.27

SKILLS REVIEW

Complete all of the Skills Review problems in sequential order to review your PowerPoint skills to begin a presentation with a template and with a blank slide; change design templates and slide layouts; add slides and text; import and format text; work with an outline; insert and change clip art; add a sound; work with drawing objects; add and revise charts and tables; make changes with the slide master; add headers and footers; and add transitions and animations.

1 Choose and Customize Templates and Layouts, and Add Slides and Text

1. Start PowerPoint. If PowerPoint is already running, click **New** on the File menu. In the New Presentation task pane, click **From Design Template**.

2. In the *Apply a design template* list box, point to the **Blends template's thumbnail**, click its **triangle button**, and click **Apply to All Slides**. Next, save the file as *Writer's Friend* in the *Skills Review* folder in your *PowerPoint Data* folder.

3. On slide 1, click the title placeholder and type **A Writer's Friend**. Click the subtitle placeholder and type **Write Like a Pro**.

4. Click the **New Slide button** [New Slide]. On slide 2, click the title placeholder and type **Just Checking**. Click the subtitle placeholder and type the following subtitles, each on a separate line:

   I said what I meant to say.
   I gave enough details.
   Details are in order.

5. With slide 2 still selected, click the **Title and 2-Column Text slide layout triangle button** in the Slide Layout task pane, and click **Apply to Selected Slides**. Go to slide 1.

6. Click the **Slide Design button** [Design]. In the Slide Design task pane, click the **Digital Dots template triangle button**, and click **Apply to Selected Slides**. Note the differences between slides 1 and 2. Select **slide 1** again, click the **Digital Dots template triangle button**, and click **Apply to All Slides**.

7. In the Slide Design task pane, click **Color Schemes**. In the *Apply a color scheme* list box, click the **thumbnail with the dark blue background**, click its **triangle button**, and then click **Apply to All Slides**.

8. Close the task pane. Save your changes and close the presentation.

2 Start From a Blank Slide and Work With an Outline

1. Click the **New button** [ ] on the Standard toolbar. Save the file as *Budget Planning* in the *Skills Review* folder in your *PowerPoint Data* folder.

2. On slide 1, click the title placeholder and type **YoYoDyne, Inc.** Click outside the slide area. Right-click the word **YoYoDyne**. When the shortcut menu opens, click Ignore All. Click the subtitle placeholder and type **Budget Planning Meeting**. Click outside the slide to deselect it; then save your changes.

3. On the Insert menu, click **Slides from Outline**. In the Insert Outline dialog box, navigate to your *PowerPoint Data* folder, select the Word file named *Budget Planning Points*, and click the **Insert button**.

4. Add subtitles to each of the new slides, as shown in Table 2.3. Save your changes to the file.

5. Go to slide 1. On the File menu, point to **Send To**; click **Microsoft Word**. In the Send To Microsoft Word dialog box, click the **Outline only option**; then click **OK**.

Table 2.3	Slide Data		
Slide 2	**Slide 3**	**Slide 4**	**Slide 5**
• Margins must rise 20%–30%.	• No new positions accepted for Q1/Q2.	• COG rose 15% last year.	• Open-door return policy must end.
• T&E must be cut 50%.	• No backfills until further notice.	• Encourage vendor competition via RFPs.	• P&L allocation must drop 50%.
• Bonus plan on hold.	• No exceptions!	• Cut loose any vendors who won't bid.	• Convince resellers to accept credits.

6. When the presentation's outline opens in Microsoft Word, save the document as *Completed Budget Outline* in the *Skills Review* folder in your *PowerPoint Data* folder. Close the file and close Word; return to PowerPoint.

7. Save the presentation as an Outline/RTF file type with *New Budget Plan Outline* as the file name. Save the file in the *RTF Files* folder in the *Skills Review* folder in your *PowerPoint Data* folder.

8. Print the Outline View of the presentation in Pure Black and White mode.

9. Save your changes to the *Budget Planning* presentation and leave it open.

3 Format Text

1. Save the *Budget Planning* presentation as *Budget Planning with Notes* in the *Skills Review* folder in your *PowerPoint Data* folder.

2. Click the **Slide Design button** . In the Slide Design task pane, click the **Compass design template triangle button**, and click **Apply to All Slides**.

3. Go to slide 1 and select the slide's title. Click the **Font Size triangle button** 12 and click **66**. Click the **Bold button** .

4. Go to slide 2 and select the slide's title. On the Formatting toolbar, click the **Italic button** . Click the **Format Painter button** .

5. Go to slide 3 and select its title to apply the formatting. Double-click the **Format Painter button** , apply the italic formatting to the titles of the remaining slides, and then click the **Format Painter button** to deactivate it.

6. Go to slide 2, click the slide's title, and then click the **Align Right button** . Then go to slide 3, click its title, and press F4 . Repeat this for the titles of slides 4 and 5.

7. Save your changes, close the task pane, and close the file.

4 Insert, Resize, and Move a Clip

1. Open *Annual Report* in your *PowerPoint Data* folder and save the file as *Customized Annual Report* in the *Skills Review* folder.

2. Go to slide 5 and double-click the clip art placeholder. When the Select Picture dialog box appears, type **people** in the *Search text* box and click **Search**. When the list of clips matching the search word appears, click the image of a welder, and then click **OK**. (If a welder image is not available, click another appropriate image.)

3. Reposition the clip by dragging it on the slide, so that its top edge is aligned with the top of the subtitle's first line and its right edge is aligned with the right end of the slide's title. Resize the clip by clicking its lower-left handle and dragging downward and to the left, until the clip's left edge is centered under the *m* in *Government*. (See Figure 2.28.) Deselect the clip.

4. Go to slide 6, point to **Picture** on the Insert menu, and click **From File**. When the Insert Picture dialog box appears, navigate to your *PowerPoint Data* folder, click the file named *Dam*, and click **Insert**.

5. Right-click the clip. When the shortcut menu appears, click **Format Picture**. When the Format Picture dialog box appears, click the **Size tab**.

6. Make sure the *Lock aspect ratio* box is checked, and then click the **Height list box** in the *Size and rotate* section and type or select 3. Click the **Width list box**, and then click **OK**.

7. Select the clip of the dam. Drag the clip to center it horizontally between the right and left edges of the slide and vertically in the space below the type. Save your changes to the *Customized Annual Report* presentation and leave the file open.

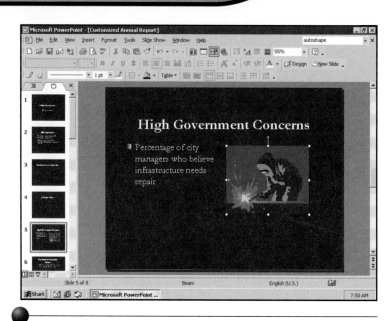

Figure 2.28

5 Add a Sound to a Slide

1. Go to slide 2 in the *Customized Annual Report* presentation. Point to **Movies and Sounds** on the Insert menu, and click **Sound** from Clip Organizer.

2. In the Results list box, scroll to the Telephone icon, click the **Telephone icon's triangle button**, and click **Insert**. Choose **No** when PowerPoint asks if you want the clip to play automatically.

3. Drag the sound icon down; center it in the blank area at the bottom of the slide.

4. Switch to Slide Show View. When the slide appears on the screen, click the **sound icon** once. When the sound is finished playing, press Esc to return to Normal View. Deselect the sound icon and close the task pane.

5. Save your changes to the file and leave the presentation open.

6 Add and Enhance Drawing Objects

1. With the *Customized Annual Report* presentation open, point to **Toolbars** on the View menu, and click **Drawing**.

2. Go to slide 2. On the Drawing toolbar, click the **AutoShapes button** AutoShapes ▾, point to **Stars and Banners**, and then click the **5-Point Star icon**.

3. Point to the end of the slide's first subtitle, click, and drag downward and to the right until a small star appears. Release the mouse button.

4. On the Drawing toolbar, click the **Fill Color triangle button** 🖍▾, and click the **yellow square** on the color palette. Click outside the slide to deselect it.

5. Go to slide 5. On the Drawing toolbar, click the **Rectangle button** ▢. Point to the upper-left corner of the clip on the slide, click, and drag to the lower-right corner of the clip to add a border around the clip. Release the mouse button.

6. Click the **Line Style button** ☰ and click the **6 pt solid line**. Click the **Fill Color triangle button** 🎨▾ and click **No Fill** in the color palette. Click outside the slide to deselect it. Save your changes to the file.

7 Add and Change Charts

1. Go to slide 3 and double-click the chart placeholder. When the datasheet appears, click the **row control box** for row 3 and press ⌨Delete.

2. Click the first cell of row 1 and replace the word *East* by typing New. In the first cell of row 2, replace the word *West* by typing **Renovations**.

3. Clear the sample text from cells A1 through D2, and type new data in those cells, as shown in Table 2.4. Leave the column headings (*1st Qtr, 2nd Qtr,* etc.) in place. Close the datasheet.

Table 2.4	Datasheet Data			
Rows	**Columns**			
	A	B	C	D
	1st Qtr	2nd Qtr	3rd Qtr	4th Qtr
1	20.4	27.4	31	28.5
2	11.5	13.9	15	13.5

4. With the chart still selected, click the **Chart Type triangle button** 📊▾ and click **Area Chart**. Click outside the slide to deselect the chart. Go to slide 4.

5. Launch Microsoft Excel, and open the file named *Proposed Contracts* in your *PowerPoint Data* folder. Click the **Chart worksheet tab**, if necessary, and click the chart's border to select it. On the Edit menu, click **Copy**.

6. In PowerPoint, on the Edit menu, click **Paste Special**. In the Paste Special dialog box, click the **Paste option**. In the *As* list box, click **Microsoft Excel Chart Object**. Clear the **Display as icon check box**, if necessary. Click **OK**.

7. When the chart appears in the slide, click its lower-right handle and drag downward and to the right about an inch to enlarge the chart. Center the chart vertically and horizontally in the available space.

8. Deselect the chart and save your changes. Leave the presentation open. Close Excel without saving the file.

8 Insert and Enhance Tables

1. With the *Customized Annual Report* presentation open, go to slide 7 and double-click the table placeholder. In the Insert Table dialog box, set the number of columns to 3 and the number of rows to 4. Click **OK**. If the Tables and Borders toolbar does not appear, open it by pointing to Toolbars on the View menu and clicking **Tables and Borders**.

2. Click the table's first cell and type **Project**, press ⌨Tab, type **Date**, press ⌨Tab, and type **Status**.

3. Click the first cell of the second row and type **I-40 Bridge**, press ⌨Tab, type **June 1**, press ⌨Tab, and type **Delayed**.

4. Click the first cell of the third row and type **Rice Mall**, press ⌨Tab, type **Aug. 15**, press ⌨Tab, and type **On Time**.

5. Click the first cell of the fourth row and type **Wayne Center**, press ⌨Tab, type **Oct. 11**, press ⌨Tab, and type **30 Days Early**.

6. Select all cells in the table. On the Tables and Borders toolbar, click the **Center Vertically button** ⊟. Select the table's first row. On the Formatting toolbar, click the **Bold button** ⓑ, and click the **Center button** ▤. Deselect the table. Go to slide 8.

7. Launch Microsoft Word and open the file named *New Clients* in your *PowerPoint Data* folder. Click the table. Then, on the Table menu, point to **Select**, and click **Table**. Then click **Copy** on the Edit menu.

8. In PowerPoint, click **Paste Special** on the Edit menu. In the Paste Special dialog box, click the **Paste option**. In the *As* list box, click **Microsoft Word Document Object**. Clear the **Display as icon check box**, if necessary, and click **OK**. (If the slide layout changes from the Title and Text layout, click **Slide Layout** on the Format menu. Then, click **Title and Text layout** in the Slide Layout task pane. Close the task pane.)

9. On the Drawing toolbar, click the **Fill Color triangle button** 🖌▾ and click the white square. Resize and reposition the table as appropriate below the bulleted item. Deselect the table.

10. Save your changes to the file. Leave the presentation open. Close Word without saving the file.

9 Make Changes With the Slide Master and Add Footers

1. In the *Customized Annual Report* presentation, go to slide 1. Determine the name(s) of the title font and the subtitle font.

2. Switch to Slide Master View by holding ⌨⇧ Shift and clicking the **Normal View button** ▣. In the left pane, select the title master. In the slide pane, select the title text and change the font to Arial. Then select the subtitle text and change the font to Times New Roman.

3. In the left pane, select the slide master. In the slide pane, select the title text and change the font to Arial. Select the subtitle text and change the font for all the subtitles to Times New Roman.

4. With the subtitle text still selected, click **Bullets and Numbering** on the Format menu.

5. In the Bullets and Numbering dialog box, click the **Bulleted tab**, if necessary. Select the **check mark bullet**, and click **OK**.

6. Switch to Normal View; scroll and check the presentation. Return to slide 1.

7. On the View menu, click **Header and Footer**. In the Header and Footer dialog box, click the **Slide tab**, if necessary. Select the **Date and time check box**, and click the **Update automatically option**. Leave the date format unchanged.

8. Select the **Slide number check box**. Select the **Footer check box** and type Peeler Construction as the footer text. Select the **Don't show on title slide check box**. Click **Apply to All**. Scroll through the presentation and review the footers. (If the footer doesn't show on any of the slides, resize the objects as necessary.)

9. Open the Header and Footer dialog box again, and click the **Notes and Handouts tab**. Select the **Date and time check box** and the **Update automatically option**. Leave the date format unchanged. Type Peeler Construction as your header text. Select the **Page number check box** and clear the **Footer check box**.

10. Click **Apply to All**, and save your updated file. Leave the file open.

10 Add Transitions and Animate a Presentation

1. In the *Customized Annual Report* presentation, switch to Slide Sorter View and select slides 2 through 8. Click the **Slide Transition button** [Transition]. When the Slide Transition task pane opens, apply the **Newsflash effect**.

2. Click the transition symbols to preview the effects.

3. Click **slide 2**.

4. On the Slide Show menu, click **Animation Schemes**. When the Slide Design task pane opens, apply the **Descend effect**.

5. Switch to Normal View, and select the object on slide 2 (the star). On the Slide Show menu, click **Custom Animation**. When the Custom Animation task pane appears, click the **Add Effect triangle button** [Add Effect], point to **Entrance**, and click **Fly In**.

6. Deselect the object and close the task pane. Save the updated *Customized Annual Report* file and close it.

LESSON APPLICATIONS

1 Moving and Sizing

Resize and reposition a clip to balance the elements on the slide.

1. Open the *Benefits* presentation in your *PowerPoint Data* folder. Save the file as *Moving and Sizing* in the *Lesson Applications* folder.

2. In Normal View, navigate to slide 8. Select the clip art, and move it down so the bottom of the image is even with the bottom of the last subtitle. Next, stretch the clip art upward, so the top of the image is even with the top of the first subtitle, while the clip's bottom edge does not move.

3. Save the changes and close the file.

SUMMARY AND EXERCISES

2 Changing Times

Apply a new design template. Customize the template by changing the font size and layout. Insert headers and footers on slides, printed notes pages, and handouts.

1. Open *Agenda* in your *PowerPoint Data* folder and save the file as *Changing Times with Header and Footer* in the *Lesson Applications* folder.

2. Apply the Network design template to the entire presentation. On slide 1, change the title font size to 54. Change the size of the slide's subtitles to 24.

3. Change the layout of slide 7 to Title and 2-Column Text. In the left column, demote the level 1 subtitle to level 2, and format it to match the other level 2 subtitles.

4. To even out the columns, move the last two level 2 subtitles from the bottom half of the left column to the right column (see Figure 2.29). Save your file.

5. Add footers to all the slides. In the footer, use a date that will update automatically and a slide number. On printed notes pages and handouts, add a date that will update automatically and a page number as a footer. Add **System Conversion** as a header.

6. Resize or reposition any objects that interfere with the footer. Then, save and close the file.

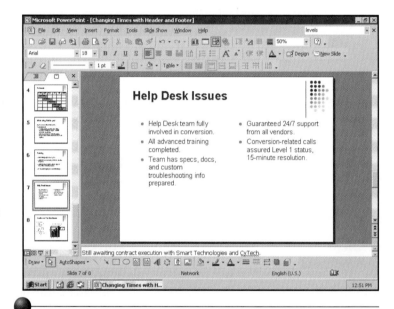

Figure 2.29

3 Be Bold!

Use the slide master to change the text styles.

1. Open the *Marketing* presentation in your *PowerPoint Data* folder. Save the file as *Customized Marketing* in the *Lesson Applications* folder.

2. In the slide master, change the title font size to 44. Then make the title text bold and italic. Change all subtitle text to Times New Roman.

3. In the title master, change the title to Arial, size 48.

4. Switch to Normal View and check the effect of these changes on each slide. Save the changes. Close the file.

4 Transition Condition

Insert, resize, and animate clip art. Apply slide transitions.

1. Open *Experience* in your *PowerPoint Data* folder and save the file as *Transition Condition* in the *Lesson Applications* folder.

2. On slides 3 and 4, use the object placeholders to insert clip art that represents the slide titles. For slide 3, look for a clip that depicts a building or some kind of construction project. For slide 4, search for a clip that depicts work. Size and reposition the clip art so that the slides look balanced.

3. Add the Fade Smoothly transition to the even-numbered slides, and set the transition's speed to Medium. Apply the Dissolve transition to odd-numbered slides, and set its speed to Medium as well. Do not apply a transition to slide 1. Preview the transitions.

4. Animate the clip art on slides 3 and 4 with the Fly In effect. Make one clip fly in from the right, and the other fly in from the top. Set the animation's speed to Medium for both clips.

5. Review your presentation in Slide Show View. Return to Normal View when you are finished. Make sure the task pane is closed. Save and close the updated file.

PROJECTS

1 New Template Design

You will be showing the *Benefits* presentation to your company's managers in the near future. Two or more recent presentations to that group were based on the same design template, so you decide it's time for a change.

Open *Benefits* in your *PowerPoint Data* folder and save the file as *Benefits—New Design* in the *Projects* folder. Review the entire presentation in Slide Show View. Then apply a different design template to the slides. On paper, note what changes the new template made. What did not change? Next, write down your reasons for choosing the new design template. What makes it appropriate for this presentation, in your view?

2 Old Favorite, New Look

You have used the *Agenda* presentation numerous times in presentations to different employee groups within Peeler Construction; in fact, some groups have seen and heard the presentation more than once. Most of the information is still current, and the template on which it's based still looks contemporary. You decide to customize the presentation, using the slide master to make most of the changes.

Open *Agenda* in your *PowerPoint Data* folder and save the file as *New Look* in the *Projects* folder. Plan a complete makeover to the slide master (don't forget the title master, too), using the information in the original presentation. Changes to consider include changing the title font, size, and special effects; changing the subtitle font; changing the background color; using different slide layouts; and inserting footers. Remember to check each change in Normal View before making the next change. Correct all spelling errors. Then save all changes and close the file.

3 I is for Interview

Training sessions on career planning are extremely popular; they attract varied audiences of career starters and career changers. You have some printed materials about job interviewing, but you would like a PowerPoint presentation to introduce or summarize the topic or reinforce main points. Here is what you have planned so far: Start your presentation from a blank slide, and then select a design template after your slides contain the basic information. Illustrate both correct and incorrect ways of behaving during a job interview. Illustrate just one point on each slide. Insert a title with the word *Do* (correct way) or *Don't* (incorrect way) on each slide that relates to interview behavior. Use several pieces of clip art. Use appropriate animation and transition effects. Start with just three points, plus a title slide. Information about job interviewing may be obtained from sources listed in Table 2.5 or other sources available to you. Save the presentation as *Interview* in the *Projects* folder in your *PowerPoint Data* folder.

Table 2.5	Web Sites and Their URLS
Web Site	**URL**
MSN Careers Page	http://careers.msn.com
Careerbuilder	http://www.careerbuilder.com
Headhunter.net	http://www.headhunter.net

4 One-Minute Presentation

The instructor of a business class has asked you to take charge of a series of seminars, which will feature local business, community, or government leaders. You must invite a local leader to come to class and speak at each seminar, and you are responsible for selecting a topic for the seminar. You will also introduce the speaker at the beginning of the seminar.

Starting from a design template, create a presentation (two to four slides) to introduce the speaker for the initial seminar. First, think of someone in your hometown you would like to invite to speak at such an event. This might be someone you know personally or someone whom you have read about in the paper. Make a short list of the person's position and qualifications—the things that qualify the person to speak on the topic you have chosen.

Plan first; think about the text, graphics, and notes your brief presentation might include. Jot down key words for the following points you need to include: the speaker's topic, importance of the topic to the audience, the speaker's name, and the speaker's qualifications for addressing the topic. Limit the content to only one minute's worth of material, including comments (notes) not shown on the slides. Save the presentation as *Introduction* in the *Projects* folder in your *PowerPoint Data* folder.

5 By Design

Your one-minute presentation went rather well at the initial seminar. You've decided to use the concept again when introducing other speakers. You realize, of course, that you will have to vary the look and feel of your presentation to fit the guest speaker, although you present the same type of information in each case.

Use *Introduction* in the *Projects* folder that you created in Project 4 as the basis for a new presentation, and save this project as *Introduction 2* in the *Projects* folder in your *PowerPoint Data* folder. (If you did not complete Project 4, use the file entitled *Guest Speaker* in your *PowerPoint Data* folder.) Select another person to introduce, and plan the text, clips, and other objects that you will use. In addition to different graphics and effects, use a different design template. Use a multilevel bulleted list on one of the slides. Insert appropriate headers or footers on the slides and handouts pages.

6 Career Presentation

Since graduating from college several years ago, you have become well established in your chosen career. You decided recently that now would be a good time to publish a Web presentation, establishing your identity in your field and promoting the work that you do. Before planning your home page, you need to visit and evaluate several Web sites.

Search the Web, using the name of your career (for example, accounting, paralegal, information technology professional, realtor, etc.) and related terms as keywords; then follow any of the first 20 links that appear helpful. Carefully examine these Web sites, noting features of the site. Plan your Web presentation. Sketch your presentation (three to six slides) on paper. One slide should contain FAQs (Frequently Asked Questions)—that is, questions commonly asked of someone in your field. Another slide or several slides should contain answers to those questions, and a hyperlink should allow Web users to jump from each question to its answer. (Remember to include links for jumping back to the FAQ slide. To review adding hyperlinks to a presentation, see the *On the Web* activity in Lesson 1 or explore Microsoft PowerPoint Help.) Preview the presentation in your browser. Save the file as a Web page named *Career Presentation* in the *Projects* folder in your *PowerPoint Data* folder.

Project in Progress

7 Build Up

Your new business, Savvy Solutions, provides writing and editing services for small and medium-sized organizations in your area. You want to create new slides for your presentation to promote your company to prospective clients. Open *Savvy Solutions-Lesson 1* in the *Project in Progress* folder in the *Projects* folder in your *PowerPoint Data* folder. (You created this file in Project 7 in Lesson 1. If you did not complete Project 7 in Lesson 1, use the file entitled *Progress* in your *PowerPoint Data* folder.) Save the file as *Savvy Solutions-Lesson 2* in the same folder. This file contains a title slide for a presentation about your company. Add two new slides to the presentation. The first new slide should list the services you provide. Format the table with some background shading and borders that complement the presentation's design template. Then add a clip art image to the slide to complement the list. The second new slide should include a chart. To create the chart, use the data in Table 2.6 to show the test results for employees of three local companies before and after you presented a business writing workshop to them. Include notes to explain the chart. Print, save, and close the revised presentation.

Table 2.6	Test Results	
Company Name	**Before**	**After**
Robinson & Wales	410	515
Portman, Inc.	475	525
Citizens Bank	460	495

Overview: **Congratulations!** Now that you have completed the PowerPoint lessons in this tutorial, you have the opportunity in this capstone project to apply the PowerPoint skills you have learned. You will create a slide show for young people who soon will apply for driver's licenses in your state. You will present this show to groups of youngsters at several different high schools in your area. As you create the case study slide show, try to incorporate the following skills into your work:

- Create a presentation from a design template, using different layouts. Insert subtitles, tables, graphics, clip art, charts, organization charts, tables, and sounds, among other elements. Import a table from a Word document into your presentation, as well as a chart from an Excel document. Use PowerPoint's drawing tools to create shapes.

- Create an outline for your presentation in Word, and then import the outline into your presentation. When you are finished, export the presentation back to Word as an outline to use in the future.

- Add speaker notes to at least half the slides in the presentation.

- Proofread and edit the text. Use the spelling feature; use the Undo, Redo, Repeat, and Find and Replace commands.

- Use Microsoft PowerPoint Help as necessary.

- Navigate the presentation effectively, and use all of PowerPoint's views to design, organize, and review your slides. Select and move slides as needed. Delete unnecessary slides from the presentation.

- Customize the presentation by making changes to the slide master. Apply a different design template to the presentation.

- Promote and demote subtitles as needed to provide the most logical arrangement of information. Insert bulleted lists.

- Change font style, size, attributes, and color. Add formatting and special effects, such as bold, italic, and underline. Use the Format Painter button when you can.

- Add headers and footers to your slides, notes pages, and handouts.

- Add hyperlinks that jump from one slide to another within the presentation, and add other hyperlinks that jump to a Web site pertinent to the presentation.

- Format, resize, and move a table.

- Add transitions and animations to your presentation.

- Use Print Preview to review your slide show, and then print a single copy of your slides, notes pages, and outline. Also print a handout that includes three slides on each page.

- Manage the files you create by setting up a new folder for them and by naming them appropriately.

- Publish the presentation for viewing on the World Wide Web.

Instructions: Read all directions and plan your work before you begin. You will be evaluated on these factors: (1) the number of skills involved in completing the case study; (2) creativity; (3) practical applications for the task; (4) appropriate use of presentation features; (5) quality of the presentation produced, including mechanical accuracy, format, and writing style; and (6) oral presentation of the slide show.

1. *Get Started.* Search the Web, using keywords such as *[name of your state]*, *bureau/department of motor vehicles, driver licensing, state licensing, government agencies/offices*, and *traffic laws.* Add an informative site to your list of favorites/bookmarks in case you need to go back to complete the research. Be sure to check other sources of information, such as a local office of your state's Bureau of Motor Vehicles, a commercial driving school, your police department, the local library, an insurance agent, or someone who teaches Drivers' Education at an area high school.

2. *Plan the Presentation.* Sketch a presentation plan. Represent each slide and show the type of information it will contain—bulleted text, clip art, graphs, tables, etc. Write key words for the text on each slide, referring to information obtained from your research. Strive for a smooth flow of information and a professional appearance.

3. *Design the Presentation.* Use the design template of your choice. You can create the presentation from a design template or from a blank slide. Save the file as *Driver's License* in the *Projects* folder of your *PowerPoint Data* folder.

4. *Add Data.* Type a title and subtitle on the title slide. Add new slides, typing a title and subtitles on each one. Try to add the main points to each slide before adding the next slide. Check the spelling throughout your presentation.

5. *Add Visual Interest.* Add graphics, colors, charts, tables, or clip art as appropriate throughout the presentation. Be sure to insert at least one hyperlink that lets you jump to a different slide in the show, and insert another hyperlink that lets you jump to an appropriate Web site (such as the department of motor vehicles for your state).

6. *Modify the Slide Master.* Study the fonts, font sizes, and font colors throughout the presentation; modify the slide master to create a more interesting presentation. Add a footer with slide numbers and the date. Enhance objects and tables with different fill effects, lines, borders, shading, etc.

7. *Add Transitions and Animations.* Add transitions and animations to some of the slides. Preview the slide show, focusing on the flow of information and the overall presentation. Adjust as needed.

8. *Produce the Presentation.* Print a complete copy of the presentation (including the slides, notes pages, and outline) for your instructor. Print a handout of the presentation for your audience.

9. *Publish to the Web.* Prepare your presentation for viewing on the Web so that your audience can view it online after you are finished presenting it in person.

MANAGING INFORMATION

Contents

E-Mail Viruses

Is Your Computer Protected?

Until recently, it was not considered possible to spread viruses within e-mail messages. Because e-mail messages are predominantly text, they could not carry viruses, which require executable code to run.

Newer-generation e-mail programs, however, support e-mail messages in various formats, including HTML. They also support attachments—you can attach a file (such as a DOC, EXE, or other binary file) to a message and send it to a recipient, who can open the file upon receiving it. These features of e-mail programs have made them more convenient and useful. However, both features have also opened the door to new types of viruses—e-mail viruses—which can be devastating to anyone who receives them.

Macro Viruses The more common type of e-mail virus—called a macro virus—relies on a file attached to the message. To create an e-mail virus, the programmer selects a popular application that has a macro language, such as Microsoft Word. Then he or she creates a document in that application and places a macro within the document. The macro can contain commands that perform various tasks, including copying and deleting files, changing system settings, creating new e-mail messages, and more. Finally, the programmer attaches the document containing the macro code to an e-mail message and sends the file to unsuspecting recipients. When a recipient downloads the attachment and opens it, the macro in the file runs automatically.

Once released, the virus looks for the recipient's e-mail address book and sends copies of the infected attachment to people in the address book. The virus also may remain on the first recipient's machine and do considerable damage, like a regular virus.

Viruses That Do Not Require Attachments
A newer and more frightening breed of e-mail virus does not require an attached file to inflict damage. This type of virus can reside directly within the text of an HTML-format e-mail message, in unseen code; these viruses are written in a programming language such as Visual Basic Script (VBScript). The first known virus of this type—called "BubbleBoy"—was transmitted in November 1999. Although the virus did not become widespread, it aroused a new sense of urgency in development and antivirus communities. To become infected with the BubbleBoy virus, the recipient did not have to do anything; it was enough simply to receive the infected message. On restarting the computer, the user activated the virus

code, and the virus made changes to the Windows Registry settings and sent copies of the infected e-mail message to everyone in the recipient's address book.

Protect Your Computer Unlike other types of viruses, there may not be much you can do to protect your computer from e-mail viruses, but you should take the following precautions:

- Do not open e-mail attachments from people you do not know or trust.

- Install a reputable antivirus program, run it frequently, and keep its virus definitions up to date. Some experts suggest using two different antivirus programs and running them on an alternating schedule.

- Check your Web browser, e-mail program, and newsreader and make sure that their security settings are set to the highest possible level. In addition, you may want to set your e-mail program not to accept messages delivered in HTML format.

- Be alert to new developments in viruses by periodically checking virus-related sites on the Web. The makers of antivirus programs, universities, and security experts host these sites.

Are you protecting your computer adequately?

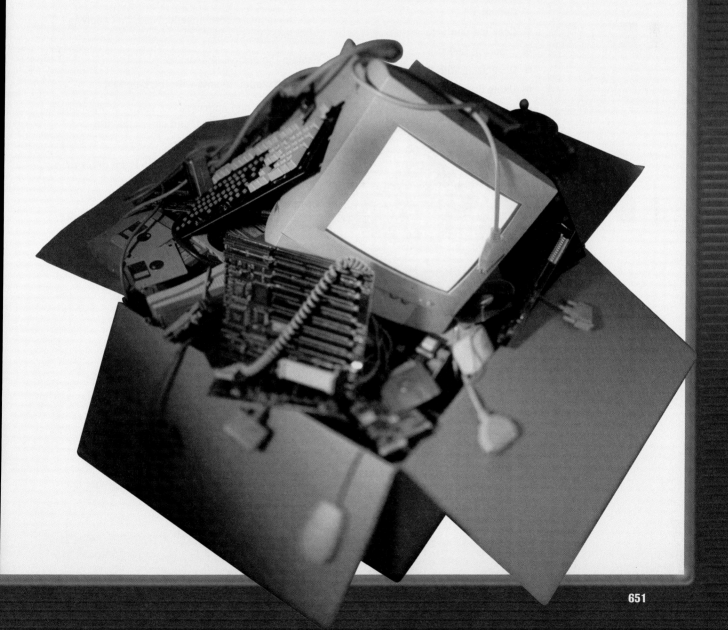

LESSON **1**

Outlook Basics

CONTENTS

- Starting Outlook and Exploring the Outlook Window
- Using the Inbox
- Scheduling With the Calendar
- Creating Contacts
- Tracking Tasks
- Organizing With Notes
- Using Outlook Today
- Using the Journal

OBJECTIVES

After you complete this lesson, you will be able to do the following:

- ▶ Describe what you can accomplish with Outlook.
- ▶ Start Outlook and navigate its window.
- ▶ Use the Inbox to create, send, read, and reply to mail messages.
- ▶ Explain the archiving process.
- ▶ Schedule appointments with the Calendar.
- ▶ Enter names and addresses as contacts, manipulate the contact information, and communicate electronically with contacts.
- ▶ Create and maintain an electronic to-do list with Tasks.
- ▶ Create, format, and sort Notes.
- ▶ Preview your day with the Outlook Today page.
- ▶ Record, view, and open journal entries.

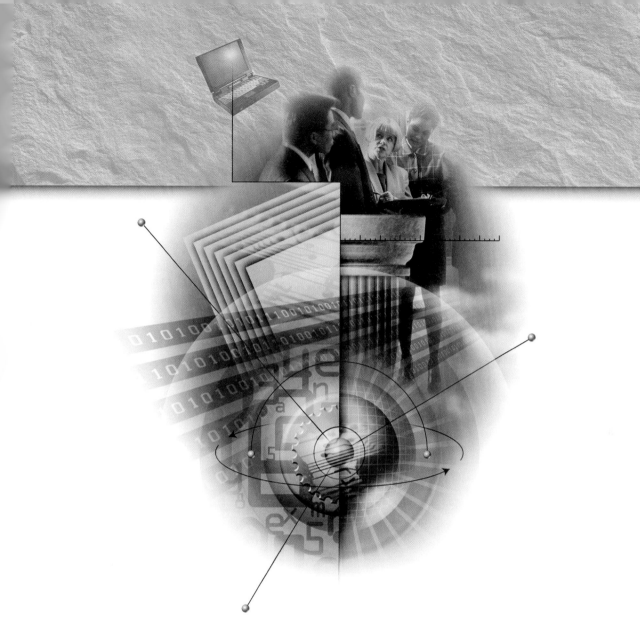

STARTING OUTLOOK AND EXPLORING THE OUTLOOK WINDOW

Microsoft Outlook is a desktop information management program in which you can organize and share many different types of information, including messages, appointments, contacts, and tasks. You can use Outlook to keep track of personal and business information, share information with other members of your workgroup, and communicate with others. You can launch Microsoft Outlook several different ways; however, the most common method is clicking the Start button ![Start].

The Outlook window contains several familiar objects, such as the title bar, menu bar, and one or more toolbars. The main part of the window is composed of two frames. The main working area is the larger frame to the right. The bar at the top of this frame, called the **folder banner,** displays the name of the open folder. The smaller frame to the left is the **Outlook Bar.** The Outlook Bar contains group names and shortcut icons. The icons serve as shortcuts to frequently used folders. You can click a bar that contains a group name, such as Outlook Shortcuts, My Shortcuts, and Other Shortcuts, to see the shortcuts within that group.

Outlook
in the workplace

E-mail now may be more popular than any other type of correspondence in the workplace. One of the reasons for its popularity is that it saves time and energy. That is the case with many of the Outlook tools that you'll learn about in this lesson.

HANDS on

Launching Outlook

In this activity, you will use the Start button 📴Start to launch Outlook.

1. **Click the Start button 📴Start, point to Programs, and click Microsoft Outlook.**

2. **The Office Assistant may appear to provide helpful information and tips. If it appears, read the message displayed and click OK. Then, right-click the Office Assistant, and click Hide. If the Outlook window is not maximized, click the Maximize button ▢.**

The Microsoft Outlook window will resemble Figure 1.1.

Figure 1.1
Outlook window

- Standard toolbar
- Folder banner
- Group name
- Shortcut icons
- Group names
- Outlook Bar
- Main working area

HANDS on

Using the Outlook Bar

In this activity, you will learn how to select the different groups on the Outlook Bar, as well as the folders within a group.

1. **If it is not already selected, click the Outlook Shortcuts group name on the Outlook Bar. A group name is selected if shortcut icons appear directly below it.**

The Outlook folders appear as shortcut icons, as shown in Figure 1.1.

2. Click the Contacts icon ▣ **on the Outlook Bar.**

The folder banner name changes to show the selected folder. Depending on whether other users of this computer have previously entered contacts, your main working area may contain names and addresses, or it may be blank. You'll learn more about *Contacts* and the other Outlook folders as you complete this lesson.

3. Scroll the Outlook Bar, if necessary, to find and click the Tasks shortcut icon ▣ **.**

Again, the folder banner changes, and the Task list is shown in the main working area, as shown in Figure 1.2. Now, you can find out which folders exist in some of the other groups.

Outlook BASICS

Using the Outlook Bar

• Click a group name to open it.

• Click a shortcut icon to open its folder.

OUTLOOK 2002

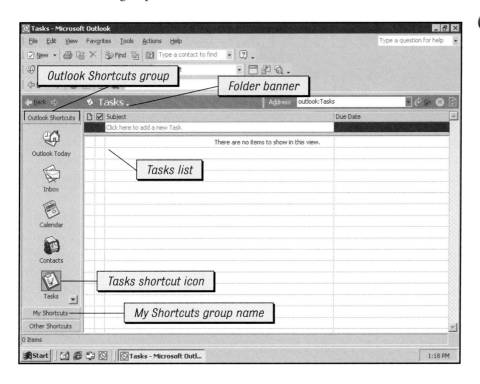

Figure 1.2
Task list

Another Way

To move to another folder, such as Tasks, point to Go To on the View menu and click the folder name.

4. Click the My Shortcuts group name on the Outlook Bar.

The My Shortcuts group name jumps to the top on the Outlook Bar, directly below the Outlook Shortcuts group name. The icons in the Outlook Shortcuts group are hidden, and the icons in the My Shortcut group are displayed. The Tasks frame is still active in the right frame, since you haven't yet selected a new icon.

5. Click the Sent Items icon ▣ **.**

The Sent Items icon is selected, and the folder banner and working area change to reflect the active folder.

6. Click the Other Shortcuts group name to see the icons contained in that group.

Now that you know how to switch from group to group and folder to folder, you're ready to learn about Outlook's folders. If you are using a computer that

WEB NOTE

You can add a Web page to your Outlook Bar for quick access. First, display the Web toolbar in Outlook, type the Web page address in its Address bar, and press ⌷Enter⏎⌷ to go to the Web page. When the Web page appears in the main working area, point to New on the File menu and click Outlook Bar Shortcut to Web Page.

Outlook Basics   **655**

has been used by others, consult your instructor before continuing with this lesson. Your instructor may provide specific instructions about deleting existing Outlook entries.

USING THE INBOX

Electronic mail, also known as e-mail, is a popular means of communication—for both work and personal use. You can send e-mail messages to anyone who has an e-mail account on the Internet or who has an account within the same network or intranet as you. The **Inbox** folder allows you to send and receive messages electronically. You'll learn how to create, send, read, and reply to a mail message.

HANDS on

Creating and Sending a New Mail Message

The Inbox allows you to access messages that others have sent to you and to create and send new messages. Since Word is the default e-mail editor in Outlook, you can take advantage of Microsoft Word's text-editing capabilities, such as automatic spelling and grammar checking, AutoCorrect features, automatic bullets and numbers, and tables—directly from within Outlook.

You can create and read e-mail messages in one of three different formats: (1) HTML, the default format, (2) Microsoft Outlook Rich Text, and (3) Plain Text. When you create a new e-mail message, you can change from the default format by pointing to New Mail Message Using on the Actions menu and choosing the desired format. To create and send a message, you must have the recipient's full e-mail address.

In this activity, you will create a mail message informing a coworker at The Pet Deli of a change in a product release date. Then you will send the message to your instructor or to a classmate.

> **1. Click the Outlook Shortcuts group name on the Outlook Bar to display the shortcut icons in this group.**
>
> **2. Click the Inbox icon ⬚.**

The folder banner changes to indicate that the Inbox is active. The main working area displays incoming messages or a message that you have no items.

> **3. Click the New Mail Message button ⬚ New ⬚ on the Standard toolbar.**

Since Word is the default e-mail editor in Outlook, Word launches; and the Untitled Message - Microsoft Word window appears, as shown in Figure 1.3, ready for you to create a new mail message.

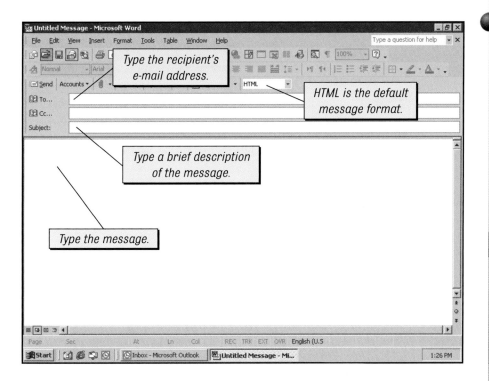

Figure 1.3
Untitled Message - Microsoft Word
window

OUTLOOK 2002

HINTS & TIPS

If you enter names and e-mail
addresses in your address book,
you can click the To button in the
Untitled - Message window to
select a recipient.

4. If necessary, right-click the **Office Assistant** and click **Hide**.

5. In the *To* box, type the e-mail address of your instructor or a classmate. (Your instructor will provide this information.)

NOTE *The Cc box allows you to send a copy of the same message to others.*

6. Press `Tab` twice to move to the *Subject* box.

7. Type New Product Release Date and press `Tab` to move to the
   message area.

Now you are ready to type the text of your message. Assume you work for The
Pet Deli, Inc., and you want to inform the recipient—a coworker—of a new product release date.

8. Type the following text:

   The release date of our new nutritional supplement has been
   changed to April 26. As you know, we are still finalizing a
   name for the supplement. Any name suggestions are welcome.

9. Click the **Importance: High button** to indicate to the recipient
   that this message carries a high importance, as shown in Figure 1.4.
   (Your *To* address will be different.)

Other commonly used buttons include the Message Flag button, which adds
special text to the message to indicate that a follow-up action is required, and
the Insert File button, which allows you to attach a file to the message.

Another Way

- To create a new mail message,
  press `Ctrl` + `N` or point to
  New on the File menu and click
  Mail Message.

- To send your message and
  check for new messages, point
  to Send/Receive on the Tools
  menu and click the appropriate
  option.

Figure 1.4
Finished mail message

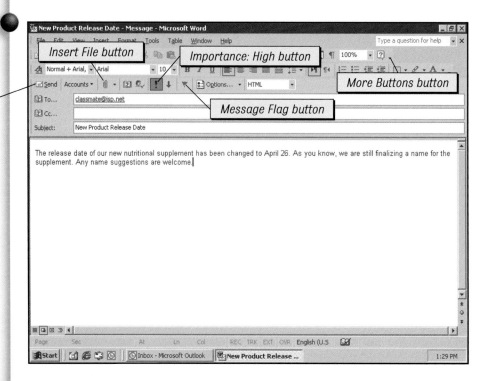

10. Proofread your message. Once you are sure that it is error-free, click the Send button ⌐Send.

In a typical Internet setup, Outlook connects to the Internet service provider, delivers the outgoing mail messages, checks for incoming messages, and then disconnects from the Internet service provider. A copy of the reply is stored in the **Sent Items** folder in the My Shortcuts group.

If you are not connected to the Internet, or your mail was not sent because of your computer setup, you may receive an error message indicating that the mail wasn't sent. If so, you may need to change some Outlook settings so that your computer can recognize and communicate with your mail program. Ask your instructor for assistance before proceeding to the next activity.

Understanding Incoming Mail

Along the top of the Inbox window are several column headings. You can double-click any of these column headings to sort messages by that column. Table 1.1 provides a brief description of the Inbox column headings.

NORTON ONLINE

Visit **www.glencoe.com/norton/online/** for more information on sending and receiving e-mail.

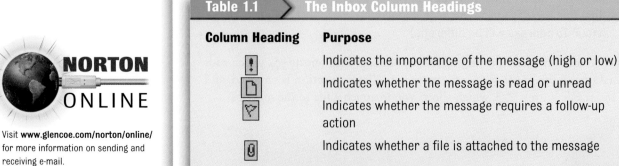

Table 1.1	The Inbox Column Headings
Column Heading	**Purpose**
!	Indicates the importance of the message (high or low)
🗋	Indicates whether the message is read or unread
▽	Indicates whether the message requires a follow-up action
📎	Indicates whether a file is attached to the message

Table 1.1 ▷ **The Inbox Column Headings (continued)**

Column Heading	Purpose
From	Displays the e-mail address or name of the sender
Subject	Displays the text in the *Subject* line of the message
Received	Shows the date the message was received
Size	Shows the size of the message

HANDS on

Reading a Mail Message

If you sent a message in the previous hands-on activity, the recipient may have responded. In this activity, you'll check for new mail and read a message, if one has arrived.

1. Click the **Inbox icon** in the Outlook Shortcuts group, if it is not active.

2. Click the **Send/Receive button** Send/Receive on the Standard toolbar.

Clicking this button checks for new mail and sends any messages you've created. The messages you receive will appear as shown in Figure 1.5. The sender's address, the *Subject* line, the date received, and the size of the message appear in the top portion of the Inbox, and the message appears in the Preview Pane at the bottom of the Inbox. (If the Preview Pane is not displayed, click Preview Pane on the View menu.)

Outlook **BASICS**

Reading a Mail Message

1. Open the *Inbox* folder and click the Send/Receive button.

2. Double-click the message you want to read.

3. Read the message.

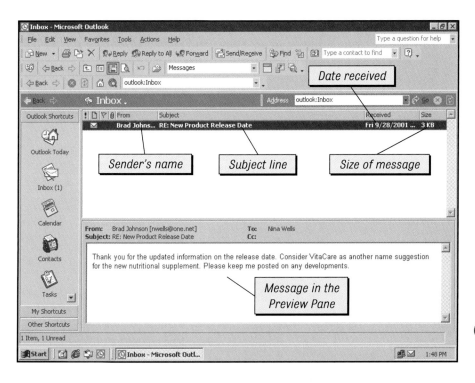

Figure 1.5
An incoming message

OUTLOOK 2002

OUTLOOK 2002

NOTE *Under perfect conditions, mail sent to you will take only a few seconds to be delivered. However, depending on your connection speed, traffic on the Internet, and other factors, a message may take a few minutes, hours, or even days to be delivered.*

You can open the message window to see more information.

3. Double-click the line of information for a new message at the top of the Inbox.

The message window appears, showing the sender's name and/or address, the date and time sent, the recipient, the name(s) of anyone who received a copy of the message, the *Subject* line, and the message.

4. Read the message.

Replying to a Mail Message

You can use the mail message window to reply immediately. When you click the Reply button ![Reply], Outlook launches Word, and the mail message automatically displays the address of the person you are replying to and the *Subject* line. You also can access the Reply button from the Inbox. In this activity, you will reply to the message you received.

1. Click the Reply button ![Reply] on the Standard toolbar.

A Word window appears with the address and subject already filled in.

2. Type the following reply:

> Thank you for the name suggestion. I will add it to the list of potential names. Will you be able to attend a team meeting on Wednesday at 1 p.m.? I hope to make a final name decision during this meeting.

Your mail message window will resemble Figure 1.6.

3. Click the Send button ![Send].

The original message that you received appears. A banner above the *From* line indicates the date and time you replied.

4. Close the mail message.

5. If necessary, click the Send/Receive button ![Send/Receive] to deliver your reply.

Your reply is sent. A copy of the reply is stored in the *Sent Items* folder in the My Shortcuts group.

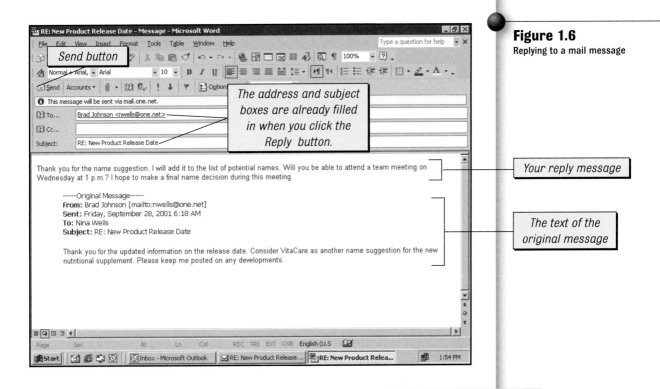

Figure 1.6
Replying to a mail message

The address and subject boxes are already filled in when you click the Reply button.

Your reply message

The text of the original message

Archiving Items

Depending on your Outlook settings, you periodically may be asked if you wish to archive old items. Use Help to better understand the archiving process.

1. In the **Ask a Question box**, type *archive* and press `Enter←`.

2. Click the **About archiving items using the AutoArchive** option.

3. In the Help window, click **Show All**. If necessary, click **Maximize** ☐. Read the information (Figure 1.7).

4. Click the **Show button** and click the **Answer Wizard** tab. In the *What would you like to do?* box, type *AutoArchive default settings.*

5. Explore the **Back up or delete items using AutoArchive** option. When you finish exploring, close the Help window.

6. Check the Archive settings for the *Inbox* folder on your computer. Do not change any of the archive settings without permission from your instructor.

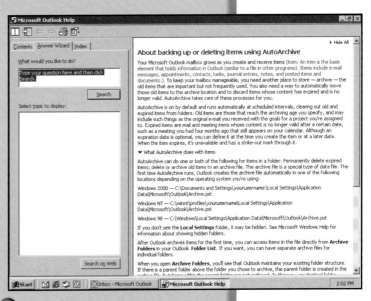

Figure 1.7
Learning about archiving

SCHEDULING WITH THE CALENDAR

The **Calendar** folder in Microsoft Outlook allows you to schedule appointments, meetings, events, and tasks. In this section, you'll learn how to set a new appointment, schedule an event, display the calendar window in a variety of views, and plan a recurring meeting.

Setting a New Appointment

Just as you can block time in a paper calendar for an **appointment,** you can do the same in Outlook's Calendar. You can give the appointment a name to describe it; you also can set the appointment's time and other characteristics. In this activity, you'll set a few appointments for your work at The Pet Deli.

1. **Click the Calendar icon** 🗓 **in the Outlook Shortcuts group on the Outlook Bar.**

The main working area will display today's calendar, as shown in Figure 1.8. If your screen does not match Figure 1.8, point to Current View on the View menu, and click Day/Week/Month. Then, click the Day button 🗓Day on the Standard toolbar. If today's calendar is not shown, click the Go to Today button Today on the Standard toolbar.

2. **In the Date Navigator, click the date for the next Tuesday.**

The appointment book for the next Tuesday appears in the center pane, and the top of the Calendar pane shows the date.

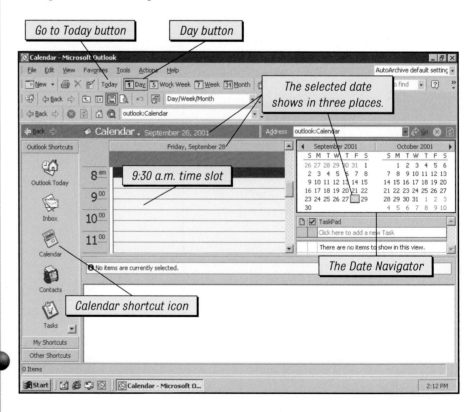

Figure 1.8
Calendar

3. Scroll down in the calendar, and click the **4:30 p.m. time slot**.

The section representing 4:30 to 5:00 is selected.

> **NOTE** *If someone has previously used the* Calendar *folder to set appointments on the computer you are using, these appointments may interfere with the completion of this section. Ask your instructor whether you may delete the previously set appointments.*

4. Type Presentation by Chris Smith and press Enter⏎.

The text that you typed appears in a highlighted bar with a bell icon that indicates that Outlook will remind you of your appointment 15 minutes before it occurs. The details of the appointment appear in the Preview Pane below the appointment book.

5. In the Date Navigator, click the date for the next Wednesday.

6. Double-click the **2 p.m. time slot**.

The Untitled - Appointment window appears, in which you can set specific attributes for an appointment.

7. On the Appointment tab, type New Product Naming Meeting in the *Subject* box and press Tab to move to the *Location* box.

Your date will be different than the one shown in Figure 1.9.

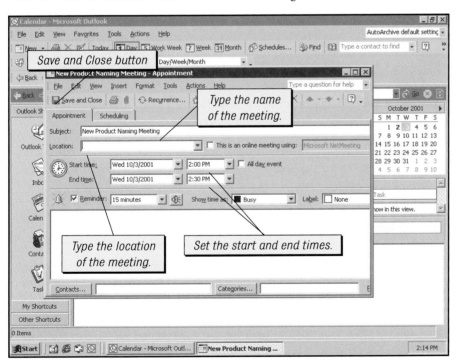

8. Type Conference Room A in the *Location* box.

9. In the *End time* area, set the end time to 3:30 p.m.

10. Click the **Save and Close button** ⊟ Save and Close on the Standard toolbar.

> **HINTS & TIPS**
>
> You can drag an appointment, an event, or a meeting to a different date and/or time. You also can edit the subject by clicking the description text and typing your changes.

Figure 1.9
Appointment window

NORTON
ONLINE

Visit **www.glencoe.com/norton/online/** for more information on using Outlook's calendar.

The new meeting is shown on Wednesday's appointment book, as shown in Figure 1.10.

Figure 1.10
New appointment indicator

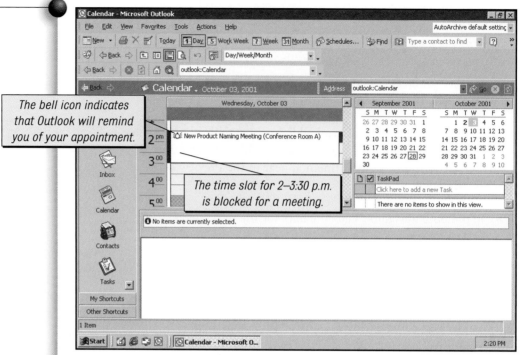

The bell icon indicates that Outlook will remind you of your appointment.

The time slot for 2–3:30 p.m. is blocked for a meeting.

You just have been notified that the presentation by Chris Smith has been rescheduled for the next Friday and that it has been extended to an hour-long presentation. You need to record the new presentation date and time on your calendar, and then delete the notation for next Tuesday.

11. In the Date Navigator, click the date for the Friday immediately following the New Product Naming Meeting.

Notice that two dates are shown in bold in the Date Navigator. A bold date indicates that you have an appointment or other activity scheduled during that day. Also notice that the Date Navigator encloses today's date in a box.

12. Drag to select the time slot for **10 a.m. to 11 a.m.**, type **Presentation by Chris Smith**, and press Enter.

To set an appointment that blocks more than 30 minutes of time, click the beginning time and drag until you select the desired block of time.

13. In the Date Navigator, click the first bold date—the date on which you set your first appointment for Chris Smith.

The Calendar jumps to the date you selected in the Date Navigator.

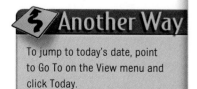

Another Way

To jump to today's date, point to Go To on the View menu and click Today.

14. Click the notation for the 4:30 p.m. presentation so that it is surrounded by a border, and then click the **Delete button** [X] on the Standard toolbar.

The appointment is deleted.

HANDS on

Scheduling an Event

An **event** is an activity that lasts one day or longer, such as a seminar, a trade show, or a vacation. An **annual event,** such as a birthday or an anniversary, occurs yearly on a specific date. Events and annual events are not indicated by blocks of time on the Calendar; instead they are indicated by a banner at the top of the appointment book for the specific day(s). In this activity, you'll set an event to remind you of a seminar.

1. **Use the Date Navigator to move to December 19 of this year. If necessary, repeatedly click a directional arrow in the Date Navigator to display the month of December.**

The date of December 19 appears above the daily calendar.

2. **On the Actions menu, click New All Day Event.**

The Untitled - Event window appears.

3. **In the *Subject* box, type** Technology Update Seminar.

4. **In the *Location* box, type** Cincinnati Convention Center in Cincinnati, Ohio. **Set the End time to December 21.**

5. **Click the Reminder triangle button, and set the time to 2 weeks.**

6. **Click the notes section at the bottom of the window and type** Confirm all travel arrangements.

The Event window should resemble Figure 1.11.

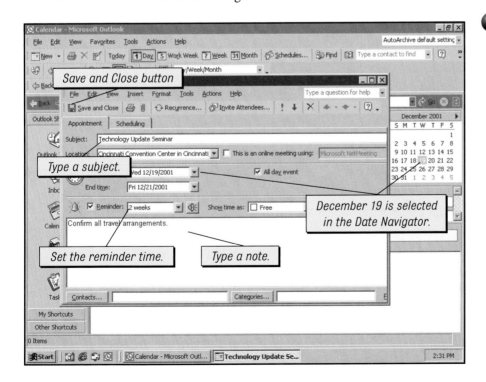

Figure 1.11
The Event window

7. Click the Save and Close button ⟨🔲 Save and Close⟩.

A banner appears at the top of the appointment book for three dates: December 19, December 20, and December 21.

HANDS on
Changing Views

At times, you'll want to look at your calendar a day at a time. Other times, however, you'll want to look at a week or month as a whole. The Calendar allows you to do just that. In this activity, you'll change the view of your calendar. You'll view an entire week, an entire month, and a five-day work week. Then you'll use the Go to Today button ⟨Today⟩ to return to today's date.

1. Click the Week button ⟨7. Week⟩ **on the Standard toolbar.**

The calendar for the week that includes December 19 appears in the center pane of the window with the event from December 19–December 21 displayed.

2. Click the Month button ⟨31 Month⟩ **on the Standard toolbar.**

The entire December calendar is displayed.

3. Click the Work Week button ⟨5 Work Week⟩ **on the Standard toolbar.**

The view changes to display the days Monday through Friday, with time slots for each day.

4. Click the Go to Today button ⟨Today⟩.

The calendar for the current work week is displayed in the center pane, and the week is selected in the Date Navigator.

> **NOTE** *No matter which view you are in, you can view details of a specific appointment by clicking the appointment; the details will appear in the Preview Pane.*

HANDS on
Setting a Recurring Meeting

A **recurring meeting** is one that occurs at regular intervals. For example, if you have a project meeting on the first Wednesday of every month, you can set one appointment and tell Outlook to automatically schedule the meeting for the same time each month. Your manager at The Pet Deli, Inc., holds a one-hour staff meeting every other Monday. In this activity, you'll learn how to schedule these recurring meetings, without manually entering an entry for each meeting.

Outlook BASICS

Changing Views

- Click the Day button to view one day.

- Click the Week button to view one full week.

- Click the Work Week button to view one work week (Monday–Friday).

- Click the Month button to view one month.

- Click the Go to Today button to move to the current day in the existing view.

1. **Use the Date Navigator to move to the next Monday from today.**

2. **In the center pane, drag to select the 9:30 to 10:30 a.m. time slot.**

3. **On the Actions menu, click New Recurring Meeting.**

The Appointment Recurrence dialog box appears.

4. **In the *Recurrence pattern* area, set the meeting to recur every 2 weeks on Monday, as shown in Figure 1.12.**

Outlook BASICS

Setting a Recurring Meeting

1. Select the meeting time of the first meeting to schedule.

2. Click New Recurring Meeting on the Actions menu.

3. Set the recurrence pattern and click OK.

4. Type a description of the meeting in the *Subject* box and click Save on the File menu.

5. Click the Close button.

OUTLOOK 2002

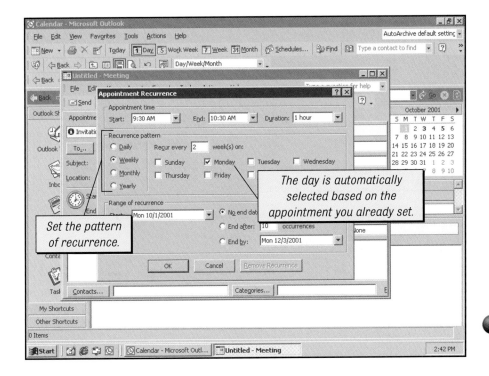

Set the pattern of recurrence.

The day is automatically selected based on the appointment you already set.

Figure 1.12
Appointment Recurrence dialog box

5. **Click OK.**

Outlook automatically assumes that you want to send a mail message to alert others of this meeting.

6. **In the *Subject* box in the Untitled - Meeting window, type Staff Meeting and then click Save on the File menu.**

7. **Since you do not need to send a message at this time to notify others of the meeting, close the window.**

As shown in Figure 1.13, the 9:30 a.m. meeting reminder appears in the box for the next Monday in the appointment book. Looking at the Date Navigator, you can see the date for every other Monday is bold, indicating that the meeting has been set on these dates.

8. **Switch to Month view. If necessary, scroll down to see the meeting reminders that occur every other Monday in several future months.**

Figure 1.13
Setting a recurring meeting

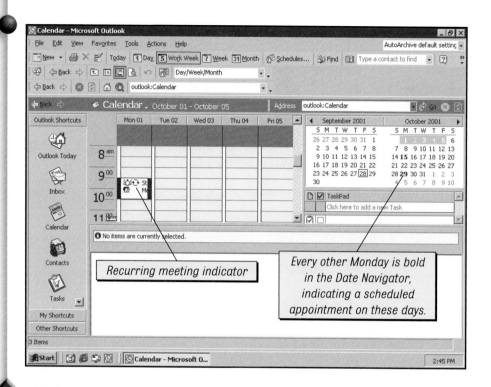

CREATING CONTACTS

The **Contacts** folder of Outlook acts as a personal and business address book. Outlook allows you to create and delete contacts; view, sort, and filter contacts; quickly send a message to a contact; and track activities entered in the Journal concerning the contact.

HANDS **on**

Creating a New Contact

You can store information about your contacts in the address book. For instance, you can store names, business and home addresses, e-mail addresses, and multiple telephone numbers. To use information without retyping it each time, you can save the data for each contact. In this activity, you will create a few new contacts.

1. **Click the Contacts icon** 📇 **in the Outlook Shortcuts group on the Outlook Bar.**

The Contacts window is displayed.

> **NOTE** *If someone previously has used the Contacts folder on the computer you are using, these contacts may interfere with the completion of this section. Ask your instructor whether you may delete the previously created contacts.*

2. **Click the New Contact button** 🗋 New ▾ **on the Standard toolbar.**

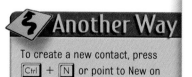

Another Way

To create a new contact, press Ctrl + N or point to New on the File menu and click Contact.

The Untitled - Contact window appears.

3. Click the **General tab**, if necessary, and then enter the following information:

Full Name:	Mr. Thomas C. Burnes
Job title:	Owner
Company:	Centerville Pet Shop
Business phone:	(513) 555-1824
Home phone:	(513) 555-8222
Business Fax:	(513) 555-9002
Mobile phone:	(513) 555-2323
Business address:	89 Centerville Avenue
	Cincinnati, OH 45222-8880

4. Click the **Business triangle button** in the *Address* area and click **Home**.

Outlook allows you to store multiple addresses.

5. Type the following home address for Thomas Burnes: 1003 Savannah Court, Cincinnati, OH 45218-1255.

6. In the E-mail box, type tcburnes@mailrtw.com, as shown in Figure 1.14.

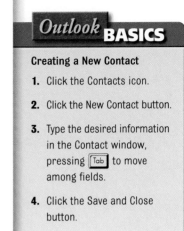

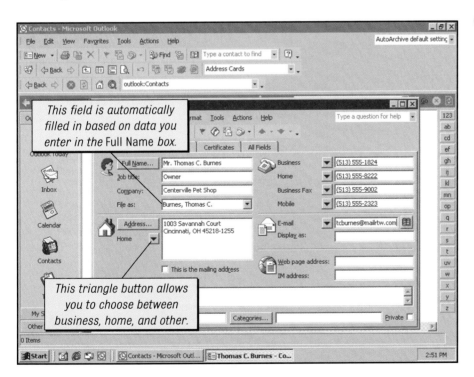

Figure 1.14
Completed Contact window

7. Click the **Save and Close button** 🖫 Save and Close on the Standard toolbar.

The contact information appears in the Contacts window.

8. Repeat steps 2 through 6 to create the following new contact:

Full Name:	Mrs. Rosa P. Santiago
Job title:	Manager
Company:	The Doggie Den
Business phone:	(859) 555-9222
Business Fax:	(859) 555-9223
Mobile phone:	(859) 555-3400
Business address:	2324 Grand Park Street Covington, KY 41011-2399
E-mail:	rsantiago@mailrtw.com

9. Since you want to enter other contacts, click the **Save and New button** to save the information for this contact and progress to a new, blank Untitled - Contact window.

10. Create new contacts from the data in Tables 1.2, 1.3, and 1.4, saving and closing each one.

When you save and close the last contact, the Untitled - Contact window reappears. The contacts appear in alphabetical order by the File As field (which displays each contact's last name, first name, and middle initial, if available).

Table 1.2	Data for New Contacts 1-3		
	Contact 1	**Contact 2**	**Contact 3**
Full Name:	Dr. Daniel Ross	Dr. Melissa Martin	Ms. Aileiah Smolty
Job title:	Owner		Manager
Company:	Dr. Dan's Animal Hospital	Valley Emergency Animal Hospital	Alley's Pet Place
Business phone:	(513) 555-3000	(513) 555-8712	(859) 555-3112
Home phone:	(513) 555-1888		
Business Fax:	(513) 555-3003	(513) 555-4322	(859) 555-6775
Mobile phone:	(513) 555-3009	(513) 555-2902	(859) 555-3337
Business address:	73 Petros Avenue Cincinnati, OH 45218-1899	13 South Street Cincinnati, OH 45220-9333	1892 Delgado Avenue Covington, KY 45011-7790
Home address:	9012 City Boulevard Amelia, OH 45102-2311		
E-mail:	DrDan@ammt.com	Mmartin@mailrtw.com	Aileiah24@ammt.com
Web page address:	www.DrDanRoss.com		

Table 1.3   Data for New Contacts 4–6

	Contact 4	Contact 5	Contact 6
Full Name:	Mr. George Cooper	Mr. Henry Alexander	Ms. Maria Gomez
Job title:		Customer Service Representative	
Company:		The Pet Deli, Inc.	
Business phone:	(513) 555-2190	(513) 555-3456	
Home phone:	(513) 555-5553	(513) 555-9026	(513) 555-7045
Business Fax:		(513) 555-1899	
Mobile phone:		(513) 555-5477	
Home address:	1384 Safeway Court Cincinnati, OH 45255-7223	23 Pinnacle Way Cincinnati, OH 45255-1824	
E-mail:		Type your instructor's e-mail address or a classmate's e-mail address.	

Table 1.4   Data for New Contacts 7–9

	Contact 7	Contact 8	Contact 9
Full Name:	Mr. James King	Mr. David Sizemore	Mrs. Andrea Giwer
Job title:		Sales Manager	
Company:		The Pet Deli, Inc.	
Business phone:		(513) 555-3456	(513) 555-3390
Home phone:	(513) 555-0033	(513) 555-1234	(859) 555-0655
Business Fax:		(513) 555-1899	
Home address:		89000 South Circle Drive Cincinnati, OH 45233-3344	17 Oak Street Covington, KY 41015-1382
E-mail:		DSizemore@petdeli.com	Agiwer@mailrtw.com

HANDS on

Modifying a Contact

Outlook allows you to change contact information easily. In this activity, you will change the information for two contacts.

Outlook BASICS

Modifying a Contact

1. Double-click the name bar for the contact you wish to change.

2. Click the appropriate tab, if necessary.

3. Click the arrow next to the information to be modified, if necessary.

4. Type the new information or edit existing data.

5. Click the Save and Close button.

1. In the Contacts pane, double-click the name bar for Thomas Burnes.

The Thomas C. Burnes – Contact window appears. You want to add a pager number for Mr. Burnes.

2. Click the **Mobile triangle button**.

3. Click **Pager** on the list that appears.

4. Type (513) 555-1185 in the Pager box, as shown in Figure 1.15.

5. Click the **Save and Close button** Save and Close on the Standard toolbar.

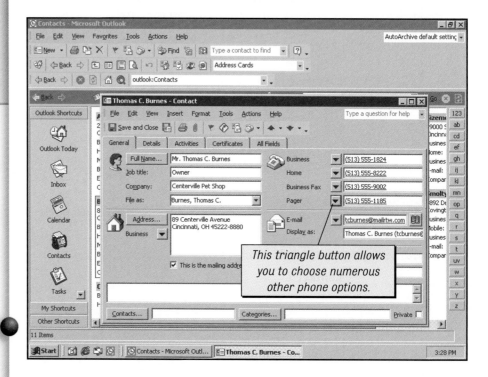

This triangle button allows you to choose numerous other phone options.

Figure 1.15
Typing a pager number

6. Double-click the name bar for Daniel Ross. If Daniel Ross' name does not appear in the window due to the number of contacts in Outlook, click the button to the right of the window that contains the letter *R* to jump to the contact last names that begin with the letter *R*.

7. When the Daniel Ross - Contact window appears, click the **Details tab**.

8. Click the **Anniversary triangle button**, and click **November 5** of the current year.

9. If necessary, click a directional arrow to scroll to the month of November.

10. Click the **Save and Close button** Save and Close on the Standard toolbar.

NORTON
ONLINE

Visit **www.glencoe.com/norton/online/** for more information on creating and modifying contacts.

Sorting and Finding Contact Information

One advantage of storing your contacts in Outlook is the ability to quickly sort and find names, addresses, and other information. You also can view the contact information in various ways. In this activity, you first will sort the contacts by company name. Then you will identify all of the contacts that are doctors.

1. **Point to Current View on the View menu and click Customize Current View.**

2. **In the View Summary dialog box, click the Sort button.**

3. **In the Sort dialog box, click the Sort items by triangle button and click Company. Click Ascending, if necessary, and click OK. If a message appears asking if you want to show the Company field, click Yes. Click OK to close the View Summary dialog box.**

The contacts are rearranged in ascending order by company name.

4. **Using the scroll bar at the bottom of the window, scroll to the first contact.**

As shown in Figure 1.16, those contacts that do not contain a company name are listed first. Your screen may contain more contacts if you did not delete entries made by previous users.

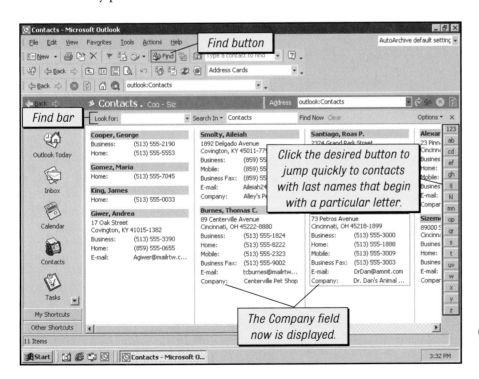

 **BASICS**

Sorting and Finding Contacts
To sort contacts:

1. Point to Current View on the View menu and click Customize Current View.

2. Click the Sort button and select the sort criteria. Then click OK.

3. Click OK.

To find information:

1. Click the Find button.

2. In the Look for box, type the data for which you are searching.

3. Click the Find Now button.

4. Click the Find button to allow all contacts to reappear in the Contacts pane.

Figure 1.16
Sorted contacts

5. Point to **Current View** on the View menu and click **Customize Current View**. Click the **Sort button** and re-sort the contacts by the File As field in Ascending order. Click **OK** to close the Sort dialog box; click **OK** to close the View Summary dialog box.

You also can find contacts whose fields contain specific information.

6. Click the **Find button** on the Standard toolbar.

The Find bar appears in the Contacts pane above the addresses.

7. Type Dr. in the Look for box, and click the **Find Now button** on the Find bar.

The two records that contain the title *Dr.* in the Name field appear: *Melissa Martin* and *Daniel Ross.* Outlook can search for this title even though it does not appear on the screen. (If entries from previous users were not deleted, more than two names may appear.)

8. Click the **Find button** to remove the Find bar from the Contacts pane and to allow all of the contacts to reappear in the main working area.

HANDS on

Sending an E-Mail to a Contact

Using Outlook, you can send mail messages to contacts without typing their e-mail addresses, and you can call them without manually dialing the telephone. In this activity, you'll create and send an e-mail message to one of your contacts without utilizing the Inbox.

1. Select the contact name for Henry Alexander. (If you can't see the name for Henry Alexander, click the button to the right of the window that contains the letter *A* to view the contact last names that begin with the letter *A.*)

2. Click the **New Message To Contact button** on the Standard toolbar.

A new mail message appears in Word, with Henry Alexander's e-mail address automatically inserted in the *To* box.

3. Compose and send an e-mail message asking Henry to send a sample package of Tiny Paws food to Aileiah Smolty at Alley's Pet Place.

NOTE *You can cut information that appears in the Address Book and paste it in your e-mail message. First, look up the address for Aileiah Smolty by clicking the Address Book button at the top of the e-mail header. In the list of names in the Select Names dialog box, select Aileiah Smolty; then click the Properties button. In the Aileiah Smolty Contact window, select the* *address, right-click, and click Copy. Close the Contact window and close the Select Names dialog box. In the e-mail message area, right-click and click Paste.*

If your computer has a modem and telephone voice capabilities, you can call a contact by selecting the contact name, clicking the Dial button on the Standard toolbar, and choosing the desired phone number.

TRACKING TASKS

Outlook not only helps track your mail messages, appointments, and contacts but also lets you track things you need to do. Outlook's **Tasks** folder is an electronic to-do list. In this section, you'll learn how to create a new task, assign a priority to the task, sort tasks, and mark a task as complete.

Creating a New Task

When you create a new **task,** it appears on your task list. You can assign a due date and a priority to any task. You also can give other details, such as a start date, percentage completed, and billing information concerning the task. In this activity, you'll create several new tasks, assigning priorities and due dates to most of them.

1. **Click the Tasks icon 🗒 in the Outlook Shortcuts group on the Outlook Bar.**

The Tasks window appears in the main working area.

> **NOTE** *If someone previously has used the* Tasks *folder on the computer you are using, these tasks may interfere with the completion of this section. Ask your instructor whether you may delete the previously created tasks.*

2. **Click the New Task button 🗹 New ▾ on the Standard toolbar.**

3. **When the Untitled - Task window appears, type** Send brochures to pet stores **in the** *Subject* **box.**

4. **Click the Due date triangle button, and click** next Tuesday **as a due date.**

5. **Change the Priority to High.**

As shown in Figure 1.17, an informational banner appears at the top of the Task tab telling you how many days you have to complete the task.

6. **Click the Save and Close button 🖫 Save and Close .**

The task appears on the task list.

7. **Create the new tasks listed in Table 1.5. When you are finished, your screen may contain other tasks in the task list if you did not delete entries made by previous users.**

Outlook BASICS

Creating a New Task

1. Click the Tasks icon.

2. Click the New Task button.

3. Type a description of the task in the *Subject* box, select a due date if desired, and select other desired options.

4. Click the Save and Close button.

Figure 1.17
Task window

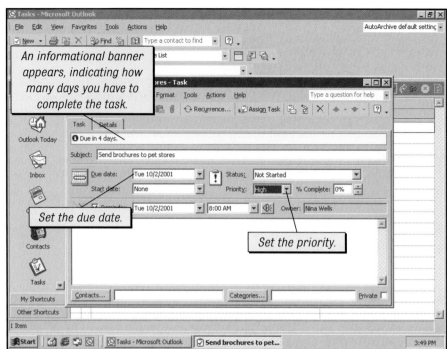

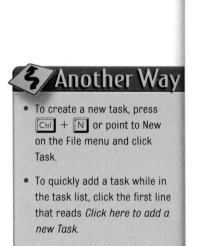

Another Way

- To create a new task, press Ctrl + N or point to New on the File menu and click Task.

- To quickly add a task while in the task list, click the first line that reads *Click here to add a new Task*.

Table 1.5	Data for New Tasks			
	Task 1	**Task 2**	**Task 3**	**Task 4**
Task	Send birthday card to George Cooper	Schedule dentist appointment	Make airline reservations for conference in Atlanta, GA	Create database of vendors
Due Date	October 15	July 2	April 24	None
Priority	Normal	Normal	High	Low

HANDS on

Arranging and Sorting Tasks

No matter in what order you add tasks to your list, if you view them in Simple List view, Outlook sorts the tasks by due date. In this activity, you will learn how to change the task list to view more information about each task and then change the sort order.

1. Point to **Current View** on the View menu and click **Detailed List**, if necessary.

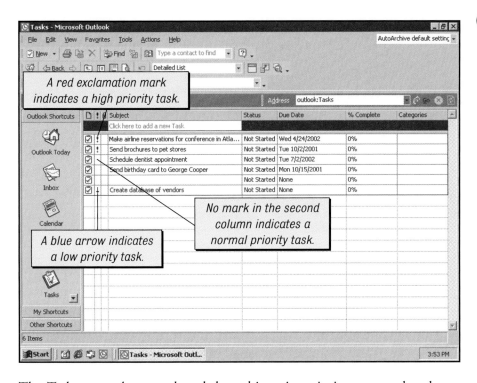

Figure 1.18
Sorting tasks by priority

The Tasks pane shows each task by subject, its priority, status, due date, percent complete, and categories.

2. Click the Due Date column heading.

The tasks are sorted by due date in reverse order.

3. Click the Due Date column heading again.

The tasks are sorted by due date.

4. Click the Priority column heading.

As shown in Figure 1.18, the tasks are sorted by priority, with the high priority tasks listed first and the low priority tasks listed last.

5. Point to Current View on the View menu and click Simple List.

The Tasks pane now shows each task by subject and its due date.

HANDS on

Deleting and Marking Tasks

When you complete a task, sometimes you will want to remove it from your task list. To do so, you can use the Delete button ✕ on the Standard toolbar. Other times, you will want to keep the task on your list but cross it off to remind you that it has been completed; this process is called **marking the task as complete.** In this activity, you'll first mark a task as complete. Then you'll delete another task.

Figure 1.19
Marking a task as complete

1. **Click the check box in the second column next to the *Send brochures to pet stores* task.**

Outlook inserts a check mark in the box and draws a line through the task and its due date to indicate that you have completed the task (see Figure 1.19).

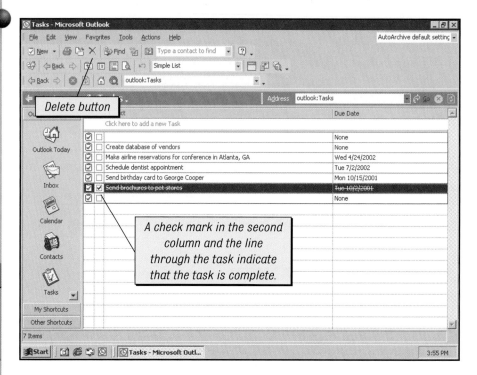

2. **Since your duties at work have increased, your manager decided to indefinitely postpone the creation of a database of vendors. To remove this task from your list, select it and then click the Delete button ⊠ on the Standard toolbar.**

ORGANIZING WITH NOTES

Outlook's **Notes** folder is an electronic version of paper self-stick, removable notes. You can use Notes to record ideas, questions, comments, or any other data you might need later. You can resize notes to fit the text on each, and you can color code notes. Outlook allows you to view your notes as icons or as lists.

HANDS on

Creating and Opening Notes

To create notes, you can start in the *Notes* folder on the Outlook Bar. If the default settings for Outlook Notes have not been changed on the computer you are using, a new note appears that is yellow in color and medium in size. In this activity, you'll create three notes. In the first scenario, assume you are speaking with a travel agent on the phone to make arrangements for two trips. You'll record the notes electronically.

1. Click the **Notes icon**  in the Outlook Shortcuts group on the Outlook Bar.

NOTE *If someone previously has used the* Notes *folder on the computer you are using, these notes may interfere with the completion of this section. Ask your instructor if you can delete the previously created notes.*

2. Click the **New Note button** [📝 New ▾] on the Standard toolbar. If the defaults have not been changed, a medium-sized yellow note will appear. The current date and time appear at the bottom of the note. Don't be concerned if the note is a different color; continue working.

3. Type the following information on the note:

   Flight #325
   Depart Cincinnati at 2:40 p.m. on 11/3
   Arrive in Boston at 4:50 p.m. on 11/3

   Flight #1288
   Depart Boston at 3:50 p.m. on 11/6
   Arrive in Cincinnati at 6:05 p.m. on 11/6

The note should resemble Figure 1.20.

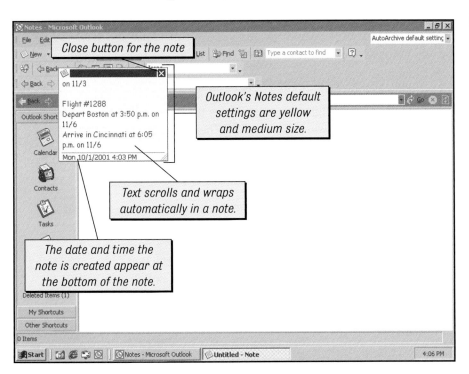

4. Click the **Close button** [✕] on the note.

The note shrinks to an icon labeled *Flight #325*.

Figure 1.20
Creating a new note

Did you know?

If you want to share the contents of a note with someone, you can e-mail it. Simply select the note and click Forward on the Actions menu. Then, enter appropriate information in the e-mail message.

5. Create two more notes containing the information in Table 1.6. Then close the notes.

Table 1.6	Data for Notes
Note 1	**Note 2**
Hotel Arrangements in Boston	Flight #890
The Raven Inn	Depart Cincinnati at 6:42 p.m. on 12/10
395 Presser Blvd.	Arrive in Dallas at 7:52 p.m. on 12/10
$195 per night	
Guaranteed late arrival on 11/3	Flight #211
Noon checkout on 11/6	Depart Dallas at 8:39 p.m. on 12/16
Confirmation #12370	Arrive in Cincinnati at 11:45 p.m. on 12/16

You now should see an icon in the Notes pane for each of the three notes you created.

HANDS on

Changing the Size and Color of a Note

You can categorize your notes by changing their colors. You also can change the size of a note to fit the text in it. In this activity, you'll open the notes you created and change their sizes and colors.

1. Double-click the **Flight #325** note to open it.

2. Drag the bottom-right corner to resize the note so that the text fits in the note, as shown in Figure 1.21. Then close the note to save it.

To organize your notes, you've decided to use yellow for all your Boston trip notes and blue for all your Dallas trip notes.

3. Right-click the **Flight #890 note**, point to **Color**, and click **Blue**, if necessary. Then, click anywhere on the screen to deselect the Flight #890 note icon. Right-click the **Flight #325 note**, point to **Color**, and click **Yellow**, if necessary. Change the Hotel Arrangements in Boston note to yellow, if it is not already yellow.

4. Open the **Flight #890 note**.

5. Resize the note so that all of the text fits on it, and then close the note.

You also can set the color and size of a note before you create it.

6. Click the **Tools menu** and click **Options**.

7. In the Options dialog box, click the **Preferences tab**, if necessary. In the *Notes* area, click the **Note Options button**.

Outlook BASICS

Changing the Size and Color of a Note

1. Double-click a note to open it.

2. Drag the bottom-right corner to resize the note. Then close it.

3. Right-click the note, point to Color, and click a color.

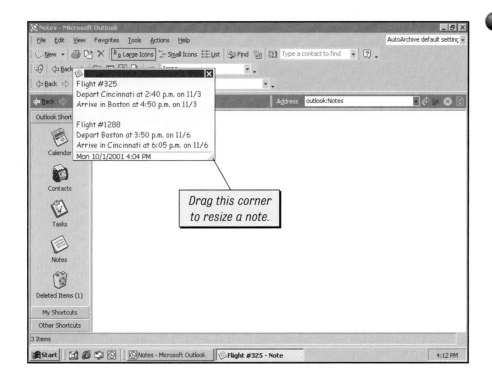

Figure 1.21
Resizing a note

Drag this corner
to resize a note.

8. In the Note Options dialog box, select **Blue** as the color and **Large** as the size, then click **OK**. Click **OK** to close the Options dialog box.

9. Create a new note to record the following hotel arrangements for your Dallas trip, and then close the note:

Hotel Arrangements in Dallas
The Portsmouth
1812 Chaplin Street
$185 per night
Guaranteed late arrival on 12/10
Check out by 2 p.m. on 12/16
Confirmation #3GH77

10. Create a note to remind yourself to take the *Pet Deli* PowerPoint presentation and 100 sample variety treat packs to Boston. Use the appropriate color and resize the note, if necessary.

Changing the View and Sorting Notes

The Icons view of notes shows the first line of text as the note title. To view more text, you can change to a different view. In this activity, you will display the notes in a variety of views. You also will sort the notes by subject and then by color.

1. Point to **Current View** on the View menu and click **Notes List**.

**Changing the View
and Sorting Notes**

1. Point to Current View on the
   View menu and click the
   desired view.

2. To sort the notes, click the
   column heading by which you
   want to sort.

The complete text of each note appears in a list in alphabetical order by
subject.

2. **To sort the notes in reverse alphabetical order by subject, click the
   Subject column heading.**

3. **Point to Current View on the View menu; click By Color to sort the
   notes by color.**

4. **Click the + of each color category to view the notes within that
   category.**

As shown in Figure 1.22, the notes now are sorted by color—thus separated
into your two trips.

Figure 1.22

Sorting notes by color

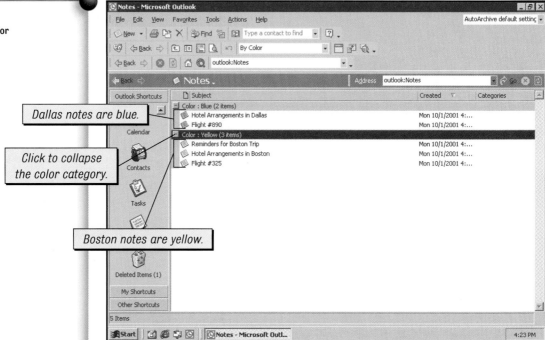

5. **Switch back to Icons view.**

The icons are rearranged by color.

HANDS on

Deleting a Note

At some point, each note you create likely will become obsolete. Rather than
filling the *Notes* folder with notes that you no longer need, you can delete notes.
You can delete notes one at a time, or you can delete groups of notes. After you
return from your Boston trip, you no longer need the notes for it. In this activity,
you will delete all of the notes related to this trip.

1. Click the first yellow note related to your Boston trip.

2. Notice where the remainder of your Boston trip notes appear. If your Boston trip notes appear in sequence in the Notes pane, hold down ⬆Shift and click the last yellow note related to your Boston trip. If other yellow notes previously were created by another user and are highlighted by your actions, or if your Dallas notes are highlighted by your actions, select only your three yellow notes by holding down Ctrl and clicking each of the other two notes.

All three of the Boston notes are selected.

3. Click the **Delete button** ☒ on the Standard toolbar.

The Boston notes are removed from the Notes pane.

USING OUTLOOK TODAY

The **Outlook Today** page gives you a quick preview of your day. When you click its icon, the main working area of Outlook displays your appointments for the day, your complete task list, and a summary of e-mail messages.

HANDS on
Getting an Overview of Your Day

In this activity, you will view the Outlook Today page to review your day at a glance. You then will learn how to mark a task as complete from the Outlook Today page and move to another part of Outlook.

1. Click the **Outlook Today icon** 🗓 in the Outlook Shortcuts group on the Outlook Bar.

The Outlook Today page appears, as shown in Figure 1.23. If other users have set additional appointments, tasks, or messages, some of the data on the page may vary.

Since you called your dentist yesterday to schedule an appointment, you can mark this task as complete. Rather than switching to the *Tasks* folder to do so, you can mark the task on the Outlook Today page.

2. Click the check box in front of the dental appointment task.

To indicate that the task has been completed, a check mark appears in front of the task, and a line is drawn through its description. From the Outlook Today page, you can move to other areas of Outlook without using the shortcut icons.

3. Click **Inbox** in the Messages column.

Figure 1.23
Outlook Today page

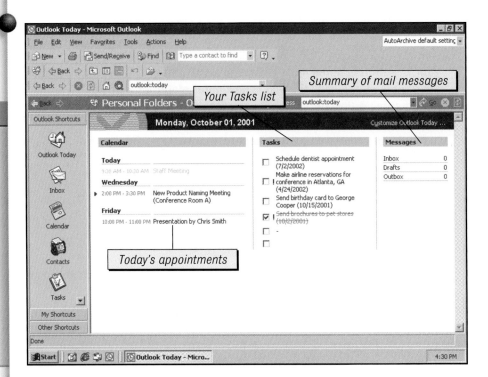

Outlook opens the Inbox, displaying any messages in it. If you have new mail, you may read it.

4. Click the Back button [◄ Back] **on the Advanced toolbar.**

Outlook returns you to the Outlook Today page.

USING THE JOURNAL

The **Journal** tracks the history of various activities. Some activities, such as opening an Office document, are automatically tracked. You can instruct the Journal to track other activities, such as mail messages sent to specific contacts. You even can create journal entries to track non-computerized activities, such as placing a phone call.

HANDS on

Creating Journal Entries

When you start the Journal for the first time, a message will appear asking what types of activities you wish to record. The activities you choose are automatically recorded in the Journal. You manually can track other activities as well. In this activity, you first will specify the types of activities to be recorded. Then you will create manual journal entries for a phone call and fax. Outlook will record another entry automatically when you create a new Word document.

1. Click the My Shortcuts group on the Outlook Bar; then click the Journal icon [icon]. Click Options on the Tools menu and click the Preferences tab, if necessary. In the *Contacts* area, click the Journal Options button.

NOTE *If a message appears indicating that you don't need the Journal to track e-mail and confirming that you want to turn the Journal on, click Yes.*

The Journal Options dialog box appears; in it, you can specify the types of activities you want to track.

2. Click the necessary options so that your dialog box looks like Figure 1.24. Then click **OK**.

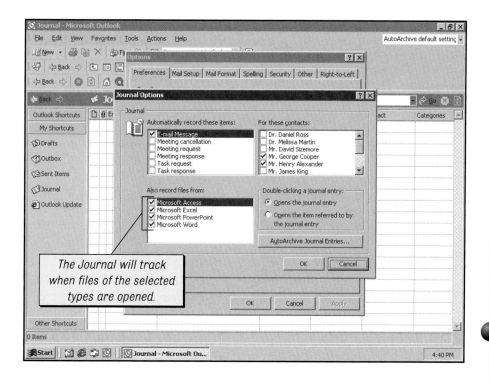

The Journal will track when files of the selected types are opened.

Outlook BASICS

Creating Journal Entries

1. Click the Journal icon.

2. If desired, click the activities in the Journal Options dialog box that you wish to track.

3. Click the New Journal Entry button and specify the characteristics of the new journal entry.

4. Click the Save and Close button.

Figure 1.24
Journal Options dialog box

3. Click **OK** to close the Journal Options dialog box. If necessary, click **OK** to close the Options dialog box.

The Journal, which appears as a timeline, appears in the main working area.

4. Click the **New Journal Entry button**  on the Standard toolbar.

The Untitled - Journal Entry window appears.

5. Type New Product Names in the *Subject* box in the Untitled - Journal Entry window. If it is not already selected, click the **Entry type triangle button** and click **Phone Call**. Then, click the **Contacts button**.

The Select Contacts dialog box appears.

6. In the *Items* area in the lower half of the Select Contacts dialog box, click **Henry Alexander** and click **OK**.

Henry Alexander appears as the contact at the bottom of the Journal Entry window.

NORTON
ONLINE

Visit **www.glencoe.com/norton/online/** for more information on using the Outlook Journal.

OUTLOOK 2002

7. Set the Start time to **7:30 a.m.** and the Duration to **30 Minutes.** In the Notes box, type Discussed names for the new nutritional supplement. I will fax the top seven names to Henry at the Cincinnati office today.

8. Click the **Save and Close button** .

You return to the main working area of the Journal. The Phone call entry is added to the Journal window.

> **NOTE** *If other phone calls previously were recorded, the* phone call *entry type existed before you created the new journal entry. Later in the lesson, you'll find your entry within that category.*

9. Open Word and create a fax to send to Henry Alexander. Switch to your Contacts list to find Henry's job title, fax number, and business phone number, and include them in the document. Create and include the seven potential names for the new nutritional supplement product. Save the Word document as *New Product Names Fax* in the *Tutorial Solutions* folder in the *Tutorial* folder in your *Integration Data* folder. Then close the document and exit Word.

10. Return to the Journal and create another journal entry recording the fax that you sent to Henry. Use the same name *(New Product Names)* in the *Subject* box and select Henry Alexander as the contact. Set the time as the time of day now and the duration as 5 minutes. Provide a description of the document in the Notes section. Then, save and close the journal entry.

When you return to the Journal window, three entry types are shown: *Fax, Microsoft Word,* and *Phone Call.*

HANDS on

Viewing and Opening Journal Entries

After you create journal entries, you can use the Journal to view the entries and to track activities. For instance, you might need to recall the date and details of a phone call that you made regarding a specific issue. If you tracked the activity, you can look through your Journal to see the date and time of the phone call as well as specifics of the conversation. In this activity, you'll view journal entries.

1. Click the **Week button** 🔲 Week on the Standard toolbar to view the Journal in Week view.

> **NOTE** *If the Week button* 🔲 Week *is not visible on the Standard toolbar, point to Current View on the View menu, and click By Type.*

2. Click the **+** next to the Fax entry type.

The fax entry type opens, and the *New Product Names* fax icon and name appear under the date the fax was sent. This journal entry indicates that the fax was sent on that date.

3. Click the + next to the Microsoft Word entry type.

The path and file name for the *New Product Names Fax* file that you created and saved will appear under the Microsoft Word category. This journal entry indicates the day that the file was created. (Your specific path and date will appear on the screen.)

4. Finally, click the + next to the Phone call entry type.

As shown in Figure 1.25, the *New Product Names* Phone call entry appears under the date you made the call.

Outlook BASICS

Viewing and Opening Journal Entries

1. Click the + next to the entry type in which the journal entry was made.

2. If desired, change the view to the Day or Week view.

3. Scroll to find the entry for the activity.

4. Double-click the entry icon to see the journal entry details.

OUTLOOK 2002

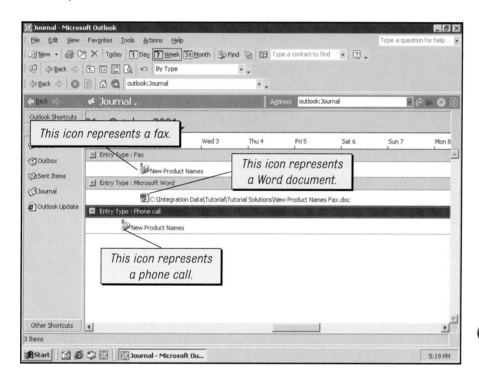

Figure 1.25
Viewing journal entries

5. Click the **Day button** [1 Day] on the Standard toolbar to change to Day view.

6. If necessary, use the bottom scroll bar to scroll to the location on the time line that shows 7:30 a.m. today.

The Phone call entry appears. The small gray bar at the top of the entry indicates the start time, and its length indicates the duration of the call.

7. Double-click the **Phone call icon**.

The Journal Entry window for the phone call appears, listing the details of your phone conversation.

8. **Close the window and scroll to the time that you opened the Word document.**

You should see the icons and names for the Word document and fax. Your manager would like a copy of the fax that you sent to Henry Alexander. Outlook will allow you to reopen the document.

9. **Double-click the Word document icon called** New Product Names Fax.

The New Product Names Fax - Journal Entry window appears, as shown in Figure 1.26. Notice that an icon representing the document appears in the bottom section of the window. Double-clicking this icon opens the document.

Figure 1.26
New Product Names Fax - Journal Entry window

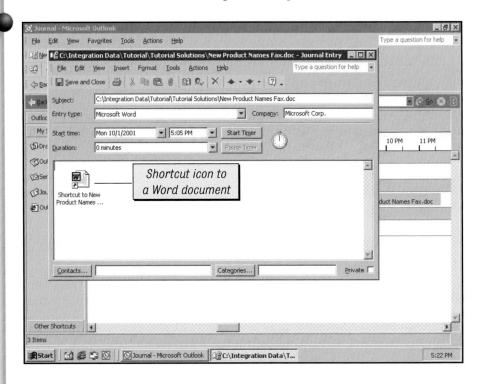

10. **Double-click the New Product Names Fax icon.**

The Open Mail Attachment dialog box appears.

11. **In the Open Mail Attachment dialog box, click Open it and then click OK.**

The *New Product Names Fax* document opens in Word.

12. **Print and close the document. Then, close Word.**

13. **When you return to Outlook, close the New Product Names Fax - Journal Entry window. Then close Outlook.**

NOTE *If you receive a message asking whether to permanently delete items and subfolders in the* Deleted Items *folder, click Yes.*

Self Check

Test your knowledge by answering the following questions. See Appendix B to check your answers.

1. The _____ folder lists a summary of appointments, mail messages, and tasks.

2. You can use the _____ folder to store names, addresses, phone numbers, and other information on various people.

3. Outlook's _____ folder allows you to track computerized and non-computerized activities.

4. You can use the _____ folder to send and receive electronic mail messages.

5. You can use the _____ folder to keep track of things you need to do and their due dates.

SUMMARY

Microsoft Outlook is Office XP's personal information manager program—an application that keeps track of your daily personal and/or business activities. Outlook organizes these activities into folders, and you can display one or more of these folders on your desktop. The *Inbox* folder is where you read, compose, and send e-mail messages. In the *Calendar* folder, you schedule, view, and edit appointments and other events. You enter information about people—addresses, phone numbers, birthdays, and so on—in the *Contacts* folder. By entering Tasks as a to-do list, you make sure that your most important obligations are done on time. You can jot down information that doesn't fit into one of the other categories as an entry in the *Notes* folder. Using Outlook Today, you can view a summary of all the information on today's activities, including appointments, tasks, and mail messages. Finally, the Journal keeps track of the times, durations, and other facts of various activities.

Now that you have completed this lesson, you should be able to do the following:

- Describe how Outlook helps you manage personal information, track activities, and share information with others. (page 653)
- Launch Microsoft Outlook. (page 654)
- Display the contents of Outlook folders. (page 654)
- Create and send an e-mail message. (page 656)
- Read an e-mail message. (page 659)
- Reply to an e-mail message. (page 660)
- Explain the archiving process. (page 661)
- Schedule an appointment in the Calendar. (page 662)
- Schedule an event in the Calendar. (page 665)
- Change Calendar views. (page 666)
- Set a recurring meeting in the Calendar. (page 666)
- Create a contact in the *Contacts* folder. (page 668)
- Modify a contact in the *Contacts* folder. (page 671)
- Sort and find contacts. (page 673)
- Send e-mail to a contact. (page 674)
- Create a new task in the *Tasks* folder. (page 675)
- Arrange and sort tasks. (page 676)
- Delete and mark tasks as complete. (page 677)
- Create and open a note in the *Notes* folder. (page 678)
- Change the color and size of a note. (page 680)
- Change the view or sort order of notes. (page 681)
- Delete a note. (page 682)
- View a summary of the current day's activities by using the *Outlook Today* folder. (page 683)
- Record entries in the *Journal* folder. (page 684)
- View and open journal entries. (page 686)

CONCEPTS REVIEW

1 TRUE/FALSE

Circle T if the statement is true or F if the statement is false.

T F **1.** An event is an activity that lasts one day or longer.

T F **2.** The *Contacts* folder allows you to send and receive messages electronically.

T F **3.** Outlook's *Tasks* folder is an electronic to-do list.

T F **4.** The *Journal* folder of Outlook acts as a personal and business address book.

T F **5.** You can create and read e-mail messages in one of three different formats.

T F **6.** All notes must be the same color and size.

T F **7.** Microsoft Outlook is a desktop information management program in which you can organize and share many different types of information.

T F **8.** The Outlook Today page gives you a quick preview of the week.

T F **9.** You easily can cut information that appears in the Address Book and paste it into an e-mail message.

T F **10.** Microsoft Outlook allows you to schedule appointments, meetings, events, and tasks in the *Calendar* folder.

2 IDENTIFICATION

Label each of the elements of the Outlook window in Figure 1.27.

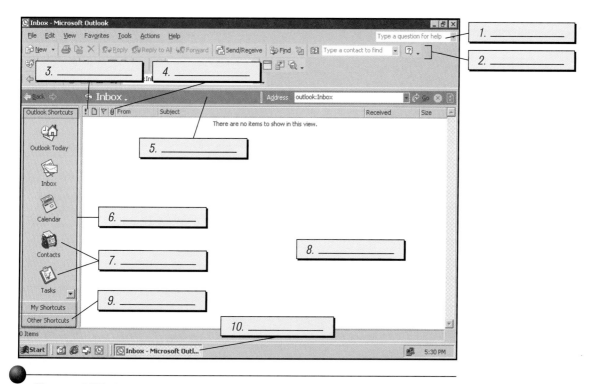

Figure 1.27

PROJECTS

You must complete all of these projects in sequence; they build upon each other and demonstrate integration among the Outlook folders.

1 Create a New Contact

Add a classmate's name, address, phone number, and e-mail address as a new contact. Assume that your classmate works at The Pet Deli, Inc., as a production manager, and include that information in the company and job title boxes. Set the Outlook options so that e-mail messages with this contact are recorded automatically. Then send a mail message to this contact, asking for information about the recommended daily serving sizes for Kibble Senior dog food.

2 Create a Journal Entry

A few hours after you send the e-mail message in Project 1, your coworker responds with the information in Table 1.7.

Since you are not sure whether the measurements of food are per meal or per day, you stop by your coworker's office to ask. You learn that the food measurements provided are the total amounts for one day. Record the five-minute conversation in your journal. Create a new Excel workbook and type the information about food amounts. Format the worksheet as desired. Save the workbook as *Daily Serving Sizes* in the *Projects Solutions* folder in the *Projects* folder in your *Integration Data* folder. Close the file and exit Excel.

Table 1.7	Kibble Senior Dog Food
Weight of Dog	**Amount of Food**
5 lbs.	1/2 cup
10 lbs.	7/8 cup
20 lbs.	1 1/2 cups
40 lbs.	2 1/2 cups
60 lbs.	3 1/4 cups
80 lbs.	4 1/4 cups
100 lbs.	5 cups

3 Create a Task and Appointments

You are preparing to hire a new assistant. First, add a task to your task list to call the human resources department; you need four brochures that explain the company's benefits to your potential assistant candidates. Then, mark next week's calendar with the interview times shown in Table 1.8. Assume that each interview will last one hour. View your appointments in Day, Week, and Month views. On a separate sheet of paper, describe the advantages and disadvantages of each of the views.

Table 1.8	Interview Times	
Candidate	**Day**	**Time**
Mauricio Espino	Tuesday	2:00 p.m.
Penny Appleton	Thursday	2:00 p.m.
Tyler Jacobs	Thursday	3:30 p.m.
Mary Ellen Zickerman	Friday	8:00 a.m.

4 Create a Note, Create a Recurring Appointment, and Complete a Task

You just learned that a new pet store is moving into the area. Create a note to record the name and location of the store: Pet Boutique, in the West Square Mall. The expected opening date is November 30 of this year. Change the color of the note to pink, since this is the color you use to indicate that a note contains information to include in your monthly report. Resize the note if necessary. Send a copy of the note to a classmate without retyping it; use Help if you can't figure out how to do this. Next, set a recurring event in your calendar to remind you that your monthly report is due on the last Friday of each month. Set the event so that you are reminded one day in advance. Lastly, since you received the brochures from human resources, mark this task as complete while you are on the Outlook Today page.

5 Write Journal Contents and Print a Mail Message From a Journal

Look at the Journal for today (or the days that you worked on this lesson). On a separate sheet of paper, list the entries made, the category of each entry, and whether the entry was automatically or manually entered. From the Journal window, open and print the mail message that you sent to your coworker asking about recommended serving amounts for Kibble Senior dog food (Project 2).

ON the WEB 6 Send a Web Page by E-Mail

One of your customers owns a shop that specializes in products made for cats. You want to tell him about a Web site for cat fanciers. With the Web toolbar displayed, type **www.fanciers.com** in the Address bar and press `Enter←`. The Cat Fanciers page will be displayed in the main working area. Then click Send Web Page by E-mail on the Actions menu. When the new mail message appears, type the address of your instructor or a classmate and type a brief message explaining that you are sending a link to a Web page in which they might be interested. Send the e-mail, and then close Outlook.

LESSON 2

Integrating Office XP

CONTENTS

OBJECTIVES

After you complete this lesson, you will be able to do the following:

- ➤ Set appointments in the Calendar.

- ➤ Copy appointments into an Excel workbook.

- ➤ Enter new contacts in Outlook.

- ➤ Use the Letter Wizard to create a letter based on an Outlook contact.

- ➤ Integrate Excel data into a letter.

- ➤ Import a database of names, addresses, and numbers into the *Contacts* folder.

- ➤ Copy text from a Word document into an Outlook journal entry.

- ➤ Send a PowerPoint presentation to Word.

- ➤ Add Word text to an imported PowerPoint presentation.

- ➤ Create a new form letter and merge it with selected Outlook contacts.

- ➤ Explore how to use Word as your e-mail editor.

- ➤ Add a Web page shortcut to the Outlook Bar.

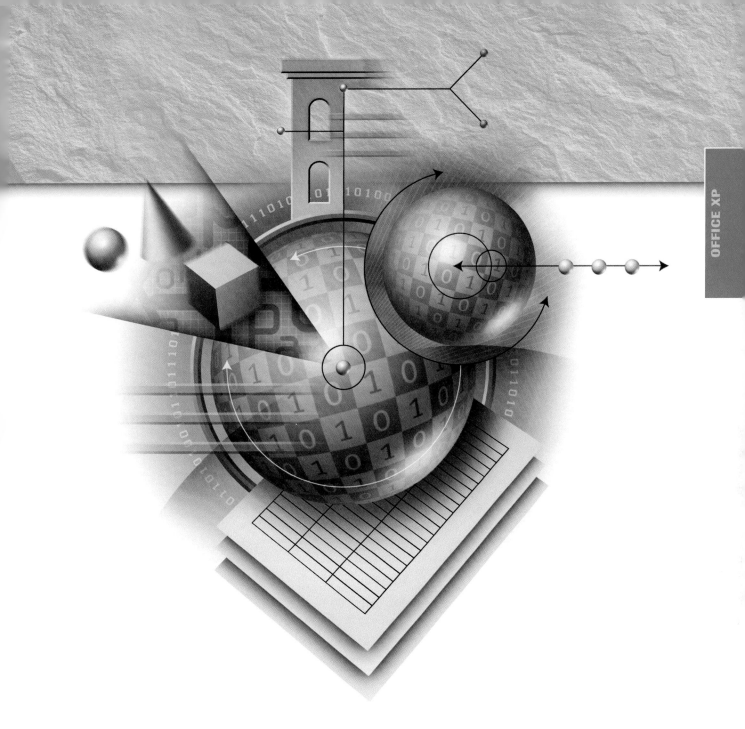

INTEGRATING CALENDAR DATA INTO A WORKBOOK

As you learned in the Outlook Basics lesson, you can use various views to look at the Outlook Calendar. You can copy data from your Calendar using any view; however, certain views allow you to see and copy more data at one time. For instance, you can use the Active Appointments view to display all your current appointments in a table format and then copy this data to an Excel worksheet.

As you work through the activities in this lesson, assume that you work for High End Consultants, a company that helps other companies increase their sales. Your first task as an associate for High End Consultants is to integrate information that you've entered in your Outlook Calendar into an Excel worksheet.

Office in the workplace

In this lesson, you'll integrate Outlook in several ways with the other Office XP programs, which can further increase your productivity in the workplace.

Setting Appointments

In this activity, imagine that you're traveling to meet with several prospective clients next month and need to mark your appointments in the Calendar.

Office BASICS

Setting Appointments

1. Open the Calendar folder in Outlook.

2. Point to Current View on the View menu and then choose Day/Week/Month.

3. Click the date on which to set the appointment.

4. Double-click the desired time slot and enter the appointment data.

5. Click Save and Close.

1. Launch Outlook and click the **Calendar shortcut icon**. Close the Folder List by clicking **Folder List** on the View menu, if necessary.

2. Point to **Current View** on the View menu, and then click **Day/Week/Month**, if necessary.

3. In the Date Navigator, click the first **Wednesday** of the next month, and switch to Work Week view. (If appointments appear in Outlook, ask your instructor if you may delete them.)

4. Double-click the **1:00 p.m. time slot** on Wednesday and set an appointment with the following information:

   Subject: Smith Corporation - prospective client appointment
   Location: San Diego, CA
   Start time: 1:00 p.m.
   End time: 3:00 p.m.
   Reminder: 1 hour

5. Save and close the Appointment dialog box.

6. Use the Calendar tool to set the other appointments in Table 2.1.

Table 2.1	Additional Appointments				
Day	**Subject**	**Location**	**Start Time**	**End Time**	**Reminder**
First Thursday of month	Farmers Mortgage Co. - prospective client appointment	San Diego, CA	9:00 a.m.	11:00 a.m.	1 hour
First Friday of month	Smith & Jones, Attorneys at Law - prospective client appointment	San Diego, CA	1:00 p.m.	3:00 p.m.	1 hour
Second Wednesday of month	Scenic View Retirement Community - prospective client appointment	Los Angeles, CA	2:00 p.m.	4:00 p.m.	1 hour
Second Friday of month	Think It Over, Wedding Consultants - prospective client appointment	Los Angeles, CA	3:00 p.m.	5:00 p.m.	1 hour
Third Monday of month	Happy Trails Moving Company - prospective client appointment	San Francisco, CA	10:00 a.m.	12:00 p.m.	1 hour
Third Tuesday of month	Rich Bank of San Francisco - prospective client appointment	San Francisco, CA	9:00 a.m.	11:00 a.m.	1 hour

HANDS on

Copying Your Appointments to Excel

Your manager asked you to provide a list of your prospective client meetings scheduled for next month. Rather than retyping all of the information, you decide to copy the data from your Calendar. In this activity, you first will view your Calendar appointments in Active Appointments view. Then you'll copy the appointments and paste them to a new Excel worksheet.

1. **While displaying the Outlook Calendar, point to Current View on the View menu, and then click Active Appointments.**

The appointments you have scheduled appear in a list, similar to the one shown in Figure 2.1. If the list is not expanded, click the plus icon next to the category name. If you did not delete previous appointments, other appointments may appear on the list.

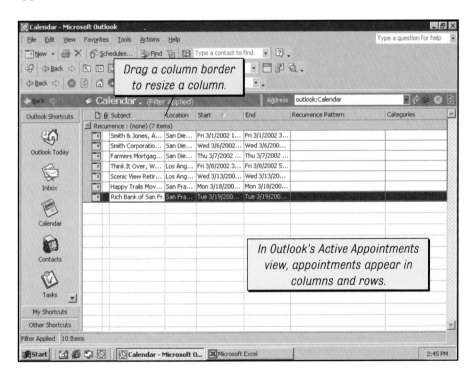

2. **Click anywhere in the first appointment row, press and hold [⇧ Shift], and click anywhere in the last row. Or, if more appointments appear than your prospective client appointments, click your first appointment, hold [Ctrl], and click each prospective client appointment.**

All of the pertinent appointments are selected.

3. **Click Copy on the Edit menu.**

WEB NOTE

You can save any part of your Calendar as a Web page. Simply click Save as Web Page on the File menu and choose the desired options in the Save as Web Page dialog box.

Figure 2.1
Active Appointments View

Office BASICS

Copying Calendar Data to Excel

1. Display the Calendar folder in Outlook.

2. Point to Current View on the View menu and then choose Active Appointments.

3. Select the appointments you wish to copy.

4. Click Copy on the Edit menu.

5. Open Excel.

6. In a new workbook, click the Paste button.

7. Format the worksheet as desired.

HINTS & TIPS

You quickly can format a range in Excel by clicking AutoFormat on the Format menu.

4. Launch Excel so that a new workbook is opened. Click the **Paste button** 📋 on the Standard toolbar.

The selected appointments are pasted to the worksheet.

5. Close the task pane, delete the Recurrence Pattern and Categories column labels if they are displayed in the worksheet, and format the worksheet as desired to improve its appearance.

6. Save the workbook as *Prospective Client Appointments* in the *Tutorial Solutions* folder in the *Tutorial* folder in your *Integration Data* folder. Leave the workbook open. Leave Excel and Outlook running.

CREATING A WORD LETTER FROM AN OUTLOOK CONTACT ENTRY

Usually, the people that you enter as contacts in Outlook are those with whom you communicate on a regular basis. For that reason, Outlook allows you to start a Word letter directly from the *Contacts* folder. When you do this, you don't need to retype the name and address of your contact; Outlook does it for you.

HANDS on

Entering Contacts

In this activity, you will enter names, addresses, and telephone numbers for a few of your Outlook contacts.

1. Switch to Outlook, and click the **Contacts shortcut icon**. Click the **View menu**, point to **Current View**, and click **Address Cards**.

2. Click the **New Contact button** 🔲 New ▾ on the Standard toolbar, and add the contacts in Table 2.2 to your address book.

Table 2.2	Data for New Contacts		
Field	**Contact 1**	**Contact 2**	**Contact 3**
Full Name:	Ms. Alicia Rodriguez	Mr. Jonathon Martin	Ms. Carol Smith
Job title:	Manager	Vice President	Senior Partner
Company:	High End Consultants	Farmers Mortgage Co.	Smith & Jones, Attorneys at Law
Business phone:	(619) 555-9322	(619) 555-1189	(619) 555-2222
Home phone:	(619) 555-1729		
Business Fax:	(619) 555-9223	(619) 555-7330	(619) 555-1111
Business address:	2447 5th Avenue San Diego, CA 92101	2845 Adams Avenue San Diego, CA 92116	1069 Front Street San Diego, CA 92101
E-mail:	arodriguez@highend.com	jmartin@farmmort.com	csmith@sj.com

HANDS on

Creating a Letter Using a Contact

In this activity, you'll use Outlook's ability to address a letter automatically. Rather than simply providing her with a printout of your worksheet, you've decided to write a letter to your manager, Alicia Rodriguez, to provide her with information about your upcoming appointments with potential new clients.

1. While viewing the *Contacts* folder, click the **name bar for Alicia Rodriguez**. On the Actions menu, click **New Letter to Contact**.

NOTE *If the Office Assistant appears, right-click him and click Hide.*

Word is automatically launched, and the Letter Wizard dialog box opens, as shown in Figure 2.2, to guide you through the steps to create a new letter.

The Letter Wizard has four pages to guide you through the steps to create a letter.

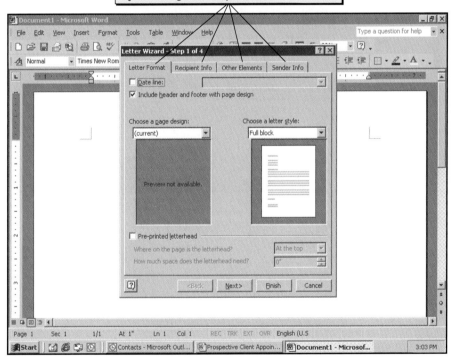

2. In the first page of the Letter Wizard (Letter Format), click the **Date line check box** to insert a date into your letter, and then click **Next**.

The second Letter Wizard page (Recipient Info) is displayed. Notice that Alicia Rodriguez's name, title, and address are automatically inserted.

3. Click **Next** to accept the default settings on the Recipient Info page.

4. Click **Next** to accept the default settings on the Other Elements page.

The fourth page (Sender Info) of the Letter Wizard is displayed.

Figure 2.2
Letter Wizard

NORTON ONLINE

Visit **www.glencoe.com/norton/online/** for more information on creating a Word letter using a contact.

OFFICE XP

5. If your name does not appear in the Sender's name box, click the **Sender's Name triangle button** and select your name, or click the **Sender's Name box** and type your name.

6. Click the **Complimentary closing triangle button**, click **Sincerely**, and then click **Finish**.

The beginning and ending of your letter are automatically generated, as shown in Figure 2.3. Your manager's name, title, and address appear at the top of the letter, and your closing and name appear at the bottom of the letter. You can type the text of your letter to replace the selected text.

Figure 2.3
Letter generated by the Letter Wizard

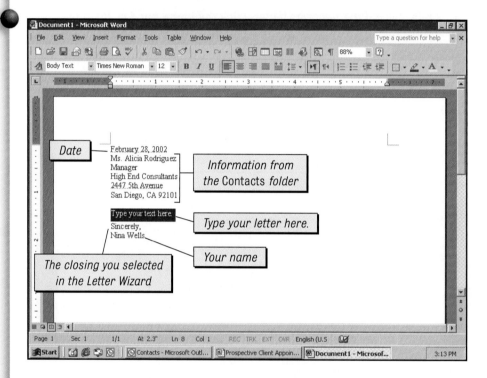

7. Type the following text to replace the selected text:

Dear Alicia,

The following table shows my *(insert the name of the next month)* appointments. As you can see, I will be traveling in the San Diego, Los Angeles, and San Francisco areas throughout the month. I am especially optimistic about the appointments that I have with Smith & Jones, Attorneys at Law and Happy Trails Moving Company.

8. Save the letter as *Letter to Rodriguez* in the *Tutorial Solutions* folder in the *Tutorial* folder in your *Integration Data* folder.

HANDS on

Integrating Worksheet Data Into a Letter

In this activity, you will copy the data from the *Prospective Client Appointments* workbook to your Word document.

1. Switch to Excel. Verify that the *Prospective Client Appointments* workbook in the *Tutorial Solutions* folder is still open.

2. Select the cells that contain your appointments *(do not select the column headings)*, and then click the **Copy button** 📋 on the Standard toolbar.

3. Switch back to the *Letter to Rodriguez* document. Place the insertion point at the end of the first paragraph and press ⏎. Then, click the **Paste button** 📋 on the Standard toolbar.

4. If necessary, format the pasted data and any other part of the letter to improve its appearance and ensure that it fits on one page.

NOTE *If your table exceeds the width of the page, change the page orientation to landscape to resize the columns in the table. Then, return the page orientation to portrait and continue formatting the document as desired.*

5. Save, print, and close the *Letter to Rodriguez* letter. Leave Word running.

6. Close Excel without saving any changes to the *Prospective Client Appointments* workbook.

INTEGRATING ACCESS DATA WITH OUTLOOK

You've learned that Access database tables and Outlook's *Contacts* folder often store similar types of information, such as names, addresses, and telephone numbers. At times, you may want to share data between Outlook and Access. You can easily do this by using Outlook's Import and Export command. When you use the Import and Export command, Office automatically sets up fields and transfers contact information.

HANDS on

Importing Database Data Into the *Contacts* Folder

Two weeks after your meeting with Smith & Jones, Attorneys at Law, you learn that you've landed an account with them. You're thrilled—and right away they put you to work. So that you can quickly contact key members of the firm, you transfer existing data (such as the people's names, addresses, and phone numbers) from Access into your *Contacts* folder in Outlook.

1. Launch Access and open the database called *Smith & Jones* in the *Tutorial* folder in your *Integration Data* folder.

2. Open the *Key Staff Members* table. Notice the names in the table. Then close the table, the database, and Access.

3. Switch to Outlook and open the *Contacts* folder.

4. Click **Import and Export** on the File menu.

The Import and Export Wizard is activated, as shown in Figure 2.4.

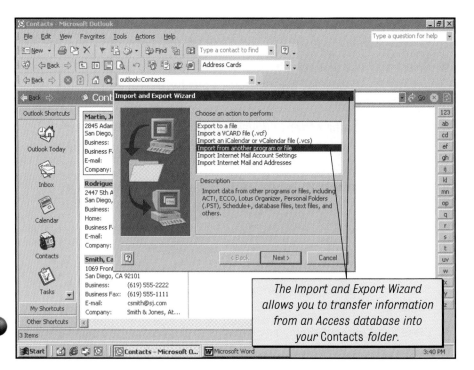

The Import and Export Wizard allows you to transfer information from an Access database into your Contacts folder.

Figure 2.4
Import and Export Wizard

**Importing Database Data
Into the *Contacts* Folder**

1. Open the *Contacts* folder in Outlook.

2. Click Import and Export on the File menu.

3. Click *Import from another program or file* in the dialog box, and then click Next.

4. Click Microsoft Access in the next dialog box, and then click Next.

5. Use the Browse button to locate and select the database to import.

6. Click OK to close the Browse dialog box and redisplay the Import and Export dialog box.

7. Click *Contacts* as the destination folder, and then click Next.

8. Click Finish.

5. In the first page of the Import and Export Wizard, click *Import from another program or file* and then click **Next**.

6. In the Import a File page of the wizard, click **Microsoft Access** on the list, and then click **Next**.

NOTE *If you receive a message informing you that this feature is not installed, ask your instructor for help.*

7. In the Import a File page of the Import and Export Wizard, click the **Browse button** and navigate to and select the **Smith & Jones database** in the *Tutorial* folder in your *Integration Data* folder. Then, click **OK**.

The name of the *Smith & Jones* database appears in the File to import text box.

Because you previously entered Carol Smith as a contact and she is included in this database, Outlook will create two Contact entries for her if you leave the default setting in this dialog box.

8. Select the **Replace duplicates with items imported option**, and then click **Next**.

9. Click *Contacts* as the destination folder (if it is not already selected) and then click **Next**.

The name of the table that you are importing *(Key Staff Members)* and the name of the *Contacts* folder appear on the next page.

10. Click **Finish**.

The Import and Export process begins. When it is finished, the *Contacts* folder will reappear and the names, addresses, and telephone numbers of the Smith &

Jones staff members are added as contacts. You quickly have imported contacts information from an Access database to Outlook.

11. If spelling, spacing, or punctuation differences cause *Carol Smith* to appear twice in the *Contacts* folder, select the name without an e-mail address and click the **Delete button**. Keep Outlook running.

SHARING TEXT BETWEEN WORD AND OUTLOOK

You can use the Copy and Paste commands to copy data from Word to just about any folder in Outlook. For instance, you can copy text from Word to the body of a new e-mail message, to a note, to a task, or to a calendar entry. Likewise, you can copy text from any of these tools into a Word document. In this activity, you'll copy text from a Word document and paste it into a journal entry.

Copying Text From a Word Document to the Journal

You recently met with Carol Smith, one of the senior partners of the Smith & Jones law firm, to discuss the objectives of the firm. You want to incorporate the information she provided during this meeting into a promotional PowerPoint presentation that you're creating for the firm. While talking to Ms. Smith, you used Word to take notes on your laptop computer. To better track the conversation, you decide to copy some of the text into an Outlook journal entry.

1. In Outlook, click the **Journal shortcut icon** in the My Shortcuts group on the Outlook Bar.

2. Create a new journal entry to record a meeting with Carol Smith. The entry should indicate that the meeting took place last Friday at 1:00 p.m. and lasted for two hours.

3. In the Notes section of the entry, type Met with Carol to discuss the law firm's objectives that should be placed in the PowerPoint presentation. The key objectives include the following:

4. Switch to Word without closing the journal entry. Open *Smith Meeting* in the *Tutorial* folder in your *Integration Data* folder.

This Word document contains the notes you took during your meeting with Ms. Smith.

5. Select all the bulleted text in the document, and then click the **Copy button** 📋 on the Standard toolbar.

6. Switch to the journal entry and press ⏎Enter twice to insert a blank line, and then click the **Paste button** 📋 on the Standard toolbar.

The bulleted list is pasted into the journal entry, as shown in Figure 2.5.

Office **BASICS**

Copying Text From Word to the Journal

1. In Outlook, open the Journal and create a new entry.

2. Switch to Word and select the text to copy.

3. Click the Copy button.

4. Switch back to the journal entry, place the insertion point where you want to paste the text, and then click the Paste button.

5. Save and close the journal entry.

Figure 2.5
Journal entry with pasted text

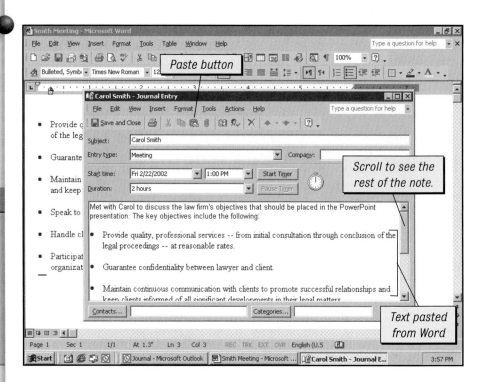

7. Save and close the journal entry. Close the *Smith Meeting* document without saving it, and then exit Word.

Did you know?

When multiple addresses are listed for a contact, you can specify the address to use as the mailing address. To do this, double-click the Name Bar to open the Contact dialog box, and then click the *This is the mailing address* box.

USING MAIL MERGE THROUGH OUTLOOK

Outlook provides a Mail Merge feature that allows you to create a new letter or use an existing one as the basis for your Outlook mail merge. Furthermore, you can develop a mail merge document that is addressed to all or selected contacts in Outlook.

In the following activities, you'll first send a PowerPoint presentation to Word. Next, you'll learn how to use Outlook's Mail Merge feature so that you can send the newly created Word document to your Outlook contacts. As you work through these steps, you'll see how helpful it can be to integrate data from Word and PowerPoint with Outlook.

HANDS on
Sending a Presentation to Word and Composing a Letter

NORTON ONLINE

Visit **www.glencoe.com/norton/online/** for more information on using Mail Merge.

One of your first projects for the Smith & Jones law firm is to create a PowerPoint presentation that introduces the firm to potential new clients. You created a PowerPoint presentation that currently includes a title slide, the firm's objectives, and a brief introduction of each partner, including their areas of practice. However, before you spend too much time developing the presentation, Carol Smith wants you to send a printout of it to each partner, asking each to verify the information in his or her introduction.

In this activity, you'll open the PowerPoint presentation and send it to Word. Later, you'll use this document as the beginning of a letter to send to each partner; you also will insert mail merge fields to automatically address the letters.

1. Launch PowerPoint and open the *Smith & Jones Introduction* presentation in the *Tutorial* folder in your *Integration Data* folder.

2. Point to **Send To** on the File menu and then click **Microsoft Word**.

The Send to Microsoft Word dialog box opens.

3. In the Send To Microsoft Word dialog box, click the **Blank lines next to slides option**, and then click **OK**.

After a few moments, your new Word document will appear and look similar to Figure 2.6.

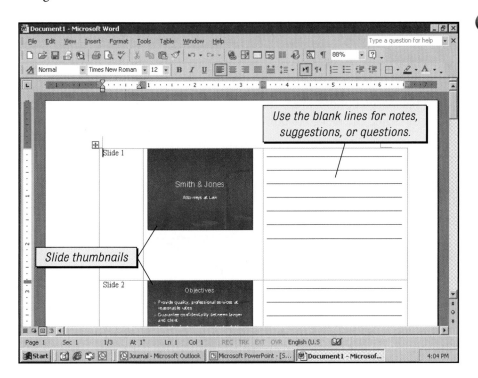

Figure 2.6
Presentation sent to Word

4. Save the Word document as *Initial Review* in the *Tutorial Solutions* folder in the *Tutorial* folder in your *Integration Data* folder. Scroll the document to see the thumbnail slides. Insert a page break above the first slide thumbnail in the document.

5. On the first page of the document, insert today's date and compose a short paragraph that asks each partner to review the printout of the presentation. Ask the partners for feedback about the overall presentation as well as the accuracy of the information about the partners.

6. Save and close the *Initial Review* document.

7. Exit PowerPoint and Word, but leave Outlook running.

WARNING *You must close the letter to use it in the mail merge process.*

Office BASICS

Sending a PowerPoint Document to Word and Composing a Letter

1. Open the PowerPoint presentation.

2. Point to Send To on the File menu, and then click Microsoft Word.

3. Click the desired option in the Send To Microsoft Word dialog box, and then click OK.

4. Move to the top of the letter and insert a page break.

5. Type the desired text for the letter.

6. Save and close the document.

HANDS on

Merging With Contacts

In this activity, you will use Outlook to create a mail merge document.

1. In Outlook, click the **Contacts shortcut icon**.

2. Click the **name bar** of the first firm partner, **Chieko Doi**, to select it.

3. Press and hold [Ctrl] and click the names of each of the other partners in the firm. (The partners include Chieko Doi, Tyler Hoffman, Jeremy Jones, Peter Macy, and Carol Smith.)

4. Click **Mail Merge** on the Tools menu.

The Mail Merge Contacts dialog box appears.

5. In the Fields to merge area of the Mail Merge Contacts dialog box, click **All contact fields**, if necessary.

6. In the Merge Options area, set the Document type box to **Form Letters** and the Merge to box to **New Document**, if necessary.

Your Mail Merge Contacts dialog box should match Figure 2.7.

OFFICE XP

Office **BASICS**

Mail Merging With Contacts

1. Select the contacts that you wish to use in the merge.

2. Click Mail Merge on the Tools menu to display the Mail Merge Contacts dialog box.

3. Use the Browse button to find and select the document you wish to merge with and click OK.

4. Click OK to close the Mail Merge Contacts dialog box.

5. Edit the document as desired.

6. Insert merge fields.

7. Save the document.

8. Issue the desired merge command.

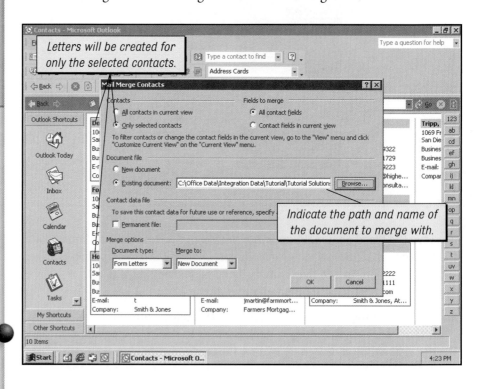

Figure 2.7
Mail Merge Contacts dialog box

7. In the Document file area of the Mail Merge Contacts dialog box, click the **Browse button**.

8. In the Open dialog box, navigate to and select the **Initial Review** document in the *Tutorial Solutions* folder, and then click **OK**.

After a few moments, your Word letter is opened so that you can insert the necessary merge fields.

9. If the Office Assistant appears, click the **Edit MailMerge document option**. Then, right-click the **Office Assistant** and click **Hide**.

10. Place the insertion point where you want to insert the first line of the addressee.

11. Click the **Insert Merge Fields button**  on the Mail Merge toolbar.

The Insert Merge Field dialog box appears, listing the available merge fields.

12. In the Insert area of the Insert Merge Field dialog box, click the **Database Fields option**, if necessary. Then, scroll through the Fields list, click the **Full_Name field**, and click **Insert**.

The Full Name field placeholder appears in your letter.

13. Close the Insert Merge Field dialog box. Press Enter⏎ and click the **Insert Merge Fields button** . In the Insert Merge Fields dialog box, click and insert the **Mailing_Address field**. Close the dialog box. Press Enter⏎ twice.

14. Type Dear, insert the First_Name field, and press Enter⏎.

Your letter should look like Figure 2.8.

HINTS & TIPS

• You can use the scroll bar at the bottom of the window to view more contacts.

• Remember to add spaces and punctuation marks as needed between merge fields.

OFFICE XP

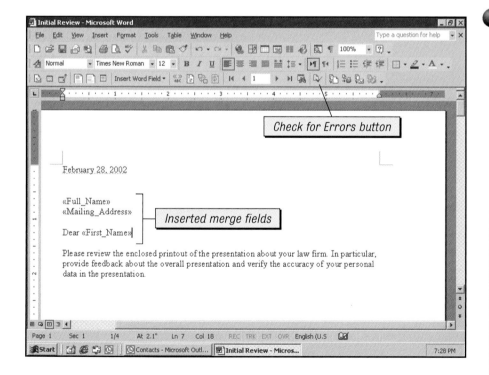

Figure 2.8
Letter with merge fields added

Visit **www.glencoe.com/norton/online/** for more information on creating a Mail Merge document.

15. At the end of your letter, type an appropriate closing (for example, *Sincerely*).

16. Press [Enter←] four times, and then type your name.

17. Save your changes to the *Initial Review* document.

18. Click the **Check for Errors button** 🔃 on the Mail Merge toolbar.

The Checking and Reporting Errors dialog box appears.

19. In the Checking and Reporting Errors dialog box, click the **Complete the merge, pausing to report each error as it occurs option**.

20. Click **OK**.

Word checks for mail merge errors and merges the letter with the selected contacts in Outlook. The first letter appears, as shown in Figure 2.9.

Figure 2.9
Merged letter

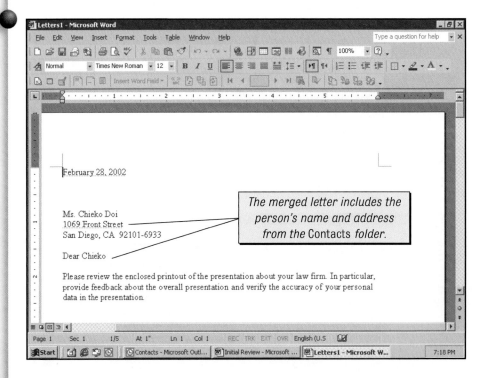

21. Print one of the merged letters, including the pages that contain the PowerPoint presentation.

22. Close the merged document without saving it.

23. Save your changes to the *Initial Review* letter and then close it.

24. Exit all open programs.

Using Word as Your E-Mail Editor

Outlook works very well to store incoming and outgoing mail messages, but did you know that you can create an e-mail message using Word as well? When you use Word as your e-mail editor, you can take advantage of its powerful features such as spell and grammar checks, AutoCorrect, and tables. To learn how to use Word as your e-mail editor, spend a few minutes researching Help.

1. **Launch Word, if it is not already open.**

2. **In the *Ask a Question* box, type e-mail editor, and then press Enter←.**

3. **On the displayed list, click About using Word as your e-mail editor.**

4. **Read the information in the Help window (Figure 2.10). Close the Help window.**

5. **If time allows, redisplay the *Ask a Question* list and click additional links related to using Word as your e-mail editor.**

6. **Send an e-mail message to your instructor or a classmate using Word as your e-mail editor. Close the Help window and exit Word.**

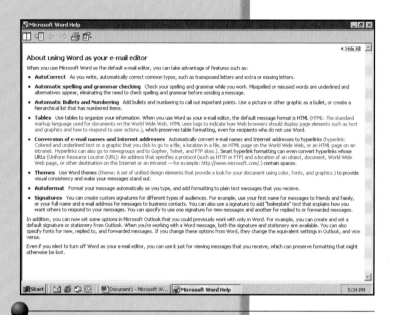

Figure 2.10
Learning how to use Word as your e-mail editor

Self Check

Test your knowledge by answering the following questions. See Appendix B to check your answers.

T F **1.** You can copy data from an Access database directly to the *Contacts* folder.

T F **2.** When you use Outlook's Mail Merge feature, you must create a new Word document; you cannot use an existing document.

T F **3.** Displaying your Calendar appointments in Active Appointments view is helpful when you want to copy the appointments into Excel, because it sets up the information in a column-and-row format.

T F **4.** You can use Outlook's Mail Merge feature only to send mail to **all** your contacts; you cannot use it to select specific recipients.

T F **5.** You can use either Word or Outlook as your e-mail editor.

NORTON ONLINE

Visit **www.glencoe.com/norton/online/** for more information on integrating Office XP.

OFFICE XP

ADDING A WEB PAGE SHORTCUT TO YOUR OUTLOOK BAR

You've worked with several of the default shortcut icons on the Outlook Bar to access the Outlook features such as the Calendar and Task list. You also can display Web content from within Outlook, and you can add your own shortcuts to Outlook.

In this activity, you continue to act as an associate at High End Consultants working to help a law firm gain new clients. To learn more about the law industry, you use Outlook to navigate to a Web page sponsored by the federal government. Additionally, since you plan to visit the site on a regular basis, you decide to add a shortcut to your Outlook Bar.

1. **Connect to the Internet. Launch Outlook. Confirm that the Web toolbar is displayed in Outlook.**

2. **In the Address bar of the Web toolbar, type** www.fjc.gov **and then press** Enter⏎ **.**

As shown in Figure 2.11, the Federal Judicial Center Web site appears in the main working area of the Outlook window.

> **NOTE** *If the Federal Judicial Center Web site no longer exists, click the Search the Web toolbar button and search for any page that contains a list of law journals or other information on legal practices in the United States.*

3. **Explore the links to display the associated information for each link. Click the Back button** ⇦Back **on the Web toolbar repeatedly until you return to the original Web page.**

So you can return to the Federal Judicial Center Web site (or other site) quickly, you want to create a shortcut to the page.

4. **Point to New on the File menu, and then click Outlook Bar Shortcut to Web Page.**

A message appears indicating that the new shortcut will be added to the bottom of the My Shortcuts group in the Outlook Bar.

5. **Click OK to confirm your action.**

Now you're ready to test your new shortcut.

6. **Click the Journal shortcut icon.**

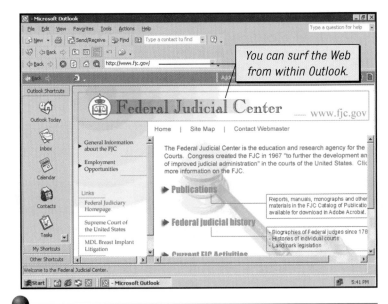

Figure 2.11
Web page displayed in Outlook's window

The contents of the Journal are displayed in Outlook's right window pane.

7. **Click the My Shortcuts button on the Outlook bar (if necessary).**

8. **If necessary, scroll down in the Outlook Bar to view the Web shortcut you added, and then click it.**

The Web page is shown in Outlook's right window pane. Now try renaming the shortcut.

9. Right-click the **Web icon** in the Outlook Bar, and then click **Rename Shortcut** in the shortcut menu that appears.

The text box next to the Web icon is displayed in Rename mode so that you can enter a new name.

10. Type Judicial Stuff and then press Enter←.

The Web icon is renamed. In "real life" you'd probably use the icon for days (or weeks) before removing it from the Outlook Bar. However, so that you can see how to delete a shortcut icon, you will remove the shortcut icon from the Outlook Bar.

11. Right-click the **Web icon** in the Outlook Bar, and then click **Remove from Outlook Bar**. Choose **Yes** in the message box to confirm your action.

12. Exit Outlook and disconnect from the Internet if your instructor tells you to do so.

WARNING *You may proceed directly to the exercises for this lesson. If, however, you are finished with your computer session, follow the "shut down" procedures for your lab or school environment.*

SUMMARY AND EXERCISES

SUMMARY

In this lesson, you learned how to integrate data among the Office XP programs. You saw how to use the Calendar, Contacts, and Journal tools of Outlook to share data with Word, Excel, PowerPoint, and Access. By tapping into the strengths of each program, you can increase your productivity and minimize the time you spend re-entering data.

Now that you have completed this lesson, you should be able to do the following:

- Schedule appointments using the Calendar. (page 696)
- Display appointments in the Active Appointments view and copy them to an Excel worksheet. (page 697)
- Enter names, titles, addresses, phone numbers, and e-mail addresses for new contacts. (page 698)
- Use the Letter Wizard to create a letter based on an Outlook contact. (page 699)
- Copy an Excel worksheet's data and paste it into a Word document. (page 700)
- Import a database of names, addresses, and numbers directly into the *Contacts* folder. (page 701)
- Copy selected text from a Word document and paste it into an Outlook journal entry. (page 703)
- Use the Send To command to transfer a PowerPoint presentation into Word. (page 704)
- Create a new form letter and use Outlook to merge it with selected contacts. (page 706)
- Use Help to learn how to use Word as your e-mail editor. (page 709)
- Create, use, rename, and delete a Web icon on the Outlook Bar. (page 710)

CONCEPTS REVIEW

1 TRUE/FALSE

Circle T if the statement is true or F if the statement is false.

T   F   **1.** Access databases and Outlook's *Contacts* folder often have similar data, such as names and addresses.

T   F   **2.** You must close a Word document before using it in an Outlook mail merge.

T   F   **3.** You must use Outlook, not Word, to create an e-mail document.

T   F   **4.** You can display the Calendar in Day, Week, or Month modes.

T   F   **5.** To link Excel data in a Word document, use Create a Link.

T   F   **6.** You can copy data from Word to an Outlook note or task.

T   F   **7.** You can display Web page contents in Outlook.

T   F   **8.** You cannot rename shortcuts in the Outlook Bar.

T   F   **9.** You can create a mail merge from Outlook.

T   F **10.** When using mail merge in Outlook, you always must send the letter to all the people in your *Contacts* folder—you can't select specific contacts.

2 MATCHING

Match each of the terms on the left with the definitions on the right.

TERMS

1. Check for Errors
2. shortcut icons
3. mail merge
4. Control key
5. Shift key
6. Letter Wizard
7. Calendar
8. Send To
9. export
10. Contacts

DEFINITIONS

a. The command that transfers PowerPoint slides into a Word document

b. Press this key to select a group of adjacent contacts

c. A way to verify that your mail merge document is error-free

d. The process used to transfer information from an Access database to the *Contacts* folder in Outlook

e. A specialized tool that guides you through the creation of a letter

f. The buttons that appear on the Outlook Bar which allow you to switch between tools

g. Press this key to select a group of nonadjacent contacts

h. An Outlook feature that allows you to create a document addressed to several contacts

i. The folder that contains names and addresses of people you communicate with on a regular basis

j. An electronic method of keeping track of appointments in Outlook by day, week, or month

SUMMARY AND EXERCISES

3 COMPLETION

Fill in the missing word or phrase for each of the following statements.

1. Outlook's _____ can be displayed by day, week, or month.

2. You can use the _____ toolbar to type names for Web page addresses.

3. You can transfer contact information from a(n) _____ database into Outlook.

4. The results of Outlook often appear in the form of increased productivity, rather than actual_____ like most of the other Office XP programs.

5. Using _____ instead of Outlook as your e-mail editor allows you to take advantage of features such as grammar and spell checks and tables.

6. To start the transfer of data from a database to the *Contacts* folder, click _____ on the File menu.

7. You can use the _____ and _____ commands to copy data from Word to Outlook tools such as Notes.

8. In Outlook, the Journal, Contacts, Calendar, and Notes icons all appear on the _____ .

9. To set up your appointments in column and row format so that you can copy them from Outlook into Excel, you should use the _____ view.

10. You can use the _____ Wizard to develop an Outlook mail merge.

4 SHORT ANSWER

Write a brief answer to each of the following questions.

1. Describe the appearance of the Word document that is created when you send a PowerPoint presentation to Word using the *Blank lines next to slides* option. What is the purpose of the blank lines?

2. Why might you copy Calendar data into an Excel or a Word document?

3. How do you set the duration of an appointment in the Calendar?

4. What is the benefit of creating a letter from within the *Contacts* folder?

5. Which parts of a letter can you use the Letter Wizard to automatically create?

6. Explain the process you use to bring names and addresses from an Access database into Outlook's *Contacts* folder.

7. Why might you copy data from Word into a journal entry? a task list? an e-mail message? Give at least one example of each.

8. Describe the process of using Outlook's mail merge feature to address letters to several contacts.

5 IDENTIFICATION

Identify each element of the Outlook window in Figure 2.12.

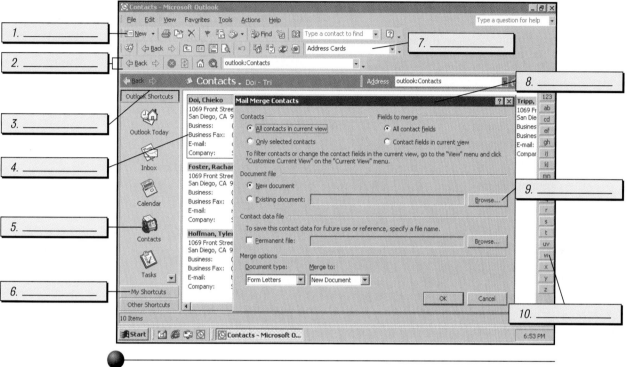

Figure 2.12

SKILLS REVIEW

Complete all of the Skills Review problems in sequential order to review your Office integration skills.

1 Set Appointments in the Calendar

1. Launch Outlook and then click the **Calendar shortcut icon**.

2. In the Date Navigator, click the date for next **Tuesday**.

3. Switch to Work Week view.

4. Double-click the **8:00 a.m. time slot** and set an appointment for a golf lesson with the following information:

   Subject: Golf Lesson with Grant Tomas
   Start time: 10:30 a.m.
   End time: 12:00 p.m.
   Reminder: 1 hour

5. Click the **Recurrence button** in the Appointment dialog box and set the appointment to recur each week on the same day for a total of eight weeks.

6. Set the additional appointments in Table 2.3.

Table 2.3	Data for New Appointments					
Day	**Subject**	**Start Time**	**End Time**	**Reminder**	**Recurrence**
Wednesday	Golf Lesson with Marta Phillips	10:00 a.m.	11:30 a.m.	1 hour	8 weeks
Thursday	Golf Lesson with Oscar Jimenez	1:00 p.m.	2:30 p.m.	1 hour	8 weeks
Thursday	Golf Lesson with Sandra Wagner	3:00 p.m.	4:30 p.m.	1 hour	8 weeks

2 Copy Appointments to Excel

1. While displaying the Calendar, point to **Current View** on the View menu and click **Active Appointments**.

2. Click the first golf lesson appointment, press and hold down ⬆Shift, and click the last golf lesson appointment. (If the appointments are not adjacent, click each appointment while pressing and holding down Ctrl.)

3. Click **Copy** on the Edit menu.

4. Launch Excel and click the **Paste button** on the Standard toolbar.

5. Delete the *Location, Recurrence,* and *Categories* columns (if necessary).

6. Format the worksheet data in an attractive manner.

7. Save the workbook as *Golf Lessons* in the *Skills Review Solutions* folder in the *Skills Review* folder in your *Integration Data* folder. Keep the workbook open.

3 Enter a Contact

1. Switch to Outlook and click the **Contacts shortcut icon**.

2. Click the **New Contact button** New and type the following information in the Untitled - Contact dialog box:

Full Name:	Mr. Eric Sims
Job title:	Golf Pro
Home phone:	(310) 555-0832
Home address:	1824 Garden View Court
	Marina del Rey, CA 90292-9705
E-mail:	ericsims@caonline.com

3. Save and close the contact.

4 Address a Letter to a Contact

1. In the *Contacts* folder, click the **name bar for Eric Sims**.

2. Click **New Letter to Contact** on the Actions menu to launch the Letter Wizard. (Click the **Word taskbar button**, if necessary.)

3. Check the **Date line box** on the first page of the Letter Wizard, and then click **Next**.

4. Click **Next** until the fourth page of the Letter Wizard is displayed.

5. Click the **Complimentary closing triangle button**, and click *Sincerely yours.* Then, click **Finish**.

6. In the letter body, type the following text:

Dear Eric,

Congratulations! All of your time slots have been filled with appointments for clients. As you are aware, golf lessons begin next Tuesday and last eight weeks. We are now accepting reservations for the next session of lessons. The following table contains the clients who have signed up for the first session.

7. Change the left and right margins for the letter to 2 inches. Also change the font to 14 point. Add additional spacing or formatting as needed to display the letter in an attractive manner.

8. Save the letter as *Letter to Sims* in the *Skills Review Solutions* folder in the *Skills Review* folder in your *Integration Data* folder.

5 Copy a Worksheet Into the Letter

1. Switch to Excel and open the *Golf Lessons* workbook (if necessary).

2. Select the cells that contain the golf lesson appointments, and then click the **Copy button** .

3. Switch to the *Letter to Sims* document. Place the insertion point below the first paragraph and click the **Paste button** .

4. Click the **Paste Options button**, and then choose **Match Destination Table Style**.

5. If necessary, further format the table and the letter to improve its appearance, as shown in Figure 2.13.

6. Save, print, and close the *Letter to Sims* document. Close the *Golf Lessons* workbook.

7. Exit Word and Excel, but leave Outlook running.

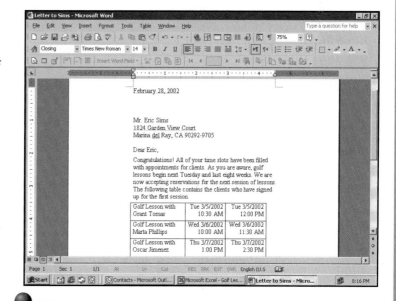

Figure 2.13

6 Import a Database Into the *Contacts* Folder

1. Launch Access and open the *Marina Golf Course* database in the *Skills Review* folder in your *Integration Data* folder.

2. Open the *Session 1 Golf Lessons* table and read the names in the table. Close the table and exit Access.

3. Switch to Outlook and open the *Contacts* folder, if necessary.

4. Click **Import and Export** on the File menu.

5. Click **Import from another program or file** on the first page of the Import and Export Wizard, and then click **Next**.

6. On the next page, click **Microsoft Access**. Click **Next**.

7. On the next page, click the **Browse button**. Navigate to and select the **Marina Golf Course database** in the *Skills Review* folder in your *Integration Data* folder. Click **OK**.

8. In the Import and Export Wizard, choose the **Replace duplicates with items imported option**, and then click **Next**.

9. Click *Contacts* as the destination folder, and then click **Next**.

10. On the final page, click **Finish**.

11. Check the *Contacts* folder to make sure the four new contacts have been added (Tomas, Phillips, Jimenez, and Wagner). Leave Outlook running.

7 Copy Text From Word to the Journal

1. Display the My Shortcuts group on the Outlook Bar.

2. Click the **Journal shortcut icon** on the Outlook Bar.

3. Click the **New Journal Entry button** and record a journal entry for a phone conversation with Eric Sims, the golf pro who works at your golf course. The entry should indicate that you talked to Eric today from 9:30 to 10:00 a.m. Without closing the journal entry, switch to Word.

4. Open the *Conversation with Eric Sims* Word document from the *Skills Review* folder in your *Integration Data* folder.

5. Select the text in the document, and then click the **Copy button**.

6. Switch to the journal entry, and click the **Notes section**. Click the **Paste button**.

7. Save and close the journal entry. Close the *Conversation with Eric Sims* document without saving it.

8 Send a PowerPoint Presentation to Word

1. Launch PowerPoint and open the *Bobcat Golf Clubs* presentation in the *Skills Review* folder in your *Integration Data* folder.

2. Point to **Send To** on the File menu and click **Microsoft Word**.

3. In the Send To Microsoft Word dialog box, click the **Notes below slides option**, and then click **OK**.

4. Save the Word document as *Bobcat Discount Letter* in the *Skills Review Solutions* folder in the *Skills Review* folder in your *Integration Data* folder.

5. Exit PowerPoint without saving any changes to the *Bobcat Golf Clubs* presentation.

9 Compose a Letter

1. With the *Bobcat Discount Letter* document still open in Word, move the insertion point to the top of the document.

2. Insert a page break above the first slide.

3. Compose a brief letter on the first page of the document that tells customers that since they signed up for golf lessons at your golf course, they are entitled to receive a 10 percent discount on any Bobcat golf clubs they buy at your pro shop.

4. Change the font to 14 points, and format the letter so that it is displayed attractively on the first page.

5. Save and close the *Bobcat Discount Letter* document. Exit Word.

10 Merge a Letter With Contacts

1. Switch to the *Contacts* folder of Outlook. Click the **name bar** of the first golf lesson student (**Oscar Jimenez**).

2. Press and hold Ctrl and click the names of the other students (**Marta Phillips, Grant Tomas, and Sandra Wagner**).

3. Click **Mail Merge** on the Tools menu. Click the **Browse button** in the Document file area of the Mail Merge Contacts dialog box.

4. Find and select the **Bobcat Discount Letter document** in the *Skills Review Solutions* folder, and then click **OK**.

5. Click **OK** to close the Mail Merge Contacts dialog box.

6. Place the insertion point to the right of *Dear* in the salutation line.

7. Click the **Insert Merge Fields button** 📧 on the Mail Merge toolbar.

8. Click **Database Fields** in the Insert area, and then double-click the appropriate **merge field (First_Name)** from the list. Close the Insert Merge Field dialog box.

9. Place your insertion point where you want the inside address to be displayed. Add the Full_Name and Mailing_Address fields for the inside address.

10. Add the date at the top of the letter; verify that appropriate blank space exists between the date and inside address and the inside address and salutation.

11. Save the document and click the **Check for Errors button** 🔽.

12. Click the **Complete the merge, pausing to report each error as it occurs option**.

13. Print one of the merged letters, including the pages that contain the PowerPoint presentation.

14. Close the merged document without saving it. Save and close the *Bobcat Discount Letter*. Exit Word.

LESSON APPLICATIONS

You must complete all of these activities in sequence; they build upon each other and allow you to integrate data among Office programs and Outlook's tools.

1 Setting and Printing Dental Appointments

You work as the office manager for Dr. Susan Beauchere, a dentist. Your staff has taken several phone calls this week for various appointments that you need to enter into the Outlook Calendar. Dr. Beauchere wants a printout of the appointments at the beginning of the week.

1. Launch Outlook and display the Calendar.

2. In the Date Navigator, click the date for two Mondays from now.

3. Set the appointments in Table 2.4 for two weeks from now. Set all reminders to 5 minutes.

Table 2.4	Data for New Appointments			
Day	**Subject**	**Location**	**Start Time**	**End Time**
Monday	Ashton Meijer: cleaning and checkup	Room 1	9:00 a.m.	9:30 a.m.
Monday	Lois Graves: cleaning and checkup	Room 2	9:30 a.m.	10:00 a.m.
Monday	Bob Clary: root canal	Room 1	10:00 a.m.	11:30 a.m.
Monday	Benito Rios: cleaning, checkup, and x-rays	Room 2	11:30 a.m.	12:30 p.m.
Monday	Sally Manchester: two fillings	Room 1	2:00 p.m.	3:00 p.m.
Monday	Parker Koenig: cleaning and checkup	Room 2	3:00 p.m.	3:30 p.m.
Monday	J. T. Stevens: crown	Room 1	3:30 p.m.	4:30 p.m.
Tuesday	Jim Doyle: cleaning, checkup, and x-rays	Room 1	9:30 a.m.	10:30 a.m.

Table 2.4	Data for New Appointments (continued)			
Day	**Subject**	**Location**	**Start Time**	**End Time**
Tuesday	Ashley Baker: two fillings	Room 2	10:30 a.m.	11:30 a.m.
Tuesday	Carl Mansberg: cleaning and checkup	Room 1	2:00 p.m.	2:30 p.m.
Tuesday	Evan West: root canal	Room 2	2:30 p.m.	3:30 p.m.
Tuesday	Umeko Shinoda: one filling	Room 1	4:00 p.m.	5:00 p.m.

4. Switch to Active Appointment view and select and copy the dental appointments.

5. Launch Excel and paste the appointments into a new workbook.

6. Format the workbook as desired and delete extra column headings. Print the worksheet for Dr. Beauchere.

7. Save the workbook as *Dental Appointments* in the *Lesson Applications Solutions* folder in the *Lesson Applications* folder in your *Integration Data* folder, and then close it.

2 Entering Dental Patients in Outlook and Sending a Letter

As office manager for Dr. Susan Beauchere, your next duty is to enter patient information in the *Contacts* folder. You are also responsible for sending welcome letters to new patients.

1. Switch to the *Contacts* folder of Outlook.

2. Enter the new patient information in Table 2.5.

Table 2.5	Data for New Contacts			
Name	**Home Address**	**Business Phone**	**Home Phone**	**Notes**
Ms. Ashton Meijer	9 Bigelow Terrace Watertown, MA 02172-2532	(617) 555-1200	(617) 555-6917	
Ms. Lois Graves	27 Irma Ave. Watertown, MA 02172-3530		(781) 555-1749	
Mr. Bob Clary	69 Parker St. Watertown, MA 02172-3913	(617) 555-3099	(781) 555-3165	Allergic to penicillin

Table 2.5	Data for New Contacts (continued)			
Name	**Home Address**	**Business Phone**	**Home Phone**	**Notes**
Mr. Benito Rios	64 Union St. Watertown, MA 02172-2525	(781) 555-8800	(781) 555-0026	
Ms. Sally Manchester	708 Mt. Auburn St. Watertown, MA 02172-1522		(781) 555-4361	
Mr. Parker Koenig	24 Whites Ave. #5 Watertown, MA 02172-4314		(781) 555-7550	
Ms. J. T. Stevens	158 Waverley Ave. Watertown, MA 02172-1105	(781) 555-1608	(781) 555-1304	
Mr. Jim Doyle	71 Putnam St. Watertown, MA 02172-1980	(617) 555-8332	(617) 555-0812	
Ms. Ashley Baker	239 Warren St. Watertown, MA 02172-9862	(781) 555-8223	(781) 555-6090	
Mr. Carl Mansberg	8 Summer St. #2 Watertown, MA 02172-3468		(781) 555-7958	
Mr. Evan West	53 Boylston St. Watertown, MA 02172-1971	(781) 555-6506		
Ms. Umeko Shinoda	212 Bellevue Rd. Watertown, MA 02172-4907	(617) 555-3828	(781) 555-0034	

3. You need to send a welcome letter to Jim Doyle, a new patient. Use Outlook to automatically address a new letter to him. In the letter, welcome the new patient and refer to a table to be inserted containing fees for common procedures.

4. Open the *Dental Fees* workbook in the *Lesson Applications* folder in your *Integration Data* folder and copy the services and fees information in it.

5. Paste the data to your letter and format it appropriately. Print and close the letter without saving it. Exit Word.

6. Close the *Dental Fees* workbook without saving it and exit Excel.

3 Importing New Contacts From a Database

Dr. Beauchere recently attended a dental conference where she met several other dentists who practice in Massachusetts. She created a small database with the dentists' names and addresses while she was at the conference. She'd like you to transfer the database information to Outlook.

1. Open the *Dentists* database in the *Lesson Applications* folder in your *Integration Data* folder.

2. Open the Contacts table and note the names of the dentists in it. Close the database and exit Access.

3. Open the *Contacts* folder in Outlook, and click the Import and Export command on the File menu.

4. Click the selections that allow you to import the *Dentists* database to the *Contacts* folder. Also make sure that no duplicates will be created. When you're finished choosing options, click Finish.

5. In Outlook, verify that the contacts were imported correctly.

4 Copying Information Into a Journal Entry

After the dental conference, Dr. Beauchere asked you to call one of the dentists that she met. Dr. Garvin Nickell gave you the name of a Web site where you can find the Principles of Ethics and Code of Professional Conduct for dentists. You'd like to share this site with your staff, but you lost the note on which you wrote the address. You call Dr. Nickell's office again and make a note in a Word file. Now you want to create a journal entry to record the phone call.

1. In Outlook, display the Journal.

2. Create a new journal entry that records a ten-minute conversation with Dr. Nickell yesterday at 1:30 p.m.

3. Open the *Ethics and Conduct* document from the *Lesson Applications* folder in your *Integration Data* folder in Word to see the notes you took during the conversation.

4. Copy the text from the Word file and paste it into the Notes section of the journal entry.

5. Save and close the journal entry. Then close the *Ethics and Conduct* file.

5 Sharing a PowerPoint Presentation With Other Dentists

You must complete Lesson Application 3 before completing this activity. Dr. Beauchere mentioned to the other dentists that she met at the dental conference that she has created a PowerPoint presentation for use by her new staff members. She wants you to send a printout of the presentation to these dentists.

1. In PowerPoint, open the *Dental Staff Training* presentation in the *Lesson Applications* folder in your *Integration Data* folder.

2. Send the presentation, including slide miniatures, to a Word document. Choose the *Blank lines next to slides* option in the Send To Microsoft Word dialog box.

3. Compose a short letter before the first slide informing the dentists that the following pages contain the PowerPoint presentation.

4. Save the letter as *Staff Training* in the *Lesson Applications Solutions* folder. Exit Word.

5. Close the *Dental Staff Training* presentation and the *Staff Training* document. Exit PowerPoint.

6. In Outlook, select Drs. Coith, Cranley, Feng, Nickell, Polasky, and Rabkin in the *Contacts* folder (you entered the data for these contacts in Lesson Application 3).

7. Use the Mail Merge feature to merge the selected contacts with the *Staff Training* document. Edit the Word document to add appropriate merge fields.

8. Print one copy of the letter, and then close the merged document without saving it. Close all documents and exit all applications.

PROJECTS

1 Keeping Track of Classes

Anthony Chao has a personal training and health counseling business that he's expanding. He also has a new partner and additional locations, and he has changed the company's name to Fitness Plus. His partner, Linda Prescott, uses Outlook, and Anthony would like to start using it as well. Your first project as an employee of Fitness Plus is to enter the karate, judo, and kung-fu classes into the company's Outlook calendar.

The next session of classes starts the second full week of June and lasts for 10 weeks. All youth classes last 45 minutes, and adult classes last 60 minutes. Use Outlook's Calendar to schedule the classes in Table 2.6.

Table 2.6	Data for New Appointments					
Class Type	Age	Level	Day	Start Time	Instructor	Location
Karate	Youth	Beginner	Monday	1:30 p.m.	Perry	Plymouth
Karate	Youth	Intermediate	Thursday	10:30 a.m.	Samantha	Shaker Heights
Karate	Youth	Advanced	Wednesday	1:30 p.m.	Perry	Plymouth
Karate	Adult	Beginner	Tuesday	4:30 p.m.	Samantha	Wellfleet
Karate	Adult	Intermediate	Monday	7:30 p.m.	Allison	Montgomery
Karate	Adult	Advanced	Thursday	7:00 p.m.	Allison	Wellfleet
Judo	Youth	Beginner	Tuesday	9:30 a.m.	Scott	Wellfleet
Judo	Youth	Intermediate	Tuesday	1:30 p.m.	Allison	Montgomery
Judo	Youth	Advanced	Wednesday	11:30 a.m.	Allison	Wellfleet
Judo	Adult	Beginner	Friday	6:30 p.m.	Rosa	Plymouth
Judo	Adult	Intermediate	Wednesday	7:00 p.m.	Scott	Shaker Heights
Judo	Adult	Advanced	Friday	7:30 p.m.	Rosa	Wellfleet

OFFICE XP

Table 2.6		Data for New Appointments (continued)				
Class Type	**Age**	**Level**	**Day**	**Start Time**	**Instructor**	**Location**
Kung-fu	Youth	Beginner	Friday	2:00 p.m.	Scott	Wellfleet
Kung-fu	Youth	Intermediate	Wednesday	3:30 p.m.	Perry	Plymouth
Kung-fu	Youth	Advanced	Monday	10:30 a.m.	Samantha	Shaker Heights
Kung-fu	Adult	Beginner	Tuesday	7:30 p.m.	Scott	Plymouth
Kung-fu	Adult	Intermediate	Thursday	8:30 p.m.	Rosa	Montgomery
Kung-fu	Adult	Advanced	Monday	5:30 p.m.	Rosa	Plymouth

After you enter all of the classes in the Calendar, the partners want you to copy them to a worksheet and print a copy to post at each studio. Transfer the information about classes to an Excel workbook, format as desired, and then print it. Close the workbook without saving it.

2 Tracking Your Employees

Anthony and Linda have asked you to add all employees of Fitness Plus to the *Contacts* folder. Use Outlook to add the information in Table 2.7 as contacts.

Table 2.7		Data for New Contacts		
Name	**Job Title**	**Company**	**Home Phone**	**Home Address**
Ms. Rosa Aponte	Instructor	Fitness Plus	(602) 555-1824	8330 N. 19th Ave. Phoenix, AZ 85021
Mr. Anthony Chao	Co-owner	Fitness Plus	(602) 555-8232	2201 E. Cactus Rd. Phoenix, AZ 85021
Ms. Samantha Deitschel	Instructor	Fitness Plus	(602) 555-7124	2333 E. Devonshire Ave. Phoenix, AZ 85021
Ms. Allison Faulkner	Instructor	Fitness Plus	(602) 555-0342	4630 E. Thomas Rd. Phoenix, AZ 85021
Mr. Scott Jacobs	Instructor	Fitness Plus	(602) 555-8245	6131 N. 27th Ave. Phoenix, AZ 85021
Mr. Perry Kahn	Instructor	Fitness Plus	(602) 555-7139	2813 W. Colter St. Phoenix, AZ 85021
Ms. Linda Prescott	Co-owner	Fitness Plus	(602) 555-0498	938 W. Glenrosa Ave. Phoenix, AZ 85021
Mr. Brent Varley	Instruction Supervisor	Fitness Plus	(602) 555-2843	350 E. Eva St., #215 Phoenix, AZ 85021

SUMMARY AND EXERCISES

3 Reporting Information to the Supervisor

You must complete Project 2 before completing this project. You've been asked by Brent Varley, the instruction supervisor at Fitness Plus, to provide a list of all the names, phone numbers, areas of expertise, and hire dates of the instructors who work for Fitness Plus. You'd like to have the instructors' names in a workbook so that you can easily add and delete information.

View the *Contacts* folder in By Company view and select the names of the instructors at Fitness Plus (you entered this instructor data in Project 2). Copy this information and paste it to a new workbook. Save the workbook as *Fitness Plus Instructors* in the *Projects Solutions* folder in the *Projects* folder in your *Integration Data* folder. Delete any columns or rows that you don't need, then add a column called *Expertise* and another named *Start Date*. Add data that indicates the areas of expertise and hire dates for each instructor as shown in Table 2.8. Sort the worksheet in ascending order by the dates in the Start Date column.

Table 2.8	Instructor Data	
Name	**Area(s) of Expertise**	**Start Date**
Rosa Aponte	Judo and Kung-fu	3/15/97
Samantha Deitschel	Karate	2/1/99
Allison Faulkner	Karate and Judo	8/15/94
Scott Jacobs	Judo and Kung-fu	12/1/92
Perry Kahn	Karate	5/1/95

Save the changes to the workbook and switch to Outlook. Use the *Contacts* folder to automatically address a letter to Brent Varley. In the letter, tell him that you are providing the information he requested and that you have sorted the instructors by the length of time they have worked for the company. Paste the data from the *Fitness Plus Instructors* workbook in the letter. Save the letter as *Instructor Information* in the *Projects Solutions* folder in the *Projects* folder in your *Integration Data* folder. Print and close the letter. Close the *Fitness Plus Instructors* workbook. Then exit Excel and Word.

4 Attracting New Customers

Many customers call and ask about the services that Fitness Plus can provide. Although many set an appointment for a tour of the facilities, some of them just wish to have information sent to them. Fitness Plus has not finalized its company brochures, but it does have a PowerPoint presentation for customers to view. You can mail a printout of the presentation to those customers who cannot visit for a tour and live presentation.

The following customers have requested information by mail. Since you'll send them information now and later follow up with a phone call or letter, start by entering the data provided in Table 2.9 into the *Contacts* folder.

Table 2.9	Data for Potential Customers	
Name	**Home Address**	**Home Phone**
Mr. Davis Ramos	5023 N. 18th St. Phoenix, AZ 85016	(602) 555-0344
Ms. Judith Zawbraski	7728 W. Crittenden Ln. Phoenix, AZ 85033	(602) 555-4002
Mr. Rinji Saga	12810 N. Cave Creek Rd. Phoenix, AZ 85022	(602) 555-2749
Ms. Abigail Freemont	9923 W. Madrugada Ave. Phoenix, AZ 85037	(602) 555-3383
Ms. Madison Alexander	1737 E. Pinchot Ave. Phoenix, AZ 85016	(602) 555-6399
Mr. Raymond Hanson	8738 W. Lewis Ave. Phoenix, AZ 85037	(602) 555-1648
Mr. Ryan Telpon	5608 W. Verde Ln. Phoenix, AZ 85031	(602) 555-7133

After entering the contacts into Outlook, open the *Fitness Plus* presentation in the *Projects* folder in your *Integration Data* folder in PowerPoint. Send the presentation to Word (with blank lines next to the slides), and compose a letter as the first page of the document. Target the letter to the potential customers and mention that you will call them in a week to answer any questions they might have. Save the letter as *Potential Fitness Customers* in the *Projects Solutions* folder in the *Projects* folder in your *Integration Data* folder. Use Outlook's Mail Merge feature to insert merge fields, and then merge the letter with the contacts you just entered. Print one copy of the letter with the presentation pages. Then close the merged letters without saving the file. Close open documents and exit PowerPoint and Word.

5 Noteworthy Impressions

Fitness Plus has an opening for an instructor trainee. Last week you interviewed three candidates. Create journal entries in Outlook to record the following interviews.

◆ David Campbell—interviewed at 3 p.m. on Tuesday. The interview lasted one hour.

◆ Sara McAllister—interviewed at 8 a.m. on Wednesday. The interview lasted one hour.

◆ Pat Burbank—interviewed at 2 p.m. on Friday. The interview lasted 45 minutes.

Immediately following each interview, you typed some notes into a Word file. Open the *Interview Notes* Word document in the *Projects* folder in your *Integration Data* folder. Copy the appropriate information from the Word file into the Notes section of each journal entry. Close all of the entries and close the *Interview Notes* file without saving it. Exit Word and Outlook.

Contents

APPENDIX A

PORTFOLIO BUILDER

WHAT IS A PORTFOLIO?

A **portfolio** is an organized collection of your work that demonstrates skills and knowledge acquired from one or more courses. The materials included in a portfolio should pertain to a specific educational or career goal. In addition to actual assignments, a portfolio should contain your self-reflection or comments on each piece of work, as well as an overall statement introducing the portfolio.

Two types of portfolios exist. The first, which shows progress toward a goal over a period of time, is called the **developmental portfolio.** Developmental portfolios help you become more aware of your strengths and weaknesses and assist you in improving your abilities. The second type, called a **representational portfolio,** displays a variety of your best work. You can show a representational portfolio as evidence of your skills and knowledge. While you may use either type of portfolio when you are seeking employment, a representational portfolio is more effective.

WHY USE PORTFOLIOS?

Portfolios offer great advantages to you, your instructor, and potential employers. They allow you to reevaluate the work you have created, by determining which assignments should be included in the portfolio and by analyzing how you can improve future assignments. If the goal of the portfolio is career related, portfolios also help you connect classroom activities with practical applications. A wide variety of genuine work is captured in a portfolio, rather than a snapshot of knowledge at a specific time under particular circumstances. Presenting a portfolio of your work to your instructor and potential employers gives them the opportunity to evaluate your overall skills and performance more accurately.

CREATING A PORTFOLIO

Creating a portfolio involves three steps—planning, selecting work to include, and providing comments about your work.

First, you should plan the overall purpose and organization of the portfolio. After you plan your portfolio, you can begin selecting pieces of work to include in it. Ideally, you should select the work as you complete each presentation; however, you can review prior work to include as well.

Table A.1 recommends documents from the activities in this tutorial that you may want to consider for inclusion in your portfolio; however, you may include additional documents, especially from the *Word 2002, Excel 2002, Access 2002,* and *PowerPoint 2002* tutorials. If two documents demonstrate identical Office XP skills, choose only one for your portfolio. If you apply your Office XP skills in another course or elsewhere, include a sample in your portfolio.

Table A.1	Possible Documents to Include in Your Portfolio	

Section/Lesson	Activity	Document Name
Word/Lesson 1	Project 7 (On the Web): Write This Way on the World Wide Web	*Web Link* (saved in the *Projects* folder in your *Word Data* folder)
Word/Lesson 2	Project 2: By Design	*Personal* (saved in the *Projects* folder in your *Word Data* folder)
Word	Case Study	(Selected documents saved in the *Reunion* folder in the *Projects* folder in your *Word Data* folder)
Excel/Lesson 1	Project 2: Make It Look Good!	*Formatted Worksheet* (saved in the *Projects* folder in your *Excel Data* folder)
Excel/Lesson 2	Project 3: Setting Goals	*Good Life Sales* (saved in the *Projects* folder in your *Excel Data* folder)
Excel	Case Study	(*Excel Case Study* saved in the *Projects* folder in your *Excel Data* folder)
Access/Lesson 1	Lesson 1 Lesson Applications 5-12 (cumulative)	*Star Realty-Lesson 1* (saved in the *Lesson Applications* folder in your *Access Data* folder)
Access/Lesson 2	Lesson 2 Project 8 (Project in Progress): Creating Forms, Queries, and Reports in the *Savvy Solutions* Database	*Savvy Solutions* (saved in the *Project in Progress* folder in the *Projects* folder in your *Access Data* folder)
Access	Case Study	*Tiny Tots Daycare* (saved in the *Projects* folder in your *Access Data* folder)
PowerPoint/Lesson 1	Project 4: Making a Model	*Advantages* (saved in the *Projects* folder in your *PowerPoint Data* folder)
PowerPoint/Lesson 2	Project 5: By Design	*Introduction 2* (saved in the *Projects* folder in your *PowerPoint Data* folder)
PowerPoint	Case Study	*Driver's License* (saved in the *Projects* folder in your *PowerPoint Data* folder)
Managing Information/ Lesson 2	Lesson 2 Hands On activities for *Creating a Word Letter From an Outlook Contact Entry*	*Letter to Rodriguez* (saved in the *Tutorial Solutions* folder in the *Tutorial* folder in your *Integration Data* folder)
Managing Information/ Lesson 2	Skills Review 8: Send a PowerPoint Presentation to Word and Skills Review 9: Compose a Letter	*Bob Discount Letter* (saved in the *Skills Review Solutions* folder in the *Skills Review* folder in your *Integration Data* folder)
Managing Information/ Lesson 2	Lesson Application 1: Setting and Printing Dental Appointments	*Dental Appointments* (saved in the *Lesson Applications Solutions* folder in the *Lesson Applications* folder in your *Integration Data* folder)

Create a list or log that provides a summary of the contents of your portfolio. (Your instructor may provide a preformatted log that you can complete.) The log can include columns in which you can list the file name, a description, when and by whom the file is reviewed, whether it was revised, and the grade you received on the assignment.

Lastly, you should prepare comments for each piece of work included in the portfolio. As you add work to your portfolio, generate comments about each piece. You may want to reflect on the skills used to create the document, or you can explain how it is applicable to a specific job for which you are interviewing. Your instructor may provide you with a preformatted comments form, or you may type your comments.

Perform the steps listed in the Hands On activity to build your portfolio.

HANDS on

Building Your Portfolio

In this activity, you will plan your portfolio, select the documents to include in the portfolio, and prepare written comments about each piece of work included in the portfolio.

1. **In a Word document, answer the following questions to help you plan your portfolio:**

   ◆ What is the purpose of your portfolio?

   ◆ What criteria will you use in selecting work to be included in the portfolio?

   ◆ What is the overall goal that your portfolio will meet?

   ◆ How will you organize your portfolio?

2. **Using Word, create a log that provides a summary of the contents of your portfolio. Follow the guidelines given by your instructor or provided in this appendix.**

3. **Remember the purpose and goal of your portfolio and select and print one document that you have completed to include in your portfolio. Enter information about the document in your log.**

4. **Prepare comments about the selected document and attach them to the printout.**

5. **Repeat steps 3 and 4 and prepare comments for other documents to include in your portfolio.**

6. **Using Word, write a paragraph or two introducing your portfolio. Include some of the information considered in step 1.**

7. **Gather the documents to be included in your portfolio and place them in a binder, folder, or other container in an organized manner.**

Self Check
Answers

Lesson	Question 1	Question 2	Question 3	Question 4	Question 5
Getting Started Lesson 1, page 37	moves	booting the system	read only	dialog	Folders
Getting Started Lesson 2, page 71	true	true	false	true	false
Getting Started Lesson 3, page 113	true	true	true	false	false
Word 2002 Lesson 1, page 163	Word Count Statistics	OVR	Thesaurus	Office Clipboard	New
Word 2002 Lesson 2, page 228	d	e	c	a	b
Excel 2002 Lesson 1, page 295	Ctrl + Home	cell pointer, active cell	cell reference or cell address	Enter	Esc
Excel 2002 Lesson 2, page 344	AutoSum	5	arguments	relative	Chart Wizard
Access 2002 Lesson 1, page 433	fields, reports	Objects	Design	primary key	referential integrity
Access 2002 Lesson 2, page 497	subform	Criteria, Or	join	expression	Report Wizard
PowerPoint 2002 Lesson 1, page 561	true	false	true	true	false
PowerPoint 2002 Lesson 2, page 629	c	d	a	b	e
Managing Information Lesson 1, page 689	*Outlook Today*	*Contacts*	*Journal*	*Inbox*	*Tasks*
Managing Information Lesson 2, page 709	true	false	true	false	true

GLOSSARY

A

absolute reference A cell reference that does not change when you copy or move it. You can create an absolute reference by placing a dollar sign ($) to the left of the part of the cell reference that you do not want to change during the copy operation. See also *relative reference*.

accessory A small program built into the Windows operating system.

action An instruction or command that you can combine with other instructions in a macro to automate a task.

active application The application that is currently running, as indicated by the highlighted button on the Windows taskbar.

active cell The cell into which you are entering data; it is identified by the cell pointer.

Active Desktop A Windows 2000 interface option that sets up your desktop to work like a Web page and to receive and display information from Internet content providers. Compare with *classic style desktop* and *Web style desktop*.

active window The window in which the cursor is located and in which the program will accept your input, as indicated by the darkened title bar.

adjacent range See *contiguous (adjacent) range*.

aggregate functions Predefined calculations that allow you to calculate totals and perform other types of common computations.

alignment The position of text, objects, or graphs in relation to the top and bottom or left and right margins.

animated object An object that appears progressively, rather than all at once, on a PowerPoint slide.

animated text Text that appears on a PowerPoint slide one subtitle at a time.

animation Motion effects that make text or objects move on the screen.

annual event In Outlook, an activity that occurs yearly on a specific day; for example, a birthday or an anniversary. Compare with *event*.

Answer Wizard One of the three tabs in the expanded Help window in Office applications. This tool is similar to the Office Assistant but provides many more topics from which to choose for further exploration. See also *Contents* and *Index*.

append To copy records from a table in another database and paste (paste append) them to a table in the current database, provided the order of the fields in the two databases is the same.

application See *application program*.

application program Specialized software program used to create or process data, such as creating text in a word processing document, manipulating financial information in a worksheet, tracking records in a database management file, or creating a presentation with a presentation or graphics program. Also called *application*. See also *program* and *software*.

application window A rectangle on the desktop containing the menus and files for an application. See also *document window*.

appointment In Outlook, an activity that you schedule in your calendar that does not involve inviting other people or reserving resources; it may be marked as *recurring* if it occurs on a regular basis. See also *recurring meeting*.

archive (attribute) A property setting that lets users modify or delete a file. Compare with *read-only (attribute)*. See also *attribute*.

argument The variable information included in a function between parentheses. For example, in the function *=SUM(A1:B20)*, the cell range of *A1:B20* is the argument.

Arial A sans serif font that commonly is used for headings.

arithmetic operators The symbols that are used to perform basic mathematical operations such as addition, subtraction, multiplication, and division.

article A message, also known as a *post*, that is distributed on a newsgroup.

ascending See *ascending sort*.

ascending sort A sort that arranges letters from A to Z, numbers from smallest to largest, and dates from earliest to most recent. Also called *ascending*. See also *sort*. Compare with *descending sort*.

Ask a Question A box at the right end of the menu bar in which you type a word, phrase, or question to access Help information quickly.

aspect ratio The width-to-height ratio of an image.

attribute A property that controls the use of a file or folder. See also *archive (attribute)* and *read-only (attribute)*.

AutoCalculate area The location in the middle portion of the Excel status bar that displays calculation results when you select a range of cells containing data.

AutoForm A form that Access builds automatically; the AutoForm gathers the information it needs by examining the selected table or query.

AutoFormats Ready-made worksheet designs provided by Excel.

automatic page break Break inserted automatically by Word where one page ends and another begins.

automatic recalculation The process of recalculating the results of formulas when the value in any referenced cell changes.

AutoReport A report that Access builds automatically, based on the selected table or query.

AutoShape A predrawn geometric shape, such as a line, block arrow, or banner, available through the Drawing toolbar in most Office applications.

AVERAGE An Excel function that computes the average value for a specified range.

B

bold A thick, heavy effect applied to text for emphasis.

booting the system Another expression for starting up; the computer often accomplishes this by loading a small program that then reads a larger program into memory. Also called *system boot*.

bottom aligned Page alignment in which text is even with the bottom margin regardless of the amount of text on the page.

browser A software package that lets the user access and navigate the major components of the Internet, such as the World Wide Web, e-mail, and so on. Also called *Web browser*.

bullet A character, typographical symbol, or graphic used as a special effect.

button A box labeled with words or a picture that you can click to select a setting or put a command into effect.

C

calculated field A field created in Query Design view in Access that displays the result of an expression rather than displaying stored data. The result is recalculated each time a value in the expression changes.

Calendar One of the default folders in Outlook; the *Calendar* folder allows you to schedule appointments, meetings, events, and tasks. See also *Contacts, Inbox, Journal, Notes,* and *Tasks.*

callout In PowerPoint, a box or balloon that holds text relating to a picture on a slide.

caption A property that can be modified to provide useful information and clarification to users of Access objects. Captions serve as column headings for fields in tables and queries, and as labels attached to controls in forms and reports.

CD drive A specialized type of disk drive that enables a computer to read data from a compact disc. See also *compact disc read-only memory (CD-ROM).*

cell A box formed by the intersection of a column and a row. Each cell can hold a single value or data entry.

cell pointer A black border surrounding a single cell in an Excel worksheet, indicating that the cell is active.

cell reference The column letter and row number combination that identifies a cell in an Excel worksheet.

center aligned Paragraph alignment in which each line of text (or an image) is midway between the left and right margins. Also, page alignment in which text or an image is midway between the top and bottom margins.

character effects Special effects (for example, shadow, subscript, superscript, or small caps) that you can add to selected text.

character spacing The amount of space between characters.

character style Formatting style that affects selected text, such as the font and size of text or bold and italic formats.

chart A graphic representation of worksheet data that displays information in the form of circles, lines, bars, or other shapes. Also called a *graph.*

Chart Wizard An interactive tool in Excel that asks a series of questions about the type of chart you want to create. It then develops a chart based on your responses.

check box A square box in a dialog box that contains a check mark when an option is selected or appears empty when the option is not selected.

choose See *select.*

classic style desktop The Windows 2000 default desktop setting that gives the user interface the same look and feel as Windows 95. Compare with *Active Desktop* and *Web style desktop.*

clear To designate (typically by clicking an item with the mouse) which option will be disabled or turned off. Formerly called *deselect.* Compare with *select.*

click To quickly press and release the left button on a mouse or trackball. See also *double-click* and *right-click.*

Click and Type Word feature that allows the user to double-click a document anywhere and then insert text or an image where the insertion point is located.

clip See *clip art.*

clip art A collection of ready-to-use graphic images that you can insert into a document and then resize, move, and modify as desired. An image also is called a *clip*.

Clipboard (1) An area in memory used by all Windows applications for temporarily storing text or graphics to be placed in a new location; (2) a task pane (in Word, Excel, and PowerPoint) for controlling and clearing items from Clipboard memory. See also *Office Clipboard*.

Clip Organizer A folder containing clip art that can be inserted into a document. See also *clip art*.

close To remove a file, a dialog box, or a window from the screen or desktop and from the computer's memory.

collapsed A state of an item in which details or subordinate items are hidden from view. A plus sign (+) in the box to the left of the item indicates that the item is collapsed. Compare with *expanded*.

column headings The gray area at the top of an Excel worksheet that contains a letter identifying each column.

command An instruction that you issue to a computer by clicking a menu option, clicking a button, or pressing a combination of keys on the keyboard.

command buttons Small, labeled rectangles in a dialog box or window that perform actions such as accepting or canceling changes.

common field A field in an Access table that has the same name and data type as a field in one or more other tables. You need to set up common fields in preparation for sharing data between tables. The common field allows Access to find matching data in different tables.

compact disc read-only memory (CD-ROM) The most common type of optical storage medium. On a CD-ROM, data is written in a series of lands and pits on the surface of a compact disc (CD), which can be read by a laser in a CD drive. A standard CD stores approximately 650 MB (about 450 times as much as a diskette), but data on a CD-ROM cannot be altered. See also *CD drive*.

comparison operator A symbol that is used to compare a value or text to characters that you enter.

Contacts One of the default folders in Outlook; the *Contacts* folder acts as a personal and business address book. See also *Calendar, Inbox, Journal, Notes,* and *Tasks*.

Contents One of the three tabs in the expanded Help window in Office applications, or one of the four tabs in the Windows Help window. This tool provides a list of general Help topics that is useful if you don't know the name of a feature. See also *Answer Wizard, Index, Search,* and *Favorites*.

context-sensitive Help Help tips and Help topics related specifically to tasks under way in the application window.

contiguous (adjacent) range An adjoining, rectangular block of cells. See also *noncontiguous (nonadjacent) range*.

copy To place a copy of text or graphics on the Clipboard. Compare with *cut*.

COUNT An Excel function that counts the number of cells in a range that contain data.

crop To trim an image.

current record The record that is active. In Datasheet view in Access, the current record is the row that contains a triangle or pencil icon in the record selector.

customize (1) To make or alter to individual or personal specifications; (2) to add a button, menu, or toolbar to an application window because it is used frequently. Also called *personalize*.

cut To remove text or a graphic and place it on the Clipboard. Compare with *copy*.

D

data Raw facts, numbers, letters, or symbols that the computer processes into meaningful information.

data access page A database object designed to be viewed in a Web browser.

data area A range that contains the data on which a chart is based.

database (1) An organized collection of data about similar entities—such as employees, customers, or inventory items—that you can filter and sort to extract specific information; (2) a collection of objects—such as reports, forms, tables, queries, and data access pages—associated with a particular topic.

Database window A window in Access that lets you gain access to all the objects (tables, forms, reports, and so on) in a particular database.

data point One value in a data series.

data series The set of related values in a row or column that you can plot on a chart.

datasheet (1) In PowerPoint, a grid of columns and rows used for entering, viewing, and editing data to create charts or graphs; (2) in Access, a tabular layout of rows and columns that allows you to add, edit, and view data in a table immediately.

Datasheet view A view in Access that displays data in a column-and-row format and permits you to view, add, delete, and edit the actual information in a database.

data type A designation that determines the type of data that can be entered into a field, such as text, numbers, and dates.

default A preset value or setting that an application program uses automatically unless you specify a different value or setting.

delete To remove text or graphics from a file.

demote To move a subtitle to the next lower indent level on a PowerPoint slide. Compare with *promote*.

descending See *descending sort*.

descending sort A sort that arranges letters from Z to A, numbers from largest to smallest, and dates from most recent to the earliest. Also called *descending*. See also *sort*. Compare with *ascending sort*.

deselect See *clear*.

design grid The grid in the Query Design view window in Access that you use to make decisions about how to sort and select your data and which fields to include in the query results.

design template A collection of formatting options that you can apply to a PowerPoint presentation. Also called a *template*.

Design view A view in Access that permits you to set up and modify the structure and appearance of database objects.

desktop (1) The working area of the screen that displays many Windows tools and is the background for computer work; (2) the most common PC model, sized to fit on a desk, with separate units for the CPU and the monitor.

developmental portfolio An organized collection of your work that demonstrates your progress toward a goal over a period of time. Developmental portfolios help you become more aware of your strengths and weaknesses and assist you in improving your abilities. See also *portfolio* and *representational portfolio*.

dialog box A rectangle containing a set of options that appears when an application requires more information from the user to perform a requested operation.

discussion server A computer that stores online discussion text and information about the location of a file that is being discussed.

disk drive A storage device that reads data from and writes data to disks.

docked toolbar A toolbar that is attached to the edge of the application window. Compare with *floating toolbar*.

document A computer file consisting of a compilation of one or more kinds of data; a file that stores the work you have created with the computer. File types include documents, worksheets, presentations, databases, graphic files, HTML files, and so on. A document, which a user can open and use, is different from a program file, which is required to operate a software program. See also *file*.

document window A rectangle within an application window that is used to view and work on a file. See also *application window*.

domain name The address of a Web site's computer.

double-click To rapidly press and release the left button on a mouse or trackball twice when the pointer is pointing to an object. See also *click* and *right-click*.

drag To move an object on screen by pointing to the object, pressing and holding the mouse button, moving the pointer to a new location, and then releasing the mouse button. Also called *drag-and-drop*.

drag-and-drop See *drag*.

drive icon A small icon or image that represents a storage device.

drop-down list A list of options displayed when you click a triangle button.

E

Edit mode A mode in Excel that is used to make corrections to data.

electronic mail See *e-mail*.

ellipsis A series of three dots to the right of a menu option indicating that a dialog box will display when you click the option.

e-mail The exchange of messages and computer files via the Internet and other electronic data networks; abbreviation for *electronic mail*.

embed To paste text or an object from the Clipboard into a file.

embedded chart A chart that displays within the same worksheet that contains the chart's data.

embedded object An object that is contained in a source file and inserted into a destination file, while maintaining a connection between the two files. Any changes made to the original file are automatically reflected in the destination file.

end mark The short horizontal line within a document that moves downward each time you begin a new line.

endnote Supporting or additional information that appears on a separate page at the end of a document. Compare with *footnote*.

event In Outlook, an activity that lasts 24 hours or longer; for example, a vacation or a seminar. Compare with *annual event*.

expanded A state of an item in which details or subordinate items are visible. A minus sign (−) in the box to the left of the item indicates that the item is expanded. Compare with *collapsed*.

expanded menu A list of all commands available on a menu that displays when a user clicks the arrows at the bottom of a short menu. Compare with *short menu.*

expression Any combination of field names, values, constants, comparison operators, functions, controls, and properties that can be evaluated to a single value.

Expression Builder An Access tool you can use to choose the fields on which you want to perform calculations and the operators you want to use in those calculations, rather than entering an expression manually.

extension A one- to three-character component at the end of a file name that an operating system uses to identify the type of data stored in the file.

F

Favorites (1) Tool used with Microsoft's browser to provide a shortcut to the location of a specific file, folder, or Web site so you can return to it later without typing the address; (2) one of the four tabs on the navigation pane of the Windows Help window; this tool lets you save useful Help topics for later review. See also *Contents, Index,* and *Search.*

field A column in a table that contains a category of data.

field code An underlying hidden code inserted into a Word document (for example, in a date/time format). These codes may be edited in the Field dialog box to create custom formats.

field properties Field settings that control the way a field looks and behaves.

field selectors In Access, the gray boxes at the top of each column that contain the captions in Datasheet view.

file A named, ordered collection of information stored on a disk. See also *document* and *application program.*

file format The patterns and standards that a program uses to store data on a disk. Also called *file type.*

file name The characters used to identify a file, limited to 215 characters in Windows 2000.

file type See *file format.*

fill color A color used to fill the interior of an enclosed space, such as a cell in a table.

first-line indentation The conventional paragraph indentation style in which the first line is indented from the left margin.

floating toolbar A toolbar that is not attached to the edge of the application window. Compare with *docked toolbar.*

focus The record that is currently selected.

folder A named location on a removable or nonremovable disk for storing and organizing files, folders, and programs. See also *subfolder.*

folder banner The bar at the top of the large frame on the right side of the Outlook window; the folder banner displays the name of the open folder.

font The design of a set of named characters. Also called *typeface.*

font size The size of text characters, measured in points. Also called *point size.*

footer Text that appears at the bottom of each page in a document, or at the bottom of each slide in a PowerPoint presentation. See also *header.*

footnote Supporting or additional information that appears at the bottom of a page. Compare with *endnote.*

foreign key A field in a related table that refers to the primary key field in the primary table.

foreign table See *related table.*

form An Access object that provides a custom layout for entering, editing, and viewing data easily and efficiently.

format A conventional arrangement of text on a page. See also *formatting.*

formatting Arranging and enhancing the appearance of a worksheet by changing the attributes, alignment, indentations, line spacing, margins, and/or paragraph spacing of text. See also *format.*

formula A group of instructions that performs a calculation and displays the result.

Formula Bar In Excel, the bar immediately below the toolbars that displays the contents of the active cell. You can enter and edit data in the Formula Bar.

Form view The view in Access that allows you to view one record at a time and display only pertinent fields in a record. Form view often is used to enter records into a database.

frames Panels in the window of a Web page that are separated by borders or scroll bars. You can scroll or resize frames without affecting other frames in the window.

function A predefined formula that performs specialized calculations. Excel includes more than 360 functions representing categories such as statistical, date and time, financial, logical, and mathematical.

G

global change A change made to the slide master that is reflected throughout a PowerPoint presentation.

glossary term A word or phrase appearing in colored text on a Help screen that you can click to display or hide its definition.

graph See *chart.*

graphic A picture, drawing, photograph, or WordArt that can be inserted into a file. Also called *image*. See also *object* and *WordArt*.

graphical user interface (GUI) An operating environment in which controls and data are visible on screen so that you can select items with a pointing device. See also *user interface*.

Grayscale mode A printer option that represents PowerPoint slide colors with black, white, and varying shades of gray. Compare with *Pure Black and White mode*.

gridlines The pattern of regularly spaced horizontal and vertical lines (the cell borders) on a worksheet or table that defines the columns, rows, and cells.

H

handles Squares or circles that surround an object or placeholder in a document and allow you to move or resize it. Also called *selection handles, sizing handles, resize handles,* or *move handles*.

hanging indentation A paragraph indentation style in which the first line of text is flush with the left margin and succeeding lines are indented.

hard copy See *printout*.

hard return A press of the Enter key to end a short line of text and force the insertion point to the next line.

header Text that appears at the top of each printed page. See also *footer*.

Help An electronic manual that provides assistance with the features and operations of an application program (for example, Word, PowerPoint, Excel, or Access). Also called *online Help system*.

hide To temporarily suppress the display of a worksheet element, such as a column or row.

highlight An enhancing tool in Word that allows you to place color over text to appear much like a highlighter. Can be used to emphasize important text or to mark text to be reviewed.

home page The main page of a Web site, which usually includes links to other pages at that site. Also called *start page*.

horizontal alignment The arrangement of text in relation to the left and right margins. Compare with *vertical alignment*.

horizontal scroll bar A rectangular bar that appears along the bottom side of a window or dialog box that is too narrow to display all of its contents; clicking or dragging in the scroll bar brings additional contents into view and allows the user to scroll information from side to side. Compare with *vertical scroll bar*.

hyperlink Text or a graphic inserted in a Help frame, a file, or a Web page that links to additional related information, another frame, a file, an Internet address, a page on the World Wide Web, or an HTML page on an intranet. Also called *link* or *jump*.

hypertext Text that contains a hyperlink.

Hypertext Markup Language (HTML) The language used to tag a document with codes so the document can be viewed on the World Wide Web. HTML includes the capability that enables Web page creators to insert hyperlinks into their documents.

Hypertext Transfer Protocol (HTTP) The set of rules that defines the way hypertext links display Web pages. HTTP allows a browser and Web server to communicate and allows the exchange of all data on the Web.

I

I-beam pointer Pointer that takes the shape of the capital letter "I" when it is moved over text.

icon A small image that represents a device, program, file, or folder.

image See *graphic*.

import To insert or add into a file; for example, inserting a graphic file into a document. Also called *insert*.

Inbox One of the default folders in Outlook; the *Inbox* folder allows you to read, compose, send, and store e-mail messages. See also *Calendar, Contacts, Journal, Notes,* and *Tasks*.

indentation Distance of text from the left or right page margins.

indent level A number that describes the position of a subtitle on a PowerPoint slide.

Index One of the three tabs in the expanded Help window in Office applications, or one of the four tabs in the Windows Help window. This tool allows you to search an alphabetical listing of Help topics. See also *Answer Wizard, Contents, Favorites,* and *Search*.

input mask In Access, a pattern you create that specifies what kind of data to enter and the number of characters allowed in a field.

insert See *import*.

insertion point The blinking vertical bar within a document that indicates where text will appear when typing begins.

Insert mode Mode in which typed text is inserted into existing text, pushing the characters after it to the right. Compare with *Overtype mode*.

Internet A worldwide system of interconnected computer networks allowing users to exchange digital information in the form of text, graphics, and other media.

Internet Service Provider (ISP) A company that provides Internet access to users for a monthly or an annual fee.

intranet A network within an organization allowing users to exchange messages and data with other users in the organization. Intranets are configured to look and function like the World Wide Web, enabling users to interact with the network by using a Web browser.

italic A thin, right-slanted effect applied to text for emphasis.

J

join An association between a field in one table or query and a field of the same data type in another table or query that tells Access how the data is related.

Journal One of the default folders in Outlook; the Journal automatically tracks the history of selected activities such as opening documents, sending mail messages, placing phone calls, etc. See also *Calendar, Contacts, Inbox, Notes,* and *Tasks.*

joystick An input device used to control the on-screen pointer; a small joystick often is found in the middle of the keyboard on a laptop computer.

jump See *hyperlink.*

justified Paragraph alignment in which both the left and right edges of text are perfectly even. Also, page alignment in which paragraphs are distributed among the top, middle, and bottom sections of a page.

K

keyword A word or phrase that defines or narrows the topic for which you are searching in Help or on the World Wide Web.

L

landscape orientation A layout that prints data across the wider dimension of the page (for example, the 11-inch dimension on 8.5- by 11-inch paper). Compare with *portrait orientation.*

language bar A toolbar that appears in the upper-right corner of the screen in Office XP programs; the language bar is used to activate handwriting and speech recognition programs for data input.

large icon An icon displayed at full size.

launch To enter a command that runs an application program.

layout The arrangement and spacing of text and graphics on a page.

left aligned Paragraph alignment in which text is perfectly even at the left margin; the standard (default) paragraph alignment.

line spacing The amount of white space between text lines.

link See *hyperlink.*

linked object An object that is created in a source file and inserted into a destination file while maintaining a connection between the two files. Any changes made to the original file are reflected automatically in the destination file.

list style Formatting style that applies similar alignment, numbering, or bullet characters and fonts to lists of text.

logical functions Specialized Excel functions that you can use to help make decisions related to numerical or statistical data. One popular logical function is the IF function.

log on To type a user name and a password when starting up a computer. See also *password* and *user name.*

M

macro A series of stored commands that you can play back all at once by issuing a single command.

manual page break Forced page break that you can insert in a document.

many-to-many relationship A relationship between tables in which a record in either table can have many matches in the other table.

margin A blank area bordering text on a page.

marking the task as complete A process in Outlook in which you keep a task on your list but cross it off to remind you that it has been completed.

MAX An Excel function that returns the highest value in a specified range.

maximize A Windows sizing feature in which an open window is enlarged to fill the screen; also, the name of the button that performs this function. Compare with *minimize.*

menu A list of commands or options displayed in an application window from which you can choose.

menu bar An area below the title bar of all application windows containing menu names that, when clicked, display a list of commands.

merge To combine a range of cells into one larger cell. When cells are merged, only the data in the upper-left cell of the range is retained and displayed. Compare with *split.*

Microsoft Outlook A desktop information management program in which you can organize and share many different types of information, including messages, appointments, contacts, and tasks.

MIN An Excel function that returns the lowest value in a specified range.

minimize A Windows sizing feature that reduces an open window to a button on the taskbar; also, the name of the button that performs this function. Compare with *maximize.*

mixed cell reference A cell reference that includes relative and absolute portions; for example, the column letter may change when the formula is copied to a new location, but the row number does not.

moderated newsgroup A newsgroup whose messages are screened by a host to ensure that their content relates to the topic of the newsgroup.

module A set of programmed statements in Access that are stored together as a unit; a module is used to automate a task.

mouse A hand-held, button-activated input device that, when rolled along a flat surface, directs an indicator to move correspondingly around a computer screen, allowing the operator to move the indicator freely to select operations or to manipulate data or graphics.

mouse pointer See *pointer.*

move handles See *handles.*

multitasking The ability of an operating system to carry out multiple operations at the same time; for example, running more than one program.

N

Name Box The box to the left of the Formula Bar that identifies the cell address of the active cell in an Excel worksheet.

navigate To move about on the Windows desktop or in an application window in a planned or preset course.

nested parentheses Multiple sets of parentheses that regulate the order in which Excel performs calculations.

newsgroup A public discussion containing a set of articles about a single topic.

newsletter columns Side-by-side column layout in which one column fills with text before text flows into the next column.

newsreader An application program used to send and receive online news articles from newsgroups.

news server A computer that supplies news articles to a newsreader program.

noncontiguous (nonadjacent) range Multiple groups of cells that are not adjoining. See also *contiguous (adjacent) range.*

Normal style The default paragraph style in Word.

Notes One of the default folders in Outlook; the *Notes* folder is an electronic version of paper self-stick, removable notes. You can use this folder to record ideas, questions, comments, or any other data you might need later. See also *Calendar, Contacts, Inbox, Journal,* and *Tasks.*

O

object (1) An element in a document, chart, or worksheet that you can manipulate independently, such as a clip art image, photo, sound file, or video clip—see also *graphic* and *WordArt;* (2) in PowerPoint, any single non-text element on a slide, such as a clip art image, table, or chart.

object area On a PowerPoint slide, a dotted area appearing below the title area which serves as a placeholder for non-text objects. See also *text area* and *title area.*

Object Linking and Embedding (OLE) A special technology used in Windows and Windows-based applications that allows you to create data in one application and re-use it in other applications. With OLE, you can copy data from one application to another and link the copy back to the original. Then, if the original data is changed, the copy is updated to reflect the change.

objects The major components of an Access database, including tables, queries, forms, reports, data access pages, macros, and modules.

Objects bar A bar that appears along the left side of the Database window in Access and represents the types of objects available.

Office Assistant An animated character in all Office programs that can answer specific questions, offer tips, and provide help with the program's features.

Office Clipboard An area in memory used by all Office XP applications for temporarily storing up to 24 items that you want to copy or move to a new location. See also *Clipboard.*

one-to-many relationship A relationship between two tables in which each record in the primary table can have zero, one, or many matching records in the related table, but every record in the related table has one—and only one—associated record in the primary table.

one-to-one relationship A relationship between two tables in which every record in one table can have either no matching records or only a single matching record in the other table.

online Help system See *Help.*

open (1) To copy a file from disk into the computer memory and display it on screen; (2) to start an application program; (3) to access the contents of an icon in a window.

operating system A collection of programs that allows you to work with a computer by managing the flow of data between input devices, the computer's memory, storage devices, and output devices. Also called *operating system software*.

operating system software See *operating system*.

option button A small circle filled with a solid dot when selected; you can select only one in a set of option buttons at one time. Formerly called *radio button*.

organization chart A diagram that depicts the structure of an organization, such as the hierarchy of managers and employees. In an organization chart, each worker's position is represented by a box; the relationships between positions are indicated by the connections between the boxes.

orientation Position of text and/or graphics on a printed page. See also *landscape orientation* and *portrait orientation*.

orphan The first line of a paragraph printed by itself at the bottom of a page.

Outlook Bar The smaller frame on the left side of the Outlook window that contains group names and icons serving as shortcuts to frequently used folders.

Outlook Today page A page in Outlook that gives you a quick preview of your day. When you click the Outlook Today icon, the main working area displays your appointments for the day, your complete task list, and a summary of e-mail messages.

Overtype mode Mode in which text replaces existing text as it is typed. Compare with *Insert mode*.

P

page (1) An area equivalent to dimensions and text capacity of standard-sized paper (8.5 inches by 11 inches); (2) see *Web page*.

page break The point at which a page ends and another begins. The page break can be inserted automatically or manually.

page footer A footer that appears at the bottom of every page of an Access report and usually includes the date on which the report is printed, the page number, and the number of pages in the entire report.

page header A header with text information printed at the top of every page of an Access report.

page orientation In Excel, the arrangement of data on a printed page. See also *orientation, landscape orientation,* and *portrait orientation*.

pane A bordered area within a window.

paragraph mark (1) In Word, an on-screen symbol (¶) marking the end of a paragraph; (2) a proofreading symbol indicating where a new paragraph should begin.

paragraph spacing The amount of white space above and below paragraphs, which is measured in points.

paragraph style Formatting style that controls all aspects of a paragraph's appearance, such as text alignment, tab stops, line spacing, and so on.

password A string of characters known only to the user, which the user must enter before accessing a computer system. See also *log on* and *user name*.

paste To insert cut or copied text or a graphic from the Clipboard into a file.

path The sequence of disk, folder, and subfolder(s) that leads from the disk drive to the location of a particular folder or file.

personalize See *customize*.

placeholder In PowerPoint, a dotted area found in a slide layout that reserves space for text or an object.

point A unit of measure (1/72 of an inch) used for text and white space. Twelve points equal a pica, which is approximately 1/6 of an inch.

pointer An arrow or other on-screen image that moves in relation to the movement of a mouse or trackball. Also called *mouse pointer*.

pointing Moving the pointer to position it over an on-screen object.

point size See *font size*.

portfolio An organized collection of your work that demonstrates skills and knowledge acquired from one or more courses. The materials included in a portfolio pertain to a specific educational or career goal. See also *developmental portfolio* and *representational portfolio*.

portrait orientation A layout that prints data across the shorter dimension of the page (for example, the 8.5-inch dimension on 8.5- by 11-inch paper). Portrait is the default orientation. Compare with *landscape orientation*.

post (1) To create and send a message to a newsgroup; (2) see *article*.

Power On Self Test (POST) A program that checks a computer system's memory, keyboard, display, and disk drives.

precedence The set of mathematical rules that determines the order in which mathematical expressions are calculated.

presentation A series of slides that can be shown on a computer, projected on a screen, or printed.

presentation program A program, such as PowerPoint, that provides tools to create presentations using text, animation, charts, clip art, pictures, shapes, and sounds.

primary key A field or set of fields that uniquely identifies each record in a table.

primary table A table in a one-to-many relationship that can have zero, one, or many matching records in the related table, but every record in the related table has exactly one matching record in the primary table. You can think of a primary table as the "one" side in a one-to-many relationship.

printout A paper copy of your document. Also called a *hard copy.*

print preview An accurate on-screen representation of the printed output—including headers, footers, and page breaks. Print preview lets you see on the screen what you will be printing before you send the output to the printer.

print scaling An Excel option that allows you to enlarge or reduce printed output without changing font sizes in order to better fit data on the page.

program Instructions written in programming code that direct the computer to execute certain functions based on additional user input. See also *application program* and *software.*

promote To move a subtitle to the next higher indent level on a PowerPoint slide. Compare with *demote.*

protocol A set of signals and commands computers use to communicate with each other.

publish To place a Web page or Web site on a Web server to make it available to others through the World Wide Web or an intranet.

Pure Black and White mode A printer option that saves printer memory and time by ignoring colors, printing all PowerPoint slides in black and white only. Compare with *Grayscale mode.*

Q

Query A question to an Access database, asking for a set of records from one or more tables or asking for data that meet specific criteria.

R

random access memory (RAM) A computer's volatile or temporary memory, which exists as chips on the motherboard near the CPU. RAM stores data and programs while they are being used and requires a power source to maintain its integrity.

range A selected cell or group of cells. See also *contiguous (adjacent) range* and *noncontiguous (nonadjacent) range.*

range reference The two cell references that specify the location of a range in an Excel worksheet. For example, A1:E25 is an example of a range that encompasses all the cells in a rectangular section of a worksheet from cell A1 through cell E25.

read-only (attribute) A property setting that lets users view and use an object, such as a file, but not modify or delete it. Compare with *archive (attribute).* See also *attribute.*

read-only memory (ROM) A permanent, or nonvolatile, memory chip used to store instructions and data, including the computer's startup instructions. ROM's contents cannot be altered.

record A row in a table that contains the set of fields for one particular entity.

record selector In Access, the box in Datasheet view to the left of a record. You can click the record selector to highlight the entire record.

recurring meeting In Outlook, a meeting that occurs at regular intervals. See also *appointment.*

Redo A command you can use to reverse the most recent Undo command. See also *Undo.*

redundancy Duplication of data in a database.

referential integrity A set of rules that Access can enforce to preserve the defined relationship between tables.

related table A table in a one-to-many relationship in which every record has exactly one matching record in the primary table. Also called *foreign table.*

relational database management system (RDBMS) A database program that lets you link, or relate, two or more tables to share data between them.

relationship The connection between two or more tables. If tables contain a common field, they can be linked through this field. When tables are related in this way, reports and other created objects can combine data from both tables.

relative reference A cell reference within a copied or moved formula that changes to correspond to its new location. By default, Excel interprets all cell references as relative references. See also *absolute reference.*

report An Access object that you use to produce polished, printed output of the data from tables or queries. You can organize the information in a report and format it in accordance with your specifications.

report header A header that appears at the top of the first page only of an Access report and usually contains the name of the table or query on which the report is based.

representational portfolio An organized collection that displays a variety of your best work. You can present a representational portfolio as evidence of your skills and knowledge. See also *developmental portfolio* and *portfolio*.

resize To change the height and/or width of a graphic.

resize handles See *handles*.

Restore Down To return a maximized window to its previous size; also, the name of the button that performs this function.

reverse video White text against a dark background.

Rich Text Format (RTF) A format in which a document can be saved; *.rtf* is the file extension for this format. In PowerPoint, you lose the graphic content of presentations saved as RTF files.

right aligned Text alignment in which all lines are flush with the right margin.

right-click To quickly press and release the right button on a mouse or trackball. See also *click* and *double-click*.

row headings The gray area on the left side of an Excel worksheet that contains a number identifying each row.

ruler A display of numbered tick marks and indent markers that indicate measurements across a document. The ruler is used to format paragraphs and position objects.

S

sans serif Description of a font without serifs (for example, Arial). Compare with *serif*.

save To transfer a file from computer memory to a storage disk (for example, a removable disk or a hard disk).

ScreenTip A note that appears on the screen to provide information about a toolbar button or other window element, a comment, a footnote or endnote, or a date or AutoText entry.

scroll arrows Buttons at each end of a scroll bar that let you scroll information in small increments when clicked—for example, when scrolling text line by line.

scroll bar A rectangular bar that appears along the right or bottom side of a window or dialog box when not all the contents are visible; used to bring hidden contents into view. See also *horizontal scroll bar* and *vertical scroll bar*.

scroll box A rectangle in a scroll bar that you can drag to display information; its location represents the location of the visible information in relation to the entire contents of the window or dialog box.

scrolling Using a scroll bar, scroll box, or scroll arrows to move around in a window or in a dialog box.

Search One of the four tabs in the Windows Help window. The Search tab lets you search for words in the description of the Help information, rather than searching by topic. See also *Contents, Favorites,* and *Index*.

search engine An Internet tool that allows a user to search for information on a particular topic.

section break In Word, a way to subdivide a document (next page break) or page (continuous break) so that each defined section may have distinctive formatting.

select (1) To designate or highlight (typically by clicking an item with the mouse) where the next action will take place, which command will be executed next, or which option will be put into effect; (2) to extract specified subsets of data based on criteria that you define. Also called *choose*. Compare with *clear*.

Select All The gray rectangle in the upper-left corner of an Excel worksheet where the row and column headings meet.

selection bar The invisible column between the left edge of the Word document window and the left margin of the page. When you click this bar, a line of text is selected.

selection handles See *handles*.

select query The most-often-used query type in Access; a select query allows you to sort, select, and view specific records from one or more tables.

serif Description of a font that has finishing strokes on the characters (for example, Times New Roman). Compare with *sans serif*.

service bureau A commercial printer that uses specialized hardware to print computer files in a variety of formats. For example, a service bureau can convert a PowerPoint presentation into a set of 35-millimeter slides.

shading Color or gradations of gray applied to cells, paragraphs, and pages, often in combination with a border.

shadow A decorative shading on text characters, used for emphasizing large-font headings.

sheet tab A tab at the bottom of an Excel worksheet area that you can click to select a specific sheet in the workbook.

shortcut menu A context-sensitive menu that appears when you right-click certain screen elements.

short menu A list of the most basic commands, which appears when you click a menu name on the menu bar. Compare with *expanded menu*.

size (1) To change the dimensions of a window or dialog box so that its contents remain visible but the window occupies only a portion of the desktop; (2) to change the dimensions of an object.

sizing handles See *handles*.

slide An image of text and graphics shown on a computer, a slide projector, an overhead projector, or on paper.

slide layout A predesigned slide containing preset placeholders for text and/or objects, which you use in developing a PowerPoint presentation.

slide master A primary background slide, used to make changes to an entire PowerPoint presentation.

slider control An indicator that you drag along a vertical or horizontal line. Dragging the indicator increases or decreases the value shown on the line.

small icon An icon displayed at quarter size.

software A collective term for programs or instructions that are stored in electronic format and tell the computer what to do. See also *program* and *application program*.

sort To rearrange records, text, or table data into alphabetic, numeric, or chronological order. See also *descending sort* and *ascending sort*.

spinner buttons A pair of controls used to change a numeric setting, consisting of an up arrow above a down arrow. Clicking the up arrow increases the setting; clicking the down arrow decreases it.

split To separate a merged cell into a range of individual cells. Compare with *merge*.

splitter bar A narrow bar separating two panes in the PowerPoint application window that enables you to resize the panes.

spreadsheet program A computer program that organizes data in a row and column format and can perform calculations and help analyze information.

start page See *home page*.

statistical functions In Excel, a group of functions that can perform statistical analysis on a range. Some of the most commonly used statistical functions include SUM, MAX, MIN, and AVERAGE.

status bar A bar at the bottom of the application window that indicates information about a selected command, an operation in progress, or other information about the program.

structure The design of objects that make up a database. These objects are used to enter, manipulate, and extract data, and they can be modified as a database grows and changes over time.

style A named set of formatting attributes for characters and paragraphs.

subdatasheet A datasheet within an Access datasheet that allows you to view and edit related or joined data in another table.

subfolder A folder nested within another folder. See also *folder*.

subform A form within an Access form that displays related records.

subject directory A list of links to topics arranged alphabetically to facilitate browsing for a specific topic.

submenu A second list of commands or options (indicated by an arrow on an initial menu).

subtitle Any text below the title of a PowerPoint slide, except text appearing in an object.

SUM A commonly used Excel function that totals the value of a specified range.

switchboard A special form that helps you navigate among the objects in an Access database. You can use the switchboard instead of the Database window to access the objects and information.

system boot See *booting the system*.

system software A computer program that controls the system hardware and interacts with application software; the program includes the operating system and the network operating system.

T

tab A control at the top of some dialog boxes and windows that displays a different screen within the dialog box or window when clicked.

table An Access object that contains data organized in records (rows) and fields (columns). All the data contained in one table usually pertains to one particular subject, such as employees, customers, or inventory items.

table of contents A list of chapter titles and headings, usually including their corresponding page numbers. Also called *TOC*.

table style Formatting style that provides a consistent look to borders, shading, alignment, and fonts in tables.

tab scrolling buttons Buttons at the bottom of the Excel application window that you use to display worksheet tabs that are not visible.

tab stop A preset (default) or user-set position on the horizontal ruler that defines the beginning of a text column or the size of a paragraph indentation.

task In Outlook, a personal or work-related duty or errand that you want to track in an electronic to-do list.

taskbar An area at the bottom of the Windows 2000 desktop that displays a button for the Start menu, icons for commonly used Windows 2000 features, a button for each application running, and a button for the clock.

task pane A window within an Office XP application that provides quick access to commonly used commands and features while you are still working on a file.

Tasks One of the default folders in Outlook; the *Tasks* folder is a personal electronic to-do list. See also *Calendar, Contacts, Inbox, Journal,* and *Notes.*

template (1) In Word, a master copy of a type of document—a model document that includes standard and variable text and formatting and may include graphics; (2) in PowerPoint, see *design template.*

text Data in an Excel worksheet, such as descriptive labels, titles, and headings, on which you cannot perform calculations. Text and values are the two types of data Excel recognizes. Compare with *values.*

text area On a PowerPoint slide, a dotted area appearing below the title area that serves as a placeholder for text, such as subtitles or bulleted lists. See also *title area* and *object area.*

text box (1) In Office XP applications, a box used to hold text (or a graphic); (2) in Windows 2000, a rectangular control that displays the name or value of a current setting and in which you can type a different name or value to change the setting.

theme A set of unified design elements and color schemes for enhancing documents, including Web pages.

Thesaurus A Word reference tool containing synonyms and antonyms.

threaded In an online discussion, a term used for a series of messages in which replies to each original message appear directly below the message.

thumbnail A miniature version of a slide or a graphical sample of a template displayed in the PowerPoint application window.

Times New Roman The standard or default font in Word for paragraph copy (a serif font).

title The first line of text on a PowerPoint slide.

title area On a PowerPoint slide, a dotted area appearing at the top of a slide that holds the main title for the slide. See also *text area* and *object area.*

title bar A bar at the top of a window that displays the name of the application, file, or device that the window represents.

title slide The first slide in a PowerPoint presentation, which displays the presentation's title. A title slide is optional.

TOC See *table of contents.*

toggle key A command or option that you can turn on and off by repeatedly clicking it.

toolbar A row of buttons representing frequently used commands that is used to execute commands quickly. Toolbars also can contain menus. See also *button.*

top aligned Page alignment in which text is even with the top margin, regardless of the amount of text on the page. This is the default vertical alignment in Word.

touch-sensitive pad An input device used to control the on-screen pointer by pressing a flat surface with a finger; it usually is found on laptop computers.

trackball An input device that functions like an upside-down mouse, containing a ball that is rolled by the thumb or fingers to move the on-screen pointer; it is used frequently with laptop computers and video games.

transition In PowerPoint, a visual effect that determines how one slide is replaced by another on the screen during a presentation.

transparent background A feature in PowerPoint in which the background color of an image is ignored and the background color of the slide shows through the image, creating the illusion that the main portion of the image was drawn directly on the slide.

triangle button A button in the shape of a small downward-pointing triangle that displays a menu of options when clicked.

typeface See *font.*

U

underline A line under text characters that is used for emphasis.

Undo A command you can use to reverse the most recent actions you've performed. See also *Redo.*

Uniform Resource Locator (URL) The address of a Web site. A URL can consist of letters, numbers, and special symbols that are understood by the Internet. See also *Web site* and *Web page.*

unnamed file A new file before it is saved; the file name is represented in the title bar as *Document#* in Word, *Book#* in Excel, *Presentation#* in PowerPoint, and *db#* in Access.

user A person who inputs and analyzes data using a computer.

user interface The rules and methods by which a computer and its users communicate. See also *graphical user interface (GUI).*

user name A name by which a user is identified on a computer. The user enters a user name as part of the log-on procedure. See also *log on* and *password.*

V

values Numbers, dates, times, and formulas on which you can perform calculations in an Excel worksheet. Values and text are the two types of data Excel recognizes. Compare with *text.*

variable information In a Word template, placeholder text that you replace with your own information.

vertical alignment The arrangement of text in relation to the top and bottom margins. Compare with *horizontal alignment*.

vertical scroll bar A rectangular bar that appears along the right side of a window or dialog box that is too short to display all of its contents. Clicking or dragging in the scroll bar brings additional contents into view and allows the user to scroll information from beginning to end. Compare with *horizontal scroll bar*.

views Different ways of looking at an Access database, depending upon the type of object you open and whether you want to work with the object's content (the data) or the object's design (the structure).

W

Web See *World Wide Web (WWW)*.

Web browser See *browser*.

Web page A parcel of information located on the World Wide Web that may contain text, graphics, animation, sound, and video. The terms *Web page* and *Web site* often are used interchangeably. Also called *page*. See also *Web site* and *Uniform Resource Locator (URL)*.

Web server A computer that publishes Web pages on the Internet so others can view them. The Web server accepts requests from browsers and returns appropriate HTML documents. A Web server has a continuous connection to the Internet or an intranet.

Web site Specific location on the World Wide Web, accessible by means of a unique address or URL. See also *Uniform Resource Locator (URL)* and *Web page*.

Web style desktop A Windows 2000 desktop setting that gives the user the same look and feel as when on the Internet. Compare with *Active Desktop* and *classic style desktop*.

Web support A feature of a computer program that allows the program to interact seamlessly with the World Wide Web.

what if analysis The process of changing values in a worksheet to observe the impact on the results.

wheel On a mouse, a button in the shape of a wheel between the left and right buttons that is used for scrolling to view information above or below the information on the screen.

widow The last line of a paragraph printed by itself at the top of a page.

window A rectangular area that displays information, such as the content of a file or the controls of an application; you can open, close, move, size, maximize, and minimize a window.

window borders The edges of a window. Frequently, you can drag the borders to resize a window.

window corner The point at which two window borders meet. Dragging the corner lets you change the height and width of a window simultaneously.

wizard An interactive tool that guides a user through an operation step by step.

WordArt Decorative text that you can stretch, skew, or rotate to fit a particular shape. See also *graphic* and *object*.

word processing program Computer program used to create text-based documents that are changed and stored easily.

word wrap Word processing feature that automatically moves the insertion point to the next line as the text you are typing reaches the right margin.

workbook A collection of related worksheets and chart sheets saved as an Excel file.

worksheet A grid of columns and rows for entering, viewing, and editing data that is used most often for entering numbers and performing calculations.

worksheet area The area of the Excel window that contains a grid of columns and rows and occupies most of the screen. This is where your data appears and where you generally enter and edit data. The column and row headings, the scroll bars, and the sheet tabs are considered to be part of the worksheet area.

World Wide Web (WWW) An Internet service that allows users to view documents containing hyperlinks to other documents anywhere on the Internet. Companies, organizations, and individuals with a special interest to share control the graphical documents. Also called the *Web*.

wrapping style In Word, the way in which lines of text break in relation to an object on the same page.

WYSIWYG An acronym for *What You See Is What You Get*, a GUI characteristic in which documents appear on screen much as they will appear on a printed page or on a Web page.

INDEX

OFFICE XP

Footers, *def.,* 222, 623, 738
  adding headers and, 623–624
  page, *def.,* 154
  headers and, using, 222–224
Footnotes, *def.,* 738
  using, 224–226
Foreign key, *def.,* 429, 738
Foreign table, *def.,* 738
Form(s), *def.,* 383, 738
  adding a record with, 384–385
  creating, 467–469
  modifying, 496
  using, 463–469, 383–385
Form view, *def.,* 383, 738
Form Wizard, using the, 467–469
Format, *def.,* 125, 738
  columns, 197–200
  datasheet, 151–154
  graphics, 212–216
  image, 213–216
  numbers, 287–288
  paragraphs, 191–194
Format Cells dialog box, 287
Format menu, 95
Format Painter button, 129
  using the, 208–209, 286
Formats, removing cell, 288–291
Formatting, *def.,* 256, 738
  changing, with slide master, 620–622
Formatting toolbar, numeric formats on the, 287
Formula(s), *def.,* 268, 326, 738
  creating, 326–328
  understanding, 326–330
Formula bar, *def.,* 260, 738
Forward button, 54
Frames, *def.,* 56, 738
Functions, *def.,* 738
  using, 330–339
  using aggregate, 484–485
  using SUM, 331–332

G

Global, *def.,* 620
Global change, *def.,* 738
Glossary terms, *def.,* 28, 107, 738
Grammar tools, using, 155–162
Graph, *def.,* 609, 738
Graphic image, inserting, 603–604
Graphical user interface (GUI), 84, *def.,* 6, 739
Graphics, *def.,* 212, 739
  copyright of, 599
  inserting and formatting, 212–216
  piracy of, 526–527
  working with, 597–601
Grayscale, 604, *def.,* 555, 739
Gridlines, *def.,* 260, 739
Grouping, using, 484–487
Groups of cells, selecting, 313–317

H

Handles, *def.,* 739
Hanging indentation, *def.,* 191, 739
Hard copy, 588, *def.,* 739
Hard return, *def.,* 136, 739
Hardware, 588
Hardware requirements, viii
Header(s), *def.,* 222, 623, 739
  adding footers and, 623–624
  page, *def.,* 154
  report, *def.,* 154
  using footers and, 222–224
Header and Footer toolbar, *illus.,* 223
Help, *def.,* 739
  exploring Favorites tab in, 58
  getting, 27–30, 107–112
    online, 38–39
    on the Web, 114–115
Help menu, 95
Help systems, understanding online, 2–3
Help topic, printing, 109

Hide, *def.,* 739
Highlight, *def.,* 205, 739
  adding, 205
History button, 55
Home button, 54
Home page, *def.,* 739
Horizontal alignment, *def.,* 191, 739
  changing, 192–194
Horizontal scroll bar, *def.,* 17, 98, 739
HTML format, saving a worksheet in, 273
HTML tags, 122
Hyperlink data type, 400
Hyperlinks, *def.,* 98, 162, 346, 739
  creating, 162–163
  inserting, 164–165
  in presentations, 562–563
  in worksheets, 346–349
Hypertext, *def.,* 59, 739
Hypertext Markup Language (HTML), 59, *def.,* 258, 739
Hypertext Markup Language (HTML) tags, 122
Hypertext Transfer Protocol (HTTP), 59, *def.,* 739

I

I-beam pointer, *def.,* 135, 739
Icons, *def.,* 9, 87, 739
  arranging, 16–17
Images, *def.,* 212, 739
  inserting, 603–604
  working with, 213–216, 597–604
Import, *def.,* 212, 418, 739
  data, 421–423
  Excel chart, 611–612
  Word table, 616–617
Importing, *def.,* 603, 739
Import Spreadsheet Wizard, using, 421–423
Inbox, *def.,* 656, 739
  using the, 656–658
Inbox column headings, 658–659

OFFICE XP

OFFICE XP